LABOR ECONOMICS AND LABOR RELATIONS

5th
EDITION

LLOYD G. REYNOLDS

Sterling Professor of Economics
Yale University

Prentice-Hall, Inc.
Englewood Cliffs, New Jersey

**FOR
ANNE,
PENNY,
AND BRUCE**

© 1970, 1964, 1959, 1956, 1954, 1949
by PRENTICE-HALL, INC.
Englewood Cliffs, New Jersey

13-517763-4

Library of Congress Catalog Card Number:
75-120143

Printed in the United States of America
Current Printing (last digit):
10 9 8 7 6 5 4 3

PRENTICE-HALL INTERNATIONAL, INC., *London*
PRENTICE-HALL OF AUSTRALIA, PTY. LTD., *Sydney*
PRENTICE-HALL OF CANADA, LTD., *Toronto*
PRENTICE-HALL OF INDIA PRIVATE LTD., *New Delhi*
PRENTICE-HALL OF JAPAN, INC., *Tokyo*

PREFACE

Labor economics and industrial relations are distinct but overlapping subjects. Labor economics is linked to the central core of economics by the theory of labor markets and wage determination; but unionism alters market structure and market results. Industrial relations is a multidisciplinary subject to which economics has made important contributions; but major contributions have come also from law, history, psychology, sociology, and industrial administration.

The effort to cover both subjects in a single text raises problems to which there is no agreed solution. While the notion of synthesizing them throughout the book is attractive in principle, it can lead to undesirable distortions in coverage. On one hand, there is a temptation to focus the economic analysis on the unionized 25 percent of the labor force, and on the other a tendency to analyze industrial relations systems in overly economic terms.

This book follows the alternative course of treating the two subjects somewhat at arm's length. This raises the question of which should come first, and again there is no "correct" answer. Each sequence has advantages and disadvantages. In this edition, I have reversed the previous sequence and have placed the economic analysis at the beginning of the book. Let me explain briefly why this now strikes me as preferable.

First, labor economics is basic in the sense that the economics of collective bargaining is included within it. Labor economics embraces everyone in the labor force, union or nonunion, floor sweepers and corporation presidents. It explores the way in which labor is allocated and compensated in "Western" economies through the operation of labor markets. For the unionized portion of the labor force, market results are modified in important respects through collective bargaining. But these modifications can be analyzed more effectively *after* one has examined the economic framework within which unions are operating.

Second, research in labor economics is shifting in a quantitative and econometric direction. Sophisticated statistical techniques are being applied increasingly to data on labor supply, employment, unemployment, and earnings. The wealth of new research material warrants both enlarging the "economic" component of this text and placing it at the beginning of the discussion.

Finally, the policy issues examined in Part I seem likely to be of greatest interest to students during the 1970s. They include such things as: the meaning of equal educational opportunity and feasible ways of attaining it; the reasons for the disadvantaged economic position of black workers and the main lines of remedial action; the problem of structural unemployment and its reduction through retraining and relocation programs; the problem of restraining wage and price increases during periods of high employment; the dimensions of poverty and new antipoverty proposals such as the negative income tax. These and other issues of labor market policy are discussed more fully than in previous editions.

Any author must realize that his own preferences on organization will not be universally shared. So I have tried to make each chapter of the book a self-contained teaching unit, which users can rearrange to suit their own preferences. The early chapters of Part II, for example, could be used effectively *before* Part I by teachers who prefer an institutional introduction to the course. Again, some might prefer to examine the economic impact of collective bargaining (Chapters 20–23) directly after the analysis of bargaining procedures in Chapters 15–16, and *before* the discussion of public control in Chapters 17–19. Such transpositions of chapters, I believe, can be made without difficulty.

I have profited by advice and help from many quarters. I am grateful especially to Dr. Mary T. Reynolds, who did the basic research and drafting of Chapters 17–19, which provide a thorough but concise introduction to labor law. Professors W. Lee Hansen of the University of Wisconsin, J. Fred Holly of the University of Tennessee, and Herbert S. Parnes of Ohio State University supplied critiques of the previous edition and made many useful suggestions for its improvement. The draft manuscript for this edition was reviewed by Professors Robert Goldfarb of Yale University, Stanley H. Masters of Rutgers—The State University, and Ronald R. Olsen of the University of Kansas. I accepted some of their suggestions and resisted others and must take full responsibility for the outcome. I am grateful also to Mrs. Olive Higgins, who labored with me through successive drafts of the manuscript, with meticulous attention to accuracy and clarity of detail.

In addition to those whom I can thank by name, I should like to express appreciation to the hundreds of students and teachers throughout the country whose suggestions have contributed to the continuing improvement of this book.

L. G. R.

CONTENTS

COLLECTIVE BARGAINING: INSTITUTIONS || AND PROCEDURES

COLLECTIVE
BARGAINING:
ECONOMIC III
IMPACT

Contents   xi

INTRODUCTION

LABOR IN INDUSTRIAL SOCIETY

1

Labor is always and everywhere the largest factor of production; and labor income always constitutes a large part of national income. Historically, this income has taken a variety of forms. In economies permitting slavery, it is mainly the subsistence of the slaves and their dependents. To the isolated peasant of Nepal, it is whatever he can produce and consume on his plot of land. Where the peasant markets part of his output, it is cash income plus his subsistence production.

Strictly, only part of the peasant's income can be regarded as labor income. Part of it is a return on his ownership of buildings and equipment, and part may be a rent arising from superior quality of his land. But where landowner, capitalist, and worker are rolled into one, these distinctions may not seem important.

Labor income becomes separable and measurable when the worker is hired for a wage or salary. His contribution to production then consists of his physical or mental effort, and the price of this effort is his wage. Modern labor economics focuses on economies in which a large part of the population consists of employees and analyzes major dimensions of the employment relation: the number of people who will offer themselves for employment, the number of hours they will work per week and per year, the deployment of the labor force among the many specialized occupations in the economy, the determination of wage rates and other terms of employment for each occupation, and the distribution of total national income between employees and others. It is concerned also with the special institutions that have grown up around the employment relation, notably trade unionism and collective bargaining, and with the degree to which these institutions modify the supply and compensation of labor. Labor economics is not confined, however, to workers who happen to be organized or to the lower occupational strata of the population. It is concerned with. *all* labor effort, with employees at every occupational level, including the effort exerted by employers and self-employed persons.

The predominance of employer-employee relations is associated with the rise of modern industry and large production units, which is still limited to certain regions of the world. Most of the world's population remains in the preindustrial era. In most countries of Asia, Africa, and Latin America, 60 to 80 percent of the labor force is engaged in agriculture. The remainder are mainly petty traders, service workers, or independent artisans. Only a small fraction of the population works in factories and other modern enterprises.

The great transformation which ushered in the industrial society began in Great Britain in the latter half of the eighteenth century. During the nineteenth century the movement spread to a dozen other countries. Accelerated industrial development began around 1830 in France, Belgium, and the United States, around 1850 in Germany, around 1870 in Sweden and Japan, and around 1890 in Canada and Russia. Today the industrialized world includes almost all of Europe (including the USSR), North America, Australia, and Japan. Mexico, Brazil, Argentina, and Chile are also nearing this stage of development.

SOME FEATURES
OF THE
INDUSTRIAL ECONOMY

Today's industrial countries differ widely in size, climate, geographic characteristics, language and cultural traditions, and form of government. Yet they also have many features in common. Similarities in the economic matrix give labor problems a family resemblance throughout the industrial world. These common features include:

1. *The Pattern of Employment.* Most of the labor force is employed in manufacturing, construction, public utilities, and govern-

ment. Agriculture employs only a declining minority; and while employment in trade remains substantial, trade is carried on increasingly by mass distributors rather than small shopkeepers. The economy is characterized by large production units, which employ hundreds or thousands of people and often use large amounts of capital equipment per worker. Occupations are highly specialized and diversified, with many jobs requiring substantial skill and training. Many people work in clerical, technical, and professional occupations, and this white-collar segment of the labor force grows considerably faster than the blue-collar segment. A description of the United States? Yes, but a description also of Sweden, the USSR, and Japan.

2. *The Level of Output and Incomes.* Large, capital-intensive production units applying modern technology yield high output per worker, and this provides higher real incomes and living standards. This accounts for the mystique of industrialization throughout the underdeveloped world. One can argue over the question how much more the American worker produces than the Soviet worker. But there is no doubt that either produces more than the average worker in Uganda or Indonesia. A large and growing national output, of course, may produce controversy over the division of the gains. How much should go to employees as against owners of capital? How much should go to each group of wage and salary earners? These issues are more intense under industrialism than in a static, agricultural society where incomes are assigned by tradition and paternal authority.

3. *The Dependent Status of Employees.* From one standpoint, the shift from self-employed farmer or artisan to employed wage earner liberates the individual. He is free to move about in search of work, to better himself, to work his way up the occupational ladder. But in other ways it reduces his independence. The wage earner must find work in order to live, while the farmer can always live after a fashion from his own output; and when he is employed the details of his work are closely regulated. Someone else specifies the times at which work is to be done, the nature of the task, the materials and equipment to be used, the pace of work, and the expected quantity and quality of output. Above the worker stand all the layers of management, from first-line supervisor to company president.

4. *Administration and the Web of Rules.* Dependence does not stop with the worker. The supervisor is himself under higher authority, and so are the general foreman, the plant superintendent, and the vice-president in charge of production. Even the company president is responsible to a board of directors. A large enterprise is bound together by an elaborate hierarchy of authority, which specifies the powers and responsibilities of everyone from company president to laborer.

It is bound together also by a network of rules governing output and cost targets; products, equipment, and production methods; types and amounts of compensation; employment, promotion, discharge; and many other things. At a particular time most of these rules are taken as fixed, and changes are occurring only at the margin; so one is apt not to realize their extent and complexity. But reading a fifty-page union contract reminds one how complicated the internal government of a large business can be. When we say that the industrial worker must learn discipline, we mean that he must know and observe this web of rules, in addition to submitting to the personal authority of the supervisor.

5. *Worker Protest and Labor Organization.* Workers new to industry often find it difficult to submit to rules that they have had no hand in creating and that may appear harsh and arbitrary. So the early stages of industrialization are usually attended by labor unrest and spontaneous individual protest. This may show up in high absenteeism and turnover, disobedience to the foreman, and underperformance on the job. There may also be sporadic strikes and riots by large numbers of workers. This was common in early British and American industry and is common today in the newly industrializing countries.

Eventually, however, protest is channeled into continuing organizations and takes a more effective if less violent form. Prominent among these organizations are the trade unions, whose tactics normally include both political action and defense of the workers' interests in the plant. Fitting trade unions into the social structure and defining their functions relative to those of industrial management and of government is a characteristic problem of industrial society.

6. *Insecurity and Mobility.* An industrial economy is by definition a changing economy. Products, methods of production, the location of industry, and the demand for specific skills are in constant flux. Without these changes the economy cannot continue to advance to ever higher levels of productivity and income.

These dynamic shifts keep open the frontier of opportunity. The new plants and industries are typically more efficient than those that they supplant. They provide more productive jobs at higher wages. But the opposite side of the coin is a high degree of personal insecurity. Plants fail and are shut down, products and services become obsolete, jobs disappear through technical change, location shifts leave stranded populations in depressed areas. The worker has to be quick on his feet to avoid being stranded and to seize new opportunities as they appear. Even if he is quick and lucky, this enforced jobhopping involves anxiety and dissatisfaction, and it leads workers and unions to be preoccupied with the problem of job security.

7. *The Pervasiveness of Labor Markets.* Under slavery or feudalism workers can be ordered to the places where they are needed. But in a complex industrial economy, coercion is inefficient, quite apart from its infringement on human dignity and independence. Even in

planned economies, direct allocation of workers to jobs has been used only in periods of national emergency. The general rule is that each worker hunts his own jobs and each plant recruits its own workers. Employers use wages as the main magnet for attracting labor, and income is a major consideration in workers' minds when choosing jobs. There are markets for labor, though usually not very efficient ones. The wage for each kind of labor is heavily influenced, if not fully determined, by supply and demand conditions in the market. This is what brings the study of labor into touch with the central core of economic theory.

In stressing the resemblance among industrial economies, one should not overlook important points of difference. There are differences, for example, in the strength and activities of trade unions. There are differences also in the balance of power among unions, industrial managers, and government officials. In some countries management still lays down the rules of industrial employment with little hindrance from any source. In others management is forced to negotiate with strong unions but is largely free of government control. In still others, government participates actively in setting terms of employment, and in some countries it has the dominant voice.

SOME KEY ECONOMIC ISSUES

What major issues arise from the employment relation? At least seven such issues can be distinguished:

1. *Maintaining Adequate Total Demand for Labor.* This is a chronic problem for economies in the early stages of industrialization, which usually have a surplus of underemployed labor in agriculture. It is a recurrent problem for industrialized capitalist economies, whose growth is interrupted occasionally by general depression. Depression cuts national output and reduces the incomes of workers along with those of most other people. It usually means a sharp reduction of new investment, the major source of economic progress and higher living standards. It reduces the opportunity for people to change jobs and make occupational progress. It leads to adoption of unwise government policies, which are presented with plausible arguments as depression remedies.

For these reasons almost everyone now subscribes to "full employment" as an economic goal. But how full is "full"? Does full employment mean an average of 2 percent of the labor force unemployed between jobs, or an average of 5 percent? Does it mean trying to maintain about as many vacant jobs as there are unemployed workers, or an actual excess of vacancies? The higher the employment target, the more likely it is that there will be consistent upward pressure on the price level. Should one worry more about unemployment or about inflation? One can scarcely expect union leaders to give the same answer as pensioners or insurance executives.

2. *Developing Effective Labor Markets.*   Ours is a market economy. To a greater degree than most other countries we have succeeded in establishing free choice of occupation by individuals, free choice of goods by consumers, and free access to markets by businessmen. The market mechanism is far from ideal, however, and labor markets are less efficient than most others.

Workers presently market their labor under serious handicaps of ignorance, misinformation, and uncertainty. Employers are not much better off in their effort to locate the best workers available. Job hunting will always be something of a game of blindman's buff because of the innate complexity of the employment process. It should be possible, however, to enlarge and improve the state employment services and to find other ways of raising the plane of competition in the labor market. A better matching of individual capacities with job requirements would improve productive efficiency and increase national output.

Efficient labor marketing is needed in any economy, developed or underdeveloped, capitalist or communist. Russia has had a continuing problem of getting workers to move to the places where new industries are expanding and to stay on the job in those places. Labor turnover has remained high despite all efforts to discourage it. Compulsory controls over the movement of labor have not been enforced seriously except in wartime. For the most part each Russian plant manager has to compete for labor in the market, using a package of wage and nonwage incentives somewhat similar to that of the capitalist employer.

3. *Training, Organizing, and Motivating the Labor Force.*   The labor market is supposed to achieve a distribution of the labor force among industries, plants, and localities which corresponds to the detailed pattern of demand for labor. But this is only a first step. Workers as they come through the hiring office are a conglomerate of isolated individuals, not a working team. They have to be trained, organized, supervised, and motivated to perform efficiently in the production process. They must be subjected to a new network of rules and controls, a new industrial discipline quite unlike that of an agricultural society.

The importance and generality of this problem has been well stated by Kerr and Siegel:

> The process of industrialization may then be seen as involving in the productive sector the addition or the changing of a complex body of

working rules . . . concerned with the recruitment of a labor force, with the training of that labor force in the myriad skills required by the advanced division of labor, with the locating of workers in some appropriate pattern of geographical, industrial, and occupational dispersion. It involves the setting of rules on times to work and not to work, on pace and quality of work, on method and amount to pay, on movement into and out of work and from one position to another. It involves rules pertaining to the maintenance of continuity in the work process (so intimately related to the maintenance of stability in the society)—the attempted minimization of individual or organized revolt, the provision of views of the world, of ideological orientations, of beliefs, the introduction of some checks on the individual insecurity inherent in an industrial order. The structuring of this web of rule must be undertaken regardless of the form of industrialization, in Russia and the United States alike.[1]

4.   *Determining Wage Rates and Labor Income.*   This set of rules has such a venerable tradition in economics that it may be singled out for special mention. The wage problem comprises at least four subproblems:

a.   *Determining the General Wage Level.*   Within the enterprise, how much of sales revenue can fairly be claimed by labor as against other operating expenses and profits? When should the company's wage level be raised, and on what grounds? Looking at the economy as a whole, what should be the level of money wages and real wages? What is a proper split-up between labor and property incomes? How fast should the national wage level be raised over the course of time, and why?

b.   *Determining Relative Wage Rates for Different Types of Work.*   How is the national wage total to be divided among the individuals comprising the labor force? Within a particular plant or industry, should the most skilled job pay 20 percent more than the least skilled, or 50 percent more, or 100 percent more? Should some industries pay higher wages than others, and how much higher? Should workers earn more in some geographical regions than in others, or more in large cities than in small towns? The relationship among wages in different occupations, industries, and areas is commonly termed the problem of "wage structure" or "wage differentials."

c.   *Deciding the Method of Wage Payment.*   The leading issue here is between payment on the basis of hours worked and payment on the basis of output ("piece work" or "incentive" payment). This issue arouses strong feeling among workers and is decided differently in different industries and countries. Piece-rate payment is used more

---

[1] Clark Kerr and Abraham Siegel, "The Structuring of the Labor Force in Industrial Society: New Dimensions and New Questions," *Industrial and Labor Relations Review,* VIII (January, 1955), 163.

widely in Russia than in the United States. Within the United States, some industries use piece rate payment exclusively, while others do not use it at all.

    d. *Deciding the Form of Workers' Income Receipts.* The national wage bill may go almost entirely into direct wage payments, or a substantial share may go into old-age pensions, family allowances, medical and hospital services, unemployment compensation, and other indirect benefits. In some European countries these indirect benefits are one-third to one-half as large as direct wage payments. In the United States, where they are less fully developed, the proportion is approaching one-fifth.

    5. *Balancing Producer and Consumer Satisfactions.* There is an obvious conflict of interest between the workers engaged in producing a particular product and the consumers of the product. It is to the workers' interest to work short hours, at a leisurely pace, amid pleasant surroundings, and to receive high wages plus ample fringe benefits. These things raise costs, however, and must be paid for by consumers through higher prices. How can one strike a proper balance between the interests of the two groups?

    Wage earners, moreover, form close to half of the consuming public and salary earners another quarter. There is thus a conflict of interest *within* the wage and salary group. People can work longer and harder as producers in order to enjoy more goods as consumers, or they can take things easier and consume less.

    Two "automatic" solutions of this problem appear in economic writings. The independent producer consuming his own product—Crusoe on his island—can presumably strike a direct balance between effort and consumption. He can judge the point at which the effort of knocking down another coconut or catching another fish would outweigh the satisfaction from eating it. Subsistence farmers, who form a large part of the world's population, are in much the same situation.

    In a complex industrial society, it can be argued that the problem is still solved by the normal working of the labor market. Each worker, by choosing his employer and occupation, can get long hours or short hours, heavy work or easy work, pleasant or disagreeable conditions. Greater effort or unpleasantness will presumably have to be compensated by higher wages. The worker will choose the combination of wages and working conditions that best meets his personal preferences.

    There is something to this line of argument, but one should not rely on it too heavily. The labor market is a rather blunt instrument even for determining relative wage rates. It is even less adequate for determining optimum hours, proper work speeds, and desirable working conditions. Despite our best efforts to improve the market mechanism, it will remain necessary to supplement it by institutional regulation.

    6. *Protecting Against Predictable Risks.* The industrial worker

depends heavily on a regular flow of money income. This dependence is increasing with the growth of credit facilities and installment buying. Anything which cuts off the weekly paycheck threatens not only the worker's dinner table but also his house, car, furniture, and household appliances.

The reasons why the stream of income may fail are well known and many of them are predictable. It is certain that everyone must grow old, and probable life spans can be predicted fairly precisely. There are good figures on the incidence of industrial accidents and on various types of disabling illnesses. We know that there is a certain minimum of unemployment even in good years. It seems sheerest common sense to develop ways of protecting workers' incomes against such contingencies. This not only benefits the people concerned but also increases the stability of the economy. There is room for argument over the desirable level of protection, the proper balance between private insurance funds and government systems, and the percentage of cost that should be borne by workers instead of by employers or consumers. The need for a comprehensive network of protective measures, however, is no longer seriously questioned.

7. *Assuring a Minimum Level of Living.* There is also increasing consensus that no member of the community should be allowed to fall below some minimum level of subsistence. Social security and private insurance systems, minimum-wage legislation, farm income supplements, and state and local relief systems are all expressions of this concern. Arguments are not so much over principle as over feasible support levels and detailed institutional arrangements.

This issue is usually discussed in a labor course because it touches many wage-earning families. But it is not exclusively or even mainly a problem of manual workers. The group below the poverty line also includes rural families living on inferior land, who have lower living standards than any sizable group in the urban population; broken homes containing no wage earner, or in which the principal wage earner is disabled; and many older people drawn from all occupational levels. Inability to work and produce, rather than low wage levels, is now the main source of poverty in the United States.

MECHANISMS OF ADJUSTMENT: INSTITUTIONS AND THE MARKET

Two main mechanisms are available for resolving these issues—the competitive labor market and institutional rules imposed by business concerns, trade unions, and government. Though these may be regarded as alternatives at a theoretical level, in practice they will always be found operating together. Even Russia, which might seem to be an extreme case of government control, has important elements of a competitive labor market. Individual establishments recruit labor as best they can, workers move about the country in search of better jobs, occupational and regional wage differentials are adjusted to lure workers to the places where labor is scarcest.

One should not assume either that market forces and institutional rules necessarily conflict. They may do so, but they may also work in the same direction, and institutional regulation may simply ratify a market decision. We shall argue at a later point that this is largely true of wage determination in the United States. Both the general wage level and relative wage rates for different jobs are determined mainly by supply and demand pressures in the labor market. Unions largely take credit for wage increases that were "in the cards" on economic grounds. It is politically necessary for a union to do this, just as it is necessary for whichever party holds power in Washington to take credit for business prosperity which it may have done little to create. But the fact that under collective bargaining the union is entitled to *announce* a wage increase does not constitute evidence that it *caused* the increase.

The question of how far labor conditions are or should be determined by institutional rules rather than by market pressures rouses strong emotions and leads people into extreme positions. One school of thought tends to glorify the market, to assert that it does or could adequately regulate terms of employment, and that institutional "interference" is bound to be either ineffective or harmful. At the other pole, some people write off the market as ineffective and defend the necessity and beneficence of institutional controls. Reality is certainly more complicated than these extreme views would suggest. The labor market seems to perform some functions quite effectively, while in other areas its performance is less satisfactory. Starting with as little bias as possible, we must try to discover where the market performs well and where it breaks down, to explain why the relative importance of market and institutional regulation differs from country to country and time to time, and to analyze what happens when the two mechanisms pull in opposite direction. This is the task of the whole book; but a few preliminary comments will help to set the stage.

The Role of the Labor Market

Elementary economics texts describe the operation of a competitive labor market and the results it might be expected to yield. The broad argument is that, given free and informed competition among workers and employers, each worker must be paid the value of his contribution to production. He cannot be paid more, because the employer could not continue to operate. He will not be paid less, because the employer would be making abnormal profits and some other alert businessman would enter the industry and bid up the price of labor. There is thus little scope for controversy or bargaining over the price of labor.

This is of course a very simplified and idealized picture. It assumes many small employers competing for labor, no collusion among employers or workers, adequate channels of information, and a number of other things. It is no secret that actual labor markets depart considerably from this competitive ideal. Many employers are large and the worker's choice is often restricted to one or a few companies; employers often get together on wage rates and on policies which make it hard for workers to change employers; channels of information are poor and there is no effective central clearinghouse for labor; the exchange of a machinist's labor for a "package" of wages and working conditions is a more complicated transaction than setting a price on a loaf of bread; workers dislike changing jobs and, when forced to do so, they hunt new jobs in a haphazard and ill-informed way; during periods of heavy unemployment the worker's bargaining power—which depends basically on his power to change jobs—is seriously reduced.

Despite these deficiencies, the labor market is a reasonably effective instrument both for determining relative wage rates and for raising the general wage level as national output rises. The great increase in real wages in the United States over the past century has not been due in any large measure to collective bargaining or government decree. It has occurred mainly because employers were able and impelled to keep raising their wage offers in the market year after year: able because development of new machinery and production methods was steadily increasing output per man-hour; impelled because the labor market forces each employer to bid against others to hold his share of the labor supply. The labor market is the main mechanism by which increases in productivity have been translated into higher wages and living standards.

The market also does reasonably well in determining relative wage levels for different plants, industries, occupations, and regions. One can always find many queer or inequitable wages rates; but viewed broadly and over the long run, the national wage structure is not unreasonable. Moreover, it is evolving over the course of time in a way that is understandable on economic grounds. Wage inequalities of every sort are diminishing and this is due mainly, though not exclusively, to changing supply and demand conditions.

Finally, the labor market is the only device we have for sorting out many millions of workers with varying skills and interests among the multitude of different jobs in the economy. Any attempt to do this by administrative methods, in addition to encroaching on personal liberty, would be hopelessly cumbersome and inefficient. Even communist countries, as noted earlier, rely mainly on wage inducements in the market to secure a desirable allocation of the labor force.

Recognition that the labor market does some things well, however, should not blind us to the things which it does poorly or cannot do at all. It is not highly effective, for example, in regulating working conditions—physical conditions, safety and sanitation, work speeds, treatment by supervisors, and other personnel policies. The market still sets limits in the sense that, if plant conditions become too bad, workers have the option of leaving. But these limits may be quite wide. Working conditions are hard for the market to evaluate and control because they are intangible, qualitative, hard for the worker to discover before he is on the job, and hard to bargain about on an individual basis. Workers conclude that the effective remedy is not individual bargaining or quitting (the market solution) but group pressure through a union.

The market cannot provide security against arbitrary demotion or discharge by supervisors, nor can it establish equitable rules concerning layoff, rehiring, and promotion. These require administrative procedures within the enterprise. The market is not very good at bringing about marked changes in employment practice, such as a shift from a ten-hour to an eight-hour day. It is not good at establishing minimum standards which, in order to survive, must be enforced on all employers simultaneously. Examples are rules concerning work by women and children, safety and health standards, and minimum wage legislation. Nor is it a good device in areas where there are substantial economies in collective action. Pensions, unemployment compensation, and other income security devices could be set up entirely by individual employers and, if enough employers adopted them, the market might force others to follow. There are clear economies, however, in applying insurance principles to the entire labor force through government security programs. Finally, the labor market obviously cannot improve itself. Organized effort is required to mitigate the structural defects noted earlier and to enable the market to perform its natural functions better.

An important and irremovable source of difficulty is that most workers regard resort to the market—i.e., a change of employers—as a disaster rather than an opportunity. They typically want to continue with their present employer. Advice that they can improve their employer's behavior by leaving him they regard as academic. They prefer to change the employer's behavior without leaving him, and for this they need union organization.

The Place of Institutional Rules

Organizational rules may be imposed to override market determinations that are displeasing to workers or employers. More importantly, however, they are a way of reaching decisions at points where the market is imprecise or ineffective. They supplement the market mechanism at least as much as they compete with it.

The main contenders for rule-making authority are the business firm, the trade union, and the state. Adherents of each of these often regard it as the normal rule-making body, entitled in principle to exclusive authority. Many businessmen still regard management as the proper group to decide on terms of employment and resent "outside interference" by unions or government. To the trade unionist, it is an article of faith that conditions of employment should be regulated by union-management agreement. Socialists tend to regard government as the logical guardian of workers' welfare.

Looking at the world as a whole, however, it is clear that no one system of rule making can be regarded as inevitable. This point has been cogently argued by Kerr and Siegel:

> Given these three contestants, there are seven general systems for distributing the essential power to make rules governing the labor force. Three of these possible rule-making relationships may be designated as monistic, in the sense that the rules . . . are set primarily by one of the contestants. . . . (1) The employer may set the rules, and . . . may follow a policy of paternalism, as in Japan before World War II, or a policy of forced worker self-dependence, as in England in the early period of industrialization. A conceivable, though much less likely actual possibility is that (2) the worker may give the directions. His "union" then becomes more or less of a producers' cooperative (as in sectors of the Israeli economy). . . . (3) The state may issue the commands, as it does in Russia and in all the nations within the Russian orbit. The "unions" there are essentially "agents of the state" with only such authority as may be granted them by the state.
>
> Three additional systems may be called dualistic, since two of the contestants share rule-making power in the industrial sector. (4) This power may be shared, as in the United States prior to the recent rise in state interest, primarily by the employer and the unions whose relationships may range from reserved tolerance to secret collusion. (5) Or the employer and the state may divide the authority between them. The power of the state may be ranged alongside that of the employer, as in Nazi Germany, or in opposition, as in Mexico or Argentina or Guatemala in recent years; or the state may vacillate back and forth as in France and Italy. . . . (6) Or the state and the worker may participate jointly in rule-making, as in the nationalized industries in Great Britain.
>
> Finally (7), the three contestants may share rule-making power in a

pluralistic system . . . as evidenced in Scandinavia, the United States, and several of the member nations of the British Commonwealth.[2]

This last situation, where all three parties have a finger in the pie, seems to be characteristic of countries with a long history of democratic government and industrial development. This group includes the Scandinavian countries, the Netherlands, West Germany, Britain, Canada, the United States, Australia, and a few others. Taking the world as a whole, it is an exceptional rather than a typical situation, though a number of other countries—France, Italy, Mexico, Japan, India—may evolve gradually in the same direction.

Though all three groups share rule-making power in these economies, each has certain areas of decision within which it has a comparative advantage and therefore a preponderant voice. Even in strongly unionized economies management retains a large measure of administrative authority. It typically has exclusive control over, or at least the right to take initial action concerning, production organization, production methods, production volume and labor requirements, recruitment and hiring of labor, assignment of workers to specific jobs, appointment of supervisors, determination of work speeds, establishment of shop rules and application of penalties for violating them, layoffs, and other personnel matters. Management acts; the union protests or appeals. The union may eventually secure a reversal of the decision, but the power to act retains much of its pristine potency.

The specific function of unionism is to police in-plant decisions and actions of management. This means negotiating a general framework of rules within which management action is confined (the union contract) and insuring equitable application of these rules to individual cases (the grievance procedure). Rules concerning the conditions under which a worker may be penalized, demoted, or discharged are of prime importance, as are rules concerning layoffs, rehiring, promotion, and other matters of job tenure. Though unions also do much to influence wages and working conditions, their distinctive function is to establish a system of industrial jurisprudence through which the individual can seek redress from harmful decisions by management.

Government has a comparative advantage in establishing minimum standards which are considered sufficiently important to be enforced on everyone. This may mean either bringing laggards up to the market level or establishing standards in areas where the market is not very effective. Government is an efficient mechanism for devising protection against loss of income through unemployment, old age, total or partial disability, and other causes. It is now generally agreed that government has responsibility for maintaining adequate total demand for labor.

[2] Kerr and Siegel, "The Structuring of Labor Force," p. 163.

Finally, only government can prescribe rules to govern union and employer conduct in collective bargaining.

The Order of Discussion

In such a complex area there is no preordained sequence of discussion. One can deal with institutional arrangements first and market phenomena later, or vice versa. Much thought and experimentation has convinced the author that it makes most sense to start with the economics of labor markets—the determinants of labor supply and demand, employment and unemployment, wage rates and income distribution. These matters are examined in Part I. The discussion is not limited to unionized workers or even to manual workers, who are now a minority of the American labor force. It covers the full range of occupations and earnings, from farm laborers to brain surgeons. It uses the standard tools of microeconomic analysis, with due attention to the ways in which labor markets differ from commodity markets. It ranges sufficiently far afield to deal with such issues as the relation between equality of occupational opportunity and the financing of higher education, and the reasons for the unfavorable occupational and income position of black workers relative to white workers. It incorporates the growing volume of sophisticated research on employment and earnings throughout the 1960s. And it explores policy issues in such areas as wages, hours, poverty, employment discrimination, economic insecurity, training and retraining, and labor market organization.

In Part II we examine trade unionism and collective bargaining as economic institutions: the development and characteristics of American trade unions, bargaining arrangements and bargaining tactics vis-à-vis employers, the content and administration of the resulting agreements, the legal framework within which collective bargaining operates, and proposals for changes in this framework by further legislation. A chapter on industrial relations in other countries underlines the point that industrial relations systems are the result of historical circumstance rather than abstract logic. Our own arrangements are not fixed or inevitable but have changed and are continuing to change over the course of time.

Part III is in a sense a synthesis of the two preceding parts. The central issue is this: how have the collective bargaining arrangements described in Part II influenced the labor market phenomena described in Part I? What has been the impact of collective bargaining on hours of work, pace of work, mechanization, productivity, the general level of wages, relative wages for different occupations, workers' job security, and individual opportunity for employment and promotion? These are tricky questions. They involve a comparison of what is with what "might have been" in the absence of collective bargaining. But what might have been cannot be determined precisely and to everyone's satisfaction. We must wrestle with the problem as best we can and try at the end to compile a reasonable balance sheet of the economic consequences of trade unionism.

Discussion Questions

1. What features of modern industrialism give rise to labor problems? What kinds of labor problems might arise even in a purely agricultural economy?
2. During the nineteenth century some writers predicted that with the growth of industry the population would soon consist mainly of manual workers. Why has this not happened?
3. "Development of strong trade unions usually takes a half century or more after the appearance of modern industry." Do you agree? If so, what reasons can you give for the slow development of union strength?
4. What are the principal "labor problems" in a general social sense? Would you expect these problems to differ substantially in the United States, the USSR, Japan?
5. Why is the labor market usually supplemented by institutional rules in determining wages and conditions of employment?
6. "The operation of the labor market has done more over the past century to improve wages and working conditions in the United States than trade unions and government together." Discuss.
7. Looking at the whole range of occupations and earnings in the American economy, which, in your opinion, are:
   (a) the most important phenomena to be explained?
   (b) the most important issues of government policy?

Reading Suggestions

The best brief introduction to the range of issues discussed in this book is probably Phelps Brown, E. H., *The Economics of Labor*. New Haven: Yale University Press, 1962. For a comparative view of the impact of industrialization on employment relations, see Kerr C., J. Dunlop, C. Myers, and F. Harbison, *Industrialism and Industrial Man.* Cambridge: Harvard University Press, 1960. On labor problems in the less-developed countries, see Galenson, Walter, *Labor and Economic Development.* New York: John Wiley & Sons, Inc., 1959. Also: *Labor in Developing Economies.* Berkeley and Los Angeles: University of California Press, 1962. On wage setting and labor mobility in the USSR see Bergson, Abram, *The Economics of Soviet Planning.* New Haven: Yale University Press, 1964.

ECONOMICS
OF THE
LABOR
MARKET

I

Economics is concerned with the way in which the productive services of land, labor, and capital equipment are brought together to produce a national output of a certain size and composition and with the way in which this output is distributed among the participants. Labor economics focuses on the supply, use, and remuneration of labor as a factor of production.

The labor aspects of production, however, are integrally related to the process as a whole. In explaining the quantity of *labor demanded* by particular firms and industries, we rely heavily on production theory. Particular demands for labor reflect demands for the products for which labor is used, plus the supplies of cooperating factors and the known techniques of production.

The determinants of *labor supply* are more nearly an exclusive province of the labor economist. The dimensions of supply include the number of persons who choose to enter the labor force, their hours of work per week or per year, the energy and motivation of the labor force, and the skills acquired through training and experience. On each of these points we have a growing body of information.

The demand for and supply of specific skills meet in the *market* to determine wage rates for particular jobs and the average wage level for the economy. Here as elsewhere in economics, demand, supply, and price are interdependent. Wages help to call forth labor supply and to determine where particular workers will seek employment. Wage rates also, given particular demand curves for labor, determine how much labor each employer will be willing to hire.

Apart from its wage-determining functions, the labor market is important in its own right. Whether employers who need labor and workers who need jobs are able to locate each other quickly, whether square pegs drop readily into square holes, whether workers' preferences and skills adapt themselves slowly or rapidly to trends in labor demand, all affect the efficiency of the economy. We shall need to examine how well our labor markets perform in these respects, and what might be done to improve them.

All the issues examined in Part I are interdependent. But since it is impossible to discuss everything at once, we shall proceed by stages. In Chapter 2 we analyze the personal decisions which underlie labor supply: decisions about whether to work at all, how many hours to work, and where to work. Chapter 3 deals with labor demand, emphasizing particularly the large shifts in demand for various types of skill over the past half century. The way in which demand and supply interact to determine the number employed and the rate of pay in each occupation is the theme of Chapter 4. We first analyze the operation of a purely competitive market and then consider the effect of various restraints on competition: restrictions on admission to some occupations, wage regulation, the "monopsony power" of large employers.

It is well known that simple theoretical models do less than full justice to the complexity of actual labor markets. The employment bargain is complex, involving many dimensions other than wages. Market institutions are poorly developed, knowledge is imperfect, access to many occupations requires expensive education and job training, and a surplus of available workers over vacant jobs may reduce the worker's bargaining power. These complications are explored in Chapter 5. In Chapter 6 we consider the main possibilities of labor market improvement: better clearinghouse facilities, more equal access to educational opportunities, retraining programs for adults who lack marketable skills, and reduction of employment discrimination on racial and other grounds.

The remaining chapters of Part I deal with the wage results which emerge from labor markets. Chapter 7 discusses the movement of the money wage level in relation to employment and prices, the possibility of "cost-push" inflation, and the question whether government can influence the wage level appreciably by persuasion or other measures. Chapter 8 analyzes the division of the national income between labor and capital and presents data on distribution trends in the major industrial countries over the past century. In most countries, the labor share of income has increased, and we suggest some possible reasons for this phenomenon. Different jobs carry widely differing rates of pay. Chapter 9 analyzes the main reasons for these differences and summarizes the information on whether they have been increasing or decreasing over time. The concluding Chapter 10 focuses on the distribution of income among households: how many families presently fall in each income bracket, the main reasons for income inequality, whether inequality is growing or diminishing, the meaning and extent of "poverty" in the United States, and the main lines of attack on the poverty problem.

THE
SUPPLY
OF   2
LABOR

There are many reasons for an interest in labor supply. An individual's decisions about education, job training, occupation, and employer are among the most consequential decisions of his life. A man's job mainly determines the size of his income, which, in turn, limits his place of residence, his general style of life, and the opportunities open to his children. Apart from income, the satisfactions (or dissatisfactions) enjoyed directly on the job are a major component of personal welfare.

WHAT
IS
LABOR?

Labor resembles nonhuman agents of production in some respects but differs from them in others. First, man is the object as well as the author of economic activity. The test of an economy's performance is the net satisfaction that it yields to the population. The relevant satisfactions (and dissatisfactions) include those associated directly with work as well as those derived from consumption. A machine used in production does not experience pleasure or pain. A human being does. In appraising a change in working hours, work speeds, or work methods, one must consider the effect on workers' satisfaction as well as on production costs and prices to the consumer.

Second, land and capital are owned by outside agents, but except under the unusual condition of slavery, the worker owns himself. He decides the direction in which his productive capacity is to be deployed. He decides (or his parents do) how much to invest in general education and vocational training, and he receives any increased income resulting from such training. Because of limited knowledge and foresight, limited facilities for educational loans, and the fact that individuals must reckon in terms of posttax income, there is probably less investment in human beings than would be desirable from a national standpoint.

In other respects, however, labor is analogous to capital. Like capital, it can be defined either as a *stock* of productive instruments existing at a point of time, or as a *flow* of services yielded by these instruments over time. In the stock sense, "labor" is the totality of people counted to be in the labor force, with whatever skills and productive capacity they possess at the moment. This is the "human capital" of the nation, a very old concept in economics. Adam Smith, in listing the components of a nation's capital included "the acquired and useful abilities of all the inhabitants or members of the society." [1] The individuals included in this stock are heterogeneous and difficult to add up in any meaningful way; but this is equally true of machines, buildings, and other capital goods.

In the flow sense, "labor" is the number of man-hours available or used in production over a period of time. Over *what* period of time? We usually say a year, and with good reason. Hours per year may change without any change in weekly hours of work because of changes in vacation allowances, paid holidays, sick leave, and other arrangements. A yearly calculation is helpful also in taking account of seasonal workers, part-time workers, and others whose activity needs to be measured over a full annual cycle.

The stock of people in the labor force is fixed at any moment, and

[1] Smith goes on to say, "The acquisition of such talents, by the maintenance of the acquirer during his education, study, or apprenticeship, always costs a real expence, which is a capital fixed and realized, as it were, in his person. Those talents, as they make a part of his fortune, so do they likewise of that of the society to which he belongs. The improved dexterity of a workman may be considered in the same light as a machine or instrument of trade which facilitates and abridges labour, and which, though it costs a certain expence, repays that expence with a profit." The parallel with modern discussions of "human capital" is obvious. (Adam Smith, *The Wealth of Nations*, II, chap. 1.)

grows rather regularly over time with the growth of population. The flow of man-hours, however, rises less rapidly than the labor force. The reason is that in a growing economy average hours worked per year typically fall as per capita income rises. Between 1929 and 1965, for example, the U. S. labor force increased by 58 percent, but available man-hours rose by only 25 percent.

While the aggregate flow of labor services measured in man-hours is a significant figure, it veils the fact that these services are extremely heterogeneous. The flow includes man-hours of corporation presidents' time, research chemists' time, bricklayers' time, farm laborers' time. This would be less troublesome if the proportion of each occupational group in the working population remained unchanged; but this is not the case. In recent decades the percentage of managerial, professional, and technical workers has risen substantially while the proportion of low-skilled workers has declined. The average *quality* of the man-hour flow has increased. Labor supply in the sense of *productive potential* has risen more rapidly than the number of man-hours would suggest.

Some economists have tried to take account of this by dividing the man-hour flow into a number of occupational levels. In adding up total hours, each level is given a *weight* corresponding to its relative wage rate. Thus, if skilled manual workers earn on the average twice as much as laborers, each unskilled hour is counted as one and each skilled hour as two. Similarly, an engineer's time might have a weight of four, and so on. Such procedures are necessarily crude. They assume that rates of pay are a good indicator of productive contribution. Besides, it is impossible to distinguish more than a few occupational levels without making the task unmanageable. Even so, these experiments are interesting and useful. As one would expect, the "adjusted" man-hour totals for the United States rise a good deal faster over time than the crude totals. This would be true in any progressive industrial economy—in France, or Japan, or the USSR.

The heterogeneity of the man-hour flow has another consequence, familiar, but still requiring emphasis. There is no such thing as *the* demand for labor, *the* market for labor, *the* price of labor. There are tens of millions of employees and millions of employing units. There are hundreds of thousands of submarkets for labor of different types in different locations, and a corresponding variety of wage rates. In principle, each of these markets is linked to others by possibilities of substitution on the part of both workers and employers. How close and effective these linkages are in practice, whether the barriers between submarkets are rising or declining over time, what might be done to improve the operation of the market network, are key issues in labor economics,

The main dimensions of labor supply, then, are the *number of people* who choose to enter the labor force, the *hours worked* per year by these people, and the *quality* of these man-hours. We proceed to examine what determines numbers, hours, and quality.

PARTICIPATION
IN THE
LABOR FORCE

Definition and Measurement

The percentage of a country's population, or of a subgroup in the population, that is in the labor force at a particular time is termed its *labor force participation rate,* usually shortened to "participation rate." Measurement of the labor force involves complicated problems, which can only be suggested here.[2] In the United States, a complete enumeration is made every ten years in connection with the decennial census.[3] Between censuses the Bureau of the Census conducts a monthly survey of a small sample of households carefully selected to represent different sections of the country. On the basis of information obtained from these households, estimates are made of the total labor force, employment, and unemployment in the country as a whole. This *Monthly Report on the Labor Force* is the standard source for current labor force information, though it is not quite as accurate as a complete census count.

An individual is counted as being in the labor force if he is able to work and either has a job or is "actively seeking" work. This apparently simple definition leaves considerable room for doubt in many cases. What about a man who says he is able to work, but whom employers judge to be so incapable that they are unwilling to hire him? What about a man who is not "actively" seeking work because he believes there are no jobs available in his area, but who would accept a job if offered? What about a coal miner in a depressed mining area,

---

[2] The reader interested in these problems and the efforts of statisticians to overcome them should consult Clarence D. Long, *Labor Force, Income and Employment* (New York: National Bureau of Economic Research, 1950); John D. Durand, *The Labor Force in the United States, 1890–1960* (New York: Social Science Research Council, 1948); and A. J. Jaffe and Charles D. Stewart, *Manpower Resources and Utilization: Principles of Working Force Analysis* (New York: John Wiley & Sons, Inc., 1951).

[3] The census is rightly regarded as one of the most accurate of statistical sources. A July 1953 issue of the *New York Herald Tribune,* however, reported that a Chicago census enumerator had added several thousand nonexistent names to his lists during the 1950 census and made up fictitious characteristics for these nonexistent people. When asked the reason for this, he replied, "I thought we had a quota to meet."

who is willing to take a mining job but no other kind of work? Added to these logical problems is the fact that the census interviewer usually sees only the housewife and has to take her word about the status of other people in the household. This leaves room for a good deal of misunderstanding and faulty reporting. Another problem is that millions of workers in the United States go into and out of the labor force quite frequently. This is true particularly of students and housewives, who may work part time or work for a few months of the year and then drop out for a considerable period.

As a result of these and other difficulties, there is a considerable range of error in published reports on the size of the labor force. While we shall follow the convention of using a single labor force figure, it would be better to think in terms of a zone around the reported figure, which in a country as large as the United States may number several million people.

Determinants of Labor Force Participation

Decisions about working are made within a cultural and legal context. In some countries it is not respectable for a woman to work outside the home. Able-bodied beggars are considered meritorious in some cultures but not in others. There may be legal requirements governing the school-leaving age for young people and the retirement age for older people.

Within such constraints, most people reach their decisions as members of *household units*. As an economic unit, the household can be regarded as seeking an equilibrium in which work, leisure, consumption, savings, and assets are optimally adjusted in terms of the family's preference system. It follows that households will differ in their labor supply behavior, i.e., in the number of family members seeking employment, the hours which each member prefers to work, the wage at which these hours will be offered, and so on. The considerations which may be relevant to supply decisions include: the number of other family members employed, total family income, the number of people dependent on this income, the age and future income expectations of family members, the family's actual and desired consumption level, its asset holdings, and its plans for purchase of additional assets, such as houses or automobiles. Labor-supply decisions are also not independent of labor demand. Decisions about seeking work are influenced by the estimated probability of actually finding a job.

Participation Rates in the United States

How have these influences worked out in terms of actual labor force participation in the United States? Table 1 shows participation

The Supply of Labor

Table 1

LABOR FORCE PARTICIPATION RATES BY AGE AND
SEX, UNITED STATES, 1890, 1947, 1967,
AND PROJECTIONS FOR 1980

Sex and Age Group	1890	1947	1967	Projected 1980
Males				
Total	89.3	86.8	81.5	80.3
16–17	61.5*	52.2	47.5	56.7
18–19		80.5	70.9	
20–24	90.8	84.9	87.5	87.2
25–34	99.0	95.8	97.4	96.2
35–44		98.0	97.4	96.7
45–54	98.2	95.5	95.2	95.0
55–64		89.6	84.4	83.7
65+	74.1	47.8	27.1	21.8
Females				
Total	21.0	31.8	41.1	41.9
16–17	26.9*	29.5	31.0	40.0
18–19		52.3	52.3	
20–24	32.1	44.9	53.4	52.6
25–34	18.0	32.0	41.9	40.3
35–44		36.3	48.1	50.0
45–54	15.7	32.7	51.8	59.5
55–64		24.3	42.4	47.3
65+	10.7	8.1	9.6	9.9
Total, both sexes	56.1	58.9	60.6	60.4

* These rates cover all persons aged 14–19, while subsequent rates cover those 16–19 only. If we had a comparable 16–19 rate for 1890, it would presumably be considerably higher than that shown.

rates for subgroups in the population in 1890, 1947, and 1967, with estimates for 1980.[4]

Reading across the table, we see the marked changes which have occurred over the years. Among men, labor force participation in the youngest age groups has declined considerably because young people on the average now complete more years of education. The sharp decline in participation rates among older men suggests that retirements are now occurring at a considerably earlier age. The most striking feature of the table is the sharp increase in the proportion of women who are in the labor force. In 1890, only one-fifth of women aged sixteen and over were at work. Today the proportion is more

[4] Data for 1890 are from Long, *Labor Force*, Appendix A. Data for 1947 and 1967 and Bureau of Labor Statistics projections for 1980 are from *Manpower Report of the President*, 1968 (Washington, D.C.: Government Printing Office, 1968).

than two-fifths, and in the age group thirty-five to sixty-four it is more than one-half. It is a curious coincidence that the greater labor force participation of some groups in the population has just about offset the reduced participation of others. The percentage of *all* people aged sixteen and over who are in the labor force is only slightly higher than it was in 1890.

The considerations affecting decisions to work or not to work differ substantially for men and for women, for young people and older people. So we shall look separately at the main subgroups in the population: prime-age men, married women, older workers, and young people. We shall also explore the disputed issue of how labor force participation responds to fluctuations in the demand for labor. The results reported come mainly from a major study at Princeton University by William G. Bowen and T. Aldrich Finegan.[5]

Prime-Age Males (Twenty-Five to Fifty-Four)

In our culture, adult males are expected to work; but not all of them do. During an average month of 1967, some 1,100,000 prime-age males were not in the labor force, compared with only 600,000 reported as unemployed. This lends interest to the question of what personal characteristics are associated with labor force participation.

The main characteristics that make a significant difference appear to be:

1. *Marital Status.* In 1960, the participation rate for married men living with their wives was 98 percent; but it was only 90 percent for the single, separated, divorced, and widowers. The main reason, Bowen and Finegan conclude, is probably that marriage is associated with personal characteristics favorable to work. Men who are able to get married and remain married are also better able to find and hold jobs. Married men also have heavier family responsibilities and greater need for income.

2. *Color.* The 1960 census data show a participation rate of 97 percent for white prime-age males, 93 percent for nonwhites. After adjusting for differences in education and other personal characteristics, there is still a two-point percentage differential; and the differential seems to have widened during the sixties. Two studies in the mid-

5 William G. Bowen and T. Aldrich Finegan, *The Economics of Labor Force Participation* (Princeton: Princeton University Press, 1969). This study is based on data from between 78 and 100 metropolitan areas for each of the census years 1940, 1950, and 1960, which were subjected to both cross-section and time-series analysis. The results for 1960, which we emphasize here, correspond in most cases to those for 1950; but 1940 shows different behavior on some points. Those interested in the wealth of detailed findings and the thorough discussion of statistical methods should consult the original source.

sixties found that the number of black prime-age males not in the labor force was larger than the number reported as unemployed. If this is true, the unemployment figures seriously understate the employment problem in the black community.

The reasons for this phenomenon are unclear. Lack of job skills and discrimination by employers doubtless provide part of the answer. When a man knows in advance that his chances of rejection are high, abandoning the search for work is a natural reaction. But there may also be other aspects of the ghetto culture that make for alienation from the world of employment.

3. *Education.* The participation rate for men with four years or less of schooling is about 90 percent; but for men with seventeen years or more it is 99 percent. Again, this must indicate differences in opportunity as well as inclination. Men whose employment chances are poor because of educational deficiencies tend to give up and drop out of the labor force. It is interesting also that since 1950 the participation rates for men with twelve years or more of education have been *rising,* while the rates for men with less than twelve years have been *falling.* This may reflect the fact, emphasized in the next chapter, that labor demand has been shifting rapidly toward technical, managerial, and other white-color jobs requiring substantial amounts of education.

4. *Other Income,* i.e., income not derived from employment. This relationship runs in the expected direction—the more income a man has from sources other than work, the lower his propensity to be in the labor force. Even in the higher brackets, however, work remains customary for the great majority. Some 84 percent of prime-age males with other income above $5,000 continue in the labor force.

These seem to be the main things which influence labor force behavior at each point in time. How does one explain the apparent tendency for the participation rate of prime-age males to decline gradually over the course of time? The most plausible explanation is the steady increase in the real income level of the American population. As wage rates and real incomes rise, more people choose not to work, or at least to work for a shorter span of years. In the earlier Long study, this inverse relation between income level and labor supply was tested in a variety of ways. The results of these tests were remarkably consistent. For the United States over the period 1890–1950, each 1 percent increase in real per capita income was associated with a decrease of about $\frac{1}{6}$ percent in the male labor force participation rate.

Married Women (Fourteen to Fifty-Four)

This is a large and growing component of the labor force. In 1967 about 16 million married women were in the labor force, of whom

three-quarters were full time workers. To understand the reasons
for the rapid increase in working wives, let us first examine *which*
wives work and which do not. The most important characteristics appear to be:

1. *Color.* Here the situation is the opposite of that for men. The
participation rate for black wives, after adjusting for education and
other personal characteristics, is about 7 percentage points higher
than that for white wives. This may be related to the traditionally
matriarchal structure of black families. It may be also that employer
discrimination in the range of occupations sought by black women is
less severe than it is for black men.

2. *Age of Children.* Participation rates rise as child care responsibilities decrease. For wives with children under six, the participation rate is the range of 15–20 percent. This rises to 35 percent
for wives with children aged six to thirteen, and to about 55 percent
when there are no children under fourteen in the home.

3. *Education.* This factor operates in the expected direction, and
even more strongly than for men. Among wives with no children
under six, those with four years of education or less have a participation rate of only 27 percent. But for those with seventeen years or
more of education, the rate is 77 percent. Bowen and Finegan estimate
that two-fifths of this difference is really a "wage effect." More education opens the door to higher occupations with greater earnings opportunities. The rest of the gap, they think, must be due to such things
as: the fact that women with very little education have difficulty
finding and holding jobs, which discourages labor force participation;
the fact that the jobs open to highly educated women are more varied
and interesting, providing considerably psychic income as well as
higher money income; and the fact that education itself may develop
a strong "taste for work."

4. *Other Family Income,* which means primarily the husband's
earnings. This effect is strong and in the expected direction. In families
whose income apart from the wife's earnings is below $3,000, about
50 percent of the wives are in the labor force. This falls to 21 percent
for families with incomes of $11,000–$15,000, and to 12 percent for
families with $15,000–$25,000.

5. *Occupational Level of Husband.* One might expect that the
"pure" effect of this factor, after adjustment for income level and
other variables, would be for the wives' participation rate to fall as
the husband's occupational status rises. To some extent this is true.
Wives of sales and clerical workers, service workers, and factory operatives have adjusted participation rates in the 38–41 percent range. For
wives of professional, technical, and managerial workers the range is
32–34 percent. Surprisingly, however, wives of laborers have a participation rate of only 32.5 percent. There is no obvious explanation

for this, except possibly that laborers marry women with limited work capacity.

6. *Labor Market Variables.* Comparing different cities at the same point of time one finds, as expected, that wives' participation rate is higher where wage rates for women are relatively high and where the industry mix contains a high proportion of "women's jobs." On the other hand, the participation rate varies *inversely* with the supply of women in the community and with the wage level of domestic servants. To the extent that working wives must hire household help, higher wage rates for domestics increase the opportunity cost of working and thus discourage participation.

The rapid increase in working wives has been one of the most dramatic labor market developments of recent decades. Between 1950 and 1967 alone the participation rate for wives jumped by more than one-half, from 24 percent to 37 percent, and the trend is still upward. How can one explain this large change in such a short period?

Several developments should have raised the participation rate for married women: a considerable rise in the earnings of women relative to men, a marked rise in educational levels, and a faster rate of increase in "women's jobs" than in "men's jobs." But there have also been important factors working in the opposite direction: the proportion of women with children under six has been higher since 1945 than before, the wages of domestic servants have risen sharply, and the real earnings of husbands have also risen sharply, which should have discouraged wives' participation via the income effect. The size of these effects is roughly measurable. But when we total them and cancel out pluses and minuses, we have still explained only about half the postwar increase in working wives.

The remaining half must be attributed to factors whose effect is harder to estimate, including: (1) A reduction in hours, including both reduction in the hours of full-time workers and greater availability of part-time work. This has made it easier for women to combine working with household responsibilities. (2) A rapid mechanization of household operations. Bowen and Finegan point out that the price of household appliances has risen more slowly since 1945 than the general level of consumer prices, while wages of domestics have risen very sharply. This has led to rapid substitution of appliances for both hired labor and the housewife's own labor. (3) A rise in income aspirations and customary standards of living. In 1950 Mrs. *A,* whose husband earned $10,000 a year, would be less inclined to work than Mrs. *B,* whose husband earned only $5,000. But in 1970, when Mr. *A* is earning $20,000 and Mr. *B* $10,000, it does *not* follow that Mrs. *B's* propensity to work will have fallen to the level of Mrs. *A* in 1950. It may be just as high as before. Income aspirations, and the propensity to work in order to meet them, shift upward over time, just as the consumption function shifts upward with increases in real income.

Older People (Fifty-Five to Sixty-Four and Sixty-Five to Seventy-Four)

While labor force participation declines continuously from fifty-five onward, there is an especially sharp break at age sixty-five. For men, the adjusted participation rate drops from 80 percent at sixty-four to 44 percent at sixty-five. Why the sharp decline at this point?

A major factor is surely the operation of the Social Security system, which now covers the great majority of employees. At the time of the 1960 Census, men became eligible for pension payments at age sixty-five. The fact that a man of sixty-five was eligible for a considerable amount of "other income," while a man of sixty-four was not, would be sufficient to account for a considerable drop in labor force participation. But this is not the whole story. Other factors in the situation are: (1) the Social Security provision that, if a man continues working beyond sixty-five, any earnings in excess of $1,680 a year lead to a reduction of pension payments. Bowen and Finegan conclude that this has had an independent effect in discouraging labor force participation, beyond the normal "income effect" of the pension system. (2) Larger companies usually have compulsory retirement plans, with sixty-five as the normal age limit. (3) There has been a long-run decline in the proportion of farmers and other self-employed workers, who have free choice of how long to continue working, as against employees who usually have no such choice. (4) The growth of compulsory retirement plans has led to a general change of attitudes. Work by people over sixty-five is no longer the expected thing, and may even be regarded as unfairly depriving some younger person of a job.

Younger People (Fifteen to Twenty-Four)

Since education is an important alternative for younger people, they require a somewhat different analysis, aimed at simultaneous explanation of labor force participation rates *and* school enrollment rates. Developments in the labor market will normally shift both of these rates, possibly in opposite directions. A period of unusually high employment, such as from 1966 to 1969, tends to lower enrollment rates by providing attractive alternatives to school, while it *raises* participation rates by making jobs easier to find. A rise in unemployment has opposite effects on both fronts.

Because of this interdependence, Bowen and Finegan develop the useful concept of *activity,* which combines the school enrollment rate and the labor force participation rate of those not in school. Young people who are neither in school nor in the labor force are classified as *inactive*. This inactive group is surprisingly large: ". . . we estimate that in April of 1960 perhaps 1½ to 2 million persons 14–24 years of age were not enrolled in school, not employed, not looking for work, and (in the case of females) not married" (p. 408). This leads them to ask: ". . . what is a teenage male who is not in school, not employed, and not looking for work, doing? The surprisingly large size of this group makes us reluctant to suggest that we have inadvertently devised a new measure of delinquency; but it is unclear what other broad categories exist, except for . . . health problems" (p. 448).

Further analysis reveals several things about this inactive group:

1. Inactivity is concentrated mainly in the ages sixteen to twenty. Before sixteen, almost everyone is in school, while after twenty the proportion who are either working or studying rises appreciably.

2. Both school enrollment rates and labor force participation rates are significantly lower for black young people than for whites. Inferior educational opportunities plus labor market discrimination may account for most of this differential.

3. There is an inverse relation between a city's wage level for jobs typically held by teenagers and the labor force participation rate of teenagers. The authors interpret this as meaning that, because of legal minimum wages and other institutional factors, the wage for teenagers is typically above what it would be in a free labor market; but the size of this wage gap varies from city to city. The higher the wage, the fewer teenagers employers will want to hire. A relatively high wage thus leads to higher teenage unemployment and to a drop in labor force participation through the discouragement effect.

4. A general rise in unemployment reduces young peoples' labor force participation rate substantially. It also raises the school enrollment rate, but not by enough to offset the first effect. Overall, there is a strong inverse relation between unemployment and the activity level of the youthful population.

The Impact of Unemployment

This issue, which cuts across all groups in the labor force, has been left to the end because it is important and because economists have been arguing about it since the 1930's. Some have argued that a rise in unemployment will increase labor force participation by wives and young people, who are forced to go to work to support the family when the husband is unemployed—the "additional worker" hypothesis. On the other side it is argued that, as unemployment rises and the chances of getting a job diminish, many workers will give up and leave the labor force—the "discouraged worker" hypothesis. An individual might respond in either of these ways; but the question is which predominates for the labor force as a whole.

Bowen and Finegan marshal convincing evidence that the discouraged worker effect predominates. The relation of unemployment to labor force participation is negative and significant for every subgroup studied. The effect is particularly strong for married women (where a 1 percent increase in unemployment [6] is associated with somewhat more than 1 percent decrease in labor force participation), for men sixty-five and over (where the decrease is 1.6 percent), and for male teenagers (where the decrease is 1.9 percent). These groups, whose attachment to the labor force is looser than that of prime-age males, are precisely the groups which one would expect to be most responsive to variations in employment opportunities.

An important implication of these findings is that, in periods of less-than-full employment, there is a substantial amount of "hidden unemployment" in the economy. Many more people would look for work if the demand for labor were higher. The amount of "labor slack" in the economy is thus larger than the unemployment figures indicate. Bowen and Finegan estimate that, in the census week of 1960, hidden unemployment was about 1.3 million persons, of whom more than half were women.

The opposite of hidden unemployment may be termed "induced participation." When the demand for labor is unusually high, jobs come seeking people. Many people who would not normally seek work will yield to the blandishments of the recruiter when he appears, literally or figuratively, on their doorstep. Bowen and Finegan estimate that the additional workers drawn into the labor force between 1963 and 1967 by the high demand associated with the Vietnam War totaled 1.9 million, of whom again more than a million were women. To ignore these expansion joints in the labor force can lead to serious miscalculations in macroeconomic policy, a point to which we return in Chapter 7.

HOURS
OF
WORK

What determines hours of work, and why do they change over time? At a particular time, hours may seem to depend entirely on institutions, law, and custom. Each employer has a fixed work schedule for his plant, and everyone must arrive and leave at the same time. In unionized establishments, weekly hours of work, plus vacations and paid holidays, which affect annual hours, are usually specified in the union contract. The workweek may be regulated by laws, such as the Fair

---

[6] There is a possibility of confusion here. If the national unemployment rate rises from 4 percent to 5 percent, we sometimes call this loosely "a 1 percent increase"; but it is of course a 25 percent increase. In the Bowen–Finegan study, a 1 percent increase means that the unemployment rate rises from, say, 4 percent to 4.04 percent.

Labor Standards Act in the United States. What scope is left for personal preference?

The labor market doubtless operates less effectively in regulating hours than in determining wages. A worker with a scarce skill can frequently bargain for an individual wage increase. An individual worker cannot bargain with his employer for a thirty-six-hour week if everyone else continues to work forty hours. The wage level of a company can move upward gradually year by year. A small reduction of hours is often not feasible. For example, in a continuous-process industry which must operate around the clock, the alternatives are to work two shifts (a twelve-hour day, as was long the custom in the steel industry), or three shifts (an eight-hour day), or four shifts (a six-hour day). Intermediate schedules are not feasible.

But this does not mean that workers' preferences are inoperative. Some establishments and industries are working considerably longer hours than others. Today, some are on thirty-hour schedules while others continue to work forty-eight hours or more. People who prefer shorter hours can to some extent shift toward shorter-hour firms. If enough people shift in this direction, the supply of labor to long-hour industries will dry up, and those industries will be under pressure to reduce hours. Workers also express their preferences through nonmarket channels. The bargains which unions strike with employers over hours reflect in some measure the opinion of the membership. Wage-hour legislation presumably also reflects widespread sentiment among the citizens.

Individual Preferences and Work Decisions

Worker preferences are sufficiently influential that it is worthwhile to examine how these preferences are formed. As usual, precise reasoning forces us to assume a higher degree of introspection and rationality than most workers probably achieve. We assume also throughout this section that there are no institutional constraints on working hours and that workers have full freedom of choice.

Decisions about working hours are usually analyzed by constructing a preference map relating income and leisure. An indifference curve on this map, such as I_1 in Figure 1, shows different combinations of income and leisure which would be equally acceptable to the worker. Put differently, it shows how much leisure the person is prepared to sacrifice for additional income of x dollars per week. This is the only precise sense in which one can speak of "desire for income." Naturally, everyone "desires" income if it can be had for nothing. The strength of this desire can be tested only by asking how much effort the worker is prepared to exert in return. The answer will differ at different *points* on the indifference curve. If the person is already working fifty hours

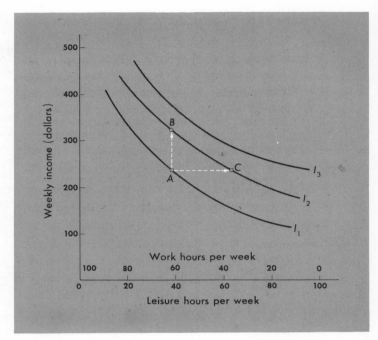

Figure 1

PREFERENCE FOR INCOME VERSUS LEISURE

a week, it will doubtless take more income to induce him to put in an extra hour than would be the case if he were working thirty hours a week. We show this by drawing the indifference curve as concave upward.

Higher indifference curves, as usual, represent successively higher levels of satisfaction. I_2 in Figure 1 is preferable to I_1. Why? Because a worker moving up from, say, point A toward I_2 can have as much income as before and more leisure (point C), or as much leisure as before and more income (point B), or some intermediate combination yielding more of both income and leisure. By the same reasoning, I_3 is preferable to I_2, and so on.

The geometry is easy. But what determines the shape of a particular worker's indifference curves? At least the following factors are relevant:

1. The household's need for income. This depends not only on the number of people in the household but on customary standards of living and on aspirations for the future. The same income may seem adequate to one household and quite inadequate to another, which has a strong drive toward a higher scale of living.

2. Income other than earnings of the worker in question, including property income and earnings of other family members. We saw that this influenced decisions on labor force participation, which can be regarded as an extreme case of the present problem (a decision not to participate is a decision to offer zero hours). One would expect "other income" to influence hours decisions in the same direction, i.e., inversely to the income level.

3. The individual's ability to use and enjoy leisure. A person who has a wide variety of spare-time interests and activities will value leisure more highly than one who does not. Ability to enjoy leisure depends also on such objective circumstances as location in a small town or a large city, in a warm or cold climate, close to or far from good outdoor recreational facilities, and on the presence or absence of radio, television, spectator sports, and other leisure time "fillers."

4. The direct satisfactions or dissatisfactions associated with the job. Other things equal, the research chemist will probably prefer to work longer hours than the garbage collector.

Knowing a worker's preference map does not tell us how many hours he will actually work. To discover this we must also know the hourly wage rate for his job. Suppose this is $5 an hour. Then if he worked the physically feasible maximum, say 100 hours per week, he could earn $500 (point A in Figure 2). If he does not work at all he will earn nothing (point B in Figure 2); and he can do anything in between. His *possibilities curve* is AB, the slope of which depends on the hourly wage rate. Given this curve, he will try to reach the highest possible indifference curve. This is I in Figure 2. His preferred work week is shown by point C, where AB is tangent to I. At this point he is working fifty hours and earning $250 per week.

We can easily demonstrate that this is the best he can do. Given the wage rate, he cannot attain any position above AB. He cannot, therefore, move to any other point on I_1. He could move up or down along AB, but then he would find himself on a lower indifference curve, indicating a lower level of satisfaction.

Suppose now that the worker's wage rises from five dollars to six dollars an hour. At first blush one might reason that he will work more hours than before. If his preference as between work and leisure has not changed, but work now yields a higher reward, he will respond by substituting work for leisure in his daily pattern. This, as we noted earlier, is called the *substitution effect*.

On the other hand, the worker is now better off than before. He can afford to buy more of everything, including leisure. This *income effect* will incline him to work less and enjoy more leisure as he becomes more affluent.

On logical grounds, one cannot say which effect will outweigh the other. Either result is possible, as illustrated in Figure 3. When the

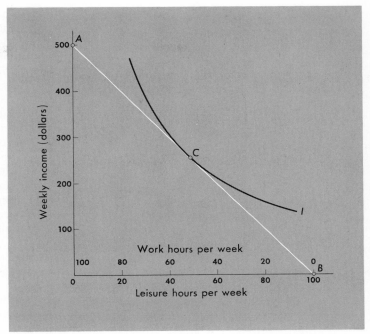

Figure 2
THE CHOICE OF A WORK WEEK

wage rises to six dollars an hour, the worker's possibility curve shifts from *AB* to *BF*. The worker will now try to reach the highest indifference curve touched by *BF*. If this has the shape I_2, his new equilibrium will be at *D,* with longer hours than before. The substitution effect has outweighed the income effect. But if the higher curve is as shown by the dotted line I_2', he will move to *D'*, which involves a shorter workweek. Here the income effect has outweighed the substitution effect.

The Aggregate Labor Supply Curve

Suppose we have a full-employment economy, thus getting around the awkward fact that labor supply is responsive to job opportunities. Suppose also that institutional conditions permit each worker to choose his preferred workweek. Then, if we know the preference system of each individual and the wage rate for each job, we can read off how many hours each person will wish to work and total these hours to obtain aggregate labor supply. This is at any moment a fixed quantity,

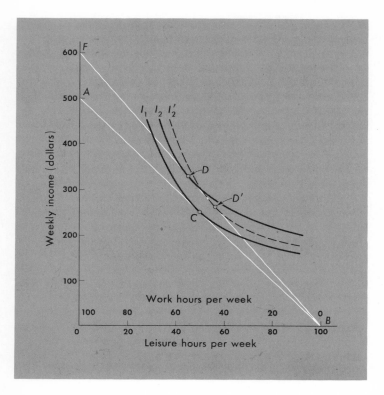

Figure 3

POSSIBLE EFFECTS OF A WAGE CHANGE

such as OS_o in Figure 4. There are a fixed number of people in the labor force, each offering a fixed number of hours, adding up to so many billions of man-hours available. The (short-run) labor supply curve is the vertical line $S_o S_o$.

The interesting question is how this line shifts over time. As real wages move upward over the decades, will this lead workers to offer more man-hours or fewer?

The answer depends on individual workers' preference systems. Suppose that a typical worker's indifference curves resemble I_1 and I'_2 in Figure 3, so that a wage increase will cause him to move from C to D', i.e., to work fewer hours. If this is the predominant worker reaction, we can draw some conclusions about aggregate labor supply. Consider what would happen in an economy with constant population and

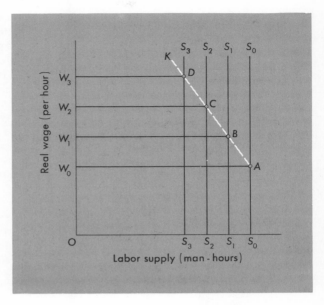

Figure 4

AGGREGATE LABOR SUPPLY
WITH STATIONARY POPULATION

constant labor force participation rates. As the wage level rises, aggregate labor supply will fall because of the reduction of working hours. A wage increase from OW_0 to OW_1, for example, might cause total man-hours offered to fall from OS_0 to OS_1 (Figure 4). A further rise of wages to OW_2 might produce a further decline to OS_2, and so on. The economy moves from A to $B, C, D,$ and so on along the dotted line AK.

The line AK is sometimes called a "long-run labor supply curve," but this is not very good usage. Strictly speaking, "supply curve" should refer to a moment of time, or at any rate to relatively short periods. The movement from A to D in Figure 4, however, may take several decades. AK is really a historical chart, showing the locus of wage-employment combinations over long periods of time. We might call it a "historical labor offer curve."

There is convincing evidence that higher real wages do in fact lead workers on balance to prefer shorter hours. There is, first, the fact that actual working hours have fallen greatly in the United States over the past century. The trend of weekly hours in manufacturing since 1890 is shown in Figure 5. Hours fell gradually until 1929, then more sharply during the Great Depression. The forty-hour work week, in lieu of the previous forty-eight-hour norm, was promulgated in the National Recovery Administration codes of 1933 and 1934 and later in the Fair Labor Standards Act of 1938. The Fair Labor Standards Act does not prohibit work beyond forty hours, but the provision that such work must be compensated at 150 percent of the normal rate gives employers a strong incentive to avoid it. Hours averaged considerably less than forty during the thirties because of depressed demand, rose well above forty during World War II under inflationary demand conditions, then settled back to an almost constant level since 1945. While there have been small cyclical variations around the forty-hour norm, the norm itself has not changed.

Hours worked *per year,* however, have continued to decline through the spread of paid vacations and holidays. Most workers now receive paid vacations of one to four weeks, and the length of service needed to qualify for these benefits has been steadily reduced. In addition seven or eight holidays are usually paid for, and this list also tends to grow longer over the years.

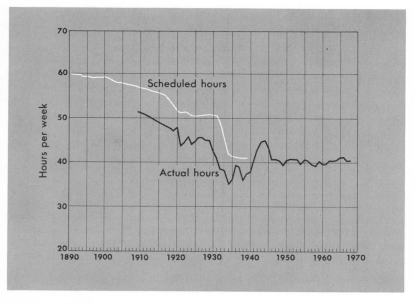

Figure 5
AVERAGE WEEKLY HOURS IN MANUFACTURING
1890–1968

The trend has been similar in other high-income economies. In Canada, for example, average weekly hours in manufacturing fell from sixty-four in 1870 to fifty-three in 1910, to forty-four in 1945, and to about forty at the present time. In all countries, workers' increasing productive power has been translated into greater leisure as well as higher incomes.

One cannot be sure that hours actually worked at any time correspond precisely with what workers would prefer. It seems certain, however, that trends in workers' preferences and in actual hours have been similar. It is unlikely that many workers today would prefer the fifty-hour week of 1900; or alternatively, that most workers would prefer only twenty-five hours, with the reduction of weekly income that this would necessarily entail. If either statement were true, one would expect more public outcry over the hours issue than there has been in recent years.

There have also been cross-section studies designed to test the wage–hours relationship for different groups of workers at the same point in time. T. A. Finegan analyzed average wage level and average hours worked by census occupational groups in 1940 and 1950. He concludes that, "In general, the findings of this study support the orthodox construct of a negatively inclined supply curve of labor. When other things are held constant, adult males with higher hourly earnings work fewer hours per week." [7] Gordon C. Winston reached similar results from an international comparison of thirty-one countries. He calculated a labor effort index for each country by combining weekly hours of work and labor force participation rates and analyzed the relation of this to per capita national income and the level of manufacturing wages in each country. The relation, as expected, was negative and statistically significant. It appeared that a 10 percent increase in income was associated typically with about a 1 percent decrease in work effort. [8]

If this negative relation does exist, why does it exist? One possible interpretation is that leisure and consumption are complementary rather than competitive. Consumption itself requires time. This is true especially of consumption of services, such as education, travel, and recreation, which bulk larger as income levels rise. The picture of a person consuming an ever wider range of goods and services, but with

[7] T. A. Finegan, "Hours of work in the United States: a cross-sectional analysis," *Journal of Political Economy,* October, 1962, pp. 452–70. Among the "other things" that must be held constant are sex, color, education (positively related with hours of work), and marital status (increased family responsibilities also being associated with longer hours).

[8] Gordon C. Winston, "An international comparison of income and hours of work," *Review of Economics and Statistics,* February, 1966, pp. 28–39. See also M. S. Feldstein, "Estimating the supply curve of working hours," *Oxford Economic Papers,* March, 1968, pp. 74–80.

decreasing leisure in which to enjoy them, is self-contradictory. It is more reasonable to regard expanded consumption as accompanied naturally by an increased amount of "optional time," and hence a reduced amount of working time.[9] Recent product innovations, such as television, may have increased the consumption value of optional time.

Some Questions of Hours Policy

The Fair Labor Standards Act, and similar acts covering intrastate workers in many states, have substantial influence on prevailing hours of work. They set the tone even for workers not directly covered by them. In a few industries hours have been reduced below the statutory level through collective bargaining. The question of whether the general level of working hours should be further reduced raises interesting policy questions.

With hours at their present level, a further reduction in hours per worker will usually mean a reduction in output per worker. This was not always true. In earlier days it often turned out that reducing weekly hours from, say, sixty to fifty-four actually increased output per man. The last hour lopped off the working day was the least productive; and the opportunity for more rest and recreation enabled men to work harder and produce more in the remaining hours. So we could eat our cake and have it—cut hours and at the same time raise output and income per worker.

That day is now past. The evidence suggests that, as hours fall from forty-five to forty to thirty-five, the reduction in hours is not fully offset by greater output per hour. Weekly output falls. This of course does not mean that hours should not be reduced, but simply that any reduction should rest on informed balancing of greater leisure against reduced income.

The issue is often beclouded by two kinds of confusion. First, it is sometimes thought that workers in an industry can gain more leisure without loss of income by an upward adjustment of hourly wage rates. Suppose the industry is operating a forty-hour week at an average wage level of $4 per hour. If hours are cut to thirty-two, while at the same time the hourly wage is raised to $5, will not workers have the same weekly income of $160 plus more leisure?

It would take an unusually strong and aggressive union to drive such a bargain. Moreover, if the union is able to get such a large hourly wage increase, why did it not do so earlier? Why should the hours' reduction make something possible that apparently was not possible before?

Suppose, however, that hourly wage rates do rise by 25 percent. And

[9] See the pathbreaking paper by Gary S. Becker, "A theory of the allocation of time," *Economic Journal*, September, 1965, pp. 493–517.

suppose, at a rather generous estimate, that output per man-hour rises 10 percent because workers put in more effort in the remaining hours. Then unit labor cost will still be 15 percent higher than before. The price of the industry's product will have to rise relative to other prices, and sales of the product will decline.

What has happened is that part of the real cost of the reduction in hours has been shifted to consumers through a rise in prices. But workers in the industry, if they consume any of the product they are making, will bear part of the cost. They may also suffer a reduction of employment opportunities depending on whether the drop in sales is larger or smaller than the drop in weekly output per worker.

If this kind of hours' reduction plus wage increase were attempted simultaneously for all industries in the economy, it seems clear what would happen: workers' weekly money incomes would be unchanged, national output would fall, the general price level would rise, and workers' real incomes would be reduced by roughly the amount of the cut in output.[10]

A second misconception is that hours' reduction is a desirable or even a necessary remedy for unemployment. This argument arises sometimes at the industry level, sometimes at the economy-wide level. Since World War II, for example, mechanization has reduced the need for production workers in a number of major industries, so that many steelworkers, auto workers, coal miners, longshoremen, and others have been left unemployed. Some union leaders argue that this unemployment can best be absorbed by shortening the workweek and sharing the available work among more people. But assuming that the existing workweek is close to the average preference of workers in the industry, unemployment does not provide a sound reason for reducing it. A forced reduction of hours would not reduce unemployment, measured in man-hours, but would simply spread this unemployment over the whole labor force. Workers would be obliged to accept shorter hours than they prefer, and to take an undesired cut in weekly income (which could not, as noted earlier, be avoided entirely by raising hourly wage rates).

The constructive approach to unemployment in a particular industry is to speed the movement of workers out of the industry through retraining and placement programs.

General unemployment represents a gap between the actual and potential output of the economy. A general reduction of hours closes

10 Not necessarily by *precisely* this amount. The reduction in hours reduces total labor supply and this, other things being equal, will raise the real wage rate relative to the rate of return to capital. So it is possible that labor may end up with a somewhat larger share of the reduced national income. The quantitative importance of this point, which will be explored further in chapter 8, is probably not very great.

this gap by reducing potential output rather than by raising actual output. It lowers the definition of "full employment" and establishes a permanently lower output ceiling. It is a defeatist solution to the unemployment problem. It would be more constructive to leave the output ceiling unchanged and to raise actual output toward it by energetic use of monetary and fiscal policy.

Suppose now that the economy is operating at full employment. How does the issue of hours' reduction appear under these circumstances? A general reduction in the workweek means a reduction in national output, and almost certainly a cut in workers' consumption levels.[11] This does not mean that hours should never be cut from their present level. Against a reduction in consumption must be set a gain in leisure and a reduction of fatigue and unpleasantness from work. The underlying issue is how workers themselves balance these considerations and what length of week they would prefer if given free choice.

There is reason to think that most workers, if faced clearly with the alternatives, would favor continuing something like the present workweek. The widespread practice of "moonlighting" (holding a second job) suggests that many workers find the hours on their primary job too short to provide the desired balance between leisure and income. Workers are generally eager to work overtime, and insistent that opportunities for overtime be allocated in an equitable way. Pressure for a shorter official week sometimes means not a desire actually to work fewer hours but a desire to work as much as before and get additional overtime pay for doing so.[12]

One experienced and perceptive union official put the matter as follows:

> Aside from the workers' desire for their paid holidays and paid vacations there is no evidence in recent experience that workers want shorter

[11] This assumes, as before, that a cut of, say, 10 percent in the workweek means a drop of 10 percent in each worker's weekly output, i.e. that output per man-hour remains unchanged. The effect on output might not actually be this severe, but it would certainly be in this direction. Nor could workers hope to escape taking some share of this cut by juggling the hourly wage level.

[12] In 1962 the International Brotherhood of Electrical Workers in New York struck for and won a basic twenty-five-hour week on New York construction jobs. This presumably does not mean electricians will sit idle the rest of the week. Some of them will continue to work longer hours on their regular job, drawing time and a half for the hours beyond twenty-five. Others doubtless do private electrical repair work or have other sideline activities. This appears to have been an income-raising maneuver as well as a work-spreading one.

It is worth noting that employers often prefer to cover production peaks by offering overtime to the existing work force rather than face the expense of hiring additional workers for short periods. See in this connection L. Moses, "Income, Leisure, and Wage Pressure," *Economic Journal*, June, 1962, pp. 320–34 and W. Oi, "Labor as a Quasi-fixed Factor," *Journal of Political Economy*, December, 1962, pp. 538–55.

daily or weekly hours. The evidence is all on the other side. Hundreds of local and international officers have testified that the most numerous and persistent grievances are disputes over the sharing of overtime work. The issue is usually not that someone has been made to work, but that he has been deprived of a chance to make overtime pay. Workers are eager to increase their income, not to work shorter hours.[13]

There is no persuasive case for general reduction of the workweek until there is clearer evidence that the bulk of wage and salary earners prefer shorter hours. Assuming that the income effect continues to operate, this time will eventually arrive, but it is not yet here. It may turn out also that, in lieu of further shortening of the standard day or week, many people would prefer further extension of holiday provisions, paid vacations, sabbatical arrangements, and the like.

Another consideration is relevant to employee welfare. We noted earlier that individuals are likely to differ widely in their hours' preferences. Housewives, and young people in school or college, may prefer to work twenty hours or less. Men with large families or high consumption goals may prefer fifty hours a week. Ideally, there should be a corresponding spectrum of job opportunities, so that each worker can find work of the duration he prefers.

While existing arrangements are doubtless not ideal, they do provide more flexibility than is often realized. First, there is the possibility of part-time work. In 1967, about 8 million people, or one-eighth of all nonagricultural workers, were on voluntary part-time schedules. Second, there is the possibility of overtime work. When business activity is high, as in the period from 1965 to 1970, many employers find it less expensive to pay overtime rates to some of their present employees than to bear the cost of recruiting and training new workers. Research studies show that those most eager to put in for overtime are workers with large families and high income needs.

Third, it is possible to hold two jobs. In 1966 some 3.6 million people, or about 5 percent of the employed population, held two jobs. Economic motivation is strongly evident here. Moonlighting increases with size of family, from 5.4 percent of married men without children to 10.3 percent with 5 or more children. It decreases as earnings on the primary job rise, from 12.5 percent for married men earning less than $60 a week to 5.5 percent for married men earning more than $200 a week. Moonlighting is especially prevalent among teachers, policemen, firemen, farmers, and service workers—all relatively low-paid groups.[14]

[13] George Brooks, formerly Research Director of the Pulp and Sulphite Workers' Union, cited in Melvin W. Reder, "The Cost of a Shorter Work Week," *Proceedings of Ninth Annual Meeting of IRRA,* 1956, pp. 207–21.

[14] For a more detailed analysis see Harvey R. Hamel, "Moonlighting—an economic phenomenon," *Monthly Labor Review,* October, 1967, pp. 17–22.

Fourth, it seems clear that many people reduce their *annual* working hours by taking time off during the year. They follow the advice of an airline television commercial to "sneak a week" now and then. T. A. Finegan found that all employed males in a recent census year averaged about forty-three weeks of work during the year.[15] They were unemployed, on the average, for two weeks and spent the remaining seven weeks in "nonparticipation." There was also much variation among individuals in the amount of time spent at work. Only about one-third of this variance was attributable to differences in unemployment, the remainder being associated with personal characteristics. Thus married men averaged more weeks of work per year than single men. Additional years of schooling, increasing age (up to age forty), and urban rather than rural residence were also associated with more weeks of work per year.

It is not clear how much government can or need do to ensure desirable flexibility in work schedules. Negatively, one can say that efforts to tailor all jobs rigidly to a standard duration have unfortunate effects in reducing the range of individual choice. On the positive side, perhaps the most important policy is vigorous pursuit of full employment. As labor markets tighten and man-hours become harder to find, employers become more willing to invent part-time jobs, allow overtime, and loosen up work schedules to attract workers with varying preferences.

LABOR
FORCE
QUALITY

Labor supply is a matter of quality as well as numbers. For economic purposes, "quality" means productive potential. One worker is of higher quality than another if he produces more, given identical equipment, work methods, and supervision.

Quality depends on *physical strength,* on *motivation,* and on *education and training.* Physical strength and energy depend partly on nutrition. Chronic hunger reduces capacity for physical and mental labor. This is still a factor even in the United States, where poverty studies have revealed serious malnutrition at low income levels. It is a major problem in many of the less-developed countries where food intake often averages less than 2,000 calories a day, and the supply of minerals and vitamins in the diet is quite inadequate.

The other main determinant of energy is medical and public health

[15] T. A. Finegan, "The work experience of men in the labor force: an occupational study," *Labor and Industrial Relations Review,* January, 1964, pp. 238–56.

facilities. In tropical countries malaria still saps the energy of a large part of the population. Internal parasites enter the system through polluted water supplies. Dysentery is common. Childhood diseases, not properly attended at the time, can lead to permanent impairment of sight, hearing, and other physical faculties. The surprising thing about workers in, say, tropical Africa is not that they produce relatively little but that they have the strength to produce anything at all. In such countries investment in training doctors and nurses, in building clinics and hospitals, in campaigns to eradicate endemic diseases, is not just a welfare measure. It has a direct impact on productivity.

Granted physical health and energy, the second question is motivation. A man may be willing to work a full week every week, eager to learn new skills and earn promotion, responsive to piece rates and other incentive systems. Or he may be irregular in attendance, unambitious and unteachable, with low income targets and aspirations. This is no longer a major problem in older industrial economies such as those of North America, Western Europe, the USSR or Japan. It is still a substantial problem in many of the less-developed countries, which are recruiting a "first generation" industrial labor force from the agricultural and service sectors.

Research studies suggest, however, that new industrial recruits in the less-developed countries learn within a few years to behave much like factory workers anywhere else.[16] If they are carefully selected, thoroughly trained, well supervised, and reasonably paid, they will stay with their jobs and work effectively. If not, they will perform poorly and drift from job to job. Poor job performance is more a reflection of inadequate personnel management than of intrinsic worker characteristics. It is a management problem rather than a labor problem.

The third component of quality is education and training. The amount of specialized skill embodied in the labor force varies greatly from country to country. Broadly, the skill characteristics of the labor force correspond to, and are induced by, the skill requirements of the economy at a particular time. As the economy advances, its skill requirements become both more diversified and "deeper," in the sense of involving more complex operations with longer training periods. The necessary skills are inculcated in the labor force, partly through on-the-job training, partly through formal education. As skill increases, output per man-hour rises. Part of the increment in output is plowed back into increased education and training, making possible still higher skill and output in the future. This circular process of "human capital accumulation" parallels the growth of physical capital in an expanding economy.

[16] On this range of issues see Lloyd G. Reynolds and Peter Gregory, *Wages, Productivity, and Industrialization in Puerto Rico* (Homewood, Ill.: Richard D. Irwin, Inc., 1965).

Measuring Labor Quality

Can we measure this kind of improvement in labor force quality?
Efforts at measurement have taken two main forms. One starts from
changes in the *educational level* of the labor force, the other from
changes in its *occupational composition*. A study of the first type, by
Professor T. W. Schultz,[17] starts from the assumption that the value of
education is equal to its cost, including the opportunity cost of the
student's own time—the amount he might have earned by working
instead of going to school. On this basis Schultz estimates that the
educational investment embodied in the labor force as of 1900 was
$63 billion, or $2,300 per worker (measured in 1956 dollars). By 1957
the total had risen to $535 billion, or about $8,000 per worker, again
measured in 1956 dollars.

The rate of increase in human capital, moreover, was considerably
faster than the increase of physical capital over this period. Total investment in physical capital in 1900 is estimated at $282 billion or
about $10,000 per worker. By 1957 these figures (in dollars of constant
purchasing power) had risen to $1,270 billion and $19,000 per worker.
Thus physical capital per worker fell somewhat short of doubling,
while educational capital per worker increased about 3½ times.

The same impression is obtained by looking at measures of educational achievement. In 1900 each member of the labor force had, on
the average, 8.1 years of education. This now has risen to 12.5 years,
and will continue to rise in the future. The increase in enrollments
has been especially dramatic at the college and graduate school levels.
In 1900 only 4 percent of young people of college age were enrolled
in college. Today the proportion is 45 percent, and is expected to
rise to 50 percent by 1980. The fact that a year of college or graduate
training is considerably more expensive (and thus, on Schultz's assumption, more productive) than a year of primary schooling helps
to account for the sharp rise of total educational investment since
1900.

Measures of labor force quality based on educational expenditures
have several shortcomings. First, education serves in part to increase
the student's capacity for personal enjoyment and responsible citizenship. This is socially valuable, but it does not add to vocational proficiency. It should be regarded as production of a consumer good
rather than a capital good. The difficulty is to separate the consumption
and capital components of education. Farmers or factory workers with
high school education are probably better producers than those with
only primary school training. But how much better? College graduates

[17] T. W. Schultz, *Education and Economic Growth,* 60th Yearbook of the National Society for the Study of Education (Chicago: The University of Chicago
Press, 1961).

are probably better business executives than high school graduates. But how much better?

One research approach to this problem is to examine the earnings of people in the same occupation but with different levels of educational attainment. If we are willing to take earnings as an indicator of productive contribution, then the contribution of education to productivity can be estimated. The few studies of this type that have been made indicate that earnings do typically rise with education, even within the same occupational level. This suggests that even general or "academic" education has some productivity effect and thus contains an element of capital formation.

But such results are open to the objection that amount of education is correlated to some extent with innate ability. Those who go on to the highest levels of education have, on the average, greater intelligence, energy, and drive than those who do not, so that even without superior education they might have been expected to perform better and earn more. It is difficult, however, to define and measure ability and to separate its effect from the independent effect of education. We return to this problem in a later chapter.

Moreover, many skills are learned partly or entirely on the job. This involves costs in terms of low or zero output during the training period, using up of materials and equipment, and time of teachers and supervisors. If we assume that training expenditures will be incurred only so long as they are repaid by subsequent higher output, then the value of on-the-job training is measured roughly by its cost. This cost should be included in any estimate of total investment in human capital.

The second main approach to measuring labor force quality starts from the occupational composition of employment. This has obviously improved over time. The percentage of farmers and laborers is much lower today than it was in 1900. The percentage of professional people, technical workers, managers, and executives is much higher. The increase in the average skill level of the labor force can be measured, provided we are willing to assume that the wage rate for each job indicates the productive contribution of workers on that job.

We then proceed as follows: instead of totaling man-hours of every type indiscriminately, we first subdivide them into occupational groups—laborers, auto workers, plumbers, schoolteachers, typists, lawyers, and so on. The subdivision can be as fine as the statistics permit. We then "weight" the number of man-hours in each group by a factor based on the relative wage rate for the group. Suppose we take the lowest-paid group in the economy (farm laborers, or whatever) as our base. Each man-hour of that kind of labor has a weight of 1. Then each hour of auto assembly-line labor might get a weight of 3, high-school teachers 4, electricians 5, college teachers 7, lawyers 10—depending on what the wage statistics show. Finally, we add up these "adjusted" man-hours for all occupations to get a figure for total labor supply.

Having done this for 1960, we redo it for 1961, 1962, and so on into the future. What shall we find? If the number of people in the more highly skilled groups, which receive heaviest weight in this procedure, is rising faster than the number in low-skilled occupation, then our total of "adjusted" man-hours will rise faster than a total of "crude" or "unadjusted" man-hours. The growing gap between the two totals over any period of years tells us how rapidly the average skill level has been rising.

There is clear evidence that the average skill level of the American labor force has risen substantially over time. John Kendrick found that over the period 1909–57 total man-hours worked in the U.S. private economy increased by 31 percent. When man-hours were weighted by skill level as described above, however, this "adjusted" total rose 56 percent over the same period—almost double the rate of increase in the crude total.[18]

Even if we measure quality by skill level, education is lurking in the background. The higher occupations require on the average more years of general education and specific vocational training. So, if the composition of the labor force is shifting toward the more skilled occupations, the average educational level will also be rising. Skill level, wage level, and years of education are highly intercorrelated.

An interesting analysis of this relationship has been conducted by James G. Scoville, some of whose results appear in Table 2.[19] Scoville classified a large number of occupations into five major classes. Class one includes jobs with the most complex skills and longest training periods, while class five includes the simplest and least-skilled occupations. From 1960 census data he obtained the average annual earnings of people at these various levels and also their average years of schooling. From the *Dictionary of Occupational Titles* used by the U.S. Employment Service he obtained the years of general educational background and specific vocational preparation supposedly required for successful performance in the occupation. The figures in the last two columns of Table 2 are thus hypothetical estimates, while the first four columns are actual measurements. Each figure, of course, is an average for many occupations falling in a particular job content class.

---

[18] John W. Kendrick, *Productivity Trends in the United States* (New York: National Bureau of Economic Research, 1961). For another set of estimates by somewhat different methods, see Edward F. Denison, *The Sources of Economic Growth in the United States and the Alternatives before Us* (New York: Committee for Economic Development, 1962).

[19] James G. Scoville, *The Job Content of the U.S. Economy, 1940–70* (New York: McGraw-Hill Book Company, 1969). The data reproduced in Table 2 appear on pages 28–31.

Table 2

RELATION OF EDUCATION
TO JOB CONTENT LEVEL, 1960

Job Content Level	ANNUAL EARNINGS		YEARS OF EDUCATION		"REQUIRED" YEARS OF	
	Male	*Female*	*Male*	*Female*	*General Education*	*Specific Vocational Training*
1	6797	4426	16.3	15.9	16.2	5.3
2	6586	4013	12.2	12.8	12.1	3.2
3	5247	3397	11.4	12.2	10.5	1.6
4	4283	2361	10.4	11.1	9.5	1.1
5	3917	2042	9.2	9.2	8.0	0.8

As one would expect, both income level and educational level rise steadily as we move from lower to higher occupational classes. So does the amount of general education and vocational training specified by employers and the U.S. Employment Service as necessary for job performance.

Whichever measurement route we adopt, it is clear that the quality of the American labor force has risen rapidly over the past several decades, and that this has contributed importantly to the rise of national output. Research into the sources of long-term economic growth has been very active since about 1955. The researchers were at first surprised to find that output, both in the United States and in other industrial countries, has risen considerably faster than the physical quantities of capital and labor ("unadjusted" man-hours) used in production. This discrepancy, which in some countries and periods accounts for more than half of the output increase, has been termed "the increase in total factor productivity" or, more simply, "the residual." A variety of factors help to explain the size of the residual, and we shall say more about them in chapter 8. But there would be general agreement that improvement in labor force quality is one of the major factors.

Discussion Questions

1. "As a country's per capita income rises, one might expect a gradual decline in the labor force participation rate. In the United States,

however, the overall participation rate is somewhat higher today than it was in 1890, despite much higher income levels." Discuss.

2. Draw an aggregate labor supply curve for the United States as of the current month. Explain why you drew the curve as you did.

3. What are the main factors influencing labor force participation by:
   (a) married women?
   (b) male teenagers?
   (c) men of prime working age?

4. How can one account for the rapid increase in women's labor force participation rate in recent decades?

5. What would be the main consequences of reducing the standard workweek in manufacturing from forty hours to thirty hours
   (a) during a period of heavy unemployment?
   (b) at a time of full employment?

6. It is sometimes argued that, when hours are reduced, workers' incomes can be maintained by an offsetting increase in hourly wage rates. Discuss the feasibility of this program
   (a) for a single industry.
   (b) for the economy as a whole.

7. "In a full-employment economy, the worker's freedom to change jobs protects him against excessive hours just as it protects him against substandard wages. Government intervention to establish a standard workweek is likely to be harmful rather than beneficial." Discuss.

8. "To take the total costs of education as a measure of investment in human capital involves serious overstatement." Do you agree? Why, or why not?

9. Compare the reliability of the educational-expenditure approach and the occupational-composition approach to deriving an index of labor force quality.

Reading Suggestions

On labor force participation, in addition to the Bowen–Finegan study, see Long, Clarence D., *The Labor Force Under Changing Income and Employment.* Princeton: Princeton University Press, 1958. Also Cain, Glen G., *Married Women in the Labor Force.* Chicago: The University of Chicago Press, 1966; and "Unemployment and the labor-force participation of secondary workers," *Industrial and Labor*

Relations Review, January, 1967, pp. 275–97. Current labor force data appear each year in the *Manpower Report of the President,* issued by the U.S. Department of Labor.

On hours of work, see the Industrial Relations Research Association symposium volume edited by Dankert, Clyde E., Floyd C. Mann, and Herbert R. Northrup, *Hours of Work.* New York: Harper & Row, Publishers, 1965.

On educational and other measures of labor force quality, in addition to the Schultz, Kendrick, Denison, and Scoville studies cited above, see Becker, Gary S., *Human Capital.* New York: National Bureau of Economic Research, 1964; Harbison, F. H., and C. A. Myers, *Education, Manpower, and Economic Growth.* New York: McGraw-Hill Book Company, 1964; and Mincer, Jacob, "On-the-job training: costs, returns, and some implications," *Journal of Political Economy,* October, 1962, Supplement, pp. 50–79.

THE
DEMAND
FOR   3
LABOR

Demand for labor can be discussed at several levels. We can analyze *total demand* for labor in the economy; or demand for particular *types of labor* (doctors, stenographers, steelworkers); or demand for labor by individual *employing units.* Each of these subjects is important, and each will be explored at the appropriate point in later chapters.

This chapter is devoted to demand at the second, or semiaggregative level. In theorizing about total demand, we often speak as though labor consisted of homogeneous units. But as soon as we look below the surface, we find that demand is highly diversified. It consists of demands for people with specific skills and experience, to perform thousands of different jobs, located throughout the breadth of the country.

Moreover, in a growing and technically dynamic economy such as that of the United States, the pattern of demand is shifting rapidly. The structure of jobs in 1970 is substantially different from that in 1940, and the job pattern of 2000 will again be quite different. The labor force is continuously being reshaped to fit the new demand pattern.

This does not happen without effort, cost, and some measure of inefficiency. The uncertainty of future demand introduces a risk element into occupational choices. Shiftability of demand increases the volume of traffic through the labor market, increases workers' costs of job hunting and unemployment between jobs, and intensifies the need for efficient labor market organization. Demand shifts also create a possibility of continuing labor shortages in expanding sectors of the economy combined with stranded workers in declining sectors, a possibility usually termed *structural unemployment*.

In this chapter we examine the main directions of demand shift and the labor market currents which they create. This will provide a background for discussion of labor market organization and policy in later chapters.

DEMAND SHIFTS
AND
LABOR TURNOVER

The volume of traffic through the labor market depends on many things, including employers' personnel policies, workers' personal characteristics and preferences, and the efficiency of labor market institutions. The largest single source of turnover, however, is the variability of enterprises' demands for labor. Seasonal and cyclical fluctuations of demand are familiar facts of life. Individual firms or even whole industries decline and disappear, while others start up or expand. Mechanization and automation eliminate as well as create jobs and gradually alter the skill composition of labor demand. Some areas of the country experience more rapid economic growth than others, setting up currents of labor migration.

Each year many workers change jobs because they have to, in addition to the many who move voluntarily. The dimensions of this movement are suggested by Figure 1, which shows monthly turnover rates in manufacturing industries over the years 1947 to 1968.[1] The chart shows average monthly hirings (accessions) by all manufacturing plants, calculated as a percentage of the workers already employed. It also shows people leaving manufacturing plants, subdivided into those leaving of their own accord (voluntary quits) and workers laid off or discharged by the employer (other separations). The bulk of the other separations are layoffs, since discharges never form more than a small percentage of employment.

Note first the substantial turnover shown by this chart. Average

[1] These figures are published currently in the U.S. Department of Labor's *Monthly Labor Review.*

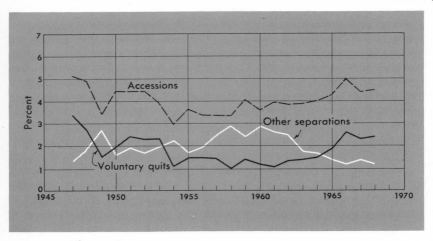

Figure 1

MONTHLY TURNOVER RATES (PER 100 EMPLOYEES)
IN MANUFACTURING INDUSTRIES, 1947–68

hirings and separations by manufacturing plants typically run about 4 percent per month, or close to 50 percent per year. This does not mean that half of all manufacturing workers change jobs every year. A good part of the movement consists of temporary layoffs followed by recall to the same job. Moreover, some very mobile workers change jobs frequently during a year and hence are counted several times in the turnover figures. The number of *movers* is less than the amount of *movement*.

But the number of *movers* is still large. Data compiled by the Bureau of Labor Statistics suggest that upwards of 10 million people, or one-sixth of all wage and salary earners, change jobs in a typical year.[2] Such a large number of job changes connote an enormous amount of human drama—experiment, risk, progress, and disappointment. Women workers are slightly less prone to change jobs than are men; but the most striking mobility differences are related to age. Mobility is highest (of the order of 25 percent per year) for young people under twenty-five, falls to less than half that for workers aged twenty-five to fifty-four, and becomes very small for older workers approaching retirement.

In some years the volume of separations rises above the volume of new hirings. This indicates a period of recession and falling employ-

[2] The 1968 *Manpower Report of the President* indicates that 11 million people were looking for work at one time or another during the previous year. This compares with a civilian labor force of 77 million, of whom 60 million were wage and salary earners outside agriculture.

ment. Note that separations exceeded hirings during the recessions of 1948 to 1949, 1953 to 1954, 1957 to 1958, and 1960 to 1961. But there is a substantial volume of layoffs even during periods of peak prosperity; and there is a large amount of new hiring even in depression. One reason is that depression and prosperity are never uniform throughout the economy. Some companies and industries are flourishing and expanding while others are encountering rough weather.

Another interesting fact which appears from Figure 1 is that layoffs and voluntary quits fluctuate in opposite directions from each other. When times are bad, workers cling to whatever job they have rather than face the risk of unemployment. When times are good and there are plenty of job vacancies, the quit rate rises because workers feel safer in leaving an unsatisfactory job and trying their luck somewhere else. Layoffs, of course, run in the opposite direction—highest in bad years, considerably lower in years of peak prosperity.

These two types of separation are basically different. From the workers' point of view, layoff or discharge is a negative, involuntary, unpleasant kind of movement. If employment opportunities could be stabilized to a greater degree, involuntary movement would be much lower than it is. Voluntary movement, on the other hand, is a hopeful thing from the worker's standpoint. It is the door to greater opportunity, the way in which the worker seeks to better his position. Even though he may fail, and land in a job no better than the one he left, it is important that he should have the chance to try. This is one of the greatest benefits from maintaining a high level of employment in the economy. Full employment assures the workers not only of a job and a means of livelihood, but it provides greater opportunity to advance to a still better job.

Observation of these millions of people flowing into and out of employment suggests some important questions. Is there more movement of labor than is strictly necessary to meet the changing requirements of the economy? How much more? Could seasonal and cyclical variations in demand be reduced by better economic policy? Given these fluctuations, could turnover be reduced by greater willingness to vary hours of work rather than number of people employed? How much could voluntary quitting be reduced by better vocational counseling, more effective public employment offices, better employer procedures in hiring, promotion, and job incentives?

INTERINDUSTRY SHIFTS

It would be useful to know how many new jobs appear each year, what kind of jobs they are, and where they are located; and also to

know the characteristics of jobs that disappear. This information we
do not have. We can draw conclusions about *net* shifts in demand,
however, by observing the behavior of employment; i.e. by comparing
the *stock* figures for two dates we can infer something about the *flows*
between these dates. An industry in which employment has risen must
have had an excess of new vacancies over vanishing jobs.[3] If employment has declined, job disappearances must have exceeded job creation. Similar conclusions can be drawn from data on the occupational
and geographic distribution of employment. It will be useful, therefore, to look at the changing pattern of employment in recent decades
and the statistical projections which have been made for the future.

Study of many countries over long periods shows that, as a country's
per capita income rises, there are systematic shifts in the relative importance of different industries. These shifts are confirmed by cross-
section comparison of countries at different income levels at the same
time.[4]

There are two main reasons for these shifts: (1) differing income
elasticities of demand (as per capita income rises, demand for medical
care rises faster than demand for potatoes); (2) differing productivity
trends. If productivity is rising unusually fast in industry *A,* its unit
cost of production will be falling unusually rapidly. This will be reflected in prices, and the products of industry *A* will become cheaper
relative to other products. This will encourage consumers to buy more
of *A*'s products than before, and less of other things.

The clearest tendency is a long-run decline in the relative importance of agriculture. The proportion of the labor force engaged in
agriculture falls from 70 percent or more in the least-developed countries to 10 percent or less in the most advanced. This does not, of
course, mean any decrease in agricultural output. It means rather such
a great rise in agricultural productivity that the population can be fed
by a much smaller segment of the labor force. One farm family, instead of feeding little more than itself, can now feed ten other families
as well.

Industries engaged in commodity production—manufacturing,
mining, construction—increase sharply in importance as economic
growth proceeds, but this increase does not continue indefinitely. After
a certain point, the proportion of the labor force engaged in these

---

[3] Note, however, that *gross* changes in demand, which determine the volume of
unavoidable labor mobility, cannot be ascertained from employment data. If employment in an industry has risen by 100,000 over a certain period, this could
mean 100,000 new jobs with none disappearing, 200,000 new jobs with 100,000
disappearing, or any similar combination.

[4] See in particular Simon Kuznets, *Modern Economic Growth* (New Haven:
Yale University Press, 1966), and Hollis B. Chenery, "Patterns of industrial growth,"
American Economic Review, September, 1960, pp. 624–54.

industries levels off and moves along on a plateau. In most advanced industrial countries this plateau level is between 30 and 40 percent of the labor force, though in a few countries (Britain, Sweden, West Germany) it approaches 50 percent.

With agriculture continuing to decline in relative importance as development proceeds, and with commodity production levelling off, what takes up the slack in the labor force? The answer is found in industries producing services of every sort—wholesale and retail trade, banking and finance, recreation and entertainment, professional and other personal services, and government. Except for domestic service, which declines in the long run, the proportion of the labor force employed in service activities rises steadily as national income rises. More than 50 percent of the labor force in Canada, and almost 60 percent in the United States, is now employed in the service industries.

The trend in the United States from 1870 to 1930 is shown in Table 1, while Table 2 gives a more detailed picture for selected years since

Table 1

DISTRIBUTION OF EMPLOYMENT
BY MAJOR SECTORS, 1870–1930

(percent)

	1870	1880	1890	1900	1910	1920	1930
AGRICULTURE	50.8	50.6	43.1	38.1	32.1	27.6	22.7
INDUSTRY	30.0	30.1	34.8	37.8	40.9	44.8	42.1
SERVICES	19.2	19.3	22.1	24.1	27.0	27.6	35.2

1929.[5] Agriculture, which as late as 1880 still employed half the labor force, today employs less than 5 percent. This has come about partly because of the low income elasticity of demand for food, partly because of a spectacular rise in agricultural productivity since 1940. Over the last three decades more than 25 million people have left the land, and those remaining are more than capable of meeting our food requirements.

The industrial sector increased in relative importance until 1920, reaching a peak of 45 percent of total employment in that year, from which it has receded to somewhat under 40 percent at present. Manufacturing has remained rather stable in the long run, at around 25 percent of the labor force, and construction has held steady at 5 per-

[5] Table 1 and the first three columns of Table 2 are from Victor R. Fuchs, *The Service Economy* (New York: National Bureau of Economic Research, 1968), pp. 19–24. The 1975 projections in Table 2 are from the 1968 *Manpower Report of the President,* p. 304.

The Demand for Labor

Table 2

EMPLOYMENT BY SECTOR AND
MAJOR INDUSTRY GROUP, 1929–75

(percent)

	1929	1947	1965	1975 (projected)
AGRICULTURE	19.9	12.1	5.7	4.7
INDUSTRY	39.7	42.1	39.6	36.5
SERVICES	40.4	45.8	54.8	58.8
INDUSTRY				
MINING	2.2	1.7	0.9	0.8
CONSTRUCTION	5.0	5.2	5.6	5.3
MANUFACTURING	22.8	26.7	25.9	24.6
TRANSPORTATION	6.6	5.3	3.5	3.7
COMMUNICATIONS AND				
PUBLIC UTILITIES	7.2	2.1	2.1	2.1
GOVERNMENT ENTERPRISE	0.9	1.2	1.6	*
SERVICES				
WHOLESALE TRADE	3.8	4.5	4.7	5.2
RETAIL TRADE	12.9	13.9	13.7	15.0
FINANCE AND INSURANCE	2.6	2.2	3.3	} 4.7
REAL ESTATE	0.8	1.0	1.1	
HOUSEHOLDS AND INSTITUTIONS	7.0	5.2	7.1	} 16.2
PROFESSIONAL, PERSONAL,				
BUSINESS AND REPAIR SERVICES	7.3	8.3	9.4	
GENERAL GOVERNMENT				
(INCLUDING ARMED FORCES)	6.0	10.6	15.5	17.7

* Included under other categories.

cent. But there has been a sharp decline in mining employment (mainly in coal) and in transportation employment (mainly on the railroads).

The really striking development since 1920, and particularly since 1945, is the rise of what Fuchs has labeled "the service economy." In 1920 the proportion of the labor force employed in service industries was less than 30 percent. Today it is nearing 60 percent and still rising. In the goods-producing industries, including agriculture, *there has been virtually no increase in total employment* since 1947. In that year some 31.3 million people were employed in the goods-producing industries. The projected figure for 1975 is only 32.8 million. This means that the 22 million net increase in the labor force between 1947 and 1975 *will have been almost completely absorbed in the service industries.*

It does not mean that no one has been hired in the goods-producing industries since 1947. Since workers retire each year, there is considerable hiring for replacement purposes. But *net expansion* has been concentrated almost entirely in the service sector. Within this sector, the most rapidly growing areas have been government service and professional, personal, and repair services. These two areas alone now employ close to 30 percent of the labor force.

What are the reasons for this growing preponderance of service employment? It is often asserted that the income elasticity of demand for services *as a group* is higher than that for goods *as a group*. After reviewing the evidence for the United States Fuchs finds little support for this view. Indeed, commodity output in real terms has risen just about as fast as output of services since 1929. The decisive factor, then, is the differing movement of output per worker in the two sectors. Fuchs finds that over the period from 1929 to 1965 output per man rose at an average annual rate of 3.4 percent in agriculture, 2.2 percent in industry, and 1.1 percent in services.[6] Put differently, the amount of labor needed for a given volume of output has been shrinking much faster in industry and agriculture than in the service industries. This leads to a steadily shrinking proportion of the labor force in the agricultural and industrial sectors.

Professor William Baumol has put this point in a dramatic parable.[7] Consider an economy with two sectors. In one sector (which we may call S for services, though Baumol does not) productivity never rises. In the other sector (which we call G for goods) productivity rises at a constant rate. Wages in *both sectors* rise at the same rate, geared to the rate of productivity increase in the G sector.

What will happen? (1) If the ratio of real output in the two sectors remains constant, the proportion of the labor force employed in the G sector will approach zero, while the proportion in the S sector will approach 100 percent. As this happens, the rate of productivity increase in the economy will also approach zero. (2) Cost (and hence price) per unit of output in the S sector will rise without limit. Output of goods whose demand is price elastic will decline and perhaps ultimately vanish. As examples, Baumol cites fine handmade goods, fine restaurants, live theatrical and concert performances, and "stately homes" requiring domestic servants. (3) Activities for which demand is income elastic and price inelastic, such as education and marketing services, will absorb a steadily increasing proportion of the labor force and of GNP. Since many of these are public-sector activities, pressure on state and local government budgets will be intense.

The rise of the service economy has other implications for economics, and especially for labor economics: (1) economic evolution is often portrayed as a movement toward ever larger and more impersonal

---

[6] *Service Economy,* p. 51.

[7] William J. Baumol, "Macroeconomics of unbalanced growth: the anatomy of urban crisis," *American Economic Review,* June, 1967, pp. 415–26.

production units. This view is based almost entirely on the (now declining) goods sector. Most service activities have relatively small scale of plant, and self-employment is common. (2) In the same vein, it is often said that the impersonal, routinized, and mechanized conditions of modern industry have squeezed the intrinsic interest out of labor, and that the worker must increasingly find his satisfactions off the job. But in the growing service sector, many activities require a high level of skill and training, involve personal contact with the consumer, and permit a wide variety of satisfying work activity. (3) Service industries employ a high proportion of white-collar workers, a high proportion (almost 50 percent) of women workers, and a high proportion (more than one-quarter) of part-time workers. This is reshaping the composition of the labor force and the character of labor markets. Economists need to devote relatively more attention to white-collar labor markets than has been true in the past. (4) Less than 10 percent of workers in the S sector are unionized, compared with more than 50 percent in the G sector. Unless unionism succeeds in penetrating the service industries, it will be a declining influence in the economy; and if it does succeed, the character of the union movement will be considerably changed.

OCCUPATIONAL
SHIFTS

A different classification of the labor force is in terms of the kind of work done—unskilled, semiskilled, clerical, professional, and so on. Trends in the occupational distribution of the labor force stem partly from the industry shifts just described. If industries employing large numbers of clerical workers, salespeople, and professional people are increasing in relative importance, these groups will form a growing proportion of the labor force. A second factor, however, is changes in work methods within particular industries. Thus manufacturing now employs a considerably lower ratio of production workers, and a higher ratio of clerical, supervisory, and other nonproduction workers than was true a generation ago. Automation of production processes in both factory and office has altered the skill composition of the labor force.

Changes in the occupational distribution of the labor force since 1930 and Bureau of Labor Statistics projections for 1975 are shown in Table 3.[8] The most striking feature of Table 3 is the growing predominance of the service-type occupations (which are largely, though

---

[8] Data for 1930 are from *Historical Statistics of the United States*, p. 76; for 1960 and 1975 from *Manpower Report of the President*, 1968, p. 304; for 1968 from *Monthly Labor Review*, April, 1969.

Table 3

OCCUPATIONAL DISTRIBUTION OF THE U.S.
LABOR FORCE, SELECTED YEARS, 1930–75

(percent)

	1930	1960	1968	1975 (projected)
SERVICE-TYPE OCCUPATIONS	36.5	55.5	59.2	62.3
PROFESSIONAL, TECHNICAL AND KINDRED WORKERS	7.1	11.4	13.6	14.8
MANAGERS, OFFICIALS AND PROPRIETORS (EXCL. FARM)	7.7	10.7	10.2	10.4
CLERICAL AND KINDRED WORKERS	9.3	14.8	16.8	16.9
SALES WORKERS	6.5	6.4	6.2	6.4
SERVICE WORKERS	5.9	12.2	12.4	13.8
GOODS-TYPE OCCUPATIONS	63.3	44.2	40.8	37.6
CRAFTSMEN, FOREMEN, AND KINDRED WORKERS	13.4	13.0	13.2	13.0
OPERATIVES AND KINDRED WORKERS	16.4	18.2	18.4	16.9
LABORERS (EXCL. FARM AND MINE)	11.4	5.4	4.7	4.1
FARMERS AND FARM LABORERS	22.1	7.8	4.5	3.6

not entirely, synonymous with "white-collar" employment) over goods-type occupations. As a percentage of total employment, the former group pulled ahead of the latter around 1955 and the gap has been widening ever since.

This is a general tendency in all advanced industrial countries. For example, Table 4 compares the occupational distribution of the Canadian labor force in 1901 and 1961. Note that more than four-fifths of women workers, and more than half of all workers, are now engaged in white-collar occupations.

There has been an especially sharp increase in demand for professional and technical skills. In the United States, professional, semi-professional, and technical workers have quadrupled in numbers and more than doubled in relative importance over the past half century. This is due mainly to a great rise in consumer incomes and living standards, which has permitted consumers to spend much more on education, health, entertainment, and other professional services. A high proportion of national income spent on professional and personal services is, in fact, almost a definition of a high standard of living. Another factor is the increasingly complex and scientific character of industrial operations, which requires large numbers of research scientists, engineers, and technical assistants. It is estimated that there were 7,000 engineers in the United States in 1870. Today there are more than half a million, and the number is still increasing.

Table 4

OCCUPATIONAL DISTRIBUTION
OF THE CANADIAN LABOR FORCE,
1901 AND 1961
(percent)

Occupation Group	MALE WORKERS		FEMALE WORKERS		TOTAL WORKERS	
	1901	*1961*	*1901*	*1961*	*1901*	*1961*
PRIMARY PRODUCTION	50.5	17.6	3.8	3.9	44.3	13.8
BLUE-COLLAR	27.4	34.1	29.8	10.8	27.9	27.9
WHITE-COLLAR	17.0	38.6	66.0	82.1	23.4	50.5
TRANSPORT AND COMMUNICATION	5.1	9.7	0.4	2.1	4.4	7.7
TOTAL	100.0	100.0	100.0	100.0	100.0	100.0

SOURCE: H. D. Woods and Sylvia Ostry, *Labour Policy and Labour Economics in Canada* (Toronto: Macmillan of Canada, 1962), p. 324.

Clerical and kindred workers have increased from 2 million in 1910 to over 13 million at present. Almost two-thirds of these workers are women, and this is the main point at which women have increased their participation in employment. The rapid growth of clerical employment reflects partly the expansion of service industries in which clerical workers are especially important—government, finance and insurance, trade, communications, and so on. It reflects also the growing size, complexity, and mechanization of industrial operations, which require more and more people to distribute and keep records on the goods produced, and relatively fewer people to produce them.

Until recently semiskilled factory operatives formed an increasing proportion of the labor force because of the growing importance of manufacturing in the economy and the accompanying mechanization of production. Increased use of hand-operated machinery created a great array of jobs which required a short period of specialized training but did not require the craftsman's all-round knowledge and experience. One should perhaps term this *incomplete or partial mechanization*. The more complete automation of many production processes since the late forties has reduced the need for semiskilled operatives, and their importance in the labor force has begun to decline.

Interestingly enough, the proportion of skilled workers in the economy has remained roughly constant over the past half century instead of declining as might have been expected. The proportion of skilled men on production work in manufacturing has indeed fallen as production processes have been subdivided, mechanized, and downgraded.

This has been offset, however, by a great increase in repair and service jobs—maintenance mechanics needed in factories to keep the more complicated machinery in good repair; automobile and airplane mechanics and repairmen; telephone, telegraph, and power linemen and servicemen; and a wide variety of other groups. Skilled building trades workers have increased in relative importance with the high level of construction activity since 1940; and foremen and subforemen, whom the census classifies with craftsmen, have also increased in number.

Farmers and farm laborers have diminished in importance with the relative decline of agriculture. Domestic service has declined sharply as high labor demand has enabled domestics to shift to better-paid jobs in manufacturing and elsewhere. There has also been a sharp decline in the proportion of the labor force engaged in urban unskilled labor, which has been more than cut in half since 1930. There is much less "back work" in industry today than there was fifty years ago, owing partly to the development of mechanical lifting and moving devices—conveyor systems, gravity feeds, mechanized hand trucks, overhead cranes, and so on. Much of the work which used to be done by people with strong muscles is now done by a machine operated by a man who needs less strength but more intelligence and experience. In this respect, then, industrial employment has become more skilled and more pleasant.

While the classification of jobs used in Table 3 is conventional, it is not entirely satisfactory. One tends to assume that all jobs in the professional–managerial categories are more skilled than those in the sales–clerical categories, and that these in turn are more skilled than most kinds of manual labor. But this is not entirely true. *Within* each of the standard occupational categories there is a wide range, from jobs requiring little skill or training up to the most complex and demanding kinds of work. For this reason James Scoville, in the study cited in Chapter 2 developed a new fivefold classification based on richness of job content—complexity of the operations involved, amount of general educational background required, and length of specific vocational training.

Scoville's classification cuts across the standard occupational classification. Thus some clerical workers (auditors, librarians) fall in class one, while others (telegraph messengers, office boys) fall in class five. Some administrative workers (personnel managers, editors) are assigned to class one, but others to lower classes down to building managers (class five). Similarly for each other major category. While this classification is admittedly experimental, it is logically superior as an indicator of skill level and training requirements, and we saw in the last chapter that it correlates well with earnings level and educational attainment.

Scoville's results, some of which are shown in Tables 5 and 6, con-

Table 5

DISTRIBUTION OF EMPLOYMENT,

BY JOB-CONTENT LEVEL

(percent)

Level	1940	1950	1960	1970 (estimated)
1	6.1	6.8	8.7	9.4
2	9.6	11.5	14.2	16.1
3	28.5	32.5	34.2	34.7
4	24.5	20.8	17.0	15.8
5	31.6	28.4	25.9	24.0

Table 6

RATE OF INCREASE IN EMPLOYMENT,

BY JOB-CONTENT LEVEL

(percent per decade)

Level	1940–50	1950–60	1960–70 (estimated)
Total	24.5	10.8	19.2
1	39.2	41.7	29.5
2	50.6	35.9	35.7
3	41.7	16.5	20.9
4	12.5	−9.1	10.3
5	12.0	10.8	10.3

firm that the skill composition of employment in the American economy has been rising very rapidly.[9] More than 25 percent of all jobs
now fall in the top two skill classes, compared with only 15 percent in
1940. There has been a corresponding shrinkage in the relative importance of the two lowest categories, from 56 percent of employment in
1940 to 40 percent in 1970. The implication of these shifts for *rates of
increase* in labor demand are shown in Table 6. The less-skilled occupations have had very low rates of increase since 1940, with class four
showing an actual decline from 1950 to 1960. Classes one and two, on
the other hand, have had very high rates of demand increase.

In order to achieve supply–demand balance over this period, it has

[9] Data are from James G. Scoville, *The Job Content of the U.S. Economy,
1940–70* (New York: McGraw-Hill Book Company, 1969), p. 54. Since the study
was published in 1969, the 1970 data are estimates, while those for earlier years
are actual magnitudes.

been necessary to deflect a high proportion of young people entering the labor force into the upper occupations, requiring more prolonged education and training. How successfully this has been accomplished and whether failure of training levels to rise as fast as demand requirements has created structural unemployment, will be examined in Chapter 5.

Automation and Skill

It is desirable to add a word on automation because of the prominence of this subject in popular discussion and the numerous misconceptions surrounding it. In popular usage, automation is a loose term covering a variety of different things. Baldwin and Shultz have distinguished (1) "continuous automatic production" or "Detroit automation"—the linking together of separate production operations along a continuous line through which the product moves unaided by human hands; (2) "feedback technology"—use of built-in automatic devices (servomechanisms) for comparing the way in which work is actually being done with the way in which it is supposed to be done and then making automatic adjustments in the work process; (3) "computer technology"—use of computing machines for recording and storing information and for performing both simple and complex mathematical operations upon it.[10]

These devices can be used separately or in combination. The hypothetical "automatic factory" of the future would employ all three in various proportions. Computer technology is farthest developed at present. Its main impact will be in the office, where it will displace a large amount of clerical labor and possibly even junior management personnel. Information technology may structure many management jobs in the future, just as Taylorism structured hourly rated production jobs in the past.

The other two types of automation are less fully developed, but have a large potential impact on factory production over the next two or three decades. Broadly speaking, these processes operate to reverse the labor force trends produced by the partial mechanization of earlier times. Old-style mechanization, as we have seen, made for a rapid multiplication of semiskilled machine tenders at the expense of skilled craftsmen. But once materials handling and machine operations have been sufficiently subdivided and routinized, they can be taken over completely by automation and the need for the semiskilled man disappears. In some industries, then, the semiskilled operative may turn

---

[10] George B. Baldwin and George P. Shultz, "Automation: A New Dimension to Old Problems," *Proceedings of the Seventh Annual Meeting of the IRRA* (1954), pp. 114–28.

out to have played a temporary and transitional role on the way from old-style handicraft production to fully automatic production.

As automation gathered force during the fifties and sixties, there were frequent expressions of alarm over its possible consequences. Here, it was said, is a "second industrial revolution," moving at a much faster pace than the mechanization of earlier decades. Whole categories of employment will be laid waste. The aggregate man-hour requirements of the economy will shrink. Reduction of the workweek and other special measures will be needed to avert massive unemployment. These predictions were disputed by others, and there was a large outpouring of literature, including a full-scale examination by a National Commission.[11] The dust has now settled to the extent of producing considerable agreement on several points.

First, there are indications that—at least in the United States—the pace of technological change has been faster since 1940 than it was in earlier decades. There is no direct measure of the rate of technical progress. But the rate of increase in output per man-hour, or perhaps better, in output per unit of combined labor and capital inputs, reflects technical progress in a broad sense. Both types of productivity index have risen considerably faster in recent decades than in earlier decades. The National Commission found also that the time lag between discovery of a new production process and its commercial application has fallen considerably. For a sample of technological innovations, the "development period" averaged twenty-four years in the era from 1920 to 1944, but only fourteen years in the period from 1945 to 1964. Expenditures on industrial research and development have risen at a sensational rate since 1945, both absolutely and as a percentage of GNP.

Second, the view that accelerated technical progress leads to *general* reductions in labor demand has been convincingly refuted. This view, always suspect on theoretical grounds, gained surface plausibility from the relatively high unemployment rates of the years 1958 to 1964. But from 1965 to 1970 the economy was consistently in a position of full, or even overfull, employment; and there is no reason why a high level of employment cannot continue after the tapering off of war demands.

Third, displacement of labor in particular firms and industries is clearly a possibility. Indeed, it seems likely that changing technology is now eliminating jobs at a (moderately) faster rate than was true before 1945. This hypothesis is difficult to test statistically. If a new

11 See the multi-volume Report of the National Commission on Technology, Automation, and Economic Progress, particularly Vol. 1, *Technology and the American Economy* (Washington, D.C.: Government Printing Office, 1966). See also Jack Stieber, ed., *Employment Problems of Automation and Advanced Technology* (New York: The Macmillan Company, 1966), proceedings of a conference held at Geneva by the International Institute for Labour Studies.

process reduces the cost and price of a product substantially, and if demand is sufficiently elastic to produce a large increase in sales, there may be no absolute decline in employment. One can still speak of "labor displacement" in the sense that the number of people employed with the new process is less than would be required for the same level of output with the old process. In some cases there has doubtless been absolute displacement as well. But these cases are confined at any time to limited sectors of the economy.

Even where total employment in a firm is not reduced by automation, the distribution of skill requirements may be considerably altered. The results of research to date suggest that the net effect of automation is usually an upgrading of skill requirements.[12] The skills eliminated tend to be of a routine or semiskilled character. On the positive side, automation increases the need for skilled workers in the machine-building industries, for skilled maintenance men to keep the automatic equipment in steady operation, for "machine watchers" who must be able to respond quickly and correctly to machine errors, and for computer programmers and other technicians. But this is cold comfort to the displaced bookkeeper or machine operative unless he is enabled to learn the new skills.

Whether an increasingly rapid shift in skill requirements leads to an increase in "frictional" or "structural" unemployment depends on the malleability of the labor force. This is partly a matter of willingness of unemployed workers to learn new skills and perhaps move to new areas. Mainly, however, it depends on the effectiveness of educational and training institutions, and of vocational counseling and placement agencies, in channeling the flow of new entrants to the labor force.

GEOGRAPHIC SHIFTS

A final important characteristic of labor demand is its geographic location. In a country as large and diversified as the United States, job opportunities may be expanding rapidly in some areas while they are

12 See, for example, George P. Shultz and Arnold Weber, "Technological Change and Industrial Relations," in an IRRA symposium on *Employment Relations Research* (New York: Harper & Row, Publishers, 1960); a March, 1962 issue of the Annals of the American Academy, devoted entirely to automation; and Roy B. Helfgott, "Electronic Data Processing and the Office Work Force," *Industrial and Labor Relations Review*, July, 1966, pp. 503–16. This study of seven large companies that had installed computerized data processing showed an overall increase of employment because of the rapid increase of workloads. There was, however, considerable displacement of labor in the lowest clerical grades, with a more than offsetting increase of employment in higher grades.

stagnating or declining in others. This may be due to the decline of
an industry (coal mining in Appalachia, agriculture in many southern
and midwestern states), to the geographic shift of an industry (textiles
from New England to the South), or to spectacular expansion of an
industry that has become localized in a certain region (automobiles
in Michigan at an earlier period, aircraft and electronics in California
in more recent years).

Recent and projected employment trends for selected states are
shown in Table 7.[13] For the nation as a whole, the labor force has

Table 7

ESTIMATED PERCENTAGE INCREASE
IN LABOR FORCE, SELECTED STATES,
1960–70 AND 1970–80

(increase, percent)

	1960–70	1970–80		1960–70	1970–80
ARIZONA	56.0	36.6	ILLINOIS	13.4	16.5
FLORIDA	40.6	33.7	IOWA	12.1	13.9
CALIFORNIA	37.7	28.1	MASSACHUSETTS	13.5	13.7
TEXAS	24.3	21.1	PENNSYLVANIA	10.4	11.1
WISCONSIN	18.0	19.0	NEW YORK	15.0	10.8
OHIO	19.0	18.4	WEST VIRGINIA	13.2	9.2
NEW JERSEY	21.2	17.0	RHODE ISLAND	9.2	7.9

increased by 21.1 percent from 1960 to 1970 and is expected to increase by 18.3 percent from 1970 to 1980. But some states are obviously
doing much better than this and others considerably worse. The expansion of employment in Florida, the Pacific Coast, and the Southwest is strikingly larger than in the Northeast. If we assume (which is
not far wrong) that the natural rate of population growth is uniform
among regions, there will clearly have to be large-scale movement of
people to the regions with highest rates of increase in employment.

The statistics of migration reveal a large amount of geographical
movement.[14] In a typical year, about 6 percent of the American people
move across county lines. About half of this is movement within the
same state, while the other half is across state lines. The movement is
broadly "economic," i.e. it is toward areas of relatively high wages and
expanding employment. Unemployed men are about twice as likely to
move as employed men. Young people are much more mobile than

13 *Manpower Report of the President*, 1968, p. 303.
14 For an analysis of migration since World War II, see Eleanor G. Gilpatrick,
Structural Unemployment and Aggregate Demand (Baltimore: The Johns Hopkins
Press, 1966), chap. 7.

older people. Mobility also increases with level of education. By occupation, much the highest migration rate is for professional people, followed at a considerable distance by sales workers and management people. The high mobility of professionals results from a combination of high education level, wide geographic scope of the market for professional skills, and good channels of market information.

On one hand, this large-scale migration connotes opportunity for personal advancement. On the other hand it involves personal and social costs and provides opportunity for mistaken choices. How far the movement could be rationalized by improved labor market institutions is an important question to be considered in Chapter 6.

SOME CONSEQUENCES
OF
DEMAND SHIFTS

Shifts in labor demand have major consequences, for workers and for the economy. First, trends in labor demand are the main force operating to reshape the pattern of employment. People learn the skills and move to the locations that production requirements impose on them. If, in the aggregate, jobs are becoming more pleasant and satisfying over the course of time, this increase in welfare should be included in any assessment of economic progress. This source of increased welfare—"producer satisfaction" as distinct from "consumer satisfaction"—has certainly been important in the United States over the past fifty years.

Second, the larger the shifts in demand, the more members of the labor force will have to change jobs one or more times in the course of their working lives. This involves costs which must be set against the advantages of a dynamic economy. An enforced job change strikes the worker as a misfortune rather than an opportunity, so subjective costs are involved. The period during which the worker is unemployed while seeking a new job involves a production loss to the economy; and the employment service activities, training programs, and other measures needed to speed the readjustment of the labor force also involve economic cost.

The dimensions of this problem depend partly on the rate at which population, labor force, and national output are growing over time. With a static labor force, a *relative* decline of employment in any sector would have to mean an *absolute* decline as well. But if total employment is rising, a redistribution of the labor force can occur without anyone losing his job. Employment can decline relatively in some sectors simply by rising less rapidly than employment in general.

In this sense a high rate of economic growth eases the difficulties of labor force readjustment.

The problem of the employed worker is different from that of the young person preparing for employment. The worker committed to a particular occupation and industry need worry only about an *absolute* decline of employment in his sector of the market. If there is no decline, his position will become increasingly secure through formal or informal seniority arrangements. Those still in the educational pipeline, however, need to know the composition of the job vacancies that will be available *at the time they enter the market.* More correctly, they should know the distribution of both prospective vacancies and prospective labor supplies, since this will determine the tightness or slackness of particular submarkets.

Finally, the magnitude of demand shifts will affect the unemployment level in the economy. A larger volume of movement through the labor market, even assuming the same average time between jobs, must itself raise the unemployment rate. In addition, there is the possibility that many of the workers who lose jobs because of demand shifts will not have the qualifications required for the vacancies that are appearing at the growth points of the economy and may on this account suffer unusually long periods of unemployment. This kind of maladjustment is often termed "structural unemployment." Structural unemployment, however, does not have to be accepted as a fact of nature. It can be attacked by various measures of manpower policy, which we shall analyze at a later point.

Discussion Questions

1. It is often said that members of the American labor force are less willing to change jobs today than they were a generation or two ago. Could one get satisfactory evidence on this point by looking at turnover statistics?

2. Would you expect the quit rate and the layoff rate to move in the same direction or in opposite directions in the course of the business cycle? Explain.

3. The rise of the "service economy" has increased the service industries' share of total employment but has apparently not increased their share of national output. Can you explain these divergent trends?

4. Over the past several decades there has been a marked shift of

demand toward jobs with higher educational and skill requirements. What kind of labor market maladjustments might result from this shift, and how could one determine whether such maladjustments have in fact occurred?

5. From your previous training in economics, can you explain why accelerated mechanization and automation need not raise the level of unemployment?

6. How is continued progress of automation likely to affect the occupational composition of the labor force?

7. "Steps should be taken to spread the growth of new industry more evenly over the country, thus reducing the need for expensive interstate migration." Do you agree? Why, or why not?

8. What are the main economic costs arising from a more-rapid, as against a less-rapid, rate of shifting in labor demand?

Reading Suggestions

The Fuchs, Gilpatrick, and Scoville studies cited above contain useful analyses of trends in labor demand over recent decades. Current data on the distribution of employment are published in the *Monthly Labor Review* and in the annual *Manpower Report of the President*.

LABOR MARKETS: THE COMPETITIVE MODEL

4

What do we mean by "the labor market"? Is it a mere abstraction, or is it something we can see and touch? How does it operate? In which respects does it resemble or differ from commodity markets?

These are complex questions, which will occupy us for the next three chapters. In this chapter we examine how labor markets would operate under simple conditions of pure competition, full information, and free choice. The next chapter describes the main ways in which actual labor markets depart from the competitive model. Finally, in Chapter 6, we consider how labor markets might be (and are being) improved by government action.

The Scope of Labor Markets

A market is not necessarily, or even usually, a single place. True, there are places which are directly involved in labor recruitment and placement—union offices in the building or printing trades, the central hiring hall for longshoremen or seamen, the local office of the state employment service in each community. But these places are not synonymous with *the* labor market, since their use is usually not obligatory and much of the flow of labor bypasses them.

The standard definition of "market" is an area within which buyers and sellers are in sufficiently close communication that price tends to be the same throughout the area. Such an area may vary in size from a neighborhood to the whole world. In the case of labor, the size of the market area varies with the skill level involved. Top administrators and professional men enjoy a national (even to some extent an international) market. The number of qualified people being small, employers find it feasible and desirable to recruit from all parts of the country. Accurate information about openings, salaries, and so on is usually available through personal contacts and professional associations. The cost of moving from one part of the country to another is small relative to potential gains in income and professional advancement.

For most manual, clerical, and subprofessional jobs, the locality is the relevant market area. A worker who is settled in one community is unlikely to know much about, or to be much interested in, jobs in other cities. Homeowners, in particular, are usually unwilling to move except in response to prolonged unemployment. Their market horizon is limited to the area within which they can readily commute to work. As auto transport has increasingly superseded public transport, however, commuting areas have become larger and more flexible. Towns that at one time were quite distinct are now merged into a common market. Moreover, nearby localities are linked by the *possibility* that people might move in response to a substantial divergence in wage levels or employment opportunities.

A locality is not a *single* market, but contains many specialized markets. In Seattle there are markets for typists, for aircraft welders, for schoolteachers, for janitors, and for hundreds of other occupations. Again, markets for "neighboring" occupations are linked by the possibility of labor transfer from one to the other. Occupationally as well as geographically, markets are linked in an intricate network, within which one can distinguish certain ridgelines at the boundaries of commuting areas and clearly defined skill groups.

In a certain sense, each employing unit can be regarded as a separate market. The specialized production jobs in a large manufacturing plant, for example, are typically filled by internal promotion rather than outside recruitment. The employer looks to present employees as his source of supply, and workers look to this "internal market" for their prospects of advancement.

EMPLOYERS'
DEMAND FOR
LABOR

Let us now look at demand for a particular kind of labor—say, the demand of automobile manufacturers for assembly-plant workers. "Demand," as you will recall from elementary economics, is a technical term with a precise meaning. Demand is *not* a single quantity. Demand is a *schedule,* showing in this case the number of workers employers will wish to hire at various possible wage rates. When we transfer this schedule to a graph, it will look like D in Figure 1. The fact that D

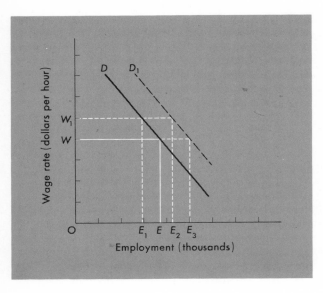

Figure 1
THE LABOR DEMAND SCHEDULE

slopes downward to the right says that—other things being equal—the lower the wage the larger the number of workers hired, and conversely.

The qualification "other things being equal" is very important. Unless we hold everything else in the system constant, we cannot define a labor demand schedule. First, the wages of all other types of labor are held constant. A movement up the vertical axis of Figure 1 means that automobile wages have risen *relative* to all other wages in the economy. Second, demand conditions for the product are held constant. Third, the known methods of production, both those actually being used and others which might be used, are assumed constant. Finally, the characteristics of the automobile workers—their education, job training, physical energy, and motivation—are taken as given.

Given all these things, we can say that an increase in the relative wage of automobile workers, say from OW to OW_1, will lead to a decline in employment from OE to OE_1. There are two reasons for this: (1) an increase in wage rates with no increase in output per worker will raise the cost of producing an automobile. This will lead to a higher price for automobiles [1] and, if the product demand curve remains unchanged as we have assumed, automobile sales will drop. The reduced production will require fewer workers. (2) An increase in wage rates makes labor more expensive relative to capital equipment and other factors of production. Employers thus have an inducement to adopt production methods which use less labor per unit of output.

The decline in employment from OE to OE_1 would be called by many people "a drop in the demand for labor." *This is incorrect.* The labor demand schedule has not changed. Employers have simply moved to a different position on the same schedule in response to the change in wage rate.

A *decrease in demand* means that the whole demand schedule has shifted downward. Similarly, an upward shift of the schedule, say to D_1, is an *increase in demand*. Such a shift will occur if there is a change in one of the things we assumed constant in constructing the demand schedule. For example, the labor demand schedule might shift upward because: (1) demand for automobiles has risen, so that more can be sold at the same price; (2) a new production method has been discovered, which enables each worker to produce more than before; or (3) the quality of the automobile labor force has risen.

This explains why, in actuality, we often see wage increases and employment increases going together. If, while the wage is rising from OW to OW_1, the labor demand curve has shifted from D to D_1, employment will *increase* from OE to OE_2. But it will increase less than it would have if wages had remained at the old level OW, in which case employment would have risen to OE_3. It remains true that there is an inverse relation between wage rate and employment level.

---

[1] The way in which this price increase comes about depends on competitive conditions in the product market. In the automobile case, where producers set their prices as a markup over cost, the price increase would follow quite directly. In a purely competitive industry, with many producers selling at a price determined in the market, the cost increase would eliminate some of the least efficient producers, which would reduce supply, which would raise the market price.

Elasticity of Demand for Labor

The slope, or more precisely the elasticity, of the labor demand schedule differs from one kind of labor to another. What determines elasticity of demand in a particular case?

The answer can be important—for example, to a union considering the possible impact of a wage change. Would an increase of 10 percent in an industry's wage level (everything else in the economy remaining unchanged) reduce employment by 5 percent? Or only by 1 percent? The answer may make considerable difference to union and employer strategy.

The demand for labor is derived from the demand for its product, and so follows the general principles of derived demand. These should be familiar to you from elementary economics, but may be restated here. Elasticity of demand for labor depends on:

1. *Elasticity of Demand for the Product.* Suppose a 10 percent wage increase raises total unit cost 5 percent and that product prices also rise 5 percent. If elasticity of demand for the product is low, say 0.5, sales will fall by only 2.5 percent. But if elasticity were higher, say 2.0, sales and employment would fall 10 percent because of the same wage increase. The more elastic the demand for the product, the more elastic the demand for the labor used in making it.

2. *The Proportion Which Labor Costs Form of Total Production Costs.* If labor is only 10 percent of the total, then a 10 percent wage increase will raise total unit costs only 1 percent. The effect on product prices, sales, and employment will be small. But if labor forms 80 percent of production costs, the impact will be greater. On this account, a skilled craft union covering only a small part of an employer's labor force is in a stronger bargaining position than a plant-wide union. The cost of buying off the craft group is small, and this lessens the employer's resistance; and the employment effect is too small to deter the union from an aggressive wage policy.

3. *The Difficulty of Substituting Other Factors for Labor in Production.* In some cases the existing technique of production may be the only known method, and the possibility of modifying it to save labor may be small. But in other cases, there may be alternative methods involving greater mechanization. At a higher wage, one or more of these methods will become profitable and will be brought into use. The greater the number of known alternative methods, and the more labor they save, the greater the elasticity of demand for labor.

4. *The Supply Curves of Productive Services Other than Labor.* (This is harder to grasp than the three previous points.) Look at it this way: one reason for lower employment at a higher wage is that production costs rise, product prices rise, sales and output are reduced,

and purchases of productive services are reduced. Suppose, however, that the industry uses some factor—say a specialized raw material with no other uses—whose supply curve is highly inelastic. As the industry's demand for this material falls, its price will go down. This reduction in the industry's costs serves as an offset to the higher costs resulting from the wage increase. So the increase in total cost and price will be smaller, and the drop in sales and employment smaller, than they would be without this cushioning factor. In this case, labor's gains are partly at the expense of the owners of this other factor.

To sum up: an industry's demand for labor will be more inelastic—that is, a wage increase will produce a *smaller* drop in employment—in proportion as: (1) demand for the product is inelastic; (2) labor costs form a small proportion of total costs; (3) the known possibilities of substituting capital and other factors for labor are small; and (4) supply of one or more nonlabor factors is inelastic.

LABOR SUPPLY
TO
AN OCCUPATION

Labor supply curves, like labor demand curves, can be constructed at different levels of generality. We can speak of the total supply of labor to the economy, or the supply to a particular occupation or industry, or the supply to an individual employer. Each of these is interesting for different purposes.

Our focus here is on supply at a semiaggregative level: the supply of automobile workers, or coal miners, or dentists, or accountants. We assume that people have free occupational choice. Any worker may enter any occupation that seems preferable to him. He is assumed also to have full information about earnings and other relevant characteristics of each occupation.

Occupational choice, and the information needed to facilitate such choice, is especially critical during the high school and college years. One can visualize young people as moving up an educational escalator, from which they step off at various points, depending on ability, finance, and preference. The decision to step off the escalator is crucial in that it limits the range of subsequent occupational choice. Those who drop out before completing high school are limited mainly to manual labor and service occupations. Those who complete high school tend to enter clerical and sales occupations, though high school completion is also normal for skilled craftsmen and foremen. Those who complete college normally go into the higher ranges of white-collar work—business management, independent proprietorship, teaching, the civil service, and a wide variety of technical and subprofessional occupations. Finally, the professions usually require graduate training beyond college, and are open only to those who come panting off the escalator after some twenty years of formal education.

The educational system thus serves as a giant sieve, sorting people out into broad occupational groups. The boundaries between these groups are not watertight—some men with an eighth-grade education have gone into business for themselves and become millionaires, while some college graduates have ended up on Skid Row. But the boundaries are reasonably firm, and people with a certain level of education tend to move within a range of "neighboring" occupations. Choice is further restricted with increasing age, because employers and educational institutions become increasingly unwilling to retrain people for something different from what they are presently doing. People over forty are usually set for life with their present occupation, and even their present employer. The flexibility of the labor force, its ability to reshape itself to changing demands, is concentrated mainly in the age level sixteen to twenty-five.

The young person (or his parents) deciding whether it is worthwhile to train for a certain occupation, is making an investment decision. For example, to become a lawyer will require four years of college plus three years of law school. The cost includes tuition and other educational expenses for these seven years. It includes also the opportunity cost of the student's time, that is the amount he might have earned by working instead of studying. The return on this educational investment is the difference between the student's prospective earnings as a lawyer and what he might have earned with only a high-school diploma, projected over his probable working life. Since we are here estimating *private* returns to the student, earnings should be estimated *after* income taxes, since this is what the individual will actually receive. Finally, the estimated increase in earnings can be reduced to a rate of return on the initial investment. The procedure is identical with that for estimating the rate of return on a million dollars put into a new factory.

If there were complete certainty about the future, full information, and no financial or other barriers to education, people would flow into each occupation until rates of return to various kinds of training were equal. In fact, many of the higher occupations appear to be "undersupplied," i.e. rates of return to training are positively correlated with levels of skill and earnings.

In 1966 the Census Bureau estimated how much individuals with differing levels of education might be expected to earn from age eighteen to retirement, based on actual earnings data for 1956 to 1966.[2]

---

[2] Bureau of the Census, *Current Population Reports*, Series P–60, No. 56, August 1968.

Here are the results:

Years of Education	Prospective Lifetime Earnings (1966 dollars)
Less than 8	188,659
8	246,525
9–11	283,718
12	340,520
13–15	393,969
16	507,818
17 and over	586,905

This does not tell us the rates of return, since estimates of educational cost were not included. Most research studies, however, conclude that the rate of return on education is above 10 percent, and that it is highest for the higher educational levels.[3]

Income is not the only criterion of occupational choice. Occupations differ in many other respects—in public esteem, in working hours and degree of effort, in regularity of employment, in the pleasantness of the work, in the scope which it offers for originality and initiative. Each person will evaluate these characteristics differently, depending on his preference system. But each person will tend to select the occupation which on balance seems to offer him greatest *net* advantage.

Suppose now that we wish to chart a labor supply curve for a particular occupation. Having just said that income is far from the only consideration in job choices, it may seem arbitrary to single it out for special consideration. But there are reasonable grounds for doing so. First, income is *measurable,* while many other dimensions of an occupation are not. Second, income is for most people an *important* consideration in job choices. Third, income is one of the more *flexible* characteristics of an occupation. Some characteristics, such as the intrinsic difficulty and pleasantness of the work, are deep-rooted and change only slowly. Income can vary from month to month. So it is plausible to take it as variable in our analysis, and to assume that other characteristics of the job are constant over the period in question.

We assume also that the characteristics of all other jobs in the economy, including their income levels, are given and constant. A movement up the vertical axis in Figure 2 is an increase in the wage for this occupation *relative* to all other occupations. The upward sloping supply curve *S* says that, the higher the relative wage for this

[3] For an interesting analysis of prospective returns to sixty-seven occupations, see Arthur Carol and Samuel Parry, "The economic rationale of occupational choice," *Industrial and Labor Relations Review,* January, 1968.

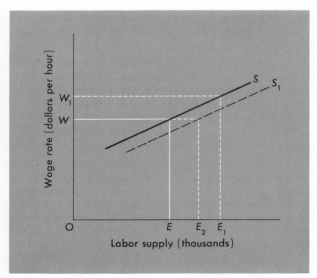

Figure 2
THE LABOR SUPPLY SCHEDULE

occupation, the more people will choose it over other occupations. A higher wage for an occupation will increase its net advantage relative to other occupations. So some people who previously did not think it quite attractive enough will now switch over and choose it in preference to something else. If the relative wage rises still higher, some more people will switch over, and so on.

A rising supply curve is still more plausible if we bring in educational and training costs. There are few occupations that do not involve some training cost, and for the higher occupations the cost is very substantial. The returns may also be substantial, but they are uncertain, so they will be evaluated differently by different individuals. People will differ in their estimate of the most likely rate of return, in their attitude toward risk and uncertainty, in their actual ability for the occupation in question, and in their confidence in their own ability. Therefore, if the true (but unknown) return to investment in training for an occupation is 10 percent, some people will choose it and some will not. But we can be reasonably sure that, if the rate of return rises to 12 percent, returns to all other occupations remaining unchanged, *more* people will choose it than previously. Supply is positively related to prospective earnings.

We must observe the same cautions in discussing labor supply which we noted for labor demand. Suppose the wage in Figure 2 rises from

OW to OW_1, everything else remaining unchanged. By looking at the supply curve, we see that the number who prefer this occupation will rise from OE to OE_1. *This is not an increase in labor supply.* It is simply a movement to another point on the same supply schedule.

An increase in supply means that the whole schedule has shifted rightward to a new location, such as S_1, so that at every possible wage more people now prefer this occupation. At a wage of OW, for example, the number wishing to enter the occupation is now OE_2 rather than OE. Why might such a shift occur? The job itself may have changed, so that its nonwage aspects are more attractive than before. There may have been a spontaneous shift in workers' preferences. Different kinds of work can become more or less fashionable, just as happens with consumer goods. Training opportunities may have been enlarged and training costs reduced, perhaps by a government-sponsored training program.

WAGE RATES
AND LABOR ALLOCATION
UNDER
PURE COMPETITION

Labor demand and supply schedules interact to determine how many will be employed in each occupation and how much they will be paid. Let us ask first how this would work out if all labor markets were purely competitive. This will provide a useful benchmark against which we can measure the effect of deviations from competitive conditions.

The Meaning of Pure Competition

Reasoning about competitive labor markets starts from several assumptions. Some of these, such as many buyers and sellers and absence of collusion, are inherent in the definition of pure competition. Others, such as maximizing behavior by workers and employers, are helpful in reaching definite conclusions. The usual assumptions are:

1. All workers in an occupation are identical as regards productive capacity and personal characteristics. One bricklayer is as good as another, from the employer's standpoint.

2. Workers have full information about job vacancies, wages, and other terms of employment in each occupation and employing unit. They also have full freedom of choice. This implies, among other things, that a young person choosing an occupation that requires training can always obtain the necessary finance to undertake training.

3. Workers act to maximize their net advantage from employment. This implies that, other things being equal, they will prefer a higher wage to a lower one.

4. Employers have full and accurate information on the cost of hiring additional labor, and on how much this labor will add to their output.

5. Employers act to maximize profit. Specifically, they will hire additional workers only as long as this increases profit. An additional worker produces output that, after deducting raw materials and other associated costs, adds something to the firm's net revenue from sales. Let us call this amount the marginal revenue product (MRP) of labor. As more and more workers are hired, their MRP will fall for two reasons: a. the physical product of additional labor applied to a fixed amount of plant and equipment will eventually decline, according to the "law of diminishing returns"; b. if the product is sold under conditions of monopoly, oligopoly, or monopolistic competition, additional output can be sold only at a lower price. If W is the wage rate for the kind of labor in question, the employer will maximize profit by adjusting his employment so that $W = MRP$.[4] If he goes beyond this, so that $MRP < W$, the extra workers will add less to revenue than they are being paid, and profit is reduced.

6. There is full freedom of exchange. Any employer may hire any worker, and any worker may work for any employer.

7. There are numerous buyers and sellers, and no collusion on either side of the market. Employers do not unite to drive down the wage level, nor do workers form unions to drive up wages.

8. There is full employment. Everyone wishing to work at prevailing wage levels can find work.

Equilibrium under Pure Competition

In this context we now ask how many people will be employed in occupation A, and at what wage rate. The demand and supply schedules for the occupation are shown in Figure 2. Then, by the usual reasoning, we can predict that the market will move toward equilibrium at point A. OE workers will be employed in this occupation at a wage rate OW. Any employer who wishes to hire this type of labor will have to pay the market wage.

Similarly, we can draw demand–supply diagrams for occupations $B, C, D \ldots$ and so on through every type of work performed in the

---

[4] This is just another way of saying that, for an individual firm, its MRP schedule is its demand schedule for labor. If we chart it on the usual demand diagram, with the wage rate measured on the vertical axis, we can determine the proper level of employment for any wage OW by running a horizontal line across to the MRP schedule.

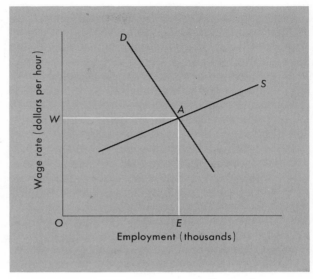

Figure 3

EQUILIBRIUM IN A COMPETITIVE LABOR MARKET

economy. There will be an equilibrium wage and employment for each occupation. Thus the structure of relative wage rates is completely determined, and so is the occupational distribution of the labor force.

This may seem no great feat until one thinks about how labor would be allocated in the absence of a competitive market. Suppose some federal official had to decide, for the American economy as of 1970, how many people should be schoolteachers, how many should be bricklayers, how many should be accountants, and so on. This would be a staggering problem. Yet a competitive market system solves the problem rapidly and inconspicuously.

We can show also that the competitive market solution is optimal, both in terms of national output and in terms of people's satisfaction from work. In output terms, correct allocation requires that the marginal revenue product of a particular kind of labor be the same in every employing unit. The need for this condition is obvious. If a bricklayer has a higher marginal revenue product in company *A* than in company *B,* then national output can be increased by shifting labor from *B* to *A.* As this goes on, marginal productivity will fall in company *A* and rise in company *B.* When it becomes equal in the two companies, nothing can be gained by further shifting.

The proof that this condition is satisfied under pure competition is straightforward. The market price of any type of labor will be the same to all producers. But each producer, to maximize profit, will employ labor only up to the point at which $MRP = W$. Since W is the same for all producers, MRP must also be the same.

Output is not everything. It is desirable also that the tasks performed by members of the community should be so allocated among them as to involve a minimum of sacrifice, because everybody is doing the work in which his net advantage is highest.[5] If this condition is met, we can be sure that no switching of two people between jobs could benefit one person without either harming the other or causing a drop in output. And this condition will be met if people are able to make a free and informed choice among jobs.

Consider Mr. *A*, whose income is below Mr. *B*'s. Then *A* must have chosen his job, in preference to *B*'s, either because, lacking aptitude for *B*'s occupation, he could not have earned *B*'s income in it; or because he sees other disadvantages in *B*'s job that more than offset the higher wage. In neither case would there be a gain from moving *A* to *B*'s job. In the first case output would fall, and in the second case *A* would feel worse off than before.

Shifts in Demand and Supply

We can show, then, that competitive labor markets yield an optimal allocation of the labor force *at a specific moment*. We can show also that the competitive market is an effective mechanism for *reallocating the labor force over time* in response to changes in demand and supply conditions.

Suppose, for example, that the supply curve in Figure 4 shifts from S to S_1. At any given wage, more people than before are now available for this kind of work. This could happen for several reasons. This could be a white-collar occupation requiring high school graduation, and the proportion of each age-group who finish high school could be rising. Or the job could have become easier or other nonwage conditions could have improved. Or certain groups (women, black workers, and so on) formerly excluded from this kind of work may now be admitted, increasing the available supply.

Remember that everything else in the economy is being held constant. Moving to the right along the employment axis means an increase in employment in this occupation relative to all other occupations. Moving upward on the wage axis means a higher wage for this occupation relative to all others. If supply shifts from S to S_1, employment will rise to OE_1 and the relative wage level will fall to OW_1.

---

[5] This point was drawn to my attention by a passage in Tibor Scitovsky, *Welfare and Competition*, rev. ed. (Homewood, Ill.: Richard D. Irwin, Inc., 1970).

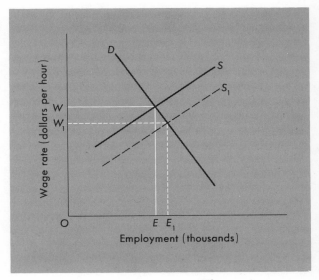

Figure 4
SUPPLY SHIFTS, WAGES,
AND EMPLOYMENT

This result may seem odd, because we hardly ever see a wage rate falling in actuality. We live in an expanding economy, in which most wages are rising continually. But this means that a particular wage can fall relatively by *rising less rapidly* than wages in general.

We conclude that *increased labor supply to an occupation, other things remaining unchanged, will raise employment and lower the relative wage in that occupation. A decrease in labor supply will reduce employment and raise relative wages.*

Now consider the effects of a shift in demand. Demand for the occupation shown in Figure 5 rises from D to D_1, the supply curve remaining unchanged. What will happen? We can predict that employment and relative wages will both rise. But employment may not rise at once if it takes time to train workers for the occupation. In the short run, with the number of trained workers fixed at OE, the equilibrium wage level will shoot up to OW_2. As new trainees enter the occupation, however, employment will expand and relative wages will subside toward the equilibrium level OW_1.

The effect of a decline in demand could be seen by sketching in a demand curve to the left of D. Employment and relative wages will both decline.

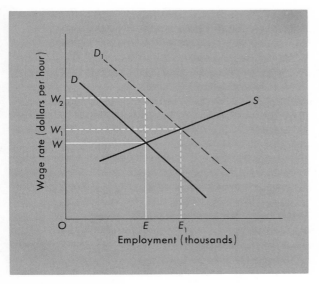

Figure 5
DEMAND SHIFTS, WAGES,
AND EMPLOYMENT

We conclude that: *increased demand for a particular occupation, other things being equal, will raise both employment and the relative wage in that occupation. A decline in demand will reduce employment and relative wages.*

Demand shifts, as we saw in the last chapter, are large and frequent in the American economy. Over a period of years, demand schedules for some kinds of labor will have risen sharply, some will have risen moderately, some will have fallen. These shifts produce both a reallocation of employment and a change in relative wage rates. The size of the wage effect relative to the employment effect depends on the elasticity of labor supply curves. A little pencil-and-paper experimentation will convince you that, if labor supply curves were highly inelastic, demand shifts would produce large changes in relative wage rates. With the same shifts in demand, more elastic labor supply curves will produce smaller wage changes and larger employment changes.

In practice, there have been large changes in the occupational distribution of the American labor force over the past half century with only moderate changes in the occupational wage structure. We can infer that most labor supply curves are quite elastic, particularly over long periods of time.

RESTRICTIONS ON COMPETITION: SOME EXAMPLES

The supply–demand apparatus is useful, not only in analyzing what would happen under pure competition, but in exploring the consequences of various interferences with competition. Such interferences do not abolish the demand and supply schedules, though they may alter the wage–employment results.

Restrictions on Labor Supply

We assumed earlier that anyone can enter any occupation, but this is not always true. If the occupation requires extended training, as in science, law, or medicine, the capacity of training institutions may limit the number who can enter. There are state licensing systems for many occupations, usually managed by those already in the field, and this can be used to restrict admissions. Some of the literary, scientific, and artistic professions require natural talents that only a few may possess.

In Figure 6, D is the demand schedule for a certain occupation, while S shows the number who would *prefer* to enter it at various wage

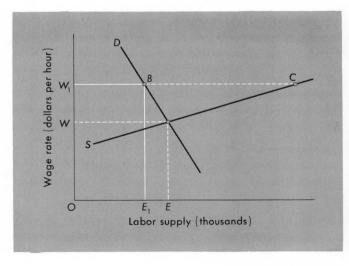

Figure 6

A RESTRICTION ON LABOR SUPPLY

levels. If entrance were free, OE people would be employed in this occupation at a wage level OW. Because of some supply restriction, however, only OE_1 people can actually get into this field. Running up to the demand schedule, we see that this number can be employed at a wage of OW_1, well above the competitive level.

Note that where supply is fixed, *the wage level is determined solely by demand*. An upward shift of the demand schedule would raise the wage rate, while a downward shift would reduce it; but in neither case would there be any effect on employment. The control of supply blocks the normal allocative function of the market.

Those who would prefer to work in this occupation but cannot gain admission, shown by the distance E_1E, will not remain unemployed. They will have to seek employment in other occupations, and the increase in labor supply to these occupations will lower their equilibrium wage. Thus the wage structure is distorted on two counts; an artifically high wage for the occupation in which the supply restriction occurs, and an artificially low wage in other occupations where entrance is unrestricted. Moreover, the forcing of people into occupations in which their marginal productivity is lower reduces national output.

Regulation of Wages

Let us use Figure 6 to illustrate a different type of market intervention. Suppose that, with the demand–supply situation as shown, some outside agency simply decrees that the wage rate shall be OW_1. At this wage, employers will be willing to hire only OE_1 workers instead of the OE workers they would have hired at the competitive wage. The number employed in the occupation is reduced, not by restriction of entrance, but indirectly via wage regulation. As before, those who would prefer to work in this occupation but are not able to do so will have to seek work elsewhere, driving down the relative wage in other occupations. Both the structure of wages and the allocation of labor are distorted.

The "outside agency" could be a trade union. We cannot assume, however, that organization of a union necessarily raises wages above the competitive level. The union might like to achieve this result; but employers have an incentive to resist. Depending on the relative strength of the parties, the bargained wage may or may not be higher than it would have been in a competitive market. In Part Three we shall examine evidence on the actual impact of unions on wage rates in the United States.

Even if a union succeeds in establishing a wage level such as OW_1, it may encounter an additional difficulty. By projecting a horizontal line from W_1 across to the labor supply curve, we see that a large number of workers (shown by the distance BC) would prefer to work in this occupation but are unable to do so. Many of them, indeed, would be willing to work for less than OW_1. This creates a possibility that nonunion employers will spring up to employ them at less than the union scale. Thus the union must not only overcome the resistance of employers who are already unionized, but must be able to organize new companies as rapidly as they appear. A high-wage policy has to be supported by an effective organizing policy.

Employers' Monopsony Power

Under pure competition, each employer is too small a buyer of labor to influence the wage. He can buy as much or as little labor as he requires at the market rate. His labor supply curve is horizontal..

Suppose, however, that the company's employment is a large part of total employment in its area. At the extreme, suppose it is the dominant employer in a "company town." In this case it can no longer assume that unlimited labor is available at a standard wage. It will normally have to raise wages to attract additional workers from other companies and areas. It is faced with an *upward sloping labor supply curve* such as S_L in Figure 7.

What does the curve S_L show? For any level of employment, it shows the wage rate—the *average cost of labor*—needed to attract that number

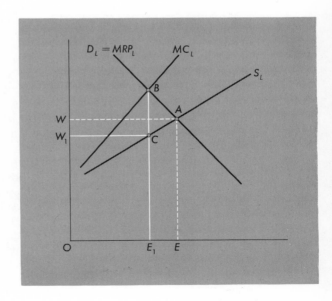

Figure 7
A MONOPSONISTIC BUYER OF LABOR

of workers. But if the average cost of labor is rising, the *marginal cost* must be rising even faster. Look at it this way: to attract an extra hundred workers, employers must offer a higher wage to those workers. But since it is impractical to have two wage levels in the same plant, they must also pay the higher wage to everyone they were previously employing. So the cost of additional labor is higher than appears at first glance. The marginal cost of labor rises along the line MC_{L}.

The employer's labor demand schedule, as we saw earlier, is identical with labor's marginal revenue productivity schedule. It is shown in Figure 7 by $D_L = MRP_L$. What will it pay the employer to do in these circumstances? To maximize profit, he should hire only up to the point at which the cost of hiring an additional worker equals that worker's revenue product. In Figure 7 this is point B, where $MRP_L = MC_L$, and corresponds to an employment of OE_1. If he goes beyond this, so that $MRP_L < MC_L$, he is losing money on each additional man employed.

Looking now at the labor supply curve, we see that OE_1 workers can be hired at a wage rate OW_1, so this will be the company's wage level. There is now a gap, shown by the distance BC, between labor's marginal revenue product (BE_1) and its wage ($CE_1 = OW_1$). This gap has been termed "exploitation" of labor [6] (a rather confusing term, because it is quite different from exploitation in the Marxian sense). The concept is symmetrical with the extra profit margin that a monopolist can extract in selling a product, usually termed the *degree of monopoly*. The degree of monopoly depends on elasticity of demand for the product. Here, the degree of exploitation depends on the elasticity of labor supply. It is easy to see that if the supply curve in Figure 7 were steeper, the MC curve would also rise more rapidly, B would be higher up on the demand curve, both wages and employment would be lower, and the gap BC would be larger. The common sense of this is that the more firmly workers are tied to a particular occupation or area, the greater is the employer's power over the wage level.

The one-company town is perhaps not as common today as in former times. In small communities, however, there are often a few substantial employers who cooperate closely on personnel matters. In such cases, a monopsony wage might result from open or tacit agreement among employers to hold down the wage level. Adam Smith thought that employers were "always and everywhere" engaged in this sort of conspiracy. While "always" is too strong, "commonly" might be accurate.

We can draw a further conclusion from Figure 7. Suppose a legal

[6] Joan Robinson, *The Economics of Imperfect Competition* (London: Macmillan & Co. Ltd., 1934), chap. 26.

minimum wage is imposed on this company. Or suppose the workers organize a union and persuade the employer to agree to a higher wage—for example, the wage OW. The employer's freedom of decision is now restricted. Any portion of S_L lying below the bargained wage is irrelevant. S_L, and therefore MC_L, becomes horizontal along the line WA. The employer will now move to the point at which this line intersects the demand curve, which will mean an employment of OE.

Thus we reach an apparently paradoxical result: starting from a monopsony situation, it is possible to raise the wage rate with no reduction in employment, and in fact with an increase in employment. Note, however, that this is true only up to the wage OW. Above this level, employment will begin to decline, though up to point B it will still be higher than the monopsonistic level OE_1.

The disagreement among economists over the economic impact of unionism is partly a difference of opinion over whether unions are more monopsony reducing than monopoly creating. Where the wage rate has been depressed by employers' monoposony power, a union may bring it closer to the level that would exist under pure competition. But a union may also, as we illustrated in Figure 6, use its power to push wages above the competitive level. Which situation is more common in practice is a question of fact.

SOME IMPLICATIONS
OF THE
COMPETITIVE MODEL

A basic and controversial question is whether, despite the restrictions on competition just described, the competitive model remains a useful tool of analysis. Does it provide a first approximation to the operation of actual labor markets?

One approach to this question is to ask what are the implications of competitive theory for labor market behavior. What would one expect to see happening if pure competition actually prevailed? At least the following:

1. Employers hiring the same kind and quality of labor in the same area would pay the same wage rate. There would be no need for any employer to go above the market level to attract labor, and no possibility of his paying below it.

2. Wage differences among occupations would be equalizing differences, i.e., differences required to equalize the net advantage of various occupations to workers on the margin of decision. A higher wage level in one occupation would normally be accompanied by offsetting costs or disadvantages.

3. Wage and employment changes would be interrelated. Any change in demand or supply conditions for an occupation would involve a change in *both* employment and relative wages. (This assumes that the supply curve to each occupation slopes upward to the right, as it must do under conditions of full employment and free occupational choice.)

4. It follows that the structure of relative wages would be rather volatile over time. Wages would adjust as needed to reallocate the labor force toward points of expanding demand, and to equilibrate demand and supply in each separate labor market.

5. Movements of labor would be in the direction of greater net advantage. Labor would tend to flow from low-wage areas, firms, and industries toward higher-wage areas, firms, and industries.

These propositions, being quantitative, are susceptible to statistical tests. Testing is not easy; but there is a growing body of sophisticated economic research in this area, which will be described at appropriate points in later chapters.

The research results, not surprisingly, turn out rather mixed. There is a substantial element of truth in each of the above propositions, but none of them is entirely true. We observe some things in reality that could not occur if the competitive model were entirely valid. The wages paid by employers of the same kind of labor often differ more widely than can be explained by differences in labor quality. The wage advantage of the higher-paid occupations is often accompanied by other advantages that accentuate the disparity instead of offsetting it. Part of the movement of labor is to worse conditions rather than better ones.

The reason for these deviations must be that the simplified market model neglects important aspects of reality. In the next chapter we outline the more important of these aspects and explore their consequences.

Discussion   Questions

1. Compare the geographic size of the labor market for: a bituminous coal miner, a computer programmer, a high-school mathematics teacher, an aeronautical engineer.

2. What assumptions are required to define a purely competitive labor market? Which of these do you think are least likely to be realized in practice?

3. Explain why a union may move the wage rate either closer to, or farther away from, the rate which would prevail under pure competition.
4. What is meant by employers' monopsony power? Under what conditions might one expect such power to be substantial?
5. What determines the elasticity of demand for a particular kind of labor?
6. What are the main factors to be considered in making a rational choice among occupations?
7. Is it plausible to assume that the supply curve of labor to an occupation always slopes upward? Explain.
8. Explain why, under pure competition, the allocation of labor among occupations and the relative wage rates for these occupations are simultaneously determined.
9. In what sense can the allocation of labor that would be achieved under pure competition be regarded as optimal?
10. Explain the meaning and the main effects of:
    (a) an increase in demand for a particular kind of labor.
    (b) an increase in supply of a particular kind of labor.

Reading Suggestions

The operation of competitive labor markets is analyzed in any text on intermediate price theory. See, for example, Ferguson, C. E., *Microeconomic Theory* (rev. ed.). Homewood, Ill.: Richard D. Irwin, Inc., 1969; Robertson, Sir Dennis, *Lectures on Economic Principles*, Vol II. London: Staples Press, 1959; Scitovsky, Tibor, *Welfare and Competition* (rev. ed.). Homewood, Ill.: Richard D. Irwin, Inc., 1970; and Stigler, George, *The Theory of Price* (3rd ed.). New York: The Macmillan Company, 1966.

LABOR MARKETS IN OPERATION

5

It is easy enough to make a list of oddities and imperfections in labor markets. But after the list has been compiled, where do we go from there? Can one show that certain characteristics of labor markets distort the allocation of labor among occupations, or interfere with free occupational choice, or reduce the level of employment, or alter the structure of relative wage rates? This is the challenge which we shall take up in this chapter. Instead of merely giving a parade of peculiarities, we shall explore their economic impact.

In the latter part of the chapter we consider the magnitude and sources of unemployment. There is a large literature on the definition and measurement of unemployment, and on how much of it can be attributed to various sources—"frictional," "cyclical," "structural," and so on. We shall sort out the issues in this area as a prelude to the discussion of labor market policies in Chapter 6.

COMPLICATIONS IN
LABOR DEMAND
AND HIRING POLICIES

We note first several features of employer behavior, which are usually not captured in simple labor market models. These include the fact that, at any moment, the firm already has a roster of employees; that the job structure within the firm may be complex, including dozens or even hundreds of specialized tasks; that applicants for work are by no means interchangeable from the employer's standpoint; and that the employer's offer consists, not just of an hourly wage rate, but of an elaborate "package" of wage and nonwage conditions.

The Firm Already Has Employees

In drawing the labor demand and supply curves of Chapter 4, we talked as though the firm was opening its doors for the first time and considering afresh whom to hire, how many to hire, and what to pay them. But most firms at any moment are going concerns, with a certain wage level and a certain roster of employees. These employees have tenure rights in their jobs, defined by company personnel policies or union contract rules; and they have reasonable expectations about their treatment by the company. This introduces an element of rigidity into the company's short-run wage and employment decisions.

Suppose the firm's labor supply curve shifts to the right. The firm could now get the amount of labor it needs at a lower wage level— conceivably, by laying off present employees and hiring unemployed workers for less money. But for reasons of organizational morale this is not a feasible policy. Potential employees are not regarded as directly competitive with actual employees. "Outsiders" cannot undercut "insiders" by offering to work for less.

Or suppose the company's demand curve for labor shifts leftward. If the supply curve to the company is upward sloping, the company should now hire less labor at a lower wage level. The company doubtless will reduce employment, though only if the decline in demand is expected to last for some time. But it will usually not cut wages, because to do so would be contrary to workers' expectations of a stable or rising wage level. The fact that a wage cut would lead some workers to quit their jobs is taken into account in the slope of the labor supply curve. But not so readily taken into account is the fact that workers who stay with the company are likely to grumble, work less effectively, possibly disrupt production by strikes or slowdowns. For this reason a wage cut is considered a desperate measure, to be undertaken only under financial pressure.

Without an absolute wage reduction, a firm can reduce its *relative* wage level by lagging behind the general upward movement of wages in the economy. But even this has to be done gradually and inconspicuously. To the extent that the company's employees "catch on," their feeling of grievance will lead to more quits and lower productivity. The quality of new recruits to the firm is also likely to suffer.

"Inside" and "Outside" Jobs

In the last chapter we spoke as though the firm were hiring a single, undifferentiated type of labor. But in a large company there will usually be dozens or hundreds of different jobs. Many of these are highly specialized, existing only within one industry or even one firm. The employer may not be able to find experienced workers in the outside market, but must provide the necessary training on the job. Moreover, employers usually consider it good personnel practice to offer present employees first choice of vacancies on "higher" jobs, and outsiders are considered only after inside sources have been tapped. Union contracts often contain elaborate rules governing which employees shall be entitled to "bid" for a particular vacancy, and how much weight shall be given to length of service, personal efficiency, and other factors in selecting among bidders.

Thus the number of jobs that are open to outside hiring may be much smaller than the number of jobs in the plant. In each production department, new workers may be hired as trainees at the bottom of the skill ladder. From that point they work their way up to more desirable and better-paid jobs as vacancies arise, and in accordance with company policies or union contract rules. Jobs on these promotion ladders are open to outsiders only in the event that no insider wants the job.

Clerical workers, and even executive personnel, also tend to come in at the bottom and work up the ladder in a similar way. The main exceptions are professional, technical, and skilled jobs requiring extended training: doctors and nurses for the company's medical department, computer programmers in the office, skilled maintenance and repair men in the plant. Vacancies on such jobs will be filled by outside recruitment.

Dunlop has termed the jobs which are normally filled by outside recruitment the *ports of entry* into the company. He emphasizes that the number of such ports is limited and may change over time with changes in company organization and collective bargaining practices. The rules and procedures governing interjob movement within the company define the *internal labor market*. Direct linkage between the internal and external markets occurs only at the ports of entry.[1]

[1] For a good statement of these concepts, see John T. Dunlop, "Job vacancy measures and economic analysis," in *The Measurement and Interpretation of Job Vacancies* (New York: National Bureau of Economic Research, 1966), pp. 27–48.

A vacancy arising anywhere in the plant will still, if total employment remains unchanged, require recruitment of a worker from outside. But the point of hiring may be quite remote from the point at which the vacancy occurred. A vacancy on a skilled production job may lead to hiring of an unskilled trainee, several insiders having meanwhile moved up the ladder. This means that the occupational distribution of new hires in the economy will differ from the occupational distribution of the labor force. New hires will be biased toward the lower end of the skill ladder.

Important consequences follow from this. A worker who has climbed some distance up a promotion ladder in one company, and is then thrown out of employment by shifts in demand, has suffered a real hardship. He is unlikely to be able to move horizontally to the same level of skill and earnings in another company. More probably he will have to start near the bottom with a new employer and work up once more. A displaced worker may also lose accrued pension rights and other benefits earned by length of service. Thus it is rational for workers to show attachment to their present jobs and to regard a forced change of employers as a misfortune.

For jobs which are ports of entry for many companies, the concept of a general labor market makes sense. Workers can move from one company to similar jobs in other companies; and each company's terms of employment must be sufficiently in line with those of other companies to attract the number of recruits it needs. For jobs that are typically filled from within, the concepts of an area-wide market and an equilibrium wage make considerably less sense. Such jobs are not fully insulated from the tides of labor demand and supply in the outside market; but they are a good deal more insulated than the port-of-entry jobs. Wage rates on them are not precisely determined by the market, but are set by rule-of-thumb procedures which will be examined in a later chapter.

Workers Not Interchangeable

The workers arrayed along the supply curve are often assumed to be equally acceptable to the employer. But in fact workers are not identical from the employer's standpoint. Most firms have an elaborate set of hiring standards and preferences, some of which may be closely related to productive efficiency, but others of which are not.

The specifications which may be important in a particular case include:

1. *Sex.* Most jobs are ticketed as "men's work" or "women's work," though practice in this respect may change gradually over time.

2. *Age.* The preferred employee is usually one with some, but not too much, work experience—someone in his twenties or early thirties. Younger people have less experience and are more prone to

change jobs, while older people are often regarded as less vigorous, less trainable, more subject to illness and accident.

3. *Color.* The fact that in the past white workers have normally been preferred to black workers of equivalent qualifications is apparent from casual observation. The reasons for this discrimination and the efforts to curb it by law will be considered in the next chapter.

4. *Education.* In some cases educational requirements are built into the job. A lawyer should have finished law school, a chemical engineer should have at least an undergraduate degree, and so on. But even where education is not strictly essential, it is normally preferred. Large companies want their potential executives to have at least a college degree, and many prefer graduate training in business administration. High school graduation is generally required for white-collar employment, and to an increasing extent even for good manual jobs.

The fact that employers' educational specifications are often higher than is required for job performance does not necessarily mean that they are irrational. Completion of a certain educational level is an indication of intelligence, energy, motivation, and future learning potential. More highly educated employees may also be considered socially more cooperative and adaptable, "nice people to have around." At any rate, employers' educational preferences are real and they confront the school dropout with substantial problems.

5. *Experience and Proficiency.* Experience enters mainly for professional, technical, and skilled manual jobs on which the employee may be presumed to continue learning and improving his productive capacity for some time. For low-skilled jobs with a short training period, the employer may actually prefer less experience to more, on the ground that the worker has less to unlearn and "we can teach him to do it our way." Even where experience is not important, however, the personnel office will usually put the applicant through proficiency tests. Prospective assemblers of radio parts may be given tests of manual dexterity, bookkeepers tests of arithmetical aptitude, typists and stenographers tests of speed and accuracy.

6. *Present Job Attachment.* A common situation, particularly in small towns and cities, is the existence of a tacit understanding among employers that they will not hire away each other's workers. These understandings, often termed "antipirating agreements," operate as follows. An applicant at plant *A* is asked what he is doing now. He replies that he is employed at plant *B* but wants to move. The personnel manager of plant *A* then calls the personnel manager of plant *B* and asks whether he is willing to release the worker in question. If the personnel manager of plant *B* says that his company still needs the worker and does not wish him to leave, plant *A* will usually decline to employ him. In line with this view, employers usually object to the public employment service registering a man for work if he is cur-

rently employed. These practices mean that a worker may be forced to cut his ties with his present employer before seeking a new one. This increases the risks of movement and reduces the number of workers willing to take the risk.

Hiring preferences, related in part to differences in labor quality, have several interesting consequences. First, "labor supply" to the firm includes only those workers whom the employer is willing to count as part of the supply; and this changes with the overall demand–supply situation. In a recession period, when many unemployed workers are available, an employer may be able to set high standards and get exactly the characteristics he prefers. But in a tight labor market he may have to reduce his requirements substantially. The available labor supply depends on how low the employer is willing to dip into the manpower barrel.

If we suppose that, when he lowers his standards of age, experience, education, and so on, he thereby gets workers of lower productive capacity, then his cost of labor *per unit of standard efficiency* will increase. There is little evidence on how far hiring specifications are in fact related to efficiency, but some relation must surely exist.

The labor supply diagram for the firm, as usually drawn, overlooks quality differences. The horizontal axis shows man-hours of standard efficiency, while the vertical axis shows the price of a standard efficiency unit. On such a diagram, the labor supply curve slopes upward to the right for a double reason. By raising the wage rate, the firm can hire more workers of standard quality. Alternatively, if it reduces its quality standards without a change in the wage rate, it will still be paying more per efficiency unit. Given full information the firm can calculate which course or which combination of the two courses will involve least cost for a given level of employment. The locus of all such points is its labor supply curve.

A further consequence is that the pool of unemployed at any time is biased toward the least-preferred members of the labor force; and a particular worker's chances of reemployment depend partly on his personal characteristics. The unemployed can be regarded as arrayed in a queue, with employers hiring from the top of the queue and working downward. At the head of the queue are male, white, high-school graduates aged twenty to forty, with good work experience and good scores on proficiency tests. Toward the tail of the queue come the teenagers, the oversixties, the unskilled, the illiterate.

The "Employment Package" Is Complex

The employer's job offer includes more than an hourly wage. Within the realm of monetary calculation, the worker has to consider regularity of employment over the week and year, which will affect his annual income; the probability of promotion to higher-paying jobs in the future; the chances of earning extra money by overtime work; and such supplementary benefits as paid vacations and holidays, pension rights, and company-financed life insurance and medical care. There is also a wide range of nonmonetary considerations, including physical or intellectual demands of the job, intrinsic interest of the work, physical conditions of work, congeniality of fellow workers and supervisors, and fairness and comprehensibility of company personnel policies.

A worker will weigh all the elements in this "package," and compare it with the packages offered by competing employers, before deciding where his net advantage lies. In principle, then, the vertical axis of our supply diagrams should show not the wage rate, but an index of total job attractiveness. But this is not a very operational idea. Many of the elements in the employment package cannot be quantified. Moreover, since different workers will attach different relative values to these elements, we should need a different weighting system—a different index—for each member of the labor force.

If we follow the alternative course of marking off the vertical axis in wage units, as we did in the last chapter, we must recognize that "labor supply" becomes a rather fuzzy concept. The supply curve seems to say that an employer who wants to hire more labor must raise his wage rate. But in actuality he can do several other things. He can improve one or more of the nonwage items in the employment package. Or he can lower his hiring requirements, thus admitting more people to the pool of candidates. Or he can increase his recruitment efforts— engage in newspaper and radio advertising, make contact with public and private employment agencies, put on more personnel staff to interview and screen applicants.

If we define supply as a function of wages only, we must recognize that such a supply curve is quite shiftable. It can be shifted to the right by an improvement in nonwage terms or by increased expenditure on labor recruitment. It will shift to the left for the opposite reasons. The employer is thus working with several variables rather than with wages alone. This point has been well put by Hildebrand:[2]

> For instance, suppose that the local labor market becomes progressively tighter. To avoid raising wage rates, the employer may intensify his recruiting efforts, perhaps improving nonpecuniary conditions as well. In some cases he may be able to simplify certain jobs, breaking them up into multiples requiring a lower grade of labor. If necessary, he may reduce his standards for hiring and for promotion, deliberately

[2] George H. Hildebrand, "External Influences and the Determination of the Internal Wage Structure," in L. J. Meij, ed., *Internal Wage Structure* (Amsterdam: North-Holland Publishing Company, 1963), pp. 277–78.

accepting candidates of lower efficiency on the premise that the enforced rise in unit labor costs will be temporary, that poorer workers can later be laid off or demoted. For the same underlying reasons, he may tolerate some rise in costs of turnover, and some fall of efficiency among the already employed, the second expressed by increases in absenteeism, tardiness, and bad work, and possibly by slow-down tactics.

Together, these responses serve as expansion joints for aborbing the shock of a change in market forces, one that enables the employer to put off raising wage rates, mainly by tolerating a decline in labor efficiency and a rise in indirect employment costs. Although unit labor cost will still rise, to some extent its course will be reversible when the market loosens up. By contrast, a rise in wage rates for practical purposes is irreversible.

BASIC
STRUCTURAL
FEATURES

The factors examined in the previous section, while interesting and practically important, do not raise logical difficulties about the supply–demand apparatus. They can be taken care of by redefining the variables on the axes or by altering the shapes of the demand and supply schedules. But beyond this is another category of difficulties, more basic in the sense that they call into question some of the central assumptions of supply–demand analysis. This category includes a low level of information and poor development of labor marketing institutions, serious obstacles to free occupational choice, lack of continuous full employment, possible interdependence of demand and supply schedules, and evidence of nonmaximizing behavior by many employers.

Information, Mobility, and Clearinghouse Facilities

The seriousness of this kind of imperfection differs among occupations. Economists and aeronautical engineers have rather good information about vacancies and salary levels in different parts of the country. Secretaries and electricians may know a good deal about jobs in their area through the union business agent or the office grapevine. Semiskilled machine operatives in manufacturing are less well informed. In general, market imperfection increases as one goes down the occupational ladder from professionals to laborers. We concentrate here on manual occupations, partly because the problems are most serious at this level, partly because most of the research studies relate to manual labor.

A key difficulty is that there is no central point at which full information is available on job vacancies and available workers in each area. The nearest thing to it is the local office of the state employment service. But for reasons to be explained in the next chapter, employers list only a minority of vacancies—with a bias toward the least-desirable or hardest-to-fill vacancies—with the employment service. Many workers respond to this, quite rationally, by bypassing the employment service and conducting their own door-to-door search for work.

Such a search is inherently difficult. The main thing a worker can find out at the plant employment office is the starting wage rate at one of the ports of entry into the company. But to make an informed decision the worker should also know the various types of fringe benefits, the probable security of employment, the prospects for promotion, the pace of work, the physical conditions of work, the quality of supervision and of personnel management in the company. Many of these things even the best-intentioned personnel manager could not tell him. He can discover them only by trying out on the job. "Shopping by working" is more informative than mere "window-shopping" for employment.

Research studies at the manual level are in broad agreement that employed workers have little information about companies other than the one in which they are presently working, this information coming to them mainly from friends and acquaintances; that much of what they think they know is incorrect; that the uncertainty arising from this limited information makes them less willing to try their chances in the market; that unemployed workers typically take the first job that seems to meet their minimum expectations, rather than conducting a full search [3] of the market; and that work experience often reveals the choice to have been mistaken, leading to quitting and renewal of the search.

The main economic effects of labor market imperfection are:

1. The time required for unemployed workers to locate a new job is increased. The amount of unemployment-between-jobs, usually termed "frictional unemployment," is larger than it would be with a higher level of information and better clearinghouse facilities. How much larger is difficult to determine. But even if the difference in unemployment rates were only 1 percent, this would amount to almost a million man-years of work—a significant cost to the economy.

2. There is mismatching of workers' abilities and preferences with job characteristics and requirements. This leads to suboptimal results

[3] An exhaustive search, of course, would not be economically rational. The costs of additional search at any point have to be weighed against the actuarial probability of getting better terms of employment by further search. On this point, see George J. Stigler, "Information in the labor market," *Journal of Political Economy* (Suppl.), October, 1962, pp. 94–105.

both in output and in workers' satisfaction from their jobs. Accurate information on both sides of the market would correct such mismatching by switches on the part of workers and/or employers. The low level of information actually available discourages switching by workers until their dissatisfaction becomes acute.

3. The necessity of learning about jobs by working on them, with the option of quitting if the experience proves unsatisfactory, raises the voluntary quit rate above what it would be with better preemployment information. This is expensive to workers, employers, and the economy.

4. The dispersion of company wage-levels is greater than it would be in a more perfect market. Even if workers made a rational search of the market, Stigler has demonstrated that the search would stop short of eliminating all wage dispersion. This is due partly to the continual fluctuation of supply–demand conditions. The faster the relative wage levels of employers are changing, the more rapidly does information become obsolete, the smaller the amount of search that it is rational to undertake, and the larger the resulting dispersion of wage levels.

Wage dispersion does not mean that wage setting is arbitrary or that employers have unfettered discretion. The fact that one employer may be paying 25 percent less than another for what appears to be the same kind of labor does not mean that he can do so *without penalty*. There is substantial evidence that the low-wage firm suffers penalties both in terms of the quality of labor it is able to attract and in terms of a higher quit rate, with consequently higher costs of recruitment and training. But it must consider that these costs are more than offset by the saving in wages, otherwise it would change its wage policy. Conversely, the high-wage employer benefits from better labor quality and lower turnover, so that his wage level is not as expensive as it appears.

Barriers to Occupational Choice

Poor information means that people will make mistakes. Some will be pleasantly surprised with the occupations they have chosen, while others will be unpleasantly surprised. But this will not alter the number entering each occupation unless there is some systematic bias in the information. If the number of people who underestimate the attractiveness of occupation A just equals the number who overestimate it, then the number of workers available to occupation A at any wage rate is unchanged. Bias could relate to the kind of work in question, some occupations being more accurately reported than others. Or it could relate to recipients of the information, some of whom are better informed than others.

There appears to be serious bias as regards the information available to low-income families about high-level occupations, i.e. occupations requiring college or graduate school training. Parents who have not themselves been to college and who do not move in middle-class circles may know so little about the higher occupations as to seriously under-estimate their advantages and so fail to consider college training for their children. In addition, their incomes are too low to bear the substantial costs of higher education. Evidence on the seriousness of this barrier is presented in the next chapter.

The consequence is that, for occupations in which higher education is either required or customary, the supply curve is shifted to the left —say, to S_1 rather than S (Figure 1). Fewer people enter the occupation

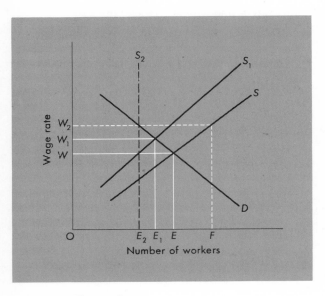

Figure 1
SUPPLY RESTRICTIONS, EMPLOYMENT,
AND RELATIVE EARNINGS

than would choose to do so with adequate information and financing. By looking at the intersection of S_1 with D, we see that this will raise equilibrium earnings and reduce the number employed.

A further possibility is that there may be limits on the number ad-mitted to an occupation. Suppose, for example, that the number of workers admitted to occupation A is fixed arbitrarily at OE_2. The sup-ply curve is then the vertical line S_2, and the equilibrium wage is OW_2. By projecting a horizontal line from W_2 to S, we see that the number who would *like* to get into the occupation at this wage level is *OF*. But only OE_2 can enter, because of the admissions bar, and E_2F must go into some other occupation instead.

There are several ways in which this might happen. If educational facilities are expensive and increasing them requires appropriations of public funds, training capacity may lag behind market requirements. This is often said to be true of medicine. Building a medical school is expensive, partly because of the associated laboratory and research facilities. Expansion of training capacity has tended to lag behind the growth of demand for medical services and the growing number of young people who would like to become doctors. Only about half of the applicants to medical school are admitted. The low level of U.S. medical school output has led to importation of large numbers of doctors from Canada, Europe, and the less-developed countries. This is an important part of the much debated "brain drain." It is possible that a similar, though less acute, situation exists in some of the other professions requiring graduate training.[4]

In some occupations admission is controlled by state licensing regulations. E.g., a law is passed providing that barbers can be admitted to the trade only after passing an examination set by a state licensing board. (For "barbers" read also beauticians, morticians, plumbers, electricians, and upwards of thirty other crafts that are licensed in one state or another.) To no one's surprise, the licensing board turns out to consist of representatives of the barbers' union and the association of barbershop owners. The number of candidates who "pass" can be held to a level that does not endanger the jobs or earnings of those already employed in the industry. While undue supply restriction is not inevitable, the machinery for restriction is certainly there. It seems likely that in most cases earnings end up higher, and the number employed lower, than would be the case under free-market conditions.

Interdependence of Demand and Wage Level

A basic assumption of demand–supply analysis is that the two schedules are independent, and that the market price does not affect the location of either schedule. There is evidence that in labor markets this is often not the case. The demand schedule is not independent of the wage rate. Specifically, a sudden increase in the wage level will often raise the demand curve as well; and without knowing the size of this shift, the effect on employment cannot be predicted.

In microeconomic theory, we normally assume that each firm is

[4] For a good recent analysis of medical demands and supplies, see Rashi Feinn, *The Doctor Shortage* (Washington, D.C.: The Brookings Institution, 1967). See also Allan M. Cartter, "The Supply and Demand of College Teachers," *American Statistical Association Proceedings,* September, 1965.

managed as efficiently as it could be. Given the known technology of production, management ensures that factor productivity is at a maximum, unit cost of production at a minimum. But this assumption is often unwarranted.[5] Many businesses are managed at suboptimal levels. A sudden wage increase, which cuts seriously into profit margins, may shock management into action. Indeed, this is often termed the "shock effect." There is, if you will, an increased input of management effort, spontaneously generated with no extra expense. The order to cut costs goes out to all corners of the firm; and part or even all of the higher wage costs may be offset by increased efficiency.

This effect first came to light in studies of the reaction of low-wage British industries to minimum-wage legislation around 1900. But it has been observed also in reactions of U.S. employers to higher minimum wages under the Fair Labor Standards Act. The writer had occasion to observe it in operation in Puerto Rico, where a rapid increase in the minimum-wage level was at least partly responsible for a rapid rise of output per man-hour during the fifties and sixties. Through plant case studies we were able to observe in detail just what management did to offset rising wage costs: more careful worker selection, better training, better incentive systems, better supervision, some capital–labor substitution, and efforts to reduce waste of supplies and materials were all involved.[6]

The same phenomenon is often evident in collective bargaining situations. A company maintains stoutly that a fifteen cent an hour wage increase will push it over the edge into bankruptcy, and its current low profit level makes this assertion plausible. The union nevertheless insists on the increase. A year later one comes along and sees the company apparently doing as well as before. Management was not necessarily being dishonest in its original claim. But after the fact, it learned to work harder in order to survive. ("What do we get out of it?" a management official once asked in a seminar discussion at Yale. A union research director replied, "Continued participation in our economic system.")

Analytically, the shock effect is similar to a change in the production function resulting from technical progress. It may take a labor-saving

---

[5] For a good sampling and analysis of the evidence, see Harvey Leibenstein, "Allocative Efficiency and X-Efficiency," *American Economic Review*, June, 1966, pp. 392–415.

[6] See Lloyd G. Reynolds and Peter Gregory, *Wages, Productivity, and Industrialization in Puerto Rico*, Part II (Homewood, Ill.: Richard D. Irwin, Inc., 1965). It may be objected that these are all normal reactions to a rise in the price of labor, and therefore would be consistent with a hypothesis that employers were maximizing profit at all times. But our case studies strongly suggest that, when wages were low, employers were not doing as much in this direction as it would have paid them to do even at those wage levels.

form, but this is not necessarily so. All of the savings might conceivably be in material inputs. Typically, labor input per unit of output will also be reduced, and total employment will probably fall. But the extent of the reduction in employment cannot be predicted by looking at the slope of a (supposedly) unchanged demand curve.

Lack of Continuous Full Employment

This is a well-known characteristic of the American economy. Precise definition of "full employment" is not easy. Most economists would agree, however, that the economy approximated full employment in the years 1951 to 1953, 1957, and 1966 to 1969. Two of these were war periods. In peacetime, whenever the economy hits full employment, it backs away rather quickly; and sometimes, as from 1958 to 1965, it has remained below full employment for a prolonged period.

The operation of a full-employment labor market differs importantly from that of a slack market. This is partly responsible for the long-standing debate between the proponents and critics of "standard" wage theory. The standard theory usually assumes full employment, as we did in Chapter 4. The critics are often saying, directly or by implication, that this situation is unusual and that things work differently when general unemployment prevails.

When unemployment is widespread, each employer has a horizontal labor supply curve. He can attract as much labor as he wishes without raising wages. The tight discipline of the labor market over relative wage rates is relaxed, and the firm's autonomy in choosing its wage level is increased.

Under full employment the situation is different. The pool of surplus labor shrinks and perhaps vanishes. A firm that wants to expand employment must compete actively in wages and other inducements. Low-wage firms find that they must come closer to the general area level even to hold their present labor force.

Many phenomena of actual labor markets can be understood only in terms of the ebb and flow of aggregate demand for labor. On the downswing large numbers of workers are laid off. Those who still have jobs cling to them more tightly, and voluntary quit rates fall. Labor force participation rates drop, as noted in Chapter 2. Many "discouraged workers" leave the labor force or fail to enter it as they normally would. Wage increases are fewer, smaller and more "ragged" as between firms and industries than they are in years of high employment.

During the upswing these tendencies go into reverse. Labor force participation increases. Workers become more willing to change jobs, and quit rates rise. There is more uniform pressure on employers to keep in step on wages. The market operates more nearly as one would predict from the competitive model.

Absence of Maximizing Behavior

The variation of company wage levels for what looks like the same kind of labor is one of the most familiar facts of labor markets. Studies carried out by the Bureau of Labor Statistics for many jobs in many cities show that these variations are particularly wide for the lower skill grades. For all the skilled occupations studied, the quartile deviation averaged 11 percent, i.e., one-half the rates for the occupation fell within a range of 11 percent on either side of the median. In the case of semiskilled occupations, however, the quartile deviation was 24 percent. The outside limits of the range of rates, of course, was considerably wider.[7]

A difficulty with such studies is lack of full comparability in the data. Even though different plants use the same job title, the work may differ considerably. "Welding" is not the same in an aircraft plant and a shipyard; and even "common labor" is not as standardized as the term implies. Moreover, workers differ in personal quality, and these differences tend to be positively correlated with company wage-levels. Such research studies as have been made, however, suggest that the quality differences are considerably smaller than the wage differences,[8] so that the high-wage employer is paying more *per efficiency unit* of labor.

A high-wage policy has other advantages to the company, some of which can be reduced to a cash equivalent. It typically lowers the quit rate. Recruitment of new workers is quicker and easier. A high-wage company can establish strict hiring specifications designed to fill the plant with "a nice class of worker." A high wage level has public relations value, inside and outside the company. For a nonunion company, it may help to ward off unionization.

Even with these qualifications, it is hard to avoid the conclusion that some employers pay more than the wage which would maximize profits. One astute observer, the late Professor Sumner Slichter, noted that "the average hourly earnings of male unskilled labor tends to be high where the net income after taxes is a high percentage of sales . . . The high correlation between sales margins and the average hourly

---

[7] For a summary of these studies, see R. L. Raimon, "The Indeterminateness of Wages of Semiskilled Workers," *Industrial and Labor Relations Review*, January, 1953, pp. 180–94.

[8] See, for example, the study of beginning rates for women high school graduates entering clerical employment in Madison, Wisconsin, cited in Chapter 8.

earnings of common labor . . . reinforces the view that wages, within a considerable range, reflect managerial discretion, that where managements can easily pay high wages they tend to do so, and that where managements are barely breaking even they tend to keep wages down." [9]

There is evidence, in short, of a good deal of unofficial "profit sharing" by business managers. An industry that can afford to pay high wages is likely to do so as a matter of policy,[10] instead of attempting to get by at the lowest level that the labor market would permit.

Such a policy is illustrated in Figure 2. S is the company's labor

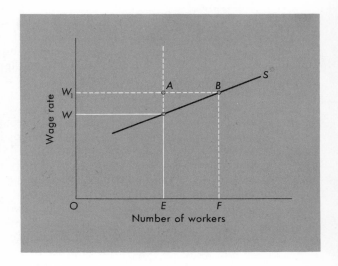

Figure 2
COMBINATION OF HIGH WAGES
AND JOB RATIONING

supply curve. Employment is OE workers, who could be hired at a wage OW. Instead, the company chooses to pay a higher wage OW_1. One consequence is that there will be a surplus of workers wishing to work at the company. By selective hiring policies, the company rations the number of jobs available (OE) among the larger number of workers available (OF). A further consequence is that, if the company wishes to expand employment beyond OE, it can do so with no increase in

[9] Sumner H. Slichter, "Notes on the Structure of Wages," *Review of Economics and Statistics,* February, 1950, pp. 81–92.

[10] Such industries tend also to be unionized industries, and it is not easy to separate out the effect of unionism. Efforts to make such a separation will be examined in Part Three.

wages by relaxing its hiring requirements. It moves along the horizontal line *AB,* and will not need to raise wages unless or until it "hits the supply curve" at *B.*

The Competitive Model and the "Vacancy Model"

This possibility has interesting implications for the reallocation of labor among firms and industries. With full employment, and with all firms operating on their supply curves, any reallocation of labor would involve a change in relative wage rates. Wages in expanding firms would rise relative to those in contracting firms.

But if many firms are in the situation of Figure 2, these results do *not* follow. Firms can expand employment simply by opening their doors. Labor can flow from lower-wage to higher-wage sectors without any change in the structure of relative wages. This has been termed a "vacancy model" of the labor market.

Research studies suggest that there is something to the vacancy model. Ulman notes that there was little correlation between percentage wage changes and percentage employment changes in fifty-seven industries over the years 1948 to 1960. What mainly happened was that industries whose wages were already relatively high in 1948 increased their wage advantage over the period. The dispersion of industry wage levels increased. These results, he concludes, run counter to the competitive hypothesis: ". . . since the relatively high-wage industries did not tend to increase employment more rapidly than the others, they did not on the average have to raise wages more rapidly, as in fact they did, in order to attract additional labor." [11]

At the same time there is evidence that *major* changes in supply–demand relations are associated with relative wage shifts, even though moderate ones may not be. Ulman notes that there was an association between wage and employment changes for the extreme cases in his sample, i.e., the 10 percent of industries in which wages rose most and the 10 percent in which they rose least. Phelps Brown also found such an association in the United Kingdom for industries in which the male labor force declined by more than 5 percent or expanded by more than 30 percent. He concludes: "Thus, within a wide range, the rate of growth of an industry seems to have imposed no particular

[11] Lloyd Ulman, "Labor Mobility and the Industrial Wage Structure in the Postwar United States," *Quarterly Journal of Economics,* February, 1965, pp. 73–97. See also Alan K. Severn, "Upward Labor Mobility: Opportunity or Incentive?" *Quarterly Journal of Economics,* February, 1968, pp. 143–51. This study lends support to the vacancy model in the sense that an industry's quit rate is strongly associated with the general unemployment rate as well as with the industry's relative wage position.

requirement on the relative earnings it offered but outside that range it did." [12]

There are two nonmarket reasons why one might expect interfirm and interindustry wage relations to show a high degree of stability despite differing employment trends. One is trade unionism, plus the tendency of union leaders to watch each other's wage gains and try to keep up with the procession. The other is sheer tradition and established expectations, whose force Phelps Brown has rightly emphasized.[13] A worker is accustomed to occupying a certain niche in the wage structure. If rates elsewhere in the economy go up, he expects that his will go up proportionately. Employers also regard this as reasonable, and try to maintain their customary standing in the wage structure.

A different test of labor market models can be had by examining geographic movements of labor, which need not necessarily follow the same rules as movement within an area. On this front, Raimon finds that interstate migration is highly correlated with state wage levels. If states are ranked by percentage population gain through migration and by average income per employed worker, the two rankings yield a correlation coefficient of 0.86. There is also, however, a close relation between a state's gain through migration and its rate of employment expansion, which could be interpreted in terms of the "vacancy model." In fact, a high wage level, a high rate of employment increase, and a high rate of immigration seem to go together.[14] This complex of phenomena is closely related to the spectacular postwar decline of agricultural employment. The states of heaviest emigration are states with considerable agriculture, and in consequence a below average income level and a below average rate of employment expansion.

UNEMPLOYMENT:
TYPES
AND SOURCES

The number of man-hours that the labor force would like to supply is usually greater than the number demanded by employers. Even when aggregate demand is very high, as in the period from 1966 to

12 E. H. Phelps Brown and M. H. Browne, "Earnings in Industries of the United Kingdom, 1948–59," *Economic Journal,* September, 1962, pp. 517–49.

13 E. H. Phelps Brown, *The Economics of Labor* (New Haven: Yale University Press, 1962), chap. 1.

14 Robert L. Raimon, "Interstate Migration and Wage Theory," *Review of Economics and Statistics,* November, 1962, pp. 428–38.

1969, between 3 and 4 percent of workers are unemployed at any moment. So we need to examine the features of the economy that give rise to unemployment.

The Level of Unemployment

Unemployment is the difference between the amount of labor offered *at present wage levels and working conditions* and the amount of labor hired at those levels. The most obvious aspect of the problem is full-time unemployment—the situation in which people are willing and able to work but have no jobs. Determining the size of this group is not as easy as may appear at first glance. How does one judge whether a worker has the necessary ability to find or hold a job? What exactly is meant by "willingness to work"? Despite these problems of measurement, we have relatively reliable information from the Census Bureau's "Monthly Report on the Labor Force," based on a sample survey of households throughout the country.

This survey also collects information on part-time workers, who are divided into (1) those who are working the number of hours they prefer, and (2) those who are working fewer hours than they prefer. The latter are said to be "working part-time for economic reasons." The amount of time they are losing, when added to that of the full-time unemployed, yields a measure known as "labor force time lost."

Figure 3 shows the movement of the full-time unemployment rate since 1948, and also the figure of total time lost, which is available only since 1956. The unemployment rate has fluctuated mostly in the range of 4 to 7 percent of the labor force. Total time lost is typically about 1 percent higher—more than this in recession years, less than this in boom years.

At the peak of Vietnam War activity in the years 1966 to 1969, full-time unemployment fell somewhat below 4 percent. This does not seem much until one translates it into 3 million people without jobs. In addition to these, there were typically about 2 million people reported as "working part-time for economic reasons."

Unemployment rates in the United States are rather high compared with those in other industrial countries. A comparison over several years, adjusted to U.S. definitions of unemployment, is shown in Table 1.[15] Canada has unemployment rates at roughly the U.S. level. The Italian rate is explained mainly by the existence of a large depressed area in southern Italy. The five other countries in the table typically have unemployment rates less than half those of the United States, with the rates of Japan and West Germany especially low. The reasons are not fully known, but probably would include the following: (1)

[15] Data are from Arthur F. Neef and Rose A. Holland, "Comparative Unemployment Rates, 1964–66," *Monthly Labor Review*, April, 1967, pp. 18–20.

Table 1

FULL-TIME UNEMPLOYOYMENT AS PERCENTAGE OF LABOR FORCE,
ADJUSTED TO U.S. DEFINITIONS, EIGHT COUNTRIES, 1959–66

	United States	Canada	France	West Germany	United Kingdom	Italy	Japan	Sweden
1959	5.5	6.0	2.8	1.6	3.1	5.7	1.9	—
1960	5.6	7.0	2.6	.7	2.4	4.3	1.4	—
1961	6.7	7.1	2.0	.4	2.3	3.7	1.3	1.5
1962	5.6	5.9	2.0	.4	2.8	3.2	1.1	1.5
1963	5.7	5.5	2.4	.4	3.4	2.7	1.1	1.7
1964	5.2	4.7	1.9	.4	2.4	3.0	1.0	1.6
1965	4.6	3.9	2.3	.3	2.1	4.0	1.0	1.2
1966	3.9	3.6	2.4	.4	2.3	4.3	1.1	1.6

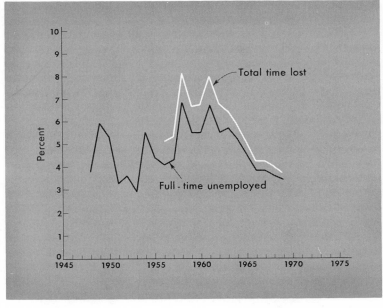

Figure 3

FULL-TIME UNEMPLOYED, AND TOTAL TIME
LOST THROUGH UNEMPLOYMENT, 1948–69
SOURCE: *Economic Report of the President,*
Jan. 1969, p. 255.

These are relatively small countries, in which people do not have to
move so far to get from declining to expanding regions. (2) Most of
them have long had active labor market policies designed to accelerate

retraining and relocation of labor. Such policies were not seriously pursued in the United States until the mid-sixties. (3) These countries have in general maintained a higher level of aggregate demand—a level that produced fuller utilization of labor and other resources.

Unemployment is distributed unevenly over the labor force. Laborers experience much more unemployment than skilled manual workers, and the latter have higher rates than clerical workers. Nonwhite workers experience substantially more unemployment than white workers—partly, but not entirely, because they fall in the lower occupational groups. Thus in 1968 unemployment averaged 3.2 percent among white workers but 6.7 percent among nonwhites. Teenagers have much higher unemployment rates than older workers. In 1968, unemployment averaged 12.7 percent for those aged sixteen to nineteen, and for black teenagers the rate was around 25 percent. Here is surely one source of riots in the core cities.

A second characteristic is the high degree of turnover within the unemployed pool. At any moment many people are entering the pool because of quits, layoffs, or a decision to enter the labor force. At the same time many others are leaving the labor force or finding new jobs. Thus the number who are unemployed *at some time during the year* is much larger than the average number unemployed at any one time. During the prosperous years from 1966 to 1969, the average number unemployed at any one time was about 3 million. The number unemployed at some time during the year, however, was upwards of 10 million.

This means that much unemployment is of rather short duration. In years such as 1966 to 1969, about half of those unemployed at any one time have been unemployed for less than five weeks, another one-quarter have been unemployed five to ten weeks, and only the remaining one-quarter have been unemployed for ten weeks or longer. In recession years, on the other hand, the proportion of long-term unemployed rises. The proportion unemployed ten weeks or more rose to about 40 percent in 1958 and again in 1961. This long-term unemployment is concentrated among the most disadvantaged groups in the labor force—older workers, handicapped workers, black workers, people with least education and lowest job skills.

Seasonal and Casual Unemployment

Turning to sources of unemployment, we may mention first seasonal and irregular fluctuations in the demand for labor. Seasonality is a familiar phenomenon, especially in agriculture and building construction. In the colder regions of the country, building activity tapers off during the winter months. In crop raising there is a peak of activity during the harvest season. The men's and women's clothing industries work hard while getting out the spring and fall styles, but slacken off in between. Seasonal industries tend to attract enough labor to meet their peak requirements during the rush season, which means that some of these people are unemployed in the slack season. In a competitive labor market, this failure to obtain a full year's work would be compensated by a higher hourly rate. But the idle time is still wasteful from a social standpoint.

In the United States during the early sixties, seasonal unemployment seems to have constituted about 15 percent of total unemployment, or somewhat less than 1 percent of the labor force. In Canada, where the climate is more severe and seasonal activities are relatively more important, the figures were roughly twice as high—30 percent of all unemployment and close to 2 percent of the labor force.[16] These figures are substantial enough to cause concern. In Canada, the Dominion government has attempted to shift some of its own construction to the winter months, has encouraged the provincial governments to do the same, and has agreed to pay 50 percent of the direct labor cost on some municipal projects not usually carried out in winter. Moreover, it has encouraged housing starts in the autumn by providing funds at reduced interest rates through the Central Mortgage and Housing Corporation. There has not yet been a thorough analysis of the impact of these programs on seasonality in the construction industry.

There are also irregular fluctuations in labor requirements in such industries as merchant shipping and longshoring. The number of ships coming into a particular port to be unloaded varies from day to day, and workers are traditionally hired each morning for that day only. Hourly wage rates are attractive. So longshoring tends to attract not merely the maximum number who might be employed on the busiest days but an even larger number. All these men hang about the docks, gambling on the chance of getting a day's work from time to time.

Correction of this situation requires reorganization of the labor market to achieve what is usually termed "decasualization." This involves establishment of a central hiring exchange from which people are dispatched to jobs, licensing of all longshoremen, and gradual reduction of the number of licenses as workers retire or leave the industry. A recent example of success in this respect is the port of New York. Before establishment of the New York Waterfront Commission in 1952, there were 44,000 longshoremen in the area, although daily employment rarely reached 20,000. Only about one-third of the longshoremen got as much as 1,200 hours of work per year. By the early

---

[16] See David C. Smith, "Seasonal Unemployment and Economic Conditions," in Arthur M. Ross, ed., *Employment Policy and the Labor Market* (Berkeley and Los Angeles: University of California Press, 1965), p. 196.

sixties, the number of licensed longshoremen had been cut in half. Over two-thirds of the remaining work force was earning in the range of $4,500–$9,000 per year, while only 20 percent earned less than $4,500.[17]

Unemployment and Aggregate Demand

The bulk of unemployment in the economy can be classified as either long-term or short-term, and can be associated either with inadequate total demand or with frictions and maladjustments in the labor market. This yields the four-way classification shown below.[18] While these categories are not entirely independent, they provide a useful framework for our discussion.

	Short-term	*Long-term*
INADEQUATE DEMAND	Cyclical unemployment	Growth-gap unemployment
LABOR MARKET MALADJUSTMENT	Frictional unemployment	Structural unemployment

Cyclical unemployment is a familiar fact of life. Although we have had two long economic expansions (from 1938 to 1945 and from 1961 to 1969) associated with war conditions, these are unusual. An upswing typically lasts only two to four years, after which the economy turns down into recession. Hours of work tend to fall. Many workers are reduced to part-time work. Many others are laid off entirely. Even the mild downswings of the periods from 1953 to 1954 and from 1957 to 1958 added about 2 million workers to the unemployed, while the downswing from 1960 to 1961 displaced 1½ million. Many people become discouraged about the prospects of finding work, and leave the labor force or decide not to enter it. Thus during recession, in addition to those visibly unemployed, there is a substantial amount of "hidden unemployment" consisting of people who would seek work if the chances of finding work were better.

---

17 For the history of decasualization in New York, see Vernon H. Jensen, "Decasualization of Employment on the New York Waterfront," *Industrial and Labor Relations Review*, July, 1958, pp. 534–50. For more recent data, see the *Monthly Labor Review*, January, 1967, p. 11.

18 While this conceptual framework is familiar, the terminology used here is borrowed from Eleanor Gilpatrick, "On the Classification of Unemployment: a View of the Structural-Inadequate Demand Debate," *Industrial and Labor Relations Review*, January, 1966, pp. 201–12.

The incidence of cyclical unemployment is very uneven. Lester Thurow has calculated the "marginal disabsorption rates"—i.e. the marginal propensity to be laid off in recession—and the corresponding marginal absorption (= rehiring) rates on the upswing for specific groups in the labor force.[19] By industry, layoffs are much heavier in construction and durable goods manufacturing than in other sectors. By occupation, layoffs hit laborers five times as hard, and skilled manual workers three times as hard, as white-collar workers. Black workers' marginal layoff rate is more than double that of white workers; and the rate for men aged eighteen to twenty-four is more than double that for those aged thirty-five to sixty-four. Layoffs are concentrated on workers with least skill, experience, and seniority.

When demand rises again, these tendencies go into reverse. Laid-off workers are recalled to work, weekly work schedules are lengthened, more part-timers are able to work full time. As the expansion continues, employment increases are fed by labor force additions, mainly of women and the more loosely attached segments of the male labor force. Movement out of agriculture and other interindustry and interarea movement continues throughout the upswing, and accelerates when male-job markets are particularly tight. As Mincer points out, ". . . the movement from unemployment to employment is least costly, interlabor force mobility more so, and geographic mobility most costly. The successive unfolding of supply adjustments is consistent with the cumulation of upward shifts in demand at the centers of expansion during the business upswing." [20]

Demand unemployment is not just a cyclical phenomenon. It would be so if each upswing carried all the way to full employment before toppling over. But this need not happen. From 1929 to 1941 the American economy remained well below full employment even at cycle peaks, and this was true again on a less dramatic scale from 1958 to 1965. An economy can experience periods of prolonged sluggishness during which demand unemployment is present continuously. In such periods there is a "GNP gap." The economy's productive capacity is rising faster than actual output, and part of capacity remains unutilized. "Growth-gap unemployment" seems a good term for this longer-run demand deficiency.

The amount of demand unemployment at any time cannot be measured precisely. Conceptually, demand unemployment is the difference between actual unemployment and the irreducible minimum that would exist because of frictional and structural factors, even at an "adequate" level of aggregate demand. But what is an adequate

[19] Lester C. Thurow, "The Changing Structure of Unemployment: an Econometric Study," *Review of Economics and Statistics,* May, 1965, pp. 137–49.

[20] Jacob Mincer, "Recent influences on the supply of labor," *Monthly Labor Review,* February, 1967, pp. 30–31.

level of aggregate demand? What is an acceptable target for full employment? It is well known that, as the level of unemployment falls, the rate of price increase tends to accelerate. So the choice of a full employment target requires a decision on what rate of inflation one is willing to accept; and on this preferences are bound to differ. Full employment is not a matter of labor force measurement but a matter of choice among (partially conflicting) economic goals.

Moreover, the level of frictional and structural unemployment depends partly on aggregate demand for labor. As demand for labor rises, the "irreducible minimum" of unemployment shrinks. But this relationship is still not well understood. We know that both "inadequate demand" and "labor market maladjustment" unemployment are present most of the time. We know that there is a complex relation between them, rather than a simple additive relation. But we do not yet know enough to decompose the unemployment existing at a particular time into its component parts.

Frictional and Structural Unemployment

Unemployment arising from characteristics of the labor market can also be divided into a short-term and a longer-term component. The short-term element is usually termed *frictional unemployment*. It includes the seasonal and casual unemployment described earlier, but it includes a good deal more than this.

Suppose demand for labor were adequate in the sense that there were always a vacant job for every worker seeking employment. (A major deficiency in present labor market statistics is lack of comprehensive information on job vacancies.) And suppose that the characteristics of these vacant jobs exactly matched the characteristics of the available workers, so that the problem of mismatching did not exist. Would unemployment then shrink to the vanishing point?

No, it would not. The reason is lack of perfect information in the labor market and lack of a central clearinghouse. Most workers in search of a job look about on their own, following up leads from relatives and friends, or simply applying at the best-known companies in the area. Even if vacancies are available, it takes time for the worker to locate the kind of job he wants; and it takes time for the company to interview applicants, administer preemployment tests, and decide whom to hire. The longer the time, the higher the unemployment rate.

Suppose, for example, that 20 percent of the labor force must find new jobs each year, and suppose that job hunting requires an average of one month. This would produce an average unemployment rate throughout the year of $20/100 \times \frac{1}{12} = 1.67$ percent of the labor force.

The number of people hunting jobs each year depends on such

things as: the amount of movement into and out of the labor force, an especially important consideration for women workers; the irregularity of particular employers' demands for labor, arising from the decline and expansion of particular industries and companies; and the extent of workers' dissatisfaction with their present jobs, leading to voluntary quitting. Under our assumption of adequate demand, the average time needed to find work would depend on the efficiency of the labor market, and would in fact be the best index of efficiency. If the job-hunting period could be cut from four weeks to two weeks by improved information and clearinghouse facilities, frictional unemployment would be cut in half. In practice, the level of demand for labor is an important determinant. Workers will find acceptable jobs faster if there are many vacancies than if there are few vacancies. When demand is high, employers also have an incentive to speed up their recruitment procedures and modify their hiring standards.

Thus there is no one answer to the question: how much frictional unemployment (including seasonal unemployment) should be taken as normal in the American economy? Three percent of the labor force is sometimes advanced as a plausible figure. Unemployment fell below this level, however, at the height of Korean War activity in the years 1952 to 1953. At the height of production activity in World War II, the unemployment rate fell to 1.9 percent in 1943, 1.2 percent in 1944, and 1.9 percent in 1945. So it is clear that, as aggregate demand rises, the level of frictional unemployment drops. What level can be regarded as acceptable is really a target rather than a datum.

Suppose now that the characteristics of the jobs available do not exactly match the qualifications of the people looking for work. To take an extreme example: suppose all the new jobs becoming available in a particular year are professional jobs requiring college training, while all the new workers becoming available are high school dropouts. Then the vacancies would presumably remain unfilled and the workers would continue unemployed. Unemployment arising in this way is termed *structural unemployment*. It is more serious than frictional unemployment in the sense that it is likely to continue for a longer time and that its reduction requires greater effort and expense.

The severity of structural unemployment in an economy at a particular time depends on:

1. *The Rapidity of Shifts in Labor Demand.* Over the past generation in the United States such shifts have been quite rapid. The direction of shift has been away from jobs with low skill and education. The number of farmers and laborers has fallen, while the number of professional, managerial, and technical workers has risen.

2. *The Speed and Accuracy of Supply Adjustments.* The fact that demand is shifting does not necessarily mean a mismatching of demands and supplies. If demand trends could be accurately forecast, if

young people preparing to enter the labor force were perfectly informed concerning them, and if the necessary educational and training facilities were always available, one could imagine a situation in which the qualifications of those emerging from the educational system just matched the pattern of new job vacancies. But these requirements can never be entirely realized. So it is quite possible that new entrants to the labor force will be undereducated, in the sense that their average educational level falls below the average educational rquirements on new jobs. And it is very likely that they will be miseducated, in the sense of oversupply of some skills and undersupply of others.

3. *The Flexibility of Skill Coefficients.* This depends on production technology. If a certain line of production requires exactly so many people at each skill level, with no possibility of substitution among skills, then a shortage of any one skill will shut down production, causing unemployment among workers whose skills are complementary to the one in short supply. If, on the other hand, a shortage of one skill can readily be compensated by substitution of others, structural maladjustments are less likely. Fortunately, a shortage (and associated high price) of one skill sets up a search for substitution possibilities. When fully trained, all-round machinists become unavailable, there is greater effort to break down jobs so that they can be performed by partly trained men. When doctors are very scarce, some of their work can be taken over by interns, nurses, and technicians.

4. *The Transferability of Skills.* This means the time required for an adult worker whose skill has become obsolete to learn a new skill that is in active demand. This depends on such things as: whether his old skill is part of a larger skill-family within which transference is relatively easy; whether his educational and training background has been broad or highly specialized; whether adult retraining facilities and programs are readily available; whether the jobs for which demand is expanding have a long or a short training period. Geographical considerations are also important. If the geographic location of new jobs is shifting rapidly, if information does not filter readily from one area to another, if costs of movement are high, the likelihood of structural maladjustments is increased.

5. *The Fixity of Employers' Non-economic Hiring Specifications.* Employers tend to specify higher educational requirements than are strictly necessary for job performance. They tend to prefer white workers over equally qualified black workers, and often to prefer male workers (who may be scarce) over women workers (who may be more readily available). These preferences soften up as demand for labor rises, but they rarely vanish entirely. They may create a problem of labor transferability on social grounds even when there is no real problem on economic grounds.

The amount of structural maladjustment in the labor market at any time is difficult, perhaps impossible, to quantify. One would need a full list of job vacancies in the economy, with the training and other requirements for each; and one would need a similar roster of the unemployed, with their skills and other relevant characteristics. Even then, transferability of labor is a matter of degree. Probably few workers are wholly nontransferable, i.e. unemployable, just as few are transferable without some retraining. Ease of transfer depends partly on workers' motivation, employers' receptiveness, availability of training facilities and programs; and some of these things are influenced by the level of aggregate demand. So just as we concluded that the level of frictional unemployment cannot be defined independently of the level of demand, we must say the same of structural unemployment.

Under the pressure of high demand, obsolete skills get "melted down" and cast into new molds. Workers have a stronger incentive to learn new skills and change localities when jobs are obviously available. Employers facing labor shortages also have a stronger incentive to spend money on training and to modify noneconomic hiring requirements. But recent experience suggests that structural unemployment does not vanish even at demand peaks. The number of unfilled job openings at the state employment services rose from around 200,-000 in 1962 to 1963 to more than 400,000 in the period from 1966 to 1968. Moreover, about 50 percent of these jobs—and 75 percent of the professional, technical, and managerial jobs—had remained open for thirty days or longer, an indication of genuine shortage. Considering that only a minority of vacancies are listed with the employment service, there were obviously widespread shortages in specific occupations at this time. During these same years there were typically about ½ million workers who had been unemployed for fifteen weeks or more. Considerable mismatching of supplies and demands is indicated.

The effect of structural unemployment is to raise the unemployment rate corresponding to a certain rate of price increase. Suppose that, at a certain level of aggregate demand, frictional unemployment alone would amount to 3 percent of the labor force. In addition, however, there are long-term unfilled vacancies equal to 1 percent of the labor force, and a corresponding number of workers who cannot fit into these jobs because they lack the necessary qualifications. Total unemployment, then, is 4 percent. Prices are rising at, say, 2 percent per year.

Now suppose the unemployed who lack qualifications could be "melted down," transformed instantaneously into proper candidates for the available vacancies. Then employment could be raised by 1 percent and unemployment reduced to 3 percent. Aggregate demand would have to be raised sufficiently to absorb the increased output.

But one could then have a higher level of output and consumption, and 3 percent unemployment, with prices rising not faster than they used to rise with 4 percent unemployment. This is clearly a net gain and probably well worth the retraining and placement costs.[21]

Discussion   Questions

1. For jobs which are typically "inside jobs," events in the outside labor market have little importance. The employer has wide latitude in determining who shall get such jobs and how much they shall be paid. Discuss.
2. The employment package includes many things in addition to wage rates. Discuss the consequences of this for:
    (a)   the construction and usefulness of labor demand-supply diagrams, and
    (b)   employers' adjustment to growing scarcity of labor during an economic expansion.
3. What are the main economic inefficiencies resulting from:
    (a)   limited information in labor markets?
    (b)   barriers to free occupational choice?
4. Suppose the full-time unemployment rate rises from 4 percent to 10 percent. How would this affect:
    (a)   the shape of labor supply curves?
    (b)   employers' hiring policies?
5. Explain the difference between a "competitive model" and a "vacancy model" of labor allocation. What kinds of research might be undertaken to test the explanatory value of these two hypotheses?
6. How would you define "full employment"?
7. On what grounds can one distinguish among "types" of unemployment? Is the size of each type of unemployment independent of the size of all other types? Explain.
8. What is meant by "structural unemployment"? What kinds of research might reveal the extent of such unemployment at a particular time?

21 There is a large volume of recent literature on structural unemployment. In addition to the Gilpatrick and Thurow studies already cited, see N. J. Simler, "Long-term Unemployment, the Structural Hypothesis, and Public Policy," *American Economic Review*, December, 1964, pp. 985–1101; Lowell E. Galloway, "Labor Mobility, Resource Allocation, and Structural Unemployment," *American Economic Review*, September, 1963, pp. 694–716.

Reading Suggestions

Most of the empirical work on labor markets has focused on manual labor. See in particular Myers, Charles A., and George P. Shultz, *The Dynamics of a Labor Market*. Englewood Cliffs, N.J.: Prentice-Hall, Inc., 1951; Lipset, Seymour M., and Reinhard Bendix, *Social Mobility in Industrial Society*. Berkeley and Los Angeles: University of California Press, 1963; Parnes, Herbert S., *Research on Labor Mobility*. New York: Social Science Research Council, 1954; and Reynolds, Lloyd G., *The Structure of Labor Markets*. New York: Harper & Row, Publishers, 1951. On the volume and behavior of unemployment, see Gilpatrick, Eleanor G., *Structural Unemployment and Aggregate Demand*. Baltimore: The Johns Hopkins Press, 1966; Long, Clarence D., *The Labor Force Under Changing Income and Employment*. Princeton: Princeton University Press, 1958; National Bureau of Economic Research, *Measurement and Behavior of Unemployment*. Princeton: Princeton University Press, 1956; National Bureau of Economic Research, *Measurement and Interpretation of Job Vacancies*. New York: Columbia University Press, 1966; Ross, Arthur M., ed., *Employment Policy and the Labor Market*. Berkeley and Los Angeles: University of California Press, 1965; and *Measuring Employment and Unemployment*, Report of the President's Committee to Appraise Employment and Unemployment Statistics, Robert A. Gordon, Chairman. Washington, D.C.: Superintendent of Documents, 1962.

IMPROVING LABOR MARKETS

6

Economists first became interested in labor markets, rather incidentally, because of an interest in wage determination. The original issue was whether labor markets are sufficiently competitive, so that the wage structure emanating from these markets could be considered approximately right, and interference with this structure by unions or government presumptively harmful. Controversy over this issue has produced a long series of empirical studies of labor market behavior, continuing to the present.

Gradually it became apparent that the labor market is important, not just as a forum for wage determination, but in other respects as well. Imperfect labor marketing can lock up in frictional unemployment people who might otherwise be productively employed. Round pegs allocated to square holes reduce national output. If educational bottlenecks unduly restrict entrance to certain occupations, the result is not just wage distortion but frustrated ambitions and economic waste. Since the job is such an intimate part of most people's lives, labor market imperfections reduce welfare more than limited information in product markets.

Labor market engineering is thus an important policy area in its own right. Moreover, while earlier labor market studies focused mainly on manual labor, it is now recognized that major issues arise at higher occupational levels. When one views manpower policy as embracing all occupational levels, and as focused on effective matching of individual skills and preferences against changing demand requirements, several basic problems come to mind.

1. There is the problem of limited information and poor clearinghouse facilities in each locality. This suggests the question of how far these deficiencies can be corrected by improvements in the U.S. Employment Service.

2. The information problem is especially critical for young people in school and college. Decisions made at this time determine the student's general occupational and income level for the rest of his life. There is every indication that these decisions at present are poorly informed and every reason to think that better occupational forecasting and occupational counseling could contribute much to economic efficiency.

3. Even if a student recognizes the advantages of higher education, he may or may not be able to pursue it, depending on availability of training facilities and on his parents' financial position. So we must look briefly at the economics of education. There are many possible ways of financing higher education, ranging from a system under which each student pays a tuition charge covering the full cost of his training to the opposite extreme of zero tuition plus full scholarships for all qualified students. How this issue is resolved has a major impact on labor supply to the higher occupations and on relative earnings in those occupations.

4. Many people who thought they had acquired a marketable skill discover in later life that their skill has been rendered obsolete by shifts in product demand, production technology, or geographical location of industry. This poses a problem of retraining adult workers so that they can enter occupations in which demand is growing, thus reducing the volume of structural unemployment.

5. We have noted at several points that black workers are seriously disadvantaged at present compared with white workers. A disproportionate number are in low-skilled and low-paid jobs, and they also suffer disproportionately from unemployment. We must analyze the main reasons for this and explore the directions of remedial action.

INFORMATION AND ORGANIZATION:
THE
LOCAL LABOR MARKET

For most subprofessional occupations—factory work, construction work, clerical and sales work, service occupations—the labor market is a locality. It is the area within which people can conveniently drive from home to work, and their movement is normally restricted to this area.

The market imperfections emphasized in the last chapter can never be removed entirely. But the fact that we shall never see a purely competitive labor market—a "stock exchange for labor"—should not deter us from doing anything at all. Much could be done to make labor markets function better, even if still imperfectly. First, however, it is necessary to ask just what we are trying to do: What are the economic objectives of labor market policy?

From a general economic standpoint, there are several shortcomings in the present movement of labor. First, there is probably too much movement—more quitting of jobs and shifting about than there would need to be if things were better organized. Unnecessary movement is a hardship to the worker and involves recruitment and training costs to the employer. Second, workers take more time to locate a new job than would be necessary in a better-organized market. Again, this is both a hardship to the individual worker and a loss of labor power to the economy. Third, there is considerable mismatching of individual abilities and job requirements. People do not necessarily end up in the jobs for which they are best suited. The ideal allocation of the labor force described in Chapter 4 is not attained.

What could be done to provide workers with better job information? Considering the importance of this matter, it is rather surprising that there is no place where a worker can get an accurate picture of the full range of occupations, wage rates, and working conditions available in the community. The nearest thing to an information center is the local office of the state employment service, which can provide information about vacant jobs registered by employers. Since employers are not required to register vacancies, however, and since many of them prefer to recruit labor directly, this gives an incomplete picture of the opportunities available. In many cities, the chamber of commerce or some other employers' organization collects periodic information on wage rates, and in some cases also on fringe benefits and other aspects of personnel policy. This information is compiled for the use of employers, however, and is not open to others in the community.

It would seem desirable that somewhere in the community, possibly at the local employment service office, there should be a roster, not simply of the jobs which happen to be vacant at the moment, but of the principal types of work offered by each employer in the community. This should include the wage rates paid, qualifications required, and other key items of information about each job; and it should be open for inspection at any time by workers interested in a change of employment. This would work some hardship on employers whose jobs are relatively unattractive and whose existence depends partly on the fact that their workers do not know about attractive opportunities elsewhere. Any competitive market penalizes those unable to meet the market price. Employers offering superior wages and conditions, on the other hand, would find it easier to recruit labor than they do at present. From a community point of view, workers would be able to seek jobs in a more informed way, the chances of each job change being in the "right" direction would be greater, and there would be a consequent gain in economic efficiency.

Central to any effort to improve labor market efficiency is the system of public employment offices. This system was established by the Wagner-Peyser Act of 1933. This act provided that states that established employment service systems and appropriated funds for their support would receive from the federal government an amount equal to that supplied by the states. In return for this grant of funds, the federal government reserved the right to prescribe minimum standards of personnel and operating procedures, which the state services must meet. Between 1933 and 1937, employment service systems were established in all the states and the District of Columbia. These state employment services were "lent" to the federal government during World War II and, as the main operating arm of the War Manpower Commission, exercised extensive influence over the movement of workers into and out of essential industries. Shortly after the end of the war, the employment offices were returned to state control. The federal government, through a small overhead organization known as the United States Employment Service continues to prescribe minimum operating standards and to share the administrative costs of the state systems.

Most cities of ten thousand or more now have a branch of the state employment service staffed by at least one full-time official, and larger cities have proportionately larger offices. Smaller towns and cities are usually served one or two days a week by a traveling official of the employment service. The function of the public employment offices is to provide a meeting place for buyers and sellers of labor. Any employer with a vacant job may place an order at the employment service, specifying the nature of the work, the qualifications required, the starting wage, and other relevant facts. Any unemployed worker may register for work at the employment service, and workers who have applied for unemployment compensation are required to register. The registration form, usually filled out with the aid of a trained interviewer, contains key facts about the worker and about his last few jobs.

The problem of the employment service official is to match orders and registrations as best he can. When an order is received, he looks through the active file of registrants for workers who appear qualified for the job in question. He makes a tentative selection, talks with the worker to find out whether he is interested in the job, and if he is interested, passes him on to the employer. The employer need not hire workers sent out by the employment service, nor need workers accept the jobs to which they are sent, though there is some pressure on workers drawing unemployment compensation. The employment service checks a few days later to find out whether the man was hired or not. If he was, this is counted as a "placement" by the local office.

The number of placements made by the state employment services in private industry remained low throughout the thirties, largely because of the low level of demand for labor. There was a great increase in placements during the war years, due partly to the active demand for labor by employers, and partly to the control regulations that required most placements in essential industries to be made through the employment service. Total placements reached a peak of more than 11 million in 1944. Placements have fallen considerably since the end of the war, but remain well above the prewar level. In recent years, nonagricultural placements have been about 6 million per year. The volume of placements naturally fluctuates with the level of business activity. The placements made by the public employment offices are also concentrated rather heavily in certain occupational groups—domestic and other personal service; farm labor, construction labor, and unskilled labor in general; and semiskilled factory work. There is relatively little placement of skilled tradesmen or white-collar workers, most of whom prefer to seek work directly.

There is no reliable way of estimating what proportion of all placements in private industry is made by the state employment services, but the proportion is probably in the neighborhood of one-fourth. Why is the employment service not more widely used? The main reason is that employers can usually fill a good vacancy quickly without resorting to the employment service. Word of the vacancy gets passed on to friends and relatives of people already in the plant, the foreman remembers someone who used to work on that job and looks him up, or the union has a suggestion to make. Thus a worker with good contacts can usually locate a job through "the grapevine," and feels little need for the employment service. Where employer and worker are able to locate each other directly, there is no need for the employment service to intervene. It exists to supplement other methods of work seeking, not to supplant them.

The employment service is hampered somewhat by the inherent complexity of the placement job. It is hard to become familiar enough with all the jobs in an area, and with the idiosyncrasies of each employer, so that one can tell whether a particular worker will be acceptable for a particular job. It is difficult also to gauge accurately the experience and abilities of each registrant. When a man says that he is a toolmaker, is he really a toolmaker or only a grade *B* machinist? A failure to judge accurately both the man and the job leads not merely to a lost placement, but also to a loss of prestige with the employer and worker involved.

The employment service is also under a certain amount of pressure to refer workers to vacancies even against its better judgment. Employers keep asking, "Why don't you send me someone?" Workers keep asking, "Why can't you find me a job?" A worker drawing unemployment compensation must be willing to accept work at his usual occupation under reasonable conditions in order to remain eligible for benefits. The only way of testing his willingness to work is by referring him to a job. The fact that the local offices of the employment service have to administer this "willingness to work" requirement has an unfortunate effect on their placement activities. It means that a large proportion of registrants at the employment service are unemployment compensation recipients. This causes many workers to look on the employment service as virtually a relief office, while others regard referral to work as simply a formality which must be gone through to earn eligibility for unemployment compensation. It also leads to employer complaints that the employment service refers many unqualified workers, and that employment service registrants constitute the least-desirable segment of the labor force.

This point can be generalized. The employment service is widely regarded as a social welfare agency whose task is to find work for the unfortunate. It is put under pressure to give priority in referrals to disadvantaged groups in the labor force—the long-term unemployed, members of minority groups, people with physical or mental disabilities. But the employment service cannot push people into employment in the face of employers' natural desire to find the most efficient candidate for each job. Ill-conceived efforts to do so may sacrifice the respect and cooperation of employers, on whose job orders the service ultimately depends.

Considering these difficulties, the efficiency of employment service operations in most states is surprisingly high. But the gap between performance and potential remains wide, and there are few areas of labor policy in which diligent effort can yield higher economic returns. There is need for clearer recognition of the service as an *economic* agency rather than a *welfare* agency. Its task is to perfect the labor market mechanism, to serve all members of the labor force rather than merely the hard-to-place, to reflect employer requirements accurately and objectively, to locate the man most suited to a particular job rather than the man who needs work most. It cannot hope to correct the distress resulting from inadequate demand for labor, or from personal handicaps, or from mistaken hiring preferences. It can hope to reduce frictional unemployment, to cut employers' hiring and training costs, and to secure a more efficient matching of individual capacities and job requirements.[1]

Effective performance of these functions calls for educational and entrepreneurial activity by the employment service. Not only the unemployed but young people on the point of leaving school and people who already have a job but want a better job should be encouraged to register. The usefulness of the service to employers must be demonstrated in action. This may require changes in internal operating procedures, such as exposure of each vacancy to several workers, and of a well-qualified worker to several vacancies. There is evidence that vigorous action along these lines can increase the service's placement volume and its acceptance in the community.[2]

There is considerable agreement that administration of unemployment compensation should be separated from employment service operations.[3] They should be in separate physical locations, and the quite different functions of their staffs should be emphasized. This would help to remove the welfare taint which has hung over the employment service in the past.

A further requirement for effective operation is adequate salaries. Employment service personnel are not on federal, but rather on state salary scales, which vary widely from state to state and are typically below the levels offered by private industry for comparable skills. An employment service officer who does a good job and becomes favorably known to employers is quickly hired for personnel work in industry. This means high turnover of employment service personnel and a tendency for the less able to remain while the best people depart. Without an attack on this problem, other efforts to improve employment service operations may be ineffective.

The focus of this section has been on movement of workers within an area, but we should note that for some occupations the market is regional or national in scope. This is true for most professional, technical, and managerial occupations, and even for some skilled manual trades.

To serve such occupations, the state employment services have organized an Interarea Recruitment System. Under this system an em-

---

[1] For an eloquent and well-reasoned statement of this view, see E. Wight Bakke, *A Positive Labor Market Policy* (Columbus, Ohio: Charles E. Merrill Publishing Co., 1963).

[2] See, for example, the account of a very successful experience in Madison, Wisconsin, in Eaton H. Conant, "Public Employment Service Operations in a Clerical Labor Market," *Proceedings of Fifteenth Annual Meeting of IRRA* (1962), pp. 306–14.

[3] See, for example, "Placement and Counseling: the Role of the Employment Service," a report to the Secretary of Labor from the Employment Service Task Force, reprinted in R. A. Gordon, ed., *Toward a Manpower Policy* (New York: John Wiley & Sons, Inc., 1967).

ployer order that cannot be filled within the locality is first cleared with other employment service offices in the state. If it remains unfilled, it is passed on to other states which seem likely to have the kind of labor in question. Employment service headquarters in these states pass the information down to their local offices, until eventually some office pulls out the card of a suitable candidate from its file of registrants. Particular attention is given to orders for professional personnel. There is a special Professional Office Network, which now includes 121 offices strategically located in cities throughout the United States.

These activities face the usual difficulties of employment service operation, and there are additional obstacles of time and distance. But these may be removed increasingly by computer hookups and other means of high-speed communication.

THE TRANSITION
FROM SCHOOL
TO WORK

During the high school years young people begin to sort themselves out into educational levels which have a heavy influence on their later occupation:

1. A certain proportion, though now only about one-quarter, drop out before completing high school. These people are consigned almost automatically to the least-skilled and poorest paid jobs in the market. They also suffer considerably more from unemployment, both before finding their first jobs and later on.[4] Some of them drift into chronic idleness. They presumably form a good part of the mysterious group of young people who are neither in school nor in the labor force (see Chapter 2).

2. The majority who finish high school divide into two streams. About 50 percent take no further education. They provide the basic supply of office workers and sales workers, as well as a large proportion of the skilled craftsmen, supervisors, and small businessmen.

3. The remaining 50 percent of the high school graduates now proceed to specialized technical schools, two-year junior colleges, or regular four-year colleges. The trend in this respect has been strongly upward over the past fifty years. In 1920 only about 8 percent of those aged eighteen to twenty-one were enrolled in college. Today the pro-

---

[4] The employment and earnings experience of dropouts compared with high school graduates is kept under continuous study by the Department of Labor and there are frequent reports in the *Monthly Labor Review*. See, for example, Vera C. Perella and Elizabeth Waldman, "Out-of-school youth—two years later," *Monthly Labor Review*, August, 1966, pp. 860–66.

portion is about 40 percent, and it is estimated that this will reach 50 percent by 1980. Of those who finish college, a growing proportion are spending additional years in obtaining an M.D., LL.B., M.B.A., Ph.D., or other advanced degree. People with college training man the professions, most technical and subprofessional occupations, and the administrative ranks in business and government.

It is in the interest of the individual that he be able to proceed to the occupational level that, considering training costs, prospective earnings, and his own abilities and preferences, yields him greatest net advantage. It is in the social interest that people be sorted out on the basis of potential productivity, each finding himself in the job for which he has comparative advantage, thus maximizing national product. The most capable potential surgeons, scientists, business administrators, and so on should be able to move into those occupations.

There is much evidence that the sorting-out process is presently rather haphazard. One important reason is inadequate information about educational and job opportunities. The level of information falls rapidly as one moves from families in the higher occupational and income levels to those in lower levels. Children of manual workers typically have a very limited range of vision. They often leave school prematurely, and wander into a blind-alley job simply because it has been suggested by a parent or relative. They may fail to consider college education even though they are well qualified and the potential rewards are high.

The child's ability and motivation also influence his progress up the educational ladder. But how do we measure ability? By the time a child is old enough to be subjected to intelligence tests, he has also been subject to five or six years of home influence. Psychologists have estimated that perhaps one-quarter of the observed variation in I.Q. scores and similar measures is attributable to home environment rather than to genetic factors.[5] There is clear evidence also that the child's progress in school is much influenced by parental interest and encouragement; and success (or lack of it) at schoolwork naturally influences decisions about staying on or dropping out. Thus families at the lower end of the socioeconomic scale tend to be caught in a vicious circle: parents with low levels of income, education, and information fail to provide a background which reinforces their child's progress through the school system, leading the child to drop off the ladder early and consign himself to a low level of occupation and income. At the other end of the scale, in business and professional families, everything conspires to propel the child through higher education and into the same occupational level as his father.

---

[5] For a good review of the relevant literature, see Harold Lydall, *The Structure of Earnings* (Oxford: Oxford University Press, 1968), chap. 4.

There have been many sample surveys indicating that, for students at the same level of measured ability, the percentage going on to college is much higher from high-income families than from low-income families.[6] Some estimates for the entire U.S. high school graduating class of 1966, prepared in the U.S. Department of Health, Education, and Welfare, are shown in Table 1. The table includes only the top

Table 1

COLLEGE ENTRANCE OF HIGH SCHOOL GRADUATES,
BY ABILITY AND SOCIOECONOMIC STATUS, 1966

Ability Group	Socioeconomic Status of Family	ENTERING COLLEGE		NOT ENTERING COLLEGE	
		Number (thousands)	Percent	Number (thousands)	Percent
HIGHEST FIFTH	1. Highest	192	95	11	5
	2.	120	79	33	21
	3.	82	67	40	33
	4. Lowest	30	50	30	50
NEXT HIGHEST FIFTH	1. Highest	109	84	21	16
	2.	90	63	53	37
	3.	78	52	70	48
	4. Lowest	34	36	60	64
TOTAL (top 40 percent)		735	70	318	30

SOURCE: *Toward a Social Report* (Washington, D.C.: Superintendent of Documents, 1969), p. 21.

40 percent of graduating seniors, ranked by measured ability, and shows the percentage who went on to college from families at various socioeconomic levels. These students were presumably all capable of college work. Yet 318,000 of them, or about 30 percent, did not go on to college; and of these two-thirds came from families in the two lowest economic groups.

Similar data for Canada, drawn from the 1961 Census of Canada and reproduced in the Lydall study, are shown in Table 2. Note again the strong association between the father's income, occupation, and educational level and the school enrollment of his children.

To a considerable extent, then, the educational system serves as a transmission belt, preserving the position of advantaged and disadvantaged families from generation to generation. But it also serves as

[6] A review of such studies, and additional analysis relevant to this section, will be found in Seymour M. Lipset and Reinhard Bendix, *Social Mobility in Industrial Society* (Berkeley and Los Angeles: University of California Press, 1963).

Table 2

RELATION BETWEEN SOCIAL CLASS OF PARENT
AND EDUCATION OF CHILDREN, CANADA, 1961

	PERCENTAGE OF CHILDREN AT SCHOOL IN AGE-GROUPS	
Occupation of Family Head (selected occupations)	*15–18*	*19–24*
MANAGERIAL	84.3	37.8
PROFESSIONAL ENGINEERS	91.9	57.0
SCHOOLTEACHERS	92.6	57.9
PHYSICIANS AND SURGEONS	94.9	73.6
ACCOUNTANTS AND AUDITORS	90.7	46.0
CLERICAL	77.8	23.9
FARMERS	66.7	15.2
CARPENTERS	68.0	15.5
NONFARM LABORERS	58.7	9.8
Schooling of Family Head (all families)		
UNIVERSITY DEGREE	93.8	63.7
SOME UNIVERSITY	88.2	45.5
HIGH SCHOOL: 4–5	84.6	34.6
3	82.4	28.9
1–2	76.4	21.5
ELEMENTARY: 5–8	66.3	14.6
1–4	51.8	8.5
NONE	45.5	6.9
Income of Family Head (employees only)		
$7,000 AND OVER	90.7	50.0
$5,000–6,999	81.7	29.4
$3,000–4,999	72.3	18.4
UNDER $3,000	60.9	12.0

SOURCE: Harold Lydall, *The Structure of Earnings,* p. 110.

a channel of opportunity. Many bright children from poor families do climb the educational and occupational ladder. Many "dumb rich kids" do flunk out and sink to lower levels. The policy problem is to increase the element of opportunity in the system and reduce the amount of sheer hereditary transmission.

Let us set aside for the moment the problem of how able youngsters can be assured of higher education, which involves issues of educational finance, and focus on young people who go directly to work after or before finishing high school. At this level the problems are largely occupational information, youth counseling, and job placement.

It is not an insuperable task to assemble information on the occupations currently available in the economy: how much each job pays, the nature of the work, the educational and skill requirements, and so on. The Department of Labor does in fact collect such information and prepares occupational handbooks for the use of employment service staff, school counselors, and others. The difficulty, however, is that the young person is making a long-range choice which may commit him for several decades. He needs to know what the occupational situation will be twenty or thirty years from now. Is a particular occupation faced with rising, stagnant, or declining demand? Are its earnings likely to rise faster, or less rapidly, than the general wage level? If demand should fall drastically, will workers in the occupation be left stranded, or are the skills involved readily convertible to neighboring occupations?

Because of the importance of such questions, one is involved inevitably in occupational forecasting, to which much talent is now being devoted in all parts of the world. An occupational forecast normally starts from a forecast of the structure of production. We estimate that Gross National Product twenty years from now will be, say, twice what it is today. Since we know something about how consumer purchases behave as consumer income rises, we can deduce what this higher income level will mean for production of each type of consumer good. Government output, now 20 percent of GNP, can be predicted from past trends in education, highway construction, military expenditures, and so on. Next—and again on the basis of past experience—we project the quantities of raw materials, intermediate products, fuel and power, capital goods, and so forth required to make possible these levels of government output and consumer goods production. So we end up with a detailed bill of goods which the economy will be producing in 1990.

The next step is to analyze the amount of labor, and the specific kinds of labor, needed to produce a unit of each kind of good—a ton of steel, a medium-sized automobile, 100 pupil-years of education. It is usually assumed that various occupations will be employed in the same proportions in the target year as in past years. If in 1970 a thousand tons of steel required twenty man-years of unskilled labor, thirty years of semiskilled labor, thirty years of skilled labor, and twenty years of white-collar labor, we assume that these same proportions [7] will hold in 1990. We then multiply the prospective tonnage of steel in 1990 by the quantities of each kind of labor required per ton, to get a picture of labor demand in the industry at that time.

---

[7] But not necessarily the same absolute amounts. In most industries output per man rises year by year, so that labor used per unit of output declines. On the basis of past productivity trends, we can build a steady shrinkage of labor requirements into our future estimates. It is usual, however, to shrink the requirements for all occupations at the *same rate,* i.e. to hold the occupational composition of the labor force unchanged.

When we have done this for each output in the economy and totaled up, we have a detailed picture of the numbers needed in every occupation in the economy in the target year.

Projections for any extended period are subject to a considerable margin of error. Technological change gradually alters the skill proportions required for any type of production. It is likely, for example, that steel production a generation from now will require relatively more engineers and white-collar workers, and relatively fewer low-skilled laborers, than it does today. But the size of such shifts is hard to predict. There is usually some substitutability among skills. If skilled craftsmen become scarce, jobs can often be redesigned to be done by less-skilled men. Finally, demand is not independent of relative wage rates, a fact which tends to be overlooked in physical man-power projections. Failure of supply of a particular kind of labor to keep pace with demand leads to a rise in its relative wage; and this leads employers to economize by substituting machinery or other types of labor for the scarce skill. Indeed, shortage or surplus of a skill cannot be defined except by reference to its wage.

A further difficulty is that, for most occupations, projections must be reduced to a local level to be really useful. A girl high school student in Scranton, Pa., needs to know the job outlook for secretaries, teachers, and so on in Scranton rather than in the continental United States. This requires estimates of shifts in the geographic location of production. For short periods ahead, each employer in an area can be asked to forecast his hiring needs at various skill levels. But such forecasts rapidly lose precision as the period is lengthened and are probably useless beyond two or three years.

Good projections of demand for each occupation could be used in several ways. First, most high school students receive some vocational education and many take courses that are primarily vocational. It is obviously desirable that vocational education be related realistically to employment opportunities. This has often not been true in the past. For many years Congress, in appropriating federal funds for support of vocational education, imposed restrictions that forced heavy emphasis on domestic science and agriculture. As late as the early sixties only one-sixth of vocational school students were classified as studying "trades and industries," where the expanding opportunities mainly lie; and only one high school out of ten offered instruction in these subjects.

The situation has been improved considerably by the Vocational Education Act of 1963 and the 1968 amendments to this act. Federal appropriations for vocational education were increased substantially and the previous occupational restrictions were eliminated. Federal support is now available for all occupations except those requiring four years or more of college training, including construction of new vocational high schools and technical colleges. This has already produced a sharp increase in the numbers being trained. Between 1964 and 1967, high school enrollments in vocational programs rose from 2.1 to 3.5 million, post high-school (technical college) enrollments rose from 0.2 to 0.5 million, and adult enrollments in part-time programs rose from 2.3 to 2.9 million. There has also been a healthy shift in occupational orientation. Between 1964 and 1967, agriculture and home economics declined from 63 percent to 44 percent of the total. In 1967, 22 percent of students were enrolled in office occupations, 21 percent in trades and industries, 7 percent in retailing and marketing, and 5.4 percent in health occupations and other technical fields.[8]

A second major use of occupational information is in counseling and placement of high school students, whether enrolled in vocational or academic programs. Most large high schools now have one or more vocational counselors, but it appears that more than half of all high school students still leave school without having had systematic occupational advice. We do considerably less well on this front than most of the European countries.

Counseling involves testing the student's aptitudes, discussing his interests and preferences, and providing accurate occupational information. During their last two years of high school, students should become familiar with the occupational structure of the economy, prospective earnings in various occupations, the nature of the work and other nonwage characteristics, the amount and type of specialized training required, the trend of demand and the chances of securing employment, employer's hiring methods and requirements, and the operation of the employment service and other placement agencies. This might be done through regular classroom courses, supplemented by class visits to stores, offices, factories, and other places of employment, and by guest lectures by employers and others familiar with particular fields. This would help students to form their own job preferences, to discuss job possibilities with school counselors in a more informed and realistic way, and to set about seeking work more effectively.

At the end of the student's school career there is need for effective collaboration between school counselors, who know most about the student's abilities and preferences, and employment service placement officers, who are in closest touch with job vacancies. Which group has formal responsibility for placement is less important than that the division of responsibility be clear and the relation one of cooperation rather than rivalry. In some localities close and effective collaboration already exists; but in other areas this is not true, and the student is left to sink or swim in the labor market.

[8] *Manpower Report of the President,* January, 1969, pp. 81–87.

Even the best counseling and placement efforts cannot remove the need for search and experimentation by the young worker himself. The congeniality of a particular kind of work, and one's proficiency at it, are best tested by experience. Many job characteristics—the personality of the foreman, the pace of work, the congeniality of fellow employees, details of company personnel policies—cannot be punched into a central data bank. Given the complexity of the employment relation, a certain amount of shopping for jobs by working at them is necessary and useful. But fuller advance information can reduce the amount of purposeless and frustrating mobility, with cost savings to both employers and workers.

FINANCING PROFESSIONAL
AND
TECHNICAL TRAINING

The highest occupational strata in the economy require four to eight years of college and postgraduate training. This training is expensive. So labor supply to these occupations depends partly on how the costs of higher education are financed. One cost—the amount that the student might have earned by working instead of studying—is almost always borne by the student and his family. But what about buildings, equipment, teachers, and the other costs involved in providing educational services? Should the student bear these costs in full, or partially, or not at all?

The problem is complicated by the fact that higher education, while partly an investment good, is also a consumer good. It increases the student's productive capacity and future earning power; but it also enlarges his interests and his capacity for personal enjoyment. It is usually thought also to confer public benefits in terms of more active and better informed citizenship. It is difficult to separate the investment component of higher education from its consumption and public-good components. This is serious, for the correct principles for financing investment in human capital may be very different from those for financing other components of education.

To avoid this problem for the moment, let us visualize a kind of professional training which is purely an investment good. There are probably types of training that approximate this definition, though it would be invidious to suggest concrete examples.

Let us next visualize three alternative systems of finance: (1) a *pay-as-you-go* system, under which each student pays a tuition charge covering the full cost of his education, and he and his parents are left to find the money where they can; (2) a *loan-fund* system, under which each student is still charged full tuition, but may borrow part or all of the necessary funds at market rates of interest, with repayment spread over a period of years following graduation; and (3) a *full-scholarship* system, under which the student's tuition and living costs are provided free of charge. Various intermediate systems are obviously possible, but it will be useful to examine these three as pure types.

Each system will produce a different supply curve to the occupation. For a given level of prospective earnings, the number choosing the occupation will be smallest under a pay-as-you-go system, largest under a full-scholarship system. Thus if the pay-as-you-go supply curve is S_1 (Figure 1), a loan-fund system might produce the supply curve S_2, and a full-scholarship system might lead to S_3.

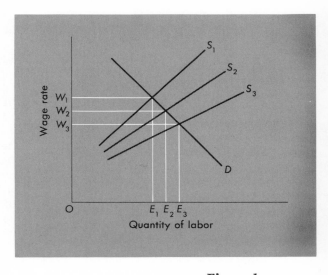

Figure 1

EDUCATIONAL FINANCE, LABOR SUPPLY,
AND RELATIVE EARNINGS

If the demand curve D is assumed independent of the system of finance, these different supply curves will lead to different equilibrium earnings for the occupation. Relative earnings will be highest (OW_1) if supply is restricted by a pay-as-you-go system, and lowest (OW_3) if supply is enlarged by full scholarships. The number engaged in the occupation will be largest (OE_3) under a scholarship system, smallest (OE_1) under pay-as-you-go.

What are the relative merits of the three systems? Can one of them be considered economically superior to the others?

Look first at pay-as-you-go. The argument for pricing human capital at full cost is similar to that for pricing physical capital at full cost. Unless supply reflects all relevant costs, and unless demand reflects informed individual preferences, there cannot be the matching of costs and benefits required for efficient allocation of resources. There is also an equity argument. The higher earnings resulting from specialized professional training come back to the individual practitioner, not to society. So he, and not society, should bear the costs of his training.

This argument is convincing, however, only if there is a capital market in which families can borrow (at a price) for human investment, just as business concerns now borrow for physical investment. In the absence of such a market, and given that many millions of families have incomes too low for self-financing, education will be underpurchased. A pay-as-you-go system without borrowing facilities would restrict professional training to children from the upper income brackets. This is both inequitable and inefficient, since it would lead to much wastage of talent.

There is a clear case, then, for an educational loan system. At a minimum, loans should be available in amounts adequate to cover living expenses as well as tuition costs. (Since a major cost of higher education is the opportunity cost of the student's time—the amount he could earn by working rather than studying—one might argue that the loan ceiling should be high enough to cover part of this cost as well.) Loans would be repayable over a period of years after graduation; but there are many possible repayment formulas. The Harvard Graduate School of Business Administration has long had a loan-fund plan, under which graduates who go into executive positions must repay the loan in full. But graduates who go into teaching, thereby consigning themselves to relative poverty, need not repay. A presidential panel has recently proposed, and Professor Milton Friedman among others has supported, an "Educational Opportunity Bank," one feature of which would be a sliding-scale repayment plan related to future earnings. This would eliminate some of the risk involved in committing oneself to repay a large fixed amount from future earnings, which, for most professions, are quite variable and uncertain.

A further policy problem is the terms on which loans should be extended. The interest rate and other terms could be made comparable with those for other loans involving equivalent risk. Alternatively, loans could be made on easier terms—an interest rate below the market level, an extended grace period after graduation, or a prolonged repayment period. To the extent that loan terms are below the market level, however, the loan contains a subsidy or scholarship element. Whether this is justifiable depends on whether scholarships in general are justifiable, a point to be considered in a moment.

It should be noted that introduction of a loan system where none has existed before will reduce the relative earnings of people already engaged in the occupation. It shifts the supply curve from S_1 to S_2 (Figure 1), and lowers the equilibrium wage from W_1 to W_2. So people who entered the occupation in earlier years, expecting a wage of W_1, will now be disappointed. Yet if their skill is specialized and not readily transferable, they will not leave the occupation. They are in the position of a company that has built a factory expecting a certain price for the product and then finds that price settles at a lower level. They must accept whatever level of earnings (technically, quasi rents) the market provides.

A system of full scholarships would have even stronger distributional effects: (1) the supply curve shifts to S_3 and the equilibrium wage to W_3, so that those already engaged in the profession take a permanent loss of income; (2) consumers of the service in question benefit by being able to get it at a lower price; (3) new entrants to the profession benefit by receiving a valuable investment good free of charge; (4) since the full cost of education is now paid from public funds, the tax burden is increased. The distributional effect depends on the kinds of tax that are levied or increased to finance educational expenditures. Progressive income taxes will shift more of the burden to higher-income groups, while sales, excise, and property taxes bear harder on low-income people. If there were heavy reliance on the latter group of taxes, the scholarship system might possibly involve a transfer from lower-income to higher-income families.

A full-scholarship system means that students are receiving a valuable investment good free of charge. Can this be justified in an economy where most other goods and services are sold at a market price? Will it not lead to relative overproduction of technical and professional education? In the case we have assumed, where the training has no consumption aspect and no external benefits to society, scholarships would indeed be difficult to justify. A case for scholarships must lean heavily on a supposition that the education in question does have these additional benefits, which are not fully reflected in money returns to the profession. There are a number of occupations—medical care, teaching, scientific research—where this is thought to be true, i.e. where the social value of the product is thought to exceed the money income of the practitioners. This is always a matter of judgment, however, and the question must be raised separately for each type of professional training.

Actual practice in the United States is mixed and in some ways quite inconsistent. Some kinds of professional training, such as legal training and (until recently) medical training in private universities, come close to pay-as-you-go standards. This is reflected in a relatively small inflow of personnel and relatively high earnings in these professions.

Loan funds were until recently rather limited, but there has been a great increase in availability of funds during the fifties and sixties. Many colleges and universities now have loan funds that allow the student to borrow up to some maximum amount, often at subsidized interest rates, and to repay over a period of years after graduation. Experience has been that most students are good credit risks and that losses through nonpayment are very small. A number of states, including New York, guarantee repayment of bank loans for educational purposes, provided they meet certain standards of interest rate and repayment terms. This should make bank credit more readily available than it has been.

There is also an increasing amount of federal activity in this area. The National Defense Education Act provides funds for loans to undergraduates specializing in science, mathematics, and modern foreign languages. Upwards of a million students have already received loans under this act. The Health Professions Educational Assistance Act provides student loan funds for prospective physicians, dentists, and optometrists. Funds under both acts are administered by individual universities, which must put into the fund at least $1 for every $9 of federal funds received.

The main question about these programs is why they are limited only to certain subjects. Can one safely assert that studying Spanish or chemistry is important to the nation, while studying economics or history is not? Why support dentistry and not engineering? Why should not loan facilities be extended to qualified students in any area? This would require a larger revolving fund but, since the money is repayable with interest, there is no cost to government beyond administrative expenses and a risk of loan default, which thus far has turned out to be negligible.

Finally, most college and university students in the United States receive substantial scholarships, arising from the fact that tuition charges are below full educational costs. This is true even in private institutions, and even more true in state institutions and community colleges. In addition to these implicit scholarships, private colleges and universities allocate substantial amounts for cash grants to students from low-income families. At the graduate level, sizable amounts of federal money have been appropriated for fellowships in medicine, the natural sciences, and some of the social sciences, and graduate students in other areas receive substantial support from foundation grants and university funds. Viewed as a whole, however, the system is rather haphazard and may oversupport some groups while undersupporting others.

One other problem of educational policy should be mentioned in conclusion. After the question of how much students should be charged for training is decided, there remains the problem of building enough educational capacity to accommodate all those who desire training on these terms. Training capacity is expensive, especially in the medical and natural sciences, and requires large appropriations of public funds.

Suppose that Figure 1 relates to the medical profession. It has been decided to rely on a system of loan finance. Looking at the Figure, we see that the relevant supply curve is S_2, the equilibrium wage is W_2, and the number who will wish to become doctors at this wage is E_2. Then enough medical school capacity should be built so that E_2 people can actually become doctors.

The difficulty is that we do not *know* the location of D and S_2, and can make only crude estimates. We do not *know* the size of W_2 or of E_2. So the policy maker faces questions such as the following:

1. Is the present level of medical earnings above or below the long-run equilibrium level? If above, there is a shortage, which needs to be filled by accelerated effort. If below, there is a surplus, which should be worked off over the years.

2. Both D and S_2 are moving to the right with the growth of population and per capita income. But at what speed are they moving, and what are the implications for equilibrium earnings and employment?

3. Since it takes close to ten years to turn out a fully trained doctor, and since school construction may also take several years, today's decisions must be based on a forecast of the probable positions of D, S_2, W_2, and E_2 ten years or more from now. But the farther ahead one tries to forecast, the greater the range of possible error. Within this range, is it better to err in the direction of overbuilding or underbuilding educational capacity?

The case of medicine has been debated actively in recent years. The preponderant opinion seems to be that training capacity has lagged behind demand, and that the number entering the profession has thus been unduly restricted. Opinion is not unanimous, however, and the problem of estimating the relevant magnitudes is highly complicated.[9]

RETRAINING
OF
ADULT WORKERS

We saw in Chapter 5 that there is substantial structural unemployment in the American economy. There are workers who have been dis-

[9] For a good analysis of the complexities, see Rashi Feinn, *The Doctor Shortage* (Washington, D.C.: The Brookings Institution, 1967). See also Elton Rayack, "The Supply of Physicians' Services," *Industrial and Labor Relations Review*, January, 1964, pp. 221–37.

placed from industries in which demand for labor is declining, such as mining and some branches of manufacturing. There are people who left school early and who are lacking in both formal education and job training. There are many who do not consider themselves in the labor force, but who would choose to work if they possessed a marketable skill.

Meanwhile demand for labor is rising in other occupations, but these are mainly either repair and service occupations or white-collar occupations. The problem is to retool the workers who lack relevant skills, so that they become available for employment in the occupations and geographic areas where work is available. Provided the cost of doing this is less than the addition to national output, a program of retraining and relocation is economically efficient.

The federal government supports large-scale activities in this area, mostly under the Manpower Development and Training Act of 1962 (MDTA). But before describing these activities we should look at the economic issues involved in any retraining effort.

The first problem is *who* is to be trained. The long-term unemployed differ in age, color, educational level, interest in work, and physical and mental capacity. Assuming that funds are insufficient to train everyone, where should one start? Should one deal from the top of the deck or the bottom?

On efficiency grounds, it might seem that one should start with the most trainable, that is, those for whom the ratio of future production gains to training costs is highest. These are likely to be the younger, better-educated, and generally more qualified members of the unemployed.

But one can also muster strong arguments for starting with the most disadvantaged. To lift people out of poverty by raising their earning power, thus reducing present disparities in income distribution, is a valid social objective. Even on narrower economic grounds, one can argue that the returns from training the disadvantaged are larger than appears at first glance. The children of the most disadvantaged workers are likely to end up disadvantaged themselves. If training the parents succeeds in breaking into this cycle of poverty, then the gains to the children are part of the return to the program.

Second, what are the most effective *methods* of training? The conventional classification is *institutional* training versus *on-the-job* training. Institutional training involves some combination of classroom instruction and practice work, often using the facilities of local vocational schools, but sometimes involving construction of new training facilities. On-the-job training (OJT) involves contracting with an employer to train workers in his plant, with the government bearing a share of the training cost. Each of these has numerous variants, and they can be combined in various ways.

The effectiveness of different training techniques can be compared by decomposing them into the specific services they provide, such as counseling, skill training, placement, and follow-up. For many people, the main contribution of the program is its informational function in leading them to job areas that are in high demand but that may require little actual training. The kind of skill in question may be a decisive consideration. For manufacturing operations involving complicated and expensve equipment, and where employers are large enough to staff training programs, on-the-job training may be indicated. But in small-scale service, repair, or construction activities, where no one employer has adequate training facilities, institutional programs may be preferable.

OJT has the advantage that people who show good ability during the training period can go directly into jobs with the employer, so that there is no placement problem. But under OJT the employer usually screens and selects the trainees, and he will naturally select the most trainable and resist the seriously disadvantaged. In a tightening labor market, he may select about the same people he would have hired in any event, so that the government subsidy is not buying anything.

Third, what should one train for? Presumably, for occupations that actually require some months of training and that cannot readily be learned without instruction. Many semiskilled machine operations, for example, can be learned in a week or two, so that special training programs are superfluous. Beyond this, training should be for occupations in which vacancies are available and placement prospects good. Under MDTA, the U.S. Employment Service is responsible for certifying occupations in which demand is rising and which are therefore suitable for training. These forecasts cannot be completely accurate; but the U.S. Employment Service at least has its finger on the pulse of the labor market.

A special problem arises where the trainees are in one area and the potential jobs in another. Suppose a town or region has an excess of labor as a result of shrinking demand, as in the coalfields of Appalachia, so that workers must move to secure employment. This poses an information problem: what other areas have suitable jobs available? The U.S. Employment Service can be helpful on this through its Interarea Recruitment System. But there are also the costs of getting to the job, and moving one's family and household. A man who has the normal reluctance to leave his home community will be even more reluctant if he has nothing in his pocket to finance the move.

On this point the United States has been less imaginative than most of the European countries. Sweden, for example, has a comprehensive system covering travel costs to the new job, a moving allowance for the family and household goods, extra costs of maintaining two households while hunting a house in the new community, and a cash advance to tide over the period until the first paycheck comes in.[10] Every combination of circumstances one can imagine is covered, the object being to remove cost as a consideration in interarea movement of unemployed workers. The amounts involved are small by our standards —some 20,000 workers assisted in a typical year, at a cost of around $2 million. But Sweden has a small population and labor force, with a normal unemployment level of only about 50,000 workers. The United States equivalent might involve relocation grants to half a million workers a year at a cost of $50 million, an activity which would probably more than repay its cost.

Fourth, how can one evaluate the benefits and costs of a retraining program? Several kinds of calculations can be made, each of which is important for different reasons:

1. *Private Costs and Returns.* How much is the worker paid during the training period, how much would he have received otherwise from earnings or transfer payments during this period, how much additional income will he receive in later years because of the training? From this standpoint, earnings must be estimated *after* income tax, since this is what the worker will actually get. An informed worker will not enroll in a training program unless the prospective private return is satisfactory.

2. *Social Costs and Returns.* These are the real resources used up in the training program compared with the resulting addition to national output. This is the basic test of worthwhileness from a public standpoint, and provides a basis for ranking training projects in order of their prospective payoff.

3. *Budgetary Costs and Returns to Government.* What cash outlay is required by the training program? What will be the offsetting savings in unemployment compensation and welfare payments? Assuming that the trainee will earn more and work more regularly in future years, how much will this add to government revenue through income taxes, and how much will it save in unemployment payments? Budgetary costs cannot be ignored, since they limit the number of projects which can be undertaken in a given year. A project with low social costs but high budget costs may prevent the government from launching a half dozen other desirable projects. Budget considerations can be overlooked only if enough funds are available, from tax revenues or borrowing, to undertake *all* projects for which social benefits exceed social costs.

Since social costs and benefits are basic, and since their estimation raises numerous problems, it will be useful to say some more about

[10] This program has been described in a number of places. See, for example, *Unemployment Programs in Sweden*, prepared for the Joint Economic Committee, 88th Cong., 2d Sess. (Washington, D.C.: Government Printing Office, 1964).

them. Trainees normally receive a living allowance during the training period. This is a budgetary cost but not a social cost, since it does not use up any productive resources. The social costs are, first, the value of the trainee's time, i.e. the amount he might have produced by working instead of studying. If we assume that, in the absence of training, he would have continued unemployed, this cost is zero; but this is not a safe assumption. A common estimating procedure is to take a control group of nontrainees with personal characteristics similar to those of the trainees, observe how much the nontrainees earned over the same period, assume that the trainees could have earned this same amount, and count this as the value of their time. In addition, the costs of training include the time of teachers, supervisors, and employment service officials; interest and depreciation on the buildings, machinery, and other equipment used in training; and paper, books, chalk, electric power, raw materials for experimental work, and other supplies used up currently in training activities.

Several problems arise in evaluating benefits. Not all of those who start a training program finish it, and not all of those who finish get precisely the jobs for which they were trained. One can argue that only graduates placed in relevant jobs should be counted. But this may yield an overconservative estimate, since even dropouts or people placed in other kinds of work have probably derived *some* value from the time spent in the program.

Now take a particular graduate, who is doing the kind of work for which he was trained. We can observe how much he is earning; and we assume that his output at least equals his earnings, otherwise he would not be employed. For this purpose earnings should be taken *before* taxes, since we are interested in the addition to national output rather than in how much of this the worker receives. The difficult problem, however, is to estimate how much more he is earning than he would have earned if he had not entered the training program. What can we use as a basis of comparison? We could take his earnings on his last job before becoming unemployed, which assumes that without training he would eventually have been reemployed in the same kind of work. Alternatively, earnings of graduates of a training program can be compared with those of a control group of people with comparable personal characteristics who have not had the benefit of training. The difference in the earnings level of trainees and nontrainees can be taken as the increase in productivity resulting from training. Neither method yields results that are beyond dispute.

This increase in output must be projected over a man's prospective working life. Suppose he is thirty-five years old, and is earning $1,000 a year more because of his training. If we take retirement age as sixty-five, and overlook the possibility of earlier death or disability, the lifetime increase in his output is $30,000. This $30,000 benefit can be reduced to a percentage rate of return on the social cost of training. This might work out at, say, 30 percent. For rational allocation of resources, the government agency in charge should make a similar estimate for all training projects that are under consideration at a particular time, and rank them in order of rate of return. It should then go down the list until either budgetary resources run out or the rate of return falls below an acceptable level. How low should this cut off point be? One possible test is the estimated rate of return on government expenditure in other areas—education, highways, water resources, and so on. Another possibility is to use the rate of return on physical capital in the private sector of the economy, currently estimated at about 15 percent.

It is worth repeating that such monetary calculations fail to capture all the indirect benefits of retraining seriously disadvantaged workers. By making these workers employable at higher levels of skill and earnings, training raises the bottom of the income structure and reduces poverty more constructively and permanently than transfer payments can do. This must surely have beneficial side effects in reducing the illness, crime, alienation from work, and social disorganization associated with slum life. It must also have favorable long-run effects on the health, education, and work attitudes of children growing up in the families whose incomes have been raised through retraining.

Turning from general principles to concrete activities, most training programs in the United States are carried on under the Manpower Development and Training Act of 1962 (MDTA), administered by a Manpower Administration within the Department of Labor. Training activities were authorized also by the Area Redevelopment Act of 1961; the Trade Expansion Act of 1962, which provided for retraining of workers displaced by tariff reductions (a provision never actually invoked) and the Economic Opportunity Act of 1964, which authorized several training programs aimed at younger people with deficient education or job skills, some of which have since been merged with the MDTA program. MDTA has been amended and enlarged several times since its initiation. Teenagers are now eligible along with older workers. Underemployed workers (plus ex-farmers and new entrants to the labor force) who wish to upgrade their skills are eligible along with the unemployed. In addition to job training proper, trainees may now get general employment orientation [11] and work designed to repair basic educational deficiencies.

[11] A recent manpower report explains the meaning of this as follows: "Training can be given as needed in communication skills, grooming and personal hygiene, the standards of behavior and performance generally expected by employers, techniques of job hunting, and even the use of the local transportation system (since many slum residents know only their own neighborhood)."

Training may be either on-the-job, under agreement with an employer, or institutional, normally using vocational school facilities in after-school hours. There are also many combined programs, in which classroom instruction is used to supplement OJT. OJT was slow to get going and was very small in the early years of the program. In 1968, however, some 60,000 workers completed OJT courses compared with 85,000 finishing institutional training; and it is expected that the ratio of OJT trainees will continue to increase in the future. Over the six years from 1963 to 1968, some 166,000 workers completed OJT courses, while 446,000 completed institutional courses.

In the early years of the program, it was criticized for skimming the cream of the unemployed, selecting the best-qualified and easiest-to-place while neglecting the seriously disadvantaged worker. In recent years there has been an effort to increase the proportion of disadvantaged people—the very young and the rather old, the nonwhites, the people with little education—in the trainee group. The MDTA administrators have also been trying to increase the ratio of OJT to institutional trainees, partly because the cash cost per trainee to the government is only about one-third as great under OJT, partly because OJT trainees have a markedly better placement record. These two objectives are somewhat in conflict, because skimming the cream is precisely what employers want to do, and they are reluctant to admit seriously disadvantaged workers to OJT programs. The enrollment data in Table 3 suggest, first, that the quality of OJT trainees is materially higher than that of institutional trainees; and second, that under both programs there has been some shift toward a higher proportion of disadvantaged workers.

Institutional training is offered only in occupations for which the employment service certifies that there is an expanding demand, and the employment service is responsible for placing trainees at the end of their course. For men, there has been heavy enrollment in machine operating, welding, automobile repairing, radio and TV repair, and work in hospitals, restaurants, and retail stores. Women have been trained as typists and stenographers, nurses' aides and hospital technicians, hairdressers and beauticians, waitresses, and a variety of other service occupations. More than 200 separate occupations are represented in the program.

Follow-up studies indicate that 70 to 75 percent of institutional trainees have secured regular work, usually in the occupation for which they were trained. For OJT trainees, the placement record is typically 90 percent or better, partly because the employer usually has vacancies into which successful trainees can be fitted after graduation. Both groups show a considerable gain in earnings, compared either with their own previous earnings or with the earnings of control groups of

Table 3

CHARACTERISTICS OF MDTA ENROLLEES
1963 AND 1968
(percent)

	INSTITUTIONAL		ON-THE-JOB	
	1963	*1968*	*1963*	*1968*
SEX				
MALE	60.3	55.4	73.5	68.3
FEMALE	39.7	44.6	26.5	31.7
COLOR				
WHITE	72.8	51.1	85.1	64.4
NONWHITE	27.2	48.9	14.9	35.6
AGE				
UNDER 22	30.9	38.3	36.1	35.1
OVER 44	10.2	11.0	7.0	10.7
EDUCATION				
8 YEARS OR LESS	10.6	19.3	11.5	15.7
9 TO 11 YEARS	31.3	40.4	28.9	34.2
12 YEARS OR MORE	58.1	40.3	59.6	51.1
PRIOR EMPLOYMENT STATUS				
UNEMPLOYED	92.1	79.8	65.1	66.5
UNDEREMPLOYED, OR OTHER	7.9	20.2	34.9	33.5
DURATION OF UNEMPLOYMENT				
0–14 WEEKS	50.2	55.3	66.0	64.8
15–26 WEEKS	17.6	15.5	9.8	12.5
27 WEEKS AND OVER	32.2	29.2	24.2	22.7

nontrainees. This is partly because they become eligible for higher-wage jobs, but a good part of the earnings increase arises from more regular employment.

There have been several estimates of the social costs and benefits of training programs. For a sample of male trainees in West Virginia, Cain and Stromsdorfer estimate that the training costs were recovered in less than a year, i.e. the rate of return was above 100 percent. Another study by Somers estimated that costs were recaptured in about eighteen months.[12] These are high returns by any test, and suggest that

[12] Gerald G. Somers, "Retraining: an evaluation of gains and costs," in Arthur M. Ross, ed., *Employment Policy and the Labor Market* (Berkeley and Los Angeles: University of California Press, 1965). See also Gerald G. Somers and Graeme H. McKechnie, "Vocational Retraining Programs for the Unemployed," *IRRA Proceedings,* 1967, pp. 25–35; Burton Weisbrod, "Conceptual Issues in Evaluating Training Programs," *Monthly Labor Review,* October, 1966, pp. 1091–97; M. E. Borus, "Time Trends in the Benefits from Retraining in Connecticut," *IRRA Proceedings,* 1967, pp. 34–46, and Gerald G. Somers, ed., *Retraining the Unemployed* (Madison: The University of Wisconsin Press, 1968).

training programs might well be expanded. This would presumably mean admitting less-promising trainees to the program, so that eventually one would reach a point at which the productivity of the marginal trainee could not be raised sufficiently to warrant the training cost. This point might provide an operational definition of "unemployability."

THE STATUS
OF
NONWHITE WORKERS

The most serious misallocation and underutilization of labor in the American economy arises from the inferior status of nonwhite workers. This underutilization is economically inefficient, socially unjust and, in the climate of the 1970s, politically explosive.

We need cite only a few well-known statistics. The first relates to the occupational distribution of white and nonwhite workers (Table 4).[13] There has been progress on this front over the past generation. Note particularly the sharp increase in the proportion of nonwhite workers in clerical, technical, and professional occupations, and the sharp decline in those employed as farm laborers and domestic servants. Progress has been due partly to the very tight labor markets in the years from 1942 to 1945, 1951 to 1953, and 1966 to 1969, during which black workers were pulled upward in the occupational structure. Legislation against discrimination in employment, pressure from civil rights groups, and increased political representation of the black community must also have contributed, but to an extent which is difficult to determine.

Despite substantial progress there is still a striking disparity in the occupational distribution. Less than a quarter of black workers are in white-collar occupations, compared with about 50 percent of white workers. The converse of this is that one-quarter of all black workers are in the lowest occupational strata—farm labor, other unskilled labor, and domestic service. Only 7 percent of white workers are employed at these levels.

A second familiar fact is the higher unemployment rate of nonwhite workers (Table 5). Since 1954, the unemployment rate of nonwhite men has been more than double that of white men. The boom years from 1966 to 1969 lowered the rate for both groups, but did little to close the gap between them. The unemployment rate among black teenagers is particularly high, and here a wide gap has developed as compared with white teenagers. Until rather recently there was little

[13] Data are from *Employment and Earnings*, Vol. 14, No. 7 (January, 1968), 47.

Table 4

EMPLOYED PERSONS BY OCCUPATION GROUP
AND COLOR 1948 AND 1967

	1948	1967		
Occupation Group	*Nonwhite (Percent)*	*Nonwhite (Percent)*	*White (Percent)*	*Nonwhite as percent of white*
WHITE-COLLAR:	9.0	24.2	49.9	48.4
PROFESSIONAL AND TECHNICAL	2.4	7.7	14.4	53.4
MANAGERS, PROPRIETORS AND OFFICIALS	2.3	2.3	11.0	20.9
CLERICAL	3.3	12.2	17.4	70.1
SALES	1.1	2.0	7.1	28.1
BLUE-COLLAR:	39.7	41.6	35.4	117.5
CRAFTSMEN AND FOREMEN	5.3	7.4	13.7	54.0
OPERATIVES	20.1	23.5	18.1	129.8
LABORERS, EXCEPT FARM	14.3	10.8	3.7	291.9
SERVICE:	30.3	29.7	10.4	212.1
PRIVATE HOUSEHOLD	15.1	9.9	1.5	660.0
OTHER	14.7	19.8	8.9	222.4
FARM:	21.0	4.5	4.3	104.7
OWNERS AND MANAGERS	8.5	1.0	2.7	37.0
LABORERS	12.5	3.5	1.5	233.3
TOTAL	100.0	100.0	100.0	

difference. In 1954, male white sixteen to seventeen year olds had an unemployment rate of 14.0 percent, while the rate for eighteen to nineteen year olds was 13.0 percent. In the same year, male black sixteen to seventeen year olds had a rate of 13.4 percent, and eighteen to nineteen year olds a rate of 14.7 percent. From this point on, however, black teenage-unemployment rates rose rapidly, while white rates were stable or declining. By 1967, these rates compared as follows: white, aged sixteen to seventeen, 12.7 percent; black, aged sixteen to seventeen, 28.9 percent; white, aged eighteen to nineteen, 9.0 percent; black, aged eighteen to nineteen, 20.1 percent.

Thurow ("Changing Structure of Unemployment") shows a much higher marginal propensity to be laid off in recession among black workers than among white workers (−1.29 percent per quarter, compared with −0.57 for whites). Part of this results from their adverse occupational distribution, i.e. a high proportion are laborers, and laborers have a high layoff rate. But even after adjustment for this factor, the layoff rate for black workers remains at −0.78, considerably higher than for whites. He concludes that "low seniority, an adverse occupational distribution, and discrimination must play a part." He

Table 5

UNEMPLOYMENT RATES,

WHITE AND NONWHITE WORKERS, 1948–68

	TOTAL			MALE		
Year	*White*	*Nonwhite*	*Nonwhite as Percent of White*	*White*	*Nonwhite*	*Nonwhite as Percent of White*
1948	3.5	5.9	169	3.4	5.8	171
1949	5.6	8.9	158	5.6	9.6	171
1950	4.9	9.0	184	4.7	9.4	200
1951	3.1	5.3	171	2.6	4.9	188
1952	2.8	5.4	193	2.5	5.2	208
1953	2.7	4.5	167	2.5	4.8	192
1954	5.0	9.9	198	4.8	10.3	214
1955	3.9	8.7	223	3.7	8.8	238
1956	3.6	8.3	231	3.4	7.9	232
1957	3.8	7.9	208	3.6	8.3	231
1958	6.1	12.6	207	6.1	13.8	226
1959	4.8	10.7	223	4.6	11.5	250
1960	4.9	10.2	208	4.8	10.7	223
1961	6.0	12.4	207	5.7	12.8	225
1962	4.9	10.9	222	4.6	10.9	237
1963	5.0	10.8	216	4.7	10.5	223
1964	4.6	9.6	209	4.1	8.9	217
1965	4.1	8.1	198	3.6	7.4	206
1966	3.3	7.3	221	2.8	6.3	225
1967	3.4	7.4	218	2.7	6.0	222
1968	3.2	6.7	209	n.a.	n.a.	n.a.

SOURCE: *Manpower Report of the President,* 1968, and Council of Economic Advisers, *Annual Report,* 1969.

argues also that over successive cycles there will be a displacement effect—high layoffs on the downswing, not fully offset by rehirings on the upswing, so that a growing unabsorbed pool accumulates. Thus far, however, there is no clear indication of this effect in the aggregative unemployment statistics of Table 5.

An adverse occupational distribution, less regular employment, and (possibly) lower rates of pay for comparable work all help to depress family incomes in the black community. The distribution of incomes of white and nonwhite families in 1947 and 1967 is shown in Table 6.[14] Here again there has been modest progress. Between 1947 and 1967 the average income of white families, measured in constant dollars, increased 75 percent, while the average for black families rose

---

[14] Bureau of the Census, *Current Population Reports,* Series P–60, No. 59, April, 1969.

Table 6

ANNUAL INCOME, WHITE AND NONWHITE FAMILIES
1947 AND 1967 (CONSTANT 1967 DOLLARS)

	1947		1967	
Annual Income	*White (percent)*	*Nonwhite (percent)*	*White (percent)*	*Nonwhite (percent)*
Under $3,000	24.1	62.4	10.8	27.1
3,000–4,999	30.4	22.4	11.9	21.5
5,000–6,999	21.8	7.9	16.0	17.7
7,000–9,999	14.2	5.1	25.1	16.9
10,000–14,999	9.5	2.2	23.6	11.7
15,000 and over			12.9	5.0
Median Income	4,720	2,418	8,274	5,141
Index (1947 = 100)	100	100	175	213

113 percent. In 1947, black families averaged 51 percent as much as white families. By 1967, this had risen to 62 percent.

But the distributions for the two groups are still strikingly different. In 1967, only 7 percent of white households fell below the poverty line as defined by U.S. federal agencies; but 30 percent of black households fell below this level. Interestingly enough, the distribution of income *within* the black community is considerably more unequal than that within the white community. In 1967, 44.7 percent of all income going to black families went to the top one-fifth, while the bottom one-fifth received only 4.4 percent. The corresponding figures for white families were 40.7 percent and 5.8 percent.

Some Sources of Disadvantage

It is too simple to regard this situation as resulting from employment discrimination alone. This is part of the story. But the situation has its roots deep in history and in the American political and social structure. Until quite recently, the black community has been almost powerless in the political arena. The white man has had a monopoly of decision making, and from this many other results have followed.

1. *Disadvantages in Education.* Until recently, school enrollment rates of black children were substantially below those of white children, with the disparity increasing as one went up the educational ladder. Far fewer entered high school, many more dropped out before completing high school, and the ratio of black college students to the eligible population was only about half that of white students. This shows up in the educational qualifications of the labor force (Table

Table 7

YEARS OF SCHOOL COMPLETED BY THE CIVILIAN LABOR FORCE
18 YEARS AND OVER, BY SEX AND COLOR, 1952 AND 1967

	MALE				FEMALE			
	WHITE		NONWHITE		WHITE		NONWHITE	
	Median Years Com- pleted	*% with 8 Years or Less*	*Median Years Com- pleted*	*% with 8 Years or Less*	*Median Years Com- pleted*	*% with 8 Years or Less*	*Median Years Com- pleted*	*% with 8 Years or Less*
1952	10.8	38.2	7.2	68.1	12.1	26.3	8.1	61.6
1967	12.3	21.4	10.2	40.4	12.4	14.8	11.5	30.0

SOURCE: *Manpower Report of the President,* 1968, pp. 259–60.

7). As recently as 1952, black male workers had on the average 3½ fewer years of schooling than white workers, while black female workers had 4 years less than white women. The median education of the black population was at primary school level, while most white workers had at least finished high school.

As a result of the large shift of black population to the Northern states, and because of intensified educational effort in all parts of the country, the gap in school enrollments is now much reduced. Thus for people under twenty-five there is no longer much difference in median years of school completed. But there is still a large residue of older people, whose poor education is a serious employment handicap. Human capital is very long-lived; and the results of educational neglect in earlier times will plague us for decades to come.

Not only have black members of the labor force received less education, but this has also been poorer education. Until recently virtually all, and even today a large majority, of black students are educated in all-black schools and colleges. These schools seem to produce an inferior educational product. Numerous studies have shown eighth-grade students performing, on the average, at sixth-grade level, and high school seniors performing at eighth-grade level. The reasons are complex, and by no means fully understood. One reason is lower expenditure per pupil,[15] leading to larger classes, less-qualified teachers, and poorer physical facilities. A further factor may be that parents,

15 See, for example, Finis Welch, "Labor-market discrimination: an interpretation of income differences in the rural South," *Journal of Political Economy,* June, 1967, pp. 225–40. This study reports average per pupil costs of $230 in white schools, $120 in black schools in rural southern areas. Differentials in urban areas and in northern states may be smaller but are probably still substantial.

who themselves have relatively little education, provide less encouragement and less supplementary training than white families at a higher educational and income level.

2. *Residential Segregation.* This factor is closely related to the schooling differentials just described. It leads to schools which are segregated *de facto* because the districts in which they are located are predominantly black or predominantly white. It leads to cultural segregation of the black community, to a separate ethos in which education may be less highly valued. The heavily black core cities have lower tax-paying ability than the white suburbs, leading naturally to lower expenditures per pupil on education, only partly offset at present by state and federal transfers.

Geography may also make it harder for adult black workers to compete for employment. Between 1940 and 1960, the total population of U.S. metropolitan areas increased by about 40 million people. But 80 percent of the increase in white population was in suburban areas, while 85 percent of the increase in black population was in the central cities. At the same time employment opportunities in the central cities have been declining, while jobs have been expanding rapidly in the suburbs. In Chicago, for example, the central city *lost* 180,000 jobs in manufacturing and 57,000 jobs in wholesale and retail trade between 1950 and 1960. In this same period Chicago suburbs *gained* 182,000 manufacturing jobs and 67,000 jobs in trade.[16]

The fact that the net increase in jobs is entirely in the suburbs while the increase in black population is almost entirely in the core cities creates obvious problems. In the lower occupational levels, the labor market operates largely through word-of-mouth tips from relatives and friends, or through random application at nearby plants. If nearby employment is shrinking, and if one's friends are located entirely in the core city, it is hard to make contact with the expanding suburban labor market. There are also physical difficulties of getting to work in an era when public transit facilities are shrinking rather than expanding. Kain's analysis of Chicago found that, of 800,000 manufacturing jobs in the metropolitan area, only one-third are within ten miles of the center of the black residential area. Rapid transit lines typically do not run near the suburban plants, and a large percentage of the black workers do not have private cars in which to drive to work.

3. *Discrimination in Employment.* Discrimination occurs when black workers of equivalent physical and mental ability, and equivalent capacity for the kind of work in question, are denied equal opportunity for employment. This can occur in several ways. Black workers may be excluded entirely from the more desirable jobs in the

[16] Kain, J. F., "Housing segregation, Negro employment, and metropolitan decentralization," *Quarterly Journal of Economics*, May, 1968, pp. 175–97.

company and restricted to those at the bottom of the skill structure. Black applicants may be excluded from training programs that would provide the skills needed for certain types of work. Craft unions, particularly in the building trades, have often resisted admission of black applicants to apprenticeship programs. In 1969, after several years of intensive federal effort, the skilled construction trades unions still included only 4 percent of black members. In the highest-paid crafts, plumbers and electricians, the proportion was only 2 percent.

Where black workers are admitted to an occupation, they may be put at the end of the queue, and hired only after the supply of qualified whites is exhausted. This may be overt and deliberate, or it may be a by-product of supposedly general hiring specifications. For example, employers often require a higher level of formal education than is really necessary for the work in question. Given the lower educational level of the black labor force, this automatically excludes many black workers who could in fact do the job satisfactorily.

We saw in Chapter 5 that many companies have only a few ports of entry into employment, of which the largest is a trainee category at the bottom of the wage structure. The important question, then, is whether the trainee has equal opportunity to move up the skill ladder on the basis of ability. Equal opportunity is denied if black workers are restricted to a separate promotion ladder, with a lower cutoff point than that open to white workers.

Discrimination is not easy to detect and to measure. Hiring practices which do not seem to discriminate may in fact do so, as in the education case just cited. On the other hand, where a certain level of education *is* required for a job, the employer may legitimately take into account quality as well as years of schooling. (This happens every day in the hiring of Ph.D.'s from graduate schools of differing quality, and is not thereby considered a discriminatory practice.)

One of the few attempts to measure the income effect of discrimination, taking quantity and quality of education into account, is Finis Welch's study of white–nonwhite income differences in the rural South as revealed by the 1960 census. He found that white workers with no education earned $1,320, compared with $1,070 for black workers with no education. This difference Welch terms "market discrimination against physical labor." The income difference widens steadily as one goes up the educational ladder. Thus white high school graduates earned $3,790 per year, compared with $1,840 for black high school graduates. Welch decomposes this difference into: $250 attributable to market discrimination against (black) physical labor; $630 attributable to inferior quality of education (using educational expenditure per pupil as a quality index); and a residual of $1,070 which he terms "market discrimination against education." This seems to mean that black workers at a specified "true" (i.e. corrected for quality) educational level have less access to the better-paid occupations than do white workers at the same level.[17]

Discrimination, correctly defined, has no productivity basis and must therefore rest on noneconomic preferences. Many employers, other things equal, simply prefer white workers to black. And white workers, partly through social prejudice, partly through fear of economic competition, resist the introduction of black employees into their plant or occupation. The relative weight of these two factors is difficult to determine, since an employer who wishes to discriminate can always find objections among his white labor force to serve as a reason.

At any event, hiring black workers involves a certain amount of disutility for most employers. This means that, at a given wage level, they will prefer white workers to black. Alternatively, the wage at which they will be willing to employ black workers is lower than that at which they will hire white workers. How this works out in the labor market depends on the flexibility of wage-determining institutions.[18] If wages were entirely market-determined, the equilibrium wage for black workers of a certain occupational level would be below that of white workers; and at this wage enough employers would prefer black workers to equate supply and demand for each group. Conversely, if a uniform wage is enforced by legislation or union contract, white workers will be hired first and any slack in aggregate demand will show up in heavier unemployment of black workers. The less the opportunity for discrimination in wages, the greater (given employer preferences) will be the discrimination in employment.

Steps toward Equal Opportunity

We have tried to underline that employment discrimination is only part of the black worker's problem—in a sense, the tip of the iceberg. If young people growing up in the black community could receive education fully equivalent to that of their white contemporaries, if residential segregation could be reduced and the black population gradually homogenized throughout our metropolitan areas, much of

---

[17] These results should not be generalized to other regions. Studies at the national level suggest that the income gap between white and nonwhite workers *declines* somewhat as educational level rises, i.e. the income of black college graduates is a higher percentage of the income of white college graduates than is true for black and white primary school graduates. Victor Fuchs' detailed studies of wage structure, which will be examined in chapter 9, also suggest that occupational segregation of black workers is especially severe in the South, and that both the absolute and relative income position of black workers is substantially higher in other regions.

[18] See the pioneer analysis of this problem in Gary Becker, *The Economics of Discrimination* (Chicago: The University of Chicago Press, 1957).

the employment problem would disappear. Conversely, while these basic problems remain, employment problems will also remain.

To discuss educational policy and housing policy, however, would carry us far beyond our space limitations. Anything that could be said in a page or two would be superficial to the point of platitude. So we restrict ourselves to policies aimed directly at equal employment opportunities.

We have already noted some difficulties in the concept of discrimination. These complications make it harder to define what an employer should not do, and also to find out whether he is doing it. For example, employers have traditionally been free to set hiring standards involving education, training, work experience, test proficiency, and so on. This has nothing directly to do with race or color. But if these standards are higher than job performance actually requires, and if possession of the required characteristics is inversely correlated with color, then they may serve as a discriminatory screening device.

Again, suppose that qualifications are formally equal but not effectively equal. An employer has a white high school graduate and a black high school graduate applying for the same position. He selects the white applicant on the ground that the *quality* of his education is superior. The black applicant charges discrimination. An outsider charged with adjudicating such a dispute would face genuine difficulties.

Does nondiscrimination imply some measure of "reverse discrimination"? Should employers devote greater effort to seeking out black applicants than they do to white applicants? Should they give systematic preference to black candidates over equally qualified white candidates so long as the available supply lasts? Even to pose such questions is to stir up argument. On economic grounds, there is no reason why one worker should be preferred to another of equal efficiency on the basis of skin color. This applies to discrimination against whites equally with discrimination against blacks. A case for reverse discrimination would have to be based on political and social grounds—for example, that this is an appropriate form of compensation for past injustices to the black population, or that it is socially desirable to raise the income level of the black population faster than nondiscriminatory hiring would do.

This issue arises also in the educational realm. In higher education at least it is being resolved increasingly in favor of reverse discrimination. Many colleges, who find that competitive admission based on objective tests would yield them only (say) 3 percent of black students, are deciding that as a matter of policy they prefer (say) 10 percent. So they are running intensified recruitment drives among black high school seniors, and lowering admission standards sufficiently to yield the desired ratio. A substantial argument can be made for this policy, even though on economic grounds one could mount a case against it.[19]

Efforts to curb employment discrimination by law date from at least 1941, when President Roosevelt issued an excutive order forbidding discrimination on government-contract work and establishing an agency within the executive branch to police this requirement. Efforts in this direction accelerated during the fifties and sixties, as the large South–North migration of black families made their economic problems more visible in all parts of the country and also increased their political leverage. The main agencies presently active in this area [20] are:

1. Every president since 1940 has established a body charged with preventing employment discrimination by government contractors. Under Presidents Kennedy and Johnson this body was called the President's Committee on Equal Employment Opportunity (PCEEO), which was considerably more active than its predecessors. The PCEEO extended its activities to all plants of companies holding government contracts, rather than only to plants directly engaged in government production. It never actually invoked its power to recommend cancellation of contracts with noncomplying companies, though such action was threatened on several occasions, but worked mainly through education and persuasion. These activities extended beyond the government contract sphere. Through a program labeled "plans for progress," upwards of 100 large corporations (including all but one of the thirty-five government contractors) agreed to accelerate their recruitment and hiring of black workers. This program had positive, though not spectacular, results. Employment data for the participating companies indicate that in the manual labor grades, employment of black workers rose slightly faster than that of white workers, while in white-collar occupations employment of black workers increased almost twice as fast. It is unlikely that this would have happened in the absence of the PCEEO program.

2. Some twenty-five states, including virtually all the northern and

---

[19] The economic arguments, however, are not entirely one-sided. In the short run, any scheme that prefers less-qualified to more-qualified people doubtless reduces efficiency. Taking a long view, however, one can argue that the heavy concentration of the black population in poor schools and poor jobs involves a large waste of talent and potential productivity. It can be argued that opening up better education and better jobs to black candidates—who may not, granted, be equally qualified—will have a substantial demonstration effect on the whole of the black community. It may raise their general level of educational aspirations and work aspirations, and incidentally incline them to join "the establishment" instead of turning their backs on it. This could have positive economic results in addition to sociopolitical results.

[20] For the past history of activities in this field, and a more detailed description of legislation and programs, see Paul Norgren and Samuel Hill, *Toward Fair Employment* (New York: Columbia University Press, 1964), and Ray Marshall, *The Negro and Organized Labor* (New York: John Wiley & Sons, Inc., 1965).

western industrial states, now have fair employment practice (FEP) laws. These are often not supported by an adequate budget and enforcement staff, and are virtually dead letters. The large industrial states, however, such as New York, New Jersey, and Pennsylvania, have sizable staffs and an active enforcement program. These state agencies have in fact borne the brunt of the antidiscrimination effort, particularly as regards small and medium-sized employers who are not conspicuous enough to be reached by federal programs.

Experience under the state FEP laws has revealed a variety of problems and difficulties. Many black workers are too uninformed or timid to launch effective complaints against their employer (or potential employer, in the case of applicants who have been refused employment). This is less true today, however, than it would have been ten or fifteen years ago. There are now civil rights groups within the black community to which an aggrieved worker can take his case and get legal assistance. Discrimination is inherently difficult to define and to prove. Some employers may be wrongfully accused, while on the other hand some justified complaints may fail for lack of evidence. In such a difficult and emotion-charged area, administrators and courts have been hesitant to apply the penalties provided by law. The main effort has been to secure voluntary compliance through discussion and persuasion. At a minimum, employers can often be convinced that it is good public relations to increase their hiring of black workers; and as many of these turn out to be well qualified and productive, employers may conclude that nondiscrimination enlarges their effective labor supply and is good economic policy.

3. The Civil Rights Act of 1964 was a major development at the federal level. This act covers many things other than employment; but Title VII makes it an unlawful employment practice for an employer "to fail to refuse to hire or to discharge any individual, or otherwise to discriminate against any individual with respect to his compensation, terms, conditions, or privileges of employment, because of such individual's race, color, religion, sex or national origin . . ." and also "to limit, segregate, or classify his employees in any way which would deprive or tend to deprive any individual of employment opportunities . . ." Similar prohibitions apply to employment agencies, labor organizations, or joint labor–management committees in charge of apprenticeship or other training programs. Title VII applies to all employers in interstate commerce with twenty-five or more employees, and to unions with more than twenty-five members.

Enforcement of Title VII is entrusted to a five-man Equal Employment Opportunity Commission (EEOC). The commission has authority to receive complaints, to try to resolve these by discussion and persuasion, and where this fails to seek enforcement through the U.S. attorney general. Civil suits may also be filed by aggrieved individuals, and the attorney general may intervene in such suits where he finds this to be in the public interest. The EEOC does not supersede existing state or local FEP laws. Indeed, when it receives a complaint from an area that has such a law, it is obliged to notify the appropriate state or local officials and to allow them a reasonable time to investigate the complaint. For states with FEP laws, then, the EEOC will operate mainly as an appeal tribunal to handle tough cases which could not be adjusted at lower levels. For states without FEP laws, on the other hand, it will operate as a court of first resort. Its authority is limited to employers engaged in "interstate commerce." The interpretation of interstate commerce, however, has become more liberal over time, and now covers more than 75 percent of all workers in private employment.

While experience under Title VII is still limited, it will probably be similar to that under previous state legislation. Penalties will be applied rarely, though perhaps not quite as rarely as in the states. The main effort will be to alter employment practices through education and persuasion.

4. The National Labor Relations Board enters the picture because the National Labor Relations Act, as amended by the later Taft–Hartley and Landrum–Griffin Acts, provides that a union must give fair and equal representation to all workers in its bargaining unit. Where black workers are employed the union may not, by internal regulations or by contract terms agreed on with the employer, deny them equal access to promotion, seniority rights, and other opportunities. A union violating this provision may be decertified as bargaining agent. It may also be charged with an unfair labor practice, and the Board may seek a cease-and-desist order in the federal courts. For the unionized sector of the economy, this presents an additional enforcement channel.

In addition to these legal procedures, much voluntary activity was generated by private and public leaders during the 1960s. For example, a national committee of businessmen chaired by Henry Ford II undertook to persuade other companies to recruit, train, and employ specified numbers of the "hard-core unemployed." These tend to be black workers with limited education, little or no experience in manufacturing, an irregular work history with long spells of unemployment, and little confidence in their ability to find and hold a regular job. This program was concentrated in the major industrial cities with a large black population, such as New York, Detroit, Chicago, and Los Angeles. A quota was set for each city, initially totaling 100,000 jobs, which after a successful first year was increased to 200,000. While the quota was not achieved in every city, in some it was more than met. It appears that two-thirds or more of these recruits proved capable enough to settle into and hold their new jobs.

The total impact of these equal-opportunity programs is hard to judge. The employment data which would be needed for a statistical test have not been collected systematically, nor has there been a careful analysis even of the data that are available. Several hypotheses seem plausible:

a. The nation's larger employers now make a more systematic effort to tap the black segment of the labor market than they used to do and have materially increased their receptiveness to black applicants. In consequence, the percentage of black workers in the labor force of these companies is substantially higher in 1970 than it was in 1960. This is true not only in manufacturing, but in public utilities, retailing, banking, and finance. It is true also of employment in federal, state, and local government.

b. There has probably been less progress in promotion and upgrading of black workers than in sheer number of workers hired. Even where hirings are impressive, the occupational distribution of black workers remains adverse, and the more attractive promotion ladders may not be equally open to them.

c. Part of what has been achieved is doubtless due to the fact that the 1960s saw the longest economic upswing in our history, with most labor markets very tight from 1965 onward. The permanence of the gains will be tested when aggregate demand slackens and unemployment rises.

d. The impact of fair employment programs has been achieved mainly through education, persuasion, and voluntary alteration of employer practices. But this does not mean that the legislative measures outlined above were unnecessary or ineffectual. Persuasion works better when government has laid down clear standards of public policy, when noncompliance with these standards leads to adverse publicity, and when legal sanctions are lurking in the background without complete certainty that they will not be invoked.

Discussion Questions

1. (a) What would be the main characteristics of an ideal system of public employment offices?
   (b) What are the practical difficulties of creating such a system?
2. (a) What are the main sources of possible error in forecasting future demands for specific kinds of labor?
   (b) Will inaccurate forecasts do much harm? Explain.

3. What are the main differences between:
    (a) estimating the *private* rate of return to investment in technical or professional training, and
    (b) estimating the *social* rate of return to such investment?
4. (a) Which of the three systems of educational finance discussed in the text do you consider preferable? On what grounds?
    (b) Would you distinguish in this respect between general liberal arts education and more specifically vocational training?
5. Suppose you are asked to design a project to determine the *social* rate of return to expenditures under the Manpower Development and Training Act. What kinds of data would you collect, and how would you analyze them?
6. What are the main reasons for the low income level of nonwhite families relative to white families?
7. What evidence would you examine to determine whether an employer has engaged in employment discrimination against nonwhite workers?
8. Are the steps taken thus far to eliminate employment discrimination adequate? If not, what additional steps would you recommend?

Reading Suggestions

In addition to the references cited in the text, see Bakke, E. Wight, *A Positive Labor Market Policy*. Columbus: Charles E. Merrill Publishing Co., 1963; Lester, Richard A., *Manpower Planning in a Free Society*. Princeton: Princeton University Press, 1966; and Ross, Arthur M., and Herbert Hill, eds., *Employment, Race, and Poverty*. New York: Harcourt, Brace & World, Inc., 1967.

MONEY WAGES, PRICES, AND EMPLOYMENT

7

As we turn from examining the structure of labor markets to analyzing how wages are set in these markets, we must first say something about the numerous possible meanings of "wages." This term is not as simple as it appears, and some of the disagreement that arises in discussing wages is due to the fact that people are talking about different things.

THE MEANING OF WAGES

The term "wages" has different connotations to the union leader, the management official, and the worker in the plant. The union leader is apt to think of wages as "that which can be bargained about with the employer," which means principally the schedule of hourly rates of pay for different jobs in the plant. The worker, however, may be more concerned with his "weekly take-home pay," or with

171

how much his weekly paycheck will buy at the store. Management is interested basically in labor cost per unit of output, which depends on the amount produced by workers in the plants as well as on how much they are paid. These differing meanings of wages must be explained before the statistics to be presented later can be fully understood.

"Rates" and "Earnings"

Most wage earners have an hourly rate of pay, usually referred to as the "base rate," but this is not necessarily the amount which the worker actually receives. Many men work on a piecework or incentive basis, under which the amount they receive depends on how much they produce. Under an incentive system a worker is expected to earn a good deal more than his base rate—indeed, it is this expectation which gives him the incentive to maintain a high rate of output. An incentive worker's earnings will also fluctuate over the course of time, as he produces more or less on a particular day. Even a worker who is paid on a time basis may receive more per hour than his base rate. He may work overtime and receive extra compensation for this. He may work on a night shift and receive a night-shift premium. Various other bonuses and supplementary payments may cause his hourly earnings to be considerably above his base rate of pay.

The distinction between base rates and hourly earnings is even more important for a plant as a whole. There are many reasons why average hourly earnings in a plant may fluctuate without any change in base rates. During the war years 1942 to 1945, for example, there was a large amount of overtime work in most industries, and this work was normally paid for at time and a half. In an effort to attract and hold workers, promotions and individual merit increases were granted much more freely than they normally would have been. Piece rates under incentive systems were unusually liberal. For these and other reasons, during the war years hourly earnings in most plants rose much more than base rates.

One reason for emphasizing this distinction is that almost all published wage statistics relate to average hourly earnings rather than base rates. The main source of wage statistics is the Bureau of Labor Statistics of the Department of Labor. Each month the Bureau of Labor Statistics publishes figures of average weekly earnings, weekly hours worked, and average hourly earnings for a large number of industries in the United States. These figures are compiled by asking a representative group of employers in each industry to report to the bureau their total plant payroll, number of employees on the payroll, and man-hours worked during a certain week of the month. From these reports it is possible to calculate the hours worked per man, and the average hourly and weekly earnings per man, during the week in question.

During periods of stable employment, changes in base rates are the main reason for changes in hourly and weekly earnings, and the three figures move very closely together. A marked change in the general level of employment, however, is likely to cause considerable discrepancy between the movement of base rates and earnings.

"Take-home Pay"

The worker himself is probably most interested in his weekly earnings, frequently referred to as his "take-home-pay." One should distinguish here between gross weekly earnings and net earnings after deductions for income taxes, social security, and other purposes. It is net earnings which the worker finds in his pay envelope, and he is apt to regard this as his real rate of pay. The worker's wife is also interested mainly in net weekly take-home. She becomes accustomed to allocating a certain number of dollars per week over the items in the family budget. A decrease in weekly take-home produces an almost immediate deterioration in the family's scale of living, while an increase provides an additional margin for saving or for the purchase of new goods that the family could not previously afford.

The weekly earnings of most workers fluctuate considerably, quite apart from any change in hourly wage rates. During good times, many workers can secure overtime work if they want it, and people with heavy family responsibilities are likely to take advantage of this opportunity. During depression periods, many workers get less than a full week's work, and their weekly take-home shrinks even without any reduction in base rates. This shrinkage of weekly take-home is regarded as a "wage cut" by most workers.

In some types of industry even weekly earnings are not a fair measure of employee welfare, because seasonal and irregular fluctuations in the demand for labor cause workers to lose a great deal of time during the year. One cannot take the full-time weekly earnings of a bituminous coal miner, a bricklayer, a garment cutter, a fruit picker, a lumber worker, or a longshoreman, and multiply by fifty-two to secure his annual earnings. In these and other seasonal industries, the pattern of production is such that the average worker may get only thirty or thirty-five weeks' work during the year. Moreover, the work is usually distributed quite unequally among the available workers. A table of annual earnings for workers in almost any industry will show figures ranging from zero up to several thousand dollars. Tables of this kind are prepared by the Social Security Board for workers in industries covered by the social security system. The variation in the annual earnings of workers in the same industry is striking.[1] Even in supposedly regular industries, many workers work much less than a full year and have correspondingly low earnings.

Money Wages and Real Wages

The worker's welfare depends, not on how much money income he receives, but on the purchasing power of this income—the amount of goods and services which he can buy with it. In this connection economists have coined the term "real wages," which means how much the money wage will buy in goods and services. The object of statistical calculations of real wages is usually to discover whether the real wage level has been rising or falling over some period of time. One may want to find out, for example, whether a certain increase in money wage rates has been accompanied by an increase in real wages, or whether the money wage increase has been canceled out by a rise in the cost of goods which workers buy. An increase in workers' average hourly earnings from $2.00 to $2.40 with no change in the retail price level is clearly quite different from a 20 percent wage increase accompanied by a 20 percent increase in retail prices. In the former case, the workers have benefited to the full extent of the increase in money wages; in the latter case they have not benefited at all.

In order to make this kind of calculation, one needs a good measure of the prices of goods and services purchased by wage earners. No completely satisfactory measure of retail price exists at the present time; indeed, it is not possible to have a perfect measure, for reasons shortly to be explained. The nearest thing to a satisfactory measure is the index of retail prices of goods purchased by moderate-income families in large cities, which is compiled and issued monthly by the Bureau of Labor Statistics.

This index, known officially as the Consumers' Price Index, measures the average change in prices of goods and services purchased by urban wage-earner and salaried clerical-worker families. It is prepared in the following way. The bureau starts from a list of goods and services normally purchased by moderate-income families. This list is based on a study of actual purchases by single persons and families of middle-income wage earners and clerical workers. The study shows which goods were bought by these families and what proportion of the family income was spent on each kind of goods. About

---

[1] This kind of evidence is not conclusive, of course, since a worker may work in more than one industry during the year. What is required is a tabulation of workers' total annual earnings in *all industries*. This tabulation cannot be obtained at present, partly because only certain industries are covered by the Social Security system.

300 items were selected for inclusion in the cost-of-living index, which themselves represent the greater part of family spending. This typical "market basket" is used to measure the average price change for all the items typically consumed by wage-earner and clerical-worker families.

Prices of items are collected by representatives of the Bureau of Labor Statistics at intervals ranging from a month to four months in fifty cities of all sizes. Each price is then reduced to a percentage of the average price for that item during the years from 1957 to 1959, which is referred to as the "base period." The indexes for the 300 items are then averaged together to obtain a single index for retail prices. It is a weighted index which reflects the relative importance of the different commodities in the consumption of those families surveyed in 1960 and 1961. In addition to a retail price index for the United States as a whole, the bureau prepares separate indexes for about twenty of the largest cities. Different cities vary considerably in their price levels, mainly as a result of differing costs of rent, heating, and utilities.[2]

Limitations of the Consumers' Price Index

There are three main reasons why even this carefully prepared index does not provide a perfectly satisfactory measure of changes in living costs. First, it measures only the cost of living *in a certain way* —the way in which certain families lived during the years 1960 to 1961. As people's incomes rise, however, there is also an increase in their standard of living, i.e. their idea of the way in which they *should* live. During a period of rising incomes and living standards, it always seems that the cost of living has risen. This rise, however, may be due solely to the fact that people are buying more commodities, rather than to the fact that commodity prices have risen; it naturally costs more to live on a higher level than before. The term "cost of living" is thus rather ambiguous, and it has been dropped entirely by the Bureau of Labor Statistics in recent years. Another difficulty is that, as people's living standards change, the list of items used in making up the index and the relative weight given to each should also be changed. It is not practicable, however, to make fresh budget studies every year. The list thus gets more and more out of date with the passage of time. The index gradually becomes a measure of the cost of living in the way in which people lived some time in the past, rather than the cost of living according to present standards.

The second limitation of the index is that it measures the change

---

[2] For an explanation of the methods currently used in computing the Consumers' Price Index, see *Monthly Labor Review,* July, 1963.

in living costs for people *at one income level.* It is true that the income group used in making up the retail price index is an important one, including about two-thirds of all people living in urban places. But what of the remaining one-third? The average change in the index would probably not be applicable either to elderly couples or unusually large families, nor to very low- or relatively high-income families. The living standards of these groups are quite different, and the cost of the items they buy will certainly not change by the same percentage from year to year.

A third limitation of the retail price index is that it does not include changes in the *quality* of items on the budget list. If an article improves in quality without any increase in its price, this improvement benefits the consumer just as surely as a price reduction. The improvement in quality, however, will not appear in the retail price index. It is probable that most goods do improve gradually in quality in the course of time. But no way has yet been found to make a precise quantitative adjustment for these quality changes.

The accepted procedure for measuring changes in "real wages" is to adjust the change in money wages over the period in question to take account of the change in retail prices during the same period.

In 1967, for example, average hourly earnings in manufacturing were 213 percent of what they had been twenty years earlier in 1948 ($2.83 an hour compared with $1.33). The consumer price index, however, had risen by 1967 to 139 percent of its 1948 level. Dividing 213 by 139, one finds that real hourly earnings in 1967 were 153 percent of the 1948 level, i.e. they had risen 53 percent over the intervening years. The limitations of the retail price index mean that such measurements have a certain margin of error. An apparent change of a few percent in real wages is of doubtful significance. An increase of 25 or 50 percent in real wages, however, clearly indicates a higher level of consumption.

Wages as a Cost of Production

Turning to the employer, we find that wages are important primarily as an element in production costs. The employer is interested in two things: how much it costs him to hire a man-hour of labor, and how much output he is able to obtain from this man-hour. It is not wages as such which matter, but wages in relation to productivity.

Published statistics of productivity relate almost entirely to average gross physical productivity. They are obtained by measuring the physical output of a plant or industry over a period of time, measuring the change in man-hours worked over the same period, and dividing the man-hour index into the output index to get an index of productivity. The procedure is comparable to that used in computing real wages. If, for example, the output of a plant has increased from

100 to 300 over a five-year period, while man-hours worked have increased only from 100 to 200, then (average gross physical) productivity has increased by 50 percent.

Such measures are often termed "the productivity of *labor*," but this is a rather misleading usage. It is quite unlikely that such a large increase in output could have come about solely through increased effort or skill on the part of the workers. It is more likely to have resulted from engineering and managerial improvements, possibly involving the installation of new mechanical equipment. Since these changes involved certain costs to the company, the increase in net productivity was probably a good deal smaller than that in gross productivity. It is wrong to regard the gross productivity increase as a net gain which can be passed on to labor in its entirety. This point will be discussed more fully in a later chapter.

The accounting systems generally used in business are constructed to yield measures of unit production cost—a reciprocal of productivity—rather than measures of productivity itself. The figure which management usually watches is direct labor cost per unit of output. This figure can be obtained by dividing the average hourly cost of labor by average gross physical output per man-hour, or more simply by dividing gross physical output into total factory payroll. An increase in output per man-hour with no change in wage rates will reduce unit labor costs, while a drop in producivity will raise unit costs.

An increase in basic wage rates, with no change in productivity, will of course raise unit labor cost; but an increase in workers' hourly *earnings* does not necessarily do so. Under a straight piece-rate system, for example, the unit labor cost to the employer remains constant no matter how much workers' earnings may increase. Under incentive systems in which workers' earnings rise less than proportionately as their output increases, any increase in workers' output and earnings means a *reduction* in unit labor cost to the employer. In discussing the relation of changes in wage rates and earnings to production costs, therefore, it is necessary always to specify whether one is assuming wages to be paid on a time basis or an output basis. The importance of this point will appear frequently in later chapters.

A CENTURY
OF
RISING WAGES

The most obvious characteristic of money wages is that they rise in the long run. Phelps Brown and Hopkins have made estimates for the United States and four other countries for the eighty years from 1860 to 1939.[3] Over this period the money wage level tripled in Germany and Britain, rose sixfold in the United States, tenfold in Sweden, and twenty-four times in France. Prices rose also, but less rapidly than wages, so that workers' real purchasing power rose substantially in all the countries. There was little relation, however, between the rate of increase in money and real wages, either as between countries or between different time periods in the same country.

Wage movements in the United States over the past century are summarized in Table 1, and year-to-year changes since 1929 are shown

Table 1

MONEY WAGES, CONSUMER PRICES,
AND REAL WAGES IN MANUFACTURING,
UNITED STATES, 1860–1968

	PERCENTAGE CHANGE IN		
	Money Hourly Wages	*Consumer Prices*	*Real Hourly Wages*
1860–70	+ 53	+41	+ 8
1870–80	− 10	−22	+11
1880–90	+ 18	−11	+32
1890–1900	+ 3	− 8	+12
1900–10	+ 29	+16	+14
1910–22	+141	+78	+37
1922–30	+ 12	0	+13
1930–40	+ 26	−16	+50
1940–50	+131	+72	+34
1950–60	+ 57	+23	+28
1960–68	+ 33	+17	+14

SOURCES: 1860–1929: Clarence D. Long, "The Illusion of Wage Rigidity: Long and Short Cycles in Wages and Labor," *Review of Economics and Statistics*, May, 1960. This study draws on basic research by the author and by Albert Rees at the National Bureau of Economic Research.
1929–1957: Albert Rees, *New Measures of Wage Earner Compensation in Manufacturing*, 1914–57 (New York: National Bureau of Economic Research, Occasional Paper 75, 1960).
1957–68: Standard Bureau of Labor Statistics series, computations by the writer.

in Figure 1. The trend of money wage rates is strongly upward. This is no recent development, but goes back as far as our records exist.

[3] E. H. Phelps Brown and Sheila V. Hopkins, "The Course of Wage Rates in Five Countries, 1860–1939," *Oxford Economic Papers*, New Series, June, 1950, pp. 226–96. The basis for the estimates, which are necessarily rough, is explained in detail in this paper.

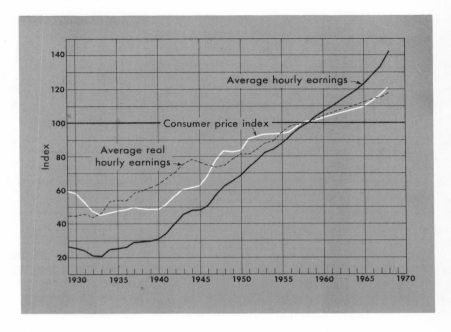

Figure 1
HOURLY EARNINGS, COST OF LIVING, AND
REAL HOURLY EARNINGS IN MANUFACTURING,
1929–68 (1957–59 = 100)
SOURCES: Same as for Table 1.

The rise was most rapid during the three war periods covered in Table 1; but a rising wage level is normal in peacetime also. From 1880 to 1914, a long period of peacetime industrial expansion, money wages rose about 70 percent. On a year-to-year basis, wage rates rose in twenty-five years of the period, remained stable in five years, and fell in only four. Since the bottom of the Great Depression in 1933, there has not been a single year in which wages failed to increase.

The price level took a dramatic turn at the beginning of this century. From 1873 to 1900, prices had drifted gradually downward, so that modest money wage increases yield substantial gains in real wages. Since 1900, however, the price level has tended strongly upward. The only periods of appreciable price decline have been during the post-World War I recession of 1920 to 1921 and the Great Depression of 1929 to 1933. The level of consumer prices today is more than three times as high as it was in 1900.

Movements of real wages are shown in the final column of Table 1.

Note that there are no minus signs in this column. There has been no period in which real wages have failed to advance; but the pace of advance has been variable. There is no visible relation between the rate of increase in real wages and money wages. Real wages rose rapidly in two periods, from 1880 to 1890 and from 1930 to 1940, when money increases were moderate. The explanation is that the price level was falling. But real wages have also risen sharply in periods such as from 1914 to 1920 and from 1940 to 1950, when prices were rising rapidly, but money wages raced ahead even faster.

It is clear that real wages have risen faster since 1914 than before; and they have risen especially fast since 1930. This is related to an acceleration of productivity in the American economy, which we shall try to account for in Chapter 8.

BEHAVIOR
OF THE
MONEY WAGE LEVEL

Until recently economists were not much interested in explaining the money wage level. The important thing was changes in the real wage level, which depended on the physical productivity of the economy. Fluctuations in money values were a veil over these real processes, and the function of the economist was to pierce the veil if not actually to ignore it. Associated with this was an expectation of price stability as the normal state of affairs. Prices might rise somewhat in boom years and fall slightly in depressions, but in the long run these fluctuations would offset each other.

Since 1940, however, the expectation of price stability has been replaced by an expectation of gradually rising prices. There has been no appreciable price decline in any of the advanced industrial countries. Instead, the price level has moved along an inclined plane, with the rate of price increase varying from year to year, but rarely falling to zero. The money wage level has risen even faster than the price level, as it must do if there is to be continued improvement in real wages.

While some economists have argued that moderate inflation is an acceptable or even desirable state of affairs, there are obviously disadvantages as well. Few would disagree with the proposition that 1 percent a year inflation is preferable to 5 percent inflation. There is active interest in how government can moderate the upward movement. And this has stimulated research into why money wages and prices behave as they do.

Behavior in Recession

The tendency for wages to be maintained during recession is not new. Even in the "good old days" of 1880 to 1914, when unionism was a minor factor in the economy, money wages fell in only four out of thirty-five years. The long and severe depression of 1929 to 1933 brought substantial cuts in wages and prices; but since 1933 there has not been a single year in which the average wage level failed to rise.

Even a nonunion employer has good reason to hesitate before cutting wages. Most of today's workers have never seen a plantwide wage reduction, and would consider it very bad behavior. Some of them would quit and advise their friends against applying for work. Others remaining on the job might be dissatisfied enough to produce less than before. The company's community reputation as an employer would suffer. So if the recession is expected to be brief and mild, as all recessions since 1945 have been, employers will find it expedient to ride out the recession at their present wage level.[4] Indeed, most employers continue to raise wages in bad years as well as good, though increases are typically smaller in recession.

Unions reinforce the tendency toward wage rigidity during recession. Refusal to take a wage cut is a cardinal tenet of union policy. The fact that union contracts run for a year or more prevents wage adjustments during the contract period. The growing tendency toward multi-year contracts, which usually contain built-in annual increases, causes the wage level to continue moving upward right through a twelve to eighteen month recession.

Professor Joseph Garbarino argues that, for this and other reasons, there is now a built-in floor for annual wage increases in the United States at around 2 to 2½ percent, even in recession years.[5]

Given this wage behavior, one cannot expect any appreciable decline of prices during recession. In the United States, the wholesale price index dipped very slightly in the 1949 recession, but the later recessions of 1954, 1958, and 1961 failed to make any dent in it. True, if the recessions had been larger and longer, the price line might have

---

[4] Without cutting wages, however, the employer may manage to reduce unit labor cost in other ways. He may be able to hire better workers at the same wage rate. Overtime declines, with a consequent drop in average hourly earnings. There may be downgrading of the labor force by making fewer promotions and replacing departing workers by lower-paid employees. On this range of issues, see Clarence D. Long, "The Illusion of Wage Rigidity: Long and Short Cycles in Wages and Labor," *Review of Economics and Statistics*, May, 1960, pp. 140–51.

[5] See Joseph W. Garbarino, "Income Policy and Income Behavior," in Arthur M. Ross, ed., *Employment Policy and the Labor Market* (Berkeley and Los Angeles: University of California Press, 1965), pp. 56–88.

buckled. But large recessions are now (happily) no longer characteristic of our economy. So the notion that price increases in good years
will be canceled out by decreases in bad years must be written off as
outdated.

Behavior in Expansion

As the economy moves up out of recession, employment can expand
for some time without serious wage pressure. The rate of wage increase
rises from its recession level, but not far enough to put pressure on
prices. The reason is that for some time the economy can draw on
existing labor reserves. Workers who were laid off in recession are recalled by their previous employers. There is a pool of unemployed in
most localities. A couple of million young people are entering the
labor force each year. There is also the reserve, noted in Chapter 2, of
people who drop out of the labor force when jobs are scarce but are
quite willing to reenter as demand rises.

Equally important is the reserve of plant capacity. In recent recessions the average operating rate of manufacturing plants has fallen to
82–84 percent of physical capacity, compared with the 90 percent
which many companies seem to consider optimal. As operating rates
rise back toward 90 percent, average fixed cost and average total unit
cost fall, and profits rise even with stable prices.

As the unemployment rate continues to fall, however, money wages
eventually rise at an "abnormal" rate, i.e. a rate which exceeds the
increase of labor's physical productivity and raises labor cost per unit
of output. The price level also moves upward. In the United States
and Canada, this seems to happen when the full-time unemployment
rate drops below 5 percent, i.e. while it is still above any acceptable
definition of full employment. One faces the awkward choice on which
so much recent discussion has centered: less unemployment and more
rapid inflation versus more unemployment and less inflation.

This dilemma was first clearly posed by Professor A. W. Phillips of
the London School of Economics. Phillips, on the basis of British data
from 1861 to 1957, concluded that there is a strong inverse relation between the rate of money wage increase and the unemployment rate;
that the relationship derived for the years from 1861 to 1913 fits about
as well for 1913 to 1948 and 1948 to 1957; that 5 percent unemployment is required in Britain to hold money wages constant; and that
with 2½ percent unemployment, wage increases would be held within
the bounds of the 2 to 3 percent annual increase in productivity.[6]

---

[6] A. W. Phillips, "The Relation Between Unemployment and the Rate of
Change of Money Wage Rates in the United Kingdom, 1861–1967," *Economica*,
November, 1958, pp. 283–99.

Samuelson and Solow have made a similar analysis of U.S. data for 1929–59, from which they derive the "modified Phillips curve" shown by the solid line in Figure 2.[7] Since it is the price level in which we

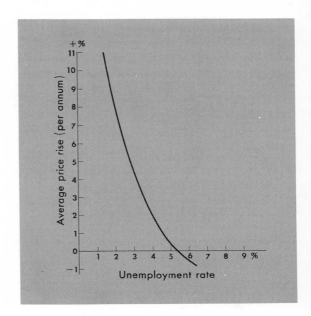

Figure 2

A MODIFIED PHILLIPS CURVE
FOR THE UNITED STATES

are really interested, the vertical axis is calibrated in price units rather than wage units. The point of zero price increase corresponds to a 2½ percent a year rise in money wages, which is considered to be within the bounds of productivity increase. The authors make an admittedly rough estimate that, with 5 to 6 percent unemployment, the price level will remain stable. If, on the other hand, unemployment were reduced to 3 percent, prices might rise 4 to 5 percent a year. The fact that price stability apparently requires a higher unemployment rate in the United States than in Britain must reflect structural differences in the two economies, but the nature of these is not clear.

In the first enthusiasm for the "Phillips curve" concept, there was a tendency to overlook the fact that it describes a phenomenon without really explaining it. The unemployment rate is an indicator, though not a very precise indicator, of supply–demand balance in the labor market. But even a cursory glance at the statistics indicates that the unemployment rate alone is not a good predictor of wage increases.

[7] Paul Samuelson and Robert Solow, "Analytical Aspects of Anti-Inflation Policy," *A.E.A. Papers and Proceedings,* May, 1960, pp. 177–94.

If one plots wage rate increases against the unemployment rate for each of twenty or thirty years, the points will show a general downward drift to the right; and one can fit a curve to these points, as in Figure 2. But the variance about the curve is large. For the postwar years in Great Britain, Phillips' study found that unemployment of between 1 and 2 percent has been associated with wage increases of anything from 2 to 8 percent a year (even excluding the Korean War increase of 10½ percent in 1950). Similarly, Samuelson and Solow found that unemployment in the neighborhood of 5 percent had been accompanied by everything from a slight wage decline in one year to a 6 percent increase in another. It seems clear that we must introduce additional variables to obtain a better explanation of wage behavior year by year.

Behind the Phillips Curve: Explaining Money Wage Increases

1. Let us ask first why the *unemployment rate* is significant. What is happening in the labor market as the unemployment rate falls, and how is this related to wage behavior?

The rate of full-time unemployment is a crude measure of excess supply in the labor market. It is crude because one should add to it the reserve of people who could be tempted into the labor market by job offers, and the extra hours that part-time workers would be willing to supply if demand were higher. One should subtract from supply the irreducible minimum of "frictional unemployment," though, as we saw in chapter 5, this is not a very precise concept. It would be useful also to know the number of *job vacancies* that employers are currently trying to fill. The ratio of available workers to available jobs would perhaps be the best indicator of the state of the market.

But while the unemployment rate does not measure the *magnitude* of excess labor supply, it does indicate the *direction of movement*. As the unemployment rate falls, labor reserves are shrinking. The next question is why this cannot go on smoothly, without pressure on wages, until the reserves are exhausted and unemployment is down to the frictional level. One important reason, surely, is the heterogeneity of labor demands and supplies. The labor reserves are unevenly distributed by skill level, customary industrial attachment, and geographic area. The expansion of demand for labor during an economic upswing is also uneven in these various dimensions. It is thus inevitable that specific labor shortages will develop even when aggregate measures still indicate excess supply, and that this will produce competitive bidding for labor.

This is especially likely to happen as regards skilled labor. Since training takes time, the short-run supply curve to the skilled crafts is quite inelastic. Moreover, recession unemployment is considerably lower among the skilled than among the unskilled. As employment expands, the skilled labor reserve may be exhausted and competitive bidding set in while reserves of unskilled labor are still ample.[8] Bottlenecks may develop also on an area basis. Areas in which labor demand is rising especially rapidly may run out of labor and have to stimulate migration from other areas by higher wage offers.

Competitive wage bidding in bottleneck sectors is then diffused throughout the economy through both market and "institutional" channels. If skilled men in a company have to be paid more, the less-skilled will usually be raised to maintain customary differentials. Areas that are losing labor may raise wages to check the flow. Workers who see others getting wage increases that they are not getting may quit their jobs, or reduce their performance on the job, thus putting pressure on their employers. Unionism can obviously serve as an important diffusion mechanism.

2. *Cost of living changes* are a second relevant factor. These could arise quite independently of wage movements—for example, from a rise in prices of imported goods in a relatively open economy. Once the price level is in motion, for whatever reason, this will influence workers' wage expectations even under nonunion conditions. Where a union is present, it will usually argue that a new contract should compensate for cost of living increases since the last contract in addition to providing a normal increase in real wages. Some unions in the United States have also secured "cost-of-living escalators," under which wages keep up with price changes month-by-month (or, more usually, quarter-by-quarter) over the life of the contract.

3. The *level of employers' profits* is a further consideration. During an economic upswing, profits tend to rise faster than output. On one side, this increases employers' ability to pay and (possibly) lowers their resistance to wage demands. On the other side, rising profits raise workers' wage expectations. Even though workers cannot look into the company's books, the rising tempo of activity in the plant will suggest that the company is doing well. Workers will then expect a share in the rising profits, and if they do not get it the "morale effect" will set in and the quit rate will rise. Again, a union seems likely to strengthen this causal chain by being better informed on company sales and profits and by using this to bolster wage demands. The employer will also be more eager to avoid a strike when profits are high than when they are low, since the cost of a shutdown will be greater.

There have been numerous attempts to test the strength of these

---

[8] See on this point two studies by Sara Behman, "The Wage-Determination Process in U.S. Manufacturing," *Quarterly Journal of Economics*, February, 1968, pp. 117–42; and "Labor Mobility, Increasing Labor Demand, and Money Wage Rate Increases in U.S. Manufacturing," *Review of Economic Studies*, 1964, pp. 253–66.

various influences by statistical analysis.[9] The approach and general findings are well exemplified by the Perry study. He explains quarterly changes in the money wage level over the years 1948–60 in terms of four variables: the unemployment rate, the cost of living index, the level of profits, and the change in profits since the preceding quarter. This last variable he takes as an indicator of *expectations*—if profits are rising, this will tend to be projected into the future, making management more willing to grant increases and workers more inclined to demand them.

Each of the four variables appears to have a significant influence on money wages.[10] One interesting feature of the results is that cost-of-living changes operate on the wage level with diminished effect. It appears that a given change in the cost-of-living will lead, three months later, to a little over one-third this percentage change in the wage rate. This agrees with the findings of other investigations, which usually place the cost-of-living effect between 0.3 and 0.5. So while there is a price-wage-price spiral, it does not seem to be an explosive spiral.

One way of viewing Perry's results is to say that, while there is at any moment a Phillips-type relation between unemployment level and rate of wage increase, the *location* of the Phillips curve is influenced by past living-cost changes, by the level of industrial profits, and by the rate of change of profits. A lower profit level shifts the Phillips curve to the left. Perry estimates that, with profits at the 1947–60 average of 11.8 percent, it would take a 5.2 percent unemployment rate to hold wage increases to 3.5 percent per year. But if instead profits were only

[9] In addition to the Behman articles already cited, see George L. Perry, *Unemployment, Money Wage Rates and Inflation* (Cambridge, Mass.: The M.I.T. Press, 1966); John Vanderkamp, "Wage and Price Level Determination: an Empirical Model for Canada," *Economica*, May, 1966, pp. 194–218; A. G. Hines, "Trade Unions and Wage Inflation in the United Kingdom, 1893–1961," *Review of Economic Studies*, 1964, pp. 221–52; A. G. Hines, "Unemployment and the Rate of Change of Money Wage Rates in the United Kingdom, 1862–1963: A Reappraisal," *Review of Economics and Statistics*, February, 1968, pp. 60–67; N. J. Simler and Alfred Tella, "Labor Reserves and the Phillips Curve," *Review of Economics and Statistics*, February, 1968, pp. 32–49; Kenneth M. McCaffree, "A Further Consideration of Wages, Unemployment, and Prices in the United States, 1948–1958," *Industrial and Labor Relations Review*, October, 1963, pp. 60–74.

[10] The basic multiple regression equation is

$$W_t = -4.313 + 0.367C_{t-1} + 14.711U_{t-1} + 0.424P_{t-1}$$
$$(0.054) \qquad (2.188) \qquad (9.068)$$
$$+ 0.796 \, \Delta P_t + e_t, \ R^2 = 0.870$$

$$(0.176)$$

where: C = the cost of living index
V = the unemployment rate
P = the profit rate
W = the money wage index

10.0 percent, wage increases could be held to 3.5 percent with only 4.1 percent unemployment. A smaller cost-of-living adjustment factor would have the same kind of effect.

Do Unions Make a Difference?

We have found good reasons for expecting the money wage level to rise before the economy reaches capacity output, and to rise faster the closer capacity is approached. This result does not depend on the existence of unions, nor does it stem from a particular theory of inflation. It is quite compatible with the traditional view that inflation arises from a high level of aggregate demand, supported by monetary expansion.

As a side comment, we may note that unit production costs tend to rise at high employment for other reasons than wage increases—for example rising raw material prices, rising prices of other industrial supplies that reach capacity early in the expansion, rising unit labor costs because of overtime work or declining quality of newly hired labor, a slowdown in the rate of productivity increase toward the peak of an expansion. To the extent that sellers have market power, and to the extent that prices are set on a cost-plus basis, these cost increases will lead to price increases. But once the price level rises, wages must rise even faster, as Perry and others have found. One is then embarked on a price-wage-price-wage spiral, which develops momentum and continues until broken by a drop in demand.

The question whether trade unionism makes a substantial difference to this process should perhaps be left until Part Three; but since we are already deep in the mechanics of money wage changes, some comments are in order here. First, there is little doubt that unionism strengthens the tendency for money wages to keep moving upward during recession. The main mechanism here is the multiyear contract, with built-in wage increases scheduled in advance. A three-year contract negotiated in a year of high profits and substantial price increases, such as 1969, will provide for large wage increases in the years 1970 to 1972. But by the time these increases become effective, demand may have fallen and the increases may no longer reflect market conditions. The momentum of a past inflationary period is thus carried forward into the future.

The more difficult question is whether unionism accelerates the rise of wages during expansion periods. There are pros and cons to this question. The nonunion employer can change wages as often as he likes, whereas under unionism adjustments usually occur once a year. So one can argue that unionism slows down the adjustment of wages to rising employment and profits. A union might be caught short, for example, if price inflation sets in just after it has agreed to a three-year contract based on an expectation of stable prices.

Cost-of-living escalators, on the other hand, may reduce the wage lag. Union officials may be better informed than the membership about increases in profits and living costs, and more aggressive in pushing for offsetting wage increases when contract-reopening time arrives. The union network may also strengthen the diffusion mechanism through which wage increases for certain groups of workers are transmitted to other groups.

It is impossible to say a priori which line of argument is more plausible. The question can be examined statistically, however, either by comparing the movement of money wages in *time periods* of different union strength (such as the years from 1920 to 1930 and from 1950 to 1970 in the United States); or by comparing wage behavior in different *sectors of the economy,* which differ in the strength of union organization. The limited testing which has been done to date suggests that unionism does accelerate the upward movement of wages in periods of rising employment. Perry, in the study cited above, made the first kind of test by analyzing manufacturing wage changes in the period from 1920 to 1928, a period of relatively weak unionism. He found that wage increases were on the average 1.43 percent per year *less* than would have been predicted from his equation based on 1948 to 1960 data. "It appears that for given values of the explanatory variables [unemployment, profit rate, etc.] wage changes were considerably greater in the recent period than in the 1920s. This may be viewed as an inflationary bias in the recent period relative to the former one, possibly attributable to the increased strength of labor's bargaining power" (p. 82).

Gail Pierson made a test of the second sort by fitting Perry-type equations separately for ten strongly unionized and several less strongly unionized manufacturing industries over the years 1953 to 1963. It appeared that the response of wages to a higher profit rate or a cost-of-living increase was significantly larger for the strongly unionized group. "To conclude . . . it appears that union strength significantly worsens the trade-off between unemployment and inflation. At 5 percent unemployment the wage-change advantage to strong unionism is in the range of 0.6 to 1.7 percentage points, indicating a rate of inflation of, say, 1 percent when prices would otherwise be stable." [11] A similar study by Kenneth McCaffree concludes that "the data presented are not inconsistent with the hypothesis that markets which are union in character tend to establish a higher rate of change of wages at any

[11] Gail Pierson, "The Effect of Union Strength in the U.S. Phillips Curve," *American Economic Review,* June, 1968, pp. 456–67.

given level of unemployment than is the case in similar non-union markets." [12]

The issue cannot be taken as settled; but there are strong indications that unionism strengthens the inflationary bias of the contemporary economy.

ISSUES
IN
WAGE–PRICE
POLICY

Choosing a Point on the Phillips Curve

Suppose we draw a Phillips curve for the American economy as of this year, using plausible values for the profit level, the cost-of-living adjustment factor, and other relevant variables. Suppose also that the federal administration, by fiscal and monetary policy, can regulate aggregate demand and employment. How hard should it push toward fuller employment? Where should it try to land on the Phillips curve?

This is a typical economic problem in that it involves a choice among objectives: higher employment and output versus greater price stability. It involves weighing the damage done by unemployment against that done by inflation.

The people who suffer most directly from unemployment are the unemployed. Even in a mild recession, a couple of million people suddenly find themselves unemployed, and their income drops far below its normal level. Another million or two find themselves reduced to part-time work. Still others find themselves demoted, or blocked from promotion, because of insufficient demand for their services. These costs fall most heavily on black workers and on young people.

The output loss is considerably greater than the employment loss. As a rough rule, each 1 percent increase in the rate of full-time unemployment is accompanied by a 3 percent reduction in GNP. At present GNP levels, an output gap of 5 percent means a loss of about $50 billion a year. This is a lot of output, which might have been enjoyed by consumers or invested to raise productive capacity for the future. The consumers who do not get this lost GNP include not only the unemployed but business owners whose profits fall in recession and farmers whose prices are depressed by inadequate demand.

Unemployment also has undesirable side effects. It increases work-

[12] Kenneth M. McCaffree, "A Further Consideration of Wages, Unemployment, and Prices in the United States, 1948–1958," *Industrial and Labor Relations Review*, October, 1963, pp. 60–74.

ers' feeling of insecurity and reduces the pleasantness of life-on-the-job. It leads to dubious policy proposals, such as forced reduction of working hours, on the ground that they are necessary to eliminate unemployment. And it hampers desirable programs, such as retraining of the low-skilled to make them more fully employable. If jobs are not available for these people after they are trained, the programs will look foolish and the graduates will become frustrated.

Inflation involves no direct loss of output or income; but it may involve considerable redistribution of income among groups in the economy. Any group whose money income rises less rapidly than the price level suffers a loss of real income. Groups whose incomes rise faster than prices are the winners in the inflation lottery.

Who are the most likely losers? There are groups of salaried people, such as college teachers and civil servants, whose pay scales are adjusted rather infrequently and tend to lag behind increases in living costs. But the main losers are probably those unable to work—the aged, the disabled, the women heads of broken homes, the people of low mental or physical capacity. These people live on pensions, relief allowances, and other transfer payments which remain fixed for considerable periods. So as the price level rises, their real income declines.

Inflation, like unemployment, has undesirable side effects. It undermines people's belief in the stability of money values. It thus undermines the basis of long-term lending, on which much of private investment and government financing depends. It may divert businessmen's energies from profit making through production efficiency to profit making through speculation on price changes.

Different individuals and interest groups will evaluate these disadvantages differently. The AFL-CIO Executive Council is unlikely to agree with the Board of Governors of the Federal Reserve System. The choice problem may be illustrated by a Phillips-type diagram (Figure 3). Suppose the highest rate of wage increase compatible with price stability is 3 percent per year. We indicate this by a horizontal line at this level. Suppose also there is general agreement that the unemployment rate should not be more than 4 percent. We draw a vertical line at this level. The box in the lower left-hand corner of the diagram can then be regarded as a preferred area. Any point within this space will command general public support.

Suppose, however, that the Phillips curve is located at *P*. It lies entirely outside the preferred area, and is in this sense a bad Phillips curve. In this situation there is no possibility of meeting both the price and employment objectives, and some trade-off must be made. Those who attach great importance to price stability might prefer to settle for point *B*. Those who are more concerned with high employment might prefer point *A*. The actual location will depend on political

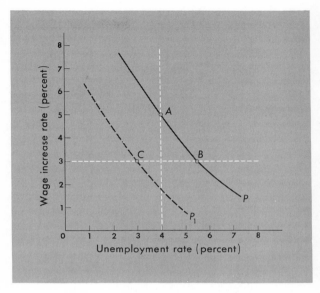

Figure 3
GOOD AND BAD PHILLIPS CURVES

pulling and hauling and will necessarily leave some groups in the economy unsatisfied.

Shifting the Position of the Phillips Curve

Suppose we were able to manipulate the position of the Phillips curve. Suppose we could shift it leftward to P_1, so that some portion of it falls within the preferred area. It might then be possible to get general agreement on a position such as C. This point is clearly preferable to A, B, or any other position on P, since it combines price stability with an unemployment rate of only 3 percent.

But can anything be done about the Phillips curve? It is deeply rooted in business pricing and profit targets, in workers' labor market reactions, in union bargaining practices. Can government expect to have much effect on it in a decentralized private economy?

Soon after 1945 several of the European countries—notably Britain, the Netherlands, and the Scandinavian countries—began to experiment in this direction. These efforts, usually termed "incomes policy," were designed to maintain high employment while at the same time moderating the advance of wage incomes, profit incomes, and the price level. They have typically involved discussion between government officials and leaders of business associations, union federations, farmers' organizations, and other organized economic groups. They have relied largely on exhortation, publicity, and voluntary cooperation rather than on legal controls.

Thus far these efforts have not been notably successful. High employment has been maintained almost continuously, but at the cost of substantial inflation. The rate of price increase, particularly in France and the Scandinavian countries, has been much above that in the United States. But the fact that the problem has not been solved does not make it any less a problem; and it is receiving much attention from government officials and private economists in all the Western industrial countries.

The United States was relatively late in taking steps to modify wage–price behavior. Not until 1962 did the Kennedy administration advance the concept of "guidelines" for wages and prices. Unlike the practice in most other countries, these guidelines were advanced unilaterally by government. They were not discussed in advance with union or management officials, who were thus in no way bound to observe them. Government had to rely on exhortation and publicity, applied mainly to key industries whose behavior was thought to have widespread economic effects.

The experiment came to an end in 1966, when counsels of moderation were swamped by the demand inflation associated with the Vietnam War. The experience of the years 1962 to 1965 is nevertheless worth reviewing, partly because it illustrates the difficulties inherent in any such effort.

The Guidelines Experiment, 1962 to 1965

The guidelines concept was stated initially in the January 1962 report of the Council of Economics Advisers, and was restated with modifications in subsequent CEA reports. The 1965 restatement read as follows:

> 1. *The general guide for wages is that the percentage increase in total employee compensation per man-hour be equal to the national trend rate of increase in output per man-hour.*
> If each industry follows this guidepost, unit labor costs in the overall economy will maintain a constant average.
> 2. *The general guide for price calls for stable prices in industries enjoying the same productivity growth as the average for the economy; rising prices in industries with smaller than average productivity gains; and declining prices in industries with greater than average productivity gains.*

If each industry follows this guidepost, prices in the economy will maintain a constant average.[13]

The Council estimated that output per man-hour for the economy as a whole was rising at 3.2 percent a year. This would warrant an average annual increase of 3.2 percent in total employee compensation. It emphasized, however, that this is only an economywide average, and that individual industries may need to deviate from the average for good cause.

> Wage increases above the guidepost level may be necessary where an industry is unable to attract sufficient labor to meet the demand for its products, where wages are particularly low, and where changes in work rules create large gains in productivity and substantial human costs requiring special adjustment of compensation . . . Wages should rise less than the guidepost rate where an industry suffers from above-average unemployment and where wages are exceptionally high for that type of work.[14]

These principles seem simple and plausible; but they are by no means as simple as they appear. It will be useful to review some of the difficulties in applying them to concrete situations.

1. Suppose we can measure the rate of increase of man-hour output in the private economy. If hourly compensation, including fringe benefits, rises at this same rate, employers' labor cost per unit of output will remain unchanged. If prices also remain unchanged, then *the division of total output between labor and capital* will be constant. The statement that hourly compensation should advance at the same rate as man-hour output implies that constancy of the labor and capital shares is desirable.

In actuality, as we shall see in the next chapter, the labor and capital shares vary with fluctuations in business activity. Labor's share typically falls during an expansion and rises during recession. Over the longer run—say, from 1900 to date—there has been a moderate but unmistakable tendency for the labor share to rise and the capital share to fall. So, the "constant shares" formula cannot be taken as a rigid rule.

2. The trend of productivity differs widely from industry to industry. In industry A, man-hour output may be rising at 6 percent a year, in industry B at only 1 percent. Suppose wage increases in each industry are guided, not by productivity changes *in that industry*, but rather by the average increase of productivity in the economy. If this is done, unit labor costs will be falling in industry A and rising in

[13] *Annual Report of the Council of Economic Advisers* (Washington, D.C., January, 1965), p. 108.
[14] Ibid.

industry *B*. Industries of type *A* should presumably cut prices, while those of type *B* will be entitled to raise them, these divergent movements averaging out to a stable price level.

One can doubtless count on rising prices in industries whose unit labor costs are increasing. But can one count on prices being reduced at an appropriate rate in the *A*-type industries? Where there is monopoly or oligopoly in product markets, prices may be maintained even though costs are falling. The sight of large and growing profits in such industries may whet union appetites and lead to outsize wage demands. If union leaders are then accused of throwing the guidelines to the winds, they can retort that employers did it first.

3. The guidelines should probably be construed as applying to average behavior over the course of a business cycle. It is natural, and probably desirable, that wages should rise less rapidly in recession than in expansion.

4. What the guidelines really define is behavior that, starting from a position of price stability, will perpetuate that stability. But suppose the applecart has already been upset, as in 1968 when the consumer price index rose 4.0 percent. What are workers entitled to expect in 1969? The usual 3.2 percent, which has already been canceled by rising prices? Or 7.2 percent (3.2 + 4.0), to enable them to catch up with last year's price increases? The latter figure will certainly help to perpetuate the upward movement of prices; but the former seems unfair, since it would mean a cut in real wages. The problem of getting back onto the rails once you have gotten off them is obviously difficult.

5. Part of the national increase in productivity comes about through the transfer of workers from low-productivity to high-productivity industries, notably from agriculture to manufacturing, in the course of economic development. This is presumably reflected in higher earnings of the transferred workers in their new occupations, and to use it also as a basis for a general increase in wage schedules would involve double counting. Increases in productivity from this source should be deducted, therefore, in calculating the tolerable rate of wage increase.

6. The guidelines apply to total *hourly compensation* rather than basic wage schedules. Compensation, however, may rise considerably faster than base rates, especially during periods of sustained high employment. The reasons include rapid increase of fringe benefits, overrating of jobs to permit higher wage offers for recruiting purposes, loosening of time standards on piecework so that hourly earnings pull farther and farther above base rates, and straight overpayment of the official scale. This tendency for earnings to diverge above official wage schedules, often termed "wage drift," has been noticeable in most industrial countries during the fifties and sixties. The moral is that the increase in basic wage schedules must be held below whatever target is accepted for employee compensation.

7. On the surface, a 3 percent (or any other) yardstick implies a uniform upward movement of employee compensation over time. But the pace of wage increases differs somewhat among occupations, industries, and regions. It is natural that wage increases should be above average in expanding companies, industries, and regions, and below average in stationary or declining areas and industries. Changes in relative wages help to speed reallocation of the labor force to the growth points of the economy. In addition, the wage structure always contains inequities and anomalies. A slice through the wage structure at a moment of time reveals groups which are underpaid and others which are overpaid, by standards of long-run equilibrium in a competitive labor market. The disadvantaged groups can catch up only if there is flexibility for specific wage rates to advance at different speeds.

The CEA recognized the need for flexibility and the desirability of above average increases in certain cases. Once this is admitted, however, it is natural that everyone will try to squeeze through the loophole of "exceptional circumstances." What standards are available for determining which cases are really exceptional, and how large an exception is warranted? Administrative bodies with wage-fixing authority, such as the National War Labor Board in World War II, have found this question extremely difficult.

In sum, there are difficult conceptual problems of how wages should move, company-by-company, and industry-by-industry, to achieve the twin objectives of price stability and optimal resource allocation. There are also serious tactical problems, notably the question of labor and management participation. Beyond this is the practical problem of how much can be expected from a purely voluntary program.

The Kennedy and Johnson administrations never attempted to apply the guidelines concept uniformly throughout the economy. Instead, they chose to intervene in selected situations, usually involving large unions and large, concentrated industries, whose decisions receive wide publicity and may be expected to have substantial economic influence.

The record contains a number of notable "successes" as well as some ignominious "failures." [15] In 1962 President Kennedy persuaded the United Steelworkers to settle for a noninflationary wage increase and, when the steel companies subsequently raised prices, his public denunciation of this action led to a withdrawal of the price increases. In 1965 the White House again intervened on the eve of a threatened steel strike and worked out a compromise wage agreement within the 3.2 percent limit. In 1965 intervention by the U.S. Maritime Commission in a maritime strike contributed to a 3.2 percent settlement. In

[15] For a detailed review of interventions by the Executive branch of the federal government, see John Sheahan, *The Wage-Price Guideposts* (Washington, D.C.: The Brookings Institution, 1967).

October 1965, President Johnson used the threat of a presidential veto to get Congress to hold civil service pay increases within the guideline limits. On the price front, when aluminum producers raised prices in 1964, President Johnson authorized release of substantial quantities of aluminum from the government's emergency stockpiles, after which the price increases were rescinded. This serves as a reminder that government does have economic instruments which can be used to support its "educational" efforts. They include use of government's position as a large purchaser to direct orders to companies that hold the price line; release of materials from government stockpiles; reduction of tariff rates or import quota restrictions; and reduction of subsidies (as in the maritime case) where cost increases are considered unwarranted.

On the other side of the ledger, the construction industry almost ostentatiously ignored and exceeded the guidelines. One widely publicized case was that of the New Jersey operating engineers. Despite intervention by the Secretary of Labor, the Council of Economic Advisers, and others, the engineers Local 825 in 1966 won a three-year contract calling for wage and benefit increases in excess of 10 percent per year. Another notable failure was the airline machinists' strike of July–August 1966. After administration officials had twisted the guidelines to permit a 4.3 percent wage settlement, which was accepted by the companies and the union leadership, the union members voted to reject the settlement and continued on strike. The final settlement was estimated to involve a 4.9 percent wage increase.

After 1965 the guidelines approach was undermined increasingly by the high aggregate demand associated with the Vietnam War. Early in 1965 the wholesale price index began to edge up after a long period of stability. The Consumer Price Index rose more than 3 percent in 1966 and 1967, and more than 4 percent in 1968. Wage demands escalated, in an effort to overtake living costs. Bargained wage increases averaged 4.8 percent in 1966, 5.6 percent in 1967, and 7.5 percent in 1968. The economy was embarked on a wage–price spiral; and while the Council of Economic Advisers continued to urge "restraint" on all parties, it became harder to translate restraint into any numerical target.

How is one to evaluate the guidelines experience? Was it only shadow-boxing? Or did it have a significant effect on price and wage behavior?

The dozen or so statistical studies which have been made suggest that wages did rise less rapidly from 1961 to 1965 than would have been predicted on the basis of unemployment levels, profit rates, and other relevant variables. Perry, for example, developed a wage equation for the years 1947 to 1960 by the method outlined above. He then used this to predict the movement of wages quarter by quarter from 1962 through early 1966. He found that actual wage increases were consistently lower than the predicted values from mid-1962 on, with the deviations increasing over time. The downward deflection of wage rate changes averaged 0.9 percent per year over the entire period, and was almost 2 percent for 1965.

In another interesting experiment, Perry separated manufacturing industries on the basis of informed judgment into a "visible" and an "invisible" group. The visible industries are highly concentrated, highly unionized, and the kind of industry government is likely to watch (steel, automobiles, aluminum, etc.). It is interesting, and possibly significant, that the "wage slowdown" of 1962 to 1965 was considerably larger for the visible group than for the other, which is compatible with the hypothesis that the guidelines had some effect on those industries.[16]

On the price side, several studies have concluded that price increases from 1962 to 1965 were also below what might have been expected. Solow, for example, estimates that the rate of price increase was 0.6 to 0.7 percentage points per year less than expected from earlier relationships.

Granted that wage–price increases were abnormally low in these years, it does not necessarily follow that the guidelines were responsible. It is possible that inflationary expectations may have been dampened by the sluggishness of the economy from 1958 to 1961, leading to less-aggressive wage and price behavior in the years immediately following. An increase in competitive pressure from imports may have restrained price increases in such areas as steel and automobiles. The economic expansion of 1962 to 1965 may have been unusually balanced and free of bottlenecks. Even considering such possible alternative explanations, however, one is inclined to agree with Perry that the burden of proof is on those who assert that the guidelines did not have an independent influence.

Alternatives for the Future

Suppose that, as Vietnam War expenditures diminish, the wage–price spiral tapers off and we enter a new period of relative stability. Should the guidelines approach be revived and pursued? Or should it be written off as useless?

This is a controversial question on which economists are far from agreed.[17] Some argue that inflation is basically a monetary phenomenon and that to attack it via money wages is starting at the wrong end.

[16] George L. Perry, "Wages and the Guideposts," *American Economic Review*, September, 1967, pp. 897–904. For a thorough review of other studies, see Sheahan, *Guideposts*, chap. 7.

[17] For a sampling of opinion, pro and con, see George P. Shultz and Robert Z. Aliber, eds., *Guidelines, Informal Controls, and the Market Place* (Chicago: University of Chicago Press, 1966). See also Robert M. Solow, "The Wage-Price Issue and the Guideposts," in F. H. Harbison and J. D. Mooney, eds., *Critical Issues in Employment Policy* (Princeton: Industrial Relations Section, 1966).

Some attach great importance to the divergent movement of specific prices and wages, which is natural in a dynamic economy, and fear that government intervention will distort these natural market adjustments. Some believe that the guidelines approach served a useful educational function and had some economic impact, and would favor continuing the same kind of effort in the future. Still others believe that standards for wage and price behavior at high employment are essential, but that they are unlikely to succeed on a voluntary basis. They would favor requiring prior notice of proposed wage and price increases in selected industries, which would then be subject to review and possible modification by a public authority.

With or without guidelines, there are various other possibilities for constructive action. The training and other manpower policies examined in chapter 6 would help to shift the Phillips curve to the left. Part of the unemployment that now persists during boom periods arises from maladjustment between the characteristics of unemployed workers and vacant jobs. More effective training programs, mobility aids, and clearinghouse facilities might make it possible to reduce unemployment to 3 percent with no more wage–price pressure than we now encounter at 4 percent.

Another possibility, suggested by Professor John Dunlop in the Shultz–Aliber symposium, is to focus government's efforts on a few key sectors. During inflationary periods, demand pressure tends to be particularly severe in certain bottleneck areas, such as steel, machinery manufacturing, and building construction. The demand pressure produces wage and price increases in these sectors, which then tend to be diffused throughout the economy. Government training and relocation programs could be aimed specifically at increasing the supply of qualified workers in these bottleneck industries. Government could try to reduce its own demand for their products. It could lower tariffs or take other actions to encourage imports. Such policies could to some extent serve in lieu of guidelines, or could be used to give government greater bargaining leverage in applying guidelines.

The one thing certain is that the problem will not go away. We do not at present have any proven technique for combining high employment (i.e. an unemployment rate in the 3 to 4 percent range) with reasonable price stability. Considering that these are both important economic objectives, inability to reconcile them is a serious defect in our institutional arrangements. Continued active discussion and experimentation are in prospect for the future.

Discussion Questions

1. Explain clearly the differences between: (a) base rate, (b) average hourly earnings, (c) average weekly earnings, (d) take-home pay, (e) annual earnings, (f) total employee compensation.
2. Does an increase in money wages necessarily mean an increase in real wages: (a) in a single industry? (b) in the economy as a whole?
3. List the main factors that influence the rate of increase in the money wage level, and explain why each is important.
4. During periods of rising prices at high employment there is usually active debate over whether prices are rising because:
   (a) aggregate demand is too high, leading to "overheating" of the economy, or
   (b) unions and companies are using their monopoly power to secure "abnormal" wage and price increases.
   Which line of argument impresses you as more nearly correct?
5. What are the main considerations in weighing the damage done by unemployment against that done by inflation?
6. It is often said that the price level will remain stable if the general wage level rises at the same rate as average man-hour output in the economy. In what ways may this definition overstate (or understate) the feasible rate of increase in basic wage schedules?
7. Do you favor any type of government action to influence specific wage and price decisions? If so, what type? If not, why not?

Reading Suggestions

There is a voluminous literature on the causes and effects of money wage behavior. Most of this is reviewed and footnoted in Perry, George L., *Unemployment, Money Wage Rates and Inflation.* Cambridge, Mass.: The M.I.T. Press, 1966. The rationale and operation of the U.S. guidelines experiment was discussed in the annual reports of the Council of Economic Advisers from 1962 through 1966. The most thorough outside review of this experiment is Sheahan, John, *The Wage-Price Guideposts.* Washington, D.C.: The Brookings Institution, 1967.

REAL WAGES
AND
LABOR'S
INCOME SHARE

8

The short-term fluctuations of money wages examined in the last chapter raise interesting questions of analysis and policy. Over a period of years, however, greater importance attaches to the movement of real wages, i.e. money wages corrected for changes in prices of consumer goods. Between 1947 and 1967, for example, average weekly earnings of employees in private industry more than doubled, rising from $45.58 to $101.99. Over the same period the consumer price index rose from 77.8 to 116.3, or about 50 percent. After adjusting for this price increase, real wages—or wages in dollars of constant purchasing power—rose by just about half.

This is a big increase. It means that employees were able to buy about 50 percent more goods and services in 1967 than they could buy twenty years earlier. And since the proportion of personal income spent on consumption remains nearly constant, actual living standards rose to the same extent.

Nor is this anything new. The level of real wages in the United States has risen continuously for the past century and more. The rate of increase varies somewhat from year to year, but the long-run trend is remarkably consistent. Real wages rise in good years and bad, when money wages are rising and when they are falling.

What accounts for this strong and persistent trend? Broadly, the real income of employees depends on the size of national output and on labor's share of national output. Real wages may rise either because national output is rising, or because labor's share of output is increasing, or for both reasons together. These considerations suggest the organization of this chapter. Let us look first at what determines labor's share of the output "pie." Then we shall examine why the pie itself has been getting larger year-by-year.

THEORIES OF
LABOR'S
SHARE

Classical Distribution Theory

Speculation about what determines the share of income going to suppliers of labor, capital, and other factors goes back to the beginning of economics. British economists of the period from 1800 to 1830, especially David Ricardo and T. R. Malthus, regarded national income as divided among wage earners, capitalists, and landowners. Wages, they thought, must tend toward a minimum level of subsistence, i.e. a level which would just enable the population to reproduce itself. If wages should rise temporarily above this level, workers would respond by having more children, and more of these children would be able to survive to maturity. This accelerated increase in labor supply would force wages down toward the subsistence level. This gloomy prognosis was termed "the iron law of wages," and did much to earn economics its label of "the dismal science."

Agriculture was regarded as subject to *diminishing returns* or *increasing* costs. As the population grows, more and more food must be produced. But this can be done only by bringing poorer land into cultivation or working the better land more intensively. In either case, if we assume no technical progress in agriculture, the amount of (say) wheat produced by a unit of labor and capital will fall. Or, putting this in reverse, the cost of producing a bushel of wheat will rise. But since the price of wheat depends on its cost of production, the price of wheat must also rise.

This has two consequences. First, rising food prices will bring an increase in landowners' incomes. Rent per acre, total rent, and rent as a percentage of national income will all rise over time. Economic growth, unaccompanied by technical progress in agriculture, means a continued enrichment of the land-owning class.

Second, *money* wages must rise in order to enable workers to buy as

much food as before and thus keep *real* wages constant, and this will
be harmful to employers of labor. The price of manufactured products
has not risen, because there has been no change in the amount of
labor required per unit of product. The manufacturers, then, are
squeezed between a constant price level and a rising wage level, and
the rate of profit must fall. It could conceivably fall to zero. But somewhere before this, the classics argued, the incentive to saving would
have vanished and capital accumulation would cease. The capital stock
would then remain constant, and the interest rate would remain constant at a low but positive level. Thus, with capital and labor both
constant, we arrive at the famous "classical stationary state."

Looking backward, it is easy to see why these predictions were not
realized in Britain. Increased imports of grain from the New World
after 1840 reduced the demands on Britain's farm land. Gradual
spread of birth control methods in the late nineteenth and early
twentieth century removed the specter of population pressure. Accelerated technical progress in all branches of the economy raised output fast enough so that workers, capitalists, and landowners could
simultaneously enjoy higher returns.

Classical reasoning remains applicable, however, in many of the
less-developed countries. Some of these countries combined severe
population pressure, inadequate food production, low rates of saving
and technical progress. It is not difficult to imagine them evolving
toward a stationary state, with the great majority of the population
living at subsistence levels.

The Neoclassical or Market Theory

By the late-nineteenth century the British economy had changed
substantially, and so had the complexion of economics. Land no longer
appeared so important or so different from capital goods. The Mal-
thusian theory of population had been generally abandoned. Economists no longer tried to determine the growth of factor supplies within
their theoretical system, but concentrated simply on factor prices. Because of these and other differences, economists writing from about
1870 on are usually termed "neoclassical."

The income distribution problem was reformulated as follows:
given fixed supplies of labor and capital, what determines the market
price of each and hence the division of national output between them?
The answer, worked out more or less simultaneously by John Bates
Clark at Columbia, Alfred Marshall at Cambridge, and several European economists, is often called "the marginal productivity theory of
distribution."

Clark, for example,[1] constructed a hypothetical economic system with the following characteristics: (1) Free competition prevails throughout the economy, in both product markets and factor markets. Prices and wages are not manipulated by collusive agreements or government regulation. (2) The quantity of each productive resource is assumed to be given. Moreover, no changes occur in the tastes of consumers or the state of the industrial arts. The same goods therefore continue to be produced year after year in the same quantities and by the same methods. (3) The *quantity* of capital equipment is regarded as fixed, but it is assumed that the *form* of this equipment can be altered to cooperate most effectively with whatever quantity of labor is available. Although this seems at first glance a queer and unreal assumption, it makes a good deal of sense for long-period problems. Over a period of decades plants *can* be adapted as they wear out and have to be replaced. If labor becomes more plentiful relative to capital, plants and machines can be redesigned so as to use greater quantities of labor. If labor becomes scarcer, equipment can be redesigned to use less labor. (4) Workers are assumed to be interchangeable and of equal efficiency. This assumption means complete absence of occupational specialization. The result is a single wage rate rather than a variety of rates for different occupations.

Clark summarized the operation of such an economy in a diagram, reproduced here as Figure 1.[2] The line *DE* represents the marginal physical productivity of labor, i.e. the amount added to the national product by the employment of additional workers. Clark showed this curve as falling steadily from the beginning. Actually, it might rise for some time, but this point is not important.

OA represents the number of workers available for employment, which we assume to be given and constant. If all these men are employed, the last man added will have a marginal productivity of *AB*. His wage rate cannot be more than *AB*, for then it would not pay to employ him. The wage rate cannot be less than *AB*, for in this event some employer, seeing a chance to make a profit by hiring the worker for less than his marginal productivity, would try to lure him away from his present employer. Competition among employers for labor will insure that the worker receives the full marginal product *AB*, but no more than this.

It follows next that no other worker in the system can receive a wage higher than *AB*. It may seem that the men above the margin— that is the men to the left of *A* on the diagram—are being cheated by this arrangement. They seem to be producing more than they are

1 John Bates Clark, *The Distribution of Wealth* (New York: The Macmillan Company, 1899).
2 Clark, *The Distribution of Wealth*, p. 201.

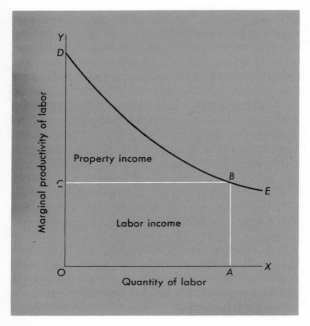

Figure 1
DETERMINATION OF
THE GENERAL LEVEL OF REAL WAGES

getting. Actually, however, under the assumption of perfect inter-
changeability of workers, no man is more valuable than any other. If
a man doing a particular important job were to drop out, a man could
be taken from the margin to replace him. Hence one cannot earn more
than another. If this were not so, and if each man were paid his
specific productivity, nothing would be left over for the other factors
of production. As it is, however, the workers as a group receive as
wages the area *OABC,* i.e. the number of workers multiplied by the
wage rate. The triangular area *BCD* goes to the owners of land and
capital.

The fact that there are thousands or millions of employers in the
economy makes no difference to the argument. In a purely competitive
labor market, each employer will be obliged to pay the market wage,
OC. He will then adjust his hiring of labor so that the marginal productivity of the last man hired is also *OC.* Thus both the wage of
labor and the marginal productivity of labor will be equal in all em-

ploying units; and it will not be possible to raise national output by transferring workers from one unit to another. Labor is ideally allocated.

Nor does it make any basic difference that there are in fact many skill levels in the economy. The assumption of a single skill level and a single wage rate is merely a convenient simplification. We could assume instead that there are several occupational levels, whose wages at any time bear a fixed relation to each other, and move up and down together. We could then regard *OC* as an average of these occupational rates. The conclusion would remain the same: the level of this average wage depends on the height of the productivity schedule and on the supply of labor.

Figure 1 was drawn for labor because labor is the subject of this book. But an exactly similar diagram could be drawn for capital. Units of capital supply would appear on the horizontal axis, and the rate of return to capital on the vertical axis. The rectangle at the bottom of the diagram would then represent property income, and the upper triangle would be labor income.

This suggests an interesting puzzle: will the two diagrams be consistent? If labor is paid its marginal product, and capital is paid its marginal product, how do we know there will be just enough output . to go around? To make sure that this will be so, we must make the further assumption that a small increase in inputs always produces a proportionate increase in outputs. A 1 percent increase in employment of labor and capital will add exactly 1 percent to output. The economy as a whole shows *constant returns to scale*. If this is true, it can be shown that paying each factor its marginal productivity will exactly use up the output of the economy.[3]

Monopoly and Monopsony Power

The competitive market explanation of factor shares has impressed many economists as too good to be true, or at least too simple to be

---

[3] The functional relation between inputs and output is termed a *production function*. The assumption described above amounts to assuming a *linear homogeneous production function of degree one*. An example is the *Cobb-Douglas function* (named after Professor Paul Douglas of Chicago and a mathematician who collaborated with him), which has the form $Y = VK^a L^{1-a}$, where V is a constant, a is a constant fraction, K is capital, and L is labor.

The fraction a shows the effect on output of a small increase in capital, everything else remaining unchanged. Similarly, $1-a$ shows the effect of a small increase in labor. It can be shown that if factor markets are purely competitive, so that each factor is paid its marginal product, *a is the capital share of national income and 1-a is the share of labor*. Since $a + (1-a) = 1$, the available product is precisely exhausted.

true, and particularly since 1930 two lines of attack have been
launched upon it. First, monopoly power is obviously present in many
product markets, and monopsony power is thought to be quite prevalent in labor markets. Second, it seems rather odd to use microeconomic
price theory to explain the *aggregate* distribution of national income,
which might well be considered a problem in macroeconomics.

The first line of criticism,[4] associated particularly with the names
of Michael Kalecki and Joan Robinson, is examined in this section.
The second line of attack, suggested by Nicholas Kaldor but since developed by numerous other economists, is considered in the next
section.

Consider first the implications of monopoly power in product markets. In Figure 2 we show the usual monopoly pricing diagram. *ATC*

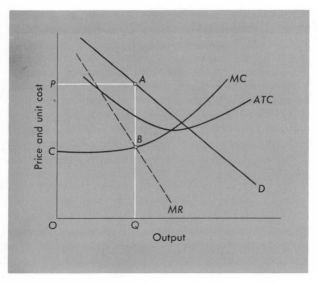

Figure 2
MONOPOLY PRICING AND FACTOR SHARES

and *MC* are the firm's average total cost and marginal cost curves,
while *D* and *MR* are its demand and marginal revenue curves. To
maximize profit, the firm will produce the output for which *MC* =
MR, in this case *OQ*; and it can sell this output for price *OP*.

4 For a review of the relevant literature and some efforts at statistical testing,
see John R. Maroney and Bruce T. Allen, "Monopoly Power and the Relative
Share of Labor," *Industrial and Labor Relations Review*, January, 1969, pp. 167–78.

Instead of price being equal to marginal cost as in pure competition, there is a gap between them equal to AB. This gap as a proportion of the price itself, that is the ratio AB/AQ, is termed the *degree of monopoly*. This measure is related to the elasticity of demand. The more inelastic the demand curve, the higher the degree of monopoly. It can be shown, in fact, that $AB/AQ = 1/e$, where e is the price elasticity of demand.

For present purposes, the important thing is that $OCBQ$, the area under the marginal cost curve, shows how much of the product price is paid for labor and other variable factors. $ABCP$ is the amount left for the fixed factors. While $ABCP$ is not precisely the capital share of output, it is very close to it. On this ground Kalecki and others have argued that anything increasing the degree of monopoly in the economy will raise the capital share, and conversely. If the degree of monopoly remains unchanged, and if business pricing practices remain stable, then the labor and capital shares will also remain unchanged.

Competition may also be restricted in the labor market. The exercise of *monopsony power* by a firm was analyzed in Chapter 4. The firm will restrict employment and output in order to profit from a lower wage level. This power to reduce the wage level is also a power to reduce labor's income share. Conversely, if the wage is raised to the competitive level by collective bargaining or legal regulation, labor's income share will rise.

There is considerable difference of opinion among economists as to how widespread monopsony power is in labor markets. But to the extent that it exists, it must operate to reduce labor's share below what it would be under fully competitive conditions.

Aggregative Distribution Theories

Finally, we must note a type of theory that does not start from the economics of the firm but from aggregative models of the economy. These models suggest that labor and capital shares are closely linked to the rate of economic growth. Nicholas Kaldor and other economists at Cambridge University have taken a prominent part in developing this line of reasoning. These theories return, in a sense, to the classical tradition of being interested in factor supplies as well as factor prices, and of trying to trace the course of events over time.

Kaldor's analysis [5] starts from the Keynesian proposition that, for any past period, saving must equal investment. He next distinguishes between saving from wage income and saving from property income. It is plausible to assume that recipients of property income have a

[5] The original statement is in N. Kaldor, "Alternative Theories of Distribution," *Review of Economic Studies,* XXIII (1955–56), 83–100.

higher propensity to save [6]—indeed, in some models of this type it is assumed that all saving comes from property income, while wage earners save nothing.

Call national income Y, investment I, the wage and property shares W and P, total saving from each of these shares S_w and S_p, and the proportion of each share which is saved s_w and s_p. Thus $S_p = s_p \cdot P$ and $S_w = s_w \cdot W$. The savings ratios, s_w and s_p, are assumed to remain constant for all levels of income.

The basic relations in the system are

$$Y = P + W$$
$$S = I$$
$$S = S_p + S_w$$

From this we can deduce that the investment level

$$
\begin{aligned}
I &= S_p + S_w \\
&= s_p \cdot P + s_w \cdot W \\
&= s_p \cdot P + s_w \, (Y - P) \\
&= (s_p - s_w) \, P + s_w \cdot Y
\end{aligned}
$$

Dividing through by Y,

$$\frac{I}{Y} = (s_p - s_w) \frac{P}{Y} + s_w$$

and $$\frac{P}{Y} = \frac{1}{s_p - s_w} \cdot \frac{I}{Y} - \frac{s_w}{s_p - s_w}$$

This means that, if the saving propensities are given and constant, *the profit share of income depends solely on the ratio of investment to output.* A high investment rate goes along with a high property share, and conversely. If we assume that wage earners do not save at all, so that $s_w = 0$, the above expression reduces to

$$P = \frac{1}{s_p} \cdot I$$

The level of property income depends solely on the level of investment and on the capitalists' own saving propensity. In Kaldor's phrase, "capitalists earn what they spend, and workers spend what they earn." Moreover, so long as s_p is greater than s_w, the system will be stable.

---

[6] Evidence is scanty, but one study for France shows the following ratios of saving to income for different economic groups: employers in industry and commerce, 36.5 percent; senior management and professions, 24.3 percent; farmers, 16.8 percent; salaried workers, 1.2 percent; industrial workers, 2.4 percent. Jacques Lecaillon, "Changes in the Distribution of Income in the French Economy," in Jean Marchal and Bernard Duclos, eds., *The Distribution of National Income* (New York: St. Martin's Press, Inc., 1968).

An increase in I raises aggregate demand. If prices are flexible, this will raise prices relative to wages and thus increase the profit share of income. But since a higher proportion of profit is saved, this will increase total saving. The process will continue until saving has risen sufficiently to offset the increase in investment. A drop in investment will set off an opposite sequence of events—lower prices, lower profits, and lower saving. Thus as long as s_p is greater than s_w, and assuming prices flexible in both directions, the system will be stable in the vicinity of full employment.

The property share of income, in short, is linked directly to the investment rate and thus to the growth rate of output. A high-level growth path, such as that of Japan since 1950, goes along with a high investment rate and a large property share of income. A low-level growth path, such as that of Britain since 1950, is accompanied by a much lower investment rate and a smaller property share. What may cause an economy to be on one or the other path is a complicated question—indeed, the central problem of modern growth theory. Kaldorians would claim only that a consistent view of the economy must link income distribution to the behavior of the grand aggregates of the economy.

The Kaldor view of aggregate income distribution is not inconsistent with the view that the wage rate in each firm and industry must equal the marginal productivity of labor; and some economists have effected a satisfactory reconciliation of macro and micro distribution theories.[7] But this involves difficult problems which fall properly in a more advanced course.

**CHANGES
IN RELATIVE SHARES:
ANALYSIS**

The division of income between capital and labor at a particular moment is perhaps less interesting than the behavior of income shares over time. In a growing capitalist economy, will labor's share tend to rise, fall, or remain constant over the decades? This is a basic issue, which has been debated since classical times. Before looking at the statistical evidence, let us analyze on what the answer will depend. Throughout this section we assume competitive factor pricing.

Total labor income is the amount of labor in use (L) multiplied by the market wage (W), which we assume is equal to labor's marginal productivity (MP_L). Capital income is the capital stock (K) multiplied

[7] See several papers in *The Distribution of National Income*, cited in fn. 6, particularly those by Martin Bronfenbrenner and Robert Solow.

by its market rate of return (P), also assumed equal to the marginal productivity of capital (MP_K). The ratio of property income to labor income, then, is

$$\frac{P \cdot K}{W \cdot L} = \frac{P}{W} \cdot \frac{K}{L}$$

The distributive shares will remain constant if this expression remains constant.

The right-hand and left-hand terms are obviously related. A change in relative factor supplies will necessarily change their relative prices. Let us chart this relation, as in Figure 3. On the horizontal axis we

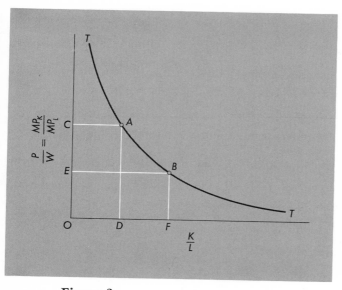

Figure 3

CAPITAL-LABOR SUBSTITUTION:
THE CASE OF UNIT ELASTICITY

measure the capital–labor ratio, K/L. Moving to the right on this axis means that each worker has more and more capital to work with. (This happens to have been the actual direction of movement in the United States and other industrial countries in modern times.)

On the vertical axis, we lay out the rate of return to capital (crudely, the rate of interest) relative to the wage rate, both defined in real terms. Moving *down* this axis means that the interest rate is falling relative to the wage rate—or, what amounts to the same thing, the wage rate is rising faster than the interest rate.

The relation between the two ratios is shown by the curve TT. Suppose we pick a point A on this curve, and lay out the rectangle $OCAD$.

$$\text{Then } OC = P/W \text{ and } OD = K/L$$

$$\text{Multiplying, } OCAD = \frac{P}{W} \cdot \frac{K}{L} = \frac{P \cdot K}{W \cdot L} = \frac{\text{Property income}}{\text{Labor income}}$$

As we move down TT, we can see whether the relative share of property income is rising or falling by observing what is happening to the size of the rectangles under the curve.

Why is it plausible to draw this curve as sloping downward from left to right? Suppose the capital stock rises with labor supply constant —a rightward movement on the X axis. This will raise labor's marginal productivity schedule (Figure 1), and hence the market wage rate. As K/L increases, P/W will fall; so the curve relating them must slope downward.

The same result follows in the more realistic case where the supply of both factors is rising but at different rates. Suppose capital supply is rising faster than labor supply. Then the marginal productivity of both factors may be rising, but MP_L will still rise faster because capital is becoming relatively more abundant. If the factors are priced competitively, P/W will decline because MP_K/MP_L is declining.

This change in relative factor prices will react on methods of production. If capital is becoming steadily cheaper relative to labor, producers will be inclined to save labor by substituting capital. This will raise the demand for capital relative to labor, and will tend to check the fall of interest rates relative to wage rates.

The outcome, if we are comparing different periods of time, will depend on how easy it is to find ways of substituting capital for labor (or vice versa). This ease or difficulty is indicated by the *slope* of TT, which is termed the *elasticity of substitution*.[8] This elasticity might have various values, and its value might be different at different points on TT. One interesting case, however, and the case illustrated in Figure 3, is that in which the elasticity of substitution is one at any point on TT. (Geometrically, TT is a rectangular hyperbola, the area under which is constant for all points.)

[8] Algebraically, the elasticity of substitution is defined as

$$\frac{\Delta \frac{K}{L}}{\frac{K}{L}} \div \frac{\Delta \frac{W}{P}}{\frac{W}{P}}$$

This means that a small increase in K/L is always exactly offset by a decrease in P/W. Thus the expression $(P/W)(K/L)$ remains constant, and hence the labor and property shares remain constant. The points D and F, for example, might represent dates thirty years apart, during which the capital–labor ratio has doubled. By our assumption, this causes the P/W ratio to fall to half its previous value. Thus $OACD$, which shows the property income/labor income ratio at the outset, has the same area as $OEBF$, which shows the ratio thirty years later. Relative income shares have remained unchanged.

The special feature of this case is that relative *rates of increase in factor supplies have no effect on income shares.* Capital supply can increase 50 percent faster than labor supply, or twice as fast, or three times as fast. Relative factor prices will always adjust, so that income shares remain unchanged. If, on the other hand, elasticity of substitution were *less than one,* the more rapidly growing factor would suffer a sharper fall in price and its share of national income would fall. Conversely, if elasticity of substitution were greater than one, the share of. the more rapidly growing factor would rise.

There is of course no reason why TT in actuality should have the shape given it in Figure 3. The elasticity of substitution could readily be greater than unity or less than unity, and could differ at various points on the curve. Statistical investigation of actual elasticities presents complicated problems. Research results to date suggest that elasticity of capital–labor substitution differs substantially from one industry to another. Most of the estimates, however, fall within a range of 0.8 to 1.2. Thus an assumption of unity for the economy as a whole seems a good working approximation for the time being.

So far we have concentrated on increase in factor supplies and have ignored the possibility of technical progress. Technical change, often referred to as innovation, shifts marginal productivity curves upward; but it is not necessarily neutral as between the two factors. It may raise the marginal productivity of labor more than that of capital, or vice versa.

Here some definitions are in order. A *labor-saving innovation* is one that raises the marginal productivity of capital more than that of labor. *It acts like an increase in labor supply.* It provides opportunities to use additional capital without depressing its productivity. Mechanization and automation in manufacturing provide an abundance of illustrations.

A *capital-saving innovation* is one that raises the marginal productivity of labor more than that of capital. *It acts like an increase in capital supply.* Transmission of messages by radio instead of telegraph wires is an example of this sort. Another is the jet airplane, which can carry more transatlantic passengers per week than a large steamship, while costing considerably less to build.

A *neutral innovation* is the borderline case between these two.

Depending on which kind of innovation predominates at a particular time and place, one can say that technical change has a *labor-saving bias* or a *capital-saving bias.*

The character of technical progress in a particular economy has an obvious bearing on factor prices and factor shares. Neutral technical progress, by definition, raises MP_K and MP_L equally, and so would not change the P/W ratio. Progress with a labor-saving bias, however, would tend to raise P relative to W, while progress with a capital-saving bias would have the opposite effect.

There has been much discussion of the character of actual technical progress in the United States over the past century. It is usually argued that progress *should* have had a labor-saving bias, because there has been a strong incentive to labor-saving improvements. With labor supply increasing slowly relative to capital, and with labor becoming relatively more expensive, the problem of economizing labor has forced itself constantly on businessmen. It would be surprising if this were not reflected in the activities of inventors, engineers, and production managers. Some technical changes drop out of the blue as a by-product of basic scientific work; and there is no reason to expect that these *autonomous* inventions will be biased in one direction or the other. But to the extent that inventions are *induced* by an effort to lower production costs, one would expect them to have a labor-saving bias.

This surmise, however, has not yet been confirmed, nor refuted, by research. It is very difficult to match the available statistics against theoretical concepts, and such evidence as we have is still indirect and fragmentary.

To sum up: the evolution of labor and capital shares over time is influenced by (1) relative rates of increase in labor and capital supplies, (2) elasticity of capital–labor substitution, and (3) the labor-saving or capital-saving bias of technical progress.

On general grounds, there is no reason why relative income shares should remain constant. But it is easy enough to find combinations of circumstances under which they would do so. This would happen, for example, if (1) L and K increase at the same rate, and technical progress is absent or neutral; (2) with technical progress still absent or neutral, factor supplies increase at different rates, but elasticity of capital–labor substitution is unity; (3) one factor, say K, increases more rapidly than the other, elasticity of substitution is too low to offset this entirely, but substitution is helped out by technical change with a labor-saving bias. Substitution and technical progress together operate to sustain returns to capital, so that P/W falls at about the same rate as K/L rises. It is often asserted that something like this has happened in the United States over the last several generations.

Some Measurement Problems

When we turn to look at the evidence, we find a number of problems and difficulties. First, we must be clear about whether we are discussing income *earned* or income *received*. Recipients of profit income receive considerably less than they earn, because part is taken by the corporate income tax. The same is true on a smaller scale of wage and salary earners. Part of their compensation goes into private and public pension funds and other deferred benefits instead of being received currently.

When we come to consider household income distribution in Chapter 10, income received is the relevant concept. But here we are considering income *earned* or *produced*. We treat the total value product of each industry as divided between employee compensation and property income. Total profits before taxes, plus interest payments, are allocated to the property share. Labor income includes fringes and supplements as well as direct wage payments. The movements of the two shares, thus defined, tells us whether the price mechanism itself is redistributing income in one direction or the other.

A second problem arises from the shifting importance of different industries in the economy. In most countries, for example, government output has been rising relative to private output. The value of government output is conventionally defined as equal to the government payroll, so that the labor share of income produced is 100 percent. Thus if government output is increasing in relative importance, the national income statistics will show an increase in labor's share, even though factor shares in the private economy have not changed. Another illustration is agriculture, which has a relatively high property share because of the importance of land and mechanical equipment. Agricultural output as a percentage of national output has been declining for many decades, and this also tends to raise the labor share and reduce the property share for the economy as a whole. Because of these biases, most studies concentrate on the private nonfarm economy.

Third, certain groups in the economy—farmers, storekeepers, and other small business proprietors—have incomes that are a blend of labor and property income. They include payment for the proprietor's capital as well as his time. One can split these incomes apart statistically—for example, by assuming that an independent retailer's time is worth as much as that of an average chain-store employee, and treating the remainder of his income as attributable to capital. But such assumptions are always debatable, and so are the estimates based on them.

Short-Run Changes in Labor's Share

In the tangled literature of income distribution, it is encouraging to find something on which researchers agree. There is general agreement that labor's share of income produced in the private economy varies counter-cyclically. As output rises during an upswing, profits rise faster than output and labor's share declines. This is usually attributed to the "capacity effect," i.e. a decline in average fixed cost and average total cost as output rises.[9] Even if the product price does not rise, this permits a wider profit margin per unit. It is sometimes explained also by a presumed lag of wages behind prices during cycle upswings; but such a lag, if it exists at all, seems too small to make much contribution to profits.

During a decline in output, these tendencies are reversed. The profit share falls and the labor share of income rises. This is noticeable in Figure 4 for the recession years 1938, 1946, 1949, 1954, and 1958.[10] One moral is that conclusions about long-run changes in labor's share should be based on averages for a period of years rather than on single-year comparison. For example, a comparison of the boom year 1951 with the recession year 1958 would seem to show a marked rise in labor's share. But this may be due entirely to differences in utilization of plant capacity.

Long-Run Changes in Labor's Share

The evidence on long-run trends is less clear, partly because of the statistical difficulties mentioned earlier. For a long time, it was customary to say that the labor and capital shares are virtually constant, and theorists worked at developing models which would explain this presumed constancy. More recent studies suggest, however, that the

[9] The underlying assumption is that, in recession years, many firms are operating to the left of the minimum point on their average total cost curves. For manufacturing, at least, there seems good warrant for this assumption. The minimum point on the *ATC* curve is usually estimated at about 90 percent of physical plant capacity. During recession years since 1945, output rates have typically been in the range of 80–85 percent of capacity.

[10] Data for Figure 4 are from U.S. Department of Commerce, *National Income by Legal Form of Organization,* and *National Income by Industrial Origin: Manufacturing,* as reported in the Survey of Current Business. Employee compensation includes wage and salary disbursements, other employee income, and personal contributions for social insurance.

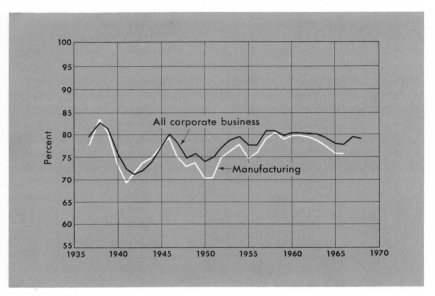

Figure 4

EMPLOYEE COMPENSATION AS A PERCENTAGE OF
INCOME PRODUCED, 1937–68

share of labor has increased moderately since 1900 or so, while that
of capital has fallen.

Three studies may be cited. A calculation by Irving Kravis, in which
the incomes of independent proprietors are allocated in a constant
proportion of 65 percent to labor and 35 percent to capital, shows
the property share of national income falling from 30.6 percent in the
years from 1900 to 1909 to 23.8 percent in 1949 to 1957.[11] Kendrick's
calculations for the private domestic economy show the capital share
of national income declining from 30.1 percent in 1899 to 18.6 percent
in 1957, with the labor share rising from 69.9 percent to 81.4 precent.[12]
Finally, Denison finds the labor share rising from 69.5 percent in 1909
to 1913 to 77.3 percent in 1954 to 1958, with property income declin-

[11] Irving B. Kravis, "Relative Income Shares in Fact and Theory," *American
Economic Review*, December, 1959, pp. 917–49. The tricky problem of splitting
up proprietors' income (which is itself declining in relative importance over time)
can of course be solved in several ways. Kravis applies three other methods in
addition to the one described. All show the property share declining, but by somewhat different amounts.

[12] John W. Kendrick, *Productivity Trends in the United States* (Princeton:
Princeton University Press, 1961), p. 121.

ing accordingly.[13] While these studies differ in detailed methodology, they all show property income shrinking from something like 30 percent at the beginning of the century to something like 20 percent today.[14]

There is similar evidence from other countries. For Canada, S. A. Goldberg has calculated that the wage share of nonfarm private business products, adjusted for shifts in the relative importance of industries, rose from 61.2 percent in the years 1926 to 1930 to 66.5 percent in the years 1954 to 1958.[15] Professor Simon Kuznets has made a wide-ranging inquiry [16] covering several of the industrialized countries for periods of up to 100 years. Some of his findings are reproduced in Table 1.

Two features of these estimates should be noted. First, they assume that the average labor income of independent proprietors was equal to the *average earnings of all employees in the economy*. This amount is then deducted from total proprietors' income to obtain the capital share. Second, the estimates are not adjusted for interindustry shifts and so, for reasons noted earlier, they exaggerate the actual increase in the labor share. The trends are so marked, however, and so consistent from country to country, that it seems reasonable to conclude that labor's share has risen even on an adjusted basis.

There is considerable evidence, then, that the capital share of income produced has been falling gradually in the long run. If true, this could be explained along the lines of our earlier discussion. In the richer industrial countries, the K/L ratio has been rising quite rapidly.

[13] Edward F. Denison, *The Sources of Economic Growth in the United States* (New York: Committee for Economic Development, 1962), p. 30.

[14] For other viewpoints on this problem, however, see Simon Kuznets, "Long-Term Changes in the National Income of the U.S.A. since 1870," *Income and Wealth*, Series II (London: Bowes and Bowes, 1952); Edward C. Budd, "Labor's Share of National Income" (unpublished dissertation, University of California, Berkeley, 1954); Clark Kerr, "Labor's Income Share and the Labor Movement," in George W. Taylor and Frank C. Pierson, eds., *New Concepts in Wage Determination* (New York: McGraw-Hill Book Company, 1957); Paul S. Sultan, "Unionism and Wage–Income Ratios, 1929–51," *Review of Economics and Statistics*, February, 1954; and Norman J. Simler, *The Impact of Unionism on Wage–Income Ratios in the Manufacturing Sector of the Economy* (Minneapolis: University of Minnesota Press, 1961).

[15] S. A. Goldberg, "Long-run Changes in the Distribution of Income by Factor Shares in Canada," in *The Behavior of Income Shares* (Studies in Income and Wealth, Vol. 27, published for the National Bureau of Economic Research by the Princeton University Press, 1964), 189–237. In a comment on this paper, Edward C. Budd concludes that the change in factor shares in Canada and the United States, using comparable definitions, was almost identical over this thirty-year period.

[16] Simon Kuznets, *Modern Economic Growth* (New Haven: Yale University Press, 1966). The data for Table 1 appear on pp. 168–70. See also several papers in Jean Marchal and Bernard Duclos, eds., *The Distribution of National Income* (New York: St. Martin's Press, Inc., 1968).

Table 1

DISTRIBUTION OF NATIONAL INCOME
AMONG FACTOR SHARES, SELECTED COUNTRIES, LONG PERIODS

	Compensation of Employees (percent)	*Income from Assets (percent)*
UNITED KINGDOM		
1860–69	54	46
1905–14	54	46
1920–29	66	34
1954–60	75	25
FRANCE		
1853	56	44
1911	66	34
1920–29	71	29
1954–60	81	19
GERMANY		
1895	53	47
1913	61	39
1925–29	79	21
1954–60	71	29
SWITZERLAND		
1924	65	35
1954–60	74	26
CANADA		
1926–29	81	19
1954–60	81	19
UNITED STATES		
1899–1908	76	24
1919–28	73	27
1954–60	81	19

Capital supply has been rising at 3 to 4 percent a year, labor supply at about 1 percent (though there is a considerable range of variation in individual countries). This tends to depress the interest rate relative to the wage rate. This tendency has been offset by capital–labor substitution and (possibly) by a labor-saving bias in technical progress. But the offsets have apparently not been fully sufficient. Not merely has the return to a unit of capital fallen relative to the return to a man-hour of labor—given the above rates of increase in factor supplies, this would have been almost inevitable. The point is that relative returns to capital have fallen [17] so much that, even when multiplied by

[17] The word "relative" should be emphasized. The absolute return to capital, in physical units, has risen moderately since 1900; but it has risen much less than real wages per man-hour. For the United States, Kendrick reports that "between 1919 and 1957, average hourly labor compensation increased at an average annual

a rapidly growing capital stock, the total capital share has diminished.

We do not enter here into the question whether the increase in labor's share has been accelerated by the growth of trade unionism and collective bargaining. It seems that union influence has been minor relative to that of factor supplies and technical change, but the reasons for this view must be deferred to Part III.

THE GROWTH
OF
NATIONAL OUTPUT

Between 1900 and 1965 real wages per man-hour in the United States rose more than fivefold, or about 2.6 percent per year. Far from slowing down, the rate of increase seems to be accelerating. For the twenty years from 1948 to 1968, it was slightly over 3 percent per year.

The modest increase in labor's income share is much too small to explain such a rapid rise of wages. Suppose we had perfect measures showing that labor's income share rose from 65 percent in 1900 to 80 percent in 1965, a 23 percent increase in labor's slice of the income pie. If the pie itself had remained unchanged, this would have allowed wages to rise less than 0.25 percent per year, instead of the actual 2.6 percent.

The main reason for rising real wages, obviously, is that the pie itself has been growing. There has been a rapid rise in total output and in output per man-hour of labor employed. A full explanation of this rise would lead us far afield into the theory of economic growth. But because of its direct bearing on wages, a few comments are in order.

Inputs, Outputs, and Productivity

Think of the national economy as a single giant producing mechanism. Into the machine at one end go certain quantities of inputs—land and natural resources, capital equipment, labor, management—and out the other end comes a stream of output, usually termed Gross National Product or GNP. If the supply of inputs is increasing year-by-year, as it has been in the United States, total output should also increase. But a 10 percent increase in output due solely to a 10 percent increase in inputs does not indicate any gain in the productivity of

---

rate of 4.0 percent—more than double the 1.5 percent average increase in the price of capital . . . The total increase over the thirty-eight years was 346 percent in the case of labor rates compared with 77 percent in the case of unit capital compensation." *Productivity Trends,* p. 117.

resources. One can speak of a gain in productivity only if total output is rising faster than total inputs.

There are many alternative concepts and measures of productivity. Partial productivity measures can be obtained by dividing output by a single input, most commonly labor or capital. When capital is used as divisor, the result is the capital–output ratio, which plays such a large part in discussions of economic growth and development policy. Using labor yields measures of output per worker or per man-hour worked. These partial measures are not very satisfactory, however, because changes in them are difficult to interpret. Suppose one finds that output per man-hour rose two percent a year over a certain period. This could have been due to increased skill and effort on the part of the workers. But it could also have been due entirely to the fact that workers were using increasing amounts of capital over the course of time. Or it could have been due to managerial improvements, or to a variety of other factors. The measurement itself provides no explanation.

John Kendrick has devised a more comprehensive productivity measure which incorporates both labor and capital. His technique is to calculate an index of the amount of labor used in production and an index of the real capital stock (including land). These are next combined by weighting each by the respective shares of labor and capital in national income, to yield an index of total factor input. This is then divided into the index of national output to yield a measure of what Kendrick terms "total factor productivity." [18]

Kendrick's measures cover the period 1889 to 1957 and show a sharp break around the year 1919. In the earlier period from 1889 to 1919, real GNP rose at an average annual rate of 3.9 percent, inputs of labor and capital rose at 2.6 percent, and factor productivity grew by 1.3 percent per year. Over the period 1919 to 1957, real GNP rose somewhat more slowly at 3.2 percent per year. There was a much greater slowdown, however, in the inputs of labor and capital, which rose at only 1.1 percent a year over this period. As regards labor, this reflects cessation of mass immigration, a reduced rate of natural increase, and a marked shortening of the workweek and work year. As regards capi-

[18] The basic relations used can be expressed as

$$\frac{Y}{Y_o} = C \left(a \frac{L}{L_o} + b \frac{K}{K_o} \right)$$

where the subscript o indicates base period quantities. a and b are the labor and capital shares of national income, and C is the measure of total factor productivity. See Kendrick, *Productivity Trends,* and the review article by Evsey D. Domar, "On Total Productivity and All That," *Journal of Political Economy,* December, 1962, pp. 597–608.

tal, it reflects the check to capital formation imposed by the Great Depression and by World War II. The amount of capital in use in 1945 was virtually the same as in 1929. Total factor productivity, then, rose by 2.1 percent a year from 1919 to 1957. The sharp decline in the growth of inputs was almost, though not quite, offset by a marked rise in the rate of productivity increase, yielding a rate of increase in output only moderately below that of the previous thirty years.

For recent decades, then, only about one-third of the increase in GNP is accounted for by increased amounts of labor and capital used in production. The remaining two-thirds is attributable to the rise in "total factor productivity." But what *is* total factor productivity? It is really little more than a confession of ignorance. It is an unexplained residual, due to "other factors" not included in the input measures.[19] If all the forces affecting the level of output were included in the production equation, then presumably any increase in output would be fully explained, and the productivity factor C could never increase. The fact that C does rise, and so rapidly, means that there are major forces at work which we have not succeeded in measuring.

Explaining the Residual

It is possible to identify some of the factors which have contributed to the residual rise in national output, even though we cannot yet measure their relative importance. They include the following.

1. *Qualitative Improvements in Labor and Capital.* The man-hours of labor in use today are not the same as those used in 1900. Today's workers are healthier, more vigorous, and longer-lived than their grandfathers. They have substantially larger amounts of education. The average member of the labor force in 1960 had spent $2\frac{1}{2}$ times as many days in school as his 1910 counterpart. Today's workers have on the average a considerably longer span of work experience in urban occupations. The fact that they work for fewer hours per week and per year than was true in 1900 probably means that they work a good deal more intensively during each hour.

A venturesome effort to quantify the effect of these improvements

[19] There have been numerous other attempts to measure and interpret this residual. While the results differ in detail, there is general agreement that the residual is large and that it accounts for most of the rise of national output in modern times. See in particular two papers by Robert M. Solow, "Technological Change and the Aggregate Production Function," *Review of Economics and Statistics,* August, 1957; and "Technical Progress, Capital Formation, and Economic Growth," *American Economic Review,* May, 1962; Denison, *Economic Growth* cited above; and B. F. Massell, "A Disaggregated View of Technical Change," *Journal of Political Economy,* December, 1961.

has been made by Edward Denison.[20] He calculates an index of labor inputs "adjusted for quality change." Over the period 1909 to 1957 this index rises by 183 percent, while the index of man-hours worked rises only 82 percent. The difference is accounted for mainly by the weight which he gives to increased education and to improved quality of a man-hour's work due to shorter hours, though increased experience is also credited with a small contribution to output. If these surmises are anywhere near correct, they would account for a major part of the unexplained residual.

Capital inputs are measured essentially by their real cost. But a new machine that costs the same and looks much the same as an older machine will often produce considerably more output. This means that technical progress is occurring; and one can say that the growth of technical knowledge is the real source of the greater output. Improved knowledge must usually be incorporated in physical capital, however, before it can begin to influence production. In recent decades there seems to have been marked improvements in buildings as well as in machinery and equipment. Because of changes in building design and space utilization, the ratio of ouput to floor space has risen sharply.

2. *Inputs Not Included in the Production Equation.* Kendrick's output measure is a measure of net output or value added. It thus takes no explicit account of raw materials, purchased energy, and other supplies consumed in the course of production. There have been important economies in the use of raw materials over the past half century. Kendrick estimates that net material product per unit of raw materials input more than doubled over the period 1900 to 1952,[21] and that this alone would account for about one-sixth of the observed increase in total factor productivity. There has also been a great increase in the amount of nonhuman energy used in production. Horsepower-hours of energy used per man-hour of work done rose from 0.72 in 1890 to 5.19 in 1950. This is related, of course, to growing mechanization of production; but it does not show up in the measures of capital input. Indeed, energy use has risen about three times as fast as capital input over the years since 1890.

[20] *Economic Growth,* chaps. 5–9. Kendrick's measure also takes account of changes in the occupational mix of the labor force. He relies mainly on a weighted index of labor inputs, in which different grades of labor are weighted by their relative wage levels. Thus a shift in the composition of employment toward skilled, technical, and professional occupations would show up as a rise in labor inputs. But employment on the same job, at the same relative wage level, which becomes more productive because of improved health, education, or training of successive generations of workers, would not be detected. It is this pervasive overall upgrading of the labor force that Denison has tried to measure.

[21] *Productivity Trends,* p. 95. This is partly due, of course, to a higher degree of processing—for example, in the case of food products—rather than to economies in the strict sense.

Another important input which does not show up in the production equation is management. Labor and capital do not manage themselves. The same plant and labor force may produce more or less, depending on how the work is organized and directed. There is reason to think that the quality of this input has risen markedly over the years. The scientific management movement of the early 1900s was the harbinger of a more systematic approach to management problems. Research on these problems has intensified steadily, leading most recently to a growing use of mathematical methods and computer techniques. University programs in business administration have grown greatly in size and sophistication, and the educational level of business executives today is much higher than in 1900. While one cannot measure the impact of these developments on productive efficiency, it has certainly been substantial.

3. *Technical Progress.* If capital accumulation consisted simply of adding more factories and more machines of the same type to produce the same products, national output would not rise nearly as fast as it does. Indeed, on this basis it would have been impossible for the American economy to generate and absorb the quadrupling of the capital stock which has occurred since 1900. With no change in production methods, the marginal productivity of capital, and consequently the returns on capital, would long since have fallen so low as to discourage further saving and investment.

An essential ingredient of economic growth, then, is continuous development of new and improved products, machines, and production methods. Some of this is done by industrial engineers and production executives as part of their day-to-day job. Some major developments come from spontaneous work by individual inventors. To an increasing extent, however, technical progress is planned by allocating part of corporation budgets to research and development activity. A large amount of basic scientific work is carried on also in universities and government laboratories. Total expenditure on research and development activities, which in 1940 was estimated at less than a billion dollars, is now approaching 15 billion dollars a year and is still increasing. The number of scientists and engineers in the labor force has risen from about 60,000 in 1900 to almost a million today. The results of scientific work are somewhat unpredictable, and one cannot say that a doubling of research activity will double the flow of useful inventions. Such a massive increase of effort, however, must be partly responsible for the apparent acceleration of productivity increase over the last several decades.

4. *Growing Size of the Economy.* Theories of production usually assume constant returns to scale. Increasing size of an industry, or of an entire economy, is not supposed by itself to change the ratio of output to inputs. This assumption is probably incorrect, and the

greatly increased size of the American economy today as compared with 1890 has probably had a favorable effect on productivity.

As an economy expands, the social overhead costs of transportation and communications networks, power facilities, and public services are spread over a larger volume of production. More and more industries are able to achieve their own optimum scale, which in the case of highly mechanized industries may be very large. A larger market permits greater industrial specialization and a fuller development of supplementary industries providing materials, components, and services. "The division of labor is limited by the size of the market," as Adam Smith observed two centuries ago.

Productivity and Wages: Some Qualifications

The notion that in the long run the rise of real wages is linked to the rise of productivity seems so obvious that it is in danger of being misunderstood. Wage changes show a good correspondence with the movement of man-hour output, as is evident from Figure 5. This correspondence holds, however, only *over considerable periods of time* and *for the economy as a whole.* One cannot expect that wage move-

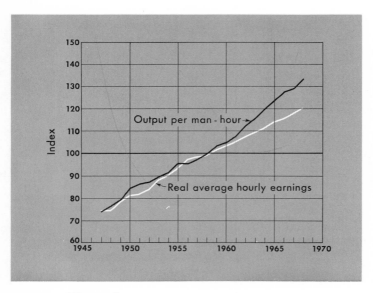

Figure 5

INDEXES OF PRIVATE NONFARM OUTPUT PER
MAN-HOUR AND NONFARM REAL AVERAGE HOURLY
EARNINGS, 1947–68 (1957–59 = 100)

ments and productivity movements will correspond within particular companies or industries.

The reason is that productivity trends vary widely from one branch of production to another. For the private economy as a whole, Kendrick's measure of total factor productivity rose at an average rate of 1.7 percent per year over the period 1899 to 1953. The rate of increase was 0.7 percent, however, in anthracite coal mining, 1.1 percent in farming, 2.0 percent in manufacturing, 3.2 percent in transportation, and 5.5 percent in electric utilities. Within manufacturing, the productivity increase averaged only 1.0 percent in lumber products but was 4.1 percent for rubber products.[22] When one considers that these rates of increase are compounded annually, it is obvious that productivity levels had pulled very far apart by the end of the period. Taking 1899 as 100, the productivity index for anthracite coal had risen by 1953 to only 147, whereas for electric utilities it had risen to 1,764.

If, then, wage changes in each industry were geared to productivity changes *in that industry,* the wage structure would rapidly be pulled apart. Wages of workers in electric power companies would rise to fantastic heights, while miners' wages would stagnate. Because of the transferability of labor on the supply side of the market, such extreme divergence of wages is unnecessary and unfeasible. In fact, Kendrick's calculations for thirty-three industry groups over the period 1899 to 1953 show no significant relation between rate of increase in factor productivity and rate of wage increase in the same industry.

What happens is rather that the wage level rises more or less evenly in all companies and industries (though not *entirely* evenly, as will appear in Chapter 9). The rate at which the wage tide rises is geared to the *average* rate of productivity increase in the economy. The impact of this rising tide on a particular industry depends on how its own rate of productivity increase compares with the general average.

An industry whose productivity rises faster than the wage level will experience a fall in unit labor costs and, probably, in unit total production costs. Under competitive conditions, this would mean a drop in prices—not necessarily in absolute terms, but relative to prices of goods in general. Even for a monopolist, a decline in unit costs will lower the profit-maximizing price. Research studies show that industries with an above average productivity increase do in fact show a decline in relative prices. Recently, for example, this has been true of electric power and of such manufactured products as plastics, radio and television sets, household appliances, tires and tubes, and synthetic fibres.[23] Partly because of these relatively low prices, output and

22 *Productivity Trends,* pp. 136–37.

23 For data on this point see *Annual Report of the Council of Economic Advisers,* 1965. See also Harold Wolozin, "Inflation and the Price Mechanism," *Journal of Political Economy,* October, 1959, pp. 463–75.

employment in such industries rise faster than in other industries. There is a marked relation over long periods between an industry's rate of productivity increase and its rate of output increase.

Industries in which output per man-hour rises more slowly than the wage level are in a less happy position. Their unit labor costs and, probably, unit total costs will be rising. This will force a relative rise in their selling prices, which in turn will tend to reduce sales, output, and employment. This seems to be the situation in many of the service industries. Barbers' productivity has not increased very much over the years; and so, as the general wage level has risen, the price of a haircut has gone up within living memory from $0.50 to $2.50—much more than the general price level. Longer hair and less frequent haircuts is a rational consumer response. In the case of products to which consumers are not strongly attached, the steady rise of costs and prices may gradually extinguish the industry. The long decline of the "legitimate theater" is a case in point.[24]

Depending on the behavior of demand, however, employment in such industries may rise rather than fall. A high rate of increase in demand can outweigh the effect of relatively higher prices and lead to an increase in output. Since labor requirements per unit of output are not falling materially, higher output will mean higher employment. Public education is a good example. Demand has been rising sharply, and so employment has risen despite a rapid advance of salary levels. The combination of rising employment and higher salaries has greatly increased educational budgets. This plus the rising cost of policing, fire protection, sanitation, and other public services whose cost is largely labor cost accounts for the severe budget pressure on state and local governments.

Discussion Questions

1. How can the real wage per man-hour *rise* even in years when national output is *falling?*
2. What did the classical economists believe would happen in the long run to the *rates of return* to land, labor, and capital?
3. In neoclassical or market theory, what determines the level of real wages at a particular time? What assumptions underlie the reasoning?
4. Explain the meaning of elasticity of substitution. Can you think

[24] The Baumol parable cited in Chapter 3 dramatizes this point effectively.

of industries in which one might expect elasticity of substitution to be

(a)   unusually high?

(b)   unusually low?

5.   What are the main factors determining whether labor's share of national income will rise or fall over time?

6.   Do recent ideas about income distribution advanced by Kalecki, Kaldor, Robinson, and others call for *substantial* modification of neoclassical reasoning?

7.   What has happened in the United States since 1900 to (a) the relative *prices* of labor and capital services, (b) the relative *shares* of labor and capital in national income? What reasons can you suggest for the apparent increase in labor's share?

8.   Explain and appraise Kendrick's concept of total factor productivity.

9.   What seem to be the main reasons for the rapid rise of total factor productivity in recent decades?

10.   "Wages depend basically on productivity. So to determine how much wages should be raised this year in a particular company or industry, one need look only at the increase in man-hour output." Discuss.

11.   How might one expect wages, prices, output, and employment to change over the course of time in an industry with zero productivity increase?

Reading Suggestions

For original statements of neoclassical distribution theory, see Clark, John Bates, *The Distribution of Wealth*. New York: The Macmillan Company, 1899; Marshall, Alfred, *Principles of Economics* (9th ed., Book VI). London: Macmillan & Co. Ltd., 1961. For more recent statements, see Hicks, J. R., *The Theory of Wages* (2nd ed.). New York: St. Martin's Press, Inc., 1966; Stigler, George J. *The Theory of Price*. New York: The Macmillan Company, 1966; and Phelps Brown, E. H., *The Economics of Labor,* chap. 7. New Haven: Yale University Press, 1962.

For statistical analysis of real wages, productivity, and relative income shares, see the studies of Denison, Kendrick, Kravis, and Kuznets cited above. See also National Bureau of Economic Research, *The Behavior of Income Shares*. Princeton: Princeton University Press,

1964; U.S. Department of Commerce, Bureau of the Census, *Long-term Economic Growth, 1860–1965.* Washington, D.C.: Government Printing Office, 1966; and Marchal, Jean, and Bernard Duclos, *The Distribution of National Income.* New York: St. Martin's Press, Inc., 1968.

DIFFERENCES IN WAGES

9

The last two chapters examined the *average* level of wages; but this conceals wide differences in individual earnings. One can still find workers in the United States earning a dollar an hour, while some business and professional people earn a hundred dollars an hour.

There are two main reasons for being interested in these wage differences. First, their size provides clues to the operation of labor markets and the efficiency of labor allocation. For example, if, relative to other occupations, people in one occupation are earning more than can be explained on a competitive basis, one is led to suspect a supply blockage or some other market imperfection, which can be explored through further research. Or suppose that, within an occupation, there are wage differences among employers greater than can be explained by differences in labor force quality. Again, one is led to explore the nature of employers' wage decisions. Much of the progress in labor market analysis has been stimulated by observation of wage differences that seemed impossible to explain on competitive grounds.

Second, the striking differences in income distribution among families in the United States arise largely from differences in the earnings of family members. Property income will be given its due weight in Chapter 10. But since about four-fifths of household income in the United States is labor income, we must look mainly to inequality of labor incomes to explain overall inequality. To the extent that one is interested either in understanding income distribution or in changing it, one is forced to explore the reasons for differences in earnings.

Occupation is one important factor determining a person's earnings. Professional men and business executives normally earn more than sales clerks. Skilled craftsmen earn more than laborers.

Even within the same occupation, however, some people earn much more than others. Harold Lydall has estimated that for the United States in 1959, about 75 percent of the total inequality of earnings resulted from differences *within* each occupation, and only 25 percent from differences among occupations in average earnings level.[1] Wage rates within an occupation are influenced by the company and industry in which one is employed, by size of city and region of the country, by education and training, by personal ability, and by numerous other factors. In addition, annual earnings are influenced by regularity of employment. On this account, dispersion of annual earnings is highest among common laborers and low-skilled service workers.

First, then, we shall examine differences among occupations. We shall try wherever possible to check general reasoning against statistical information; but this is not as easy as it might seem. We should like to compare the *price* of different kinds of labor, per unit of time; but the data are hardly ever available in this form. Most of the data on manual workers relate to *average hourly earnings,* which as we saw in Chapter 7 are considerably different from *wage rates.* Information about white-collar earnings is much less abundant, and usually takes the form of *weekly or monthly salaries,* with hours often unspecified. The only information available for the whole range of occupations is on *annual earnings,* and this is available only every ten years from the decennial census. In between censuses, the Census Bureau conducts sample surveys that yield average annual earnings for broad occupational groups, but not for specific occupations within these groups. Annual earnings, which are much influenced by time worked during the year, do not correspond at all closely to the price of labor; but we are nevertheless forced to rely heavily on them.

A further difficulty is that most of our data cover only *current money payments* to employees, where we should really be comparing *total employee compensation.* Total compensation includes such things as employer contributions to Social Security and to private pension plans; medical, hospital, and life insurance benefits provided by the employer

1 Harold Lydall, *The Structure of Earnings* (Oxford: Oxford University Press, 1968), pp. 103–4.

under group plans; and vacations, paid holidays, and other payments for time not worked. Such supplementary payments have grown considerably faster than wages since 1945, and now form about a quarter of total employee compensation in the larger companies of the country.[2]

If supplementary payments varied in the opposite direction from current money payments, then wage data would exaggerate the true size of differentials in compensation. There is much evidence, however, that the actual relation is positive—larger supplements accompany higher earnings. Indeed, not merely do supplements vary positively with earnings, but the *ratio of supplements to earnings* also varies positively.[3] This means that wage differentials progressively understate true compensation differentials as one goes up the occupational ladder. When one reaches the top executive levels in large corporations, direct salary payments form only about one-third of total compensation.

OCCUPATIONAL
WAGE
DIFFERENCES

General Principles

The theory of occupational differentials in a competitive labor market was developed in Chapter 4, and we need only remind the reader of what was said there. Occupations differ in numerous important dimensions—in the inherent pleasantness or unpleasantness of the work, in the social esteem it enjoys, in regularity of employment, in costs of learning the occupation, and in the chances of success or failure. Some of these characteristics are irremovable, while others change only gradually over long periods. The most flexible element in the system is rates of pay. Given free choice of occupations, then, the wage structure would adjust itself so as to equalize the *net advantage* of various occupations to people on the margin of decision, including young people entering the labor force. *Wage differences would be equalizing differences* and would serve to offset differences in job characteristics that cannot be readily changed.

Since the competitive labor market is a hypothesis rather than a reality, we cannot say precisely what a competitive wage structure would look like. One suspects that wage differences would be smaller than they presently are, but how much smaller is difficult to judge.

[2] See the further discussion of this point in chap. 22 and the references there cited.

[3] On this point see Robert G. Rice, "Skill, Earnings, and the Growth of Wage Supplements," *AEA Proceedings*, May, 1966, pp. 583–93.

There are several reasons why earning differentials may differ from what they would be in competitive equilibrium. First, as Phelps Brown has correctly insisted, custom and tradition have a strong influence on wage setting.[4] He cites the interesting example of the British construction industry, where over six centuries the wage of a laborer has tended to be about two-thirds that of a craftsman—sometimes departing from this norm for a while, but later returning to it. The medieval notion of the "just price" has largely disappeared. But the concept of the "just wage" dies harder. It would seem odd to most people if sanitation workers were to earn more than electricians, or if civil servants were to earn more than business executives. Occupations are layered one above the other in social status, and this ranking does not change much over the years. The notion that a man is entitled to earn enough to live "according to his station" is perhaps more prevalent in Europe than in the more fluid societies of Canada or the United States; but even here it lurks in the background of thinking about relative wages.

Second, there are barriers to movement from one occupational level to another. Once a man has left school and has been at work for some years, he is usually "locked in" to a narrow range of occupations. He may move a short distance up the occupational ladder, but any large movement is difficult. It is easier for children of families at one level to move to a higher level via the educational system. But even here there are the barriers described in Chapter 6: parental ignorance and short-sightedness, inability to finance costs of higher education, and capacity limits of educational institutions.

The importance of such barriers was emphasized particularly by J. E. Cairnes, writing in mid-nineteenth century Britain:

> What we find, in effect, is not a whole population competing indiscriminately for all occupations, but a series of industrial layers, superposed on one another, within each of which the various candidates for employment possess a real and effective power of selection, while those occupying the several strata are, for all purposes of effective competition, practically isolated from each other . . . the average workman, from whatever rank he be taken, finds his power of competition limited for practical purposes to a certain range of occupations, so that, however high the rates of remuneration in those which lie beyond may rise, he is excluded from sharing them. We are thus compelled to recognize the existence of noncompeting industrial groups as a feature of our social economy.[5]

---

[4] See particularly his *Economics of Labor*, chap. 5, and the references cited there.

[5] J. E. Cairnes, *Some Leading Principles of Political Economy Newly Expounded* (New York: Harper and Brothers, 1874), pp. 64–68.

If Cairnes' noncompeting groups were in fact watertight compartments, then relative earnings would be determined in the same way as the terms of exchange between two trading nations. Earnings would depend on the supply of labor within each group, presumably determined by birth- and death rates, and on the trend of demand for the skills supplied by each group. Suppose, for example, that unskilled laborers have a high birthrate and that demand for laborers is rising slowly, while professional people have a low birthrate and demand for their services is rising rapidly. The earnings gap between them would then widen steadily in the course of time.

In the contemporary United States, the walls between occupational compartments are rather permeable, and this tends to check such divergent movements of earnings. But mobility is by no means complete, and so Cairnes's reasoning retains considerable force.

Third, reasoning about wage differentials under pure competition typically relates to equilibrium positions. It aims to answer the question: given the characteristics of each job, the level of demand for each job, the preferences of each member of the labor force, and free choice of occupation, *and* given that these conditions remain unchanged long enough for each person to reach his preferred position, where will relative wages "settle down"?

In actuality, however, supply adjustments for higher occupations take considerable time, because of the length of training periods; and meanwhile, demand will probably have shifted once more. If upward shifts of demand are frequent, if these shifts are not perfectly anticipated, and if supply adjustments are slow, supply may never catch up with demand. Relative earnings may differ permanently from what they would be if equilibrium could be attained.

Fourth, many wages are influenced by union wage policies and collective bargaining negotiations. Unions can sometimes (though not always) raise the wages of their members relative to other groups in the economy. In some parts of this chapter we shall comment on possible union influences, but a full analysis of the evidence must wait until Part Three.

Occupational Differences in the American Economy

Turning to the size of occupational differences in the United States, look first at Table 1.[6] This shows the annual earnings from wages or salaries of male workers at various occupational levels who were employed from fifty to fifty-two weeks during the year. Using data for

[6] Data for 1967 are from the Bureau of the Census, *Current Population Reports,* Series P–60, June 1969. Data for 1939 and 1955 are from a 1960 census monograph by Herman P. Miller, *Income Distribution in the United States* (Washington, D.C.: Government Printing Office, 1966), p. 82.

Table 1

MEDIAN WAGE AND SALARY INCOME,
MALE YEAR-ROUND WORKERS,
BY MAJOR OCCUPATION GROUP,
1939, 1955, AND 1967

MEDIAN ANNUAL INCOME

Occupation Group	1939		1955		1967	
	Dollars	*Index (laborers = 100)*	*Dollars*	*Index (laborers = 100)*	*Dollars*	*Index (laborers = 100)*
PROFESSIONAL AND TECHNICAL	2,100	212	5,382	174	10,023	190
SELF-EMPLOYED	n.a.	n.a.	n.a.	n.a.	16,018	301
SALARIED	n.a.	n.a.	n.a.	n.a.	9,773	184
MANAGERS, PROPRIETORS, AND OFFICIALS	2,254	227	5,584	180	9,711	182
SELF-EMPLOYED	n.a.	n.a.	n.a.	n.a.	7,636	143
SALARIED	n.a.	n.a.	n.a.	n.a.	10,381	195
CLERICAL	1,564	157	4,162	134	6,939	130
SALES	1,451	146	4,937	160	7,910	149
CRAFTSMEN	1,562	157	4,712	152	7,557	142
OPERATIVES	1,268	128	4,046	131	6,409	120
SERVICE, EXCEPT PRIVATE HOUSEHOLD	1,019	103	3,565	115	5,584	105
FARM LABORERS AND FOREMEN	365	37	n.a.	n.a.	2,694	51
LABORERS, EXCEPT FARM	991	100	3,105	100	5,323	100

year-round workers rather than all workers should eliminate most of the variation arising from irregularity of employment. Earnings are still not the same thing as rates of pay, because of the inclusion of overtime, bonuses, and other supplementary items. But they are the best indicator we have covering the whole range of occupations.

The year 1939 provides a pre-World War II base for comparison. The year 1955 is the first postwar year for which data are available on year-round workers. Data for 1967 are the most recent available at this writing. For each year, the earnings of higher occupational groups have been reduced to a percentage of laborers' earnings, to facilitate comparison of changes in occupational differentials.

The rank order of incomes in Table 1 is about what one would expect. Within the professional group, independent practitioners average much more than salaried workers. The main reason is that the salaried group is heavily weighted with schoolteachers, whose median earnings are still relatively low despite the rapid advance in recent years. Within the business group, on the other hand, the opposite relation holds: salaried executives earn substantially more than independent proprietors, most of whom operate stores, service establishments, and other small businesses. The reasons for this difference have not been thoroughly investigated. Is the self-employed proprietor less capable, on the average? Does he value independence so highly that he deliberately sacrifices income to achieve it? Or is he a perennial optimist, always expecting to make more than he actually does make, and never learning from experience?

Looking at trends over time one notes that, during the period of very high employment and substantial inflation from 1939 to 1953, the two top occupational groups lost considerable ground relative to manual labor. Since 1955, on the other hand, the earnings of professional men have risen faster than those of any other group, and the relative position of the professional group has improved considerably. But this is not true of the business group, whose relative earnings remain well below the prewar level. Clerical workers have lost ground continuously, and their premium over the common laborer is only about half of what it was in 1939. Within the manual group, the earnings of skilled and semiskilled workers have fallen moderately relative to those of laborers. Farm workers continue to be by far the lowest-paid group in the economy, though their relative position has been somewhat better in the sixties than in the thirties.

Table 2 shows the relative weekly earnings of major occupational groups in Canada at various dates. Note first that the earnings hierarchy is broadly similar to that in the United States. Note also that the income advantage of the higher occupational groups diminished considerably between 1931 and 1951. This happened also in the United States. Indeed, this trend toward smaller occupational dif-

Table 2

WEEKLY EARNINGS OF MALE WAGE
AND SALARY EARNERS, CANADA, 1931–51

Occupation Group	INDEX OF AVERAGE * WEEKLY EARNINGS *(laborers = 100)*		
	1931	*1941*	*1951*
MANAGERIAL	345	283	226
PROFESSIONAL	268	212	185
CLERICAL, COMMERCIAL, FINANCIAL	171	156	139
SKILLED	176	147	145
SEMISKILLED	137	130	135
LABORERS, NONPRIMARY	100	100	100
LABORERS, AGRICULTURAL	50	63	49

* Mean earnings for 1931; median earnings for 1941 and 1951.
SOURCE: H. D. Woods and Sylvia Ostry, *Labour Policy and Labour Economics in Canada* (Toronto: Macmillan of Canada, 1962), p. 425.

ferentials and the reasons behind it provide the main theme of this section.

The decennial census makes possible a more detailed analysis of annual earnings. Table 3 gives data on a few groups selected from a longer list of 321 occupations.[7] The number at the left gives the rank of each occupation on this list. The earnings index gives average annual earnings in the occupation as a percentage of laborers' earnings. The final two columns contain educational and employment information that has some bearing on earnings.

Table 3 reveals that, within each broad occupational category, there is a wide range of earnings for specific occupations. In the professional group, for example, doctors are number 1 on the list, but high-school teachers are 117 and clergymen are 245, just above semiskilled factory workers. The highest paid skilled craft, airline pilots, are number 6; but painters, because of irregular employment as well as lower skill, are number 259. In the sales category, advertising agents and salesmen are number 87, but retail sales clerks are 251.

This means that the broad groupings, instead of being layered neatly one above the other as Table 1 suggests, show a great deal of overlap. Airplane pilots earn more than most professional and managerial people. Tool-and diemakers earn more than most clerical workers. Factory operatives earn more than retail clerks.

[7] The full list appears in Max A. Ratzich, "A Ranking of U.S. Occupations by Earnings," *Monthly Labor Review*, March, 1965, pp. 249–55. The earnings figures, derived from the 1960 census, cover the calendar year 1959. While they are now out-of-date as regards absolute level, the relative ranking has probably not changed materially.

The education column reveals a marked relation between average earnings and years of formal education. Note, however, the low rank of sales clerks despite their high school training, and the low rank of high-school teachers and clergymen even after college and some

Table 3

A RANKING OF U.S. OCCUPATIONS
BY ANNUAL EARNINGS

Rank	Title	Median Earnings 1959	Earnings Index (Laborers = 100)	Median Years of Schooling	Percent Employed Full Year
1	Physicians	14,561	477	17.5	77.9
2	Managers, self-employed, banking and finance	12,757	418	14.3	80.0
5	Lawyers and judges	10,587	387	17.4	86.4
6	Airplane pilots and navigators	10,274	337	13.5	82.7
8	College presidents and deans	9,704	318	17.4	86.4
10	Managers, salaried, manufacturing	9,090	298	13.1	92.6
17	Economists	8,649	283	16.8	88.3
60	Electrotypers and stereotypers	7,042	231	11.7	84.4
63	Foremen, manufacturing	6,932	227	11.8	90.6
76	Tool- and diemakers	6,503	213	11.7	77.2
87	Advertising agents and salesmen	6,286	206	13.3	79.8
104	Locomotive firemen	5,969	196	11.7	60.7
117	Teachers, secondary schools	5,827	191	17.2	46.9
149	Stenographers	5,379	176	12.6	80.0
153	Actors	5,349	175	14.1	28.3
161	Policemen and detectives	5,272	173	12.2	90.2
169	Clerical workers, public utilities	5,200	170	12.2	83.2
245	Clergymen	4,008	131	17.1	87.8
248	Operatives, manufacturing	3,938	129	9.4	61.6
251	Salesmen and sales clerks, retail	3,897	128	12.1	67.9
259	Painters	3,708	121	9.1	37.7
273	Spinners, textile	3,450	113	8.1	65.9
298	Charwomen and cleaners	2,539	83	8.9	48.3
303	Farmers (owners and tenants)	2,155	71	8.7	79.2
307	Garage laborers, car washers and greasers	1,906	62	9.4	44.6
316	Farm laborers	1,080	35	7.9	41.0

graduate training. The employment column indicates that the low ranking of some occupations results partly from their failure to provide regular employment throughout the year. Note that 86 percent of lawyers and college presidents, but only 37 percent of painters and 28 percent of actors reported steady year-round employment.

We proceed now to take a closer look at several major occupational groups: professional people, salaried business executives, clerical and sales workers, skilled and unskilled manual workers, and farmers. In each case we shall be concerned with the present earnings position of the group, but even more importantly with trends in this position. Has the relative earnings level of the higher-paid groups been improving or deteriorating over time? Have occupational differentials in the economy been widening or narrowing? Can the evidence be interpreted satisfactorily in terms of the general principles set forth above?

The Professions

Professional workers, and particularly the self-employed professionals, have the highest average incomes in the economy. Doctors earn almost five times as much as laborers, lawyers almost four times as much, economists three times as much.

There is of course wide variation around these averages. A top surgeon may earn $100,000 a year, while a country doctor earns $10,000 or less. Similarly for lawyers, engineers, and others. Ph.D.'s in nonteaching activities earn more than those in teaching positions; [8] and teaching salaries vary widely from the top universites to the smallest colleges. Thus a person training for one of the professions cannot be sure where he will eventually arrive on the income scale. If most people are risk averters, this uncertainty is a disadvantage which will deter entrance and cause *average* incomes in the professions to be higher than otherwise. If, on the other hand, Adam Smith was right in thinking that most people have an "overweening conceit" in their own ability and good fortune, the reverse will be true.[9]

The other key characteristic of the professions is their long training

---

[8] This is true, at any rate, in the natural and social sciences, though the reverse seems to be true in the humanities. For an interesting analysis, see Orley Ashenfelter and Joseph D. Mooney, "Graduate Education, Ability, and Earnings," *Review of Economics and Statistics*, February, 1968, pp. 78–86.

[9] "The over-weening conceit which the greater part of men have of their own abilities, is . . . remarked by the philosophers and moralists of all ages. Their absurd presumption in their own good fortune, has been less taken notice of . . . There is no man living who, when in tolerable health and spirits, has not some share of it. The chance of gain is by every man more or less over-valued, and the chance of loss is by most men undervalued." *The Wealth of Nations*, Book 1, chap. 10.

period. Most of them require six to eight years of higher education. To the extent that the student or his parents bear this training cost, and to the extent that he makes an economic calculation, he must expect to recover it with interest over his working life. This consideration warrants an earnings differential for the professions; and the appropriate size of this differential can be calculated roughly from data on educational costs and market rates of interest.

Most professions seem to yield a larger earnings differential than could be explained either by training costs or by scarcity of natural ability. Considering that they are also preferable on other grounds, such as steadiness and security of work, prestige, independence, and intrinsic interest, one is bound to ask why. Custom and tradition may provide part of the answer. But it seems probable also that fewer young people get through the educational bottleneck than would do so under conditions of perfect information, adequate financing, and free occupational choice. Even in the United States, the cost of higher education still bars many people; and for some professions, at least, there are not enough university places even for those able and willing to bear the cost.

If this is an important part of the explanation, one might expect to observe a relation between the size of the professional differential, country by country, and the proportion of young people admitted to higher education. Professor Tibor Scitovsky has tested this hypothesis [10] and found it to be well supported by the evidence. As a measure that could be obtained for many countries, he took the salary of a highly paid natural scientist (the head of the national meteorological service), as a multiple of an office messenger's pay. This showed a good inverse relation to higher educational enrollments as a percentage of population. The less-developed countries, with low educational enrollments, typically showed the meteorologist receiving 10 to 20 times as much as the messenger, and in India and Pakistan the multiple was near 30. In the developed countries, on the other hand, the multiple was typically in the range of 3 to 5.

Looking at events over time, college enrollments have been rising relative to population in most countries; and as predicted, the ratio of professional earnings to average earnings of the population has been falling. Some of the evidence for the United States is summarized in Table 4. The course of events has been broadly similar in Canada, the United Kingdom, France, Germany, and the Scandinavian countries.[11]

The one significant exception is the medical profession in the United States, which has been widening its advantage over other occupations.

[10] Tibor Scitovsky, "The Trend of Professional Earnings," *American Economic Review,* March, 1966, pp. 25–42.
[11] Scitovsky, "Professional Earnings," pp. 35–40.

Table 4

PROFESSIONAL EARNINGS
AS MULTIPLES OF PER CAPITA INCOME
OF OCCUPIED POPULATION, UNITED STATES

Year	Physicians	Dentists	Lawyers	Professors	Top Civil Servants
1910				3.7	6.1
1929	2.9	2.4	3.1	3.7	6.1
1939	3.2	2.4	3.3	4.3	7.1
1950	3.3	2.0	2.2	2.0	2.8
1958	4.2	2.8	2.4	2.1	4.1

There has been much discussion of a shortage of doctors in the United States, and of the failure of supply to keep pace with rising demand. The concept of shortage is tricky, and some of the indicators usually presented are not necessarily convincing.[12] There does not seem, for example, to be a shortage in the sense that people cannot get as much medical service as they are willing to buy at prevailing prices. Price rations supply, as it does elsewhere in the economy. Again, it is interesting but not conclusive that the number of doctors per 100,000 population is no larger today than it was in 1920. There is no natural law that a certain physical ratio is correct (bushels of potatoes grown per 100,000 population have fallen considerably since 1920). Only on certain assumptions about income elasticity and price elasticity of demand for medical services can one argue that the doctor–patient ratio should have increased.

The most convincing indications of supply restriction are perhaps the following:

1. The number of young people who, weighing income and other considerations, believe it worthwhile to become doctors is much larger than the number admitted to the profession. The ratio of medical school admissions to applications has been falling, and is now less than one-half. Considering that the applicants have presumably completed a college premedical course, many qualified people must have been rejected.

2. In recent years the output of medical graduates has been insufficient to staff the internship and residency positions which are a normal step in postgraduate medical training and an important part of hospital operations. About one-quarter of the internships available have remained unfilled. And of those that are filled, the proportion filled by foreign medical graduates has risen from 10 percent in 1950

[12] For a careful appraisal of the evidence, see Rashi Fein, *The Doctor Shortage: An Economic Diagnosis* (Washington, D.C.: The Brookings Institution, 1967).

to about 25 percent at present. We have been maintaining our supply of medical services partly by large imports of doctors from other parts of the world, including the less-developed countries.

3. The widening earnings differential is a further indicator of supply difficulties. It is true that training costs have been rising, as a growing percentage of doctors enter specialties requiring some years of apprenticeship beyond medical school. This might warrant some widening of the earnings gap, but scarcely at the rate observed in recent years.

There are strong indications, then, that the market for medical practitioners is out of equilibrium, and that investment in additional training capacity would yield high social returns. Because of the high cost of medical school construction, most of this will necessarily be public investment.

Business Management

It is clear from Table 1 that the *average* salary level in business is quite moderate. But here, even more than in the professions, there is wide variation of salaries within the group. Thousands of minor executives work for $10,000 a year; but the president of a major corporation may get $500,000.

It is the fact of the high salaries at the top of the business pyramid which calls for explanation. They are scarcely determined in a competitive market, for intercompany movement at the top executive levels is rare. On the contrary, a man normally achieves top rank by spending many years in the company and moving up to successively higher levels in the hierarchy. Top executives, in effect, determine their own salaries, within limits of accepted business practice and stockholders' tolerance.

There is quite a close relation between top executives' salaries and *size* of company, as measured by assets, sales, or profits.[13] This can be rationalized on the ground that large companies require greater effort and ability. It may result also from the rules of thumb used in salary setting. A common principle is that those at one level in the hierarchy should receive a standard premium—say 50 percent—above those at the next lower level. The larger the company, the more levels in the hierarchy, and the higher a figure one comes out with at the top.

The actual compensation of top executives is not easy to determine. With a 70 percent marginal income tax rate, an extra $100,000 in salary for the company president may enrage the stockholders without

[13] See, for example, the analysis in Wilbur G. Lewellen, *Executive Compensation in Large Industrial Corporations* (New York: National Bureau of Economic Research, 1968). Lewellen found that correlations of salary level with company size over the years 1940 to 1963 were almost invariably significant at 1 percent level.

greatly benefiting the executive. So there has been a strong trend, particularly since 1950, toward paying executives in forms that are either nontaxable or taxable at less than the personal income tax rates. The commonest forms are pension rights, other types of deferred compensation to be paid after the executive's retirement (when he will presumably be in a lower tax bracket), and issuance of stock options.[14]

To determine total compensation, then, one has to estimate the present value of these future rights. Wilbur Lewellen has made estimates for the five top executives of the fifty largest manufacturing corporations over the period 1940 to 1963. He finds that, on average over the years 1955 to 1963, the *chief officers* (presidents or board chairmen) of these companies received the equivalent of $210,663 *after taxes*. Of this, salary and bonuses constituted $80,833 (38 percent), pensions $31,288 (15 percent), deferred compensation and profit sharing $23,645 (11 percent) and stock options $74,897 (36 percent). The *top five executives* of these companies during the same period averaged $128,940 after taxes, of which salary and bonus was about one-half. This was about double the posttax earnings of the top five executives of these companies in 1940, which averaged $59,740.

Has the salary premium of business executives declined in the course of time? Both Table 1 and the Lewellen study suggest that such a relative decline has occurred. Lewellen finds that posttax earnings of top executives doubled between 1940 and 1963. This is well below the increase for all gainfully employed persons. Over this same period, however, the posttax earnings of junior executives, as indicated by starting salaries of M.B.A. graduates, increased about four times. Thus top executives lost ground, both relative to junior executives and to the working population in general.[15]

The implication is that salaries of beginning executives are heavily influenced by market forces, and that demand for executives has more or less kept pace with the rising supply of college and M.B.A. graduates. But top executive salaries, as noted earlier, have a strong conventional element, which may lead them to move more sluggishly. The sharp increase in the level and progressiveness of personal income tax-

---

14 The rules governing use of stock options are set by federal legislation and are somewhat complicated. Essentially, however, a stock option is a right to buy a certain number of shares of the company's common stock at a specified price, normally near the market price at the time the option is issued. The option may be exercised at any time within five years after issue. If the price of the stock rises subsequently, the executive can benefit by using his option to buy stock below the market price and later reselling it at a profit (though he must hold it for at least three years after buying). Any profit is considered a capital gain rather than ordinary income, and is taxed at a maximum rate of 25 percent.

15 In Britain, on the other hand, the relative position of business managers seems to have changed little since 1914. See Guy Routh, *Occupation and Pay in Great Britain, 1906–60* (Cambridge: Cambridge University Press, 1965), p. 107.

ation since the mid-thirties may also have had considerable influence. If top executives had maintained their relative posttax position in the face of these increases, it would have meant pushing pretax compensation up to levels unacceptable to stockholders and the general public. The more effective publicizing of top executives' compensation under SEC regulations may also have had a cautionary effect.

Clerical and Sales Workers

As we move down the ladder to routine white-collar work, the educational system again occupies the center of the stage, but now at the high school rather than the college level. High school graduation has been a traditional requirement for white-collar employment; and conversely, graduates have tended to feel themselves entitled to white-collar work.

The rapid rise in the percentage of each age-group that completes high school is thus a significant supply development. Only 18 percent of the children born between 1886 and 1890 ended up as high school graduates 17 to 18 years later. Of those born between 1936 and 1940 62 percent completed high school. Interestingly enough, the main reason is a steady increase in the percentage of youngsters who *finish primary school and enter high school*. The ratio of *high school graduates to high school entrants* has risen only moderately over the years.[16] We are now approaching a situation in which three-quarters or more of each age cohort will have completed a high school course. For the majority, this will have been an "academic" or a "commercial" course, oriented toward white-collar activity.

At the same time, demand for sales and clerical workers has been rising rapidly. Between 1930 and 1968, employment in these occupational groups rose by 138 percent, while total employment rose only 55 percent. Only professional and technical workers show a higher rate of demand increase.

While both demand and supply schedules have been shifting to the right, the supply shift has clearly been more rapid. In addition to the increasing number of high school graduates, there is the marked increase in labor force participation by adult women noted in Chapter 2. Most of these women have white-collar skills and expectations, and so swell the labor supply in this area.

This leads to a prediction that white-collar earnings will have fallen relative to manual earnings over the past several decades. While the evidence is fragmentary, it tends to support this hypothesis. An early study by McCaffree concluded that the premium for white-collar

---

16 For an interesting analysis of enrollment and graduation trends, see Beverly Duncan, "Dropouts and the Unemployed," *Journal of Political Economy*, April, 1965, pp. 121–34.

work had been falling gradually for at least fifty years prior to 1939, mainly because of the rapid increase in the number of high school graduates.[17] In 1939, however, the annual earnings of white-collar workers were still about 40 percent above those of all manual workers. This advantage was further eroded by the inflation of the years 1940 to 1949. During periods of rapid inflation, there is a tendency for wage increases to be given as *equal absolute amounts* to all skill levels in the labor force, and this reduces the *percentage* difference between them. Thus by 1950 skilled manual workers had pulled ahead of the white-collar group, and even semiskilled workers were getting quite close to them. This continues to be true today. The relative earnings position of white-collar workers seems to have been lowered permanently as compared with the pre-1940 years, and some further decline may be expected in the future.

Routh's study of British occupational differentials also reveals a marked decline in relative earnings for men clerical workers, but only a slight decline for women. The comparison is as follows, using unskilled earnings as the base:

	1913–14		1960	
	Men	*Women*	*Men*	*Women*
CLERICAL	144	160	127	151
SKILLED	144	157	148	141
SEMISKILLED	109	174	108	122
UNSKILLED	100	100	100	100

The data for intervening years indicate that the relative decline of white-collar male salaries in Britain occurred in two jumps, during the sharp inflations of World War I and World War II. Since 1950, the clerical workers have, if anything, improved their position relative to manual workers. This seems also to have been true in Canada,[18] where salaries have risen rather faster than wages in the postwar period.

Skilled and Unskilled Labor

For manual occupations we have information on wage rates over a considerable period in the past. This shows both short-term and long-

17 K. M. McCaffree, "The Earnings Differential Between White-Collar and Manual Occupations," *Review of Economics and Statistics,* February, 1953, pp. 20–30.

18 For a review of wage trends in Canada since 1946, see George Saunders, *Wage Determination in Canada* (Ottawa: Economics and Research Branch, Department of Labour, 1965).

term movements in the differential between skilled and unskilled wages. The differential appears to narrow in boom periods and to widen again in depression. Differentials narrowed especially fast during the years 1916 to 1920 and 1940 to 1949, periods of inflation and full employment associated with the two world wars. Inflation and severe labor shortage seem to raise low wage rates faster (percentagewise) than higher rates and thus reduce the percentage spread between them. After the end of each war boom differentials have tended to widen again, but have not rebounded all the way to the prewar level. Thus the long-run tendency has been for occupational differentials to decline.

Nor is this tendency characteristic only of the United States. For Britain, Professor Fogarty reports that "skill and responsibility differentials have narrowed markedly since 1913 and especially since 1938, but the process has been stepwise and not continuous. . . . Differentials between skilled and unskilled manual workers narrowed sharply in the first World War, widened a little in the years of deflation after it, and stabilized again from 1924 to 1939. There was then another sharp squeeze during the second World War and the years of acute inflation and shortages till 1949. Differentials then once again leveled off, and there has been no further general change till the present." [19]

The American data have been examined in detail by Ober.[20] He calculates that in 1907 the average wage level of skilled workers in manufacturing was roughly double (105 percent above) that of unskilled workers. The advantage of the skilled workers fell to 75 percent in the years 1918 to 1919, 65 percent from 1937 to 1940, 55 percent from 1945 to 1947, and to something like 45 percent in the early fifties. Similar trends are observable in most other lines of industry. In building construction, for example, union rates for craftsmen were almost exactly double (98 percent above) those of laborers in 1914. This figure fell to 80 percent in 1923, 70 percent in 1938, 54 percent in 1945, and 38 percent in 1952. Speaking roughly, one can say that sixty years ago it was normal for craftsmen to receive wage rates twice as high as those for common laborers in the same industry. Today it is normal for them to receive one-third to one-half more than laborers. The gap in *earnings* remains wider than this, however, because of differences in regularity of employment, overtime earnings, and other things.

[19] M. P. Fogarty, "Portrait of a Pay Structure," in J. L. Meij, ed., *Internal Wage Structure* (Amsterdam: North-Holland Publishing Co., 1963), pp. 12–13.

[20] Harry Ober, "Occupational Wage Differentials, 1907–1947," *Monthly Labor Review*, August, 1948, pp. 127–34. See the review of this and other evidence in Lloyd G. Reynolds and Cynthia H. Taft, *The Evolution of Wage Structure* (New Haven: Yale University Press, 1956), chap. 12; and also Melvin W. Reder, "Wage Differentials: Theory and Measurement," in *Aspects of Labor Economics* (Princeton: Princeton University Press, 1962), pp. 257–311.

The long-run decline of skill differentials can be explained reasonably well on a demand–supply basis. The demand for unskilled labor has suffered a relative decline. Laborers form only half as large a percentage of the nonfarm labor force as they did in 1910, while the percentage of skilled workers has changed very little. This decline in demand has been overborne, however, by an even sharper decline in supply. In the past high rural birthrates, plus a steady decline of labor requirements in agriculture, produced a large surplus of farm population, which moved into the lower levels of the urban labor force. The rate of migration from farms has not fallen (it has been consistently about 5 percent per year since 1940), but the absolute numbers have fallen because the farm population has been shrinking. Again, in the first quarter of this century European immigrants numbered more than a million a year. Most of these come from a rural background and entered American industry at the unskilled level. Because of changes in our immigration laws, the number of immigrants is now much smaller, and preference is given to occupational skills that are scarce in the United States.

Perhaps most important of all has been the broadening of educational opportunities already mentioned. The three-quarters of each age-group who now finish high school certainly do not look to unskilled labor as a career. So recruitment is restricted to dropouts who can find no better alternative. Thus a shrinkage in supply of farm boys, immigrants, and poorly educated Americans has combined to shift the supply curve of unskilled labor to the left. Such a shift, accompanied by a smaller leftward shift of demand, seems adequate to account for a rise in relative earnings of the unskilled.

Most of the mature industrial nations, indeed, show a trend toward smaller occupational differentials, and many of them now have smaller spreads than the United States. In Britain and Western Europe, rates for skilled craftsmen are typically in the range of 20 to 30 percent above laborers' rates in the same industry. In all cases there has been a considerable shrinkage of differentials compared with the years before World War II.

The USSR, interestingly enough, has somewhat wider differentials than Western Europe and the United States.[21] Sizable differentials have been found useful in recruiting labor into skilled occupations in a rapidly expanding industrial economy, under conditions of relatively free occupational choice. This practical consideration has overborne an ideological preference for greater income equality.

---

[21] For a discussion of Soviet wage-setting practices and actual wage scales, see Walter Galenson's articles "The Soviet Wage Reform," *IRRA Proceedings*, 1960, p. 225, and "Wage Structure and Administration in Soviet Industry," in J. L. Meij, ed., *Internal Wage Structure* (Amsterdam: North-Holland Publishing Co., 1963); and M. Gardner Clark, "Comparative Wage Structures in the Steel Industry of the Soviet Union and Western Countries," *IRRA Proceedings*, 1960, pp. 266–88.

Even wider skilled–unskilled differentials are characteristic of the less-developed countries. In the less-developed countries skilled men almost invariably earn 50 percent more than the laborers' wage, and often two or three times as much.[22] In these countries, facilities for both general and vocational education are very limited. The number of skilled craftsmen at the outset of modern development was small. In a country that succeeds in accelerating its growth rate, partly by investing in manufacturing, roads and highways, electric power, and other modern industries, the demand for craftsmen—especially building trades' workers—will rise rapidly. The response of supply is slowed by training-bottlenecks. At the same time there is a surplus of unskilled labor in both the cities and countryside. Wide occupational differentials are a natural consequence.

For the same reason—rapidly rising demand accompanied by educational restrictions on supply—the less-developed countries show unusually wide premiums for white-collared work. In Chile, Gregory found that office workers in manufacturing averaged 2½ times as much as manual workers. In government service in Uganda, Knight reports that holders of primary school certificates received twice as much as unskilled workers of whom no education was required, while high school graduates received five times as much. Taira presents data on the relative earnings of unskilled laborers and bank tellers. In nine developed countries, the ratio of tellers' to laborers' earnings varied from 0.8 to 1.7. In the less-developed countries, however, tellers typically earned two to four times as much as laborers, the ratio rising as high as 5.9 in Chile, 6.5 in Nigeria, and 6.9 in Guatemala.[23]

In the long run one would expect the differentials between white-collar and manual, and skilled and unskilled, workers to narrow as a *consequence* of economic growth and educational improvement, as has happened in the more-developed countries. But "long run" may mean two or three generations.

Farm Labor and City Labor

It is no secret that farm people earn less than city people. This is clearly true of hired labor. The hourly cash earnings of farm workers have never in modern times been even half as high as average hourly

[22] For relevant evidence, see Koji Taira, "Wage differentials in developing countries: a survey of findings," *International Labour Review,* March, 1966, pp. 281–301; J. B. Knight, "The determination of wages and salaries in Uganda," *Bulletin of the Oxford Institute of Economics and Statistics,* Vol. 29, No. 3 (1967); Elliott J. Berg, "Major Issues of Wage Policy in Africa," in Arthur M. Ross, ed., *Industrial Relations and Economic Development* (London: Macmillan & Co. Ltd., 1966).

[23] See the Knight and Taira articles cited in fn. 22, and Peter Gregory, *Industrial Wages in Chile* (Ithaca: New York School of Industrial and Labor Relations, 1967).

earnings in manufacturing, and during the Great Depression they fell to one-quarter.

It is more pertinent, however, to look at the incomes of farm operators, who constitute the bulk of the farm labor force. How do farmers' incomes compare with city workers' incomes? This is a complicated question. Farm families usually own their own homes and produce part of their own food. What cash value should be attached to these items? How much of the farmer's income is a return to his labor, and how much should be considered a return to his ownership of land, farm buildings, livestock, and machinery? With whom should the farmer be compared? The standard comparison is with average earnings of factory workers. It is possible to argue, however, that farming is either more (or less) skilled than the average of factory occupations. One can argue also that the farm labor force differs in quality,[24] measured by such indicators as age and educational level, and that this would warrant some difference in earnings.

The most serious difficulty, however, is that farmers' incomes differ widely, so that comparison of averages is not very meaningful. The top one-fifth of farm operators receives more than half of all cash farm income, while the bottom one-fifth receives only about 3 percent.

Professor Luther Tweeten has made the following analysis [25] of differences in farm income:

Economic Class	Number of Farms (thousands)	Average Size (acres)	Productive Assets per Farm (dollars)	Gross Income (dollars)	Operator Labor Income (dollars)
1	105	2,491	301,981	113,851	17,384
2	228	838	115,947	32,721	8,373
3	490	420	69,259	17,873	4,702
4	590	282	45,397	10,610	2,861
5	541	174	27,410	6,690	2,389
6	307	90	12,436	2,346	537
Noncommercial farms	986	111	18,533	4,784	2,496

The right-hand column of this table shows farm operators' labor income. This is derived by deducting from gross farm income all costs

[24] For a good analysis of this issue, see D. Gale Johnson, "Comparability of Labor Capacities of Farm and Non-Farm Labor," *American Economic Review*, June, 1953, pp. 296–313.

[25] Luther G. Tweeten: "The Income Structure of Farms by Economic Class," *Journal of Farm Economics*, May, 1965, pp. 207–21. The income data are for 1960, but the *relative* position of different income classes would not be very different today.

of purchased materials *plus* an allowance for interest on the value of farm property.

Classes 1 and 2, including about 10 percent of all farms but making more than half of all farm sales, are clearly doing well. Their incomes are well above those of industrial workers. Another 15 percent of farms, in Class 3, are near the industrial level. If we defined income to include capital gains from rising land values, these farms would show up still more favorably.

But look at the million and a half farms in Classes 4 to 6 (not to mention the million classified as "noncommercial," many of which are sidelines to urban activities). Their incomes do not approach those of urban workers by any reasonable test. Present prices of farm products, while quite adequate for the larger and more highly capitalized farms, do not yield a decent living to the small farmer.

American agriculture has for many years been an overexpanded industry. Productivity has risen rapidly since 1940, and potential supply has tended to outpace the sluggish growth of demand. There has been a continuing need for land and labor to be withdrawn from the industry, and for the remaining land to be consolidated into larger and more efficient production units.

These adjustments have in fact taken place. Average farm size has risen. There has been a massive migration out of agriculture, amounting to more than 25 million people since 1940. Land under cultivation has fallen, partly spontaneously, partly through government programs that pay farmers for not-cultivating. But the adjustments have not been large enough or fast enough to eliminate substandard incomes for most of the farm population. The agricultural industry has struggled toward equilibrium without as yet being able to reach it.

The gap between rural and urban incomes is a worldwide phenomenon. It exists in acute form in most less-developed countries. Even in the developed countries farm incomes are typically only 50 to 75 percent of urban industrial incomes.[26] The main exceptions to this rule are Denmark and New Zealand, which have highly productive agricultural economies geared to food exports.

WAGE DIFFERENCES
WITHIN
AN OCCUPATION

While a man's occupation is basic in determining his earnings level, there are substantial differences even among members of the same occupational group. There are *geographic differences* among regions

[26] For a review of the evidence see Simon Kuznets, *Modern Economic Growth* (New Haven: Yale University Press, 1966), chap. 3.

of the country and among different sizes of community in the same region. There are *intercompany differences* within the same geographic area. There are often wage differences between *men and women* doing the same kind of work. Let us look briefly at the size of such differences in the United States.

Geographic Differences

There is evidence of sizable geographic variation in wages. In gauging these differences, however, one must be careful to compare like with like. For example, the average annual earnings of all employed persons in the South are substantially below those in other regions: but this is due partly to the greater importance in the South of agriculture relative to industry, of light industry relative to heavy, of small towns and cities relative to large cities, and of nonwhite workers relative to white workers. The industry mix and labor-force mix would produce lower *average earnings* in the South even though *wage rates* were identical for similar workers in similar occupations. Only after adjusting for such differences can one judge the size of geographic differentials proper.

A careful analysis by Victor Fuchs reveals, first, that there are sizable wage differences by size of community,[27] after adjusting for age, sex, color, and education of the labor force. Average hourly earnings rise steadily as one moves from rural areas through communities of increasing size up to the largest metropolitan areas. In the southern region, cities of more than a million population pay 40 percent more than towns of less 10,000. In regions outside the South, the largest cities pay about 30 percent more than small towns. These differences are much larger than the differences in living costs revealed by Bureau of Labor Statistics surveys, so that there is a sizable difference in *real* wages.

How are these size-of-city differences to be explained? One possibility is that cost-of-living comparisons fail to capture all the costs and disadvantages of big-city life, such as the greater expenditure of time in getting from home to work and the reduced availability of costless outdoor recreation. Another possibility is that there may be differences in labor force quality that are not captured by such objective measures as age and education. It may be true, as tradition has it, that those who migrate to the big city to seek their fortunes are more capable and energetic than those who remain at home.

[27] Victor R. Fuchs, *Differentials in Hourly Earnings by Region and City Size, 1959* (New York: National Bureau of Economic Research, Occasional Paper 101, 1967). See also Victor R. Fuchs and Richard Perlman, "Recent Trends in Southern Wage Differentials," *Review of Economics and Statistics*, August, 1960, pp. 292–300; and James N. Houff, "Area Wages and Living Costs," *Monthly Labor Review*, March, 1969, pp. 43–46.

Still another possibility, as Fuchs points out, is "the existence of a disequilibrium in the supply of labor and capital. Surplus labor from agriculture may tend to move first to the small towns, and then later to the larger cities. Capital may be more readily available in the larger cities. If there is disequilibrium, we should observe a tendency for labor to migrate from small to large cities, and for industry to move in the reverse direction" (p. 34). Such labor and capital flows are actually occurring, but they are apparently too slow to eliminate intercommunity differences in wages.

For regional comparisons, the country may be divided into the northeast and north central states, the mountain and Pacific Coast states, and the southern states. The highest wages in the country are found in the western states, which average about 5 percent above the northeast and north central regions. The largest contrast, however, is between the South and all other regions combined. On a gross basis, the non-South averages about 25 percent above the South. But after adjusting for differences in labor force characteristics—age, education, sex, color—and for differences in city size (the South has a lower percentage of big-city population) Fuchs estimates that the true regional differential is only 9 percent.

A striking feature of the North–South differential is its variability among different kinds of industry and different categories of labor. For example, in some manufacturing industries (furniture, food products, hosiery) the South has hourly wage rates 20 to 30 percent below the northern level. But in other industries (glass, rayon, bituminous coal, basic steel, pulp and paper) there is virtually no regional difference. The influence of unionism is clearly observable in some of these industries.

Galloway has made an ingenious effort to explain the North–South differential in manufacturing, which he estimates at 14–15 percent after adjusting for differences in industry mix.[28] He first tests and rejects the hypothesis that lower southern wages arise from greater monopsonistic exploitation of labor by employers. A detailed analysis of 150 branches of manufacturing shows that labor's share of value added is on the average almost identical for South and North. Nor is there any systematic difference in the relation of wage rates to the marginal value product (MVP) of labor in each industry.

It does seem, however, that labor's marginal value product is systematically lower in the South than in the North. This is accompanied by a lower capital–labor ratio in the South. Each worker has less capital to work with and, for this and possibly for other reasons, produces less than a northern worker. The basic condition for closing the wage

[28] Lowell E. Galloway, "The North–South Wage Differentials," *Review of Economics and Statistics*, August, 1963, pp. 264–72. The data, unfortunately, are now somewhat out of date. It would be interesting to repeat Galloway's calculations with more recent data.

gap, Galloway concludes, is that the capital–labor ratio should rise faster in the South than in the North. This condition was being met during the 1950s, and it would be interesting to examine whether this was true also in the sixties.

The North–South differential is *inversely* related to levels of skill and education, i.e. it declines as one moves up the occupational ladder. Fuchs finds that white workers with zero to four years of schooling receive only 70 percent as much in the South as in the North. But white workers with high school education and above received 90 percent as much. This is compatible with a hypothesis that the geographic scope of the labor market broadens as one moves up the occupational ladder. Mobility and potential mobility serves to iron out geographic wage differences more effectively at higher occupational levels than at lower ones.

The regional differential is much wider for nonwhites than for whites. Even after standardizing for age, education, and city size, black male workers earn only 74 percent as much in the South as in the North, while white male workers earn 93 percent as much. The explanation may be partly that there are differences in skill level which are not captured by the years-of-education measure. Southern nonwhites may receive a lower quality of formal education, and also less on-the-job training. Further, market discrimination against nonwhite workers, while present in all regions, may be more severe in the South than elsewhere. This may force nonwhite workers down to occupational levels lower than would be predicted from their educational attainment, while at the same time lowering the market wage for these occupations because of supply pressure.

Continuing our comparisons with Canada, we may note that, in lieu of a north–south differential, Canada has an east–west differential (Table 5). Ontario and the Prairie provinces operate at rather similar wage levels. But British Columbia, the California of Canada, pays substantially higher wages. British Columbia has rich natural resources, sparse population, high investment per worker, and is an area of immigration from other provinces. At the other end of the country, wages in Quebec and the Maritime provinces are well below those in the central provinces, even after adjusting for differences in the composition of industry. Investment and output in these areas are growing relatively slowly, population is relatively abundant, and there is substantial emigration to other regions.

Interemployer Differences

If one compares men of the same occupation in the same city, one still finds considerable wage variation among companies. This may be decomposed into two parts: differences in the wage levels characteristic

Table 5

AVERAGE HOURLY EARNINGS
IN CANADIAN MANUFACTURING, 1939 AND 1959

	1939		1959	
Region	Dollars per hour	Index (Maritimes = 100)	Dollars per hour	Index (Maritimes = 100)
BRITISH COLUMBIA	0.52	141	2.09	138
PRAIRIES	0.50	135	1.74	115
ONTARIO	0.51	138	1.82	121
QUEBEC	0.41	111	1.54	102
MARITIMES	0.37	100	1.51	100

SOURCE: Woods and Ostry, *Labour Policy and Labour Economics,* p. 469.

of particular industries, and differences among companies within the same industry.

A striking example of the former sort was pointed out by Professor John Dunlop,[29] who noted that the union scale for truck drivers in Boston was almost twice as high for magazine and newspaper publishers as for scrap metal dealers. This is particularly interesting because truck driving is a standardized and interchangeable occupation and because all these rates were negotiated by the same union. Dunlop interpreted these differences as stemming mainly from differing competitive conditions and ability to pay in the various industries: ". . . the product market tends to be mirrored in the labor market and to determine the wage structure. The differentials are not transitory; they are not to be dismissed as imperfections."

Though the spread in this case was unusually large, some differentiation of wage level by type of industry is characteristic of all local labor markets. What is behind this? Why are some industries high-wage and others relatively low-wage? Slichter, Dunlop, Garbarino, and others have suggested that the following conditions make for a high industry wage level: [30]

1. A low ratio of labor costs to total costs, so that wages are not a major factor in management calculations of cost and profit. Oil refining is an outstanding example of this sort.

[29] John T. Dunlop, "The Task of Contemporary Wage Theory," in George W. Taylor and Frank E. Pierson, eds., *New Concepts in Wage Determination* (New York: McGraw-Hill Book Company, 1957), pp. 135–36.

[30] See in particular Sumner H. Slichter, "Notes on the Structure of Wages," *Review of Economics and Statistics,* XXXII (February, 1950), pp. 80–91; John T. Dunlop, "Productivity and the Wage Structure," in *Income, Employment and Public Policy,* Essays in Honor of Alvin H. Hansen (New York: W. W. Norton & Company, Inc., 1948); Joseph Garbarino, "A Theory of Interindustry Wage Structure Variation," *Quarterly Journal of Economics,* LXIV (May, 1950), pp. 283–305.

2. A rapid rate of increase in man-hour output. In a fully competitive economy, as noted in Chapter 8, one might expect all wages to rise at a rate roughly proportionate to the average of man-hour output in the economy as a whole. Productivity changes in a particular industry would not directly affect its wage level. In actuality, however, the specific rate of productivity increase in an industry does have an impact on its wage behavior. Industries with high rates of increase tend to lead the wage parade, while those where productivity is stagnating lag behind.

3. A high ratio of profits to sales. Conditions (2) and (3) are likely to accompany a rapid increase in demand for the industry's products and a rapid expansion of plant capacity. An industry in this situation cannot merely afford to raise wages from a profit standpoint but may be forced to raise wages to attract large numbers of new workers to its expanded plants.

4. A high degree of output concentration in a few companies and "cooperative" pricing arrangements. This prevents the profits of industrial expansion from being eroded by price competition. Behind the shelter of protected prices, management can decide how the gains of rising productivity are to be distributed among consumers (perhaps in product improvements rather than price reductions), stockholders, and workers. In principle, profits belong to the owners and should go into dividends or be plowed back into company expansion. But the employees are closer to the seat of power and can usually cause more trouble for management than stockholders can. Management may well decide, therefore, to pay the stockholders customary but not necessarily rising dividends and to use part of profits to maintain a better-than-average wage level. This wins worker goodwill and community prestige, eases recruitment problems, pacifies the union, and makes management's life easier in various ways.

There is evidence, in short, of a good deal of unofficial "profit sharing" by business managers. An industry that can afford to pay high wages is likely to do so as a matter of policy, instead of attempting to get by at the lowest level that the labor market would permit.

Reder points out, however, that the statistical evidence is not entirely conclusive. He emphasizes also the importance of distinguishing clearly between *relative industry wage levels at a point of time* and *relative rates of change in industry wage levels in the course of time.* Cross-section comparisons at a point of time seem to show some influence of industry profit rates, concentration ratios, rates of increase of productivity and employment in the recent past, and so on. If one analyzes changes over fifty or sixty years, however, there is little relation between the rate of wage increase in an industry and rates of increase in employment, capital in use, productivity, or profits. The results are thus close to those of theoretical models of a competitive labor market, where in the long run an industry's relative wage level would change only because of changes in the skill mix used or in geographical location. It is interesting also that the relative ranking of industries seems to remain rather stable over long periods, and that there is no clear evidence of a decline of interindustry differentials over time.[31]

Cross-section studies of local labor markets also reveal sizeable wage differences among companies in what is supposedly the same industry, especially under nonunion conditions. Assuming that the industry is competitive, how do some companies manage to pay more than others and survive? Closer examination sometimes reveals that the companies are producing different types or qualities of product, and are not actually competing in the same product market. Another plausible hypothesis is that company wage levels are inversely related to managerial ability. The higher-wage companies get more output per worker through better management, so that their unit labor costs are not necessarily above those of lower-wage companies.

A further consideration is that workers differ in intelligence level, muscular coordination, physical and nervous endurance, and willingness to exert sustained effort. The higher-wage plants may be able in the long run to attract, select, and retain workers of superior efficiency, while low-wage plants are forced to accept the leftovers. If the labor market does operate as an efficient sifting device, employers' costs *per efficiency unit of labor* will be smaller than the difference in nominal wage rates.

Evidence on this last point is scanty. Professor Leonard Weiss, in what was really an interindustry rather than an intraindustry analysis, concluded that industries with a high degree of market concentration pay somewhat higher wages than less concentrated industries.[32] But he also found that "once personal characteristics are introduced, the relationship between concentration and earnings is no longer significant. . . . The monopolistic industries do get superior 'quality' for the incomes they offer." He emphasizes, however, that "quality" was defined in terms of characteristics that employers seem to prefer, such as education and race. It is not certain that the *productivity* of workers in the preferred categories is above that of other workers.

Eaton H. Conant analyzed the aptitude test scores and hiring salaries of female high school graduates placed as typists by the state employment service in Madison, Wisconsin.[33] He found a statistically

[31] For an excellent summary of the evidence on these matters, see Reder, *Wage Differentials.*

[32] Leonard W. Weiss, "Concentration and labor earnings," *American Economic Review,* March, 1966, pp. 96–117.

[33] Eaton H. Conant, "Worker efficiency and wage differentials in a clerical labor market," *Industrial and Labor Relations Review,* April, 1963, pp. 428–33.

significant difference between the test scores of girls hired by employers in the top third of the salary range (which at this time was
about $185–$250 per month) and those hired by employers in the
bottom third of the range. The average quality differential, however,
was only about 5 percent, and was sufficient to account for only about
10 percent of the difference in starting salaries.

It seems a reasonable hypothesis that, while high-wage firms are
able to hire somewhat more productive workers, the productivity differential typically falls short of the wage differential. In addition,
however, the high-wage firms can select workers with preferred personal characteristics, and this may be considered to bring nonpecuniary
benefits.

Men and Women Workers

Do women receive less than men for precisely comparable work?
They should not, if the Equal Pay Act of 1963 were fully effective; but
such effectiveness cannot be taken for granted.

One difficulty with the question is that it relates to a somewhat
unusual situation. Most occupations are predominantly "men's work"
or "women's work." Even where both men and women are employed
in an occupation, they do not necessarily work side by side in that
occupation *in the same establishment*. Donald McNulty, who analyzed
eleven occupations employing substantial numbers of men and
women,[34] found that for most occupations two-thirds to three-quarters
of the people were employed in establishments employing only men
or only women for the occupation in question. In these segregated
establishments, the occupational wage level in men-only establishments was usually one-quarter to one-third higher than in the women-
only establishments. In the minority of establishments where men and
women shared the same occupation, differentials were considerably
smaller—of the order of 8 to 14 percent. Direct discrimination is obviously difficult. The presence of male co-workers tends to pull
women's wages up toward the male level.

An analysis of census and Bureau of Labor Statistics data by Henry
Sanborn reaches similar conclusions.[35] When comparison is narrowed
to men and women in the same occuption in the same plant, the dif-

34 Donald J. McNulty, "Differences in Pay Between Men and Women Workers,"
Monthly Labor Review, December, 1967, pp. 40–43. The study covered accounting
clerks, order clerks, payroll clerks, office boys and girls, tabulating machine operators, elevator operators, janitors, and shipping packers.

35 Henry Sanborn, "Pay Differences Between Men and Women," *Industrial and
Labor Relations Review*, July, 1964, pp. 534–50.

ferential in earnings is typically less than 10 percent, and such difference as remains is not necessarily discriminatory. Where workers in
an occupational class move up within a rate range with increasing
experience, the fact that male workers usually have longer average
length of service may give them some wage advantage. The higher
quit rates and absentee rates of women workers impose hiring costs
on the employer, which may be reflected in a lower market wage.
There may also be productivity differences, though evidence on this
point is scanty. Sanborn reports an analysis of pieceworkers' earnings
in the shoe and furniture industries, indicating that women pieceworkers earned (and presumably produced) about 10 percent less than
men; but one would expect relative productivity to vary with the kind
of work in question, so that this result cannot safely be generalized.

One can argue that any sizable wage differential, not offset by
productivity differences or hiring costs, is inherently unstable. If
women and men are substitutable in an occupation, and if the cost
of female labor per efficiency unit is (say) 10 percent less than that of
male labor, the inducement to substitute women will be strong. As
employers proceed to substitute, the occupation will rapidly become
an all-women's occupation.

For the most part men and women do different types of work, and
jobs that have become identified as "women's work" carry considerably lower wage rates than men's jobs. This is due partly to differences
in job content. Manufacturing operations performed by women are
typically light and low-skilled, while men do most of the work that is
physically exhausting or requires long training. But women receive
less partly because they are willing to work for less. Most women
workers are either supplementary wage earners in a family or single
people without dependents. The paycheck is not as critically important to them as it is to a male family head. The supply curve of female labor is thus lower than that of male labor, and employers are
able to pay women less than they would have to pay men of the same
efficiency to do the same work.

This adverse position of women workers cuts in two directions.
From one point of view, it seems unjust that a worker of standard
efficiency should receive less simply because she is a woman rather
than a man. But from another standpoint the fact that women can be
paid less than men gives employers an incentive to hire women wherever possible. Willingness to work for less has been a major factor
helping women to penetrate more and more areas of employment. If
women were forced to demand the same wage level as men for each
type of work, justice might be served but the expansion of employment opportunities for women would be less rapid.

Discussion   Questions

1. Explain the main reasons why occupational wage differences would exist in a purely competitive labor market.
2. To what extent are occupational differences in the United States today explainable in terms of competitive forces?
3. Suppose you were asked to organize a research project to determine whether there is a shortage of medical practitioners in the United States. How would you define "shortage," and what kinds of data would you analyze?
4. Do you expect that earnings of sales and clerical workers will continue to decline relative to those of manual workers? Why, or why not?
5. How can one explain the large difference in earnings between farm and factory workers?
6. Discuss the statistical problems involved in measuring the true wage differential between the southern and northern states.
7. Outline the main reasons for differences in wage rates for similar jobs:
    (a)   between northern and southern states;
    (b)   between large cities and small towns.
8. "Strict enforcement of the law that women workers shall be paid as much as men for the same job might do more harm than good to women members of the labor force." Discuss.

Reading   Suggestions

In addition to the Fuchs, Lydall, Meij, Reder, and Reynolds-Taft studies cited in the chapter, see relevant chapters in Pierson, Frank E., and George W. Taylor, eds., *New Concepts in Wage Determination*. New York: McGraw-Hill Book Company, 1957; Phelps Brown, E. H., *The Economics of Labor*. New Haven: Yale University Press, 1962; and Robertson, D. J., *The Economics of Wages*. New York: St. Martin's Press, Inc., 1961. There is a very large article-literature, much of which is footnoted in these sources. Current information on median annual earnings by broad occupational categories is published by the Bureau of the Census in its *Current Population Reports* series. Detailed occupational data, comparable to that in Table 1, from the 1970 census should become available in the early 1970s.

INEQUALITY,
POVERTY,
AND PUBLIC POLICY   10

In Chapter 8 we considered the distribution of income between the owners of labor and capital; and in Chapter 9 we saw that labor income is quite unequally distributed. Now we want to examine how these and other factors affect the size distribution of income among households.

The Census Bureau makes frequent sample surveys of household incomes from which estimates can be made for the population as a whole. In 1967, families living together had a median income of almost $8,000. In addition, there were about 13 million individuals not living with relatives, and these people had a median income of only about $2,400. The average for this group is low because many of them are young people just entering the labor market or older people dependent on pensions and social security payments. It is best for most purposes to concentrate on the family units, which include almost 95 percent of the total population.

The distribution of family incomes in 1967 (Table 1) was obviously quite unequal. There were still some 6 million families, or about one-eighth of the total, with incomes below $3,000 a year. At the upper

Table 1

DISTRIBUTION OF FAMILIES
AND UNRELATED INDIVIDUALS
BY INCOME LEVEL, 1967

Total Income	Families (thousands)	(percent)	Unrelated individuals (thousands)	(percent)
Under $1,000	1,031	2.1	2,559	19.5
1,000 to 1,999	2,189	4.4	3,248	24.8
2,000 to 2,999	2,981	6.0	1,664	12.7
3,000 to 3,999	3,155	6.3	1,273	9.7
4,000 to D,999	3,243	6.5	997	7.6
5,000 to 5,999	3,879	7.8	928	7.1
6,000 to 6,999	4,145	8.3	719	5.5
7,000 to 7,999	4,414	8.9	517	3.9
8,000 to 9,999	7,661	15.4	529	4.0
10,000 to 14,999	11,147	22.4	451	3.4
15,000 AND OVER	5,989	11.9	229	1.7
TOTAL	49,834	100.0	13,114	100.0
MEDIAN INCOME	7,974		2,391	

SOURCE: Bureau of the Census, *Current Population Report*, Series P-60, No. 59,
April, 1969.

end of the distribution another 6 million families had incomes of
$15,000 or more.

This inequality of household incomes is found in every type of
economy. Distributions for other industrial countries would not look
very different from Table 1. Inequality is even greater in most of the
less-developed countries, where small groups of high-income landowners, businessmen, and government officials exist alongside masses
of poor peasants and laborers. Although we have no data for the
USSR and other socialist countries, their distributions would probably be more nearly equal than those in the United States, partly because of the absence of property income.

THE DETERMINANTS
OF
HOUSEHOLD DISTRIBUTION

What explains the pattern of household distribution at a particular
time, and changes in this pattern over time? For the most part, people
receive income by providing productive services to the economy. How
much an individual receives depends on how much capital and labor
power he owns and on the price that these services command in the mar-

ket. This enables us to classify the determinants of income distribution into four groups: the distribution of wage–salary income; the distribution of property income; the relative size of the labor and capital shares; and a variety of other considerations, which include the relative size of the farm population, the number of wage earners per family, and the extent of government transfer payments to low-income groups.

1. *Income from Labor.* Close to four-fifths of income produced in the United States goes to those who provide labor services. So the distribution of labor income is the most important single determinant of overall income distribution.

We saw in Chapter 9 that the labor market establishes widely differing wage rates for different occupations, from domestic servants at the bottom to surgeons and concert pianists at the top. In a dynamic economy, these occupational differences may either widen or narrow in the course of time. If they are narrowing, as they seem to have done since 1900 in the industrial capitalist countries, this will reduce inequality in household incomes.

Annual earnings depend not only on hourly wage rates but on hours worked during the year; and this produces shifts in income distribution over the business cycle. In a recession year more people are partly or wholly unemployed and drop down to lower income brackets. Inequality of income increases. During prosperity, these people are reemployed, their annual incomes rise, and inequality is reduced.

2. *Income from Property.* Most income-yielding property is held by a small minority of the population. The top 5 percent of income recipients in the United States receive more than two-thirds of all dividend payments and about half of all property income. The concentration of property income is much greater than that of labor income. The top 5 percent of income recipients get only about 10 percent of total wage and salary payments.

3. *The Labor and Property Shares.* Since labor income is more equally distributed than property income, the relative size of the labor and capital shares affects overall distribution. If labor's income share is rising, as seems to have been happening for reasons noted in chapter 8, this makes for a more equal distribution of household incomes.

4. *Additional Considerations.* Several other considerations deserve brief mention. First, income levels in agriculture are substantially below those in urban occupations. So people have been leaving agriculture, and when they do they typically raise their income level. Thus the shrinkage of the agricultural sector reduces the proportion of low-income families in the population.

Second, a household may include more than one wage earner. Particularly striking is the growing tendency, noted in Chapter 2, for married women to reenter the labor market after they are past the peak of child rearing. If married women's propensity to work were randomly distributed over all income brackets, it would not alter the national income distribution. But this is not the case. We noted in Chapter 2 that there is a clear inverse relation with the husband's income level, i.e. the lower the husband's income, the greater the likelihood of the wife working. The fact that double incomes are more common at the lower occupational levels tends to pull up the bottom of the income distribution and to reduce inequality.

Third, many millions of people in the United States receive transfer payments from the government. These include pension payments under the Social Security system, government payments to farmers, unemployment compensation, aid to the blind and to dependent children, and general public relief. The more generous these transfers are, the fewer people will fall into the lowest-income brackets.

LONG TRENDS
IN
HOUSEHOLD DISTRIBUTION

What has happened to household distribution in the United States and elsewhere over the past several generations? Has inequality been increasing or decreasing?

It makes considerable difference whether we examine incomes before or after personal income taxes. If one is interested in the results which emerge from the market mechanism, one should look at the distribution of pretax incomes, and this is what we shall mainly do. In terms of ability to consume, however, it is posttax income which matters. Posttax incomes are more nearly equal than pretax incomes, because of the impact of the personal income tax.

But the *pretax* distribution has also gradually become more equal. Evidence of this for the United States and a number of other countries has been assembled by Professor Simon Kuznets.[1] As an indicator of inequality he takes the percentage of national income received by the top 5 percent of households or tax units. Some of his results are summarized in Table 2. Note that for every country the share of the top income group is lower in the post-World War II period than in earlier periods. For some countries the decline of inequality can be traced back to before 1900. In other countries it seems to have begun with World War I, and in the United States the decline began still later, during the 1930s. The general direction of movement, however, is consistent for all countries. It is interesting also that the share of

[1] Simon Kuznets, *Modern Economic Growth* (New Haven: Yale University Press, 1966), pp. 208–11.

Table 2

PERCENT OF PRETAX INCOME
RECEIVED BY TOP 5 PERCENT
OF CONSUMING UNITS,
SELECTED COUNTRIES, LONG PERIODS

United States		*Netherlands*	
1929	30	1938	19
1935–36	26.5	1949	17
1944–47	21	1954	13
1955–59	20	*Denmark*	
		1870	36.5
United Kingdom		1903	28
1880	48	1925	26
1913	43	1939	24.5
1929	33	1955	17.5
1938	31		
1947	24	*Norway*	
1957	18	1907	27
		1938	20
		1948	14
Germany-West Germany			
1913	31	*Sweden*	
1928	21	1930	30
1936	23	1935	28
1950	24	1948	20
1959	18	1954	17

pretax income received by the top 5 percent is now so nearly similar in the Western industrial nations.

Additional detail for the United States is provided by Table 3.[2] This shows, for selected years over a 40-year period, the share of personal income received by the lowest 20 percent of income recipients, the next 20 percent, and so on up to the top 20 percent and top 5 percent of families. It is clear that there was a marked shift toward greater equality over this period. The proportion of personal income received by the top 5 percent of families fell from 30 to 15 percent, that of the top 20 percent from 54 to 41 percent.

The shift toward equality was particularly strong during the thirties and forties. The Great Depression brought a reduction of property incomes and an increase in transfer payments to those at the bottom of the income structure. The forties brought a marked reduction in wage differences among occupations. Since the late forties the trend

[2] Data for 1929–62 are from Bernard F. Haley, "Income Distribution in the United States," in the I.E.A. symposium volume, *The Distribution of National Income* (New York: St. Martin's Press, Inc., 1968). Data for 1967 are from the Census Bureau source cited in Table 1.

Table 3

DISTRIBUTION OF FAMILY PERSONAL INCOME
AMONG CONSUMER UNITS IN VARIOUS YEARS

	PERCENT DISTRIBUTION				
Quintiles	*1929*	*1935–36*	*1947*	*1962*	*1967*
LOWEST ⎫	13	4	5	5	5
SECOND ⎭		9	11	11	12
THIRD	14	14	16	16	17
FOURTH	19	21	22	23	24
HIGHEST	54	52	46	45	41
TOP 5 PERCENT	30.0	26.5	20.9	19.6	15.3

toward equalization has slowed down, and some statistical measures fail to reveal any significant change in income distribution. When we look below the aggregates to specific age and sex groups, we find that income inequality among adult males has continued to decline quite rapidly during the fifties and sixties. But this has been partly offset by the fact that women and young people, whose income distribution is less equal than for adult men, have formed a growing proportion of the labor force.[3]

The reasons for the long-run trend toward greater equality are to be found in the determinants listed above, most of which have been operating in an equalizing direction. Occupational wage differences have been shrinking. Inequality in property ownership, while still high, is not as high as it was fifty years ago.[4] The property share of income has been falling and the labor share rising. The low-income agricultural sector is an ever smaller part of the total economy. Government transfer payments, which were very small in 1930, have risen rapidly since that time.

It is dangerous to project past trends into the future, but it does seem that future changes are more likely to be toward equality than away from it. As the educational system catches up with the rising demand for professional and managerial workers, we may see a further reduction in occupational differentials. Social security and other transfer payments are likely to be liberalized. Even property income may gradually become more evenly distributed throughout the population.

[3] See T. Paul Schultz, "Secular Trends and Cyclical Behavior of Income Distribution in the United States, 1944–1965," in Lee Soltow, ed., *Six Papers on the Size Distribution of Wealth and Income* (New York: Columbia University Press, for the National Bureau of Economic Research, 1969).

[4] Simon Kuznets, *Shares of Upper-Income Groups in Income and Savings* (New York: National Bureau of Economic Research, 1953).

Is Inequality Still a Problem?

It is important to distinguish between *inequality* and *poverty*. It is clear that there is still a problem of poverty in the sense that many families do not have enough income to attain a decent minimum standard of living. There would be widespread agreement that families below some minimum level should be brought up to that level.

Suppose now that this has been done. All families below $4,000 a year or some other figure have been brought up to that level. Is there any reason to worry about the distribution of incomes *above* this basic minimum? If the poorest families can live decently, does it matter whether some television stars and corporation executives earn (before taxes) a half million dollars a year? Should we be concerned about inequality per se?

The standard arguments on this issue are well known. On the egalitarian side, it is usually argued that a dollar brings less satisfaction to the $50,000-a-year man than to the $5,000-a-year man. Thus a transfer of income from higher to lower income brackets is likely to increase total consumer satisfaction. (This is stoutly denied by others, however, who maintain that one's capacity to get enjoyment from spending money increases with practice!) It is argued also that the envy engendered by wide differences in living standards involves a loss in community satisfaction. I may be content with my $5,000 a year if no one else around me has more than double that amount, but quite unhappy if others in the community have ten or twenty times as much.

Against egalitarianism it is argued that envy and the desire to climb to a higher income bracket perform an indispensable economic function. If incomes are too equal, no one will have an incentive to train for the higher occupations and perform efficiently in them. The fact that most of the personal saving is done by the top income groups is used as an argument for inequality by those who believe our economy suffers from a shortage of capital and as an argument for equality by those who believe that oversaving threatens us with depression. And so it goes.

One could probably get widespread agreement on the desirability of establishing equal *opportunity* for young people to train for professional and managerial occupations within the limits of their native ability. This would produce some further reduction of occupational differentials. If we could establish equality of occupational opportunity and could eliminate poverty, the writer would be content to let upper bracket incomes fall where they may. But he would not undertake to convince other people that they should rest content.

The question of how far equality should be pursued as an end in itself is a political issue which has divided men for centuries. In modern times, this has turned increasingly into an argument over the tax system. Egalitarians favor steeply progressive income taxes and heavy reliance on federal spending, which is financed mainly from income taxation. Those who believe income equalization has gone too far, or is in danger of going too far, favor state and local spending, excise and sales taxes, and a less steeply graduated personal income tax. The economist can try to predict the consequences of moving in one direction or another. But taxation is still an inexact science, and the predictions are not very reliable. Even if they were better, they could not alone decide an issue which involves political and ethical judgments.

WHO ARE
THE
POOR?

Suppose we agree that poverty is today a more urgent problem than inequality per se. How do we define and measure it? How many people in the United States are poor, and who are they?

The definition of poverty is necessarily conventional. When one gets above the minimum of food, clothing, and shelter necessary for physical survival, the adequacy of consumption levels becomes a matter of judgment. Where one sets the poverty line depends on one's beliefs about how people should be entitled to live. Moreover, conceptions of an adequate living standard change over the course of time. Conditions which were widely prevalent and accepted at one time may be regarded as unacceptable a generation later.

For this reason, Victor Fuchs has suggested that poverty be defined on a relative rather than an absolute basis. Any family whose income is less than, say, half of the median family income in the country might be regarded as poor. In support of this approach, Fuchs argues: "Firstly, it explicitly recognizes that all so-called 'minimum' or 'subsistence' budgets are based on contemporary standards . . . and have no intrinsic or scientific basis. Secondly, it focuses attention on what seems to underly the present concern with poverty, namely, the first tentative gropings toward a national policy with respect to the distribution of income at the lower end of the scale. Finally, it provides a more realistic basis for appraising the success or failure of antipoverty programs." He points out that, if poverty is defined as an income of less than $3,000 a year (in constant 1965 dollars), the proportion of families who are poor fell from 30.0 percent in 1947 to 16.5 percent in 1965. The proportion of families with incomes less than one-half the median, however, remained virtually constant at about 20 percent.[5]

Most scholars and policy makers, however, continue to use an absolute standard of poverty. In the early sixties, this was commonly set at $3,000 for a family of four. Any such standard must be kept up-to-date, however, as living costs change. A bundle of consumer goods costing $3,000 in 1960 would cost close to $4,000 today. The standard must be adjusted also for differences in family size. In the case of farm families, the fact that the family usually owns its home and grows part of its food should be considered.

After making these adjustments, the Census Bureau estimated that about 13 percent of Americans were living in poverty in 1968.[6] This is an encouraging decline from earlier estimates of 31.7 percent in 1947 and 21.4 percent in 1959. But 13 percent is still about 25 million people.

The main reason why the percentage of impoverished families has fallen is the steady rise of per capita income in the American economy. As the average level of income rises, the proportion *below* any bench mark figure will decline. So why not wait for the problem to solve itself? If family incomes continue to rise at the present rate for another generation, will poverty not disappear automatically and without special effort?

This argument is valid *for people who are able to participate fully in the market economy.* The trouble is that most of the poverty group are not in this category. More than half of them are people who cannot work at all because of age, disabling accidents, mental or physical deficiencies, or the need to care for dependent children. For these people the continuing rise in the national wage level is irrelevant, since they cannot earn wages. Most of the remainder are people who are seriously disadvantaged in the labor market because of limited education and training, racial discrimination, geographical remoteness from centers of expanding employment, and other reasons. Potentially employable they may be; but in actuality they have no jobs or only irregular and precarious jobs. Because of their tenuous connection with the labor market, they are left behind in the rising tide of affluence which benefits their fellows.

The steady rise in average income levels will certainly continue to reduce the percentage of impoverished families; but it will not eliminate poverty within the foreseeable future. There is a hard core, amounting to perhaps 10 percent of our population, who can be lifted above the poverty line only by programs directed specifically to that end.

[5] Victor Fuchs, "Comment," in Soltow, *Six Papers,* pp. 198–202.
[6] Bureau of the Census, *Current Population Reports,* Series P–60, August, 1969.

Who are today's poor, and why are they poor? The outlines of the picture are shown in Table 4.[7] The first column shows the *number* of

Table 4

CHARACTERISTICS OF
POOR HOUSEHOLDS, 1967

Characteristics of Head of Household	Number of Poor Households (millions)	Incidence of Poverty (percent)
HEAD 65 YEARS AND OVER	3.8	36.3
UNRELATED INDIVIDUALS	2.7	53.4
FAMILIES	1.1	20.3
HEAD UNDER 65 YEARS	6.4	12.2
UNRELATED INDIVIDUALS	2.2	27.0
WHITE	1.6	24.4
MALE	0.5	18.0
FEMALE	1.1	29.0
NONWHITE	0.5	40.1
MALE	0.2	29.4
FEMALE	0.3	51.7
FAMILIES	4.2	9.5
WHITE	2.8	7.1
MALE	2.0	5.4
FEMALE	0.8	25.3
NONWHITE	1.4	29.9
MALE	0.7	20.9
FEMALE	0.7	54.9
TOTAL, ALL HOUSEHOLDS	10.2	16.2

poor households with various characteristics. The second column shows the *percentage* of all households with a certain characteristic who were living in poverty in 1966. Thus, the third figure in that column says that 20.3 percent of families with heads aged 65 and over were poor in that year.

Note that, of some 10 million poor nonfarm households, 4 million were headed by people aged 65 or over. These are older people who either failed to qualify for Social Security or whose Social Security payments are too small to lift them above the poverty line. More than one-third of these elderly people are living in poverty.

[7] Data for this table are from the Report of the Council of Economic Advisers, 1969, p. 157. For other analyses of the poverty population, see Lester C. Thurow, "The causes of poverty," *Quarterly Journal of Economics*, February, 1967, pp. 39–57; and James N. Morgan, Martin H. David, Wilbur J. Cohen, and Harvey E. Brazer, *Income and Welfare in the United States* (New York: McGraw-Hill Book Company, 1962).

Another 3 million poor households are headed by women under 65. These are women who have been widowed, divorced, or abandoned by their husbands. Many of them are unable to work because of the need to care for small children. Again, more than 40 percent of all households in this category are impoverished.

This leaves about 3½ million households headed by men under 65. The sources of their poverty are not so clear. Many of these men, probably close to a million, are disabled and unable to work. The remainder are presumably men at the bottom of the labor force in terms of education and skill. Some are able to get little or no work and constitute the hard-core unemployed. Others are employed in the lowest-paid jobs in the economy, where even full-time work fails to yield an adequate income.

In every category the poverty percentage is much higher for non-white than for white households. Thus, for families with male heads under 65, the proportion of poor is 5.4 percent for white families, 20.9 percent for nonwhite families. For families with female heads under 65, the poverty percentage is 25.3 for whites, 54.9 percent for non-whites. This is partly a reflection of low employability. Black workers, especially those reared in rural areas of the southern states, have been particularly disadvantaged as regards education and the kinds of work skill needed for urban occupations.[8] But it is also partly a reflection of continued hiring discrimination by employers. Black workers tend to get the least-attractive and lowest-paid jobs, even when their qualifications would entitle them to something better.

Old age, broken families, low employability, and color are the ingredients of the poverty problem. These characteristics are not mutually exclusive, but overlap in a complicated pattern. At a rough estimate, 30 to 40 percent of presently impoverished families contain employable members, and might be lifted out of poverty by better job opportunities. For the majority, however, transfer payments provide the only feasible source of income.

Poverty is clearly a complex problem, calling for action on many fronts. Some lines of action—drawing low-income families off the land, reducing general unemployment, retraining the disadvantaged, measures to cope with the "depressed area" problem—were examined in Chapter 6 as part of our discussion of manpower policy. The basic rationale of these policies is to achieve a better deployment and use of the labor force and to raise national output. But at the same time

---

[8] Thurow, "Causes of Poverty" notes that in 1960 some 48.5 percent of non-white family heads had less than eight years of education, compared with only 19.2 percent of white family heads. He estimates that educational differences alone account for nearly half of the difference in incidence of poverty between white and nonwhite families.

they can be expected to raise families with one or more employable members out of the poverty category.

We proceed to examine three other lines of action:

1. Minimum wage legislation. A sizable percentage of poor families have at least one employable member, whose earnings are crucial for the family's income level.

2. Social insurance systems, designed to offset losses of income resulting from unemployment, old age, illness, disability, and other causes. Again, these aim at protection of regular workers, and cannot do much for people outside the labor force. In large measure they transfer income *within* the wage-earning population as between times of earning and not earning. But this is highly important, and prevents millions of people from falling into the poverty group when for one reason or another they are unable to work.

3. Public assistance payments, which are the last resort of those who lack work ability and are unprotected (or inadequately protected) by social insurance. Such transfers are already substantial, but they fail to reach everyone and are usually too small to lift a family above the poverty level. We shall examine proposals to increase and standardize such transfers.

POVERTY REMEDIES:
THE
MINIMUM WAGE

The United States has had a federal minimum wage since the passage of the Fair Labor Standards Act of 1938, commonly known as the Wage Hour Act. This set a minimum wage for workers engaged in interstate commerce, exclusive of agriculture and a few other types of industry. The standard workweek was set at forty hours after 1940, with limited exceptions for certain seasonal industries. Employers were required to pay time and a half for work beyond this limit.

The original minimum wage levels, 25 cents an hour in 1938 and 40 cents an hour in 1945, rapidly became obsolete because of the rapid rise of money wages since 1945. The Fair Labor Standards Act has accordingly been amended several times, raising the minimum to $0.75 in 1950, $1.00 in 1956, $1.25 in 1963, and $1.60 in 1968. At the same time the concept of what constitutes "interstate commerce," and the consequent definition of workers covered by the act, has been considerably broadened. Virtually all workers in mining, construction, manufacturing, public utilities, and government service are now covered. In addition, trade and service enterprises with annual sales of $250,000 or more are covered, and so are workers on large farms (roughly, farms with seven or more wage workers).[9]

Under the most recent amendment, some 41 million out of a total of 50 million nonsupervisory wage and salary earners were covered by the act.[10] The main groups still excluded are some 7 million workers in trade and service establishments that do not meet the dollar volume criterion for coverage, plus 2 million domestic servants and 1 million wage workers on smaller farms.

Thirty-eight states, including all the major industrial states, also have minimum wage laws covering intrastate activities; but in fourteen states the law covers only women and minors. The minimum wage is often not specified in the act, but is left for administrative determination on the basis of recommendations by industry wage boards. The minima vary considerably from state to state, being lower in states where the general wage level is low. The minima are generally below, and sometimes substantially below, the federal minimum.

The federal minimum has typically been set well below the *average* level of hourly earnings at the time. The intent is not to raise the general level, but to bring up workers who are judged to have lagged too far behind the general advance of wages. Typically, each amendment has set a new minimum at around 50 percent of actual average hourly earnings in manufacturing. As the general money wage level continues to rise, the percentage relation of the minimum wage to average earnings declines. When it has fallen to one-third or so, Congress gets busy again and raises the minimum.

The 1966 amendments, however, were more aggressive in this respect than earlier amendments. The new $1.60 minimum was 60 percent of average hourly earnings in manufacturing in 1966. The increase in average hourly earnings between 1963, when the $1.25 minimum became effective, and early 1968, when the $1.60 became effective, was about 21 percent. The increase in the minimum, however, was 28 percent. Moreover, the act brought in 9 million new workers from trade, services, and other industries that have traditionally operated well below the manufacturing wage level.

The impact of the minimum wage system is uneven. It has virtually

[9] The minimum wage for farm workers, however, is only $1.30 an hour rather than $1.60. In addition, nonagricultural enterprises that were covered for the first time by the 1966 amendments, employing some 9 million workers, are allowed to approach the new minimum more gradually than enterprises previously covered. For them, the minimum was set at $1.15 in February, 1968, $1.30 in February, 1969, $1.45 in February, 1970, and $1.60 in February, 1971.

[10] For a detailed analysis see Susan Kocin, "Basic Provisions of the 1966 Fair Labor Standards Act Amendments," *Monthly Labor Review,* March, 1967, pp. 1–4; and Edward C. Martin, "Extent of Coverage Under the Fair Labor Standards Act as Amended in 1966," *Monthly Labor Review,* April, 1967, pp. 21–24.

no effect on durable goods manufacturing, construction, or public utilities. But it does affect trade, services, and low-wage branches of manufacturing, such as cigars, fertilizers, sawmills, seamless hosiery, men's and boys' shirts, footwear, and canning. Within this sector, it impinges on the least-skilled groups and on the lowest-wage areas of the country. The effect on plants in the southern states is considerably more severe than in the North. Much of the pressure for continued increases in the minimum comes from unions that have succeeded in organizing most northern plants in their industries but have not been equally successful in the South. Their only effective tool for bringing pressure on the southern wage level and sheltering union plants from lower-wage competition is through the minimum wage.

There is no doubt that the Fair Labor Standards Act has achieved its direct purpose of raising wages in the lowest-wage areas and industries. Unskilled workers must be brought up to the new minimum; and this often leads to increases for higher job classifications, in order to give them a reasonable differential over the unskilled. Studies of the 1956 and 1963 increases indicate that, in low-wage branches of manufacturing in the southern states, plant-wide average hourly earnings were often increased by 10 to 20 percent.

If wages are raised, and if the labor demand curve has its usual shape, one would expect an adverse effect on employment. The higher wage level will encourage capital–labor substitution, so that less labor is demanded per unit of output. Moreover, output itself will fall because of the higher level of production costs, which under either monopolistic or competitive assumptions leads to higher product prices and reduced sales. Unemployment may show up particularly in the demise of marginal producers who cannot survive at the new wage level.

An exception to this occurs where the employer is a monopsonistic buyer of labor. In this case, as explained in Chapter 4, he has an incentive to restrict employment in order to hold wages below the level for comparable work in other markets. Here a forced increase in the wage rate can, in principle, raise wages and employment simultaneously. The one-company town is the traditional example.

Reliance is also sometimes placed on the "shock effect" discussed in Chapter 5. This assumes that, in labor markets where supply conditions permit a low wage rate, management is apt to become lazy and inefficient in its use of labor. A forced increase in wage rates will rouse it from its lethargy and lead to improvements in personnel and production management. These may be sufficient to raise labor's marginal physical productivity schedule by as much as the wage rate, so that unit labor costs are no higher than before.

This may indeed happen. But the conclusion that *employment* will remain unchanged does not follow. Consider first a purely competitive industry. A company in which management adjusts as described will end up with unchanged employment; but because of the rise in labor's marginal productivity, its output will be greater than before. This is all right, since by definition a competitive producer can sell as much as he wishes at the market price. But this is not feasible *for the industry as a whole.* If total industry output rises, demand remaining unchanged, the price of the product must fall. This lower price is unprofitable, since unit production costs have not changed. The least-efficient producers will presumably vanish from the industry, and employment will decline.

Now consider a monopolist, who is following the marginal revenue = marginal cost rule for maximum profit. The minimum wage raises his *MC* curve by, say, 10 percent. Now by strenuous economizing he raises labor's physical productivity by 10 percent and forces the *MC* curve back to its previous level. His equilibrium output, price, and profit are the same as at the beginning. But his employment is lower, because labor requirements per unit of output have fallen.

What the "shock effect" argument really demonstrates is that a forced wage increase need not permanently reduce an industry's output level or profit level. But this is quite different from saying that employment will remain unchanged. Management's economizing efforts usually involve using less labor per unit of output, so that employment declines.

Empirical testing of employment effects is not easy, because it is hard to disentangle the effect of higher wages from the effect of other things which are happening simultaneously. Even crude tests, however, usually show a drop in employment or a marked deceleration of the increase of employment, following an increase in the minimum wage. After the 1956 increase to $1.00 an hour, for example, the Bureau of Labor Statistics analyzed wages and employment in southern plants in five low-wage branches of manufacturing. They found that earnings increases of 10 to 20 percent in these plants were accompanied by an average decline of 8 percent in employment during the year following the increase in the minimum.[11]

There have also been more sophisticated statistical studies. J. M. Peterson examined [12] the relation between percentage change in average hourly earnings and percentage change in man-hours for individual establishments in the men's seamless hosiery industry, after the 1950 minimum wage increase. He obtained a correlation coefficient of −.476 (significant at the 1 percent level). A similar negative relation appeared in the sawmill industry and in men's cotton garments. The

[11] Effects of the $1 Minimum Wage in Five Industries," *Monthly Labor Review,* May, 1958, pp. 492–501.

[12] J. M. Peterson, "Employment Effects of Minimum Wages, 1938–1950," *Journal of Political Economy,* October, 1957, p. 429.

larger the forced increase in a plant's wage level, the less favorable was its employment experience.

David Kaun used Census of Manufactures data for 1947, 1954, and 1958 to test the effect of the 1950 and 1956 minimum wage increases.[13] For a number of low-wage industries—textiles, seamless hose, men's and boys' suits and shirts, sawmills, millwork—he found a strong relation between plant wage levels *before* a minimum wage increase and the change in nonlabor inputs over the period immediately following. Plants with the lowest initial wage levels showed the largest increases in nonlabor inputs, suggesting accelerated capital–labor substitution following the increase in minimum wage.

Kaun also tested the effect on marginal producers by assuming that individual proprietorships and partnerships are apt to be smaller and more marginal than corporations. For tobacco, textiles, clothing, and leather products his hypothesis was confirmed for both periods. Proprietorships and partnerships showed a decline in number of establishments, value added, and production workers employed after each of the minimum wages increases.

After surveying these and other studies, Kaufman and Foran conclude that the bulk of the evidence supports the theoretical expectation that a relative wage increase in certain establishments and industries is associated with a relative decline of employment in those industries.[14] This does not necessarily mean a rise in unemployment for the economy as a whole. So long as part of the economy is not covered by the minimum wage system, workers displaced in the covered sector can seek employment in the uncovered sector. This increase in labor supply will depress relative wage rates in the uncovered sector and produce a wider wage gap between the two sectors.

If all occupations were covered by the minimum wage, however, the effect would be to raise the general standard of employability and to squeeze some workers out of the labor force. There are always people who, because of youth and inexperience, advancing years, limited intelligence, or physical handicaps are unable to produce at the normal rate. Where there is no legal minimum, employers can hire these people at a wage proportionate to their productivity. With a minimum wage, this is no longer possible. The employer cannot afford to keep on his payroll anyone who cannot produce enough to be worth the minimum wage. Workers of low productivity are discharged. If they then leave the labor force, they will not be counted as unem-

13 David E. Kaun, "Minimum Wages, Factor Substitution, and the Marginal Producer," *Quarterly Journal of Economics*, August, 1965, pp. 478–86.

14 Jacob J. Kaufman and Terry G. Foran, "The Minimum Wage and Poverty," in Sar A. Levitan, Wilbur J. Cohen, and Robert J. Lampman, eds., *Towards Freedom From Want* (Madison, Wisconsin: Industrial Relations Research Association, 1968), pp. 189–218.

ployed. But the practical result is the same—they become dependent on private or public support. Minimum wages tend to set a higher standard of employability, to draw a sharper line between the employable and the unemployable, and to increase the number of the latter group.

Thus the effect of the minimum wage is ambivalent. Among those who remain employed under it, some may be lifted out of the poverty group by higher minima. But for those whom it rules out of employment, the poverty problem is accentuated. The line between haves and have-nots is more sharply drawn.

POVERTY REMEDIES: SOCIAL INSURANCE

We use this term to cover *income rights earned in the course of employment* under governmentally administered programs. While a worker is employed, he and/or his employer pay a certain percentage of his earnings into special trust funds. When he reaches retirement age, or becomes unable to work because of disability, or is temporarily unemployed, he is entitled to draw benefits from these funds at a specified rate.

While these benefits are termed "transfer payments" in the national income accounts, they differ in principle from relief payments. They are an earned right rather than a charitable contribution; and their size depends mainly on the worker's previous employment and earnings rather than on family need per se. For workers with a regular employment history, social insurance serves the important function of redistributing income *over time,* as between periods of earning and not earning. Many families are thereby held above the poverty level, particularly in old age. On the other hand, social insurance by its nature cannot help those who cannot or do not work regularly.

All the developed industrial countries and many of the less-developed countries have social insurance systems. The major programs in the United States are the federal Old-Age, Survivors, Disability, and Health Insurance system (usually called OASDHI, or simply "social security" after the Social Security Act of 1935 which established it); and the federal–state unemployment compensation systems, initiated by the same act. There are also programs for veterans' pensions and benefits, workmen's compensation for industrial accidents, and a number of other purposes. In addition to these public programs, most employers maintain private pension programs; and in some industries supplementary unemployment benefit systems have been established by union–management negotiation.

Social insurance is a complicated subject, which is now usually treated in special textbooks and courses.[15] We can do no more here than outline the two major programs, and then consider the bearing of these programs on the poverty problem.

The OASDHI system now covers wage and salary earners in virtually all nonagricultural industries, and self-employed people may join the system at their own option. The system is financed by equal employer and employee contributions, each of which is currently 4.8 percent of the employee's earnings up to a maximum of $7,800 per year. This tax base has been raised several times as the general wage level has risen, and the payroll tax rate has also risen as pension payments have increased. Total benefit payments under the program were about $25 billion in 1967, and have been rising at a rate of several billions per year.

A worker is fully insured if he has earned at least $100 from covered employment in each of forty calendar quarters. He is covered for all except disability benefits if he has earned at least $100 from covered employment in one calendar quarter out of every four between 1950 (or, if he becomes of age after 1950, between the time he comes of age) and the time he reaches sixty-five. Disability benefits require, in addition, work in covered employment during five of the last ten years. A covered worker is entitled to benefits (1) on reaching age sixty-five (or, in case of women workers, age sixty-two); (2) if he is totally disabled before reaching sixty-five; or (3) in the event of death before sixty-five, his surviving dependents are entitled to specified benefits. In addition, low-cost medical care for covered workers over sixty-five was provided by the Medicare amendment of 1965.

Benefit rates are calculated on the basis of the worker's average earnings over a period of years preceding his retirement, with a minimum of $64 and a maximum of $189.80 per month. Benefits as a percentage of earnings fall as income rises, which favors the lower-income groups. A worker who barely qualifies will get at least the minimum monthly payment, which may be five to ten times the amount he has earned through payroll contributions. A worker earning $250 a month will get less in absolute terms than a man earning $500 a month, but he will get more *relative to his contributions*. A certain amount of income redistribution is thus built into the system.

If the worker has a dependent wife, his benefits are increased by

15 See, for example, Eveline Burns, *Social Security and Public Policy* (New York: McGraw-Hill Book Company, 1956); William Haber and Merrill I. Murray, *Unemployment Insurance in the American Economy* (Homewood, Ill.: Richard D. Irwin, Inc., 1966); Valdemar Carlson, *Economic Security in the United States* (New York: McGraw-Hill Book Company, 1962); Margaret S. Gordon, *The Economics of Welfare Policies* (New York: Columbia University Press, 1963); Robert J. Meyer, *Social Insurance and Allied Government Programs* (Homewood, Ill.: Richard D. Irwin, Inc., 1965).

50 percent. Thus a single person drawing benefits at the maximum rate would receive $2277.60 a year, while a couple would receive $3416.40 a year. At present price levels, this would not be quite enough to lift them above the poverty line. And of course most retired workers draw less than the maximum, so that the system falls well short of eliminating poverty for the aged population. One recent estimate suggests that about 25 percent of retired people over sixty-five would be above the poverty level even without OASDHI payments. For another 35 percent, the OASDHI payments are sufficient to raise them above the poverty line. But this still leaves 40 percent, or some 5 million retired people plus their dependents, who are drawing all they are entitled to under the program and are still living in poverty.

The continuing rise of consumer prices since 1945 has imposed serious hardship on the aged population. Prices rise almost every year, while pension levels are adjusted at relatively rare intervals. Thus payments are always lagging behind income requirements, and meanwhile the elderly feel the sharp bite of inflation. Because of the Social Security Act, however, the situation is now much better than it was in the days when the great majority of older people would have been classified as poor, most of them lived with and on their children, and the remainder had no alternative but charity.

Unemployment compensation legislation has been passed separately in each state, within federal standards established by the Social Security Act and subsequent amendments to that act. The coverage of unemployment compensation is somewhat less than that of the old-age pension system, but is still very extensive, including more than three-quarters of all wage and salary earners. The main uncovered groups are state and local government employees, domestic servants, and workers on farms and in agricultural processing establishments.

The system is financed by a payroll tax levied on employers, varying from around 1 percent in some of the more rural states to around 3 percent in the leading industrial states. In most states, however, the tax applies only to the first $3,900 of each worker's earnings. Thus the tax base, tax rates, and annual outgo of the unemployment compensation system are considerably lower than under OASDHI. The obvious reason is that, while everyone grows old, not everyone suffers unemployment. Since 1945 the average unemployment rate has been low enough, so that benefits could be financed with a relatively small tax intake.[16]

16 This is not meant to imply that benefits are high enough, or that the system's finances are in satisfactory shape. One problem is that unemployment levels vary considerably from state to state. Thus states with relatively high unemployment, such as Michigan, Ohio, and Pennsylvania, have large compensation payments even in good years. In some states the unemployment compensation reserve fund is now less than one year's benefits, and the problem of how to bolster reserves is a serious one.

When a covered worker becomes unemployed through no fault of his own (i.e. when he is laid off, but not when he quits "without reasonable cause" or when he is discharged for cause), he is entitled to weekly benefits from the compensation fund. The weekly benefit is calculated as a percentage, usually 50 percent, of his average weekly earnings in some recent period. The reasoning behind this is that high-wage workers need more to maintain their customary standard of living than do low-wage workers. In addition, however, there is a flat maximum above which benefit payments may not rise in any event; and for this reason many workers are not able to get even 50 percent of their normal earnings. *Example:* a man normally earns $150 a week and, under the 50 percent principle, would draw unemployment compensation at $75 a week. The law in his state, however, sets a $50 a week ceiling on benefits. He will receive this maximum, but it amounts to only one-third of normal earnings instead of one-half.

The states have tended to raise their ceilings less rapidly than the money wage level has risen. The result is that a high proportion of benefit recipients receive the maximum, and even so average benefits paid are closer to one-third than to one-half of normal earnings. To restore the original intent of the system, sixteen states have now provided a "flexible maximum," which is recalculated annually or semiannually on the basis of actual weekly earnings in the state. The general rule is to set the figure at 50 percent of actual statewide earnings. Even at this level, workers who earn more than the statewide average will find their benefits restricted by the ceiling.

There is a limit also on the number of consecutive weeks for which a worker may draw benefits. The intent is to cover relatively short periods of unemployment suffered by regularly employed workers, but not to get involved in financing chronic or long-term unemployment among workers of low employability. In most states, a worker's maximum benefit period is calculated on the basis of his prior weeks of employment under the system, so it is shorter for some than for others. There is also a general maximum, usually twenty-six weeks, which may not be exceeded in any event.

The twenty-six-week maximum is reasonably adequate in good years. In most years only about 15 percent of the people who have spells of unemployment remain unemployed for more than twenty-six weeks. This percentage rises in recession years, however, so in such years there has been pressure to extend payments for a longer period. In the recession year 1958, Congress voted a federal fund from which the state unemployment compensation systems could borrow to extend benefit payments up to a maximum of thirty-nine weeks. In 1961 a different approach was adopted. The federal government took responsibility for financing the extended benefit payments, and Congress voted to recover the costs by a flat payroll tax of 0.4 percent on all covered employers during 1962 and 1963. About $800 million was paid out in 1961 to 1962 under this provision. Because it seemed unsatisfactory to have special legislation for each recession year, the 1966 amendments to the Social Security Act made extended benefits a regular feature of the system. A specified increase in unemployment either at the national level or within a particular state "triggers" an automatic extension of the benefit period to thirty-nine weeks for qualified workers who have reached the twenty-six-week limit; and there is also an "off" indicator which brings extended benefits to an end. The cost is covered by a federal payroll tax.

There must be some limit to benefit amounts and benefit periods to protect the insurance character of the unemployment compensation system and prevent it from deteriorating into general relief. At the same time, these limits—plus the fact that some workers are still uncovered—mean that unemployment compensation falls far short of replacing the earnings lost through unemployment. Lester has estimated that, over the years 1948 to 1959, compensation payments amounted to only 20 percent of total wage losses.[17] Because of more recent liberalizing amendments, the percentage is probably higher today, but even so it can scarcely be above 30 percent.

To a large extent, then, unemployed workers still finance their own unemployment. How do they adjust to a large and often unexpected drop in weekly income? [18] First, they defer purchase of consumer durables and any other expenses that can be postponed. Second, they use up their savings and other assets and go into debt by borrowing money and running up store bills. Third, a considerable proportion receive help from relatives and friends. By these expedients the great majority (90 to 95 percent) of unemployment compensation recipients are able to avoid going on relief. There is severe pressure on their consumption level, however, and this pressure increases with the duration of unemployment.

POVERTY REMEDIES:
INCOME
SUBSIDIES

Social insurance systems are oriented toward the regularly employed, and provide benefits that are somewhat proportionate to previous employment and earnings. Apart from the two major programs just described, there are special pension systems for federal civil servants, railroad workers, and veterans of the armed forces.

[17] Richard A. Lester, "The Economic Significance of Unemployment Compensation, 1948–1959," Review of Economics and Statistics, November, 1960.

[18] For a summary of research studies on this point, see Haber and Murray, *Unemployment Insurance,* pp. 187–92.

In addition to these insurance systems, there are several programs of public assistance oriented toward the nonemployable. Some of these are *categorical* programs, under which eligibility depends on certain personal characteristics. This includes old-age assistance for people not qualified for Social Security or whose benefits are seriously inadequate; aid to dependent children in families where the husband is not present; and aid to the blind. These programs are supported by matching federal grants to the states, but the states set benefit levels and administer the programs. Some 7½ million people are currently receiving benefits under these programs, of whom 4½ million are dependent children in upwards of a million families. The benefits are typically too small, however, to lift the recipients above the poverty line. For example, average monthly payments to the aged in a recent year varied from $35 in Mississippi to $109 in Minnesota; and the *percentage* of people aged sixty-five and over receiving state assistance varied from 3 percent in New York and New Jersey to 26 percent in Colorado. Average monthly payments to dependent children ranged from $9 in Mississippi to $47 in New Jersey and Minnesota.[19]

The last resort for those who fit into none of these categories is general public assistance. General assistance is financed entirely from state and local funds. The amounts paid vary widely from state to state, and even in the more generous states are well below the poverty line. Administration is cumbersome, bureaucratic, and degrading to the recipients. This is in a sense deliberate, since the main objective is to keep people off relief and to conserve funds rather than to alleviate poverty. Another unfortunate aspect of relief systems is that, if a member of a family on relief earns any money, the relief payment is reduced by a corresponding amount. This amounts to a 100 percent tax on income from work, and greatly reduces the incentive to seek employment.

How far do social insurance and public assistance programs go in lifting low-income families above the poverty line? Some interesting estimates on this point have been made by Professor Christopher Green.[20] He estimates that, in a recent year, about 13½ million families were below the poverty line *before* taking account of transfer payments. When transfer payments are added to family income, however, only about 9 million families were still poor. Thus about one-third of the original group had been lifted out of poverty through the transfers.

The dollar amounts involved, as estimated by Green, are shown in Table 5. It should be remembered that the transfer income of $13.8 billion shown on line (4) was only about half of total transfer pay-

[19] George F. Break, *Intergovernmental Fiscal Relations in the United States* (Washington, D.C.: The Brookings Institution, 1967), p. 81.

[20] Christopher Green, *Negative Taxes and the Poverty Problem* (Washington, D.C.: The Brookings Institution, 1967), chap. 2.

Item	*Before-Transfer Poor*	*Families Who Remained Poor After Transfers*	*Families Made Nonpoor by Transfers*
(1) INCOME NEEDED IN ORDER NOT TO BE POOR	$32,734	$22,476	$10,258
(2) BEFORE-TRANSFER INCOME	14,764	8,582	6,182
(3) BEFORE-TRANSFER POVERTY GAP (1) — (2)	17,970	13,894	4,076
(4) TRANSFER INCOME	13,848	6,280	7,568
(5) TOTAL MONEY INCOME	28,730	14,969	13,761
(6) TRANSFERS AS A PERCENTAGE OF BEFORE-TRANSFER POVERTY GAP, (4) ÷ (3)	77.0	45.2	185.7
(7) TRANSFERS AS A PERCENTAGE OF TOTAL MONEY INCOME, (4) ÷ (5)	48.2	42.0	55.0

ments of $27.0 billion in this year. It includes only income going to families who without transfer would have been below the poverty line. The remaining half went to families who would have been above the poverty line in any event, but who were nevertheless entitled to benefits because of coverage by unemployment compensation, OAS-DHI, or other retirement systems.

Look especially at the center column, which shows the position of the million families who remained poor even after transfer payments. Taking account of family size and other factors, these families would have needed $22.5 billion of income to reach a level at which they would no longer be considered poor. From earnings and other private sources they had income of $8.6 billion, leaving a "poverty gap" of $13.9 billion. Government transfer payments to this group totaled $6.3 billion, or about 45 percent of the poverty gap. This percentage is probably higher today, however, because of the continued sharp increase in welfare payments.

While existing transfer programs are helpful in ameliorating poverty, they are by no means sufficient to eliminate it. One surprising fact is that a majority of poor families do not receive relief or other forms of public assistance. Green estimates that only about a third of the poor families and a fourth of the poor persons received public assistance in 1963. This could be caused by failure to fall into any of the groups eligible for categorical assistance. It could be caused also by a family having a house or other assets which it is unwilling to sell to qualify for relief; or existence of relatives who can be called on for support (most states require that such possibilities be exhausted before relief will be given); or failure to meet state and city residence requirements; or simply unwillingness to apply for relief, which carries a social stigma.

Alternative Income Subsidy Measures

Several kinds of action might be taken to close the remaining poverty gap. These are not mutually exclusive, but could be used in various combinations, depending on judgments about economic equity, political acceptability, and administrative efficiency.

First, benefit schedules under existing transfer programs could be raised. Much the largest of these programs is the OASDHI pension system. Monthly pensions could be set high enough to bring retired single persons (or a retired couple, as the case might be) up to the poverty line; and there could be provision for automatic escalation of pension rates to cover increases in the consumer price index. This would of course involve larger payments to a substantial proportion of pensioners who are already above the poverty level because of private resources; and this added expense—unnecessary from a poverty standpoint—might be considered a disadvantage. Similarly, an increase in unemployment compensation benefit rates, while it may be quite justified on other grounds, would be only incidentally an antipoverty measure. Green estimates that two-thirds of unemployment compensation payments go to families above the poverty level.

Public assistance payments, on the other hand, go almost entirely to poor families. An increase in benefits under these programs would have a direct effect on the poverty gap. Because of the heavy pressure on state and local budgets, a substantial part of any such increase would have to come from federal sources.

Second, low-income families could be subsidized in kind rather than in cash. Government could provide goods and services either free or at prices below full cost. We already do a good deal of this. Government now spends well over a billion dollars a year on payments to doctors, hospitals, and nursing homes for medical care of indigent patients. More than half of this comes from federal funds, but the states and localities also contribute. The need for this particular subsidy may diminish, however, as medical care of the aged is taken over increasingly by OASDHI funds under the medicare program. Public housing projects provide rentals below full cost for families below specified income levels. More recently, low-income families have been assisted to buy houses through federally subsidized interest rates on home mortgages. Substantial amounts of food are distributed to low-income families through the food-stamp programs of the Department of Agriculture. The school-lunch program provides schoolchildren, regardless of income, with milk, citrus juices, and other requirements for adequate nutrition.

Such programs are sometimes criticized as an unwise infringement by government on consumers' freedom of choice. If government wishes to raise the living standards of the poor, why not simply give them more cash and leave them to spend it as they please? Is it not reasonable to suppose that consumers will get greatest satisfaction by choosing the goods they individually want? If they choose beer rather than housing, whose business is it but their own?

One can make a strong case for free choice in the market as the general rule. But there are at least two important qualifications. First, consumption of some items by one family has strong external effects on other families. The amount I spend on education or preventive medical care affects my neighbors now and may also affect the welfare of future generations. So one can justify subsidies designed to induce consumers to buy more of such goods than they would consider to be in their individual interest. Second, in some fields the market does not seem to operate very effectively in meeting consumer preferences. Urban housing is a leading example. It is doubtful that the desire of inner city residents for better housing, even if supported by adequate incomes, could by itself bring about slum clearance and the construction of new housing in such a way as to prevent development of future slums. Effective action has to involve sizable tracts of land, substantial financing, and the joint planning of housing, schools, parks, transportation, and facilities. This provides a rationale for public stimulus and supervision, though not necessarily for public subsidy.

Third, the burden of taxation on the lowest-income groups could be reduced. While the poor do not pay much income tax, they pay heavily in sales, excise, and property taxes. Musgrave has estimated that taxes take about 27 percent of incomes below $2,000 a year, and 28 percent of incomes in the $2,000–3,000 bracket. This could be offset by giving poor families a direct payment—a "tax credit"—amounting to say, 30 per cent of their money income. Green estimates that this would raise 3.3 million families, or about one-third of the poor, above the poverty line. The main administrative problem would be accurate determination of household income, which might require the services of the Bureau of Internal Revenue. The main equity problem is that this kind of transfer, being proportionate to income, would do most for the "best-off poor" and least for the "poorest poor."

Fourth, a proposal going farther in this same general direction is that for a "negative income tax." It is argued that this device has the advantages of transferring income only to the lower-income groups,

in amounts tailored to their need, and with no qualifying requirements except proof of the family's income level. If adopted uniformly
throughout the the United States, it could potentially eliminate any
need for local relief, categorical assistance, and other special programs.

While a variety of plans have been proposed,[21] they have several
common features:

1. A *basic allowance* or income guarantee. This is the amount paid
to a family whose other income for the year is zero. It is the family's
minimum disposable income. It could be adjusted to family size according to a prescribed scale.

2. An *offsetting tax*, which the family would pay on its income from
work or other sources. The main issue here is the rate at which other
income should be taxed—one-third, one-half, two-thirds, or whatever.
The higher the tax rate, the less the scheme would cost the federal
government, but the smaller also would be the incentive to work and
earn income. There would, however, be more incentive than exists
under present relief systems, which impose a 100 percent tax on earned
income.

3. The *net benefit* to the recipient is the basic allowance less the
offsetting tax. At low income levels, the government would be making
net payments to the family—hence the term "negative income tax."
As the family's other income rises, the net benefit would decline.
Eventually one reaches a *break-even* point, at which the offsetting tax
just equals the basic allowance, and the family neither pays nor receives anything.

By combining various basic allowances with various tax rates one
can derive numerous concrete programs. Suppose, for example, one
set a basic allowance of $2,500 for a family of four and a tax of 50
percent on other income. Then family income would behave as shown
in Table 6. The break-even point under this program would occur at
an income level of $5,000. Income above that level would be subject
to normal rates of personal income taxation.

How much would a negative income tax plan cost the government?
This depends heavily on the basic allowance schedule and on the rate
of offsetting tax. It depends also on how "other income" is defined.
For example, should Social Security and public assistance payments
be counted as other income subject to tax? What about the rental
value of an owner-occupied house, or the value of food grown and

---

[21] See, for example, Milton Friedman, *Capitalism and Freedom* (Chicago: The
University of Chicago Press, 1963); James A. Tobin, Joseph A. Pechman, and Peter
M. Mieszkowski "Is a negative income tax practical?", *Yale Law Journal*, December,
1967, pp. 1–27 (reprinted copies available also from The Brookings Institution);
Christopher Green, *Negative Taxes;* and George H. Hildebrand, *Poverty, Income
Maintenance, and the Negative Income Tax* (Ithaca, N.Y.: New York State School
of Industrial and Labor Relations, 1967).

Table 6

OPERATION OF A NEGATIVE INCOME TAX SYSTEM

Basic Allowance	*Other Income*	*Tax Payment*	*Net Benefit*	*Disposable Income*
(1)	(2)	(3)	(1) − (3) (4)	(2) + (4) (5)
2,500	0	0	2,500	2,500
2,500	1,000	500	2,000	3,000
2,500	2,000	1,000	1,500	3,500
2,500	3,000	1,500	1,000	4,000
2,500	4,000	2,000	500	4,500
2,500	5,000	2,500	0	5,000

consumed on farms? Finally, adoption of a negative income tax plan would reduce the need for existing programs of categorical assistance and general relief. Scaling down of these programs would yield a substantial tax saving. Thus the net cost of the negative income tax would be considerably less than its gross cost. After making assumptions on these points, which can be checked in the original source, the Tobin-Pechman-Mieszkowski paper estimates that the net cost of the most plausible programs would lie in the range of $10 billion to $20 billion.

An uncertain and disputed aspect of such a program is its effect on work incentives. Availability of "other income" tends, as we saw in Chapter 2, to reduce labor force participation. Depending on the generosity of the guaranteed income allowance, a family head employed at a low wage level might increase his family income by leaving his job. The fact that anything he might earn would be taxed at, say, 50 percent would also operate as a disincentive to work.

There would presumably be an effort to offset this effect by providing that a family with an employable member who refuses suitable work shall be disqualified from benefits; but administration of such a regulation raises numerous problems. What is "suitable" work? At what wage rates and other conditions? How far from home? Could a person without work skills be required to undergo training? In the case of women family heads, what degree of child-care responsibility would be accepted as an excuse from the work requirement?

The practical alternative to a guaranteed income plan, however, is not complete absence of income support, but rather a continuation of the present welfare system. Under the present system, money earned by a welfare client is usually deducted in full from his welfare payment. This 100 percent tax on earned income means that people who remain on welfare have no incentive whatever to work at the same time. On the other hand, the low level of welfare payments in most states provides an incentive to get off welfare and into employment.

Overall, one cannot say a priori whether a guaranteed income plan would have stronger or weaker disincentive effects than the welfare system. Much would depend on structural features of the two programs which were being compared. Nor do we know enough about the labor force behavior of the low-income population to draw any factual conclusions at this stage. In two areas of the country, an experimental negative income tax plan has been put into operation on a trial basis, with a view (among other things) to testing its labor force and employment effects; but the results of this research are not yet available.

In late 1969 President Nixon recommended to Congress a complete overhaul of the existing welfare system, which incorporated some features of the guaranteed income idea. While Congress has not acted on the program at this writing, a description of it may indicate the direction of current thinking.

For the largest category of welfare recipients—families with dependent children and no employed member—the program would establish a guaranteed annual income, uniform throughout the country, financed by the federal government, and adjusted to family size. For a family of four, this basic figure would be $1,600 per year. In addition, each state would be required to contribute at least 50 percent, but not more than 90 percent, of the amount it is presently spending on welfare in order to supplement the federal benefits. The result would be a sharp increase in benefit levels in the bottom half of states. For example, in the lowest state which now pays a family of four about $40 per month, the payment would rise to $140 per month. At the same time, the financial burden on the states and localities would be reduced, part of present costs and all new costs being transferred to the federal budget.

The program would apply also to the "working poor," some of whom are now employed at wage levels yielding little more than they would get on relief. A family of four with an employed member would be guaranteed the same $1,600 per year; and the first $720 of its earnings would be disregarded in setting this allowance. For each dollar of earnings above $720, the guaranteed payment would be reduced by 50 cents, disappearing entirely when annual earnings reached $3,920.

The operation of such a system is illustrated in Figure 1. The path of family income as earnings increase would be $ABCD$. Point A is the amount guaranteed if earnings are zero. At point B, corresponding to earnings of $720, subsidy payments begin to fall by 50 cents for each dollar of earnings. At point C the income subsidy ceases, and from then on total income equals earned income along the 45-degree line OD.

The monthly payments would be made by the Social Security Ad-

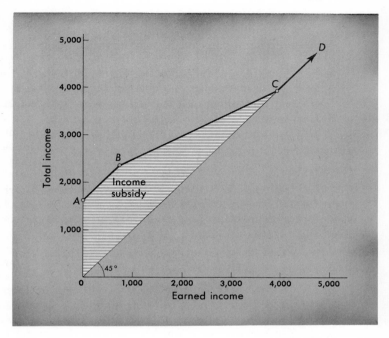

Figure 1

OPERATION OF A GUARANTEED
INCOME PLAN

ministration, on the basis of income statements submitted by the recipients. Since almost all organized employment is now covered by Social Security, with the authorities receiving reports from employers on each worker's earnings, it would be easy to check these individual statements against the records. City welfare departments would presumably continue to operate, but would no longer have any financial duties. They would be free to concentrate on positive functions such as family counseling, vocational guidance, and psychotherapy, instead of policing family income and expenditure.

Discussion Questions

1. "Inequality of family incomes is a persistent fact of our economy." Explain the main reasons for the present inequality of family incomes in the United States.

2. Would you expect family income distribution to be more equal, or less equal, in 2000 than in 1970? Explain.
3. Do you think government should take steps toward further equalization of incomes in the United States? Why, or why not? If your answer is positive, what specific measures would you advocate?
4. "As wage and income levels continue to rise in the American economy, the poverty problem will largely take care of itself." Discuss.
5. Assume that there will continue to be minimum wage legislation in the United States, but that the undesirable effects noted in the text should so far as possible be avoided. What does this suggest about the construction of minimum wage laws?
6. "It is not a good idea for government to provide poor families with food, housing, medical care, or what not at cut-rate prices. Where subsidies are desirable, it is better to give a cash subsidy and let people spend it as they prefer." Discuss.
7. Describe the main ways in which transfer payments to the low-income population might be increased, and appraise their relative merits.
8. How would a negative income tax system operate? Do you think it would be desirable to institute such a program?
9. What were the merits of the 1969 Nixon proposal for welfare reform? What did Congress do with the proposal? What do you think of what they did?

Reading Suggestions

In addition to the references cited in the chapter, see Wilcox, Clair, *Toward Social Welfare*. Homewood, Ill., Richard D. Irwin, Inc., 1968. Current data on the size and characteristics of the poverty population are published each year in the *Report of the Council of Economic Advisers*. Current data on household income distribution are published by the Bureau of the Census in its *Current Population Reports* series.

COLLECTIVE BARGAINING: INSTITUTIONS AND PROCEDURES

This section of the book includes three subsections, each consisting of three chapters. After a brief survey of industrial relations systems in other countries (Chapter 11), we examine the growth of American trade unions over the past century and a half (Chapter 12). The growth of union membership has slowed considerably since 1950, and the percentage of the labor force in unions has fallen. The prospects for future growth depend largely on union ability to organize workers in white-collar employment and in the southern states, and we examine union prospects in these areas. Chapter 13 analyzes the internal government of trade unions, the extent of membership influence on union policy, and efforts to protect members' rights against arbitrary action by the leadership.

Turning to union–management relations, we first examine the central objectives of union and management officials (Chapter 14). These objectives are in conflict, not only because the union usually wants more money, but also because unions strive to limit management's discretion in personnel and production decisions. The parties are locked in a power struggle, the outcome of which has important economic consequences. Chapter 15 describes the procedures used in negotiating "union contracts," and in administering these contracts from day to day through the "grievance procedure." In Chapter 16 we examine the concept of "bargaining power," the tactical maneuvers used by union and management negotiators, and the reasons why negotiations sometimes end in a deadlock. A deadlock usually leads to a strike, so we discuss the frequency of strikes and their economic cost.

Collective bargaining operates within a framework of legal rules, imposed partly by state and federal statutes, partly by rulings of administrative bodies such as the National Labor Relations Board, and partly by court decisions. Chapter 17 describes the way in which public policy has evolved from strong hostility toward unions before 1930, through a brief prounion period from 1933 to 1947, toward greater neutrality combined with increasingly detailed regulation of industrial relations. In Chapter 18 we outline the main principles of contemporary labor law. The treatment is necessarily too brief to do justice to such a complex subject. But it may serve to indicate the main issues, the points on which the law seems quite definite, and the areas in which the rules are still unclear and evolving.

In Chapter 19 we examine frontier areas of public policy, of which two are especially important. First, what can be done about "emergency strikes" which cut off an essential service such as railroad transport, electric power production, food deliveries, health and sanitation services? Such strikes cannot be allowed to continue for any length of time. Yet the disputes which give rise to them must somehow be resolved. We examine the main devices which have been used in this area, and also some new and experimental proposals. Second, we consider the status of unionism and collective bargaining in public employment. Public policy has been slower to accept unionism in this area than in private industry. Yet the same employment problems exist, unions of government employees are growing rapidly, and strikes and other interruptions of service are frequent. We examine recent state and federal legislation in this area and the problems which remain unsettled.

INDUSTRIAL
RELATIONS
SYSTEMS:
A COMPARATIVE
VIEW

11

Trade unions exist in all parts of the world. There are unions in Senegal, in Pakistan, in Chile, in Rumania. But what a union is and what it does varies greatly from country to country. Collective bargaining in the American sense is limited largely to northern and western Europe, the United States, Canada, Australasia, and Japan. Even within this range of countries, there are marked differences in union strength and bargaining procedures. In the USSR and the East European countries, trade union functions reflect basic differences in political structure. In most countries of the "third world," unions are weakly organized, highly political, and rather ineffectual.

It will be instructive to look briefly at these intercountry differences. Without this we are apt to conclude erroneously that American practices are natural and inevitable. The American industrial relations system, like any other national system, has been shaped by a specific politico–economic matrix. Some features it has in common with other countries, but some are peculiar to the United States. Our practices are no more "natural" than those of Sweden, Italy, Australia, or

Japan; and we shall understand them better by looking at them in world perspective.

What do we mean by an "industrial relations system"? [1] We mean such things as:

1. The politico–economic matrix which surrounds employer–employee relations: the industrial structure of the country, the characteristics of the labor force, the looseness or tightness of the labor market, management's personnel policies, and the balance of power in the political system.

2. The characteristics of trade unions: whether workers are organized by plant, by craft, or by industry, whether power resides mainly in local or national unions, the degree of membership attachment, the strength of union finances and leadership.

3. Trade union tactics: whether they concentrate mainly on controlling the employer through collective bargaining or on influencing government through political action.

4. The structure of collective bargaining: the size of bargaining units, the subjects regulated by agreement, the duration of agreements, the method of resolving disputes over the application of the agreement, the use of strikes and other forms of economic pressure.

5. The framework of public control, which determines what the parties may bargain about and what tactics they may use.

We could embark on a Cook's tour of countries, trying to give a thumbnail sketch of each country's system in a few pages. But this might become tedious, and the number of interesting countries is too large to handle in this way. It seems preferable to discuss each of these structural characteristics in general terms, drawing on material from individual countries for illustrative purposes.

THE POLITICO–ECONOMIC MATRIX

When we say that an industrial relations system reflects the setting in which it has developed, what do we mean? What aspects of the setting are important, and why are they important? This subject could easily become a chapter in itself. We limit ourselves to a few topics of particular importance.

The Size of Employing Units

Where people work for themselves as farmers, storekeepers, or artisans, the problem of employment relations does not arise. Beyond

---

[1] For an effort to answer this difficult question, see John T. Dunlop, *Industrial Relations Systems* (New York: Holt, Rinehart and Winston, Inc., 1958).

this, unionism is associated with establishments *of substantial size.* Small workshops employing only a handful of workers are not very susceptible to union organization. Railroads, steel mills, government departments, and other large employing units are much more susceptible. This seems to be as true in India, Japan, or Uganda as it is in the United States or France.

In small shops the employer has somewhat the role of a family head. He is apt to know his workers rather intimately, and to take some part in their family festivities and social life. The simplicity of production organization does not require elaborate rules of procedure. Instead of formalized personnel policies, one has day-to-day decisions by the employer to meet situations as they arise.

The situation is different in an enterprise with hundreds or thousands of employees. The top manager, whose orders may be filtered through several layers of subordinates, is less of a person and more of an abstraction. It seems natural that his impersonal power should be countered by forming a separate workers' organization. The fact that there are many employees enhances their combined power—for example, by making them harder to replace in the event of a strike.

A large organization must either (a) have definite rules for production and personnel management, in which case workers can reasonably argue that they should have a voice in setting the rules; or (b) in the absence of definite rules, the differing decisions of individual foremen are likely to create injustices, or at least to provoke charges of injustice from the workers under them. This creates an atmosphere in which the argument for a union capable of protecting workers against arbitrary action becomes quite persuasive.

The size of the potential union "base" in a particular country is readily determined. First, subtract from the national labor force all farmers and other self-employed persons. (In the less-developed countries of Asia, Africa, and Latin America, the great bulk of the gainfully employed are self-employed.) Then subtract those working for employers with fewer than, say, twenty employees. This leaves as (potentially) organizable the government employees; workers in transportation, power, and other public-utility type enterprises; workers in sizable manufacturing and mining establishments; construction workers on large projects; possibly some agricultural workers on large farms or plantations.

Even in India, with its relatively large industrial base, this organizable area includes only about 5 percent of the labor force. In some countries of tropical Africa, the proportion would be only 1 or 2 percent. In the more-developed Latin American countries, it might approach 10 percent. So even if *all* potential union members were actually enrolled, total membership would be relatively small.

At the opposite pole, the country with the highest percentage of its workers in large establishments is probably the United States.

Three-quarters of our manufacturing workers are in establishments with upwards of 100 employees. If one adds to this miners, public utility workers, government employees, and half of those in construction, trade, and services, it appears that two-thirds of the American labor force is in what might be considered the normal area of union operation. The proportion is high also in Canada, Britain, several of the Western European countries, and Japan.

Characteristics of the Labor Force

A key characteristic of the industrial labor force in many countries is its newness. People very recently out of the bush or the rice paddy are being trained for employment in the "modern" sector of the economy. There is much evidence that, given proper training, supervision, and incentives, these new recruits can become efficient industrial workers within a few years. It seems to take longer, however, for them to develop attitudes and traditions that are compatible with strong union organization.

In the older industrial countries, the lag between the appearance of industry and the appearance of widespread unionism was long indeed. Britain's Industrial Revolution began before 1800, and there was limited unionism among skilled workers throughout the nineteenth century; but not until the 1890s was there mass unionization among the less skilled. The United States was building textile mills in the 1810s, and had a large industrial base by 1870; but again, large-scale organization of semiskilled and unskilled workers dates only from the 1930s. Japan was already industrializing in the 1880s and nineties; but widespread unionism developed only after 1945, and then partly under the impetus of U.S. occupation policies.

One should not turn these examples into a historical law. The lag between industrial development and widespread unionization may well be shorter in today's industrializing countries. But one should not be surprised that few of these countries yet have sizable union movements.

Many employees in newly industrializing countries do not yet have a permanent commitment to industrial employment. In sub-Sahara Africa, the tradition of migratory labor is still strong. A young man may travel hundreds of miles to find employment in a Johannesburg mine or a Nairobi factory. He works there for two or three years, after which he returns home with his bicycle, transistor radio, and other modern necessities, and perhaps with enough money to pay a bride-price to his prospective father-in-law. Even in India, with its longer industrial tradition, it is reported that Bombay textile-mill workers return frequently to their native villages for family ceremonials and religious festivities. While they have one foot in the industrial economy, their social security still lies largely in their family and village connections.

The educational level of factory workers in the less-developed countries is low and many are illiterate. Even if the impetus to unionism is present, it is hard to find people capable of running a meeting, keeping the union's books, or drafting written agreements with the employer. Partly for this reason, most union officials in India are "outsiders," often lawyers who have no direct connection with the industry. One of these men may serve a dozen or more local unions, giving each a minimal share of his time. This is a general problem throughout Africa, Asia, and many parts of Latin America.

Another important factor is the social status of the worker and his attitude toward the employer. In some countries the class stucture is rigid and traditions of class hostility are strong. This is true, for example, in France, Italy, and most parts of Latin America. Union and political leaders preach constantly to the worker that the employer is his enemy. He is not to be reasoned with, he is to be overthrown. Most employers look down on their workers with equal distaste. This makes for guerilla warfare in industrial relations rather than for peaceful bargaining.

In some countries, the gap is widened by caste and racial cleavages. How can a high-caste Hindu negotiate on equal terms with workers from the lowest strata of Indian society? How can a South African mine owner negotiate with African workers who by definition are second-class citizens? (In the independent African state of Zambia, on the other hand, unions of African copper miners negotiate quite effectively with the foreign-owned copper companies.)

Japan has an unusual and strong tradition of worker attachment to the company. Young people normally enter an enterprise on leaving school and expect to remain with it for the rest of their working lives, moving up the wage ladder primarily on the basis of age. Under these conditions, as Professor Alice Cook points out, ". . . workers generally are reluctant to undertake actions which may endanger their job security or, equally important, their relationships with the firm. Strikes . . . tend, as one union leader put it . . . to differ from their counterparts in the West since 'it is not our intention to hurt the enterprise, but rather to call the attention of the public to our grievances.' The delicate arrangement of feelings, sentiments, and obligations which constitute the Japanese concept of loyalty are not to be seriously or lengthily disturbed by any anti-enterprise action." [2]

---

[2] Alice H. Cook, *Japanese Trade Unionism* (Ithaca: Cornell University Press, 1966), p. 8.

Tightness of the Labor Market

The labor market is often biased in favor of the employer, in the sense that there is a surplus of available workers over available jobs. Where this surplus is large, the conditions for unionism are unfavorable. In many of the less-developed countries, there is substantial underemployment in the cities and an almost bottomless reservoir of underemployed farmers in the countryside. Those who have jobs in the modern sector, usually at wage rates well above what can be earned in agriculture, are a privileged class. They are not eager to jeopardize their jobs, and they are in a poor position to bargain, since they could be replaced instantly from the unemployed. This is undoubtedly one reason for the relative weakness of unionism in the less-developed countries.

The same phenomenon was evident in earlier times in the presently "developed" countries. Japan, from the 1870s onward, had a large flow of labor from country to city and a consistent labor surplus in industry. Only in the 1950s did the reservoir finally run dry, and then only because of a sharp drop in the birthrate. This must be partly responsible for the fact that unionism was not a prominent feature of Japanese industry until after 1945. The United States had from the 1840s to the 1920s, in addition to a high rate of natural increase, a large influx of European immigrants created an ample supply of low-skilled labor. This seriously hampered union organization outside the skilled crafts.

But while unemployment is harmful to unionism in one way, it is helpful in another. It reduces the bargaining power of the individual worker, which consists essentially in his ability to change jobs. If there is either temporary unemployment or a continuing labor surplus, most workers will have difficulty in finding other jobs. How, then, can the worker protect himself against the employer *without quitting?* How can he ward off wage cuts and other adverse acts by the employer in bad years? One obvious way is to join his fellow workers in a mutual assistance pact, a trade union.

From this point of view, permanent prosperity might undermine union strength by reducing the worker's need for protection. Thanks partly to improvements in economic knowledge and national economic management, unemployment has been very low in the Western European countries since 1945. Except for the period from 1958 to 1964, it has been unusually low in the United States. In many countries labor has been so scarce that employers have bid up wages above the official union scale. The threat of wage cuts, layoffs, and so on has receded. It is thus natural for many workers to conclude that the union is not adding much to what they could win on their own. This may partly account for the fact that, both in the United States and Western Europe, the unionized percentage of the labor force tended to decline during the fifties and sixties.

The Political Structure

Finally, we must note the important influence of power relations among economic interests. The American-Western European systems of industrial relations have developed in a specific and rather unusual political context: a plural society with multi-party government, administrations changeable at the will of a broadly based electorate, economic groups which have independent bases of power and interact with the political regime in a complicated pattern.

Most countries do not have this kind of structure. About half of the less-developed countries have military governments in which, while one general may replace another, the military remains in control. Most of the remaining less-developed countries have one-party governments, with other parties either prohibited or in a permanent minority position. Only in India, the Philippines, Chile, and a few other countries does one find a functioning multi-party system. In a one-party state one can scarcely expect unions to enjoy much independence. They may be forbidden, they may be ignored and overridden, they may be (as in Argentina under Perón, Brazil under Vargas, or Italy under Mussolini) absorbed into the authoritarian structure of government and thus enabled to survive in emasculated form.

The situation is different again in the U.S.S.R. and the Eastern European countries. There are trade union organizations which perform important functions. But their method of operation is conditioned by their being embedded in a one-party political system, with all producing enterprises owned by the state and subject to a central economc plan.

UNION
ORGANIZATION

We now bring the unions onto the scene and raise such questions as: What is the meaning of union membership, at various times and places? Is there a tendency for some kinds of workers to become unionized earlier than others? Do workers most commonly organize by *occupation*, by *company*, or by *industry?* What are the main *levels* (local, regional, national) of organization, and what determines the balance of power among these levels?

The Meaning of Union Membership

Union membership is normally *permissible,* and it is normally *voluntary;* but neither statement is invariably true. In nineteenth-century Britain and the United States, judges imbued with laissez-faire economics often ruled that a union was an illegal combination in restraint of trade. Only after decades of legal and political struggle was the right of unions to exist clearly established. Even today there are countries in which to join a union is to commit a crime.

It is usually left to the union organizer to persuade workers to join; but this may be accompanied by various types of external pressure. American unions have devised the "union shop" clause, under which new workers hired by the company must join the union within a specified period. The union shop is common also in Japan, perhaps because of American influence during the occupation period, or perhaps because of the strong enterprise attachment already noted. The worker's lifetime commitment to the enterprise includes a similar commitment to the union organization within the enterprise. The union shop is not found, however, in such strongly unionized countries as Britain, Australia, Germany, and the Scandinavian countries, where worker solidarity is strong enough to make social pressure an effective weapon. In Britain, a nonunion man in a unionized shop is "sent to Coventry"; no one will speak to him, no one will eat or drink with him, no one will work alongside him.

Another specifically American concept is that of "exclusive jurisdiction" by a single union over a certain category of workers. AFL leaders of the eighties and nineties felt that the trade union movement was too fragile to weaken itself further by interunion competition. The principle of exclusive jurisdiction was accordingly written into the constitution of the Federation, and remains a cardinal principle of the AFL-CIO today. Each national union has a certain job territory within which it alone is permitted to enroll members. Disputed areas, which two or more unions claim are within their territory, are usually adjusted by negotiation under Federation auspices.

In most other countries, each union organizes wherever it is able. In Britain, union "territories" have grown up every which way over a century and a half of history. It is common to find half a dozen unions with members in the same plant. This happens also in countries where the union movement is split along political or religious lines. Thus in a French factory one may find members of a communist union, a socialist union, a Catholic union, even an independent union. This obviously creates complications in dealing with the employer. In Britain, unions with overlapping territories in the same industry have usually solved the problem by forming confederations for collective bargaining. In France and Italy, too, unions with differing political outlooks often collaborate in bargaining negotiations.

American unions require their members to pay regular monthly dues, and members may be dropped for nonpayment. A common union contract provision is the "checkoff," under which the employer deducts union dues and transmits them directly to the union. Dues paying is also a regular practice in Canada, Australia, Britain, Germany, Scandinavia, and Japan. But that is about it. In Italy and France, even those who consider themselves "members" pay dues only sporadically and intermittently. The percentage of dues-paying workers is still lower in most of the less-developed countries.

In such countries, "union membership" becomes hard to define. Does it mean the number of people who have a nominal affiliation with the union, who will attend a mass meeting or participate in a "quickie" strike? In this case the total numbers may be impressive. Or does it mean the number who contribute regular financial support? This may be a small fraction of the first total. In countries other than the few cited above, the number of members claimed by union leaders gives an exaggerated impression of union strength.

A union whose dues are low or nonexistent is seriously handicapped. It cannot accumulate enough funds to support its members during a strike. Nor can it afford to pay for full-time, salaried leadership. A practical reason for strong communist influence in the trade unions of many countries is that the Party usually has money while the unions do not. The Party functionary, with a secure payroll behind him, can offer his time free of charge for union affairs; and a union with no other source of professional leadership may accept the offer.

The Propensity to Organize

The propensity to become unionized has not been thoroughly studied, but the evidence would probably support two hypotheses: first, unionism typically originates with the best-off workers rather than the worst-off. The skilled craftsmen organize earlier and more strongly than the less skilled. In the United States, the earliest unions were among printers, carpenters, and journeymen cordwainers (shoemakers). The first unions in Great Britain consisted of building and printing trades' workers, who were followed shortly afterward by unions of tailors and wool combers. The prosperous condition of the wool combers is indicated by the fact that they normally came to work in top hats and long coats. In Sweden, the first unions were formed by the printers, the next by the carpenters, and the next by the skilled metal trades' workers. These crafts have a tradition extending almost unbroken from the medieval guilds. Proud of their skill, financially able to pay dues, with a fraternal feeling based on common training and experience, these men are quick to resent and resist any worsening of their conditions of employment.

Second, there are indications that some *industries* are more union-prone than others. This seems to be true of coal and metal mining, where workers often live together in remote areas and work under unusually difficult conditions. It is true also of the transport industries. Even in countries where unionism is not generally strong, the railroad workers, dock workers, and merchant seamen are usually organized. This may be due partly to conditions of life and work in these industries, partly to the economic power of those who can bring transportation to a standstill.

Bases of Organization

In some industries most of the work force falls in a single occupational group. Most coal mine employees are miners, and their basis of organization is clear. But in many industries this is not true. An automobile assembly plant employs laborers, assembly line workers, machinists, tool- and diemakers, patternmakers, electricians, carpenters, and a variety of other skills. This raises a question whether the dominant principle of organization shall be by occupation or by industry. Should all workers in the plant belong to a single union, or should there be multiple unions representing the various skill groups?

This has been a continuing issue in the American labor movement, particularly during the 1930s when the new CIO industrial unions were challenging the older craft-based AFL. Arguments were advanced purporting to show that one basis or the other was logically correct. Actual union structure from country to country, however, has been shaped more by history and practical expediency than by logical principles.

Very broadly, one can say that the industry principle predominates, and has tended to predominate increasingly with the passage of time. In the United States, Britain, and a few other countries one finds separate unions for each craft in industries where skills are clearly identifiable, such as printing, building construction, and railroad operation. Most countries, however, have single unions of railroad workers, construction workers and so on (though sometimes with subunits for the various crafts). In Sweden, Germany, France, and other European countries with a long union tradition, where a variety of union forms had grown up over the years, there has been a deliberate effort to merge these into a smaller number of units along industrial lines.

In manufacturing, where most of the labor force is semiskilled and craftsmen are a minority, organization by industry is almost universal. This is generally true of mining, public utilities, and transportation.

Government employees tend also to be organized in broad, industry-type unions, though quasi-professional groups such as teachers often prefer to maintain a separate identity.

In some countries one finds multi-industry unions covering a complex of related activities. In Italy, for example, both employers and workers are organized by "categories" of employment. The "metal-mechanical category" covers steel, automobiles, shipbuilding, electrical apparatus, and a variety of other metal-fabricating industries. In West Germany the Metal Workers' Union, which has almost a quarter of total union membership in the country, includes workers in iron and steel plants, automobile factories, foundries, machine shops, electrical equipment factories, and many others. In Britain, the giant Transport and General Workers' Union takes in members from a wide range of industries.

Multi-industry unionism is not common in the United States, where the AFL-CIO has usually defined jurisdiction along industry lines or along narrower craft lines within an industry. The United Steelworkers, however, embraces a wide range of steel-fabricating industries. The United Automobile Workers extends beyond automobiles into aircraft and other industries, where it often encounters the even more wide-ranging Machinists' union. The Teamsters, while it has a solid core of truck drivers, has ranged far afield to take in members only distantly related—or not related at all—to transportation.

Levels of Organization

The basic units of the trade union world are local units: but these can be set up in two different ways. First, a local may include only employees of a single company. This is the main basis of organization in the United States. (Where employers are numerous and small, however, the same local may include employees of different companies, as is usually true of the building trades' unions, the retail clerks, and so on.) In Japan, too, where worker attachment to the enterprise is very important, the enterprise union is typically the basic unit. Its company-oriented character is indicated by the fact that it usually includes white-collar workers up to the lower levels of management, and that many union officers are from the white-collar group.

In most countries, however, union organization is basically territorial. The local branch includes all members of a particular union, regardless of employer, in a particular city or district. There may be sublocals for members in a particular plant, but these groups do not have the independence and vitality of the U.S. plant local. This weakness, in most countries, of *union organization within the plant* is a serious handicap in handling issues arising at the plant level.

In France, Italy, Latin America, and some other countries the situation is complicated by political and religious cleavages. Thus instead of a single construction workers' local in a French city, one may have a communist-oriented local, a socialist-oriented local, and a Catholic-oriented local. Each of these will have members who work side by side for all construction employers in the area.

The superstructure of the union world is constructed along both industrial and geographic lines. The local union of construction workers belongs to a national union of construction workers, representing workers in this industry throughout the country. At the same time the construction workers' local will usually belong to a federation of all local unions in its city; and above this may be broader federations on a state or regional basis. At the top of the structure is an overarching federation, uniting both the industrial unions and the geographic federations in a single body. Thus in the United States most unions are affiliated with the AFL-CIO, in Britain with the Trade Union Congress (TUC), in Sweden with the Landsorganisationen (LO), in Germany with the Deutsche Gewerkschaftsbund (DGB). In France and Italy, because of the political cleavages noted above, there are three top federations, each with a full panoply of national industrial unions and territorial federations.

Where does power reside in this complex structure? The answers differ from country to country. Broadly, the relative importance of industrial as against territorial units is linked to the relative emphasis on collective bargaining as against political action in a particular country. If one wants to bring pressure on the city council, the local federation of all unions in the city is the strongest instrument. At the national level, top federations such as the AFL-CIO are useful for lobbying and other political activities. For negotiating a contract with all steel producers, on the other hand, it is the United Steelworkers which matters; and here the national industrial union comes to the center of the stage. Thus in countries where collective bargaining is well established, the national industrial unions are the core of the trade union world. In countries where labor activities are more politically oriented, the geographic federations are relatively more important.

UNION STRATEGIES:
POLITICAL
ACTION

Unions pursue their objectives in two main ways: by bargaining with employers and by political action. On a world scale, the latter technique is more widely used. In almost every country the trade unions are associated with one or more political parties; and they function as a pressure group to secure minimum wage laws, social security laws, and other things of benefit to their members. Direct bargaining with employers is the predominant activity in only a handful of countries: Britain, Germany, the Scandinavian countries, Canada, the United States, Mexico, Australia, New Zealand, possibly Japan. Even in these countries, political action is of substantial importance.

This bifurcation of union strategy raises fascinating questions, about which little is known: what determines the distribution of union effort between politics and collective bargaining in a particular country? How is this related to the importance of government in the country's economy? To what extent do unions turn to politics because they are too weak to deal directly with employers? Does growing union strength in a country produce a shift of emphasis toward collective bargaining?

Political action is of two main types: (1) union support of a political party, with a view to changing the control of government; (2) union efforts to secure favorable action from whatever government is in power, through pressure, lobbying, and negotiation. We proceed to consider each of these lines of activity.

In terms of union–party relations, countries can be divided into four groups: (1) one-party countries, in which the party is dominant and unions play a subsidiary role; (2) "Labor-party countries," in which most unions are affiliated with a moderate socialist party on the British pattern; (3) fractionalized countries, in which there are several left-wing parties, with union support divided among them; (4) neutral countries, in which the unions have no official party affiliation.

One-Party Systems

The leading example of this situation is the Soviet-type economy, in which the Communist Party is the only recognized political organization. This is a relatively small, carefully selected, élite group, to which top figures in all branches of national life normally belong.

There are trade unions in these countries, with a typical structure of plant locals, industry-wide organizations, and national federations. The question whether these are "genuine" unions is perhaps a semantic one. They are certainly different from our unions, reflecting the institutional differences in the society. Most people are public employees, and a "strike against the government" is viewed with even more disfavor in the USSR than in the United States. Wage schedules for the entire economy are centrally determined. Individual plant managers operate within financial and other limits laid down by higher authorities, so that bargaining with them cannot have the same meaning as bargaining with the Ford Motor Company.

The top union federation, however, is involved in framing wage schedules and national regulations on hours, health and safety standards, vacations, bonuses, and so on. The local union, as will be explained in a later section, plays an important role in handling worker grievances. Its leverage comes from the fact that the elected union officials are natural leaders in the plant and often members of the Communist Party. A plant manager who is unreasonable and uncooperative in labor matters will find his shortcomings discussed in the local party meeting, and reports may go back to Moscow, through both party and union channels, that will do him no good.[3]

Labor Party Countries

These are countries in which a moderate socialist party operates with trade union support. The group includes Britain, Australia, New Zealand, and the three Scandinavian countries.

The nature and closeness of affiliation varies from country to country. In Denmark, individuals can join the party only by enrolling in the party club of their district. In Norway and Sweden, it is common for local unions to affiliate as a group. About half the membership of the Norwegian Labor Party, and about two-thirds that of the Swedish Social Democratic Party, comes from unionists who have affiliated in this way. In some countries national unions may affiliate for their entire membership. In Britain, for example, some eighty national unions are affiliated with the Labour Party, and these unions provide more than four-fifths of the Party's members. Where block affiliation is practiced, there is normally a legal provision that individual union members who favor another party may claim exemption from contributing money to support of the affiliated party.

Unlike the one-party countries, where the party is dominant and the unions subordinate, the union–labor party relation is conceived as an association of equal partners, with each organization performing its own functions under its own leadership. Galenson [4] has described the relationship in Britain as follows:

> The question frequently asked in other countries is whether the trade unions control the Labour Party or the Labour Party controls the trade unions. In fact neither interpretation would be true. Naturally the trade unions have an influence on Labour Party policy, but theirs is one influence among several and it is not uniform in character. On the whole

[3] The best available description of labor relations in the U.S.S.R. is Emily C. Brown, *Soviet Trade Unions and Labor Relations* (Cambridge: Harvard University Press, 1966).

[4] Walter Galenson, ed., *Comparative Labor Movements* (Englewood Cliffs, N.J.: Prentice-Hall, Inc., 1952), p. 190.

it is probably more negative than positive: It would be difficult for the Labour Party (or a Labour Government) to disregard any strong and widely held trade union opinion, but policy, except in those matters with which the trade unions are intimately concerned, is rarely initiated by the trade union wing of the Party. The trade unions for their part are usually careful not to act in such a way as to injure the Labour Party's prospects, but there is no merging of identities . . . it is not uncommon for the Trades Union Congress and the Labour Party to take a different view upon a subject, although they then endeavour to reach an agreement, or at least to avoid any violent conflict in public.

This does not mean that the relation is an easy one. The party, to win a national election, must present a program which will attract middle-class and white-collar voters as well as manual workers. Once in office, it is responsible for governing in the national interest. This may lead it to take positions that its union supporters regard as against their own interest. But if it goes too far in this direction, it will weaken its union base and will no longer be able to govern.

This dilemma is well illustrated by the problem of wage policy. In the era of high employment and continuing inflation since World War II, even labor governments have sought means of restraining the onrush of money wages. But it is hard to explain to union members why "their" government should be trying to hold down their wage increases. The result has been considerable union–party tension and considerable vacillation in policy. Another example is the 1969 effort of Labor Prime Minister Harold Wilson to impose restraints on unauthorized ("wildcat") strikes, which in longshoring and elsewhere have done considerable harm to Britain's export trade. Union officials, of whom more than a hundred sit as Labour members of Parliament, took strong exception to this proposal, and the government withdrew it rather than face serious intraparty strife.

Fractionalized Countries

In many countries several left-wing parties compete for union support. There are often "right-wing" and "left-wing" socialist parties. Even the more disciplined communist group may be divided into pro-Moscow, pro-Peking, and (in Latin America) pro-Havana factions. Each group has its supporters in the union world.

The union–party relation is usually not a formal affiliation, but a looser and more personal relationship. Some union leaders move over to become party leaders, and conversely. A union collaborates with its chosen party in organizing demonstrations, providing election workers and election finance, and selecting candidates for office. The party provides trained leadership and other free services to the union. Strikes and demonstrations are called over political as well as economic issues.

In France and Italy, the largest union federations have close links with the Communist parties of those countries. Several factors help to account for this. In both countries class lines are firmly drawn and class feeling is bitter. Employers typically look down on their workers to an extent that is difficult to imagine in the United States. They are bitterly opposed to dealing with trade unions, and collective bargaining is poorly developed. The unions are weakly organized, poorly financed, and the attachment of workers to them is so loose that one can scarcely speak of "union membership" in the American sense. A union may be able to call out a large number of workers for a short strike, but it cannot get these same workers to pay dues or participate in ordinary union activities. Seeing no way of rising through their own efforts and apparently blocked from advance through collective bargaining, not surprisingly, the workers turn to political activity. Economic and social reforms in these countries have been achieved almost entirely through legislation rather than through private collective bargaining. It is not surprising, then, that the political parties dominate the trade unions, and that the party with greatest popular appeal is the one that denounces employers in the strongest terms.

The situation is similar in many of the Latin American countries. The social gulf between employer and employee is wide, unions are rather weak and often led by men with primarily political interests, collective bargaining is poorly developed, and improvements in wages and other terms of employment are sought mainly through government. These conditions tend to produce a strong political orientation of the labor movement. Periodically, trade unions are suppressed by military or other dictatorships. In between, union strength is fragmented by rivalry among numerous left-wing groups.

An interesting exception is Mexico, where the unions are "in" rather than "out." Unions participated actively in the Mexican Revolution a half century ago, and are now a pillar of the dominant political party, which has governed continuously since the revolution. The leading union federation (the CTM) and most of its affiliates are solidly proadministration, though there is a communist-led minority. CTM leaders help to choose presidential candidates, are consulted on all relevant legislation, and appear frequently as legislators and administrators.[5]

In India there are four major federations, affiliated with the Congress, Communist, and two other political parties. As noted earlier, many union leaders are outsiders not employed in the industry, whose main interest is in using the union as a political base.

[5] See two books by Robert J. Alexander: *The Labor Movement in Brazil, Argentina, and Chile* (New York: McGraw-Hill Book Company, 1962); and *Organized Labor in Latin America* (New York: The Free Press, 1965).

In Japan there are right-wing socialist, left-wing socialist, and communist parties, each with its union supporters. In spite of the fact—or perhaps because of the fact—that workers have a rather paternalistic relation with the companies employing them, there is a strong "class struggle" atmosphere in Japanese politics. Antagonisms and frustrations that are muted within the enterprise break out in the political arena.

Union Neutrality in Politics

The leading example here is the United States. In modern times, left-wing political groups have not attained significant strength. Union groups with an ideological outlook. such as the Knights of Labor and the Industrial Workers of the World, have had little influence since World War I. The Socialist Party polled its largest presidential vote in 1912, but its strength has declined since then and is negligible at present. The Communist Party achieved some influence in the depressed conditions of the 1930s. A number of communists volunteered as organizers in the early CIO campaigns, and later served as officers of the new unions. After 1945, however, the foreign-policy split between the United States and the USSR produced a similar split between American communists (who continued to support the Soviet position) and noncommunist labor leaders. During 1949 and 1950, eleven national unions with some 900,000 members were expelled from the CIO on grounds of communist control. The present AFL-CIO constitution contains strong provisions against domination of unions by communists or members of other totalitarian groups, and communist influence has fallen to a very low level.

The earlier AFL and the present AFL-CIO have also refused to ally themselves permanently with either of the major political parties. They pick and choose among candidates from one election to the next, depending mainly on the individual's voting record on labor issues. Since the New Deal era, however, there has been a strong tendency to support the Democratic candidate in Presidential elections.

In West Germany also there is a single major union federation, which is officially neutral among parties. This was not always so. Before World War II the German labor movement was divided among communist, socialist, and religious groupings. This fragmentation of the labor movement is believed to have weakened the basis of democratic government, contributing to Hitler's rise to power in 1933. Burned by this experience, postwar union leaders have resolved to avoid ideological cleavages in the interest of a united labor movement. In day-to-day politics, German unions lean toward the Social Democrats; but there is no direct party affiliation.

Unions as Pressure Groups: American Experience

Political neutrality does not mean political inactivity. American unions take a strong interest in passing prolabor legislation and in seeing that this legislation is effectively administered. Since we shall have no occasion elsewhere in this book to discuss these political activities, it may be appropriate to use American experience for illustrative purposes.

1. *Endorsement and Support of Candidates.* State and local labor groups in the United States have been endorsing political candidates for more than fifty years; and the top AFL-CIO leadership frequently endorses presidential candidates. Approval of a candidate lays a foundation for financial support. Union contributions to election campaigns have been restricted in a series of acts culminating in the Taft–Hartley Act of 1947, which prohibited political contributions in elections, primaries, or conventions involving federal offices. Some state legislatures have enacted similar bans on union activity in state elections. This has forced the unions to operate through quasi-independent political affiliates, such as the AFL-CIO Committee on Political Education. This Committee collects donations from union members for political activity and maintains a separate treasury. Below the national Committee on Political Education are state and local committees which interest themselves in elections at those levels, and which actually spend a good deal more money than the national body.

Contributions of unpaid time by union members are probably as important as cash contributions. Of particular importance is the systematic organization that actually gets out the vote. Door-to-door canvassing must be carried out in advance of election day. Lists of qualified voters must be checked to see that maximum registration is achieved. On election day, more lists must be checked, telephone calls made, and automobile transportation and even baby-sitting provided, to be sure that registered voters get an opportunity to vote.

There is little evidence that the labor vote can be "delivered" in the sense that union members will necessarily vote as their leaders advise. For example, much of the substantial vote for George Wallace in the 1968 presidential campaign is thought to have come from blue-collar workers. All that an organization can do is to ensure that those who are believed likely to vote the "right" way actually turn up at the polls.

2. *Lobbying and Legislation.* It is not enough to elect friendly candidates. It is important also to have continuous contact with the legislature while it is in session. Thus we find the AFL-CIO and many of the larger national unions maintaining permanent legislative representatives in Washington. In most state capitals legislative representa-

tion is a part-time function of officers of the state labor federation and of individual unions.

Some kinds of legislation are of interest to organized labor as a whole. Examples are labor relations statutes which define the legal rights of unions and employers; unemployment compensation, old-age pensions, and other social security measures; laws concerning minimum wages and maximum hours; tax legislation; provision of funds for education, public housing projects, medical care, and other items of mass consumption.

In addition to such general objectives, many unions have specific problems in their respective industries. Only a few illustrations need be given. The railroad industry has been faced for decades with increasing competition from trucking, shipping, and air transport. The railroad unions have therefore advocated legislation designed to protect the competitive position of the railroads. They have supported proposals for increased taxation and regulation of trucking, opposed subsidies to shipping, and opposed the St. Lawrence waterways program. They have also tried to meet the problem of declining employment by sponsoring train-limit and full crew laws. They have tried to reduce the legal workday on the railroads from eight to six hours. They have taken an active interest in legislation governing industrial relations on the railroads, and played a large part in the enactment of the Railway Labor Act of 1926 and amendments to this act in 1934 and 1951. They have promoted legislation requiring the railroads to install such safety devices as airbrakes, automatic couplers, and automatic signal systems. They have also been active in promoting state and federal employer liability laws.

The seamen's unions have been mainly responsible for legislation to improve the working and living conditions of seamen on shipboard. They have also advocated the maintenance of a large American merchant marine by shipping subsidies and other methods. The United Mine Workers has been mainly responsible for mine safety legislation. It has also been the strongest sponsor of legislation to regulate prices and output in bituminous coal, a competitive industry faced with chronic overcapacity. Unions in low-wage industries, such as textiles and certain types of clothing, have been the strongest supporters of minimum-wage legislation. Most of the unions in manufacturing have lined up with employers in support of tariff protection and other advantages for their industries. Unions of government employees work mainly through legislation, since their wages and working conditions are governed by legislative enactment. The barbers' union has promoted state legislation limiting weekly hours of work, requiring licensing of barbers in order to control entrance to the industry, and legalizing price-fixing arrangements to prevent "unfair competition."

3. *Labor and Public Administration.* The impact of a law de-

pends partly on how it is administered; and so unions take an active interest in the personnel and policies of administrative agencies.

Organized labor thinks of the state and federal departments of labor as the voice of labor inside the administration. Since the creation of the U.S. Department of Labor in 1913, it has been taken for granted that the secretary of labor will be someone acceptable to the unions, and a certain number of ex-labor leaders will usually be found at lower levels in the department. In many of the state governments, union leaders have regularly been appointed to head the state labor departments. One finds also an increasing number of independent regulatory agencies dealing with labor matters, notably the National Labor Relations Board and the state labor relations boards in many states. Labor is naturally concerned that both the members and the key employees of these agencies should be sympathetic to labor's interests. The attitude of adminstrative officials, the interpretation placed on statutory provisions, and the vigor or lack of vigor in enforcement are often of key importance.

The fact that many appointments of trade union officials and sympathizers are made to administrative posts is significant, but it is easy to overstate the importance of such appointments. Regardless of his origins, anyone who spends any length of time in public service tends increasingly to identify himself with the public interest—or at least to take a viewpoint broader than that of the pressure group that originally put him in his job. Probably the expectation of the pressure group that an administrator recruited from its own ranks will give it an inside track is about balanced by the expectation of the chief executive that such a man will be useful in persuading organized labor to swallow unpalatable policies.

UNION STRATEGIES: COLLECTIVE BARGAINING

An important union activity in most countries, and the major activity in some, is negotiating with employers over wages and other terms of employment. This procedure is called *collective bargaining*, and its outcome is a *collective agreement* or *union contract*.

The arrangements for collective bargaining, like the structure of trade unions themselves, vary widely from country to country. We may note differences in the coverage of collective agreements, the content of these agreements, arrangements for handling grievances at the plant level, and use of the strike weapon.

The Area of the Collective Agreement

The collective agreement may cover a small number of workers or a very large number. It may be limited to employers of a single company or even a single plant. Alternatively, it may cover all workers of a certain type in a particular district, or all workers in an industry throughout the country. In a few countries, top union and management federations negotiate on broad issues for the whole union membership. Single-company agreements are important in a few countries —the United States, Canada, Japan, Chile. On a world scale, however, the dominant form is the multi-employer agreement, negotiated with an employers' association. For local trade and service industries, building construction, and manufacturing industries catering to a local market, this may be a citywide agreement. For national industries— mining, transportation, public utilities, most manufacturing—it will usually embrace workers and employers throughout the country. This is almost the exclusive form of bargaining in Germany, Holland, Italy, and the Scandinavian countries. It is the dominant form in Britain and France. It is prevalent practice also in Australia, in Mexico, and in the French-speaking areas of Africa. Even in the United States, the great majority of union members in building construction, garment manufacture, coal mining, transportation, retailing, and service industries (altogether, upward of 6 million workers) are covered by local or national multi-employer agreements.

There are several pressures making for multi-employer agreements. Where employers are numerous and small, as in retailing, hotel and restaurant employment, local trucking, or building construction, the individual employer is in a weak position to resist union demands. It seems clear that employers can increase their bargaining power by forming a common front. Even where employers are larger, they are in competition with each other; and labor costs are usually an important factor in this competition. Each employer has an interest in seeing that rival employers have to pay as much for labor as he does. Again, the logic points toward joint negotiation and a uniform wage scale.

Government intervention in the bargaining process also makes for larger bargaining units. These are more convenient from an administrative standpoint, and so government agencies usually prefer them. In Australia, for example, industrial disputes tend to end up before a government arbitration board, with power to make a binding decision. The procedure is rather time-consuming and expensive. So employers and unions, instead of processing dozens of small cases, usually band together to seek decisions with broad coverage.

In a number of countries, including Italy, France, Holland, Germany, and the French-speaking African countries, there is provision for legal "extension" of the terms of a collective agreement. An agreement that covers more than 50 percent of workers in an industry, or that has been negotiated by "representative" associations of employers and workers, is given the force of law throughout the industry. This places a premium on industry-wide negotiations covering enough workers to claim representative status.

The most highly centralized negotiations occur in the Scandinavian countries. These economies are small and compact, everyone who is anyone lives in the capital city, leaders of all economic and political groups are well acquainted with each other. The top union and employer federations have strong disciplinary powers, and a union or employer group that engages in a work stoppage without federation approval receives no financial support. The bargaining season opens each year with consultation among top officials of the union federation, their opposite numbers in the employers' federation, and government economic officials who can judge the impact of prospective wage increases on the national economy. The object is to hammer out broad guidelines for the subsequent negotiations in each industry.

The individual industries are not strictly bound by the guidelines, and the ultimate wage increases tend to average out higher than the top leaders had originally intended. But the procedure probably does moderate the pace of wage movements, and may also facilitate agreed readjustments of *relative* wages in the economy—for example, by restraining some of the highest-paid groups while the lower-paid are brought nearer to their level.

The Content of the Agreement

This varies greatly from country to country. Broadly, the larger the coverage of the agreement, the simpler are likely to be its terms. The European and British agreements, which cover an entire industry or even several industries, usually set only a minimum wage level. Individual employers may pay more than the minimum and, in the tight labor markets which have prevailed since World War II, they have usually done so. Rates for particular jobs, and other details of the wage structure, are not covered by the national agreement.

Such broad national agreements should logically be supplemented by more detailed agreements at lower levels; but the extent to which this is done varies from country to country. In Britain, there has been a considerable movement toward local agreements to set standards above the minimum. In most countries, however, local agreements are fragmentary. This is due basically to union weakness at the plant level, which leaves the employer in a dominant position. He conforms to the minimum standards laid down in the national agreement; but he declines to be bound beyond this.

Collective agreements in the United States are probably the most detailed and complex in the world. In addition to covering wages and hours, they usually include provisions for the union shop or some other form of union security; provisions governing layoffs, promotion, and discharge of employees; clauses requiring compensation for workers displaced by technical change; provision for health care, pensions, and other "fringe benefits"; and provision for handling employee grievances arising during the life of the contract. Canadian agreements, many of which are negotiated by U.S.-based unions, tend to resemble U.S. agreements. Mexico also has rather complex and complete union contracts. In other countries, however, most of the items included in U.S. agreements do not appear.

The reasons for this include: (1) Some of the matters covered in U.S. contracts are covered in other countries by legislation. Examples are pensions, medical care, unemployment compensation, and other social insurance benefits. (2) Some items may not be of interest to unions in a particular country for special reasons. British unions, for example, are not interested in the union shop because they are able to isolate nonunion workers by social pressure. (3) Union weakness is a major contributing factor. Employers throughout the world are strongly opposed to being restricted on matters of employee selection, promotion, and discipline, and on questions of production methods and technical change. It takes a strong and aggressive union to impose such restrictions. In most countries the trade unions are not strong enough at the plant level to win concessions on these points.

Grievance Procedure

Once a collective agreement has been signed, the employer is bound by its rules. But suppose the employer next week breaks the rules? Or suppose a question arises as to what a particular rule really means? How are such day-to-day problems to be settled?

American collective agreements normally provide that any worker who thinks he has been treated improperly under the contract may take the matter to his union representative. The representative discusses it with the man's supervisor, and the case is appealed if necessary through higher union and management levels. If there is still no agreement, the case is usually referred to an outside arbitrator whose decision is final. This is termed the "grievance procedure." Its object is to provide for orderly day-to-day administration of the contract, and to avoid the possibility of strikes over individual grievances.

To anyone familiar wth the American system, it is startling to find that few other countries have this kind of grievance procedure. (Canada and Mexico are exceptions, their agreements resembling U.S. agreements on this point as on others.) One reason is that few union movements have enough money to afford paid local officials. In Britain, for example, the grass roots union representative is usually a "shop steward," who tends to become the *de facto* negotiator, grievance settler, and strike caller in the plant. But the stewards, who are locally elected and unpaid, are not really under the control of the national union. This fact, plus the absence of local contracts with a clear grievance procedure, helps to account for the large number of "quickie" strikes in Britain. This is a common situation in other countries. Local grievances fester and accumulate until they spill over into strike action.

A complicating factor in several European countries (and in some of the ex-British and ex-French areas of Africa and Asia) is legal provision for "plant committees" or "works councils." These are elected by all workers in the plant and have legally defined functions. While unions often sponsor candidates in these elections and thus try to infiltrate the plant committees, the committees themselves are not part of the union machinery. Yet they have grievance-handling and negotiating functions which in the United States would clearly be union responsibilities. For example, the German plant committees have: (1) a right of *co-decision* on "social matters," which include working conditions, methods of remuneration, establishment of piece rates, work schedules, vacation schedules, welfare services, and industrial discipline; (2) a right to be *consulted* on "personnel matters," such as recruitment, promotion and layoff.

From one standpoint, the existence of these committees reduces the need for union–management negotiation at the plant level. From another standpoint, they provide employers who wish to ignore the union with an effective means of bypassing it by carrying all issues to the plant committee.

We may add a word on the grievance-handling functions of local unions in the USSR. All workers in a Soviet plant are *de facto* union members, and participate in electing a factory committee which has the following functions: (1) the committee has a right to be *consulted* on production plans, plant expansion, and mechanization that might lead to displacement of labor; also, it must be consulted on appointments of managerial personnel; (2) the committee must *agree* on matters of overtime work, discharge of employees, penalties on any member of the factory committee, vacation schedules, distribution of housing, allocation of profits retained by the enterprise, and "all details of the wage system and production standards."

Grievances of individual workers are processed through the following stages: (1) an effort is made to work out the problem directly with management; (2) unsettled cases go next to a commission on labor disputes, which has an equal number of members from the factory committee and from management; (3) a worker can appeal from this body to the full factory committee, but management has no appeal right; (4) the final appeal is to a district court. The emphasis of the system is on quick settlement, with deadlines of ten days or less for each stage of the procedure. Workers who are found to have been discharged illegally are ordered reinstated with back pay.

This machinery could be merely window dressing for one-man rule by the factory manager; but it does not seem to be so in practice. Managers often complain that they are hampered by pressure from the factory committee, and some express antiunion sentiments not unlike those heard in the United States. Removal of managers with a poor record in labor matters is not uncommon.

The Strike Weapon

The main weapon used to enforce union demands is the strike. There are several kinds of strike. First, there are strikes of indefinite duration over the terms of a new agreement. If negotiations do not produce a meeting of minds, the men walk out and stay out until, after further negotiations, a settlement is finally reached. This kind of strike seems to be declining gradually in the older unionized countries. In part, this may reflect the strength of union and employer organization. In Sweden, for example, a union whose strike is approved by the central labor federation can draw on the full resources of the federation. Similarly, employers are reimbursed by the employers' federation for profits lost during the shutdown. Neither side can starve out the other and a strike, once called, could continue forever. But just for this reason large strikes involving a whole industry are very rare.

Unions in most countries have low dues, small financial reserves, and cannot afford a long strike. A common device in such countries is the *scheduled strike,* called for a definite and short period, after which the union automatically returns to work. This is a standard technique in Japan. In France, Italy, and Latin America, there are frequent one- or two-day stoppages, sometimes involving a large segment of organized labor. This kind of strike seems to accompany union weakness in collective bargaining and heavy involvement in political party activity.

A third type is the "quickie" or "wildcat" strike, an impromptu stoppage over a localized issue. In the United States, union contracts normally prohibit this kind of strike and provide that detailed grievances shall be settled peaceably through the grievance procedure. But many such strikes do occur each year. Local union leaders and members who feel that the machinery is moving too slowly often take matters into their own hands. Quickie strikes are even commoner in countries where collective agreements do not include a grievance procedure. Such strikes are usually short; but if they occur again and again in the same plant, they can seriously disrupt production.

A special problem is strikes of public employees. In most of the "mixed economies," government now employs a substantial percentage of the labor force. Government employees are often strongly unionized; but a strike by public employees is usually considered illegal, as constituting an attack on the sovereignty of the state. Strikes nevertheless occur—either openly or in the disguised form of "calling in sick," observing every rule in the book, or otherwise slowing down production. How to resolve disputes where the rules of private bargaining do not apply is a growing issue in the United States.

THE FRAMEWORK
OF
PUBLIC CONTROL

We have noted a variety of ways in which government enters the industrial relations scene. Government regulates the general level of employment, with important effects on employers' and employees' bargaining power. Government often regulates wage rates and other terms of employment in greater or less detail. Government determines the legal status and powers of trade unions. It may regulate the procedures for union–management negotiation and the permissible content of collective agreements. It always limits use of the strike and other economic weapons and often prescribes procedures for resolving unsettled disputes. What government does, or fails to do, in each of these respects, affects the climate of industrial relations.

Government and the Level of Employment

In the advanced industrial countries, whether capitalist or socialist, government now takes responsibility for regulating aggregate demand so as to maintain a high level of employment. The success of this effort is attested by the fact that, within the developed world, there have been virtually no declines in national output since 1945. Economic fluctuations now take the form of accelerations or decelerations in a positive growth rate.

The importance of this change is difficult to overestimate. Trade unionism dates from an era in which national economies were racked by frequent depressions. Under the pressure of falling demand and prices, many employers felt obliged to cut wages, raise output standards, lay off workers, and make other cost-reducing changes. Individual workers, with no alternative employment opportunities, were virtually powerless to resist such changes. Unionism appeared an important, even an essential, device for maintaining employment standards during recession. Briefly, we may call this the "wage-protective function" of unionism.

Under continuous high employment, all this is changed. Vacancies are plentiful, employers compete actively for labor, the freedom to change jobs is real. Each employer must keep his terms of employment reasonably in line with those of other employers. It is perhaps an exaggeration to say that the worker is *fully* protected by the market; but he is much better protected than under conditions of serious unemployment.

To a considerable extent, then, the "wage-protective function" of unionism is now obsolete. This does not mean that unionism is obsolete, because unions provide a variety of other services. The nature of these services will become clear in the following chapters.

Government and the Wage Structure

In many countries government engages in extensive wage regulation. But wages are also the most important single issue in collective bargaining. To the extent that government takes over responsibility for wage decisions, the importance of collective bargaining is diminished, and union activities are directed toward influencing the wage-setting agencies.

France, for example, has an elaborate structure of legal minimum wages, providing graduated minima for higher occupational classifications, and geographic adjustments for different regions and sizes of city. These legal scales are the bony framework inside the actual wage structure. The French system has been imitated in most of the French-speaking countries of West and Central Africa. In India and some other ex-British colonial areas, government also has a decisive influence on the level and structure of wages.

Australia has a complex system, including two kinds of agency—the wage board and the arbitration tribunal—and including agencies of the various state governments as well as the Commonwealth government.[6] Wage boards have been set up to establish minimum wages in sectors where unionism is weak or absent. In strongly unionized industries, wage disputes usually end up before one of the arbitration tribunals, whose awards are binding. Purely private wage agreements are less numerous and important than in the United States, and union

[6] On the Australian system, see Kenneth F. Walker, *Industrial Relations in Australia* (Cambridge: Harvard University Press, 1956); and J. E. Isaac and G. W. Ford, eds., *Australian Labour Relations Readings* (Melbourne: Sun Books, 1966).

officials spend much of their time preparing and presenting cases before official bodies.

Most countries also have an elaborate body of social legislation covering such things as hours of work, health and safety standards, retirement pensions, unemployment compensation, and medical and hospital care. To the extent that these matters are arranged by government, they do not have to be bargained about with employers. Government decrees are in this sense competitive with union contracts; and the greater their importance, the more will union activity be directed into political channels.

The Status of Unions and Collective Agreements

In various countries unions are treated as: (1) prohibited organizations; (2) purely private associations; (3) organizations recognized, and in some measure controlled, by government; (4) official organs of the state.

At one extreme, British unions have traditionally been regarded as purely private bodies. They have the right to exist and to win concessions from employers through their economic power. But government does not intervene to protect, certify, or control them.

More commonly, unions win the right to represent a certain body of employees through certification by a government agency. In the United States, the National Labor Relations Board certifies bargaining representatives through procedures described in a later chapter. Similar procedures operate in Canada. In most of the Western European countries, a government agency determines which is the "dominant" union in a particular industry, and this becomes the group authorized to negotiate with employers. In most of the less-developed countries a union must be registered—"acquire a legal personality," as is said in Latin America—before its activities can have legal status.

Government recognition tends to bring varying degrees of public control. In some countries, including the United States, there is an elaborate body of law concerning internal union government, collective bargaining procedures, and legally permissible tactics of unions and employers.

There is a similar variation in the legal status of collective agreements. In Britain, these are purely private agreements between the parties. In the United States and some other countries, they have more nearly the status of a commercial contract, and one party can sue the other for damages resulting from violation of contract. Such suits are not common, but the courts will recognize them. In still other cases, the agreement has virtually the effect of a government decree. In Germany, Italy, France, and the French-speaking countries of

Africa, an industry agreement negotiated by a "representative" union may be extended by decree to all employers and workers in the industry. In such countries figures on the coverage of collective agreements can be quite misleading. Wide coverage may result mainly from government procedures rather than from large union membership.

Adjustment of Industrial Disputes

There is a distinction here between disputes over the terms of a new contract and those over grievances arising under an existing contract. The former are disputes over *interests,* the latter disputes over *rights;* and the two are often treated differently in public policy. A common provision is that disputes over interests may be carried to the length of a strike after other possibilities have been exhausted, while disputes over rights must be settled by private arbitration or referred to a government tribunal. The reason is that, in disputes over what a certain contract clause means, or over whether a worker actually did the things for which he was discharged under the contract, judges and arbitrators can make findings of fact and rely on established precedents in similar cases. In a contract dispute over whether the wage increase should be twenty cents or twenty-five cents an hour, it is harder to find principles that an outside arbitrator can apply and that the parties are willing to accept.

The largest and longest strikes typically occur over new contract terms. In this area, there are several degrees of government intervention:

1. *Voluntary Conciliation.* Most governments maintain experienced staffs who stand ready, with the consent of the parties, to step into a dispute and try to work out settlement. In the United States this kind of help is available from the U.S. Mediation and Conciliation Service in the Department of Labor, and from similar services in most of the larger states.

2. *Compulsory Conciliation.* Under which the parties *must* permit a government mediator to try and settle the dispute before taking strike action. This is a common procedure in Canada; but the situation varies from province to province, because main authority over industrial relations is vested in the provincial governments. In the United States, compulsory conciliation applies by statute to the railroad and airline industries, and can be applied to major disputes in other industries by presidential decision.

There is a wide variety of possible procedures. Conciliation may be undertaken by a single mediator, by a permanent conciliation board, or by a board appointed specially for each case. The board may or may not have a duty to file a report on the issues in the case, and this report may or may not be made public. The parties are sometimes required to wait for a certain length of time after a report has been filed (a "cooling-off" period) before taking strike action.

3. *Compulsory Arbitration.* This is a procedure under which, after negotiation and conciliation have been exhausted, an unsettled dispute must be referred to a government arbitration board. The board's award is binding, and a strike against it is illegal. The country with longest experience of compulsory arbitration is Australia, which has a system dating from the 1890s. Some of the Canadian provinces have compulsory arbitration procedures. There is no regular provision for compulsory arbitration in the United States, though in a recent railroad strike Congress passed a special law sending the dispute to arbitration.

Experts have been arguing the merits of compulsory arbitration for decades. Broadly, the argument for it is that it provides a civilized way of settling disputes through a judicial process, without the loss of production and income associated with a strike. As a practical matter, the party that is weaker in a particular situation may be able to get more through a government board than through direct bargaining; and unions or managements have sometimes supported the procedure for this reason. Against compulsory arbitration it is argued that the parties know their own interests better, and are better able to write a workable agreement, than any outside body; and that if an outside board is available, the parties will cease to bargain seriously with each other and will refer all issues to the board. Even in Australia, after seventy years of experience, there is substantial difference of expert opinion on the merits of the arbitration system.

DISTINCTIVE FEATURES
OF AMERICAN
INDUSTRIAL RELATIONS

The theme of this chapter has been variety in institutions and procedures. Viewed in world perspective, many features of the American system appear unusual rather than typical. These features include:

1. The concept of exclusive jurisdiction.
2. Substantial importance of craft organization.
3. Substantial importance of single-company agreements.
4. Complex agreements specifying employment conditions in considerable detail, and restricting employers' managerial authority at many points.
5. Strong grass roots organization, with plant-based locals the predominant form.

6. Well-developed grievance procedures culminating in arbitration.
7. Predominance of collective bargaining over political activity.
8. Absence of political party affiliation.
9. Limited government influence on wage rates, fringe benefits, and other terms of employment.
10. Extensive legal regulation of collective bargaining procedures and tactics.
11. Absence of provisions for compulsory settlement of contract disputes.

Why have these characteristics developed in the United States to a greater degree than elsewhere? This question should be kept in mind as we examine the American system in more detail in the following chapters.

American unionism is often termed "business unionism," because of the concentration on driving bargains with employers, the relative neglect of political action, and the disinterest in—or even scorn for—abstract ideologies. The conventional wisdom has it that this represents a "mature" stage of union development. Unions that are deeply involved in party politics, as in France, Italy and many of the less-developed countries, are simply immature unions which, as they develop further, will shed their ideological trappings and concentrate increasingly on collective bargaining. Is this a valid theory of union evolution? Or does it simply reflect a cultural bias, a natural feeling that others should behave as we do? On these questions, too, we might well for the time being keep an open mind.

Discussion Questions

1. "Unionism is a carryover from the period before full employment. Under conditions of substantially full employment, it no longer serves any major function and may be expected to decline in future importance." Discuss.
2. "Russian unions, which lack the ability to strike, have no real leverage over management. They are most nearly comparable to the 'company unions' that flourished in the United States before 1930." Do you agree? Why, or why not?
3. In most countries, unions including all workers in an industry and collective agreements covering all firms in the industry are the general rule. What are the main reasons for this pattern of organization?

4. Does major involvement in political party activity represent an "immature" stage of union development? Explain.
5. Unions in the less-developed countries are generally regarded as weaker than those in the advanced industrial countries. What are the main reasons for, and the main indications of, this weakness?
6. American collective agreements cover many more subjects, and have a more detailed grievance procedure, than agreements in most other countries. What would you surmise to be the main reasons for this difference?
7. What limitations, if any, do you think government should place on the right to strike?

Reading Suggestions

For a general survey of the issues raised in this chapter, see Dunlop, John T., *Industrial Relations Systems.* New York: Holt, Rinehart and Winston, Inc., 1958; Dunlop, John T., Frederick Harbison, Clark Kerr, and Charles Myers, *Industrialism and Industrial Man.* Cambridge: Harvard University Press, 1960.

There are a large number of monographs on particular countries or groups of countries. Especially worth reading are Alexander, Robert J., *The Labor Movement in Brazil, Argentina, and Chile.* New York: McGraw-Hill Book Company, 1962; Brown, Emily C., *Soviet Trade Unions and Labor Relations.* Cambridge: Harvard University Press, 1966; Cook, Alice H., *Japanese Trade Unionism.* Ithaca: Cornell University Press, 1966; Galenson, Walter, ed., *Labor and Economic Development.* New York: John Wiley & Sons, Inc., 1959; Galenson, Walter, ed., *Labor in Developing Countries.* Berkeley and Los Angeles: University of California Press, 1962. Isaac, J. S., and G. W. Ford, eds., *Australian Labour Relations Readings.* Melbourne: Sun Books, 1966; Lorwin, Val R., *The French Labor Movement.* Cambridge: Harvard University Press, 1955; Myers, Charles A., *Labor Problems in the Industrialiaztion of India.* Cambridge: Harvard University Press, 1958; Roberts, B. C., and L. G. de Bellecombe, *Collective Bargaining in African Countries.* New York: St. Martin's Press, Inc., 1967; Sturmthal, A F., ed., *Contemporary Collective Bargaining in Seven Countries.* Ithaca: Cornell University Press, 1957; and Walker, Kenneth, *Industrial Relations in Australia.* Cambridge: Harvard University Press, 1956.

THE EVOLUTION OF AMERICAN UNIONISM

12

More than fifty years ago Sidney and Beatrice Webb defined a trade union as "a continuous association of wage earners for the purpose of maintaining or improving the conditions of their working lives." This chapter is concerned with the development of such associations in the United States since their origin around the year 1790.

REASONS FOR THE DEVELOPMENT OF UNIONS

The history of American unionism is frequently dated from 1792, when a local union was formed by the journeymen cordwainers (shoemakers) of Philadelphia. Within the next ten years unions of shoemakers, carpenters, and printers were founded in Baltimore, Philadelphia, Boston, New York, and several other cities.

What accounts for the appearance of these associations? They cannot be traced to particular oppression of workers at that time. On the contrary, most workers were better off in 1800 than they had been in 1780. It is significant also that unions did not appear at first among the most exploited groups—the cotton-mill workers, and home workers on piece rates—but among skilled tradesmen, such as the printers, carpenters, and shoemakers. In the United States, as in most other industrial countries, the relatively skilled and prosperous workers organized first. The first unions in Great Britain, for example, consisted of building- and printing-trades workers, who were followed shortly afterward by unions of tailors and wool combers. In Sweden, the first unions were formed by the printers, the next by the carpenters, and the next by the skilled metal-trades' workers.

Neither can the rise of unionism be traced to the introduction of machine production. None of the industries organized during the period 1790 to 1830 had been significantly affected by machine methods. An important stimulus to union organization in some industries was the broadening of the domestic market for manufactures which resulted from the improvement of transportation facilities. This expansion meant intensified competition in the sale of goods—shoes made in Philadelphia competed increasingly with shoes made in New York, Baltimore, and other cities. The merchant capitalist appeared, playing off small masters against each other and forcing them to cut wages in order to survive. This activity threatened the journeymen's customary standard of life and forced them into defensive organizations.

The growth of the market also fostered division of labor and development of larger production units. Even without mechanization of production, this meant that it took more capital to set oneself up in business and that it was increasingly difficult for journeymen to rise to the master class. The gulf between worker and employer widened. For the first time there appeared a group of permanent wage earners, who had little expectation of becoming masters in the future. Moreover, greater specialization of tasks reduced the element of skill in the production process. The semiskilled operative made his appearance and the need for fully skilled craftsmen diminished. This threat to the craftsmen's skill was unpleasant in itself and also threatened his earning power.

The extension of the market for manufactures can scarcely explain the rise of unionism in industries such as printing and building construction, which continued to cater to purely local markets. While product markets in these industries remained local, however, the labor market broadened steadily as improved transportation increased the mobility of labor. Printers, carpenters, and bricklayers began to move about the country in considerable numbers and were sometimes used by employers to undercut local wage scales. Some means had to be found for controlling this competition. Moreover, in local-market as well as national-market industries, employers were sometimes led by business depression or price competition to make a direct onslaught on established wage scales and working conditions. The development of local unions was a natural protective response to this pressure.

Until after the Civil War, almost all unions were local unions of workers in a particular trade or industry, and they were confined largely to a few cities along the Atlantic seaboard. These early unions were strikingly modern in objectives and methods. From the beginning, regulation of wages was the main issue and the strike was the main weapon. There was little, it is true, which could be termed "collective bargaining" during this period. In the beginning, the union simply decided on its "price" (i.e. wage rate), and the members pledged themselves not to work below this price. A little later, it became customary for a union committee to visit each employer and request his adherence to the union rate. Those who refused to agree were struck. There was still no written agreement with employers, and the procedure could scarcely be called bargaining. The wage scale was determined unilaterally by the union, and employers were given the choice of conforming or not conforming. When nonconforming employers were struck, the "walking delegate," who at first was an unpaid worker but later became a paid official, went from shop to shop to make sure that all union members were out. Strikebreakers were termed "rats," and later "scabs." The locals of the same trade in different cities exchanged lists of scabs and agreed not to admit them to membership. This activity was almost the only contact between local unions in the early days. Strikes were financed by levies on the membership. They were relatively peaceful, and, except in depression periods, most of them were successful.

Another policy of the earliest trade unions was not to work with nonunion men. The union shop, like the union wage scale, was enforced directly through a pledge by unionists "not to work for anybody who does not pay the rate nor beside anyone who does not get the rate." Nonunionists were also boycotted socially; union men would not live in the same boarding houses or eat at the same places as nonunion men. Thus the union shop, which is sometimes pictured as a new invention, actually dates from the earliest days of unionism in this country. Apprenticeship regulations were another major concern of the early unions. Their main purpose was to prevent employers from replacing journeymen with learners, runaway apprentices, and women, at wage rates below the union scale. The number of apprentices which an employer might train was usually limited to a certain proportion of the number of journeymen employed. They were required to serve a specified period of apprenticeship, and only journeymen who had completed this apprenticeship were admitted to the union and allowed to work in union shops.

These unions, though few in number, were sufficiently strong and aggressive to arouse consternation among employers. Editorial writers denounced unionism, employers' associations were formed to combat it, and conspiracy cases were launched against the unions in the courts. The antiunion arguments, like the union tactics of the day, have a surprisingly modern ring.[1] One hundred and fifty years have brought little change in the issues at stake and the arguments advanced on either side. Many of the arguments put forward today might easily have been copied from newspapers and speeches of a hundred years ago.

An important characteristic of these early unions was their inability to withstand business depression. They sprang up and flourished in good years but were nearly all wiped out during depression periods. After the Civil War, however, the situation began to change. The depression of the years 1873 to 1878 reduced union membership from about 300,000 to 50,000; but it did not wipe out unionism completely, as earlier depressions had done. With this development, and with the foundation of the American Federation of Labor (AFL) in 1886, we enter a new period of trade union history.

UNION GROWTH

IN

MODERN TIMES

The growth of unionism in the twentieth century is shown in Figure 1 and Table 1. Figure 1 shows the estimated number of union members year-by-year since 1897. The black line includes Canadian members of American unions, who have numbered about 1 million in recent years. The white line for recent years includes only members within the United States.[2]

Table 1 shows union membership as a percentage of nonagricul-

---

[1] The master carpenters of Boston, for example, when confronted in 1825 with a demand for a ten-hour day, replied that they could not believe "this project to have originated with any of the faithful and industrious sons of New England, but are compelled to consider it an evil of foreign growth, and one which we hope and trust will not take root in the favored soil of Massachusetts. . . . And especially that our city, the early rising and industry of whose inhabitants are universally proverbial, may not be infected with the unnatural production." John R. Commons and associates, *History of Labor in the United States,* Vol. I (New York: The Macmillan Company, 1918), 160. See also the antiunion statements on p. 271 of this same volume and those contained in E. W. Bakke and Clark Kerr, eds., *Unions, Management, and the Public* (New York: Harcourt, Brace & World, Inc., 1948), pp. 272–80.

[2] Data for the old series, 1897–1960, are from the Bureau of Labor Statistics, *Handbook of Labor Statistics,* 1950, p. 139, and Bureau of the Census, *Statistical Abstract of the United States,* 1962. Data for the new series, 1956–66, are from the Bureau of Labor Statistics, *Directory of National and International Labor Unions in the United States* (Bulletin 1596, 1967).

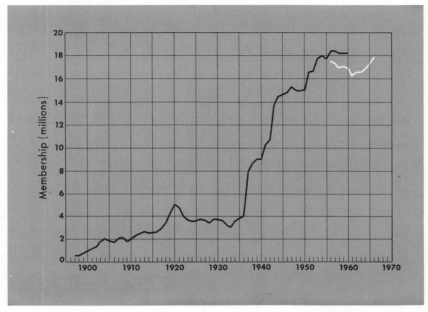

Figure 1

TRADE UNION MEMBERSHIP
IN THE UNITED STATES, 1897–1966

Table 1

UNION MEMBERSHIP AS A PERCENTAGE
OF NONAGRICULTURAL EMPLOYMENT,
SELECTED YEARS, 1880–1966

	AVERAGE ANNUAL UNION MEMBERSHIP			AVERAGE ANNUAL UNION MEMBERSHIP	
Year	*Thousands*	*Percent of Nonagricultural Employment*	*Year*	*Thousands*	*Percent of Nonagricultural Employment*
1880	200.0	2.3	1933	2,857	11.5
1890	372.0	2.7	1939	8,980	28.9
1900	865.5	4.8	1945	14,796	35.8
1910	2,140.5	8.4	1956	17,490	33.4
1920	5,047.8	16.3	1960	17,049	31.4
1930	3,392.8	8.8	1966	17,940	28.1

tural employment for selected years since 1880.[3] Again, the years up to 1945 includes Canadian members, while the figures from 1956 onwards exclude them. Note that while the number of union members has increased slightly since 1956, the organized percentage of the labor force has fallen.

From 1880 until the early 1930s union membership rose gradually and intermittently, going up in prosperity periods and falling back in depression. Unionism was confined largely to the skilled crafts and did not succeed in penetrating the basic manufacturing industries. Except for a brief spurt during and after World War I, union membership never rose above 10 percent of nonagricultural employment. Membership declined gradually during the complacent twenties, and more sharply during the severe depression of 1929 to 1933.

The New Deal era brought a great upsurge of union strength. Between 1933 and 1939 union membership tripled, and unions for the first time became firmly established in steel, automobiles, and most other branches of manufacturing. Organization spread from the skilled crafts to the semiskilled and unskilled. The reasons included a federal administration favorable to unionism, new legislation guaranteeing the right to organize and improving the legal status of trade unions, a substantial recovery of employment from 1933 to 1937, and the vigorous organizing efforts of the Congress of Industrial Organizations (CIO).

By 1939 the organizing drive was losing momentum, and union membership might once more have stagnated or declined had it not been for World War II. During the war years administration policy remained favorable to unionism, and union leaders were enlisted both in the production drive and in the effort to stabilize wages and prices. The sharp increase of employment in war industries was favorable to enrolling more union members. Employers were more concerned with recruiting labor and getting out production than with fighting the union, and employer resistance to organization subsided for the time being. So another 5 million union members were added. Unions came to include more than a third of the nonagricultural labor force and about 60 percent of all manual workers in the economy.

In retrospect, 1945 appears as a high watermark in union penetration of the economy. Membership spurted briefly during the Korean War, but has stagnated since that time. Since the labor force has continued to grow, the percentage of nonagricultural workers who are union members has been falling. What accounts for this stagnation of membership during a period of sustained prosperity? What does it

[3] Data through 1945 are from Lloyd Ulman, "American trade unionism—past and present," in Seymour E. Harris, ed., *American Economic History* (New York: McGraw-Hill Book Company, 1961), pp. 393 and 421. Data from 1956 on are from Bureau of Labor Statistics, Bulletin 1596.

portend for the future? Is unionism over the hill, or will there be a fresh upsurge at some time in the future? We shall comment on these questions at the end of the chapter. But first we must examine the structure of union organization and how this has changed over the course of time.

THE EVOLUTION
OF
UNION STRUCTURE

There are four main types of organizational units in the trade union world: local unions of workers in a particular trade or industry; city-wide and statewide federations of local unions, regardless of industry; national unions of workers in the same trade or industry; and peak federations of these national unions, such as the AFL-CIO.

The organizational structure may be visualized more readily by looking at a particular union. The printers' Local Number 6 in New York City is a branch of the International Typographical Union, and holds its charter and authority only from the international union. At the same time, Local Number 6 is a member of the New York City Federation of Labor and the New York State Federation of Labor. At the national level, the Typographical Union is affiliated with the AFL-CIO.

These organizational units did not develop overnight, nor did they develop simultaneously. They represent successive stages of development, comparable to strata in a geological formation. The first local union was the Philadelphia shoemakers' union, founded in 1792. Next in order of development came the city federations of local unions, the first of which were founded in New York, Philadelphia, and Baltimore in 1833. The first national union that has had a continuous existence up to the present day was the International Typographical Union, founded in 1850. The first federation of national unions that has had a continuous history to date was the American Federation of Labor, founded in 1886.

Numerous other forms of organization have also been tried during the past 150 years. There have been attempts to combine people from different trades and industries into a single local union, and to combine these "mixed locals" into an all-inclusive national organization. The outstanding example of this type of organization was the Knights of Labor, which flourished briefly during the 1880s. There have also been attempts to merge federations of local trade unions, local labor political clubs, and miscellaneous labor groups into a federation such as the National Labor Union, which flourished during the late 1860s.

The reasons for the failure of these movements will be discussed below. Briefly, they suffered from a lack of homogeneity of interest among the underlying membership. Because of diversity of the membership, a chronic shortage of funds, an absence of systematic organizing tactics, and a lack of interest in continuous bargaining with employers, they made only slight headway on the economic front. Their activities were oriented mainly toward politics, and here they tended to dissipate their energies in broad middle-class reform movements of little immediate interest to wage earners. The organizational forms that we find in existence today are the survivors, which have proved their ability to survive by the concrete functions they perform.

These different organizational units are not of equal importance in the labor world. The key unit around which all else revolves is the national union of workers in a particular trade or industry. The national union is more important than the locals of which it is composed, and it is also more important than the federation with which it is affiliated. This has not always been the case, and we need to ask how the national union has come to occupy its present key position.

THE DOMINANCE
OF THE
NATIONAL UNION

The beginnings of local unionism around the year 1800 have already been described. These isolated locals soon found that they were in a relatively weak position compared with that of a strong employer. Consisting of workers in only one trade, with limited funds and no outside support, they often crumbled when forced to strike against a large employer or employers' association. The need for some kind of defensive alliance with other unions was felt almost from the beginning.

Such an alliance can be formed on either of two bases. The local may join with local unions of other trades in the same *area* to form a city-wide or statewide organization; or it may join with other local unions in the same *trade or industry* to form a national trade union. The first efforts were in the former direction. City-wide federations, called at the time "trade assemblies," sprang up in Philadelphia, New York, and Baltimore in 1833, as we have noted, and in ten other cities during the next two years. The main function of these groups was mutual aid in strikes. Funds were obtained by taxing each local so many cents per member per month, and the tax was sometimes raised to meet emergency situations. A local wishing to go on strike usually had to secure approval either by a majority or by two-thirds of the member locals in order to draw strike benefits from the common fund. The trade assemblies also functioned as boycott organizations, lobbyists, propaganda bureaus, publishers of labor newspapers, and in some cities sponsored an independent labor party. The usefulness of the city federation is proved by the fact that it has persisted, with some change of functions, to the present day.

Why did the local unions find it necessary to go beyond this and to establish national unions of their respective trades and industries? One important reason was the nationalization of the market for many goods. Hoxie has laid down the principle that union organization tends to parallel the organization of the industry. In an industry in which employers compete on a national basis, the isolated local soon finds itself competing with local unions in other plants of the industry. In this sort of competition, wages tend to be leveled down to the lowest rates prevailing anywhere in the country. In some trades, too, migration of journeymen from one city to another early became a problem. The local unions of printers, for example, began to exchange lists of scabs, to regulate the conditions under which printers from one area might secure work in another area, and to provide "tramping benefits" to support the brother in the trade during his journeys in search of employment. A permanent national organization facilitated these exchanges and made it possible to enforce uniform apprenticeship and membership rules. With the passage of time, improved transportation facilities made it easier for delegates to assemble at national conventions and for organizers from the national office to travel throughout the country.

National unions date for all practical purposes from the Civil War. Two so-called national unions of shoemakers and printers were formed in 1835 and 1836, but they were confined to the Atlantic Coast and were wiped out almost immediately by depression. Three permanent organizations appeared during the 1850s: the printers (1850), molders (1859), and machinists and blacksmiths (1859). The first period of intensive national organization, however, was from 1863 to 1873. During these years some twenty-six new national unions were formed, many of which have survived to the present day. The present unions of locomotive engineers, locomotive firemen, carpenters, cigar makers, bricklayers, and painters date from this period.

The national unions showed much greater resistance to depression than the earlier local unions. The depression of the years 1873 to 1878 caused a great decline in union membership, but at least eleven nationals are known to have survived these years and eight new nationals were founded during the depression. The reasons for the greater permanence of a national union are not difficult to see. Even though many of its local unions are wiped out during a depression, the national headquarters can continue on a reduced scale and serve as a center for reviving the lost locals when prosperity returns. Moreover, a national union tends constantly to expand to the limits of its trade or industry. Its officers have the duty of organizing the unorganized; their prestige, and even their continuance in office, depend on successful performance of their function.

The national unions not merely survived, but gradually took over more and more functions from the local unions and the city federations. They early began to build up war chests to aid in financing strikes. To prevent dissipation of these funds, it was necessary to forbid local unions to call strikes without the sanction of the national union. The national officers thus became involved in disputes between local unions and employers, with a view to preventing strikes except where absolutely necessary. From this it was a natural step for national officers to begin participating in the negotiation of new contracts with employers. This action was desirable also in order to keep some reasonable relation among the wage schedules and other contract terms secured by the various locals. These tendencies, to be sure, have been strongest in industries with a national product market. In industries where competition is confined to a locality, such as building construction, the local unions have retained a large measure of autonomy.

It was natural also that national officers with an intimate knowledge of the trade or industry should take over the work of organizing new locals. The great majority of full-time union organizers now draw their pay from the treasuries of the national unions. The benefit functions of the unions also became centralized increasingly in the national office. Uniform rules for sickness benefits, death benefits, strike benefits, and other types of payment were established throughout the union, and funds were paid to the national treasurer and were disbursed by him.

The expanding functions of the national unions tended to transfer the loyalty of local unions from the city federations to the national union of their trade. Most workers naturally have a sense of closer kinship with others in their own trade or industry. This feeling was now reinforced by the material benefits received from the national organizations. Dues payments to the national organization and cash benefits received from it soon amounted to many times the amounts paid to the city federations. The national unions benefited by the truth expressed in the maxim, "where your treasure is, there will your heart be also."

The predominance of the national union was strengthened also by the turn that the labor movement took in the eighties away from political action and toward direct bargaining with employers on the economic front. Had the labor movement taken a strongly political turn, the outcome might well have been different. The city, state, and national federations are the natural units for political action. For reasons to be discussed below, however, political action has played a minor role in the labor movement over the past century. The state and city federations have accordingly fallen to a subordinate position. They continue to meet regularly, give a certain amount of support to member locals in strikes and organizing campaigns, approve legislative demands of member locals and lobby for them in city councils and state legislatures, conduct educational and propaganda activities, and in some cases support candidates for public office. The local union's real loyalty, however, is to the national union of its trade or industry. It is to the national union that it looks for support, and in any conflict of principles or policies it is the policies of the national union that will prevail.

The cornerstones of the trade union world today are the great national unions, which have a more lasting significance than any federation based on them. It was a question of less importance than one might think whether the old AFL and CIO survived as separate organizations, or whether they agreed to merge into a new federation, as actually happened. The important thing is the growth and development of the national unions of steelworkers, automobile workers, textile workers, machinists, teamsters, carpenters, painters, mine workers, and other key groups.

PEAK FEDERATIONS:
THE
AMERICAN FEDERATION OF LABOR

Federation of these national unions into an overarching labor organization dates from the 1880s. Several attempts at national federation were made in earlier years, notably by the ill-fated Knights of Labor established in 1869. This heterogeneous organization cut across industry lines and included large numbers of low-skilled workers, who joined enthusiastically but were easily discouraged and quick to drop out. The national unions of skilled craftsmen eventually concluded that they would do better to form their own federation. The American Federation of Labor, founded in 1886, quickly assumed a leading role in the trade union movement. It was a hard-hitting organization, led by Samuel Gompers and other energetic men in their thirties, who almost immediately launched the first successful strikes for the eight-hour day. The AFL also had a distinctive philosophy of unionism which appealed strongly to most organized workers.

What were the cardinal points of this trade union philosophy? The first element that may be noted is group consciousness. Before this time workers had not distinguished their interest from those of farmers and other middle-class people. They had joined in political reform movements that also drew support from these other groups. All this was changed by Gompers and his followers, most of whom had been reared as Marxian socialists. Although they later abandoned most of the tenets of Marxism, they retained a conviction that the interests of workers are distinct from those of other groups. Gompers argued that the workers must defend their own interests and must refuse to be drawn into middle-class reform movements. He asserted also that there is little hope of the workers' climbing out of their class through producers' cooperatives, antimonopoly campaigns, or other methods.

A second principle was that of organization by trades. Gompers believed that to lump together different trades, as the Knights of Labor had done, reduced the cohesiveness of the union. Greatest solidarity was obtained when each craft had its own union. The desirability of strong national unions, buttressed by large treasuries and extensive benefit systems, was stressed from the beginning. The Cigar Makers' Union, under Gompers's leadership, showed the way in this direction in 1879 by adopting a high scale of dues and benefits, and by giving the national officers complete control over the local unions. The Cigar Makers' organization was used as a model by most other national unions during the next ten years, and its prestige contributed to the election of Gompers to the AFL presidency. The marked success of British craft unions cut on this same pattern, and the influence of British immigrants in American unions, also helped to shape AFL thinking in these formative years.

Early AFL leaders insisted also that each national union must be autonomous within its own field of operation. The federation entered the scene only to define and enforce the jurisdictions of the member unions, and to perform certain political and educational functions. The federation, in short, was a confederation of sovereign bodies. Its chief power was that of granting jurisdiction over particular trades or industries: jurisdiction granted to one union must be observed by others, and dual unionism must be suppressed at all costs. This attitude toward dualism sprang partly from the unfortunate experience of the national unions in competition with the Knights of Labor during the 1880s. It sprang also from the fact that the AFL had to contend with strong and determined employer opposition. The existence of two unions in an industry gave the employer a chance to play each against the other, and the labor movement therefore has a strong practical interest in preventing dual organization. The bitterness of the rivalry between AFL and CIO from 1935 to 1955 can be understood only in terms of this long-standing taboo on dual unionism.

The third cardinal principle was that labor's objectives should be pursued mainly on the economic front through collective bargaining with employers. In spite of the socialist training of its founders, the AFL soon came to accept the main outlines of the capitalist order.

Gompers believed that unions should not try to overthrow capitalism, but to get as much as possible for the workers by collective bargaining within the confines of the existing system. When someone asked Gompers what the aims of the federation were, he is reported to have answered, "More, more, more—now!" When another AFL leader was called before a Congressional committee in 1883 and asked about the ultimate objectives of trade unionism, he replied as follows: "We have no ultimate ends. We are going on from day to day. We are fighting only for immediate objects . . . we are opposed to theorists . . . we are all practical men." [4] There has never been a better summary of the traditional AFL position.

The device of the union contract or collective agreement, which had been used by a few unions in the eighties, became during the nineties the accepted method of dealing with employers. The AFL hammered out and wrote into union contracts a new conception of the union as a continuously operating organization, rather than a sporadic protest and strike movement. The union was to be a partner, though perhaps only a junior partner, in the conduct of industry. It was to be active every day in the year, representing the interests of its members on all fronts, winning small gains which would eventually mount up to an impressive total.

A corollary of the AFL's emphasis on collective bargaining was the avoidance of political organization, or at least of anything approaching an independent labor party. The labor movement had experimented with labor parties and political action since at least 1830. Gompers and his group felt that these activities had not gotten anywhere in the past and had served mainly to split the unions and divert them from their real business. They believed that the unions could get what they wanted through pressure on the established political parties—voting for candidates who had shown themselves to be "friends of labor," getting union demands written into party platforms, lobbying in Congress and the state legislatures, and so on. Along with this avoidance of labor politics went a suspicion of intellectuals and of their tendency to foist abstract programs on the workers. There has been in the United States nothing of that close connection between intellectuals and the labor movement which exists in most European countries. Union leaders have had a similar distrust of socialists and other radical groups that attempt to divert trade union energy to revolutionary ends. This point of view is well expressed in Gompers's statement to an AFL convention:

> I want to tell you Socialists, that I have studied your philosophy, read your works upon economics. . . . I have heard your orators and watched the work of your movement the world over. I have kept close

[4] J. B. S. Hardman, *American Labor Dynamics* (New York: Harcourt, Brace & World, Inc., 1928), p. 99.

watch upon your doctrines for thirty years; have been closely associated with many of you, and know what you think and what you propose. I know, too, what you have up your sleeve. And I want to say
that I am entirely at variance with your philosophy. . . . Economically,
you are unsound; socially, you are wrong; and industrially you are an
impossibility.[5]

All in all, then, the AFL provided a model of organization well
suited to the requirements of the skilled trades. It stimulated the
formation of new national unions. It acted as a stabilizer of union
membership during depression periods. It shook the labor movement
free of an incubus of unfruitful ideas and presented a practical operating program which proved very successful in winning gains on the
economic front. Except for the short-lived Industrial Workers of the
World, which flourished just before the first World War, the story
of American unionism for almost fifty years was the story of the AFL.

THE RISE OF
INDUSTRIAL
UNIONISM

While the growth of union membership from 1880 to 1930 occurred
largely within the skilled trades, there was also some development of
unions that included all workers in a particular industry. The most
important of these were the United Mine Workers, the Amalgamated
Clothing Workers, and the International Ladies' Garment Workers.

In many areas of the economy the issue of craft versus industrial
organization does not arise. In some cases—barbers, musicians, teachers
—craft and industry are virtually synonymous. But the issue does arise
acutely in large-scale, mechanized manufacturing industries. In most
of these industries, 80 to 90 percent of the plant labor force is semiskilled or unskilled. The remaining 10 to 20 percent of skilled workers
are the plant aristocracy: the loomfixer in textile mills, the machine
tender and his assistants in paper mills, the toolmaker and machinist
in metalworking plants, the cutter in garment shops. Most large
plants also employ considerable numbers of carpenters, electricians,
pipe fitters, and other skilled tradesmen on maintenance work. The
question is whether each of these skilled groups should have its own
local union, affiliated with a national union of its trade, leaving the
low-skilled workers as a headless remnant; or whether all workers in
the plant should belong to a single local, whose bargaining strength
would be enhanced by including the skilled men.

[5] *AFL Convention Proceedings, 1903,* pp. 188–98.

So long as organizing conditions were unfavorable, this issue was largely academic. But the favorable political and economic climate after 1933 presented the labor movement with an unprecedented opportunity to penetrate the manufacturing industries. The question of how to go about it became practical and immediate. Two points of view quickly developed within the AFL. A minority, spearheaded by the leaders of existing industrial unions, demanded an aggressive organizing drive and the chartering of industrial unions in the mass production industries. Craft union leaders, however, representing a majority of the federation's membership, urged a more cautious policy. They were skeptical of the organizability of the low-skilled workers; and they wished to preserve the right of existing craft unions to enroll members of their trade who worked in manufacturing plants.

This difference of opinion came to a head in the national AFL conventions of 1934 and 1935. The industrial unionists were led by Lewis of the Mine Workers, Hillman of the Clothing Workers, and Dubinsky of the Ladies' Garment Workers. After being outvoted at the 1935 convention, six unions set up a Committee for Industrial Organization devoted to organizing industrial unions in the basic manufacturing industries and then bringing these new unions into the AFL. The AFL Executive Council, however, scenting a threat of dual unionism, first suspended and then expelled the unions that had formed the CIO. These unions then banded together in 1938, along with the new unions that they had fathered in the meantime, to form a rival federation—the Congress of Industrial Organizations.

The success of the CIO organizing drives is now a matter of history. During the late thirties one antiunion citadel after another capitulated. The list of employers organized by the CIO between 1936 and 1941 reads like a roster of Who's Who in American industry: Ford, General Motors, Chrysler, General Electric, Westinghouse, United States Steel, Bethlehem Steel, Republic Steel, Youngstown Sheet and Tube, Goodyear, Firestone, Goodrich, the major oil companies, the larger radio and electrical equipment manufacturers, the "big four" meat-packing companies, and so on down the list.

Why was the CIO able to organize industries that had hitherto presented an impenetrable front to unionism? The most important factor was probably a favorable government attitude toward unionism throughout the Roosevelt era. Unions that formerly had to strike to win union recognition could now use the election procedures of the National Labor Relations Board, and the board also protected them against harassing tactics by the employer, which were now forbidden as "unfair labor practice." The CIO organizing campaigns were aggressive, well financed through donations from the sponsoring unions, and led by experienced and capable organizers, many of whom had grown up in the rough school of the United Mine Workers. A final factor was the prolonged rise in business activity after 1933. Except for the relapse of 1937 and 1938, employment and production rose steadily from 1933 to 1945. This provided a favorable setting for union organization.

RIVALRY
AND REUNION:
1935 TO 1955

The rise of the CIO was paralleled by a great growth in AFL membership. The AFL, like its rival federation, benefited from prosperity and the favorable attitude of government, and made good use of its opportunities. The AFL pulled ahead of the CIO in total membership by 1940 and widened its lead in subsequent years. There were several reasons for this. First, the craft unions continued to enlarge their membership. There was a striking growth of such old-line unions as those of the teamsters, machinists, carpenters, electrical workers, and hod carriers. Second, the AFL went into competition with the CIO in organizing manufacturing plants on an industrial basis. It sponsored industrial unions in the automobile, textile, boot and shoe, meat-packing, pulp and paper, and men's clothing industries. The AFL Electrical Workers, formerly confined mainly to the construction industry, later recruited many workers in plants manufacturing electrical equipment, competing in this area with the International Union of Electrical, Radio and Machine Workers, CIO. The International Association of Machinists entered into competition with CIO unions in the metal and machinery industries, particularly aircraft manufacture. The marked success of the AFL unions in this rivalry is suggested by Table 2.

Third, several of the unions instrumental in forming the CIO, including the Mine Workers and the Ladies' Garment Workers, later withdrew from the CIO and rejoined the AFL. Fourth, the AFL proved more successful than the CIO in expanding into retail trade, service, and other industries. The CIO remained largely confined within basic manufacturing.

Finally, in 1949 and 1950 the CIO expelled a number of important left-wing unions following the refusal of their officers to sign the non-Communist affidavits required by the Taft-Hartley Act. The eleven unions expelled included the powerful United Electrical, Radio and Machine Workers, with a membership of 600,000. In all, nearly a million workers were involved. The CIO organized new unions to take over the jurisdictions of the ousted unions, and claimed to have recaptured 70 percent of their former members by 1950. Nevertheless

Table 2
MEMBERSHIP GROWTH
IN SELECTED AFL AND CIO UNIONS
1940–1956

Union	Affiliation	1940	1951	1956
BOOT AND SHOE WORKERS UNION	AFL	30,800	50,000	40,000
UNITED SHOE WORKERS OF AMERICA	CIO	53,627	60,000	60,000
UNITED BROTHERHOOD OF CARPENTERS AND JOINERS	AFL	305,867	750,000	850,000
INTERNATIONAL WOODWORKERS OF AMERICA	CIO	58,682	117,251	88,517
INTERNATIONAL BROTHERHOOD OF ELECTRICAL WORKERS OF AMERICA	AFL	209,700	500,000	675,000
UNITED ELECTRICAL, RADIO, AND MACHINE WORKERS OF AMERICA	CIO, Ind.	206,824	*	100,000
INTERNATIONAL UNION OF ELECTRICAL, RADIO, AND MACHINE WORKERS OF AMERICA	CIO	—	*	397,412
AMALGAMATED MEAT CUTTERS AND BUTCHER WORKMEN	AFL	70,000	195,000	310,000
UNITED PACKING HOUSE WORKERS OF AMERICA	CIO	90,000	132,000	150,000
INTERNATIONAL BROTHERHOOD OF PAPER MAKERS	AFL	24,300	70,000	
UNITED PAPER WORKERS OF AMERICA	CIO	—	50,000	
MERGED TO UNITED PAPER MAKERS AND PAPERWORKERS	AFL-CIO	—	—	130,000
SEAFARERS INTERNATIONAL UNION OF NORTH AMERICA	AFL	18,700	70,000	75,000
NATIONAL MARITIME UNION OF AMERICA	CIO	52,000	43,000	40,000
INTERNATIONAL BROTHERHOOD OF TEAMSTERS, ETC.	AFL	393,700	1,000,000	1,368,082
INTERNATIONAL ASSOCIATION OF MACHINISTS	AFL	190,100	699,298	949,683

* Split over Communist issue; membership unknown.
SOURCE: Ulman, *Trade Unionism*, p. 412.

the expulsions and reorganization were a setback for the CIO in its competition with the AFL.

As a result of the growth of the CIO and the growth of industrial unions within the AFL, there was a marked increase in the percentage of all union members who are in industrial unions. Only about one-third of the AFL membership was in industrial unions in 1933. By 1952, more than two-thirds of the combined CIO and AFL membership were in industrial or semiindustrial unions.

The cleavage in the labor movement after 1935 had disadvantages on both the political and collective bargaining fronts, and leaders on the two sides worked sporadically to close the breach. Negotiations looking toward unity were conducted by joint committees in 1937, 1939, 1942, 1943, 1947, and 1950. For a number of reasons, however, all of these discussions bogged down. Until 1945 both groups were making good gains in membership and unity was not a primary concern. Each group continued skeptical of the other's chances of survival, and hoped for victory in a straight competitive struggle. There was a mistaken idea that reunion must be preceded by an ironing out of all jurisdictional problems between overlapping unions in the two federations. The CIO tended to insist that its affiliates be taken into any merged federation "as is"; but the AFL typically insisted that the new unions, which in a sense were "outlaw" from their point of view, must have their jurisdictional status regularized before admission. There were substantial differences of political outlook between the two federations. Finally, personal bitterness among John L. Lewis, William Green, Philip Murray, and other leaders who had been involved in the original split was an obstacle to unity.

By the early fifties many of these circumstances had changed. Organizational and membership stability had been achieved on both sides. Instead of expanding into new territory, the unions found themselves engaging in intensified competition for workers already organized. Interunion "raiding" of membership increased to an uncomfortable degree. The political climate had also become increasingly unfavorable to unionism. In 1947 the Taft–Hartley Act imposed new federal restrictions on trade unions and restrictive state laws continued to multiply. A Republican president was elected in 1952 despite both AFL and CIO opposition. Many labor leaders concluded that unity was essential to protect established positions and fight off political attacks.

In late 1952 Presidents William Green of the AFL and Philip Murray of the CIO died within a month of each other. The new presidents George Meany and Walter Reuther, quickly reactivated the twenty-four man Joint AFL-CIO Unity Committee. Over the next two years this body succeeded in hammering out, first a "no-raiding agreement" between most of the national unions on both sides, and later the terms of a full merger. The key to the final agreement was a decision that all national unions in both groups would be taken into the new federation "as is." Mergers and other methods of eliminating overlapping jurisdiction would be encouraged but were not made compulsory. In December 1955, the AFL and CIO held their last separate conventions and then met jointly for the first convention of the new American Federation of Labor and Congress of Industrial Organizations.

The superstructure of the AFL-CIO is complicated, since it adds together the top management structure of the two predecessor bodies.

In addition to a president and secretary-treasurer there are twenty-seven vice-presidents, distributed on an agreed basis between former AFL and former CIO affiliates. In addition to the trade departments of the old AFL (Building and Construction Trades, Metal Trades, Union Label Trades, Maritime Employees, and Railway Employees) there is now an Industrial Union Department, open to all unions organized wholly or partly on an industrial basis. This serves to maintain something of the identity and spirit of the old CIO.

Merger of the central AFL and CIO organizations was intended to stimulate merger of subordinate bodies on both sides. In the case of national unions, merger was to be encouraged but not enforced. A few mergers have since been consummated, but there is no indication that the structure of the major unions will be seriously altered. The state and city federations of local unions, where parallel AFL and CIO organizations had grown up, were definitely ordered to merge.

The old AFL had quite limited powers over the affiliated national unions, and this remains basically true of the AFL-CIO. Two significant differences, however, should be noted:

1. The old AFL attach great importance to avoiding overlapping jurisdiction among the national unions, and asserted the right to draw clear jurisdictional boundary lines. This principle of exclusive jurisdiction was abandoned in 1955 for the sake of labor unity, and all national unions were taken into the new federation with the territory that they had managed to occupy at that time. Another new feature in the situation is the election procedures of the National Labor Relations Board, which give workers the ultimate right to decide whether they shall be represented by one union or another. The AFL-CIO retains the right to define the jurisdiction of new affiliates, to mediate jurisdictional disputes among its constituent unions, and if necessary to make decisions in such disputes. It has no enforcement powers, however, short of the drastic step of expelling an offending union. As a practical matter, jurisdictional controversies are now resolved mainly through National Labor Relations Board elections and through a large network of bilateral agreements between unions in neighboring fields.

2. The AFL-CIO constitution goes farther than its predecessors in prescribing standards of conduct for the national unions. No union which is controlled or dominated by communists, members of other totalitarian movements, or racketeers ("corrupt influences") may remain affiliated with the federation. The executive council has power to investigate situations where such control or domination is alleged, to make recommendations or give directions to the union in question, and to suspend the union from membership by a two-thirds vote. Council actions may be appealed to the biennial convention, which has final authority to reinstate or expel the accused union. But the threat of expulsion, while it may have some effect on small unions, is

ineffective against the more powerful organizations. The outstanding example is the Teamsters' Union, which simply ignored federation orders to eliminate corruption, and accepted expulsion in 1957 with equanimity. Since then the union has continued to flourish on its own, while the federation had been deprived of valuable revenues and support.

The national unions, then, remain largely autonomous in managing their internal affairs and continue to be the real power centers of the labor movement. The national unions are not members of the AFL-CIO in the sense that Minnesota is part of the United States. Their position is more like that of countries within the United Nations, which by threatening to withdraw can veto actions contrary to their interests. They confer power on the federation much more than they draw power from it.

The independence of the major national unions was strikingly illustrated in 1968. President Walter Reuther and other officers of the United Automobile Workers had long been critical of the top AFL-CIO leadership, charging failure to penetrate the unorganized sectors of the economy as well as social and political conservatism. In 1967 Mr. Reuther resigned from the AFL-CIO Executive Council. In 1968, after inconclusive discussions looking toward reform and "revitalization" of the federation, the United Automobile Workers voted to withhold its dues payments. This led to its suspension, followed by a formal disaffiliation from the federation. The United Automobile Workers subsequently formed a loose mutual-aid alliance (the Alliance for Labor Action) with the Teamsters, with an open-ended invitation to any other groups which might wish to join.

Thus while total union membership has held its own since 1955, the number of unionists affiliated with the AFL-CIO has declined. Two of the three largest national unions are not presently affiliated, and there are several other large independent groups, including the United Mine Workers, the United Electrical, Radio and Machine Workers, and the Mine, Mill and Smelter Workers.

THE
TRADE UNION WORLD
TODAY

It is appropriate to close this survey of union development by indicating the centers of union strength at the present time. It is apparent from Table 3 that membership is highly concentrated in a few large organizations.[6] Three unions—the Teamsters, Automobile Workers,

---

[6] Bureau of Labor Statistics, *Directory of National and International Labor Unions in the United States* (Bulletin No. 1596, 1967).

and Steelworkers—have more than a million members each. The ten
largest unions have about 8½ million members, or almost half of all
union members in the country. At the bottom of the scale are about

Table 3

UNIONS REPORTING 100,000 OR MORE MEMBERS, 1966

TEAMSTERS, CHAUFFEURS, WAREHOUSEMEN AND HELPERS (IND.)	1,651,240
AUTOMOBILE, AIRCRAFT, ÅND AGRICUTURAL IMPLEMENT WORKERS (IND.)	1,402,700
STEELWORKERS	1,068,000
ELECTRICAL WORKERS, INTERNATIONAL BROTHERHOOD OF	875,000
MACHINISTS	836,163
CARPENTERS AND JOINERS	800,000
RETAIL CLERKS	500,314
HOD CARRIERS, BUILDING AND COMMON LABORERS	474,529
GARMENT WORKERS UNION, INTERNATIONAL LADIES'	455,164
HOTEL AND RESTAURANT EMPLOYEES AND BARTENDERS	449,974
CLOTHING WORKERS, AMALGAMATED	382,000
MEAT CUTTERS AND BUTCHER WORKMEN	353,059
BUILDING SERVICE EMPLOYEES	348,500
ENGINEERS, OPERATING	330,000
COMMUNICATIONS WORKERS	321,117
ELECTRICAL, RADIO, ÅND MACHINE WORKERS, INTERNATIONAL UNION OF	320,000
PLUMBING AND PIPE FITTING	284,707
STATE, COUNTY AND MUNICIPAL EMPLOYEES	281,277
RAILWAY AND STEAMSHIP CLERKS	270,000
MUSICIANS, AMERICAN FEDERATION OF	252,487
PAINTERS, DECORATORS, AND PAPERHANGERS	200,569
GOVERNMENT EMPLOYEES, AMERICAN FEDERATION OF	199,000
LETTER CARRIERS	189,628
RAILROAD TRAINMEN	185,000
TEXTILE WORKERS UNION OF AMERICA	182,000
PULP, SULFATE, AND PAPER MILL WORKERS	171,118
RETAIL, WHOLESALE, AND DEPÅRTMENT STORE UNION	170,500
RUBBER, CORK, LINOLEUM, AND PLASTIC WORKERS	170,437
ELECTRICAL, RÅDIO, AND MACHINE WORKERS OF AMERICA, UNITED (IND.)	170,437
OIL, CHEMICAL AND ATOMIC WORKERS	165,329
IRON WORKERS, BRIDGE, STRUCTURAL AND ORNAMENTAL	162,000
MINE WORKERS OF AMERICA, UNITED (IND.)	*
BRICKLAYERS, MASONS AND PLASTERERS	149,000
PAPERMAKERS AND PAPERWORKERS	144,300
POSTAL CLERKS	143,146
MAINTENANCE OF WAY EMPLOYEES	141,000
BOILERMAKERS, BLACKSMITHS, FORGERS AND HELPERS	140,000
PACKINGHOUSE WORKERS	135,000
TRANSPORT WORKERS	135,000
TEACHERS, AMERICAN FEDERATION OF	125,000
RAILWAY CARMEN	125,000
FIRE FIGHTERS	115,000
PRINTING PRESSMEN AND ASSISTANTS	114,000
TYPOGRAPHICAL UNION	106,646
SHEET METAL WORKERS	100,000

* Membership not reported, but probably not above 150,000.
SOURCE: Bureau of Labor Statistics (Bulletin No. 1596; 1967).

one hundred national unions with less than 25,000 members each. Although this group includes half of the unions in the country. it includes only about 5 percent of all union members.

The degree of union penetration varies widely among sectors of the economy. In mining, construction, and transportation the great majority of wage earners are union members. In manufacturing a substantial majority are members, though the ratio varies in different branches of manufacturing—high in steel and automobiles, low in textiles. These four sectors—manufacturing, mining, construction, and transportation—account for more than 80 percent of total union membership. In the trade and service sectors, on the other hand, unionism has made much less progress.

The geographical distribution of union membership reflects in part the distribution of employment. States that have many workers in manufacturing, construction, and transportation also have many union members. Five states (New York, California, Pennsylvania, Illinois, and Ohio), each with more than a million union members, account for about half of total membership.

In addition to the distribution of employment, however, regions differ in their susceptibility to union organization. The most recent survey shows the highest ratio of union members to nonagricultural employment in the state of West Virginia (44 percent), followed by Michigan and Washington (40 percent), Pennsylvania, New York, Indiana, Illinois, Ohio, Missouri, and Montana (34–37 percent). Union organization is strongest in the Middle Atlantic, East North Central, and Pacific Coast states. The Mountain and West North Central states, the South, and the Southwest are weakly unionized. The ratio of union members to nonagricultural employment is lowest in North and South Carolina (7 percent), South Dakota (10 percent), Mississippi (12 percent), Florida, Georgia, North Dakota, and Texas (14 percent), Virginia and Oklahoma (15 percent).

The weakness of unionism in the South is not just a matter of the industry mix. The same industries are less unionized there than in other parts of the country. An interesting calculation, made in 1953 near the peak of union strength, showed that union membership in the southern states was only 57 percent of what it would be *if each industry were as strongly unionized in the South as in the nation as a whole.*[7] The reasons for this weak showing include unusually active employer resistance to unionism, a generally unfavorable attitude in state legislatures and the courts, a new industrial labor force recruited largely from agriculture, and the complicating factor of racial divisions in the work force.

[7] Leo Troy, "The Growth of Union Membership in the South, 1939–1953," *Southern Economic Journal,* April, 1958, pp. 407–20.

MEMBERSHIP STAGNATION
AND
THE FUTURE OUTLOOK

The most striking feature of the past twenty years is the stagnation of union membership. After a period of rapid expansion, membership has stopped growing and the percentage of the labor force in unions has dropped. In the traditional strongholds of manufacturing, mining, and transportation, most unions have lost members since the midfifties. The unions that have managed to swim against the tide and increase their membership are largely outside these areas. They include the Teamsters; Retail Clerks; Retail, Wholesale, and Department Store Employees; Letter Carriers; State, County, and Municipal Employees; Musicians; Building Service Employees; Plumbers; and Electrical Workers (IBEW).

There are several reasons for the leveling off of union membership. In the midfifties the most easily unionized people—manual workers in large establishments in cities of the Northeast and Pacific Coast—had already been substantially organized. As unionism presses out into white-collar employment, smaller establishments, smaller cities and towns, and more heavily agricultural regions, it encounters increasing resistance.

The composition of employment has been changing in ways unfavorable to unionism. The number of production workers in manufacturing has been cut by technological improvements, and employment in mining and transportation has fallen sharply. The sectors with a strong uptrend of employment are trade, government, finance, and services; but in these largely white-collar areas unionism has only a slight foothold. Geographically, industry has tended to move from the Northeast to the South and Southwest, and from metropolitan areas to smaller communities, i.e. to areas in which union organization seems inherently more difficult. For the time being, unionism seems to be confined within a shrinking area of the economy.

There has been a marked change in public attitudes and in the political climate over the past generation. The low wages, heavy unemployment, and other hardships of the 1930s have receded into the past. No longer can unions count on public sympathy for the underdog. On the contrary, they now attract part of the criticism and distrust of concentrated economic power formerly reserved for big business. The Taft–Hartley Act of 1947 and the Landrum–Griffin Act of 1959, apart from their direct effect on union operations, are symbolic of a changed climate of opinion which makes organization more difficult.

In addition to these external influences, some observers assert that the labor movement itself has become bureaucratic and complacent, and that the internal pressure for expansion has slackened. While lip service is still given to the principle of organizing the unorganized, most union officers are in fact content to settle down within the area won in the past.

Further expansion of union membership, however, will have to come from moving outside existing frontiers. Geographically, the main frontier now lies in the South. Occupationally, the frontier lies mainly in white-collar employment. The prospect for further union growth, therefore, depends on the answer to two questions: Will unions be able to increase their coverage of employment in the southern states? Will the percentage of white-collar workers in unions rise substantially?

Prospects in the South

The organized percentage in the South has remained consistently at about half of the level in other regions.[8]

	PERCENT OF NONAGRICULTURAL EMPLOYMENT ORGANIZED		
	1939	*1953*	*1964*
SOUTH	10.7	17.2	14.4
NONSOUTH	21.5	34.1	29.5

When one looks beneath such averages, however, the situation is very uneven. In Kentucky, where coal mining is important, the organized percentage is above 25. But in North and South Carolina, where the weakly unionized textile industry is important, only about 7 percent of nonagricultural employees are union members.

There is a similar unevenness among industries. Communications workers, longshoremen, mine workers, and the skilled crafts in printing, building construction, and railroad operation are about as well organized in the South as in other regions. Within manufacturing, the southern unionized percentage is high (i.e. in the range of 75–95 percent) in basic steel, automobiles, aircraft, electrical equipment, rubber products, pulp and paper, and oil refining. These are oligopolistic industries in which most of the national output is produced by a few companies. Plants are large and mechanized, employee relations are impersonal. Southern plants are often owned by companies that operate throughout the country. Once a union has established collective bar-

---

[8] Ray Marshall, *Labor in the South* (Cambridge: Harvard University Press, 1967).

gaining relations in a company's northern plants, it is relatively easy to extend this relation to its southern plants.

In light manufacturing—food, beverages, textiles, clothing, boots and shoes, wood and furniture products—the situation is quite different. Here the unionized proportion is typically below 30 percent, and in the important textile industry it is only 14 percent. These industries are relatively small-scale, and are often located in small towns or rural areas. Competition in the product market is severe, and labor costs are a large part of total costs. Thus employers have a strong economic incentive to resist the increase in labor costs which might result from unionization. In some cases, notably textiles, southern producers dominate the industry, depriving the union of a northern beachhead from which to expand.

Looking toward the future, several tendencies should be favorable to union organization:

1. The structure of manufacturing in the South is becoming more diversified. In 1939, the hard-to-organize light manufacturing industries provided three-quarters of southern manufacturing employment. Today the proportion is only one-half, and still falling. There has been a rapid increase of southern branch plants of companies in heavy manufacturing, many of which are unionized from the outset. The strongly unionized building trades are also growing as a proportion of total employment.

2. In the South, as in other regions, the percentage of the labor force employed in agriculture has dropped sharply since 1940. This drying-up of the labor reservoir in agriculture removes a major source of "cheap labor" and a ready supply of strikebreakers to combat union organizing drives.

3. As the South becomes increasingly urban and industrial, with rural attitudes declining in importance, the ideological and political climate should become less hostile to unionism than it has been in the past. This is one aspect of the vast "homogenization" of American society, the gradual erosion of regional differences.

There are other tendencies that may make union organization more difficult. Ray Marshall notes [9] among other things, "the tendency for plants to locate in smaller communities; the scattering of workers from the plant gates, making it more difficult to contact them; rising living standards and changed patterns of living . . . the workers' rising educational levels which make them more questioning of both management and unions . . . technological changes which increase employment in non-union areas and increase management's ability to operate during strikes; management's growing sophistication in fighting unions where it wishes to avoid them; the growing disenchantment with unions by intellectuals and union staff people . . ."

[9] Marshall, *Labor in the South,* p. 351.

It is hazardous to predict how these conflicting tendencies will balance out in the future. There may possibly, over the next generation, be a moderate reduction in the gap between the percentage organized in the South and in other parts of the country; but there seems little reason to expect a large reduction.

Prospects in White-collar Employment

We noted in chapter 3 the rapid rise of white-collar employment in all the industrial countries. These white-collar workers are by no means immune to union organization.[10] The percentage in unions, however, varies widely among countries, from a high of about 60 percent in Sweden to only about 11 percent in the United States. Comparative analysis of the industrial countries suggests several conclusions:

First, it appears that white-collar workers are best organized where unionism in general is strong. In Sweden and Austria, both strongly unionized, the percentage of white-collar workers in unions is unusually high. In West Germany and the United Kingdom, where the degree of unionization is somewhat lower, white-collar unionism is also weaker. The United States stands at the bottom of the range in both respects.

Second, the percentage of white-collar workers organized is always (with the possible exception of Japan) below that for blue-collar workers. In Sweden, for example, about 80 percent of blue-collar workers are union members, compared with 60 percent of white-collar workers. In West Germany the respective percentages are 42 and 23. In the United States they would be about 40 and 11.

The reasons for this differential, which is especially large in the United States, are not entirely clear. There seems no inherent reason why unionism should not be as advantageous to white-collar employees as to anyone else. Sales and clerical jobs now pay little more, on the average, than manual labor. In government agencies, banks, insurance offices, and elsewhere, large numbers of white-collar people work together under something like factory conditions. Problems of salary levels, fringe benefits, fair treatment by supervisors, job tenure and promotion, threatened displacement by automation and technical change are presumably no less compelling for them than for manual workers.

On the other side stands the traditional feeling of white-collar workers that they are different from, and in some sense superior to, the manual worker; and that trade unionism is *his* institution rather than

---

[10] For a good survey of evidence from a number of countries, see Adolf Sturmthal, ed., *White-Collar Unions* (Urbana: The University of Illinois Press, 1966).

theirs. White-collar people normally have a superior educational background. At the supervisory, technical, and professional levels, which set the tone of the white-collar world, the orientation toward management is typically strong. These people do enjoy an income advantage, and they also have chances of promotion and professional advancement, based primarily on individual performance rather than seniority. So they tend to think in terms of individual progress rather than group action.

The lower ranges of white-collar employment, the routine sales and clerical workers, do not share these advantages. But most white-collar workers at these levels are women. Young women usually expect to be married before long, and older women are usually supplementary earners rather than family heads. So while issues of employment are important for them, they are not fighting issues as they may be for men. The lower propensity of women to join unions shows up clearly in the statistics. In Britain, for example, 36 percent of male white-collar workers are union members, but only 25 percent of women are in unions. In West Germany the percentage of white-collar workers in unions is 31 for men, but only 15 for women. While data have not been assembled for the United States, they would undoubtedly show a similar discrepancy.

A third conclusion is that white-collar employees show a greater propensity to organize in public employment than in private employment. In many countries the largest and strongest white-collar unions are those of teachers and civil servants. In Sweden, the United Kingdom, and Japan, about three-quarters of government white-collar employees are unionized. In West Germany, which has a special civil servants association limited to white-collar workers, the percentage organized is very high. Even in the United States, five of the ten white-collar unions with membership above 100,000 are unions of government workers.[11]

This greater propensity to organize among government employees has not been fully explored. It may be due partly to the large size of the employing unit and the impersonal, bureaucratic character of the employment relation. Research studies indicate that large plants and companies are more union prone than small ones, and this tendency may operate in public as well as private employment. The fact that government, by definition, is a monopoly and not subject to product-market competition may be important. Next, there is the well-known sluggishness of civil service pay scales, which often remain unchanged for years at a time, while private wages and consumer prices are moving upward. In an economy which seems to have a persistent in-

[11] Sturmthal, *White-Collar Unions*, p. 340. These unions are the Postal Clerks, Letter Carriers, Teachers, Government Employees, and State, County, and Municipal Employees.

flationary bias, civil servants may well find it advantageous to substitute collective bargaining for unilateral salary determination. Finally, unions of public employees are in an unusually strategic position to bring pressure on government. They can work through political channels as well as through bargaining. Strikes of public employees are unlawful, but by no means unknown; and even without striking, there are ways of reducing the normal level of service, attracting publicity, and bringing pressure on public officials.

What does all this signify for the United States? Is the proportion of white-collar workers in unions likely to rise substantially over the years ahead? The best prospects seem to be in public employment. At the federal level, union prospects were strengthened by an executive order of 1962, affirming the right of employees to join unions and providing for varying degrees of recognition corresponding to differing degrees of union strength. Where a union has been chosen by a majority of employees in an appropriate administrative unit, it may be granted exclusive recognition, and then has the right to negotiate a written agreement. The status of unionism in state and local employment varies from state to state; but here too there has been a movement toward acceptance of union organization and collective agreements as a normal feature of employee relations. Seventeen states now have comprehensive labor relations laws for public employees.

The public school systems of the country alone employ some 2 million teachers. The American Federation of Teachers has upwards of 100,000 members, but has been overshadowed by the much larger National Education Association. The National Education Association has traditionally included school administrators as well as teachers, has emphasized improvement of professional standards, has opposed strike action, and has tried to differentiate itself clearly from collective bargaining organizations such as the American Federation of Teachers. Under the stimulus of teacher unrest and intensified competition with the more aggressive American Federation of Teachers, these attitudes have changed considerably. Resolutions have been passed favoring "professional negotiations," which do not seem to differ substantially from ordinary collective bargaining. Local National Education Association branches have appeared on the ballot as competitors of the American Federation of Teachers in collective bargaining elections. While strikes are still not favored, there has been considerable use of "sanctions," including discouraging National Education Association members from accepting employment in school systems that have not met the salary or other terms requested in negotiations. The National Education Association, in short, is behaving more and more like a union; and one scholar has suggested that this may lead in time to an American Federation of Teachers–National Education Association merger with frankly collective bargaining objectives.[12] Several mergers have already occurred at the local level.

A similar development has occurred within the American Nurses Association. As early as 1943 the California branch of the American Nurses Association began to act as collective bargaining agent for its members, and other state units have since followed this lead. While the association's official statements emphasize that "collective bargaining is not to be confused with labor unionism," the distinction does not seem very substantial. The agreements negotiated by the American Nurses Association cover such standard subjects as wages, sick leave, vacations and holidays, and some of them provide a form of union shop.

Another area in which union expansion may be expected is wholesale and retail trade. Gradual replacement of the small retailer by large supermarkets, chain stores, department stores, and discount houses has created favorable conditions for union organization. The largest union in the field, the Retail Clerks' International Association, has a membership of about half a million, with particular strength on the Pacific Coast and in the large food chains nationally. Total union membership in wholesale and retail trade is estimated at more than a million. But this is still small relative to the 10 million nonsupervisory employees in this sector.

Overall, it seems likely that the percentage of white-collar workers in unions will rise gradually over the years ahead. The expansion of white-collar membership may be about sufficient to offset the decline of employment and union membership in some branches of manufacturing, mining, and transportation. In this event, the unionized proportion of the labor force may level off in the range of 25–28 percent for the foreseeable future.

Discussion Questions

1. To what factors can one attribute the beginnings of modern trade unionism around 1800?
2. In a depression, workers would seem to need special protection against wage cuts and loss of jobs. Why, in spite of this, has union membership usually declined in depression periods?

[12] Michael H. Moskow, *Teachers and Unions* (Philadelphia: Wharton School of Finance and Commerce, Industrial Research Unit, 1966).

3. Explain why skilled workers have usually been the first to form stable trade unions.
4. What explains the dominance of the national union over other forms of trade union organization in the United States?
5. The rise of the CIO was pictured at the time as a victory of "industrial unionism" over "craft unionism." What do these terms mean? Is this a correct interpretation of CIO development?
6. The AFL in its later years forged steadily ahead of the CIO in total membership. Why was this? Did it indicate a decline of belief in industrial unionism?
7. "The formation of the AFL-CIO was a merger of two radically different organizations which had different problems, goals and philosophies." Discuss.
8. Should union strength be defined in terms of the number of union members, or the percentage of the labor force in trade unions? Using the definition you prefer, would you expect union strength in 1975 to be greater or less than today? Explain.
9. "Union organization in a newly industrialized area is always slow and difficult. This is the basic reason for the limited progress of unionism in the South." Discuss.
10. How would you appraise union prospects in the area of white-collar employment?

Reading Suggestions

Classic studies in the history of American unionism include Commons, John R. and associates, *History of the Labor Movement in the United States* (4 vols.). New York: The Macmillan Company, 1918; Perlman, Selig, *A History of Trade Unionism in the United States.* New York: The Macmillan Company, 1937; Taft, Philip, *The A.F. of L. in the Time of Gompers.* New York: Harper & Row, Publishers, 1957. The standard source for British unionism is Webb, Sidney and Beatrice Webb, *The History of Trade Unionism.* London: Workers Educational Association, 1919.

More recent studies relevant to this chapter include Bakke, E. Wight, and Clark Kerr, eds., *Unions, Management and the Public,* rev. ed. New York: Harcourt, Brace & World, Inc., 1960; Section 1, "Sources of the Union Movement"; Section 2, "History of Unionism in the United States." Bernstein, Irving, "The Growth of American Unions," *American Economic Review,* XLIV (June, 1954), 301–18;

Marshall, Ray, *Labor in the South*. Cambridge: Harvard University Press, 1967; Sturmthal, Adolf, ed., *White-Collar Unions*. Urbana: The University of Illinois Press, 1966; Ulman, Lloyd, *The Rise of the National Trade Union*. Cambridge: Harvard University Press, 1955.

THE GOVERNMENT
OF
TRADE UNIONS

13

Collective bargaining is a relationship between organizations—the business firm and the trade union. The internal structure of these organizations affects the relations between them and helps mold the daily life of the worker. In this chapter we examine first the broad outlines of union government at the national and local levels. Next we shall consider some common criticisms of internal union management, and then review the efforts which have been made to correct these deficiencies through legislation.

MANAGING
A
NATIONAL UNION

A national trade union operates under a written constitution, which may run to forty or fifty closely printed pages. These constitutions are much more detailed than the charters of business corporations or of most other organizations. The duties and powers of union officers, the rights and duties of members, and all procedures for the conduct of union business are usually set forth at length.

The supreme governing body is usually the national convention. Most unions hold their conventions every year or every two years, though sometimes conventions are four or five years apart. The convention consists of delegates from the affiliated local unions. Each local is usually represented in proportion to its dues-paying membership, which means that the locals from the larger plants or cities have a dominant voice. The convention has a number of functions and powers. It listens to reports by the national officers on their activities since the last convention, discusses these reports, and approves or disapproves them. It elects officers to serve until the next convention. It is free to debate any question of union policy or organization, and has power also to amend the basic constitution of the union.

The national convention provides a forum in which the views of local unions throughout the country can be expressed. Most of the delegates are local union officials. Many locals pass resolutions at their local meetings for submission to the national convention and frequently instruct their delegates on the stand they should take. The convention provides an opportunity for leaders of a particular local to learn about the problems facing other locals and the national organization as a whole. It thus widens the viewpoint of local leaders and makes them more cognizant of the part they play in a national institution. The convention debates also allow able local officials to display their leadership ability, thus giving them a channel into national office. Almost all national union leaders rise from lower ranks in the union, and must demonstrate their ability repeatedly before they attain high office.

The initiative in bringing business before the convention does not rest entirely, or even mainly, with the delegates. The national officials work out in advance their own policy proposals and seek support for them from the convention. The officers are also usually seeking re-election for another term. The union convention is therefore "stage-managed" in much the same way as the national convention of a political party. The top union officials appoint the key convention committees—the credentials committee, the resolutions committee, the committee on officers' reports, and so on. They determine the order of business and the time allowed for discussion of various subjects, and the union president from his position in the chair can do a good deal to influence the course of discussion. Much of the important business of the convention is done in private through individual discussions and committee meetings, and many key decisions are made in advance of any discussion on the convention floor. The delegates occasionally revolt and take decisions out of the hands of the union leaders. The leaders are usually astute enough, however, to appraise correctly the feeling of the delegates on each issue, and to shape their proposals so as to be sure in advance of a favorable vote. Their control is not arbitrary, but is based on a well-developed talent for keeping an ear to the ground.

A number of unions, primarily craft unions that have been in existence for many years, use the referendum procedure, either alone or in conjunction with conventions. In some unions all national officers are elected by referendum vote of the membership, and all constitutional amendments must be ratified in the same way. In some cases, even though there is a national convention, all policy decisions of the convention must be submitted to a referendum vote. A few unions provide for initiation of new legislation directly by the membership. A petition signed by a certain number of union members or endorsed by a certain number of locals compels the national officers to submit the proposition in question either to the convention or to a referendum vote.

Administration of Unions

Administration of the national union's affairs is entrusted to an executive board, consisting usually of a president, secretary, treasurer, and numerous vice-presidents who are responsible for particular geographical areas or segments of the industry. Subject to any constitutional limitations, the executive board has full power to act for the union during the period between conventions.

The executive board, or in some cases the president acting for the executive board, appoints the salaried staff of the union and directs its day-to-day work. In the larger unions, the salaried staff includes several hundred people. At national headquarters there are usually departments for research, legal problems, education, the union magazine, organization, and other functions, plus a clerical staff to handle bookkeeping and correspondence. If legislation is important to the union, and if national headquarters is not located in Washington, there will be a branch office in Washington staffed by a legislative representative and frequently several assistants.

The field organization of the union usually consists of several regional or district offices, each headed by a regional director. If the union has jursidiction over several industries, as in the case of the Textile Workers' Union, there may be a regional director for each industry. Under the regional directors are the field representatives or "organizers," who organize new local unions and assist existing locals in their dealings with employers. The field representatives are the cement that binds the locals to the national union. They move around their regions constantly, keep in close touch with grass roots sentiment, report back to national headquarters, and at the same time interpret national union policies to local officials and the rank and file.

The salaries of most union officials are modest by business standards. A few of the larger unions pay their presidents $50,000 or more per year, but this is unusual. Most union presidents would be in the range of $25,000 to $50,000. Most second-echelon union officials would fall in the range of $15,000 to $25,000 per year. Local officers frequently serve without pay. Salaried local officers and field representatives usually do not receive much more than they could make by working in the plant. The practical reason for this is that union members are envious of anyone appointed to a job paying more than they earn themselves, and it is therefore poor politics to let the salaries of lower-level officials get much out of line with the members' earnings. In addition to salary, union officials usually receive allowances for travel and other necessary expenses.

Almost all of the top officials of American unions began as workers in the industry and rose to their present positions through the union's ranks. A man begins as a worker in the plant, is elected shop steward or shop committeeman, goes on to become an official of the local union, rises to international representative or district director, and finally becomes an officer of the international union.[1] A man rarely leaps from nowhere to high office in the union, just as he does not often became a candidate for president of the United States without having served his time in lesser political positions. Disappointing as it may be to college graduates who wish to contribute their talents to the labor movement, there is virtually no way of winning elective office in a trade union except by starting in the plant and coming up through the ranks.

In addition to its administrative functions, the executive board exercises supreme judicial authority during the period between conventions. It hears appeals of union members from actions of local officials, mediates disputes between local unions or factions within a local, and has broad authority to discipline local officials for maladministration or violation of the union constitution. Decisions of the executive board can usually be appealed to the next national convention, but there are a few cases in which this is not true. The president of the American Federation of Musicians, for example, has the right to perform any act on behalf of the union, including making amendments to the union constitution, with no appeal by the membership.

---

[1] See Eli Ginzberg, *The Labor Leader* (New York: The Macmillan Company, 1948), particularly chaps. 5 and 6. See also Jack Barbash, *Labor Unions in Action* (New York: Harper & Row, Publishers, 1948); C. A. Madison, *American Labor Leaders* (New York: Harper & Row, Publishers, 1950); and Florence Peterson, *American Labor Unions—What They Are and How They Work*, rev. ed. (New York: Harper & Row, Publishers, 1952).

There are historical reasons for this provision, connected with the unstable and migratory character of musicians' work, which created a special need for strong central authority. Instances of this sort, however, are very rare in the union world.

Union Finances

Dues paid by the members are the main source of union income. While dues have tended to rise with wage levels, it remains true that "in most unions the monthly dues can be earned in less than two hours of work."[2] The highest dues are usually charged by unions of skilled workers whose earning level is higher. In the craft unions, too, dues frequently include an insurance premium to cover sickness, retirement, death, and other benefits provided by the unions. Dues are collected by the local union and divided between it and the national union in some specified proportion. The commonest basis is a 50–50 division, but in some cases the national office takes as little as 25 percent, and in a few cases it takes more than 50 percent.

As the functions of the national union have grown, there has been a tendency for its share of dues payments to increase. The level of dues has also risen in the course of time. Wage levels have also risen greatly, however, and it is doubtful whether dues are now as large relative to earnings as they were ten or twenty years ago. It is hard for national union officials to get dues raised fast enough to keep up with rising wage levels and the growing needs of the union. Convention delegates, who are tractable enough on other issues, frequently kick over the traces when it comes to approving a dues increase which they know will be unpopular with the members.

A secondary source of revenue is initiation fees for new members. These fees are generally less than 25 dollars and in many cases around 5 dollars. Only seven of the eighty unions Taft studied, all seven in the building trades, had initiation fees averaging as much as 75 dollars. There is considerable variation among local unions, which are usually allowed to set their own initiation fees within outside limits specified by the national. Reports by about 39,000 local unions under the Landrum–Griffin Act showed 325 locals with fees of 250 to 500 dollars, and 17 with fees ranging from 500 to a peak of 1,400 dollars.[3]

Where does the money go? A union economist has estimated that about one-third of national union expenditures goes for organizing purposes, with benefits to members accounting for 22 percent, adminis-

2 Philip Taft, *The Structure and Government of Trade Unions* (Cambridge: Harvard University Press, 1954), p. 81.

3 Albert Rees, *The Economics of Trade Unions* (Chicago: The University of Chicago Press, 1962), p. 127.

trative expenses 15 percent, and strike benefits 13 percent.[4] Publications, research and legal expenses, and other minor items account for the balance. The major expense item for a local union is salaries of local officers, business agents, and clerical help.

The finances of the national union are carefully safeguarded. Officers who handle funds must be bonded, and there is usually a requirement that checks be signed by at least two officials. The union's books are normally audited at least once a year, and a statement of receipts and expenditures is usually printed either in the union magazine or in the proceedings of the national convention. Most national unions also require that the books of local unions shall be inspected periodically by a traveling auditor from the national office. Despite these precautions, embezzlement of local union funds still occurs occasionally, though it is very rare at the national level. Taft found that in any given year a certain proportion of local unions, ranging between 1 and 3 percent, will report shortages in their accounts. Some of this is of course due to inexperience and poor bookkeeping rather than deliberate misappropriation. After considering amounts recovered from surety companies and other bonding agencies, net losses are a very small percentage of total dues collections.[5]

Government of Local Unions

The government of local unions may be described more briefly. The local union is usually a branch of a national organization, though there are a few unaffiliated locals that have chosen to go their own way. An affiliated local operates within the constitution of its parent organization, which defines what it can and cannot do. In many unions, for example, a local cannot sign a contract with an employer until the contract has been approved by the national executive board. A local is usually forbidden to call a strike without national approval. If it does anyway, it is not entitled to funds or other support from the national organization and may be subject to disciplinary action.

The business of a local union is carried on in weekly or monthly meetings of the membership. Where plants are very large, as in the automobile industry, some locals are so large that it is physically impossible to have a single meeting, and a delegate system has to be used. The typical local union, however, has at most a few hundred members, who can be brought together in a single meeting and can take a direct hand in union affairs if they wish to do so.

Only a small proportion of union members actually take an active and continuous interest in union affairs. On important occasions—the

[4] Cited in Jack Barbash, *The Practice of Unionism* (New York: Harper & Row, Publishers, 1956), p. 79.

[5] Taft, *Structure and Government of Trade Unions*, chap. 3.

election of officers for the coming year, the formulation of demands to be presented to the employer, the ratification of a new contract, or the taking of a strike vote—a large percentage of the membership will appear at the meeting. In between crises, however, attendance shrinks to perhaps 5 to 10 percent of the membership.[6] The day-to-day work of the union is carried on by a few "wheelhorses" who are willing to put in the necessary time. These are the professional politicians of the labor movement, corresponding to the ward and precinct leaders in a political machine. This active minority, however, is in close touch with the remainder of the membership. Even though only two men from a certain department of the plant show up at the meeting, they probably have a good idea of what the other men in the department are thinking. They also carry back and explain to their fellow workers the decisions which were taken at the meeting. There is thus a great deal of informal representation of the inert majority, and the government of the union is more democratic than might appear at first glance.[7]

The officers of the local union usually work in the plant along with the rest and receive no pay for their union activities. Exceptions are sometimes found in large locals, where union office may become a full-time job. The local officers carry on the day-to-day work of keeping the union running, persuading new workers to join, collecting dues, handling grievances arising in the plant, and so on. On major problems, such as the negotiation of a new contract, the handling of a strike, an important grievance, or an arbitration case, they are usually advised and assisted by a national field representative.[8]

The Local and the National

Over the past fifty years there has been a general tendency toward greater centralization of authority and responsibility in the national union. The main reason is increased centralization of bargaining

[6] According to one survey the "normal" attendance in medium-sized established locals, i.e. of 200 to 4,000 members, is 2 to 8 percent. See George Strauss and Leonard Sayles, "The Local Union Meeting," *Industrial and Labor Relations Review*, VI (January, 1953), 206–9.

[7] See George Strauss and Leonard Sayles, "What the Worker Really Thinks of His Union," *Harvard Business Review*, XXXI (May–June, 1953), 94–102, and "Patterns of Participation in Local Unions," *Industrial and Labor Relations Review*, VI (October, 1952), 31–42.

[8] See George Strauss and Leonard Sayles, "The Unpaid Local Leader," *Harvard Business Review*, XXX (May–June, 1952), 91–104; Joel Seidman, Jack London, and Bernard Karsch, "Leadership in a Local Union," *American Journal of Sociology*, LVI (November, 1950), 229–37; and Eli Chinoy, "Local Union Leadership," in A. W. Gouldner, ed., *Studies in Leadership* (New York: Harper & Row, Publishers, 1950), pp. 157–73.

negotiations with employers, which stems in turn from the broadening of competition in product markets and the increasing scope of employer organization. It is significant that local union autonomy is greatest in industries where the product market remains local, as in building construction, newspaper printing, local trucking, and the like. In such industries as steel, automobiles, clothing, and coal mining, on the other hand, competition is national, bargaining is in effect national, and union organization is correspondingly centralized. Key negotiations with major companies are conducted by the national officers, national field representatives typically sit in on local negotiations, all agreements are required to conform to national standards, and local policy decisions are closely monitored. A large national staff —a union "bureaucracy"—has been developed to service the local unions. Another significant tendency is the growth of intermediary bodies between the local union and the national office—regional or district councils on a geographical basis, conferences to deal with a major industry subdivision or a single major employer, and the like. For a million-member union operating in a variety of industries and in all parts of the country, some intermediate organization of this sort is essential.

Two aspects of local–national relations should be noted particularly, since they have given rise to considerable controversy and occasional charges of abuse. First, local union officers are subject to disciplinary action by the national officers. If the officers of a local are accused by members of violating the national constitution, mishandling union funds, or other misdeeds, they may be brought to trial before the national executive board. If the verdict is against them, they may be removed from office and the national union may appoint a trustee or receiver to manage the affairs of the local until the situation can be rectified and new officers installed.

National officers are reluctant to take such drastic action because of the possibility of local opposition and schism, and in most unions the receivership device is used very sparingly. The commonest reasons for national intervention are financial irregularity, intense factionalism in the local, failure to organize the trade or locality, failure to reopen agreements on time, strikes in violation of contract commitments, communist domination and use of the local for political purposes, and toleration of racketeering in the local.[9] National intervention, in short, is typically a method of protecting the membership against incompetence, venality, or oppression by local leaders. The receivership device can also be used, however, to suppress local union democracy, to

[9] For detailed evidence, see Taft, *Structure and Government of Trade Unions,* chap. 4.

get rid of critics of the national machine, and to loot the local treasury. This has led to government regulation of trusteeships and receiverships, which will be considered in the next section.

A second issue concerns the adequacy of present procedures for protecting the "civil rights" of the individual union member. A member may be accused of having violated some working rule of the union, such as accepting pay below the union scale, doing piece work contrary to union policy, or working overtime without permission; or of misbehavior on the job—fighting, drinking, failure to perform job duties, or refusing to follow reasonable instructions of the shop steward. Less frequently, but more dangerously, he may be accused of antiunion activity, defaming a union officer, and so on. There certainly is such a thing as antiunion activity and the union constitution must provide against it, but such charges can also be a way of getting at men whose only real offense is criticism of the officers in power.

Any charge against a member is heard and decided initially at the local level, either by a trial committee or by vote of the entire membership. The penalty, if guilt is established, is typically a fine appropriate to the offense. Expulsion from membership is regarded as a drastic measure and is rarely used. Either the member or his accusers may appeal the decision to the national president or the executive board, and there is usually a final right of appeal to the next national convention. Taft's study of the records of eight national unions indicates that the right of appeal is used quite frequently. The president and executive board typically review anywhere from twenty-five to one hundred appeals per year. The handling of appeals by national officers appears to be careful and conscientious. The ratio of reversals or modifications of local decisions is quite high—often between 30 and 50 percent of all cases considered. Even when a member's guilt is reaffirmed on appeal, the size of the penalty is frequently reduced. Emotion and personal vindictiveness run higher at the local level than in the national office. Taft concludes:

> The cases that arise out of what might be termed civil rights are relatively few . . . disciplinary penalties are usually imposed for the violation of trade rules and rather infrequently over issues such as free speech or publication of unauthorized materials. It is difficult for outsiders to evaluate the reasonableness of penalties, but the information does indicate that they are seldom severe or unwarranted. . . . On the whole, there is no evidence that the appellate machinery does not function effectively, that it is vain or useless, or that it would be improved by government supervision.[10]

[10] Taft, *Structure and Government of Trade Unions*, p. 180.

PROBLEMS OF
UNION STRUCTURE
AND ADMINISTRATION

The internal procedures of trade unions have produced a variety of criticisms and complaints. In a minority of unions, officers have used their positions for self-enrichment and have been guilty of gross breaches of trust. More generally, it is charged that the officers typically dominate union affairs, and that members who oppose the leadership have inadequate protection against retaliation and arbitrary penalties. The proven instances of corruption, and the more general accusation of autocratic government, have led to increasing public control over union affairs. Let us first consider the criticisms before proceeding to the remedies.

Financial Malfeasance

Direct embezzlement of union funds mainly occurs at the local rather than at the national level and is relatively rare. The most important methods of self-enrichment are more subtle. They involve use of the union officer's position of power to secure special perquisites, while at the same time damaging—or at any rate failing to advance— the interests of the membership.

The union leader may negotiate a "sweetheart contract," in which he settles for less than the union's strength would have allowed, receiving a kickback from the employer in return. Or he may own a share in the business with which he is negotiating on behalf of the union. Or he may set up a business of his own to sell supplies or services to the union at inflated prices. Or he may arrange for the union health and welfare fund to place its insurance with a company in which he has a financial interest.

Congressional investigations have turned up a wide variety of such practices. Here are a few examples:

1. Loans may be secured from the union to finance the officers' personal investments. Dave Beck, former president of the Teamsters Union, was found to have borrowed $270,110 from union sources. Vice-president Frank Brewster, operating at a lower level, confined his borrowings from the Western Conference of Teamsters to $77,660.[11]

2. Ownership of securities or other interests in a business with

[11] Hearings before the Select Committee on Improper Activities in the Labor and Management Field (*cited hereafter as "McClellan Committee"*), 85th Cong., 1st sess., pursuant to Senate Resolution 74, part 4, pp. 1357, 1370.

which the union deals in collective bargaining. In 1950 Peter Weber, business manager of Local 825 of the Operating Engineers, secured a one-eighth interest in Public Constructors, Inc., a company under contract with the union, in exchange for a loan of $2,500. By September, 1957, the book value of these shares had risen to $108,677.[12] This is one way in which a company could bribe a union official to go easy on the company in bargaining or to avoid pulling strikes on company projects.

3. A less direct form of the same thing is interest in a business selling services or supplies to, or otherwise dealing with, a company involved in bargaining with the union. Mrs. Dave Beck purchased 40 percent of the stock of K and L Distributing Co., which distributed beer for Anheuser-Busch, Inc., a majority of whose employees are members of the Teamsters' Union. The territory of K and L was enlarged and it received preferential shipments of beer as a result of Beck's influence. Later the investment was sold at a 60 percent profit. A later Teamster president, James Hoffa (or his wife), held a substantial interest in companies that rented equipment to trucking concerns under contract with the Teamsters.[13]

4. Ownership of an interest in a business that buys from, sells to, or otherwise deals with the union itself. Dave Beck bought two lots that adjoined the Teamsters' Joint Council in Seattle for $39,000 and then sold them to the union for $139,000. He also, through a front man, had a hand in the National Mortgage Company, which handled $9,000,000 of Teamsters' funds.[14]

5. Other business transactions with employers. The McClellan Committee hearings revealed that a number of union officials had sold equipment to, received loans from, or received other special payments from employers with whom they negotiated. These payments were presumably intended to influence the officers' conduct in organizing and collective bargaining.

These practices are concentrated in certain of the conservative craft unions. Unions with a strong welfare tradition, such as the Clothing Workers, Ladies' Garment Workers, and the newer industrial unions organized by the CIO, have been almost completely free of corrupt practices.

Racketeering

"Racketeering" is not a very precise term, but may be taken to include extortion from workers or employers under threat of physical

[12] McClellan Committee Hearings, part 2, pp. 8134–40.
[13] McClellan Committee Hearings, part 7, pp. 2058–68, and 2099–2102; part 13, pp. 4933–50, and 4966–71; part 13, pp. 5543–57.
[14] McClellan Committee Hearings, part 5, p. 1671; part 7, pp. 2106–12.

violence, typically involving alliance with gunmen and local criminal syndicates. It has flourished principally in New York, Chicago, and a few other large cities, and in highly competitive industries catering to a local market, such as restaurants and other service establishments, local trucking, and building construction.[15]

The position of the union business agent in the construction industry is rather unusual. The business agent acts as an employment agency, and his control of jobs gives him power over the union membership. He also negotiates with employers, polices the terms of union contracts, and usually has the right to call an immediate strike where he believes the contract is being violated. This power enables him to make things easier or harder for the employer. An inopportune strike may prevent a contractor from finishing a building on time and subject him to a large penalty. The selling of "strike insurance" to employers has sometimes yielded incomes for union officials. The practice is by no means general in the building trades, but it has happened.

Racketeering sometimes results from the invasion of a union by gangsters who turn the union to predatory purposes. Instances of this sort were especially numerous after the repeal of prohibition in 1933. Many gangsters had been employed in the bootlegging industry. When liquor became lawful, these men were left unemployed and had to find some other use for their talents. In Chicago and New York, in particular, they turned to control of local unions as a source of revenue. The main attempt was to control transport unions—drivers of milk wagons, coal trucks, oil trucks, laundry trucks, and so on. Control of transportation enables the gang to "shake down" the businesses that depend on transportation for their existence. In some cases rival gangs tried to win control of the same union, and pitched battles were fought in Chicago for control of the milk-wagon drivers' and certain other locals. It was estimated that in the mid-thirties about two-thirds of the union members in Chicago were paying tribute in one way or another to the Capone organization. It must not be forgotten, of course, that a large proportion of the businessmen of the city were also paying tribute to the same organization.

An aggravated and long-standing example of racketeering involves the longshore industry in the Port of New York. Hearings before a special Crime Commission of New York State in 1952 revealed that numerous locals of the International Longshoremen's Association had been taken over forcibly by men with criminal records; that both rival gangsters and rebels within the union had been silenced by violence and even murder; that union funds had been spent and union business conducted with no effective control by the membership; that large

[15] See on this point the interesting analysis in Philip Taft, *Corruption and Racketeering in the Labor Movement,* Bulletin 38 (1958), New York School of Industrial and Labor Relations (Ithaca).

amounts of money had been extorted from shipowners and other businessmen in the port by threats of strike action, damage to merchandise, and other forms of violence; that longshore workers had been forced to pay for their jobs through "kickbacks," "presents," and other payments to those in control; and that the gangsters involved had good political contacts in the cities surrounding the port.

As a consequence of the inability or unwillingness of top International Longshoremen's Association officials to correct these conditions, the AFL expelled the union from Federation membership in 1953, and chartered a new longshoremen's union in the hope of winning away members from the expelled organization. The International Longshoremen's Association won a subsequent National Labor Relations Board election by a narrow margin, however, and has continued to maintain control of the port. Perhaps a more significant development was the establishment of a joint Waterfront Commission by the states of New York and New Jersey as a result of the 1952 hearings. The Commission has endeavored to abolish the notorious "shape-up system" and to substitute hiring through Commission employment offices, to reduce the amount of surplus labor on the docks by issuing longshore licenses only to reasonably regular workers, and to weed out racketeers by refusing licenses to men with criminal records. These measures may gradually weaken the economic basis for racketeering and provide a climate in which honest unionism can develop and survive.

Racketeering is a law enforcement problem rather than a problem of trade union government. The practices just described are already unlawful and can continue to exist only where the law is not enforced. Racketeering in unions is usually carried on in collusion with local political organizations and often with local business interests as well. It is not specifically a union sin, but stems from a generally low level of political and business morality.

Mills concludes that racketeering has been most prevalent in small-scale industries where intense competition has prevailed and where business has not yet grown large enough to maintain its own cartel arrangements. "In the main, these have been the building trades, cleaning and dyeing, restaurants, the garment trades, furriers, trucking, theaters, produce and live poultry markets.[16]

It should be reemphasized that racketeering is not of great quantitative importance in the labor movement. In most cases, union leaders maintain control of the organization by peaceable and lawful methods, by skillful use of the normal tactics of machine politics. This leads us to another line of complaint against trade unions—a complaint, not of wrongdoing, but of serious defects in internal structure.

[16] C. W. Mills, *The New Men of Power* (New York: Harcourt, Brace & World, Inc., 1948), p. 129.

Leadership Domination

Union government is democratic in the sense that officers at all levels are elected from below and are formally responsible to the membership. But in union elections, unlike elections for public office, there is usually only one recognized party. The Typographical Union, which has an old and successful two-party system, is a rarity in the trade union world. Normally all the political machinery of the union is controlled by the people in office, who naturally use it to remain in office. People who oppose them are "factionalists," "dual unionists," "union busters." The concept of a loyal opposition is not recognized.[17]

Strong leadership in a union seems unavoidable and even desirable for at least two reasons. The union is in part a fighting organization. It reaches crises in negotiating with employers that can be met only by a strike. It may have to fend off attacks by employers, government agencies, or others that threaten the very existence of the organization. Hardman has aptly said that a union is part army and part debating society; [18] but it cannot be both things at once. Debate is all right before the battle is joined; but while the battle is on, someone must have authority to issue commands. A strike may be won or lost by a single decision, which has to be made so quickly that the members cannot be consulted, and on which the members might not be able to give an informed judgment in any case.

In addition to threats from without, unions are often threatened by factional strife within their own ranks. Unions are especially susceptible to penetration by doctrinaire political groups who are more interested in the establishment of their ideology than in the strength of the union. When a politically minded minority captures control of a union, the result is frequently the atrophy and eventual disappearance of the organization. Union officials must have sufficient authority to prevent schism and to defend the union against internal as well as

---

[17] For discussions of this problem see Will Herberg, "Bureaucracy and Democracy in Labor Unions," *Antioch Review*, III (Fall, 1943), 405–17; Joseph Kovner, "Union Democracy," Industrial Relations Research Association, *Interpreting the Labor Movement* (1952), pp. 83–88; Joel Seidman, "Democracy in Labor Unions," *Journal of Political Economy*, LXI (June, 1953), 221–31; Joel Seidman, *Union Rights and Union Duties* (New York: Harcourt, Brace & World, Inc., 1943); Philip Taft, "The Constitutional Power of the Chief Officer in American Labor Unions," *Quarterly Journal of Economics*, LXII (May, 1948), 459–71; and Philip Taft, "Democracy in Trade Unions," *American Economic Review Supplement*, XXXVI (May, 1946), 359–69.

[18] See J. B. S. Hardman, *American Labor Dynamics* (New York: Harcourt, Brace & World, Inc., 1928), particularly the articles by Hardman and Muste. See also Sylvia Kopald, "Democracy and Leadership," in E. W. Bakke and Clark Kerr, eds., *Unions, Management and the Public* (New York: Harcourt, Brace & World, Inc., 1948), pp. 180–84.

external enemies. This is admittedly a delicate matter. It is hard to distinguish between a legitimate criticism of union officers and a movement to subvert the union's purposes. The charge of "union wrecking" has been used to crush a minority whose only real offense was differing with the leadership. One must recognize, however, that there is such a thing as antiunion activity by those professing allegiance to the union, and that a means of defense is necessary.

A striking feature of trade union government is the long tenure of office by national union officials, particularly national presidents.[19] John L. Lewis of the Mine Workers, David B. Robertson of the Locomotive Firemen, and William Hutcheson of the Carpenters were union presidents for more than thirty years. Daniel Tobin of the Teamsters, William Mahon of the Street Railway Employees, and George Berry of the Pressmen held office for more than forty years.

Long terms of office have advantages for the union as well as disadvantages. A union needs skilled and experienced leadership. Running a large union requires a detailed knowledge of the economics of the industry, wide acquaintance with management people and political officials, skill in speaking and writing, administrative ability, and experience in negotiation and in the management of men. A leader who is competent and experienced in these respects is a valuable asset to the union. This is a major reason for the long tenure of office by national union leaders. It is true, of course, that many union officials are continued in office beyond the point at which their usefulness has begun to diminish. After a man has been a union official for many years, there is scarcely anything else to which he can turn for a living. The union members, recognizing this fact and appreciating the leader's past services, are usually reluctant to "turn the old horse out to grass."

On the other hand, long tenure of office presents certain problems. The viewpoint and objectives of the union leaders tend to diverge more and more from those of the rank and file. The leaders become increasingly interested in sheer perpetuation of the organization, in "union-oriented demands" rather than "membership-oriented demands." Union-shop and checkoff clauses are a case in point. The members would frequently trade such objectives for immediate benefits. The leaders also become more skeptical about the possibility of rapid progress. The union members exaggerate business profits and believe that more money can always be had for the asking. The leaders know that this is not so. They tend to become conservative in their demands, to moderate the zeal of the membership, to settle for less than the members think possible. To the rank and file, this attitude

[19] Mills, *The New Men of Power,* p. 64.

often appears as a "sell-out" to the employers; to the leaders, it means being realistic and practical.

The dilemma is this: in order to protect the long-run interests of the union, the leaders must have enough power to pursue union-oriented objectives, to make compromises with employers, and to override excessive and ill-advised demands by the membership. Given this power, however, it is difficult to prevent them from slighting the interests of the memberships if they choose to do so.

Another problem is that union officers—like officeholders in industry, government, and elsewhere—become attached to their jobs and bend a good part of their energies to staying in office. The methods used are those of machine politics anywhere. The union leader makes friends with as many members of the organization as he can, performs various services for them, distributes salaried positions in the right quarters, stage-manages the union conventions, and makes full use of oratory and the other political arts. All this he does in perfectly good faith. He becomes convinced after a few years that he can run the union better than anyone else, and in many cases he is right. Indeed, unless he is able to "deliver the goods" year in and year out, no amount of political machination will suffice to keep him in office.

Where a strong leader has remained in office for twenty or thirty years, it will usually be found that he is an exceptionally able person with a profound grasp of the union's problems, and also that he has kept in close touch with membership opinion. The main function of the leader's political machine is not to suppress opposition, but rather to give an accurate report of rank-and-file sentiment which will enable the leader to develop a program commanding general approval. It will be found also that the successful and long-lived leader has achieved substantial gains for his membership in terms of wages and conditions. He is in most cases overwhelmingly popular with the rank and file. Such leaders as Lewis of the Mine Workers, Petrillo of the Musicians, Hoffa of the Teamsters, and Hillman of the Clothing Workers certainly used astute political manipulation to perpetuate their control. At the same time they have been tremendously popular with union members and could easily have been reelected at any time in the freest referendum.

The Meaning of Trade Union Democracy

In what significant sense may this structure of control be regarded as "democratic" or "undemocratic"? If one asks, "Are the forms of democracy observed?" the answer must be "Yes." Union constitutions are thoroughly democratic. The system of government is normally a one-party rather than a multiple-party system, but this is characteristic of virtually all private associations.[20]

If one asks, "Do the members determine union policy?" the answer is usually "No." Policy is determined by the national leaders and to a lesser extent by local leaders, within rather wide limits set by the members' interests and attitudes.

If one asks, "Are unions by and large operated in the interest of the members?" the answer is predominantly "Yes." Most union officers are honest and men of good will. They would rather do a good job for their members than not, and this is sensible also from a political point of view. It helps to keep the machine popular and reelection easy.

If one asks, "Can the members get rid of their leaders and install new ones whenever they wish?"—perhaps the most searching test of democratic control—the answer is "Yes and no." Contests over local office are frequent and the turnover of local officers is high. At the national level, it is possible to revolt against and overthrow an entrenched machine, but is it certainly not easy. It requires organization and hard work, and involves a good deal of personal risk for leaders of the insurgent faction.

The most damaging criticism of union government in the United States is that it fails to recognize the right of legitimate opposition and to provide adequate protection for the dissenting member. A salaried union official who finds himself on the losing side of an internal power struggle is almost certain to be out of a job. A member who opposes the leadership will in some unions find himself exposed to physical violence. In others he will be expelled, with possible loss of employment; and if he appeals his case through union channels, he may find the very people he has opposed sitting in judgment upon him.

REGULATION
OF
INTERNAL UNION AFFAIRS

Self-Regulation

The labor movement itself has taken some steps toward meeting these criticisms. The United Automobile Workers in 1957 established

---

[20] The only two-party system that has operated over a long period of time is found in the International Typographical Union. This is an unusual situation that is scarcely likely to develop in other unions. For a good analysis of the International Typographical Union case, see Seymour M. Lipset, J. S. Coleman, and M. Trow, *Union Democracy in the International Typographical Union* (Glencoe, Ill.: The Free Press, 1956).

a Public Review Board, composed of leading lawyers, professors, and clergymen. Members can appeal decisions of the union's international executive board to this outside body, and the review board can take up cases on its own motion. If the board finds that a worker's membership rights have been violated, it can revoke the penalties imposed on him, and the union is pledged to abide by the decision. The board has heard several dozen cases, upholding the union's executive board in about three-quarters of these, and reversing it in the remainder. It is regrettable that only two other unions, the Upholsterers and the Packinghouse Workers, have thus far adopted this promising technique.

The AFL-CIO constitution of 1955 pledged the organization "to protect the labor movement from any and all corrupt influences." An Ethical Practices Committee was appointed, which drew up six codes of ethical practice covering (a) issuance of local union charters; (b) operation of health and welfare funds; (c) the barring of racketeers, criminals, communists, and fascists from union office; (d) prevention of conflicts of interest between union officers and their organizations; (e) the setting up of adequate accounting and financial controls; and (f) establishment of minimum standards for union elections and disciplinary procedures. Any national union that after hearings is found guilty of violating these codes may be directed to mend its ways. If it declines to do so, the AFL-CIO Executive Council may suspend it from membership by a two-thirds vote. Suspension can be appealed to the next AFL-CIO convention, which has the ultimate right of expulsion. The executive council may also charter a new union to compete with the expelled organization and try to take over its membership.

This procedure has a good chance of success where there is a "clean" faction in the union that is willing to mobilize against a corrupt leadership. The Bakery Workers, whose president had been guilty of malpractice but where corruption was not deeply entrenched, was expelled at the 1957 convention and a rival union was chartered. The new union quickly took over the bulk of the membership in the industry. But where corruption is of long standing and is tolerated by the membership, as in the Teamster and Longshoremen cases, federation action can accomplish little. The Longshoremen were expelled by the AFL in 1953 and a rival union was chartered, but the new union did not succeed in winning mass support. The old union was eventually cleaned up somewhat and was readmitted to the federation in 1961; but this was due mainly to reforms instituted by the New York–New Jersey Waterfront Commission. When the powerful Teamsters Union was expelled in 1957, the federation did not even venture to charter a rival union, and the Teamsters continued to flourish as before. This case has done much to discourage AFL-CIO efforts against corruption.

Court Regulation

A member who has suffered damage from some union action can always go to court and seek redress under the common law. The legal status of unionism and collective bargaining is the subject of a later chapter; but we may comment here on court attitudes toward internal union affairs.

The courts have traditionally regarded a trade union as a private association, comparable to a lodge or social club. Like any club, the union could admit people or bar people as it saw fit, and could set up any rules it liked for internal government. So long as the union observed its own constitution, the courts would not intervene; and they were disinclined to intervene in any event. Only when it came to handling of union funds did the courts become interested, for here property was involved and analogies were available from trust and corporation law.

With the growing economic power of unions, however, this view has become less and less appropriate. Most collective bargaining agreements now provide for a union shop or its equivalent, under which a worker is expected to be a union member as a condition of continued employment. All workers are bound in any event by the conditions of employment which the union negotiates. A worker excluded from the union is thus bound by the actions of an organization in which he has no voice. Rules concerning admission, discipline, and expulsion can threaten a man's livelihood. So the courts have moved toward the view that a union resembles a public utility or government agency, and that its internal procedures are a matter of public concern. The new view is well stated in a California court decision:

> Where a union has, as in this case, attained a monopoly of the supply of labor by means of closed shop agreements and other forms of collective labor action, such a union occupies a quasi-public position similar to that of a public service business and it has certain corresponding obligations. It may no longer claim the same freedom from legal restraint enjoyed by golf clubs or fraternal associations. Its asserted right to choose its own members does not merely relate to social relations; it affects the fundamental right to work for a living.[21]

Following this doctrine, the courts have become more willing to probe into union affairs and to require not merely that the union abide by its own rules, but that the rules themselves should be reasonable. Courts have held, for example, that a closed-shop union must admit black workers to membership or else give up the closed shop;

---

[21] Cited by Joseph R. Grodin, "Legal Regulation of Internal Union Affairs," in J. Shister, B. Aaron, and C. W. Summers, eds., *Public Policy and Collective Bargaining* (New York: Harper & Row, Publishers, 1962), p. 192.

that union disciplinary procedures must meet the test of due process of law; that a union member may not be tried by people having a direct interest in the controversy; and that the union cannot prescribe support of a particular political candidate or otherwise regulate the member's private life.

An aggrieved member, then, may be able to bring a successful suit against the union under common law; but as a practical matter few people are willing to do this. Courts make most people nervous, lawyers are expensive, lawsuits are slow, and long before the worker can get redress he may be out of a job and even out of town. There has consequently been a demand for legislation to spell out standards of good union conduct, to ward off injury to members before it occurs, and to place enforcement responsibility on public officials. After exposure of serious malfeasance in the Teamsters and a number of other unions in the McClellan Committee hearings, Congress passed the Labor-Management Reporting and Disclosure Act of 1959, usually referred to as the Landrum–Griffin Act.

Statutory Regulation: The Landrum–Griffin Act

This act endeavors to do several things: (1) a "bill of rights" section guarantees the right of each member, subject to reasonable rules, to attend and participate in union meetings, vote in union elections, and nominate or support candidates for union office. (2) Every union covered by the act must file a copy of its constitution and bylaws with the Secretary of Labor. Every union must also file an annual financial report, and union officers must report personal financial transactions with the union. These reports are open to the public. (3) The taking over of local unions through the trusteeship device is regulated. (4) Union elections and voting procedures are regulated in considerable detail, and there is provision for appeal of disputed elections to the Secretary of Labor. (5) Embezzlement of union funds is made a federal offense, and other financial restrictions are placed on union officers and employers.

This complicated statute, whose practical effects are still unclear, will be examined further in Chapter 17, which traces the development of American public policy toward unionism and collective bargaining.

Discussion Questions

1. What are the dangers and advantages of strong control over local unions by national unions?
2. What advantage does a national union derive from affiliation with

the AFL-CIO? Is expulsion of a national union from the federation an effective disciplinary measure?
3. In what ways have some union officers used their positions for personal advantage? What remedies for this situation have been attempted, and what others might be tried?
4. "Unions are democratic in form, undemocratic in substance. Policy is determined by the leaders, and membership participation is at a minimum. There is urgent need of reforms to return the unions to membership control." Discuss.
5. Draw up specifications for a perfectly democratic national union.
6. "There is an inherent conflict between maximum democracy in a union and maximum effectiveness of the union in serving membership interests." Discuss.
7. Why do national union officers usually remain in office for long periods? Is this an undesirable tendency?
8. Why has racketeering occasionally developed in trade unions, and what remedial measures can be taken?

Reading Suggestions

An authority on the subject of union government is Professor Philip Taft. See in particular his studies: *Corruption and Racketeering in the Labor Movement.* Ithaca, N.Y.: New York State School of Industrial and Labor Relations, Cornell University, 1958; and *The Structure and Government of Labor Unions.* Cambridge: Harvard University Press, 1954.

Other general studies include Barbash, Jack, *Labor's Grass Roots.* New York: Harper & Row, Publishers, 1961; Galenson, Walter, *Trade Union Democracy in Western Europe.* Berkeley: University of California Press, 1962; Kerr, Clark, *Unions and Union Leaders of Their Own Choosing.* New York: The Fund for the Republic, 1958; Leiserson, William, *American Trade Union Democracy.* New York: Columbia University Press, 1959; Sayles, Leonard R., and George Strauss, *The Local Union: Its Place in the Industrial Plant.* New York: Harper & Row, Publishers, 1953; Estey, Martin S., Philip Taft, and Martin Wagner, eds., *Regulating Union Government.* New York: Harper & Row, Publishers, 1964.

A series of case studies of individual unions, sponsored by the Center for Study of Democratic Institutions, have been published by John Wiley & Sons, Inc. Volumes in this series include Horowitz, Morris

A., *The Structure and Government of the Carpenters' Union;* Kramer, Leo, *Labor's Paradox—The American Federation of State, County, and Municipal Employees;* Perlman, Mark, *Democracy in the International Association of Machinists;* Romer, Sam, *The International Brotherhood of Teamsters;* Rothbaum, Melvin, *The Government of the Oil, Chemical, and Atomic Workers' Union;* Seidman, Joel, *The Brotherhood of Railroad Trainmen;* Stieber, Jack, *Governing the UAW;* and Ulman, Lloyd, *The Government of the Steel Workers' Union.*

COLLECTIVE BARGAINING: UNION AND MANAGEMENT APPROACHES

14

It is often said that collective bargaining is a relationship between a political organization, the trade union, and a business organization. Before plunging into the details of bargaining procedures, it is desirable to take a broad look at the objectives of the organizations involved. What is the general outlook and thrust of the trade union movement? On the other side of the table, what is the management group trying to accomplish? How does the appearance of a union on the scene alter management organization and policies?

TRADE UNION OBJECTIVES

What are the unions really after? It is surprising how many different answers have been given to this question. Union leaders frequently deny that they have any general objectives and assert, in Strasser's words, that they are simply "going on from day to day." Many management leaders nevertheless believe that, even if there is no deliberate union policy of displacing management in the long run, this is at least the unintended consequence of union development.

Scholars have also given a variety of answers. Some have maintained that there are several varieties of unionism, each with its own ideology and objectives. Thus R. F. Hoxie distinguished between uplift unionism, business unionism, revolutionary unionism, and predatory unionism.[1] These he regarded as distinct and permanent types, which would continue to coexist indefinitely in the labor movement. Selig Perlman, on the other hand, regards business unionism as the central type which most unions tend to approach in the long run.[2] In Perlman's view, a union dominated by mutual benefit activities or revolutionary politics is simply an immature union, which, if it survives, will move in the direction of business unionism.

Union Participation in Management

Judged on a world scale, American unions appear relatively conservative. They have tended to avoid entanglement in left-wing politics. They show little interest in overturning capitalism or making drastic changes in the political order. They concentrate mainly on winning limited gains through direct bargaining with employers.

Even though labor's objectives appear limited, however, may not its eventual consequences be revolutionary? May not union encroachment on management functions eventually reduce the private business manager to complete impotence? Some management people suspect that union leaders are secretly aiming at this objective. Others see it as a possible unintended consequence of union operations.

This fear is expressed in such statements as the following:

> Restriction on management freedom is a big issue. This isn't breast-beating. We've got heavy responsibilities for making quick, accurate and effective decisions. Sometimes there are considerations that we can't divulge or that wouldn't be understood if we did. We're held responsible for the success of them, but the union isn't. It takes complicated maneuvering to run a business, and all the parts have to be kept working together. You have to have a good deal of free play in the rope for that. Sometimes there is a particular restriction that gets your goat, but on the whole it's the overall sense of being closed in on, and the anticipation of more of the same, that gets you. It's the cumulative effect of one area of freedom after another being reduced and the promise of still

[1] R. F. Hoxie, *Trade Unionism in the United States* (New York: Appleton-Century-Crofts, 1923).

[2] Selig Perlman, *A Theory of the Labor Movement* (New York: The Macmillan Company, 1928).

more that give us real concern, but you make adjustments and go on to every particular one. It's not impossible, but you wonder how long it can go on and leave you able to meet your responsibilities.[3]

Officials of American trade unions strongly deny any such long-range program. Their outlook is represented by such statements as these:

> The union doesn't want to run the business. It doesn't want to take over management. At the same time, while we don't attempt to usurp management's prerogatives, we do attempt to mitigate them so that their exercise cannot endanger the security and well-being of the workers.
>
> If the unions are planning a drive to secure a greater voice in management, I haven't heard of it. Of course, it may work out that our program may lead into socialism, as they worry about, but it won't be because we planned it that way. The basic motivation is security. As long as management's decisions don't adversely affect the security of the workers or their unions, we are glad to let the management run the business—we don't want any part of that responsibility.[4]

These disclaimers, granted their sincerity, are not sufficient to dispose of the matter. They leave open the question of how far unions may eventually feel obliged to go in order to protect the security and job interests of their members. Almost any kind of business decision —about plant location, products, methods of production, pricing, marketing methods, finance—affects the company's ability to pay wages and the volume and regularity of employment which it affords. Must unions try to limit management's discretion on all these matters? May they not feel obliged, in order fully to protect the interests of their members, to assume virtual management of industry?

One approach to an answer is to examine the content of union–management agreements in the United States. The bulk of the clauses in a typical contract relate either to recognition of the union as an institution, and provision for orderly dealings between union and management representatives, or to matters of personnel administration—wage rates and supplementary benefits; hours and work schedules; hiring, promotion, layoff, and discharge; health, safety, and other aspects of working conditions; work speeds and work assignments. Some unions have also taken considerable interest in production methods, usually with a view to creating additional employment by prescribing time-consuming methods of work, or to protecting workers against displacement by new machinery.

[3] E. Wight Bakke, *Mutual Survival* (New York: Harper & Row, Publishers, 1946), p. 29.
[4] Bakke, *Mutual Survival*, p. 90.

Most aspects of management, however, have been left largely untouched by collective bargaining. Few unions have sought any voice in selection of products, determination of production volume and inventory policy, choice of market channels and sales methods, determination of prices and other terms of sales, competitive relations with rival companies, methods of financing new capital requirements, dividend policy, and other aspects of financial management. Personnel decisions have been brought squarely within the orbit of collective bargaining. Production, sales, finance, and general executive coordination of the business have been affected only tangentially.[5]

Is this only because many American unions are relatively new? May they not penetrate more deeply into management functions as they grow older and stronger? It is instructive to look at some of the long-established unions in the United States. In industries such as building construction, printing and publishing, railroad transport, and coal mining, trade unions have been in continuous operation for a hundred years. The unions are powerful, they bargain with management on a multitude of issues, and they have tied management's hands at many points where management would have preferred to remain free. Management continues, however, to have the dominant voice in production, marketing, finance, and other matters of business strategy. It has by no means been eliminated from the scene. Nor is there any indication that the scope of collective bargaining will expand much beyond its present limits.

The evidence suggests that a union, after an initial period during which it extends its membership to the limits of the industry and gradually widens the scope of collective bargaining, settles down to keeping its fences mended and wielding established authority without seeking further expansion of that authority. The long-run result is not displacement of management by the union, but an equilibrium between the expansive power of unionism and the resistance that management never ceases to offer.

Union Objectives in Collective Bargaining

A further test of union objectives is provided by union activities in the short run. What kinds of demands do unions make on employers year-by-year? What provisions do they try to get written into collective agreements?

Union demands in collective bargaining can be classified under the following headings: maintenance of the organization; rationing of scarce job opportunities; improvement of working conditions; and

[5] For a more detailed analysis, see Neil W. Chamberlain, *The Union Challenge to Management Control* (New York: Harper & Row, Publishers, 1948), chaps. 4 and 5.

development of a judicial system of deciding disputes over rights of individual workers.

The right to maintain a union organization is basic, since without this nothing else can be accomplished. The union's right to exist is usually challenged by employers at the outset, and conflict over this issue may continue for decades before the union is finally accepted as a permanent feature of the industry. During this time the union spends much energy in fending off employer attacks, developing experienced leadership and stable organizational forms, and persuading workers of the need to join the union, pay dues, and support union objectives. The right to organize is one of the few tenets that is accepted implicitly by all unionists everywhere and that will never be compromised. Even after the union's survival is no longer in doubt, much attention is still given to keeping the organization intact and strong.

A second facet of union activities, so important that Perlman has found in it the key to union policy, involves the control of job opportunities. Workers old enough to have lived through a depression are deeply convinced that there is never enough work to go around. Beyond this, there is clearly a shortage of "good" jobs, and the number of people trying to get into these jobs far exceeds the number of vacancies available. This poses the problem of who is to get the good jobs and who is to be left on the street or pushed into undesirable kinds of work.

In economic theory, this problem would be solved through employers' appraisal of workers' efficiency. The employer would select the "best man for the job" at a given time. In principle, he would be free to change his opinion from month to month—to promote or demote, to hire or discharge, on the basis of his most recent evidence concerning relative worker efficiency. It is not surprising that this solution does not commend itself to most manual workers. It implies great insecurity of job tenure, a constant threat of displacement if the employer can find someone else to do the job better. It also implies that nothing but efficiency should be taken into account in hiring and firing. Most workers would not agree. What about length of service, age, family responsibilities, membership or nonmembership in the union, and other considerations?

Faced with an assumed scarcity of jobs, and faced with the insistent demand of workers for security of job tenure, the union develops policies designed to maintain or increase the total number of jobs in its industry, to ensure that union members get first chance at these jobs, and to see that the different kinds of jobs are distributed among workers in a fair and reasonable way. The distribution of the available work is too vital to be left to the sole discretion of the employer, and steps are taken to control it by rules which the union has helped to formulate. In Perlman's words,

The group then asserts its collective ownership over the whole amount of opportunity, and, having determined who are entitled to claim a share in that opportunity, undertakes to parcel it out fairly, directly or indirectly, among its recognized members. . . . Free competition becomes a sin against one's fellows, anti-social, like a self-indulgent consumption of the stores of a beleaguered city, and obviously detrimental to the individual as well. A collective disposal of opportunity, including the power to keep out undesirables, and a "common rule" in making bargains are as natural to the manual group as "laissez-faire" is to the business man.[6]

The feeling that people already engaged in an occupation have a right to protection against outside competition, that experience on a job constitutes a kind of property that deserves equal protection with other forms of property, is strongest among the skilled crafts. Almost a century ago the leaders of a British craft union put the point as follows:

Considering that the trade by which we live is our property, bought by certain years of servitude, which gives us a vested right, and that we have a sole and exclusive claim on it, as all will have hereafter who purchase it by the same means. Such being the case, it is evident it is our duty to protect, by all fair and legal means, the property by which we live, being always equally careful not to trespass on the rights of others.[7]

A third set of union objectives has to do with improvement of wages, hours, and other terms of employment. On this front, the unions are riding a flood tide. National output per capita has been rising for many decades in most countries of the Western world, and continuing improvement in wages and working conditions has come to be taken for granted. The unions may speed up this process in some respects. At any event, they usually take credit for the improvements which occur in the course of time, even though most of these may already have been in the cards; and they strengthen the workers' conviction that progress is normal and right. When an economist tells him that things are bound to get better for him because of the mysterious working of economic forces, he may have doubts; but when the union tells him that things will be better next year because this is his right and the union will demand it, he is likely to believe. Thus normal economic progress takes on the aspect of a social movement, of something which is organized, planned, and inevitable.

It is above all in bargaining over terms of employment that unionism reveals its flexible and pragmatic character. There are no general principles determining how large the demands should be at a particular time, or what should be their specific character. At one time the

6 Perlman, *A Theory of the Labor Movement,* p. 242.
7 Webb and Webb, *The History of Trade Unionism,* p. 564.

unions will push for reductions in hours, at another time for pension plans or medical care funds, at other times for straight wage increases. In one year the wage demand may be ten cents an hour, in another twenty-five cents, as circumstances seem to warrant. The only firm principle is that the movement must always be in the same direction —forward.

A fourth sphere of union activity involves the process by which the general rules stated in the union contract are interpreted and applied to individual workers. The union is concerned, not only with a voice in making the rules, but with seeing that they are equitably applied and that the rights of individual workers are fully protected. The grievance procedure through which this is typically done in the United States is described in Chapter 15.

A Concluding Comment

Let us return now to the general question raised at the beginning: "What are the unions after?" To a singular degree the American trade union movement is a movement without ideology. Its objectives are not deduced from broad principles of politics or economics. Union leaders have no picture in mind of an ideal future society which will remain unchanged for all time.

It is clear that unionism brings important social changes. The trade union becomes a leading community institution, more central in the lives of many workers than the lodge, the company, the political party, or anything else. Other basic institutions must, so to speak, move over to make room for it. The union comes to play an important role in industrial management, particularly as regards wages and hours, working conditions, job tenure, and other personnel matters. Perhaps most important, unionism brings a considerable shift in the balance of political power in the community. It exerts effective pressure in the direction of what has come to be termed "the welfare state" and bars any return to the governmental policies of the nineteenth century. In a strongly unionized democracy, every political party must take account of labor's interests in order to survive.

One of the most important ways in which unionism tends to conserve and strengthen the social structure is by strengthening the worker's attachment to his job, his work group, and his employer. It provides him with a club, a fraternity, which helps to gratify the natural desire for social bonds with one's fellows. It provides a channel through which he can seek redress of grievances against supervisors or others, so that he has the feeling of living in a self-governing society rather than in an autocracy. It dramatizes the gradual improvement of wages and other conditions from year to year. It strengthens his security in his job and, through the influence of seniority rules, makes it more likely that he will stay with the same employer in the long run. In all these ways unionism gives workers a "stake in the system," a sense of belonging and participation, a feeling that the existing setup of industry is reasonably satisfactory, and an antipathy to proposals for radical change.

Some observers would disagree with this characterization of unionism as a conservative movement. In the light of the drastic changes in western capitalism over the past 200 years, however, and in the light of the revolutionary political movements now sweeping the world, the demands and achievements of the trade unions seem modest. Certainly they appear to be well within the range of tolerance both for private capitalism and democratic government.

THE
FUNCTION AND OUTLOOK
OF
MANAGEMENT

Turning to management, we may begin by examining the economic function of the business firm. The picture of the business concern in economic textbooks is considerably simplified, partly because of the emphasis which economists have placed on the theory of pure competition. Under purely competitive conditions, the prices which must be paid for all factors of production are strictly determined by the market, and the prices of the company's products are similarly determined. The only decision left to management concerns the method of production to be used. On closer investigation, however, it turns out that management has no real choice even in this respect. By the definition of pure competition, new producers are free to enter the industry at will. Unless a particular company uses the most efficient possible methods, therefore, it will not be able to keep pace with rival producers. It will find itself losing money and will eventually have to go out of business. Under purely competitive conditions, in short, the business concern is a puppet maneuvered by the general forces of supply and demand. Management discretion and judgment do not exist.

In practice, however, we know that management does do some managing. There is scope for initiative and judgment. The main reason is that actual business concerns operate under conditions of imperfect competition. They are sheltered in greater or lesser degree from the full sweep of market forces.

The price of labor, for example, is not completely determined by market forces; it can be altered within limits by management decision or union–management negotiation. Prices of purchased materials and equipment are frequently open to bargaining. The types, specifications, and prices of the products which the company sells can usually be adjusted within limits. Production methods can be altered somewhat. The upshot is that competing companies in the same industry may show quite different levels of cost and profit. Every industry has its high-cost and low-cost producers. This is due partly to factors other than management; but managerial skill and ingenuity do make a difference.

The extent of management's freedom, however, should not be exaggerated. First, management is bound by the simple accounting principle that you cannot make something out of nothing. A wage increase, to take the most relevant example, has to come from somewhere. Either product prices must be raised, or the volume of sales must be expanded, or money must be saved on material costs, selling expenses, or some other nonlabor item. If none of these things is done, profits will be reduced by the amount of the wage increase. Accounting logic allows no other possibilities.

Second, management is put under pressure by certain long-run tendencies that characterize our type of economy. The long-run tendency of wages is upward, for reasons which were discussed in Part One. Any company must count, year after year, on finding more money to pay for the labor it uses. At the same time, however, the company is subject to downward pressure on the prices it can charge, because of the existence of rival producers and products, and because of continuing technical progress which makes better products possible at lower costs. Management is caught in a scissors between a steady expansion of its costs and at least a potential shrinkage of its revenues.

The only escape from this dilemma lies in managerial efficiency and inventiveness. In order to survive in a competitive world, management must continually search for new or improved products, better methods of merchandising, improved machinery and production techniques, and more efficient administrative organization within the company. These things can be neglected for a year or two, but any company that neglects them for ten or twenty years is headed for economic extinction.

These basic characteristics of business management help to account for certain attitudes which influence the process of collective bargaining. Top management officials feel that the essence of their job lies in adjusting the conflicting pressures impinging on the company from competitors, customers, stockholders, wage earners, and others. The conflicting character of these pressures means that management cannot afford to respond fully to any one of them. It may, for example, have to resist certain union demands in order to ensure reasonable prices to consumers or reasonable returns to stockholders. Further, management people are inclined to feel that they, along with the scientists and engineers, are responsible for most of the improvement in products and production methods which constitutes economic progress and has made possible present living standards. Union demands are sometimes resented as an effort by a group which has contributed little to higher productivity to "cash in" on the fruit of management's labors.

The Significance of Profit

Our economy is sometimes described as a "profit system," or as being guided by "the profit motive." Economists often assume that each business concern tries to make as large a profit as possible. How much is there to this, and what is its significance for collective bargaining?

There is a large literature on the motivation of corporate executives and the objectives of the business firm. There is widespread agreement that to maximize profit at each moment of time is an impossible task, mainly because of continual changes in product and factor markets. Executives aim rather to achieve a "reasonable," or "normal," or "safe" level of profit.

Why is this considered necessary? First, profit provides a margin of security for the company. The higher the company's profit margin, the farther it can fall if business turns bad before encountering actual losses. Second, profit is important as a return to present and prospective investors in the company. Stockholders who find their dividends falling off seriously are likely to become discontented with the management and may try to do something about it. More important, a low rate of profit may make it difficult or impossible for the company to raise funds for expansion by floating new securities. Third, profits are themselves a source of funds for expansion of plant and purchase are now the main source of capital for expansion. A low rate of profit may mean that the company will have insufficient funds to finance projects that would help to increase profit. Fourth, profits are an index of management success. A management that is not able to turn in as good a profit rate as other companies in its industry, or that finds its profit rate declining from year to year, is apt to feel this as a criticism of its own performance. Even though the profit rate may have no direct bearing on executive salaries, any manager likes to feel that he is "up to par" with others in his profession.

Some of the difficulties of collective bargaining arise from the difference in the way profits are regarded by management and by union officials. In the eyes of management, profit is not merely a legitimate form of income but an essential element in the operation of a private enterprise system. The expectation or hope of profit is a major incentive to managerial efficiency and serves to call forth capital investment in new enterprises. Realized profits are a major source of funds for expansion of existing businesses. A positive rate of profit is thus an essential condition for economic growth and development.

Most union leaders would not quarrel with this in principle. Their enthusiasm over profits is more restrained than that of management people, however, and their idea of a "reasonable" rate of profit is apt to be more modest. They sometimes talk as though the net income of a company were a simple surplus performing no function in the economy, a pool into which the union can dip at will without any economic consequence. Management people object strongly to this as a simplified and incorrect view of the situation.

There is also a general feeling among management people that profits are none of the union's business anyway. Management believes that the company should pay "fair wages," which usually means fair in comparison with what other employers are paying for similar work. If management can pay fair wages and still make large profits, this is purely management's business. Union officers and members, on the other hand, feel that high profits should be shared with workers in the enterprise through better wages. The workers have helped to produce these profits, it is argued, and hence should be entitled to a share in them. When a company is taking losses, however, the two parties usually switch sides in the argument. The union is apt to argue that the company should still pay fair wages and that its losses are of no concern to the union, while the company may now argue that losses should be taken into account.

A further source of difficulty is that the relevant profit figure in collective bargaining is the estimated profit for the year ahead. Past profits are bygones. The union and management are bargaining over how much the company can afford to pay *next year*, not *last year*. This involves forecasts of future sales volume, product prices, material costs, and numerous other things. Sales volume, which depends so largely on general business conditions, is especially hard to forecast in many industries, and a small change in volume may make a large difference in the firm's profit position. Faced with these uncertainties, management typically tries to play it safe, to leave some margin for a possible downturn in business, to make a conservative estimate of probable profits. Union leaders, on the other hand, have a strong interest in taking a rosy view of the future, estimating profits at a high level, and trying to get wages set accordingly. The union, in short, is constantly trying to get management to stick its neck out farther than management likes to do.

This is a serious complication in the path of collective bargaining. If sales and profits for the next year could be known with certainty, if management could be sure just how much it was giving away and how much it would have left after paying a specified rate of wages, negotiations would be much simpler than they actually are.

MANAGEMENT
AND THE UNIONS:
SOME SOURCES OF TENSION

In the modern corporation, pursuit of efficiency requires coordination of the efforts of hundreds or thousands of individuals. The business manager is not just an expert in production techniques. He is the leader of an organization, the captain of a team. Successful performance of his functions requires that he have wide latitude in making decisions, and that he have "cooperation" or "teamwork" from those under him.[8] To most management people, teamwork seems to mean mainly fealty—a willing acceptance of managerial decisions and an earnest effort to execute them. It leaves room for tactful and "constructive" criticism of particular decisions, but no room for any challenge to management's right to make these decisions. The ideal situation is one in which the manager functions as a benevolent monarch. No one questions his authority, but his exercise of authority is so just and reasonable that his subordinates esteem rather than fear him. The feeling that one has been fair even when one did not have to be is probably one of the greatest satisfactions obtainable from a management position.

All this leads to a characteristic management view of satisfactory industrial relations, which has been summarized by Bakke in four major principles:

Industrial relations are primarily and basically a matter of relations between management and employees, its own employees.

The first objective of industrial relations, like that of every function of management, is the economic welfare of the particular company.

Industrial relations arrangements must leave unimpaired management's prerogatives and freedom essential to the meeting of management's responsibilities.

All parties to industrial relations should be businesslike and responsible.[9]

Trade unionism challenges these cardinal points in management's philosophy. It interposes between employer and employee the trade

[8] E. Wight Bakke and Clark Kerr, eds., *Unions, Management and the Public* (New York: Harcourt, Brace & World, Inc., 1948), pp. 242–43.

[9] Bakke, *Mutual Survival,* pp. 2–3.

union, which many managers believe is more interested in its own growth and power than in the economic welfare of either workers or the company. It refuses to accept survival and profitability of the company as the sole aim of business management. It interferes with management's effort to achieve lowest money cost of production, and with the freedom of maneuver which most managers consider essential to successful performance of their functions. At point after point the union says, "You cannot do that," or, "You must consult us before doing anything." Many management people see in this a deliberate policy of union encroachment on management functions. They ask themselves where the process will end, and whether they may not be forced eventually to abdicate control of the plant to the union.

Management opposition to unionism is based partly on self-interest. Being human, managers dislike a reduction in their authority just because it is a reduction. Unionism also makes the manager's job harder by increasing the number of people whose agreement must be secured for a given decision, and by presenting the risk that agreement may not always be secured. If a lower executive of the company refuses to comply with a decision of top management, he can be removed from office; but management cannot fire the union or its officials. Unionism increases the number of conflicting pressures which converge on management. Between the insistent demands of organized workers for more money, customers for lower prices, and the board of directors for larger profits, the manager may be ground to pieces. In all these ways, unionism increases the amount of frustration, personal insecurity, and nervous wear and tear to which management is subjected.

It is too narrow a view, however, to regard management opposition to unionism as entirely self-interested. Most managers believe that unionism, by limiting managerial initiative and discretion, strikes directly at the roots of economic progress and rising national income. Unionism thus tends in the long run to reduce rather than raise the real income of the working class. This conviction is held just as firmly and sincerely as the conviction of union leaders that they are leading a drive for social progress.

Another element in the differing outlook of managers and unionists is the difference in their personal background and experience. Two-thirds of the top management officials in American corporations come from business and professional families. Three-quarters of them have been to college. Only a small percentage have engaged in manual labor at any stage of their careers.[10] The day-to-day problems of the

---

[10] Based on a sample survey of 8,300 top management people in 1952. See W. Lloyd Warner and James C. Abbeglen, *Occupational Mobility in American Business and Industry* (Minneapolis: University of Minnesota Press, 1955); and Mabel Newcomer, *The Big Business Executive* (New York: Columbia University Press, 1955).

plant worker are something they have read about in business school casebooks, but have not experienced directly. Contrast this with the background of the union official, almost invariably a former worker, short on formal training but long on plant experience. It is not surprising that the two groups view the world of industry differently and have different conceptions of "proper" personnel management.

The general outlook of management toward unionism, then, is critical and sometimes hostile. Concrete strategies, however, differ greatly from one situation to the next. They range all the way from forcible opposition and a determination to get rid of the union at one extreme, through various shades of reluctant acceptance, to positive cooperation with the union at the other pole. The commonest situation is one which might be termed "defensive endurance," a feeling that "if this is what our workers want, I guess we'll have to go along with it. But we don't understand why they want unionism. There's nothing in it for them. Perhaps they'll eventually see the light and the whole thing will go away."

Underlying this outlook are two assumptions which may be termed the "harmony of interests" assumption and the "management can do it better" assumption. The first asserts that there is no real divergence of interest between employer and employees. Prosperity for the worker depends on prosperity for the company. Management and workers have an equal interest in harmonious coordination of the enterprise and maximum productive efficiency. We shall have occasion in later chapters to examine both the element of truth in such statements and the qualifications which must be attached to them. Regardless of the truth of the matter, however, this attitude is sincerely held by large numbers of management people. It leads them to a conclusion that unions are stirring up conflict where no real conflict exists, and that they are useless or even harmful.

The second assumption flows logically from the first. It asserts that all legitimate interests of the employee can be protected adequately by management itself. The union can do nothing which management, with its greater technical skills and more reliable information, could not do even better. If the workers accept unionism, then, this must be due to some failure of management to organize itself effectively and to "put across" its story to employees. Unionism, in short, results from managerial failure and nothing else.

Managements in this frame of mind accept unionism as a punishment for their sins and because it is legally obligatory. They continue, however, to regard it as an alien growth against which management must protect itself at every turn. They try to build dikes against the advance of union influence, to restrict the area of collective bargaining, to resist union intrusion on "managerial prerogatives."

These attitudes, however, are not immutable. After twenty or thirty years of collective bargaining (in some cases, only after the rise of a new generation of top executives!), a company may come round to a different view of unionism. It finds that the union, while it limits management at many points, can also be used to further the broad objective of profitable operation of the enterprise. Information about the economic situation and problems of the company, for example, may be accepted more readily by workers if funneled through the union organization than if disseminated directly by management. Union leaders who know the company's problems and have confidence in management may be able to "sell" the membership on new company policies and to elicit worker cooperation in production which could not be obtained in any other way. The grievance procedure to be described in the next chapter provides a sensitive instrument which top management can use to detect disturbances in lower levels of the organization. There are numerous ways in which a positive acceptance of the union, an effort to integrate it into the administrative structure of the enterprise instead of treating it as a thing apart, can contribute to efficient management.

Companies which take this point of view are still a minority. There are more of them today than there were a generation ago, however, and the number will probably continue to increase gradually in the future.

ORGANIZATION
FOR
INDUSTRIAL RELATIONS

Two kinds of management officials are involved in handling industrial relations: "line" officials who are directly responsible for production, and "staff" officials who function mainly in an advisory capacity.

In a manufacturing company, for example, line authority runs from the company president through a vice-president in charge of production to the superintendent of a particular plant. Under the superintendent are division heads, department heads, and so on down to the foreman. If the foreman has many workers to supervise, he may be aided by one or more assistant foremen or group leaders. The number of layers of supervision in the plant depends mainly on its size. The management of forty or fifty thousand people in a single plant, as in some of the giant automobile factories, require a complicated hierarchy of production officials. This makes it difficult to get effective upward and downward communication, and to ensure uniformity of policy throughout the organization; and this gives rise to complicated problems in union–management relations.

The most important staff group involved is the industrial relations department. This group is charged with developing and recommending policies on such matters as employee recruitment and selection; training; employee rating and promotion; transfer, downgrading, and layoff; discipline and discharge; wage policies and wage administration; hours of work and shifts; services for employees; employee health and safety; and employee participation in production problems. There may also be a separate industrial engineering department responsible for analysis of job methods, time study, determination of output standards, and application of wage incentive systems.

People in the production line of command are responsible for issuing orders about what is to be done, how it is to be done, and who is to do it. They authorize changes in production schedules, methods, and personnel. They initiate layoffs, new hirings, discharges, promotions, and transfers of workers. Members of the industrial relations staff recommend overall company policies on these matters, check on how they are working in practice, and suggest changes as needed. But no orders can be issued until the production manager or some other line official has been sold on the policy in question. Indeed, people all the way down the chain of command must be sold on a policy to make it fully effective. Not least important is the foreman, who gives direct orders to the work force. The modern foreman has been shorn of much of the authority he once possessed, but he still has considerable power to sabotage policies that he does not understand and accept.

In theory, then, line officials are the doers, while staff officials look over their shoulders as advisers. The actual relation, however, is more complex and variable; and it is defined through day-to-day decisions in the plant rather than by the lines which appear on the organization chart. Suppose a foreman discharges a worker. The labor relations officer assigned to the department considers the discharge unwise and so reports to his superiors. There follow further discussions, perhaps between the industrial relations director and the plant superintendent. Eventually the decision is confirmed or reversed. If line officials find that too many of their decisions are reversed at higher levels under pressure from the industrial relations staff, they will become more hesitant about making decisions; and the *de facto* authority of the industrial relations department will have increased. Personalities are also important. If the industrial relations director is capable, assertive, and able to win the support of top management on disputed issues, the authority of those working under him is increased.

Union Impact on Management Organization

In preunion days, most managements did not attach major importance to the industrial relations function. The director of industrial relations, in those days commonly called personnel director, was usually not an outstanding man and did not rank high in the management hierarchy. In large measure the line officials made personnel policy through their day-to-day decisions, which the personnel department had little power to influence. Many managements, either deliberately or through inadvertence, left wide latitude in decision making to lower levels of supervision. Thus actions on a particular subject might vary widely from one department to another; and top management might know little about what was actually happening at the grass roots.

The coming of a union changes the situation drastically. Personnel actions are no longer solely a matter of management discretion. They are governed by provisions of the union contract, and the union is there to police observance of the contract. It has its own information network throughout the plant, can detect discrepancies in management's actions, and is then likely to demand that the most favorable practice in any department be extended to all other departments—a tactic commonly known as "whipsawing." Moreover, unsettled grievances between the union and management are normally referred to an outside arbitrator, under procedures to be described in the next chapter. So management must try to ensure that its decisions are consistent and will stand up under outside review.

Unionism, in short, compels *management by policy* rather than by off-the-cuff decisions. A newly unionized company usually reacts in three ways. First, it has to strengthen its industrial relations department, both because there is more work to be done and because top-flight people are needed to deal with the professional union leaders. Second, it may decide that personnel decisions should be made at higher levels of management, in order to ensure uniform interpretation of company policies and union contract provisions. Third, this normally means that industrial relations officials will have greater voice in decisions and line officials will have less. Some managements, indeed, have panicked to the point of virtually abolishing line authority over personnel actions and work standards, and turning these matters over to the industrial relations department for handling.

While greater centralization of decision making and greater staff authority are natural first reactions, they have their own disadvantages. Foremen know what is happening on the plant floor and are in closest touch with the facts on which correct personnel decisions should be based. They are also the people in charge of production. To hold them responsible for production results while depriving them of disciplinary authority over the work force is scarcely feasible in the long run. So in recent years many companies have been moving back toward decentralization, toward pushing decisions down to the plant floor, and toward reconstituting the authority of line supervisors.[11]

[11] See on this point Sumner H. Slichter, James J. Healy, and E. Robert Livernash, *The Impact of Collective Bargaining on Management* (Washington, D.C.: Brookings Institution, 1960), chap. 29.

Both line supervisors and industrial relations people are involved in applying personnel policies to concrete situations and in handling grievances brought by the union. The problem is to work out the most effective cooperation between them. This must take account of characteristic differences of outlook arising from their differing functions in the organization. Line officials are naturally more production-oriented, while industrial relations people are more labor-relations-oriented. This does not necessarily mean that the former are "tougher" in holding the line on plant discipline and work standards. Foremen will often make special deals with a worker to secure his cooperation in getting out a rush production job, and it may be the staff people who have to insist on strict adherence to company policy. It is probably fair to say that the industrial relations people typically take a longer-range view and are more concerned with how decisions made today will affect company relations with workers and the union next month or next year.

But foremen and supervisors can also be trained to take a long-range view and to be concerned with the policy implications of specific decisions. This is essentially an educational task, a task of inculcating understanding and acceptance of the company's overall personnel policies. A foreman who has been trained in this way can and should be given the right to make initial decisions on all personnel matters arising in his department, which includes the right to make mistakes. It is important also that correct decisions based on established policy should be ratified and defended at higher levels of management. A foreman who finds his decisions constantly overturned because of union pressure or second-guessing by staff officials will soon cease to make any decisions and will pass all problems up the line. This is a common reason for "clogging up" of the grievance procedure and accumulation of problems in the front office.

Discussion Questions

1. Is there a genuine danger that trade unions, while not taking responsibility for industrial management, may become so strong as to prevent existing managements from functioning effectively?

2. "The idea that the political objectives of trade unions are 'liberal' or 'reform' objectives is an illusion. The political programs of American trade unions have been precisely as selfish as those of business associations, farm groups, and other economic interests." Discuss.

3. "Trade unionism is basically a conservative institution, and does more to perpetuate private enterprise than to destroy it." Discuss.
4. "The profit motive no longer operates in the simple manner assumed by economic theory. The managers of a large corporation are interested in profit, to be sure, but their interest is quite different from that of the small owner-operator." Discuss.
5. What features of management's job produce a natural opposition to trade unionism?
6. "Whether the plant is already unionized, or whether it is merely liable to unionization in the future, management is forced to engage in a long-drawn-out competition with unionism for the attention and loyalty of its employees. In such a competition, the union has certain natural advantages that usually bring it out ahead in the long run." Discuss.
7. What does a management stand to gain, and to lose, by accepting the union as a permanent feature of its operations and trying to establish a cooperative relationship with it?
8. "A wise industrial relations director does not try to exercise authority—only influence." Discuss.
9. How is a company's problem of managing its industrial relations altered by the appearance of a trade union?
10. A foreman considers a worker in his department guilty of behavior warranting discharge. The union asserts that the discharge is unjustified. Analyze the proper functions of the foreman, an industrial relations officer attached to the department, the plant superintendent, and the plant director of industrial relations in handling this case.

Reading Suggestions

A classic study of union objectives is Perlman, Selig, *A Theory of the Labor Movement.* New York: The Macmillan Company, 1928. A more recent study is Lester, Richard A., *As Unions Mature.* Princeton: Princeton University Press, 1958. For analysis of management organization and objectives, see Slichter, Sumner H., James J. Healy, and E. Robert Livernash, *The Impact of Collective Bargaining on Management.* Washington, D.C.: The Brookings Institution, 1960; and two volumes by Pigors, Paul, and Charles A. Myers, *Personnel Administration.* New York: McGraw-Hill Book Company, rev. ed., 1969; and *Readings in Personnel Administration.* New York: McGraw-Hill Book Company, 1956.

COLLECTIVE BARGAINING PROCEDURES   15

Trade unions try to advance the interests of their members mainly by negotiating agreements, usually termed "union contracts" or "collective agreements," with employers. The processes by which these agreements are negotiated, administered, and enforced are included in the term "collective bargaining." The word "collective" indicates that the agreement is negotiated on behalf of a *group* of workers. The workers present a united front to their employer, and the terms of the bargain apply uniformly to all members of the group. Different employers may also band themselves together for the purpose of negotiating an agreement with a union. Such an agreement is frequently said to be "collective on both sides."

From the union's standpoint, the object of collective bargaining is to prevent unilateral action by the employer. This is accomplished by requiring him to sign a contract fixing conditions of employment for a specified period and establishing a procedure for handling disputed issues arising during the period. Collective bargaining is thus an employer-regulating device, a method of guaranteeing certain rights and immunities to the workers by limiting the employer's freedom of action. The employer must now apply uniform procedures to all workers in the group; these procedures can be changed only at fixed intervals after negotiation with union officials; and any charge that the agreed procedures have been violated can be taken up through a series of appeal courts (the grievance procedure). There is thus created what Slichter has termed a "system of industrial jurisprudence," a body of common law rights and obligations binding on workers, union officials, and management officials alike.

Collective bargaining includes two different kinds of union–management negotiation. General negotiations are entered into at regular intervals, usually every two or three years, to revise the basic agreement between the parties and extend it for a further period. At this time any term of the contract—wage schedules, work assignments, rules concerning layoff and promotion, union security provisions, and all the rest—may be reopened for discussion. These negotiations are usually carried on by top union and management officials. After the agreement has been signed, there are frequent discussions between lower union and management officials throughout the plant for the purpose of clarifying particular provisions and applying them to concrete situations. The method of resolving these day-to-day disputes, usually termed the "grievance procedure," is specified in the contract itself. While the negotiations for a new contract are more dramatic, the day-to-day negotiations may be equally important. Through them the contract is enforced, or, in the case of a new or weak union, not enforced. Through them the general provisions of the contract are given specific meaning and application.

These two aspects of collective bargaining—contract negotiations and the grievance procedure—will be discussed in turn. The present discussion is concerned with bargaining *procedures* rather than the substantive issues over which bargaining occurs. The main issues in bargaining will be discussed in Part III.

BARGAINING STRUCTURE

The Labor Management Relations Act requires an employer to bargain with representatives of a majority of his employees "in an appropriate bargaining unit." But what unit is appropriate? At one extreme, a single employer may bargain with representatives of a single skilled craft. At the opposite extreme, an employer's association may bargain with an industrial union over terms for all employees in the industry throughout the country.

We should distinguish first between the *election unit,* the *negotiat-*

ing unit, and the *impact unit.* The election unit is laid down by decisions of the National Labor Relations Board. The normal method of securing union recognition is to file a request with the National Labor Relations Board for certification as bargaining representative. If the union's claim to represent a majority of the workers is challenged by the employer, or if more than one union is seeking to represent the same workers, the board will conduct an election to determine the employees' wishes. In order to do this, it must decide on the appropriate bargaining unit. Depending on the wishes of the parties and on general board principles to be discussed in Chapter 18, it may select a single craft, or all employees in a plant, or several plants of the same company, or employees in a group of companies.

The *negotiating unit* will normally not be smaller than the election unit, and may be considerably larger. Even if elections have been held plant by plant, the union may prefer company-wide negotiations or may prefer to negotiate jointly with a group of employers. When an agreement is reached, it is applicable to all workers in the negotiating unit. The size of negotiating units thus determines the coverage of union contracts.

The *impact unit* may be still larger. A common union technique is to single out one leading employer—say, Ford or General Motors in the case of the United Automobile Workers—as the initial target in a particular year. After negotiations have been completed, the union insists that other employers in the industry sign up on the same terms under penalty of a strike. Under this technique, usually termed "pattern bargaining," the impact unit is the industry even though the bargaining unit is a single company.

Our main interest here is in the size of negotiating units. The most recent Bureau of Labor Statistics survey indicates that there are about 150,000 union contracts in the United States. The great majority of these units are small, covering only one company and a small number of workers. At the other pole, however, are 1,733 contracts covering one thousand or more workers each; and these contracts cover more than 8 million workers, or about half of all workers under contract. These large units are usually termed "major agreements." The nine largest, each with more than 100,000 workers, cover almost 2 million workers in all.

The commonest type of agreement outside of manufacturing is the multi-employer agreement, including either all employers in a certain locality (building construction, printing, retailing, hotel and restaurant work, and other service industries), or all employers in a major region or in the entire country (coal mining, railroads, over-the-road trucking, merchant shipping).

In manufacturing, the single-company agreement is the dominant form. Multi-employer agreements are found in a number of manufacturing industries, however, including men's and women's clothing, baking, canning and preserving, brewing, glassware, pottery, lumber, furniture, and leather goods. And even where the union negotiates separately with each company, it can achieve some of the results of a multi-employer unit through the pattern-bargaining technique.

The main pressure for multi-employer agreements stems from competition among employers in product markets. If different companies organized by the same union are in competition with one another, the bargains between the union and various companies cannot be kept separate. The union cannot raise the labor costs of some plants so much above the general level that these plants are forced out of competition. Employers paying the highest wage rates in the industry are likely to demand that the union bring low-wage plants up to their level. Union members also compare wage rates in different plants. Members of one local who find their rates below those of certain other locals will be quick to protest and to demand that they be brought up to levels prevailing elsewhere. Apart from this political pressure, it seems natural to union officials that wages and conditions should be standardized for competing plants. The concept of "the standard rate," of "equal pay for equal work," is deeply engrained in union thinking. For all these reasons, unions seek some measure of uniformity among employers in the same competitive area.

While the area of product market competition has great influence on the size of bargaining units, it is not the only determinant.[1] Other important influences include:

1. *The Nature of Bargaining Issues.* Some issues, notably wages, have market-wide implications and tend to be resolved through large negotiating units. Other issues, such as safety rules, plant working-conditions, details of pension and insurance plans, application of seniority provisions, and time standards on piece-rate jobs are best handled at the company or even the plant level. When market-wide issues are predominant, there will be a tendency toward larger bargaining units and more centralized decision-making power within the union and management groups. But when local issues assume major importance, there will be pressure for local bargaining and decentralized decision making.

2. *Representational Considerations.* The union is comprised of work groups, defined on a plant, department, occupation, age, or ethnic basis. These groups have common but also divergent interests. Up to a point, they can gain by pooling their strength in larger and larger bargaining units. But this involves losses in autonomy and attention to specific interests of the group. Thus in Weber's words,

---

[1] See on this point Arnold R. Weber, "Stability and change in the structure of collective bargaining," in Lloyd Ulman, ed., *Challenges to Collective Bargaining* (Englewood Cliffs, N.J.: Prentice-Hall, Inc., 1967), pp. 13–36.

"each group will press for, or acquiesce in, the expansion of the worker alliance as long as the rate of substitution between the gains derived from the increment to bargaining power are greater than the perceived losses associated with the denial of autonomy in decision making. At some point, this rate of substitution will become negative, and tensions will develop within the union and the associated bargaining structures for the accommodation of special group interests or the fragmentation of the alliance." While representational considerations are especially important on the union side, they arise on the management side as well. The interests of different companies in a bargaining unit are not identical, and there are numerous examples of companies which have withdrawn from an employers' association or have defected from the association's position in a particular negotiation when they found this to their advantage.

3. *Tactical and Power Considerations.* "Bargaining power" is hard to define but easy to recognize. Each side seeks a bargaining structure that will enhance its bargaining power. A common power-enhancing tactic is "whipsawing." When a company deals with several unions, it may try to settle first with the union judged to be in the weakest bargaining position, and then to extend these terms to the other unions. A union may tackle a company from which it believes it can secure the best terms, and then try to extend this "pattern" to other companies. The obvious reply to whipsawing is counterorganization. This maneuvering and countermaneuvering tends to enlarge the size of bargaining units.

4. *Public Policy.* This is a final influence expressed particularly through election district decisions of the National Labor Relations Board. Depending on his estimate of where the union has penetrated most effectively, the employer may wish to include certain departments or plants and exclude others. The union's preference may be different. If two or more unions are involved, they may differ on the proper scope of the unit. The National Labor Relations Board officials, after hearing the parties and considering the pattern of bargaining elsewhere in the industry, must decide what is appropriate.

A particularly controversial issue has been that of craft versus industrial units. After 1935 the National Labor Relations Board often encountered situations in which a CIO industrial union urged a single unit covering all employees, while one or more AFL craft unions urged that groups of skilled workers be carved out as separate units. For some years the board showed a marked preference for industrial units —sufficiently so to permit the major companies in steel, automobile, electrical manufacturing, and other mass production industries to be organized on this basis. Yielding to AFL criticism and pressure, however, the board by the early forties was permitting craft groups to vote separately whenever they showed any marked inclination to do so. The

Taft–Hartley Act increased the possibility of "craft severance" by providing that the National Labor Relations Board may not refuse a craft group's claim to separate representation simply because of some previous board decision concerning the bargaining unit. The general policy at present is that where there are indications that a skilled group may prefer separate representation, the board will allow them to vote separately from the rest. If a craft union wins out, it will be certified as bargaining representative. This policy has not been applied, however, to steel, aluminum, and a few other mass-production industries where the board has held that production processes are so highly integrated as to make craft severance impracticable.

During the critical period from 1935 to 1950, the board's preference for company-wide bargaining units contributed to the development of the many large units we observe today.

Product Market Competition and Negotiating Units

Since the area of the collective agreement is strongly influenced by the area over which employers compete in the sale of their products, it will be well to explore this relation in greater detail. The basic distinction here is between local-market industries and industries in which competition is regional or national.

Where competition is limited to the immediate locality, city-wide agreements are likely to develop. This is the typical situation in building construction, hotel and restaurant work, newspaper and job printing, milk and bread delivery, local trucking and warehousing, retail trade, laundry and dry cleaning, and other local industries.

The individual employer in these industries is typically small and is in a weak position to negotiate separately with the union. So after a little experience, employers often decide to pool their strength in a bargaining association. The result is a single agreement, reached by bargaining between representatives of the employer association and representatives of the union.

After the master agreement has been concluded, its administration and enforcement are usually left to the union and individual employers. In areas that have gone farthest in the direction of master agreements, however, such as San Francisco, the employers' association sometimes takes a continuing interest in the administration of the agreement. Several of the San Francisco associations maintain expert staffs to assist their members in processing grievances and handling other problems that arise during the life of the contract. A few have even gone so far as to forbid members to settle grievances without association approval. The purpose of this policy is to prevent the union from "whipsawing" the employers, i.e. securing more favorable treatment on a certain point in some plants than in others, and then using this as an argument to bring all plants up to the most favorable settlement achieved anywhere.[2]

A master agreement with the union has several advantages from the employers' standpoint. It enables employers to meet the union on more equal terms. It also places employers on an equal competitive footing as regards wage rates and other items in labor cost; the "chiseler" can no longer undercut the employer who pays a "decent" wage. Moreover, the agreement with the union can often be used to police price-fixing and other monopolistic practices within the industry. Union and employers, instead of fighting each other, can unite with mutual benefit to levy tribute from consumers.

This situation has occurred from time to time in building construction. The building contractors' association generally agrees to employ only union men, thereby strengthening the building trades' unions. The unions on their side agree to work only for members of the association. In some cases there has also been a tacit agreement that the unions will not supply labor to a contractor found guilty of departing from the established methods of figuring bids in the industry, i.e. of cutting prices. The two main channels of competition—free price setting and free entrance of new firms to the industry—are thus effectively blocked.

Industries such as laundering and dry cleaning have frequently achieved the same result by allying themselves with the deliverymen, who usually belong to a local of the Teamsters' Union. Firms that cut prices or engage in other "unethical" practices forbidden by the association are brought into line by strikes or threatened strikes. It has not been unknown for "accidents" to happen to the property of uncooperative employers; clothes get lost or misdelivered, acid gets spilled in the wrong places, or delivery trucks break down mysteriously.[3] In agreements between the Barbers' Union and the master barbers' association of a city, the price which must be charged for haircuts, shaves, and other services is frequently included in the agreement, so that any price-cutter is guilty of a violation of contract and is struck automatically.

It should not be inferred that unions are mainly responsible for local price-fixing arrangements. In many cases, price agreements existed long before the union made its appearance. The union does, however, strengthen such agreements by providing an additional method of disciplining price-cutters.

[2] Clark Kerr and L. H. Fisher, "Multiple-Employer Bargaining: The San Francisco Experience," in R. A. Lester and Joseph Shister, eds., *Insights into Labor Issues* (New York: The Macmillan Company, 1948).

[3] See in particular: C. L. Christenson, "Chicago Service Trades," in Twentieth Century Fund, *How Collective Bargaining Works*, chap. 15; and C. L. Christenson, *Collective Bargaining in Chicago* (Chicago: The University of Chicago Press, 1933).

While there is strong pressure in local market industries to standardize terms of employment *within* each locality, there is no similar pressure for equalization *among* localities. Bricklaying in Pittsburgh does not compete with bricklaying in Minneapolis, and there is no reason why the union scale should be the same. Union scales in building, printing, and similar industries vary a good deal throughout the country, and national union control over local settlements is loose.

Turning to companies that operate on a regional or national basis, one finds a variety of situations. First, there are the "natural monopolies" in transportation, power, communications, and so on. Here the bargaining unit is typically coextensive with the company. Each of the unionized electric power companies negotiates separately. So does each regional affiliate of the Bell Telephone system, though the union has pressed unsuccessfully for national negotiations. The main counterexample is railroading, where national negotiations have been customary for decades.

Second, there are some important nonmanufacturing industries where competition is regional or national. This is true, for example, of bituminous coal mining. It is increasingly true of major commercial construction, and of road and highway construction. Over-the-road trucking is another example. Longshoring is localized in each port, but there are coast-wide linkages arising from the movement of ships from port to port and the possibility of varying transportation routes to achieve a cost advantage. In such cases the union normally bargains with an employers' association covering a state, region, or occasionally the entire country. The basic pressure is the usual one of product-market rivalry. In some cases, however, the bargaining unit has been influenced by other factors. The national contract for over-the-road truckers, for example, resulted partly from the effort of Teamster President Hoffa to obtain firm national control over the union.

In manufacturing, competition is usually regional or national, and the union must take an interest in securing similar contract terms from competing employers. But this effort takes different forms in different industries. In small-scale, highly competitive industries such as men's and women's clothing, hosiery, pottery, or canning, multiemployer bargaining is the general rule. Where there are many small employers, the union cannot find any firm prominent enough to establish an industry "pattern." On the other side, small employers cannot feel much confidence in their own strength and tend to band together for mutual protection. Both employers and the union find a master agreement convenient in enforcing minimum labor standards and "putting a floor under competition."

Quite different is the situation in heavy manufacturing, where companies are large and oligopoly the prevalent market form. Here employers usually feel powerful enough to go it alone, and also have a traditional resistance to industry-wide bargaining. While the unions often argue that industry-wide bargaining is desirable in principle, they have not pressed the point because pattern bargaining serves their purposes reasonably well.

The Electrical, Radio, and Machine Workers' Union, for example, attempts to establish an industry pattern by dealing first with Westinghouse or General Electric. The United Automobile Workers directs its initial pressure at one or other of the "Big Three" companies. The Pulp, Sulphate, and Paper Mill Workers traditionally open negotiations with the Great Northern Paper Company. The United Steelworkers negotiates first with the largest basic steel producers before proceeding to the hundreds of smaller companies.

The steel case may serve to illustrate both the procedures and problems of pattern bargaining. The contract terms to be presented to employers in a particular year are worked out initially by the Executive Board of the United Steelworkers. They are then presented for discussion to a Policy Committee, consisting of some 250 delegates from all parts of the country. After the program has been ratified by the Policy Committee, negotiations for a new contract are begun simultaneously with representatives of the major basic steel producers. After a settlement is reached with the major producers, the union proceeds to sign similar contracts with the other basic steel companies.

Negotiations with the hundreds of smaller companies engaged in steel fabricating are left mainly to district and local officials of the union. International headquarters, however, distributes to local officials a mimeographed list of the demands which are to be made on all employers. With respect to many contract terms, these instructions specify minimum as well as maximum terms of settlement. They tell local officials not only what they should demand to begin with, but also the minimum which they must get in order to have the agreement approved by the international office. The union's objective here is to prevent "whipsawing" by employers. If the union accepts a poor settlement in one plant, word will spread rapidly throughout the industry, and the case will rise to plague the union in another plant a thousand miles away.

In spite of this effort toward uniformity, the contracts signed with the fabricators show considerably more variation than the contracts with the basic steel companies. Wage levels in the smaller companies are both lower than those in basic steel and more variable from company to company.[4] The underlying reason is that the fabricators are operating in hundreds of specialized and distinct product markets—for

[4] On this point, see George Seltzer, "Pattern Bargaining and the United Steelworkers," *Journal of Political Economy,* August, 1951, pp. 319–31; and David H. Greenberg, "Deviations From Wage-Fringe Standards," *Industrial and Labor Relations Review,* January, 1968, pp. 197–209.

wire, for pipe, for structural steel shapes, and so on—which may differ widely in demand trends, profit margins, and severity of competition. The union has to tailor its demands to these different situations. Thus the pattern tends to fray at the edges when transferred to product markets other than that for which it was designed.

This tendency is observable also in other industries. The United Automobile Workers develops its wage pattern for a particular year in negotiations with the major auto manufacturers. When it tries to transfer this pattern to the hundreds of automobile parts manufacturers, however, it runs into resistance. The parts manufacturers, who must bid for orders from the Big Three against strong competition from rival producers, have lower and more variable profit margins than the auto manufacturers themselves. The union adjusts to this by allowing greater intercompany variation of wages. The United Automobile Workers also has members in a variety of other industries, notably the West Coast airframe plants. At one stage the union attempted to apply the pattern of automobile wage changes to the aircraft plants as well, thus going beyond an *industry-wide* pattern to a *union-wide* pattern. This effort failed, however, because of the different market situation of the aircraft producers and also because of a different organizational situation in which some aircraft plants have been organized by the Machinists' Union.

An interesting question about oligopoly manufacturing is why employers are willing to accept single-company bargaining. Why do they not band together to resist the union's demands? Why will the other automobile companies, for example, allow the unions to single out one company to enforce concessions which will then be demanded of everyone? No outsider can say. Traditional intercompany rivalry in product markets, fear that any concerted action may fall foul of the antitrust laws, and emotional resistance to "industry-wide bargaining" may all play some part. These attitudes may change in the course of time. Already there are limited arrangements in some industries for "strike insurance," i.e. payments to a struck company by other companies in the industry that continue to operate, to compensate the target company for its loss of sales and profits.

Centralization and Decentralization in Bargaining

From the thirties until the mid-fifties, the trend was strongly in the direction of larger bargaining units and greater centralization of negotiating power in the hands of top union and management officials. More recently, however, a reaction has set in. There has been pressure for greater attention to the interests of workers in particular plants or occupational groups, and a greater voice for the union membership in decision making. We may note particularly the increased influence of skilled craft groups in negotiations, the relegation of numerous issues to settlement at a local level, and a growing tendency for union members to reject settlements negotiated by their leaders.

1. *Skilled craft representation.* During the rush to unionize mass production manufacturing in the thirties and forties, skilled craftsmen were usually blanketed into plant-wide or company-wide units, where they formed a minority of the membership. Moreover, the new industrial unions during this period concentrated on bringing up the bottom rather than the top of the wage structure. It was common practice to negotiate a uniform cents-per-hour increase for everyone in the plant. Percentagewise, this meant larger increases for laborers than for craftsmen, and a reduction of the percentage differential between the two groups. This was an important source of craft discontent and of pressure for greater craft autonomy.

The effectiveness of this pressure varies from industry to industry, depending partly on the ratio of skilled workers to total employment. Where the percentage is high, as in electric utilities (48.5 percent skilled), the skilled men tend to dominate the union without ceremony. At the opposite pole, as in meatpacking (10 percent skilled), they are too weak to make their voice heard. The interesting cases are those in which skilled workers form a substantial minority, not sufficient to dominate, but large enough to be influential. This group includes rubber products (18 percent), beverages (20 percent), electrical machinery (26 percent), motor vehicles (28 percent), and primary metals (35 percent).

Adjustment of the union machinery to accommodate craft interests takes a variety of forms.[5] Proceeding from weaker to stronger forms, we may note: (a) formation of a Skilled Trades Department (or Council), which conducts its own conventions and manages apprenticeship programs of special interest to craftsmen. Existence of such a department does not per se confer any special voice in wage negotiations. (b) Formal participation in decision making—for example, through a specified number of skilled representatives on the union's wage policy committee or negotiating committee. The United Automobile Workers, for example, deals with General Motors through a General Motors Council (there are corresponding councils for Ford and Chrysler). Under this are eleven subcouncils, two of which represent craft groups. Each subcouncil elects one representative to the National Committee of the General Motors Council, which represents the union in company-wide negotiations. In some unions, including the Brewery Workers and the Paper Workers, separate craft locals assure the skilled

[5] For a detailed discussion, see Arnold R. Weber, "The craft-industrial issue revisited: a study of union government," *Industrial and Labor Relations Review,* April, 1963, pp. 381–404.

groups of representation on the joint committees created to negotiate with employers.

(c) Most drastically, skilled groups may be given the right to approve or disapprove contract terms applying to them, and may autonomously exercise their right to strike. Since a strike of the skilled men would shut down the plant, this gives them an effective veto power. Only the Brewery Workers and the United Automobile Workers have gone this far, and there are still some controls and reservations. In the United Automobile Workers, craftsmen can vote separately only on issues that affect them alone (which would *not* include wage differentials vis-à-vis other occupational groups), and even this requires approval by the International Executive Board.

2. *Local Negotiations.* A large manufacturing corporation may include dozens of plants, with quite different production operations and problems. Each plant has local problems of working conditions, work speeds and time standards, adjustment to technical change, application of seniority rules, scheduling of overtime work and vacation periods, calculation of fringe benefits, and so on. In the 1958 United Automobile Workers–General Motors negotiations, some 11,600 "local demands" were presented by the union. In the 1961 negotiations this had grown to 19,000 local demands, and in 1964 to 24,000. It is impossible to resolve these issues in a single national negotiation focused on general wage and benefit adjustments. Yet unless they are resolved there will be growing membership discontent, with a probability of wildcat strikes and slowdowns.

It is common practice, therefore, to provide for several levels of negotiation. In basic steel, there are industry–union, company–union, and plant–union committees at work simultaneously, and issues are sorted out for assignment to one or other of these levels. In the rubber industry, there is a company-wide master agreement plus local supplements negotiated at the plant level. The master agreement must be ratified by a majority of plants, each of which has a voice in proportion to its employment. Even if the master agreement is ratified, a local union can still strike over its local supplement. In the automobile industry, too, local unions have a qualified right to strike over local issues; and in some years there have been many such strikes even after national issues had been settled. The companies charge that this is a deliberate union tactic, designed to win maximum concessions at all levels. The union replies that it is a necessary adjustment to pressure from members and local union leaders.

The feasibility of permitting local issues to be resolved through strike action depends partly on characteristics of the industry. If a company's plants are carrying out parallel and independent operations, some can carry on while others are shut down. In the automobile industry, however, there is interdependence between parts suppliers and assembly operations. Strikes in a few plants can cripple the flow of materials and compel a company-wide shutdown. The auto companies will probably insist more and more that local issues be resolved *before* the master agreement is concluded.[6]

3. *Membership Ratification of Contract Terms.* The ratification of new contract terms by membership vote is normally the last stage in negotiations, and we shall discuss it in the next section on negotiating procedures. Here we note only that it provides an opportunity for grass-roots' participation and veto of union leaders' actions, and that this veto power has been used increasingly in recent years.

CONTRACT NEGOTIATIONS

Collective bargaining is a highly stylized game, with ground rules which are understood and observed by both parties. These include rules about the timing of negotiations, the selection of the negotiators, the agenda for discussion, the main stages of negotiation, and the ratification of a new contract. We are concerned here solely with procedures, not with results. In the next chapter we shall examine why the outcome may be more favorable to the union or to management, the meaning and determinants of "bargaining power," possible reasons for a deadlock in negotiations, and the cost of the strikes which result from such deadlocks.

Timing of Negotiations

Union contracts in the United States run for a specified period, usually either two or three years; and the approach of the contract expiration date triggers the beginning of new negotiations. There is nothing inevitable about this procedure. In Britain, for example, agreements have no expiration date, and negotiations may be requested by either party at any time. The U.S. procedure is simply a convention, which concentrates bargaining activity into periodic intervals, with periods of relative quiet in between.

The contract usually provides that, if either party wishes a change in contract terms, it must give notice to this effect so many days before the expiration date. Such notice is almost invariably given, since it is rare for a contract to be renewed without change. There is also a legal provision that the federal mediation service must be notified

---

[6] On this range of issues, see E. Robert Livernash, "Special and Local Negotiations," in John T. Dunlop and Neil W. Chamberlain, eds., *Frontiers of Collective Bargaining* (New York: Harper & Row, Publishers, 1967).

sixty days before the contract expiration date so that it may have an opportunity to keep in touch with negotiations in important cases.

A further ground rule is that, if agreement on terms of a new contract is not reached before the old one expires, a strike results automatically—"no contract, no work." This sets a deadline for the discussions, and negotiations become more intensive and more serious as this deadline approaches. The union may decide, however, to ignore this rule and to keep its members at work while negotiations continue. This might happen, for example, if the expiration date comes at a time of low activity in the industry, when a strike would put little pressure on employers. Or, if the parties feel that they are very close to agreement when the deadline arrives, the old contract may be extended for a short time by mutual agreement.

Selection and Authority of Negotiators

The next important point is that negotiations are conducted by *delegates* of the parties, who usually do not themselves have power to conclude an agreement. This obviously complicates the bargaining process. Terms that the negotiators themselves would consider acceptable may be vetoed by higher company officials or the union membership. It also enlarges the room for tactical maneuvering. A negotiator on either side may resist certain terms on the ground (genuine or alleged) that he would not be able to "sell" these terms to his superiors.

Who are the negotiators, and how are they selected? On the union side, it will be simplest to begin with a local union negotiating with one or more employers in its area. As the expiration date of the old contract approaches, the demands to be served on the employer will probably be discussed at a general membership meeting. A committee will then be appointed to put the demands into better shape and to draft proposed terms for a new contract. In doing this they must weigh and balance numerous considerations: what they know about the financial situation of the company and the business outlook; instructions or advice from national union headquarters; what has been happening to wages in other companies in the locality, and also in other companies in the same industry; the wishes and expectations of union members; differences of interest among different groups within the membership; and how far the members appear willing to back up their demands by strike action. Union leaders must demand and win enough to keep the members reasonably content; yet they must not set their sights so high that the organization is forced into a strike that members are reluctant to support. Strikes are rarely popular with the rank and file, and a local cannot strike more than once every few years without a decline in morale and effectiveness.

After the drafting committee has done its best, the proposed contract terms are taken back to another membership meeting. There they are discussed at length, perhaps revised, and eventually approved. A negotiating committee is then selected to meet with management. This will normally include the chief officers of the local, but may include other members as well. The national union representative for the area normally sits in on the negotiations and frequently plays a leading role. At some point prior to or during negotiations a strike vote of the membership will usually be taken. This does not necessarily mean that a strike is going to occur. The purpose is to strengthen the union representatives' hand by advance authorization to call a strike if negotiations with the employer break down.

After the union negotiators feel they have won as much as they can from management, they must come back to the membership for approval of the new contract before it becomes valid. In many unions the contract must also be approved by the national office. Participation by a national union representative is designed partly to ensure that the terms will be in conformity with national policy.

Preparation for regional or national negotiations, or for bargaining with a major pattern-setting employer, is considerably more complicated. National union officers normally take a leading role in such negotiations. Proposed union demands are hammered out by the national executive board, and then submitted for discussion to a conference of delegates from the local unions and district organizations. Depending on bargaining practices, this conference may cover the entire industry throughout the country, or all local unions dealing with a particular employer, or some other grouping. After revision and ratification of demands by the conference, the union negotiators begin discussions with management representatives. At the end of the process, the proposed contract terms must usually be reported back to the conference for further discussion and approval. Membership participation in national negotiations is typically indirect and vicarious. In local negotiations, local officers bear the brunt of the discussions with national representatives serving as advisers. In national negotiations, national officers play the leading role, with local representatives serving as critics and advisers.

On the management side, contract negotiations are usually conducted by a small group of top management officials. In a small or medium-sized company, the president may serve as chief management negotiator. In large organizations, this responsibility is more likely to fall on the executive vice-president or some other line official. The chief counsel and the treasurer frequently participate and several top production officials normally sit in on the negotiations. The industrial relations director and members of his staff take part as expert advisers.

Where the industrial relations director is a forceful individual with high status in the company, he may even serve as chief company spokesman.

The management representatives, like the union negotiating committee, begin to formulate their position well in advance of the start of negotiations. An effort is made to anticipate the main union demands and to determine a position on them. Management may itself want to take the initiative on certain points. Management initiative in presenting demands, instead of simply responding to union demands, is commoner today than it was ten or twenty years ago. Anything that requires a major change in company policy, such as agreement to a union shop, must normally be ratified in advance by the board of directors or the executive committee. Proposals involving money also require advance ratification. The management representatives go into negotiations with instructions that they may not raise the company's labor costs by more than a certain figure. If they are unable to reach agreement with the union within the specified limits, they must go back to the board for further discussion.[7]

Where there is multi-employer bargaining, representatives of the various companies involved will be called together for a preliminary conference. If there is a formal association, members of the association staff may take a prominent part in working out proposals to the union. Important conflicts of interest may have to be faced and resolved. Some companies, for example, may be in a comfortable profit position and able to afford substantial wage increases. Other companies closer to the margin may feel obliged to fight any increase in costs. These and other differences must be compromised in order to present a united front to the union. After policy has been determined, the actual conduct of negotiations is usually delegated to a small committee of the most experienced and influential company representatives.

The Agenda for Discussion

Negotiations in the international field are often two-stage negotiations. The parties first must agree on what they are going to discuss. Each side tries to put on the agenda items on which it hopes to score gains and to keep off the agenda items that might be harmful to its interests or on which it is determined to make no concessions. Only

---

[7] In one case that came to the author's attention, the management negotiators were instructed by the board of directors that they could not concede more than five cents an hour. Agreement on this basis appeared impossible, so the vice-president conducting the negotiations came back to the board with an earnest plea that he be allowed to go up to eight cents. After he had made an eloquent statement of his case, the president burst out laughing and said, "Why, that's fine! We were willing to go to ten cents all along!"

after the agenda is settled do the parties proceed to substantive negotiations.

In collective bargaining, on the other hand, these two stages are merged. There is no advance agenda. At the first negotiating session, the union representatives present their full list of demands, and the management representatives list the changes they would like to see in the new contract. The agenda is obtained simply by combining the "shopping lists" of the parties, and substantive discussion of these items begins at once. Occasionally one side objects that a certain topic "is not a proper subject for collective bargaining"; but such objections have not been very successful. In general, either side may raise any issue it chooses, and all these issues become part of the bargaining agenda.

We should note one legal point, which will be discussed further in Chapter 18. The National Labor Relations Act requires that both parties should "bargain in good faith." Suppose the union makes a demand on a point that management believes is within its sole discretion. Management says, "We do not want to discuss that issue." The union files a charge with the National Labor Relations Board that the employer has refused to bargain in good faith. The National Labor Relations Board then decides whether it is an issue that the parties must discuss, with a view to possible compromise and settlement, or whether it is an issue on which one or the other party may stand pat. The former is termed a *mandatory* subject of negotiation, while the latter is *permissive* only; and it is important whether an item falls in one category or the other.

The agenda usually includes dozens or scores of items. This leaves room to trade concessions on some items against gains on others. The agenda can be divided broadly into: (a) *cost items,* including basic wages, fringe benefits, and rules that directly affect labor costs, such as overtime. These items can be reduced to a cents-per-man-hour equivalent and totaled, so that one can speak of a "20-cent package," or a "30-cent package"; (b) *noncost items,* such as union security arrangements or the seniority system, where the cost effect is so indirect that no measurement of it is attempted. Cost items are readily tradable against each other, since each side can measure approximately what it is yielding or getting. Trading between cost and noncost items is also possible, as indicated by the union official who said, "Every year I sell the union shop for a nickel."

A complete draft settlement, including tentative provisions on all major items, is known as a "package"; and both sides usually adhere to what may be termed "the package convention." The items on the agenda are discussed one at a time—many of them more than once—with each side indicating the concessions and trades it might be willing to make. It is understood, however, that agreement on each item is tentative until agreement has been reached on the total package. If this proves impossible and negotiations break down, each party is free to withdraw these tentative concessions and start bargaining all over again. Realistically, however, the statements that have been made in the course of negotiations cannot really be erased from people's minds.

Stages of Negotiation

While the course of negotiations is never the same in any two situations, one can distinguish several standard phases. The first of these —presentation of initial demands—typically reveals a wide gap between the positions of the parties. The union wants the moon, while management does not want to concede anything. In some cases, however, the initial statements of the parties may be close to their final positions. This may be true, for example, in a "pattern-following" company, where the union is prepared to insist on acceptance of terms already conceded by a leading company.

Next comes a period of probing, which in a large negotiation may last for weeks, during which each side questions the other's demands at length. Clause by clause questioning of the other party produces various kinds of information: the detailed contents of a particular proposal, the reasons it is considered necessary, the kinds of factual data that have been assembled to support it, sometimes a preliminary indication of the firmness with which the demand is held.

At this stage the negotiating group is usually scaled down to more manageable size—a few key people on each side who have authority to make concessions and decisions. Discussion can move more rapidly in such a group, and can also be more frank and informal. Each side continues to probe the other's position while trying to protect its own freedom of maneuver. There may be indications of willingness to make concessions on certain items. Some of the less-controversial issues may be resolved and set aside, subject to the general rule that no one subject is regarded as settled until all items in dispute have been settled. For the key issues in dispute, each side may eventually indicate one or more "packages"—combinations of terms—that it would consider acceptable. The contents of these package proposals are significant in indicating which demands the parties are really serious about.

The packages put forward by the two sides, however, are likely still to be some distance apart. What forces further concessions and final compromise is the approach of the deadline date, after which a strike will occur. It is no accident that many contract settlements are reached after all-night conferences on the eve of a strike. The imminence of a strike, with the attendant costs and uncertainties for both sides, forces each party to reexamine its position realistically and to ask, "Is it really worth it?" This usually leads to a lowering of union demands and a raising of management offers to the point where they overlap and settlement becomes possible. Between 98 and 99 percent of the contract negotiations carried out in the United States each year result in agreement without a strike. The possibility of a strike, however, is a central feature of the bargaining process and the main force making for ultimate agreement.

A work stoppage, while marking a crisis, does not bring an end to negotiations. The issues in dispute must still be resolved. The only difference is that the costs of a stoppage, which previously were potential, have now become actual. As the strike lengthens and costs mount on both sides, there is growing pressure on the parties to make further concessions so as to bring the strike to an end. Occasionally a strike ends in closing down of the enterprise; and occasionally it just dies quietly, with the strikers trickling back to work or being replaced by strikebreakers. But the normal outcome is an agreement on new contract terms. A strike is one route to agreement.

Ratification of Agreements

At the end of the road comes ratification of the agreement by company and union. A few unions empower their negotiators to reach a binding agreement. In others, including the United Steelworkers, the agreement is ratified by a policy committee operating at one remove from the membership. By far the commonest procedure, however, is ratification by membership vote. A recent study found that more than 90 percent of union officers and members consider this to be the correct procedure.

Ratification by referendum vote involves the possibility of rejection. While there are no statistics on the frequency with which members reject the terms recommended by their leaders, experienced observers place it at 5 to 10 percent of the cases. There is also general agreement that the percentage has increased considerably over the past decade.

Rejection does not always mean what it appears to mean. The union negotiators may pretend to agree to certain terms, submit them to the membership, but openly or secretly urge the members to reject them. The membership vote is a bargaining gambit, used to justify additional demands. In other cases the negotiators may submit a tentative agreement to the members without any recommendation, simply to test membership sentiment. A negative vote in this case is an instruction to the negotiators to try for more.

But there are also genuine rejections. The union leaders believe that the terms they have secured are reasonable and acceptable, they recommend them to the members, and the members proceed to vote them down. Where this happens, it is usually because the package lacks certain components highly valued by the membership. Contracts have been voted down because of provisions relating to work assignments, seniority rights, shift preferences, rotation of job assignments, work scheduling, and specific working conditions. The commonest reason for rejection appears to be a failure of communications within the union, so that the leaders' conception of what is acceptable fails to accord with reality. In some cases factional strife within the union is a contributing factor. Leaders aspiring to union office urge members to reject terms recommended by those in office, as a step toward displacing the existing leaders.

Membership rejection may mean a strike where none was anticipated, or continuation of a strike that the leaders were willing to settle. This raises the dilemma discussed in Chapter 13 with respect to "union democracy." Greater membership influence on the terms of the agreement carries with it the possibility of greater industrial strife. What balance do we prefer as between grass-roots democracy and industrial peace?

A study of the problem by Professor Clyde Summers concludes that membership ratification serves a constructive purpose in explaining and legitimizing a proposed agreement. Even those who vote against it will usually accept the principle of majority rule. Conversely, if an agreement is imposed by the negotiators and turns out to have unpopular provisions, it is likely to generate "quickie" strikes and other forms of protest. But proper use of ratification votes requires procedural safeguards. Misuse of the procedure, as a bargaining ploy or as an abdication of leadership, should be avoided. The vote on ratification should be tied to a vote to strike (which is often not true at present), so that the price of rejection is clearly evident; and those who vote on the issue should be the ones who will actually have to strike, which again is not always the case.[8]

The Technique of Continuous Negotiation

A prominent feature of contract negotiations in the United States is their crisis atmosphere. Discussion usually begins only a few weeks before the contract expiration date, and not until a few days before the deadline do the negotiators begin to reveal their basic positions. Hence the familiar sight of weary negotiators working right down to the deadline in day-and-night sessions, and finally signing an agreement at the last possible moment. This may not work too badly for wage

---

[8] Membership of a local, for example, may include workers in several plants, while the negotiation in question involves one plant only. If the proposed agreement is submitted to a vote of the entire local, employees in other plants are free to vote it down without having to strike in consequence. For a review of this and other problems see Clyde Summers, "Ratification of agreements," in Dunlop and Chamberlain, *Collective Bargaining*.

issues, where the positions of the parties can be stated and compromised in quantitative terms. But it is not a good way of resolving more intricate problems, such as rewriting the company's seniority rules, or compromising management's desire for flexibility in production methods with the union's desire to protect the job security of its members.

There has been a growing tendency, therefore, to refer such problems to special committees, whose mission is to work on them continuously between contract negotiations, and to have agreed proposals ready in advance of the next contract deadline. These are sometimes tripartite bodies, including neutrals as well as union and management representatives. In other cases they include labor and management representatives only. In either event they have leisure to undertake thorough exploration of the issues, to commission special studies and expert reports, to test the acceptability of various possible solutions, and to draft clauses for inclusion in the next contract.

After the long and bitter steel strike of 1959, the parties agreed to set up two special committees. The controversy over management's right to change established working methods was referred to a tripartite study group, the labor and management members of which were to agree on a single neutral member to serve as chairman. It proved impossible to agree on a chairman, and this venture came to nothing. More successful was a "Human Relations Research Committee," which included union and management representatives only and which was assigned to look into matters touching on job security, particularly "seniority, including maximum practicable protection for long-service employees against layoffs and for recalls after layoffs." This committee worked continuously from 1960 to 1962, and both parties give it much of the credit for the fact that the 1962 negotiations were concluded three months before the old contracts expired. The 1962 agreement provided that the committee should be continued and should work on additional problems of job security, such as subcontracting of work by the steel mills to outside contractors.

The committee subsequently became an issue in the campaign for the union presidency between incumbent David McDonald and challenger I. W. Abel. It was charged that McDonald had lost touch with the membership and that, through the Human Relations Committee and on the advice of staff officials, he was making decisions that bypassed the regular negotiating procedure. Control over such decisions, it was argued, should be "returned to the membership." Mr. Abel won the presidency and the Human Relations Committee was officially disbanded. But the problems posed by technical change in the industry remain. So there continue to be regular meetings between a top-level committee of union and management representatives, including the men responsible for the triennial negotiations—a group which looks remarkably like the old Human Relations Committee.

It is not surprising that the technique of continuous negotiation should have been used most frequently to deal with problems arising from technical change. Here basic interests of both parties are deeply involved. Management feels that without freedom to close and open plants, to introduce new machinery, and to make other changes in production methods it cannot control costs and maintain the company's competitive position. The union wants to protect workers' rights in their jobs, which it considers akin to property rights, and to hold displacement or downgrading of workers to a minimum. Compromise of these interests is possible, but workable compromises require inventiveness and the drafting of intricate contract provisions. The substantive problems of technical change, and the lines of compromise which seem gradually to be emerging, are examined in Chapter 21. We are concerned at this stage with procedure only, with the advantages of handling complicated problems through leisurely and thorough analysis rather than hurried improvisation.

These advantages are sufficiently clear that many companies and industries are now considering some system for negotiation between contract deadlines. One may expect a considerable spread of this technique over the years ahead.

ADJUSTMENT
OF
GRIEVANCES

Collective bargaining does not end with the signing of an agreement. Union and management officials must live under the agreement during the ensuing year, and the agreement must be applied to concrete situations arising in the plant. Contract provisions must at best be rather general. They are often unduly vague, even self-contradictory, because of unwillingness of the parties to face and resolve an underlying difference of opinion. It is easier to compromise on a vaguely worded clause that each party may interpret differently. The necessities of plant administration, however, compel specific decisions in particular cases. For this reason virtually all collective agreements contain a grievance procedure providing for adjustment of disputes arising during the life of the contract.

The grievance procedure serves a variety of functions in a collective bargaining relationship.[9]

9 For a good discussion of this matter, see Van Dusen Kennedy, "Grievance Procedure," in Arthur Kornhauser, Robert Dubin, and Arthur M. Ross, eds., *Industrial Conflict* (New York: McGraw-Hill Book Company, 1954), chap. 21. See also Slichter, Healy, and Livernash, *Impact of Collective Bargaining*, chaps. 22–26.

1. The most obvious function is that of interpreting the terms of the agreement and applying them to particular cases. Two or more sections of the agreement may be in conflict. Which is to govern? The contract may be silent on a particular problem, so that grievance adjustment involves closing a gap in the agreement. The language of a particular section may be unclear. What does the section actually mean? Even where the wording is clear, its application to a particular case frequently involves a finding of fact. The agreement may say that smoking on duty is a valid reason for discharge. A foreman discharges a man on this ground. The man says that the foreman's charge is incorrect. Was the man smoking or was he not? Shall he be discharged or not?

2. The grievance procedure is also a means of *agreement making* in two senses. To the extent that it reveals problems that are not covered clearly enough or not covered at all in the existing agreement, it helps to build up an agenda of issues for the next contract negotiation. Further, the body of decisions on past grievances itself forms part of the agreement in the broadest sense. There gradually develops, case by case and precedent by precedent, an impressive body of shop law. In old-unionized industries such as railroading and coal mining, this body of precedents is much larger than the formal union agreement and is understood by both sides to be in effect incorporated in the agreement.

3. The grievance procedure can be a sensitive device for locating sore spots in the plant organization and for pointing up inadequacies of particular foremen or union committeemen. The fact that an unusual number of grievances is filed in a particular department or on a particular issue may be more significant than the intrinsic merit of the grievances. Several leading students of industrial relations have urged the wisdom of taking a clinical rather than a legalistic view of the grievance procedure, of seeking to remove sources of conflict rather than to score points or win cases.

4. Where relations between the parties are good, the grievance procedure may be used to adjust virtually all day-to-day difficulties between workers and supervisors, whether covered explicitly by the agreement or not. It can become an orderly and systematic way of examining any disputed personnel action.

5. Conversely, where relations are poor, the procedure may become an instrument of conflict. It may be used ". . . not to settle problems between worker and supervisor or union and management but to promote the interests of either or both parties in connection with a future test of strength. . . . In unusually incompatible relationships the grievance process may operate as a sort of guerilla warfare during which the parties keep sniping at each other and endeavor to keep

their forces at a martial pitch in preparation for the open conflict which will follow expiration of the contract." [10]

Most grievances relate to rights and duties of individual employees. Discharges, or even less severe disciplinary penalties, are frequently appealed. The application of complicated seniority rules to a particular worker may be questioned. Any choice by a supervisor that involves giving preference to one worker over another—distribution of overtime work, assignment to day work rather than night work, assignment to a preferred type of work and work location—may become a subject of grievance. Classification of a worker or his job for wage purposes—whether a job should be rated as Machinist A rather than Machinist B—may be disputed. On occasion, considerable numbers of workers may become involved in a grievance case: it is alleged that the assembly line is being run too fast, or that a foreman is speeding up those under him, or that work loads throughout a department are too heavy, or that piece rates on a certain operation have been set too low. A multitude of such issues, each of them minor from a top management standpoint but important and emotionally explosive to the workers concerned, get worked out peaceably through the grievance process.

The procedure for handling grievances varies with the nature of the industry. In building construction, for example, the work sites are scattered, jobs are often of short duration, and disputes have to be adjusted quickly or not at all. Each union normally has a *business agent* who makes frequent visits to building sites in his area to check that only union men are employed, to ensure that other contract terms are being complied with, and to hear any complaints by the members. The business agent goes over any grievances with the employer then and there. If no agreement is reached, the men simply leave the job. This is quite different from the long-drawn-out grievances procedures in manufacturing or railroading.

In most manufacturing industries, the basic union official concerned with grievances is the *shop steward* or *grievance committeeman*. He is usually elected by the union members in his department, and is normally a plant employee; but he is allowed time off from his job to handle grievances, which in a large department can become almost a full-time job. The time spent in handling grievances is often paid for by the company, but in some cases the union bears the cost.

The normal first step in a manufacturing plant is for the worker who is "grieving" to consult his shop steward, who discusses the matter informally with the foreman. The great bulk of grievances is and must be disposed of at this level. If this is not done, higher union and management officials face a hopeless burden of cases, settlements are long delayed, and the procedure becomes a source of annoyance rather

10 Kennedy, "Grievance Procedure," p. 282.

than relief. An experienced foreman eventually learns the wisdom of bargaining things out informally with the union, trading concessions that he can afford for offsetting concessions from the union when he really needs them.

A grievance that is not adjusted between the steward and the foreman is generally reduced to writing and then goes to the shop committee on one side and the plant superintendent on the other. The next appeal stage may be discussion between a national field representative and the labor relations director of the company. The final step before arbitration may be discussion between a vice-president of the company and a national union representative. The number of stages in the grievance procedure varies somewhat with the size of the company, and the complexity of its organization. Where the procedure is working properly, the case load is gradually whittled down at successive levels, leaving only a small percentage of "hard core" cases for the final arbitration stage.

The Arbitration of Grievances

Unions generally favor arbitration as the final step in disposing of unsettled grievances. Many newly unionized companies in the thirties and forties opposed it because it allowed outsiders to intervene in personnel decisions. Experience has gradually convinced most managements of the value of the procedure and its use has increased steadily. Today between 90 and 95 percent of union contracts provide for arbitration as the final step in the grievance procedure.

Both management and the union take a risk under arbitration that they may lose decisions on matters that they consider important. Arbitration has the decisive advantage, however, of making possible a final settlement of grievances without a stoppage of work. Arbitration is also in some cases a convenient face-saving device, particularly for the union. Union officials sometimes have to push a case up through the grievance procedure to satisfy a group in their membership, even though they know that the members' demands are unreasonable. If such a case goes to arbitration and is decided against the union, the blame can be put on the arbitrator. Part of the arbitrator's function is to serve as a "shock absorber" for decisions that are unavoidable, but for which one side or the other is reluctant to take responsibility.

It should be noted that we are talking here about voluntary arbitration, agreed to in advance by the parties and limited to interpreting an existing agreement. The arbitrator under a grievance procedure is there solely to say what the existing agreement means. He has no authority to change the terms of the agreement or to rule on issues not covered by the agreement.

There are several types of voluntary arbitration clauses. The commonest practice is for the parties to appoint an arbitrator each time the occasion arises. It is frequently provided that, where the parties cannot agree, the arbitrator shall be designated by the American Arbitration Association, the head of the Federal Mediation and Conciliation Service, the head of the state department of labor, or some other public official. In some industries it is customary to use three-man or five-man arbitration boards; each party appoints one or two members to the board, and these members select a neutral chairman. In large companies, or in agreements between a union and employers' association, there may be enough arbitration work to justify hiring a permanent arbitrator on a full-time or part-time basis. Such an official is frequently termed an "umpire" or "impartial chairman." This arrangement exists, for example, in the agreements between the Ford Motor Company and the United Automobile Workers, the General Motors Corporation and the United Automobile Workers, United States Steel Corporation and the United Steelworkers, the Hosiery Workers' Union and the Association of Full-fashioned Hosiery Manufacturers, the International Ladies' Garment Workers' Union and the several ladies' garment manufacturers' associations, and the Pacific Coast longshore employers and the Longshoremen's Union.

A properly constructed grievance procedure capped by arbitration should in principle render work stoppages unnecessary during the life of the agreement. In recognition of this fact, most contracts contain clauses denying or limiting the right to strike during the contract year. For example, "Under no circumstances shall there be any strike, sympathy strike, walkout, cessation of work, sit down, slow down, picketing, boycott, refusal to perform any part of duty, or other interference with or interruption of the normal conduct of the company's business during the term of this agreement." [11] What happens if a worker engages in a "wildcat" or "outlaw" strike during the term of the agreement? Some contracts do not contain any penalty provisions. Many contracts, however, provide that instigators of an outlaw strike may be subject to discharge, and that participants may be fined or suspended from work for a time. If there is disagreement over whether a man did instigate a work stoppage, this is taken up through the grievance procedure in the usual way.

Twenty years ago wildcat strikes were a serious problem in many manufacturing companies. Newly organized workers were still enjoying the excitement of being able to talk back to the boss. Finding that the grievance procedure operated slowly, they often tried to get quick settlement of a disputed issue by direct action. In some plants the slowdown and the "quickie" strike virtually replaced the official

[11] Agreement between the Turbo Engineering Corporation, Trenton, New Jersey, and Local No. 731, United Automobile Workers.

grievance procedure. Managements inexperienced in labor relations got into the habit of yielding on disputed issues to avoid interruptions of production; and this success of wildcat tactics encouraged their continued use.

By the late fifties, however, increased experience and a different economic climate had brought a change in management attitudes. Companies found that constant yielding on work speeds, output standards, and shop discipline had raised production costs to a dangerous extent. With the ending of the postwar boom in the mid-fifties, costs once more became a matter of concern. Many employers, therefore, decided to stand up to the situation. They began to penalize participants in outlaw strikes; and they refused to settle disputed issues while such a strike was in progress, insisting that work be resumed first and the normal grievance procedure followed thereafter. Once management resistance was apparent, most of the unions accepted it in good spirit. The national unions had never sanctioned the unofficial tactics of their more exuberant local members, and now took steps to tighten internal union discipline. The problem of outlaw strikes receded to minor proportions.

Discussion Questions

1. What procedures and activities are covered by the term "collective bargaining"?
2. Why may there be differences in the size of the election unit, the negotiating unit, and the impact unit? Can you think of cases in which the three are identical?
3. Explain clearly, giving examples, why the scope of product markets has an important influence on the size of negotiating units.
4. Why are multi-employer bargaining units less common in manufacturing than in nonmanufacturing industries?
5. "The divergent interests of local and occupational groups pose a serious problem for a union engaged in nationwide bargaining."
   (a) Why is this a problem?
   (b) What are some of the steps that have been taken to deal with it?
6. What are the main functions of the grievance procedure in collective bargaining? What are the characteristics of a satisfactory grievance procedure?
7. "Without the strike threat in the background, real collective bargaining cannot exist." Discuss.

8. "The union officers, who know most about the issues under discussion, should have full authority to conclude agreements with employers. Membership ratification is not really necessary and can have harmful results." Do you agree? Why, or why not?

Reading Suggestions

Comprehensive discussions of collective bargaining include Chamberlain, Neil W., *Collective Bargaining.* New York: McGraw-Hill Book Company, 1951; Dunlop, John T., *Collective Bargaining: Principles and Cases.* Homewood, Ill.: Richard D. Irwin, Inc., 1955; Dunlop, John T., and Neil W. Chamberlain, eds., *Frontiers of Collective Bargaining.* New York: Harper & Row, Publishers, 1967; Kuhn, James W., *Bargaining in Grievance Settlement.* New York: Columbia University Press, 1961; Macdonald, Robert M., "Collective Bargaining in the Postwar Period," *Industrial and Labor Relations Review,* July, 1966, pp. 553–57; and Slichter, Sumner H., James J. Healy, and E. Robert Livernash, *The Impact of Collective Bargaining on Management.* Washington, D.C. The Brookings Institution, 1960.

BARGAINING POWER, DEADLOCKS, AND STRIKES

16

Why do the terms of settlement come out as they do? Why are they sometimes more favorable to management's position and in other cases more favorable to the union? Can one develop any theory of bargained wage rates comparable to the theory of market-determined wages?

APPROACHES TO BARGAINING THEORY

We assume at the outset that the bargain can be expressed in quantitative terms. Without this we cannot graph the positions of the parties or frame hypotheses capable of statistical tests. This is, of course, a considerable simplification of reality. Conversion of demands to a common denominator is easiest for wages and other monetary benefits, such as pensions, paid vacations, or health care. But what about a demand for a union shop? Or a demand for a change in the bargaining structure, which one side or the other believes will work to its advantage in future negotiations? Such demands are often considered "matters of principle," which are not capable of compromise. We assume nevertheless that any principle has its price, and that all the items in the settlement "package" can be reduced to dollar equivalents.

The Contract Zone

Consider a single buyer of a certain kind of labor confronting a single union, a situation known as *bilateral monopoly.* In Figure 1, D

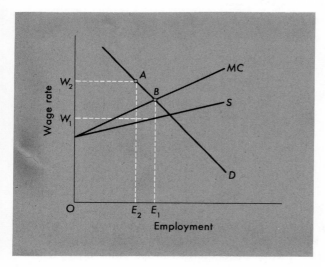

Figure 1

THE CONTRACT ZONE UNDER BILATERAL
MONOPSONY

is the employer's labor demand curve, while S and MC are his labor supply and marginal cost curves. The diagram is identical with that for the monopsonistic buyer of labor in Chapter 4. We now face two problems: (1) what are the outside limits within which the bargained wage must fall? (2) what determines where it will fall within these limits?

The limits within which the bargain must fall is usually termed the *settlement range* or the *contract zone.* Its location depends on the policies of the parties. As regards the employer, we usually assume that he will try to maximize profit. In the present case, by the reasoning used in Chapter 4, this will mean operating at point B. The most profitable employment is OE_1, where the marginal cost of additional labor (shown by MC) just equals the marginal revenue product of additional labor (shown by D). We see from the supply curve that OE_1 workers can be recruited at a wage OW_1.

Concerning the union we cannot be so definite. Union negotiators will certainly give some weight to employment as well as wages. They may be influenced also by political and "pattern-following" considerations. They may feel compelled to win as much from one plant or company as they have won from others in the industry. Or they may try to match the gains of other unions with which they feel somewhat in competition. But the weight of such considerations will vary from case to case.

The determinants of union wage policy are examined more fully in Chapter 22. Here we need assume only that the union negotiators do have a policy, i.e. that they can select a wage that is preferred to any other wage. Suppose this preferred wage is OW_2 in Figure 1. Have we now defined the limits of the contract zone? Not necessarily. The contract zone cannot be *wider* than W_1W_2 because neither party would want to go outside these limits; but it may be narrower. Suppose the union considers a wage of OW_1 so unattractive that it would strike indefinitely rather than accept it. Then the bottom of the contract zone, the lowest wage that the union could be forced to accept, will be above OW_1. Similarly the wage OW_2 may be so high that the employer would close down permanently rather than pay it, so that the top of the zone is below OW_2. But there will normally be a contract zone, and it will often be wide enough to leave substantial scope for bargaining.

At this point earlier economists, such as Edgeworth, were inclined to leave the matter. They said, in effect, "We cannot answer the second question raised above. Within the limits of the contract zone, the actual wage rate is indeterminate." But this means only that *the market variables usually included in economic theory* are insufficient to determine the outcome. A wage rate does get decided, after all, through the negotiating process. In this sense the outcome *is* determinate.

The Hicks' Approach

Not all economists were happy with the Edgeworth pronouncement; and intermittently they have tried to find paths to a determinate solution. One such attempt, by Professor Sir John Hicks of Oxford, is sketched in Figure 2. The central idea is that there is a functional relation between the wage that one or the other party will accept and the length of strike that would be necessary to establish that wage. The horizontal axis in Figure 2 is a time axis, along which various

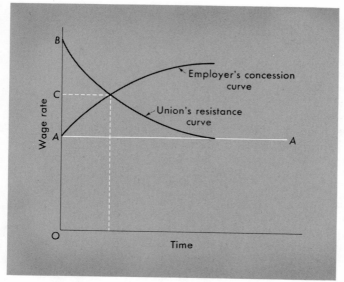

Figure 2

HICKS' SOLUTION OF THE BARGAINING PROBLEM

possible lengths of strike can be measured. *OA* is the wage that the employer would prefer if the union were not in the picture. He will concede more, however, in order to avoid a strike; and up to a point, his concessions will rise with the length of strike he anticipates. Thus we derive the *employer's concession curve*, each point on which shows the maximum amount the employer would pay rather than face a strike of specified length. This curve eventually levels off, i.e. there is an upper limit beyond which the employer will not go under any circumstances.

The union's preferred wage would be *OB*, provided this could be obtained without a strike; but the prospective costs of a strike may lead it to accept less. The *union's resistance curve* shows the minimum that the union would accept rather than face a strike of the length indicated, and this minimum declines as the prospective strike becomes longer. The resistance curve eventually intersects *AA*, i.e. there is some maximum length of strike beyond which the union would prefer simply to accept the employer's terms.

It seems natural to think that the intersection of the two curves yields a determinate solution to the bargaining problem. *Both* parties would agree to the wage *OC* rather than face a strike *OS* weeks in length. But what does Figure 2 really tell us? If it applies to the negotiation period *before* a strike has been called, then the determinate solution rests on assumptions about knowledge and foresight. *If* each party knows the other's curve, and *if* each expects that a strike when called would last at least *OS* weeks, the path to settlement is clear. But these assumptions are not very plausible. The essence of collective bargaining is uncertainty about the other party's intentions and about the course of events if negotiations break down.[1]

Alternatively, the Hicks' diagram might be interpreted as charting the course of events over time *after* negotiations have broken down and a strike has begun. With each succeeding week of strike, the union's minimum demand falls and the employer's maximum offer rises, until after *OS* weeks agreement is reached at *OC*. This may or may not be a useful way of looking at the history of a strike; but it does not provide a theory of negotiation in advance of strike action.

The Concept of Bargaining Power

This is a slippery concept, which can be defined in different ways. One interesting definition, developed by Professor Neil Chamberlain,[2] starts from the concept of the *inducement to agree*. Two parties, *A* and *B,* are in a bargaining situation. *A* makes an offer to settle on certain terms. *B*'s inducement to agree is defined as the cost of disagreeing on *A*'s terms/the cost of agreeing on *A*'s terms. This will usually be a positive fraction, greater than zero, but not necessarily greater than one. Only if and when it becomes greater than one—that is, when the costs of continued disagreement exceed the benefits to be gained—will *B* be willing to accept *A*'s offer.

The size of the ratio depends partly on the terms. By making his terms more and more attractive, *A* can raise *B*'s inducement to agree and eventually bring about a settlement. Concession is one route to agreement. But there are other things that *A* can do without altering his offer. *A* may try to persuade *B* that the cost of accepting *A*'s terms is less than it seems, thus reducing the denominator of the ratio. Or he may, by bluff or threat, cause *B* to raise his estimate of the cost of disagreement, thus raise the numerator.

---

[1] Hicks recognized this difficulty: "If there is a considerable divergence of opinion between the employer and the Union representatives about the length of time the men will hold out rather than accept a given set of terms, then the Union may refuse to go below a certain level, because its leaders believe that they can induce the employer to consent to it by refusing to take anything less; while the employer may refuse to concede it, because he does not believe the Union can hold out long enough for concession to be worth his while. Under such circumstances, a deadlock is inevitable, and a strike will ensue; but it arises from the divergence of estimates, and from no other cause." *The Theory of Wages* (New York: St. Martin's Press, Inc., 2d ed., 1966), pp. 146–47

[2] Neil W. Chamberlain, *A General Theory of Economic Process* (New York: Harper & Row, Publishers, 1955), pp. 80–82.

This leads to a definition: "Bargaining power can be defined as the capacity to effect an agreement on one's own terms; operationally, one's bargaining power *is* another's inducement to agree. If X and Y are in a contest over the terms of their cooperation, X's bargaining power is represented by Y's inducement to agree . . . while Y's bargaining power is X's inducement to agree . . ." [3] While the two are inversely related, Y's bargaining power tending to be less as X's is greater, the relation is not a simple reciprocal. It is possible, for example, that at some point in a union–management negotiation *both* parties may find themselves with an inducement to agree greater than one. All that is necessary for a settlement, however, is that *one* party find itself in this position.

While Chamberlain's concept is useful, and has been adopted in one form or another by most later writers, it carries us only part of the way. We need to examine the costs of agreement and disagreement in more detail and to look at the tactics that the parties may use to manipulate these magnitudes.

The Bargainers' Utility Functions

It is useful to think of each bargainer as having in mind not a single wage target, but a variety of possible settlements yielding varying degrees of satisfaction. Let us call this the *utility* of the settlement to the negotiator in question. In Figure 3, let the vertical axis measure utility and the horizontal axis various sizes of wage increase. O indicates the existing wage level. Then the utility function of, say, the union negotiators will have a shape such as U_L. Any increase of less than OB would yield negative satisfaction. Increases above OB yield increasing satisfaction up to OL, at which U_L reaches a maximum. Still larger increases, in the range LC, would be acceptable but would yield decreasing satisfaction for reasons to be noted in a moment.

The union negotiator must consider not only the potential benefits of various wage settlements but also the potential costs of attaining them. The costs are mainly strike costs, and are positively related to the size of the wage demand. The larger the increase on which the union insists, the more likely is it that a strike will occur and the longer its probable duration. The cost function, then, will be upward sloping to the right, as indicated by AS. By deducting this potential cost from the potential benefit of each wage increase we derive the *net* utility function U'_L.

Note that U'_L reaches a maximum at an earlier point, L' instead of L. It also becomes negative at an earlier point, C' instead of C. We conclude that, when costs are brought into the picture, the range of

3 Chamberlain, *Economic Process*, p. 81.

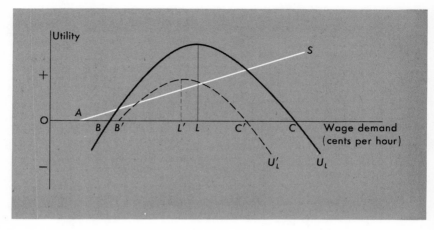

Figure 3
THE UNION NEGOTIATOR'S
UTILITY FUNCTION

outcomes that could benefit the union becomes narrower, and its *preferred* increase (OL') is lower. Moreover, an increase in the probability of a strike or in its estimated cost will increase the slope of AS —the steepness of the *strike gradient,* if you will. Any such shift will move L' still farther to the left.[4] Thus if management can convince the union that probable strike costs are greater than it originally thought, this will reduce the union's (preferred) wage demand.

In Figure 4 we construct a similar picture of the management negotiator's gross and net utility functions. Since the logic is identical with the foregoing, we can abbreviate the discussion. Note that management's cost function slopes upward to the *left—*the *smaller* the increase management is willing to concede, the greater the probability of a strike and the greater its estimated cost. Introduction of costs, then, raises management's preferred settlement from OM to OM'. Moreover, any increase in the strike gradient FS will move M' still farther to the right.

The net utility functions, U'_L and U'_M, are most significant for bargaining. Several features of these functions should be noted. First, they are utility functions for the *negotiators* rather than for the organizations they represent. One can scarcely think of a corporation feeling varying degrees of satisfaction from a wage bargain; but one can do this for the executives in charge of negotiations. Second, each

---

[4] L' is the point at which the rates of increase in benefits and costs are equal, i.e. the slopes of AS and U_L are equal. An increase in the slope AS will shift L' leftward to a point where the slope of U_L is greater by a corresponding amount.

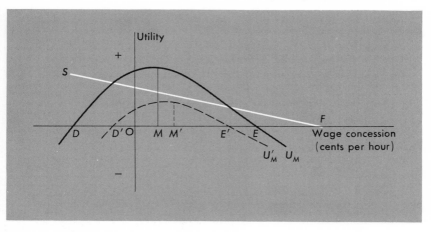

Figure 4
THE MANAGEMENT NEGOTIATOR'S
UTILITY FUNCTION

negotiator's utility function is *unknown* to his opponent. If each party knew at the outset where the other side stood, most of the phenomena observed in collective bargaining would never arise. Third, the utility functions *shift* in the course of negotiations. A major tactical objective in bargaining is to shift the opponent's utility function in a way favorable to oneself.

The points corresponding to the maxima of the net utility functions can be interpreted as "strike points." The union will call a strike rather than accept an increase of less than L'. Management will take a strike rather than concede more than M'.

The Contract Zone Once More

We concentrate now on these strike points rather than on the net utility functions as a whole. Remember that neither party knows the true position of the other. Indeed, to discover this is a major objective in bargaining. So, with a slight change in lettering, let us call the union's real strike point or minimum wage demand L_R, and management's real maximum offer M_R. And let us use L_N and M_N for the nominal or "shadow" positions put forward by the parties.

Several possible relations among these quantities are shown in Figure 5. The union's real demand might be below the employer's real offer, as in Figure 5(a). The range $L_R M_R$ is a *positive contract zone,* any point within which will be acceptable to both parties. This does not mean, however, that a bargain can be struck immediately. The nominal positions of the parties are far apart. It may take much hard bargaining before the true positions are disclosed; and it is even pos-

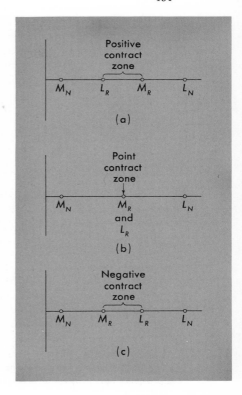

Figure 5

POSSIBLE POSITIONS AT
THE OUTSET OF BARGAINING

sible to have a deadlock and a strike because of the difficulty of "backing down" from the nominal positions. If and when the true positions are revealed, there is still a problem of just where the bargain will be struck within the range $L_R M_R$. We return to this in discussing negotiating tactics.

Second, the true positions of the parties might coincide, as in Figure 5(b). This is what Boulding terms the "bare bargain" case, since agreement is possible at one point only. Again, the existence of a point of (potential) agreement does not ensure that this point will be reached quickly or at all.

Finally, in Figure 5(c), the union's demand is above management's offer. The range $M_R L_R$ is a *negative contract* zone in the sense of a gap between the true positions of the parties. But this does not mean that a breakdown of negotiations is inevitable. Indeed, we know that the great majority of contract negotiations are concluded without a shutdown. One reason is that, in the course of negotiations, the positions M_R and L_R are shifted toward each other by tactical maneuvers of the parties.

With this framework in hand, we can give more operational content to the concept of bargaining power. The union's ability to win increases is higher (a) the higher the value of M_R at the outset of negotiations, and (b) the greater the union's ability to shift M_R upward over the course of negotiations.

BARGAINING POWER

AND

NEGOTIATING TACTICS

Determinants of Bargaining Power

"Bargaining power" may seem to imply personal forcefulness, shrewdness, or tactical skill. So we should emphasize that bargaining power depends mainly on objective circumstances, economic and organizational. Such famous negotiators as ex-President John L. Lewis of the Mine Workers and ex-President James Hoffa of the Teamsters achieved their results, not mainly by superior poker-playing ability, but because they actually held the necessary cards.

The determinants of bargaining power can be classified into those that affect the estimated benefit of a settlement at various levels; those that affect the estimated cost of continued disagreement; and those that affect negotiators' attitudes toward risk.

Look first at benefits. The union negotiator's prime concern is with stability of his organization and security of his own position within it. He must win a settlement that the members will vote to accept; but beyond that point the benefit from additional gains declines. If a union is united, well disciplined, ready to follow its leaders' advice, this strengthens the credibility of the union negotiator. But if the union is too well disciplined, this may increase the employer's bargaining power by allowing the union negotiator to accept a low settlement. An extreme example is the "sweetheart contract," in which union officials trade economic concessions for employer support, forming a union–management alliance in which the members' interests are secondary. Up to a point, dissidence and political rivalry within a union may increase its bargaining power by raising the union negotiator's demands.

Economic factors also influence the union negotiator's estimate of benefits. Particularly important is elasticity of demand for the type of labor in question. If a 10 percent wage increase will reduce employment by only 1 percent, it will be more attractive than if the prospective drop in employment were 5 percent.

The management negotiator's estimate of benefits will depend mainly on economic circumstances, and especially on how large a wage increase is judged necessary in terms of labor recruitment and employee morale. If the company is catching up from an abnormally low wage level, or if its demand for labor is rising rapidly, or if aggregate demand for labor is unusually high, then M_R will lie farther to the right than otherwise and the union's bargaining power will be greater. Opposite conditions will reduce union power.

These comments are intended merely to suggest that union and management policies are shaped by objective circumstances, which are largely economic in character. A fuller discussion of policies on both sides must be deferred to Chapter 22.

The costs of a shutdown are a key factor in the power relation between the parties. In part, these costs depend on the nature of the product and the industry. If the company is producing a service or a perishable commodity, sales lost during a strike can never be regained. In an industry that produces a durable good and that normally operates below capacity, such as coal mining, what is not produced during the strike will be produced later on. But if potential imports are important, as in steel or automobiles, a shutdown may mean a loss of sales to foreign producers; and if U.S. customers find the foreign goods acceptable, this loss can become permanent. In the construction industry, builders normally contract to complete a building by a certain date, with a substantial penalty charge for each day beyond this. A strike called close to the completion date thus becomes very expensive.

Apart from these intrinsic industry characteristics, each party may maneuver to reduce strike costs to itself and raise costs to its opponent. The United Automobile Workers prefers that a strike, where one eventuates, be confined to one of the auto companies. This reduces the cost to the union, since most of its members continue to work and pay dues while only a minority are drawing strike benefits. And it increases the cost to the company, since if Ford alone is shut down many customers will switch to Chrysler or General Motors.

In some cases this tactic has led employers to band together and insist on industry-wide bargaining. In other cases companies have established a system of "strike insurance." The airline companies, whose strike hazards are increased by the multiplicity of unions with which they bargain, have a mutual assistance pact dating from 1958. A company that is shut down by strike is entitled to receive 25 percent of its "normal air transport operating expense" for the duration of the strike. The method of calculating benefits, and of assessing the cost against other airlines, is specified in great detail.[5] Transfers under the program have been substantial, totaling about $30 million in the years 1960 to 1965. In 1967 the five major tire producers formed a

[5] For the detailed provisions, see Vernon M. Briggs, Jr., "The Mutual Aid Pact of the Airline Industry," *Industrial and Labor Relations Review*, October, 1965, pp. 3–20.

similar agreement, details of which have not been made public, and used it to sustain a two-month strike against three of the companies. The American Newspaper Publishers' Association provides strike insurance for a specified premium. An annual premium of $50,000, for example, buys strike benefits of $20,000 per day of strike. The association of American railroads has a similar scheme operated through Lloyd's of London.[6]

An interesting power tactic developed by the Teamsters' Union is the "open-ended grievance procedure." Unlike the usual grievance procedure terminating in arbitration, Teamsters' contracts provide that any grievance that cannot be adjusted by discussion between the parties may become a subject of strike action. This increases the union's leverage in contract negotiations. An employer who does not accede readily to union demands may be informed none too gently that he is likely to have an unusual number of grievances in the year ahead. The union's ability to cut off the flow of freight from other unionized companies is also a powerful bargaining weapon.

A shutdown brings losses to workers and the union as well as to the employer. Striking members are usually excused from dues payments and entitled to draw strike benefits, so that a long strike drains the union treasury. On this score, union bargaining power fluctuates over time. A union that has just been through an expensive strike has reduced bargaining power because the treasury is low and the memory of lost paychecks is fresh in the members' minds. As time passes, the union's ability to strike recovers and its bargaining power rises.

The prospective losses are usually serious enough to serve as a substantial deterrent to both sides. But how can one estimate the probability that insisting on a certain position will actually lead to a strike? It is here that uncertainty becomes critical. If the union negotiator knew the management negotiator's utility function, he would know that up to some point the probability of a strike is zero, and that above some point a strike is a certainty. But the union negotiator does not know where these points are. So he will estimate the probability of a strike at something between zero and one, rising toward the upper limit as the wage demand becomes larger.

In an uncertain situation, attitudes toward risk influence the outcome. A cautious bargainer may settle for less than he could have gotten. A negotiator who enjoys taking chances may try to see just how far he can go, sometimes overstepping the mark. Instances of both sorts can be found in the history of collective bargaining. This determinant, unlike those discussed previously, depends partly on the personalities of the negotiators. Increasing experience, however, is

---

[6] John S. Hirsch, Jr., "Strike Insurance and Collective Bargaining," *Industrial and Labor Relations Review*, April, 1969, pp. 399–415.

likely to moderate extremes of behavior. Negotiators who persist in being too cautious or too reckless will find themselves eliminated from the game.

The Tactics of Negotiation

How does the union (or management) negotiator endeavor to improve the opponent's offer? We noted earlier that the first step in negotiations is usually "the big demand"—deliberate overstatement by the union of how much it wants, deliberate understatement by management of how much it will concede. One reason for this is the process by which demands are formulated. On the union side, every member is entitled to put forward proposals. The list of proposals is bound to be long and some of them are bound to be impracticable. Rather than take responsibility for weeding out the list and convincing the members that certain things are unfeasible, union officials find it politic to shift this unpleasant task to the employer. They put as many of the members' demands as possible into their initial program, knowing full well that many of them will be shot down by management, or traded off in the course of negotiations.

A long and ambitious list of demands has other advantages. It conceals one's true demands and "keeps the other fellow guessing," which is an important element in bargaining strategy. It provides ample room for negotiation and maneuver, for trading elimination of some items against concessions on others. It serves as protection against a marked change in economic conditions during the course of negotiations. Some negotiations go on for months, during which prosperity may change to recession or vice versa. If one's initial demand turns out to be less than would be feasible several months later, one is bound to be criticized for ineptitude or worse. Finally, some demands are put in with no expectation of immediate gain, but with a view to a genuine push on the matter in subsequent years. The Automobile Workers and Steelworkers unions began talking about a "guaranteed" annual wage in the mid forties, and were met with complete and outraged opposition by employers. In 1955, this demand finally bore fruit in both industries in the form of "supplementary unemployment benefit" programs. Pensions, health and welfare funds, and numerous other union proposals have had a similar history.

Presentation of long and "impossible" lists of initial demands, then, should not be taken as an indication of greed or unreasonableness on either side. It is the normal opening gambit in the chess game.

While initial demands are expected to be large, they must not be so large as to lose credibility. If the union's minimum demand is twenty cents an hour, it may be good strategy to ask for forty cents. But to ask for a dollar an hour would not be taken seriously and would be equivalent to saying nothing. Similarly, in a period of rising prices and profits such as from 1966 to 1969, a company insistence on no wage increase would not be credible and could arouse anger rather than amusement.

While the big demand is usual, it is not invariable. In rare cases management states its maximum offer at the outset and adheres to it firmly thereafter. This technique is often termed "boulwarism," after a former vice-president of the General Electric Company, who was one of its early exponents. In this case, M_R and M_N are identical. If the union's (true) demand is above M_R, it must do all the adjusting required for a settlement. If the union is unable or unwilling to adjust, management will take a strike rather than yield.

This tactic is resented by union leaders, not because it necessarily leads to smaller wage increases, but because it is a refusal to play the bargaining game and to allow the union to take any credit for the settlement. Management is saying to its employees, "We are prepared to make a fair adjustment in wages for the year ahead. We will not give a penny more because of the presence of a union. So what is the union really doing for you?" The probable result is increased antagonism between union and management officials, and more frequent breakdown of negotiations. Union resistance to this tactic has contributed to several work stoppages at General Electric, including a three-month strike in the winter of 1969–70.

Starting from the initial positions, each negotiator is trying to accomplish certain things. The union negotiator is interested in: (a) representing (or in some measure misrepresenting) his own preferences; (b) trying to discover management's preferences; (c) trying to shift management's preferences; and in some cases (d) attempting to alter the preferences of third parties such as the general public, or executive and legislative officials. The management negotiator is trying to accomplish the same things vis-à-vis the union.

The available tactics are persuasion and coercion. The union may try to persuade management that a certain wage increase will be more beneficial than management thinks—because labor productivity will rise along with wages, because the economic outlook is brighter than management expects, and so on. Management may argue that the benefit of a large increase is *less* than the union thinks, because it would reduce employment or even force the company out of business.

Such arguments amount to saying to the other party, "You don't really know your own interests." This is not likely to be very palatable. But persuasion should not be dismissed as entirely ineffective. It may convey factual information that the other party did not have at the outset, possibly leading to a shift of preferences. The rationalizations set forth by one side may also provide the other with a ladder by which to climb down gracefully from a position that no longer seems defensible.

The object of coercive tactics is to change the other party's estimate of the costs of disagreement. The union negotiator implies that a strike will result unless certain minimum terms are met. The management negotiator may state that the company will have to shut down or move to another location if the increase exceeds some maximum.

Following Carl Stevens,[7] we may distinguish between "bluff" and "notbluff." Notbluff consists in announcing what you intend to do ("we will strike at anything less than ten cents an hour"), with the intention of actually doing it if the contingency develops. The difficulty is that even though your intention is firm, the other party may not believe it. So one can have the following sequence of events: the union announces a certain demand. The employer, if he believed the strike threat, would be willing to concede rather than take a strike. But he does not believe it, and refuses to concede. The result is a "strike that nobody wants."

Bluff consists in announcing a certain course of action even though you do *not* intend to follow it if the contingency arises. Again, there is a problem of credibility. To be effective the bluff must be believed. If the bluff is called and the bluffer backs down, this will reduce his credibility in future negotiations.

One possible method of increasing credibility is *commitment*. Thomas Schelling has argued [8] that a negotiator can strengthen his bargaining position by committing himself in such a way that he cannot later retreat without disastrous consequences. The union negotiator can whip up membership sentiment behind certain minimum demands, take a strike vote, mobilize a strike fund, and make other visible and dramatic strike preparations. The management negotiator may state that the board of directors will not go beyond a certain limit, thus laying their credibility on the line along with his own.

This is a dangerous tactic, because events can get out of hand. What started out as a tentative commitment on one or both sides may harden into a firm commitment, leading to a strike that was not necessarily in the cards at the outset. It is a little like playing a game of "chicken" with the steering wheel locked in position.

Tactical maneuvering on both sides over a period of weeks usually leads to concessions that bring the stated positions of the parties closer to their true positions and also bring the true positions closer together. Making concessions is delicate, since it may be interpreted as weakness, and so concessions are usually signaled indirectly. One side may simply remain silent about a point on which it has been insisting; or it may suggest that the point be set aside for the time being, implying that eventual agreement will not be too difficult. One

7 See his *Strategy and Collective Bargaining Negotiation* (New York: McGraw-Hill Book Company, 1963).

8 Thomas C. Schelling, "An Essay on Bargaining," *American Economic Review,* June, 1956, pp. 281–306.

party, having made such an implicit concession, may then wait for the other to take reciprocal action, so that negotiations proceed through a series of moves and countermoves.

Eventually the approach of the contract expiration deadline forces a final reexamination of positions. As the probability of a shutdown rises, the costs of shutdown are estimated more carefully and taken more seriously. It is no accident that many contracts are renewed at the eleventh hour after hectic all-night bargaining sessions. The fact that it *is* the eleventh hour moves the parties toward a possible agreement.

There are several possible cases:

1. The final positions of the parties may still fail to overlap, even after shutdown costs have been fully weighed. In this case the parties will continue to go through the motions until the deadline, but a strike is inevitable.

2. The final positions may have shifted sufficiently so that they coincide. Here agreement appears easy. Remember, however, that neither party knows the true position of the other. The stated positions are probably still some distance apart. Someone must take the first step toward a solution; and this step, like any concession, is subject to misinterpretation.

Consider the following sequence: the company states it will give no more than ten cents but is actually willing to give fifteen rather than face a shutdown. The union is still asking for twenty cents but is willing to take fifteen. As the deadline nears, the union reduces its nominal demand to the true figure of fifteen cents. The management negotiator takes this as indicating that "the union is caving in," and reduces his maximum offer to twelve cents. The union does not cave in, and a strike follows.

This problem, which Stevens terms "coming clean without prejudice," is quite difficult. A strike remains a possibility until settlement has been reached; and if there is a strike, bargaining will continue from the final announced positions of the parties. This may lead one or both parties, even at the eleventh hour, to announce positions somewhat more favorable to themselves than the true positions. Thus overt agreement may not be reached despite the existence of covert agreement.

3. The final positions of the parties may overlap, yielding what we termed earlier a positive contract zone. The union would take ten cents, but the employer would concede fifteen; so any settlement between these figures is feasible. What will determine the actual figure? There are various possibilities. One party, under the pressure of the strike deadline, may reveal its true position, in which case the bargain will be struck at that level. Here the party that moves first loses. Perhaps more commonly, the parties will cast around for precedents that might justify a settlement at some intermediate level. Under "pattern bar-

gaining," the level already accepted by comparable companies may point the way toward compromise. The standard "wage criteria" employed in collective bargaining may also suggest a certain figure as plausible.

These wage criteria deserve brief comment. The criteria most commonly urged in negotiations are: (1) the wage currently paid by other employers for the same type of labor; (2) wage increases in the recent past by other employers of the same type of labor; (3) cost-of-living increases since the date of the last wage increase; (4) the average rate of increase in labor productivity and real wages in the economy; and (5) the recent and prospective movement of labor productivity, unit labor cost, prices, and profits in the company for which the bargain is being made—"ability to pay."

These criteria are often derided on several grounds: that each yields a different figure, so that they do not point to a unique solution; that some of them are not proper criteria; that the union and management positions are in fact shaped by other considerations; and that the supposed criteria are used merely to "dress up" or rationalize these positions.

This view, however, is too extreme. The wage criteria do serve several useful functions: (1) Some of them—current wage levels of other employers competing for the same grade of labor, cost-of-living changes, the average movement of wages in the economy—are valid criteria, both in the sense that they would be operative in a nonunion economy and in the sense of having significant influence on union and management positions; (2) In a bargaining setting, the criteria chosen and the strength with which they are asserted provide useful clues to the true positions of the parties; (3) The arguments developed in support of one or another criterion may provide a line of retreat for a party that wishes to make concessions. Here the fact that different criteria point in different directions and can be used to justify a range of possible settlements is a positive benefit. (4) Finally, they can rationalize an eventual compromise figure within a positive contract zone. If different criteria yield increases varying from zero to twenty-five cents an hour, a negotiator who agrees to twelve cents can claim some objective justification.

STRIKES,
STRIKE COSTS,
AND STRIKE PREVENTION

It has been said that war is a continuation of diplomacy by other methods. Similarly, the strike is a continuation of bargaining by other methods. Why do strikes happen? How much harm do they do? Under what circumstances, if any, should unions and managements be prohibited from "slugging it out"? What methods might be developed for settling disputes without a stoppage of production?

Why Strikes Occur

In an average year of the 1960s, about 1¾ million workers were involved in strikes. This was about 10 percent of union members, and 3 percent of all employed workers. Strike activity was below average from 1960 to 1965, but rose substantially during the inflationary years from 1966 to 1969. The average length of strikes was about three weeks. The amount of time lost through strikes, as a proportion of total working time in the economy, varied from about 0.12 percent in the years 1961 to 1963 to 0.25 percent in 1967 and 1968.[9] How far this represents an actual loss in output will be considered in a later section.

Why did these strikes occur? It is customary to classify strikes according to the leading issue in a particular dispute—so many strikes over wages, so many over working conditions, and so on. This is not a meaningful classification. The issues involved in a dispute are always interrelated, and to single out one as the primary issue is an arbitrary procedure. Moreover, the important thing is not what the issue was, but why the parties were unable to reach agreement on it. In order to discover the "causes" of strikes, one must discover the kinds of circumstances in which agreement between the parties becomes impossible.

Drawing on our previous analysis, we can distinguish between *avoidable* and *unavoidable* strikes. An avoidable strike is one in which the true positions of the parties overlap, so that an omniscient observer could prescribe a solution acceptable to both. An unavoidable strike is one in which the final positions of the parties fail to overlap, so that each prefers a shutdown to further concessions.

In the last section we noted several reasons why a potentially avoidable strike may nevertheless not be avoided. First, inexperienced or clumsy negotiators may stake out firm positions from which it is later difficult to retreat, may misread the signals from the other side, may be unable to surmount the tactical difficulties of graceful concession, and so on. Second, even the tactics of experienced negotiators may misfire on occasion. The notbluff that is not believed can lead to a strike that no one wants. So can excessive commitment to a threatened course of action, which may build up an equally firm commitment on the other side. Third, there is the tactical difficulty of "coming clean" about one's true position in the crucial final stages of

[9] *Monthly Labor Review,* May, 1969, p. 123.

negotiation. This can lead to an impasse even when there is a positive contract zone.

Unavoidable strikes, where the contract zone is still negative when the deadline arrives, may also occur for several reasons. First, the basic issue may be not the terms of the new contract, but the framework of bargaining itself. We noted earlier that the size of the bargaining unit, the degree of cooperation among employers and unions, and the timing of contract expiration dates can influence the balance of power between the parties. One party may decide that the time has come to force a change in the bargaining framework that will improve its bargaining position in future years. Such a power struggle is less easily compromised than a dispute over terms of employment.

An example is the 114-day strike of the Printers' Union against the New York newspapers in 1962 and 1963. Prior to this time the employers' contract with the Newspaper Guild had expired five weeks before that with the printers and other pressroom crafts. The newspapers first negotiated new wage terms with the guild, which then became the pattern for other employee groups. The printers felt that this deprived them of any independent negotiating power. They demanded, and eventually won, a common contract expiration date that enabled them to enter negotiations on an even footing.

Second, one party may attach positive value to a strike. An employer may think that a prolonged strike will break the union and free him from the necessity of collective bargaining. A union leader may consider an occasional strike desirable to maintain the members' morale and to impress the employer with the union's willingness to fight. Unused weapons become rusty. A union that never strikes may lose its ability to make the strike threat credible and may have to accept unfavorable settlements in consequence.

Third, we have assumed that all terms of the contract can be reduced to a dollar equivalent, which can be compromised by small stages. But this is not always true. It is hard for the employer to concede "half a union shop." A demand that does not have a clear dollar dimension, that must be granted in full or denied in full, and that is considered a matter of principle by one or both sides, can readily lead to an impasse.

Fourth, the negotiators are delegates of their respective organizations. Even where their own judgment would lead them to compromise, they may be prevented from doing so by institutional constraints. An absentee corporation president or board of directors may order a plant manager to take a position that the latter knows will lead to a strike. A union leader may privately consider the union's demands untenable; but to retreat might jeopardize his own position and split the union. A rival leader, for example, may have convinced the bulk of the membership that the demands are attainable. If the negotiator settles for less, he will be accused of a "sellout," the settlement will be voted down by the membership, and a strike will result in any event.

Finally, a strike may result from misjudgment of the costs of disagreement. Even where compromise is possible, one side may be unwilling to compromise because it has a low opinion of the other's strength and thinks it can win its point easily and quickly. The employer may underestimate the membership, solidarity, and financial strength of the union; the union may underestimate the determination of the employer to resist further concessions. One frequently finds an employer who, by conceding wage increases and restrictive working rules year after year, has got his production costs seriously out of line with those of competing companies. He may finally decide to hold the line and prevent further cost increases. Union leaders, however, have got in the habit of securing easy concessions from him and will not take him seriously. When they find out too late that he is serious, they are confronted with a strike.

To discover which of these situations was responsible for a particular strike requires careful analysis of the circumstances. The union normally makes the first overt move, and the public therefore tends to regard it as the aggressor. The employer can cause a strike by doing nothing; the union has to take the positive step of calling out the workers. But all one can conclude from the fact of a strike is that there was a failure to reach agreement. The reasons for the failure can be learned from an "inside" knowledge of the people and issues involved.

The Role of Mediation

Most of the strongly unionized countries, including the United States, maintain staffs of experienced, full-time neutrals, usually called "mediators" or "conciliators," to assist in resolving industrial disputes. Some countries require that mediators be given a chance to settle a dispute before strike action is lawful. In the United States, except for the railroad and airline industries and for the "emergency dispute" provisions of the Taft–Hartley Act and some state acts, use of mediators is entirely voluntary. But when the Federal Mediation and Conciliation Service or a state mediation body proffers its services, the offer is rarely refused.

The work of mediation is difficult to describe, since it is probable that no two mediators operate in the same way. One cannot find anywhere a clear definition of the job, and some experienced mediators deny that such a definition is possible. The mediator has no authority. He can intervene only if both parties are willing, and any settlement to which he may contribute must be acceptable to both parties. He is neutral in the sense of not desiring an outcome favorable to one party or the other. His activities, however, are bound to influence the outcome; and he does have a positive interest in peace, in getting a settlement. How far he can legitimately go in furthering this interest raises tactical and even ethical questions.

The mediator may come in at an early stage of negotiations, at the critical eleventh-hour stage, or after a strike has begun. Whenever he enters, he tends to become the main communication channel between the parties. A common technique is to separate the parties physically, while the mediator carries information and proposals back and forth between them.

The possible functions of the mediator can be analyzed in terms of our earlier discussion of negotiating tactics. First, he may be able to convey additional information. He may try to persuade the parties that they have misestimated the benefits of agreement or the costs of disagreement. Even this modest function raises tactical issues. Is the mediator's main responsibility to convey accurate information, or to bring the parties to a settlement (which might be aided by some degree of misinformation)?

Another common function is to "save face" for one or both parties when they have gotten locked into a position from which there seems no graceful retreat. As Stevens points out, ". . . the mediator may supply a party with arguments which the party may in turn use to rationalize a position (or retreat from a position) vis-à-vis his own constituents . . . the mere fact of a mediator's entrance into a dispute provides the parties with a means of rationalizing retreats from previously held positions, particularly if the mediator can be made to appear to take a part of the 'responsibility' for any settlement." [10]

The mediator may help in a situation where a "notbluff" by A, which is not believed by B, creates the possibility of an unwanted strike. Each party is more likely to believe the mediator than to believe the opposing party. The mediator may be able to convince B that the notbluff is genuine, thus averting the strike danger.

The mediator's function in the event of a bluff is less clear. Consider this situation: A is bluffing. B, if he believed the bluff, would make concessions sufficient to settle the dispute. If the mediator can convince B that A is *not* bluffing, this will contribute to a settlement. What is more important for the mediator: to be truthful or effective? Another possibility, of course, would be for the mediator to convince A that his bluff is not believed and that he should abandon it.

As the strike deadline approaches, it becomes increasingly important that each side reveal its true position; but this raises the tactical difficulty of "coming clean without prejudice." Each side fears that,

[10] *Strategy and Negotiation,* p. 130.

if it reveals that it is willing to compromise, this will be interpreted as weakness and will cause the other side to stiffen its position. They may be willing, however, to reveal their true positions to the mediator. When the mediator discovers that the potential compromises coincide or overlap, he may call the parties to a joint session and propose a settlement that each has privately indicated it will accept.

Where positions overlap and there is a positive contract zone, the question arises of where the bargain should be struck within this zone. In this situation the mediator can help to focus the attention of the parties on one solution as most plausible, incidentally providing a rationalization for it and taking a measure of responsibility. The union negotiator can now go back to his members and say, "We were holding out fine, but that unmentionable mediator made us give in."

Finally, an ingenious mediator can sometimes think of compromise proposals that have not occurred to either of the parties. This is particularly useful in demands that have become "matters of principle." In the early days of World War II top union officials, in return for a no-strike pledge during the war, demanded the union shop as a standard contract clause. Employers also pledged themselves to keep the peace, but were strongly against the union shop demand. There appeared to be a deadlock. After much discussion the public members of the National Defense Mediation Board came up with an ingenious compromise—the "maintenance of membership clause"—which both sides were willing to accept. This provided that no one must become a member of the union, but that those who chose to do so must thereafter retain their membership for the duration of the contract in question.

The Federal Mediation and Conciliation Service and the state services are able to adjust the great majority of the disputes in which they intervene without a stoppage of production. Many of these disputes would probably have been settled in any event, but some would not, and there is little doubt that the benefits from mediation work are worth its cost. An important recent development is a tendency for the Secretary of Labor, who in recent administrations has been an experienced neutral drawn from academic life, to undertake mediation of major disputes. The status as well as the personal skills of these cabinet members has helped to settle some disputes in which lower-level intervention would have been ineffective.

Frequency of Strikes

The number of strikes fluctuates with the movements of the business cycle. Strikes fall off during depression and the percentage of strikes won by the union also declines. Rees concludes from this that union strategy rather than company strategy dominates the scene and that strikes behave as one might expect on economic grounds—they are more frequent when the chances of success are high, and vice versa.[11] If employers could choose when to have strikes, the number would presumably rise during depression when employers are relatively strong.

There are also marked differences in the strike-proneness of individual industries. Kerr and Siegel, on the basis of strike statistics from eleven countries for varying periods of time between 1919 and 1950, found a consistently high propensity to strike in mining, shipping, longshoring, lumber, and textiles. The lowest strike propensities were found in clothing, public utilities, hotel and restaurant service, trade, railroad transportation, and agriculture.[12] They attribute the high incidence of strikes in the first group of industries to:

1. An isolated position of the worker in society. Workers in these industries typically form an "isolated mass," living apart from other people in company towns, at sea, in the woods, and so on. All do the same work, have the same grievances, and mingle only with each other. There is little or no opportunity to rise to higher occupational levels. The employer is often landlord and governor as well. Under these circumstances, all grievances focus on the (usually absentee) employer. The union becomes a kind of working-class party or even a subgovernment. "The strike for this isolated mass is a kind of colonial revolt against far-removed authority, an outlet for accumulated tensions, and a substitute for occupational and social mobility."

Workers in the low-strike industries are in an opposite situation in these respects and are integrated successfully into the larger community.

2. A subsidiary but important factor is the nature of the work and the workers. "If the job is physically difficult and unpleasant, unskilled or semiskilled, and casual or seasonal, and fosters an independent spirit (as in the logger in the woods), it will draw tough, inconstant, combative, and virile workers, and they will be inclined to strike."

Is there any tendency for strike activity to increase or decrease in the course of time? Are some countries more strike prone than others? These questions have been investigated by Ross and Hartman,[13] and some of their results are summarized in Table 1. Looking at the period since World War II, one notes sizable differences in the level

---

[11] Albert Rees, "Industrial Conflict and Business Fluctuations," in A. Kornhauser, P. Dubin, and A. M. Ross, eds., *Industrial Conflict* (New York: McGraw-Hill Book Company, 1954), chap. 15.

[12] Clark Kerr and Abraham Siegel, "The Interindustry Propensity to Strike—an International Comparison," *Industrial Conflict*, chap. 14.

[13] Arthur M. Ross and Paul J. Hartman, *Changing Patterns of Industrial Conflict* (New York: John Wiley & Sons, Inc., 1960).

Table 1

MEASURES OF STRIKE ACTIVITY IN SELECTED COUNTRIES

	PERCENT OF UNION MEMBERS INVOLVED IN STRIKES (ANNUAL AVERAGE)		DAYS OF WORK LOST THROUGH STRIKES PER UNION MEMBER (ANNUAL AVERAGE)	
	1900–29	*1948–56*	*1900–29*	*1948–56*
DENMARK	6.3	1.4	2.0	0.2
NETHERLANDS	7.0	1.3	2.1	0.1
UNITED KINGDOM	16.1	5.9	4.3	0.2
GERMANY	14.2	2.6	2.2	0.2
NORWAY	27.0	1.2	9.4	0.2
SWEDEN	22.7	0.3	8.9	0.1
FRANCE	27.1	62.4	4.2	1.7
ITALY	—	35.2	—	0.9
JAPAN	30.3	21.5	—	1.1
INDIA	—	37.2	—	3.2
UNITED STATES	33.2	15.4	—	2.4
CANADA	14.7	6.3	4.4	1.3
AUSTRALIA	18.2	25.2	2.6	0.9
FINLAND	24.5	13.9	8.1	5.8
SOUTH AFRICA	24.4	1.4	3.2	0.1

of strike activity. Britain, Germany, and the Scandinavian countries have had very low strike rates. This is not an indication of union weakness, but rather the reverse. As Ross and Hartman point out:

> The distinction between the ability to strike and the need to strike must be strongly emphasized. We are not suggesting that Swedish or Norwegian unions, for example, are unable to strike or that they have disowned the principle of the strike. On the contrary, resort to strikes may be least necessary where threats are most effective.[14]

Italy, France, and India, where unions are relatively weak, have had high proportions of union members involved in strikes. But in some countries that have many strikes (France, Italy, Australia), the average strike lasts only two to three days, so that time lost is not great. Canada and the United States have had moderately high rates of strike activity in the postwar period, the American rate being typically about double the Canadian one.

In most countries the level of strike activity today is well below the level in earlier decades; and in some of the most strongly unionized countries resort to strikes is approaching the vanishing point. Ross and Hartman suggest three main reasons for this "withering away of the strike":

> First, employers have developed more sophisticated policies and more effective organizations. Second, the state has become more prominent as an employer of labor, economic planner, provider of benefits, and

14 *Patterns of Conflict,* p. 19.

supervisor of industrial relations. Third, in many countries (although not in the United States), the labor movement has been forsaking the use of the strike in favor of broad political endeavors.[15]

Dunlop has suggested several additional factors.[16] In some industries—oil refining, chemical plants, telephone communication, electric utilities—technical progress has made it increasingly possible for supervisors and technicians to keep the plant in operation during a strike. This obviously reduces the usefulness of the strike weapon. In other industries—rail and bus transportation, maritime transport, steel, automobiles—strikes have led customers to shift to other sources of supply, including imports. This increases the cost of a stoppage to both parties, which discourages its use. In other newly unionized areas, such as atomic energy, military procurement and construction, public-school teaching, and public employment generally, strikes are either illegal or severely frowned on by public opinion.

The Cost of Strikes

Here one must distinguish between *private* and *social* cost, between cost to the parties and cost to the national economy. The striking workers lose some wages and the company loses some profit. These are losses that the parties consider it worthwhile to bear rather than settle on adverse terms. The loss to the economy consists in a reduced output of goods and services available for consumption or investment.

A strike may not involve any loss in national output. In a seasonal industry, a strike may simply change the location of the "slack season." A strike in men's clothing factories early in the spring season means only that the factories will have to work longer at the end of the season to make up for lost time. In this case there is not even a loss of income to the parties, merely a postponement of income to a later date.

The impact of strikes is mitigated also by the fact that most industries in most years operate below full capacity. This is true, for example, of the basic steel industry. Every three years when the steel contract expires, raising the possibility of a strike, users of steel stock up heavily in advance and the industry works full blast for a while to meet these orders. If a strike actually develops, steel buyers can "sit it out" for two or three months by drawing on inventories. After the end of the strike, the mills may again work full blast for a time to restore inventories throughout the industry. But the main effect is a shift in the *timing* of production rather than the *amount* of production.

---

[15] *Patterns of Conflict,* p. 42.

[16] John T. Dunlop, "The Function of the Strike," in John T. Dunlop and Neil W. Chamberlain, eds., *Frontiers of Collective Bargaining* (New York: Harper & Row, Publishers, 1967).

A similar shift occurs when a union strikes selectively against part of an industry. If Ford is shut down, Chrysler and General Motors will sell more cars. Ford and its workers have less income, but other companies and their workers have more income. This assumes, of course, that the other companies have unused capacity and can absorb the additional business. If all plants are operating at full capacity throughout the year, a strike anywhere in the industry will reduce national output.

The main output losses occur in two situations. First, in industries producing services for immediate consumption, production lost today is lost forever. If I do not buy a newspaper or a subway ride today, I am not going to buy two tomorrow to catch up. The seriousness of such losses depends on the kind of service in question. A strike of radio announcers would not affect most people's lives materially. A strike of hospital attendants, public-school teachers, garbage collectors, or truckers delivering perishable food to market is a more serious matter. In some cases, availability of close substitutes may mitigate the impact on consumption.

Second, there are industries, such as electric power production and rail transportation, whose continuous operation is essential to steady production in other industries. A strike in such an industry may, by crippling production in many other industries, cause a disproportionate drop in national output. Strikes in merchant shipping and longshoring can have a serious effect on countries that depend heavily on foreign trade.[17]

The fact that some strikes are serious but most strikes are not is reflected in our national policy. As a general rule, government does not intervene in strike situations beyond offering mediation services. At the same time there has been an effort to develop special procedures for "emergency disputes," designed to avert strikes that cause serious public inconveniences. The methods used, and their effectiveness, are examined in Chapter 19.

Discussion Questions

1. What is meant by the statement that, under collective bargaining, a company's wage level becomes indeterminate?
2. Explain the merits and limitations of J. R. Hicks' approach to wage bargaining.

---

[17] Donald E. Cullen, *National Emergency Strikes* (Ithaca: New York State School of Industrial and Labor Relations, 1968). Chap. 2 surveys research studies that have tried to measure the losses caused by specific strikes.

3. Explain the meaning, and outline the main determinants, of bargaining power.
4. Construct a bargaining situation all elements of which would contribute to maximum bargaining power for the union negotiator.
5. Can the tactical skill of a negotiator appreciably influence the outcome of bargaining? Explain.
6. Why may it be impossible to reach a settlement even when the eleventh-hour positions of the parties coincide or overlap?
7. What is an "unavoidable" strike? What are the main reasons for such a situation?
8. "A mediator cannot really be neutral. His main interest and responsibility is to achieve a settlement. Any tactics that contribute to this end are justified." Discuss.
9. Why does the United States have a higher level of strike activity than Britain, Germany, or the Scandinavian countries?
10. Under what circumstances will a strike reduce national output?

Reading Suggestions

The best modern statements of bargaining theory as applied to union–management negotiations are probably Pen, J., *The Wage Rate Under Collective Bargaining.* Cambridge: Harvard University Press, 1959; and Stevens, Carl M., *Strategy and Collective Bargaining Negotiation.* New York: McGraw-Hill Book Company, 1963. See also Ashenfelter, Orley, and George E. Johnson, "Bargaining Theory, Trade Unions, and Industrial Strike Activity," *American Economic Review,* March, 1969, p. 35–49. A more general study, with suggestive implications for collective bargaining, is Boulding, Kenneth E., *Conflict and Defense.* New York: Harper & Row, Publishers, 1963. The role of mediation is well analyzed in Stevens, Carl M., "Mediation and the Role of the Neutral," in Dunlop, John T., and Neil W. Chamberlain, eds., *Frontiers of Collective Bargaining.* New York: Harper & Row, Publishers, 1967, pp. 271–90.

For statistical studies of strike activity, see Knowles, K. G. J. C., *Strikes—A Study in Industrial Conflict.* Oxford: Blackwell, 1952; Ross, Arthur M., and Paul T. Hartmann, *Changing Patterns of Industrial Conflict.* New York: John Wiley & Sons, Inc., 1960; and Oxnam, D. W., "The Incidence of Studies in Australia," in Isaac, J. E., and G. W. Ford, eds., *Australian Labor Relations Readings* (Melbourne: Sun Books, 1966), which contains international comparisons as well as Australian data.

PUBLIC POLICY: DEVELOPMENT AND ADMINISTRATION

17

Unionism everywhere operates in an environment of legal and political controls. Through statute, through administrative regulation, and through judicial decision, the larger community enforces its will in "public policy"—a large and amorphous body of rules, yet a potent force.

Around the world there are quite different types of public policy towards unionism. At one end of the spectrum unions exist and operate free of government controls, as private bodies. At the other end unions are brought into a close relationship with government agencies, so that economic decisions on wages and related matters are carried out under direct government supervision. The United States is somewhere in the mid-range. Historically, American public policy has moved from a position of complete freedom of action and absence of direct government controls to one of increasingly detailed regulation of union activities.

As the American continent was settled and developed, legal institutions inherited from the English system altered as they adjusted to the problems of governing on a continental scale. Unions learned how to develop and exercise political power. They engaged in a continuing conflict with employers on the political level no less than in collective bargaining. Each side adopted in turn the weapons and tactics of the other. The prize was control over the rules of the game, for these rules affected the growth, power and operation of organized labor. The relative fortunes of each side fluctuated, and the balance of power tilted with changes in the external environment.

Elements of consistency can be identified amid the zigzags of policy. These include, first, a consistent assertion of the public interest; the two sides could not be left completely free to fight out their differences. Second, American policy has implied a basic approval of conflict, as a healthy and creative force, which should be curbed only as it becomes disruptive. Third, there appears a consistent narrowing of the area of conflict. Fourth, there is a consistent invocation of the principle of equality of treatment.

Major shifts in labor policy are marked by acts of Congress and the state legislatures. The legislature is the proper body for defining social policy; but under the American Constitution the judicial and executive branches of government have elements of independent authority. American courts, through judicial review, have a considerable power of veto. The courts say that they merely interpret the law and the Constitution; but as one student of labor law has said, this only means that they are reserving the freedom to change their minds. Landmarks of policy change thus appear in Supreme Court decisions. The tremendous power of the American president, and to a lesser extent of the state governors, means that the executive branch also has a powerful voice in labor policy. The National Labor Relations Board, the National Mediation Board, and other agencies charged with administering the statute law of industrial relations have elements of independent power, and some of their major decisions stand for a long time.

This fragmentation of power and rivalry between separate units of government, which could happen in few other countries, has made it possible for the contest between labor and management to be shifted from one arena to another, as one side saw some advantage to be gained. Loss of ground at the bargaining table may be regained by an appeal to the government. "Law" becomes a weapon in the struggle for power.[1] The intrusion of government ever deeper into industrial relations has created an increasingly large, complex and often contradictory body of rules.

[1] Archibald Cox, "The Role of Law in Labor Disputes," *Cornell Law Quarterly*, Vol. 39 (1954), 592.

JUDICIAL CONTROL
OF
UNION ACTIVITIES

A review of the turning points in American labor policy begins with a long period of a century or more when the power of the judiciary was unchallenged. Trade unions have been subject to comprehensive government control through the courts from the very beginnings of union organization.

There are two main types of legal rule: statutory rules enacted by the legislature, and common law rules which are unwritten and are based on consistent lines of previous court decisions. The courts have the final word in administering both types of rules. Statutory law is applied first by administrative agencies, such as the National Labor Relations Board, but decisions of the board can be appealed by the losing party to the lower courts and eventually to the Supreme Court. Thus the practical effect of a law is tested in a series of hearings, first administrative and then judicial, and in the end the judges often decide what the statute means.

Common law rules, on the other hand, are rules which have developed solely or primarily through the accumulation of judicial decisions. Instead of interpreting the language of a statute, the court decides a dispute on the basis of a line of precedents, a logical sequence of decisions in previous cases where the court finds elements of similarity. In the absence of statutory law, judicial application of common law principles shaped the growth of unionism for almost a century.

To enforce their decisions the courts have three types of legal remedies. The first of these is criminal prosecution. If it can be shown that union members have broken laws concerning theft, trespass, assault and battery, arson, and other crimes, or even that they have violated local ordinances prohibiting loitering, obstructing traffic, or disturbing the peace they may be subject to fine and imprisonment. The number of workers who have been punished for real or alleged misdemeanors runs into the hundreds of thousands. The second type of remedy is civil suit for damages. If union members cause damage to an employer's property, suit can be brought against the workers and in some circumstances against the union. The third and perhaps most important type of remedy is the injunction. This is a court order restraining the party against whom it is issued from doing specified acts. If the person goes ahead and does these things anyway, he may be ruled in contempt of court and punished by fine or imprisonment. The speedy and powerful character of this procedure has caused it to be widely used in labor cases.

The long period of judicial control was repressive and negative in character. Judges for the most part concluded that unionism was an undesirable activity which, if it could not be prevented altogether, should be held within narrow limits. This view was due partly to the nature of law itself and partly to the personal predilections of the judges. Law is necessarily a conservative force. It exists to protect established rights. The common law of Great Britain, carried over in large part into American practice, gives special weight to rights connected with property ownership. Unionism, however, attacks the rights of the owners of industrial enterprises to manage them as they see fit. It seeks to curb property rights in order to establish new rights of workers in their jobs. The common law also regards freedom of contract and freedom of trade as desirable social objectives. The union, however, exists to restrict competition and establish a quasi-monopolistic position for its members. Unionism thus seemed contrary to the spirit of the common law, and it was easy for judges to find rules and precedents that would repress the activities of organized labor.

The judges' legal training in common law principles was buttressed by their political preferences. They came mainly from the propertied class, mingled more freely with employers than with workers, and tended naturally to sympathize with the interests of property owners. Their political thinking was influenced also by the classical economics, which could find no useful place for joint action by wage earners.

But unionism had developed in response to important economic and social needs. Policies that were merely negative could not continue indefinitely. The spread of industrialization required a reduction of labor disputes and an environment of labor peace rather than violence and unrest. Repressive judicial policies left the underlying economic problems unsolved. As the size of the industrial working class increased, a power base was built up for the emerging labor organizations.

The Doctrine of Criminal Conspiracy

In the early nineteenth century a number of court cases declared union activity of any sort illegal as a criminal conspiracy under the common law, punishable by fine or imprisonment. In other cases it was held that union actions designed to raise wages or reduce hours were lawful, but that other objectives such as the closed shop were unlawful. The basic legality of trade unionism was not settled until the case of *Commonwealth* v. *Hunt,* decided in 1842. In this case, Chief Justice Shaw of Massachusetts held that union activities were not per se unlawful, their legality depending rather on the objectives they sought to attain. Workers who were powerless as individuals could, he said, combine lawfully for mutual assistance. They might increase their control over their own livelihood by bargaining as a group with their employer. He held further that the closed shop was a legitimate union objective and that a strike to obtain it was not illegal. The case was not appealed to the Supreme Court of the United States, perhaps because it was recognized as a policy that would reduce labor violence and thereby benefit the expanding industries of Massachusetts. Labor peace required some show of equal treatment before the law. At any rate, the doctrine of criminal conspiracy disappeared from American labor policy after this decision.

Trade Unions "Lawful for What"?

Unions thus came to be regarded as lawful associations, but the question remained open as to what kinds of activity a labor union could legally pursue and what actions were forbidden to it. To this question the courts applied the common law rule that harm intentionally inflicted on another is actionable unless it can be shown that the harm was justifiable. This idea arose out of business disputes, where the courts developed a line of precedents ruling that pursuit of economic self-interest by normal business methods is sufficient justification for harm done incidentally and without malice to the interests of others.

A strike or boycott clearly harms the employer and frequently other groups and individuals as well. This provides a ground for finding such activity unlawful unless the union can justify it as necessary to promote the economic interests of the workers. A judgment of fact must be made as to what tactics really advance the economic interests of the workers and under what conditions their claims are strong enough to justify the damage inflicted on the employer and on third parties. In the absence of a legislative statement of policy, the courts decided these questions case by case.

During this period the common law of labor relations developed somewhat differently in the different states. The courts of New York, for example, allowed considerably more scope for union activities than did the courts of Massachusetts or Pennsylvania. But in most states legitimate union activity was narrowly confined to peaceable strikes for improved wages, hours, or working conditions. Strikes for the closed shop, sympathetic strikes in aid of workers in related industries or trades, strikes against one employer to compel him to bring pressure on another employer (secondary boycotts), and many other types of activity were held unlawful. Once the objective of a strike had been ruled illegal, even peaceable actions in support of the strike came under the ban. And where the object of the strike was lawful, a court might nevertheless find that the tactics used were unduly coercive or injurious.

In the efforts of employers to seek court protection against strikes and boycotts, the favored weapons were criminal prosecution of union leaders and suits for damages. But in the 1880s a speedier and more effective instrument was developed—the labor injunction, which spread rapidly and continued unchecked until the 1930s.

"Government by Injunction"

The injunction was originally a court order designed to prevent threatened physical damage to property, under circumstances in which later action through regular court processes would be too slow. This device also came from English law.[2] The injunction was presumed to be a temporary restraining action to prevent irreparable damage to tangible property interests. It "froze" the relative position of two antagonists until the dispute could be settled in court. But once applied to *economic* damage, and to *intangible* property, in practice the necessity of later legal action was forestalled. The injunction is one of the speediest of legal remedies. Requiring only the judge's signature and backed by the court's full authority of fine and imprisonment, it could close down a picket line and bring a strike to a halt within a matter of hours.

When American courts extended the idea of safeguarding property interests to such intangibles as "justifiable expectation of profit" from the continuous operation of a business, the entire strategy of the union was undercut. Under such an interpretation it could be shown that any strike was *ipso facto* injurious to property. American courts also tended to accept unsubstantiated allegations that the strikers were threatening physical damage, and to take affidavits from only one side of the controversy. This was a clear abuse of the equity procedure, which should obviously be applied without favoring one antagonist over the other. Yet the existence of many such cases has been well documented.

The injunction procedure operated usually as follows.[3] The company would go to a judge, usually one already known to be antiunion, and present a written complaint, stating that the union was threatening imminent damage to the employer's property and that this damage could be prevented only by issuing an order restraining the union from certain specified actions. Many injunctions were actually drawn

[2] The injunction developed as one of the remedies in "courts of equity," which in England are separate courts with separate judges and a body of precedents different from the "courts of law," where disputes between two adversaries are tested in open trials with judge and jury. But American courts sit simultaneously as trial courts and equity courts, the judge applying the different bodies of precedent according to the type of action taken by the plaintiff.

[3] The classic study is Felix Frankfurter and Nathan Greene, *The Labor Injunction* (New York: The Macmillan Company, 1930).

up by a company attorney and simply signed by the judge. Even if the judge decided to take evidence from the union, this would be limited to an affidavit replying to the employer's charges; the union could not call witnesses or present oral testimony. After considering the employer's and possibly the union's statements, the judge decided whether to issue the restraining order.

The temporary injunction, or "restraining order," was usually drawn in sweeping terms, restraining anyone from interfering with the employer's business in any way. Judges occasionally went into detail, specifying that there must be only one picket at each plant entrance, that he must be standing so many feet from the gate, and so on. But the general vice of injunctions was their vagueness. Drawn in broad terms, anyone who supported the strike in any way could be held guilty of a violation, tried without a jury for contempt of court, and severely punished.

In theory there was a later hearing by the court, at which witnesses were heard, after which the temporary injunction was either vacated or made permanent. But the strike was usually won or lost in the intervening months. Even when the injunction was not strictly enforced, its application to a labor dispute brought the weight of law down against the strikers. With the union stigmatized before the public, its members became demoralized and intimidated, its treasury melted away, and its drive was weakened. In the more usual case where the injunction was broadly drawn and vigorously enforced by the police, it was an almost unbeatable method of strikebreaking.

An indirect result of the injunction procedure was to stimulate union interest in political activity. Many state judges were elected, and the others were appointed by elected officials. Unions saw the point of taking an active role in this process. They also appealed repeatedly to Congress and the state legislatures to pass statutes legalizing trade union activities and forbidding the courts to interfere with them. These efforts were largely unsuccessful. Few laws were passed, and even these were unfavorably interpreted in hostile court decisions.

LEGISLATIVE POLICY:
FIRST
PHASE

When organized labor turned to the state legislatures and to Congress for support, Samuel Gompers and other labor leaders were confident that they could hold their own with employers if only the courts would give labor unions the same treatment they gave businessmen in business disputes. The economic power of thousands of workers organized into unions would be sufficient, if only they were not tied

down by antistrike injunctions, to meet and outlast the economic resources of the employers. The policy of "union self-help," unassisted
by direct government regulation, had a relatively brief existence. Indeed, some students of unionism believe that it never had a fair trial.

The Antitrust Acts of 1890 and 1914

Legislative action in labor relations is part of a general trend toward increased government regulation of industry. After a century
of rapid industrial development, in which business competition was
restrained only by the courts under the common law rules of contract
and tort, the legislative branch of government began to assert the
public interest in a series of antitrust laws, which attached criminal
penalties to agreements that created monopolies and market controls.

The Sherman Antitrust Act of 1890 was the first major step toward
a federal economic policy, and its basic structure has been copied with
variations each time Congress has approached an economic problem.
First, there is a statement of social policy that defines the purpose of
Congress in broad and sweeping terms. Second, activities within the
scope of this policy are specified, and a list of prohibited actions is set
forth. Third the attorney general, as chief law enforcement officer of
the United States, is directed to take positive action against offenders
by bringing a criminal action or seeking an injunction. Fourth, private
individuals injured by violations of the new policy are permitted to
bring civil suits for damages under the act—in effect, a new category
of tort is created for the courts to apply.

It is well to remember that the Sherman Act was passed at a time
when giant corporations threatened to dominate the industrial scene,
driving small competitors out of business, cornering the market on
scarce raw materials, and driving up prices paid by the consuming
public. The power of government, in contrast, was relatively weak.
State governments were often controlled by an alliance of business
interests with corrupt political bosses. The federal government was
far less important in American life than the state governments. There
was no direct challenge to the interstate power of the supercorpora-
tions except the growing power of the labor unions.

The Sherman Act sought to prohibit monopolistic control over the
production and marketing of commodities. It applied, under the federal Constitution, only to "interstate trade and commerce"—that is, to
activities not wholly within a single state. It is not certain whether
Congress ever meant the Sherman Act to apply against big unions as
well as big corporate interests. At any rate, the Supreme Court in 1908
did apply the act to union activities in the *Danbury Hatters* case.[4] The

---

4 *Loewe* v. *Lawler,* 208 U.S. 274 (1908).

United Hatters Union, in a drive to organize the manufacturers of felt hats, had called a strike against Loewe, a small hat producer in Danbury, Connecticut. It tried to force a settlement by cutting off the flow of orders for his hats from merchants in other states. Loewe successfully sued the union membership for triple damages, and the award of the court (which amounted to half a million dollars) sent a shock wave of fear through organized labor.

Within a few years the Sherman Act was amended by the Clayton Act of 1914. The unions believed that they had scored a great victory, for Congress wrote into this act a long list of normal strike activities, forbidding the federal courts to issue injunctions against such acts so long as they were "peacefully" and "lawfully" carried on. Samuel Gompers and other AFL leaders called the act a Magna Charta of American labor. But it soon appeared that the legislators had drafted the act in less than precise terms. The new law did not say plainly that the Sherman Act should not apply to labor unions. Instead, it referred to "labor, agricultural, or horticultural organizations, instituted for the purposes of mutual help, and not having capital stock or conducted for profit." Moreover, the ambiguous words "lawfully" and "peacefully" opened up a loophole wide enough to drive a truck through, which the Supreme Court soon did, in the 1921 case of *Duplex* v. *Deering.* The Court nullified the act for all practical purposes, by limiting its application to disputes where employer and workers were in the direct relationship of master and servant. Leaders and friends of organized labor might rage, but the decision stood as a precedent for all federal courts, which would be changed only by a later Supreme Court decision or by an act of Congress.[5]

However, in the *Duplex* case Justice Brandeis wrote a carefully reasoned dissenting opinion, which for the first time systematically related the legal issues to underlying economic and social problems. He reproved the majority of the Court for going beyond its proper role, reminding them that, "The conditions developed in industry may be such that those engaged in it cannot continue their struggle without danger to the community. But it is not for judges to determine whether such conditions exist, nor is it their function to set the limits of permissible contest and to declare the duties which the new situation demands. This is the function of the legislature."

Two subsequent decisions indicate that the Supreme Court was beginning to see the logic of this statement, though it was not yet ready to take a balanced view of labor relations. Labor disputes were continuing and violence was, if anything, increasing. The record of judicially controlled policy was a poor one, having brought no peace

[5] *Duplex Printing Press Co.* v. *Deering,* 254 U.S. 443 (1921).

to the industrial arena and being widely regarded as unfair. The 1922 *Coronado Coal* case arose out of a highly destructive strike by the United Mine Workers against a mine owned by the Coronado Coal Company. The company, ignoring the clear grounds for a damage suit in the state courts, elected to sue the union in federal court for triple damages under the Sherman Act. The Supreme Court ruled against the company, distinguishing the case from the *Danbury Hatters* and *Duplex* cases by noting that the strike had shut down only the *mining* of coal and had not directly interfered with interstate marketing or distribution. The company then brought a new suit, at which a disgruntled union official testified that the union's *intention* had been to eliminate competition between union-mined and nonunion-mined coal in interstate markets. On this showing, the Court ruled against the Mineworkers.[6]

A few years later, in the *Bedford Cut Stone* case of 1927, the Court applied the Sherman Act to a secondary labor boycott by the national stonecutters' union, and struck down their attempt to organize the Indiana limestone quarries by refusing to handle nonunion Indiana limestone.[7] In these four cases the entire program of organized labor was threatened. If strikes and boycotts were to be interpreted as restraints on interstate commerce, the logical extension of this view would lead to workers being forced to work at whatever terms the employer set, since few industries by this time did not have some interstate aspect.

In this period another weapon was added to the antilabor injunction and the antilabor interpretation of the antitrust laws. This was the "yellow-dog contract," a promise that the employee would not join a union, which many employers began to require as a precondition of employment. In the absence of statute law, employers were free to exact whatever terms of employment they could; workers were legally presumed free to accept or reject the job as offered. Such an antiunion pledge was usually informal and, since the employer did not promise a fixed period of employment in return, it is doubtful whether it could properly be called a contract. In the *Hitchman* case in 1917, however, the Supreme Court granted an injunction against the United Mine workers to forestall organization of a mine in West Virginia where miners had secretly signed up with the union after having given the employer an antiunion promise. The union was forbidden to induce workers to violate their legitimate contract with the employer. This was a landmark decision in the use of the in-

[6] *United Mine Workers* v. *Coronado Coal Co.,* 259 U.S. 344 (1922); and *Coronado Coal Co.* v. *United Mine Workers,* 268 .U.S. 295 (1925).

[7] *Bedford Cut Stone Co.* v. *Journeymen Stone Cutters' Association,* 274 U.S. 37 (1927).

junction, and still more in the buildup of belief that Court control of industrial relations was weighted heavily against the workers.[8]

The Railway Labor Act of 1926

Meanwhile the railroad industry had taken the first step toward recognizing the value of collective bargaining and peaceful settlement of labor disputes. Arbitration boards, made up equally of labor and management representatives with a neutral referee, had come into use on a voluntary basis. When these were incorporated into the machinery of the Railway Labor Act of 1926, the country's first important piece of labor legislation was on the books.[9]

A National Mediation Board was created to handle "major disputes," which the law distinguished from "minor disputes" arising under existing contracts. The latter were to be handled by adjustment boards or, in the event of deadlock, passed up to the National Mediation Board. In 1934 the act was amended to strengthen the settlement machinery by creating a National Railroad Adjustment Board for the arbitration of disputes arising under existing contracts. Not until 1957, however, was it finally settled that the board's authority over such disputes is final, when the Supreme Court ruled that a railroad union cannot resort to a strike over matters pending before the National Railroad Adjustment Board.[10] In 1936 the coverage of the act was extended to airline transportation. Subsequent amendments have, in 1951, permitted the negotiation of union shop or maintenance of membership contracts, which had been prohibited by Congress in 1934; and, in 1966, created machinery for appointing presidential "emergency" boards to handle disputes that, in the judgment of the National Mediation Board, threaten an interruption to "essential transportation service" either in the railroads or airlines.

Successful operation of the Railway Labor Act has always depended on the cooperation of the powerful railroad unions. The leaders of these unions were involved in the drafting of the original act and in subsequent amendments. To some extent, union pressure has been transferred from the employers to the legislative committees.

The Norris–LaGuardia Act of 1932

The last phase of the period in which labor leaders favored government neutrality closed with the passage of the Norris–LaGuardia Act

[8] *Hitchman Coal Co.* v. *Mitchell*, 245 U.S. 229 (1917). For a comprehensive review of these issues and cases see Charles O. Gregory, *Labor and Law*, 2d rev. ed. (New York: W. W. Norton & Company, Inc., 1958), chaps. 7, 8, and 10.

[9] The amended Railway Labor Act can be found at U.S. Code, Title 45, chap. 8.

[10] *Brotherhood of Railway Trainmen* v. *Chicago River and Indiana Railroad Co.*, 353 U.S. 30 (1957).

of 1932. This legislation set up for the first time a national policy in labor relations. Carefully drafted, its provisions specifically removed the judicially built obstacles to union organization and peaceable union activities.

The act, which is still in effect, declares that as a matter of sound public policy the individual worker would "have full freedom of association, self-organization, and designation of representatives of his own choosing, to negotiate the terms and conditions of his employment, and that they shall be free from the interference, restraint, or coercion of employers of labor, or their agents, in the designation of such representatives or in self-organization or in other concerted activities for the purpose of collective bargaining or other mutual aid or protection." Activities that the courts are forbidden to enjoin are listed: (1) a concerted refusal to work; (2) membership in or support of a labor organization; (3) peaceable urging of others to leave work; (4) publicizing a trade dispute by any method not involving fraud or violence; (5) peaceable assembly; and (6) payment of strike benefits and aid to anyone interested in a labor dispute who is party to a lawsuit. Moreover, "yellow-dog contracts" were made unenforceable in the courts.

The issuance of labor injunctions by the federal courts was further controlled by procedural requirements. The employer was required to prove that the regular police force was either unwilling or unable to protect his property. He also had to be innocent of violating any labor law. The judge, in issuing a temporary injunction, had to hear witnesses from both sides and could not rely solely on affidavits. A jury trial was permitted if contempt of court proceedings followed issuance of an injunction.

These provisions were essentially negative and neutral. The intent and effect of the law was to remove certain legal restraints by which trade union action had been controlled, and to leave the unions free to exert their full economic power against the employer. The Norris–LaGuardia Act was followed by antiinjunction acts in most of the major industrial states (Wisconsin had passed a similar law in the preceding year). The state courts would thus tend to follow the policy and procedures laid down by Congress for the federal courts.

GOVERNMENT INTERVENTION: PROTECTIVE LEGISLATION

A major change in direction came only three years later, with the passage of the National Labor Relations Act of 1935, commonly known as the Wagner Act from its principal sponsor, Senator Wagner of New York. From this date onward, government was to take an active part in labor relations.[11]

What made the difference after 1935? Government had scarcely been absent from collective bargaining in the preceding century. The judicial branch had taken an active hand from the beginning; the legislative branch had laid down basic rules to govern the contest. But the Wagner Act took the additional step of creating an administrative agency to implement the legislative policy and to oversee the collective bargaining process.

This step was the result of experience. In other areas of federal economic policy it had been found that mere passage of a law, with enforcement left to the initiative of the attorney general and the decisions of the courts, was not enough. A useful instrument had been devised in the quasi-administrative agency, which performs the adminstrative functions of fact finding, just as a division of the Justice Department would do, but which also makes a preliminary judgment between contesting parties in which it exercises judicial power, subject to review by the federal courts. Such boards had dealt successfully with other policy areas in which the subject matter is specialized, technical, and controversial. Members of such boards are appointed by the president, with senatorial confirmation, for a fixed term of years. Appointments are timed so that a change in party control does not bring an automatic reversal of policy. This provides policy continuity, stability, and a degree of detachment from the shifting winds of politics.

Passage of the Wagner Act, and its subsequent approval by the Supreme Court, mark a change in direction so revolutionary that it can only be understood by recalling the atmosphere of the early 1930s, when worldwide depression had brought stagnation to the American economy. Underlying the provisions of the act was a belief that the economy could be managed by government without being completely controlled; and that unionization would bring higher wages and greater purchasing power, which would contribute to economic recovery.

The philosophy of the Wagner Act was essentially as follows: it is desirable that terms and conditions of employment be regulated by collective bargaining. It is also desirable, therefore, that workers should organize strong and stable unions as rapidly as possible, without the crippling effects of bitter organizational strikes. This objective will not be accomplished if government follows a hands-off policy, since employers have many effective methods of resisting union or-

[11] The National Labor Relations Act of 1935 can be found in 49 Stat. 449; the Taft–Hartley amendments are in 61 Stat. 136 (1947), and the Landrum–Griffin amendments in 73 Stat. 519 (1959). The full text of the act with amendments is found in 28 U.S.C. 151 *et seq.*

ganization. It is necessary, therefore, that government should restrain the use of certain types of coercion by employers for a long enough period to allow unions to be formed throughout industry.

Workers were not required to join unions, but the union organizer was to be given full freedom in presenting his case to them, while the employer was required to remain silent and inactive. The act took the position that a worker's decision concerning union membership is none of the employer's business. The role of government, through the National Labor Relations Board, was to ensure that union organization was not hindered by employer action. It was assumed that, if employer pressure were removed, most workers would choose to join unions. The growth of union membership from about 4 million in 1933 to 15 million in 1948 seems to confirm the accuracy of this forecast, though it must be remembered that high employment and excess demand for labor during and after World War II also did much to promote unionization.

The Wagner Act gave employees the right to organize unions, to bargain collectively through representatives of their own choosing, and to engage in other concerted activities for the purpose of mutual protection. Employers were prohibited from engaging in "unfair labor practices," which included: (1) interference with, restraint, or coercion of employees in the exercise of their rights under the act; (2) domination of, interference with, or financial support of a union organization; (3) discrimination to encourage or discourage union membership, except where a closed or union shop was established by agreement with a majority of the employees; (4) discrimination against an employee for filing charges or giving testimony under the act; and (5) refusal to bargain "in good faith" with the legal representative of the employees.

The act provided that, where doubt existed as to the majority status of a union, the matter could be decided by a secret ballot of the workers involved, or by some other suitable method. Such elections and other fact-finding aspects of the act were to be administered by a National Labor Relations Board, which was also given responsibility for prosecuting unfair labor practices by employers.

The Supreme Court's long record of antilabor decisions created expectations that the Wagner Act would be declared unconstitutional. But the Court had finally decided to accept the authority of Congress and the president in determining national economic policy. The great popularity of President Roosevelt, and his unprecedented landslide victory in 1936, were doubtless a factor in the Court's change of attitude.

At any rate, the constitutionality of the Wagner Act was upheld by the Supreme Court in 1937, in the case of *National Labor Relations Board* v. *Jones & Laughlin Steel Corporation,* by a vote of five to four.[12] For a decade thereafter, it was the unchallenged law of the land. It was still not generally accepted by employers, however, and in the early years there were serious difficulties in administering the act. The staff was inadequate and inexperienced for handling the flood of unfair labor practice charges that came in 1937 and 1938. But the board developed informal and increasingly effective administrative procedures and, by concentrating its effort on key cases, was able to bring about widespread observance of the act. In the twelve years from 1935 to 1947 over 45,000 unfair labor practice cases and over 59,000 representation cases were handled either formally or informally. Collective bargaining became the accepted method of conducting industrial relations.

Acceptance of the Wagner Act soon led to passage of "little Wagner Acts" in many of the industrial states. State labor relations acts were enacted by Utah, Wisconsin, New York, Pennsylvania, and Massachusetts in 1937, Rhode Island in 1941, and Connecticut in 1945. These state laws are important, because the Wagner Act (and its successors) cover only establishments engaged in interstate commerce. A third or so of the nonagricultural workers in the country are subject primarily to state regulation.

Government protection of union-organizing activities, combined with the rising level of employment after 1933, led to a rapid increase in union membership. The CIO, which was not in existence when the Wagner Act was passed, quickly unionized most workers in the mass production industries. This was not accomplished, however, without a number of large and bitter strikes, culminating in the wave of sit-down strikes during 1937. Regardless of the reason for these strikes, middle class opinion tended to label the sit-down as a sign of "radicalism" in the new unions. Instances of violence or irresponsibility during strikes, and occasional malfeasance by union officials were publicized by newspaper editors, columnists and commentators. Public opinion, particularly in small towns and rural areas, became increasingly critical of union objectives and tactics.

The strongest criticism of the Wagner Act, if one ignores the attacks of those who rejected it altogether, was that its treatment of unions vis-à-vis management was inequitable. Employer tactics were severely restricted, but no comparable restrictions were imposed on the unions. There was also criticism that the rights of individual employees were not sufficiently protected under the act. This objection is not surprising, since the purpose of the act was to favor collective action in all cases where a majority had voted for it.

[12] *National Labor Relations Board* v. *Jones and Laughlin Steel Corp.*, 301 U.S. 1 (1937).

GOVERNMENT
INTERVENTION:
RESTRICTIVE
LEGISLATION

The unfavorable public reaction did not lead to repeal of the federal and state labor relations acts, though this was the hope of many employers. It resulted rather in the passage of additional laws intended to control certain types of union activity. In an effort to achieve a workable balance of power between unions and employers, government was projected ever farther into the labor relations scene.

The first of the new acts, which Killingsworth has termed "restrictive laws" as contrasted with "protective laws" on the Wagner Act model, was passed as early as 1939, when Pennsylvania amended its state labor relations act. In the same year Wisconsin repealed its act, substituting a new measure with controls on union activities; and Minnesota and Michigan passed new labor relations acts of a restrictive type. Kansas and Colorado followed in 1943, and Utah in 1947. In addition to these comprehensive labor relations acts, the years 1937 to 1947 saw a multitude of state acts imposing specific restrictions on trade unions. These laws dealt, among other things, with sit-down strikes, use of force and violence in strikes, mass picketing, jurisdictional strikes, sympathy strikes, strikes in the absence of an agreement, strike votes, picketing in the absence of a labor dispute, picketing of agricultural premises, picketing by nonemployees, primary and secondary boycotts, refusal to handle nonunion materials (the secondary labor boycott), coercion or intimidation of workers by trade unions, prohibition of the closed or union shop and the dues checkoff, licensing of unions and their officers, registration and submission of information by unions to the state government, filing of financial reports, control of membership requirements, control over expulsion of workers from membership, regulation of strikes in public utilities, and regulation of strikes in public employment. By the late 1940s there was scarcely a state that did not have one or more union control laws on its statute books.

The Taft–Hartley Act of 1947

The movement toward restrictive laws was less rapid on the federal level. Numerous amendments to the Wagner Act were introduced in every session of Congress; but the Democratic majority in Congress and the opposition of President Roosevelt prevented enactment.

During the war years amendments were pressed less vigorously, since labor disputes were handled under special emergency provisions by the National War Labor Board.

After the war the campaign to curb union power gained momentum. When government control of wages ended with the war, there was no accepted plan for resolving the difficult issues of wages and hours in the reconversion period. Unions demanded higher wage rates to compensate for reduced earnings due to shorter workweeks and less overtime pay. Serious strikes over this issue occurred in the steel, coal, and automobile industries in 1946, and there was also a nationwide railroad strike. Public alarm over these strikes was partly responsible for election of a Republican majority to Congress in 1946. In 1947 Congress passed the Labor–Management Relations Act of 1947, commonly known as the Taft–Hartley Act after its two principal sponsors.

The new law was in form an amendment of the Wagner Act, most of the provisions of the earlier law being carried over intact. But there were many new provisions, and the total effect was to establish a different philosophy of labor relations. The Wagner Act assumed that most workers prefer to join unions; that the interests of unions and their members are identical; that restricting certain employer tactics will ensure sufficient equality of bargaining power between unions and management; and that, once the parties have been brought to the bargaining table, they should be left free to write whatever contract provisions they choose. Government should not try to shape the content of collective agreements.

In contrast, the Taft–Hartley Act reflects a distrust of collective action, regardless of majority sanction. Its outlook may be summarized as follows: (1) Workers may or may not wish to join unions. Their right to stay out should be protected against coercion from any quarter, including the unions; and workers already in unions should be given reasonable opportunity to get out if they so desire. (2) The interests of members and of the union organization are not necessarily identical. Workers need protection against the union as well as against the employer. Government may have to regulate internal union affairs for this purpose. (3) Unions are not necessarily the weaker party in collective bargaining. In some areas of the economy the employer may be the underdog. To ensure true equality of bargaining power, the law must restrain unfair tactics of unions as well as of employers. (4) There is a public interest in the terms of union contracts. It may be necessary to prohibit some contract provisions; government is entitled to scrutinize bargaining results as well as bargaining procedures. (5) The public also requires protection against crippling strikes in essential industries, and special procedures are needed to deal with such strikes. (6) Union political power should be specially controlled; it is necessary to prohibit unions from contributing to federal election campaigns.

The Taft–Hartley Act thus moved away from the policy of protecting unions toward a policy of protecting employers, individual workers, and the general public. A variety of restrictions were imposed on union operations. The unions strongly opposed the act and later worked energetically to secure its repeal. These efforts were unsuccessful, however, and the Taft–Hartley Act continues as the main federal legislation governing labor relations.

Most provisions of the act can be related to three professed objectives:

1. To equalize bargaining power by restraining certain tactics of both unions and employers. To this end the act lists certain unfair practices on the part of unions, paralleling the list of unfair employer practices which was carried over intact from the Wagner Act. Unions may not interfere with the individual employee's right not to participate in collective bargaining. They may not attempt to cause employers to discriminate against nonunionists, except as may be required by a valid union shop agreement. They may not refuse to bargain collectively with an employer. They may not engage in secondary boycotts or jurisdictional strikes, nor in strikes to force recognition of one union when another has already been certified as bargaining representative. They may not extract money from an employer for work not needed or not actually performed.

2. Second, the act attempts to protect individual employees against the union in a variety of ways. Union contracts may no longer establish a closed shop or any other system of preferential hiring. A union may not charge excessive dues or initiation fees. While it remains free to discipline and expel members, it cannot cause the employer to discharge a worker under a union shop contract if the worker was denied membership or dropped from membership for any reason other than nonpayment of dues and initiation fees. In addition, employees are given a way of getting rid of a union that they no longer wish to represent them. If 30 percent of the employees in a bargaining unit file a petition requesting decertification of the union representing them, the National Labor Relations Board must conduct a secret ballot to determine the wishes of the majority.

The checkoff system of collecting union dues is regulated by a proviso that dues can be deducted from the paycheck only with the written consent of the individual employee. Employer payments to union welfare funds are only permitted if certain conditions are observed, such as separation of the welfare funds from general union funds and joint union–management administration. The act provides further that union funds may not be used for political purposes.

3. A third professed objective is to protect innocent bystanders against the consequences of interunion or union–management strife. The innocent party may in some cases be the employer. Under the Wagner Act, an employer sometimes found himself caught in the cross fire of two rival unions, each seeking to organize his plant and each threatening to shut it down, unless granted recognition. Since the employer could not petition for a National Labor Relations Board election to settle the issue, his hands were tied. The Taft–Hartley Act accordingly provides that employers as well as unions may petition the National Labor Relations Board for a representation election. A similar situation often arises in jurisdictional disputes where two unions —say, the carpenters and machinists—each demand that the employer assign a certain type of work to its members under penalty of shut-down. The Taft–Hartley Act forbids strikes in such situations and provides that they may be decided by the National Labor Relations Board unless the rival unions work out their own arrangements for settlement. This has stimulated the growth of private settlement machinery, notably as between the various building trades' unions.

We have already noted the act's restrictions on the secondary boy-cott, an old union device of putting pressure on one employer so that he will exert pressure on another employer whom the union is really after. The practical effect of this provision, as applied and interpreted by the courts, will be examined in the next chapter. While secondary boycotts have not been eliminated by the act, they have probably been considerably reduced.

Strikes often cause inconvenience to another neutral party, the consuming public. The Taft–Hartley Act contains no limitations on strikes in general, but it does provide a procedure for use in so-called "national emergency" disputes. Strikes that, in the opinion of the president, imperil the national health or safety are made subject to injunction for a maximum period of eighty days. The president is authorized to appoint a special board of inquiry, which makes a preliminary investigation prior to the time an injunction is sought, and must turn in a final report when the injunction has been in effect for sixty days. If the parties, with the aid of the Federal Mediation and Conciliation Service, have not been able to settle the dispute by this time, the National Labor Relations Board is required to poll the employees as to whether they are willing to accept the employer's last offer. After this step the injunction is dissolved and the president may, if he wishes, refer the dispute to Congress and recommend a course of action concerning it. The board of inquiry is specifically prohibited from recommending terms for settlement of the dispute. These provisions do not apply to government employees, who are prohibited by the act from striking; nor do they apply to railroad workers, for whom a special procedure is provided by the Railway Labor Act.

The Landrum–Griffin Act of 1959

In the decade from 1947 to 1957 there was continued complaint of corruption and high-handed procedures in trade union government. Such practices may not have been widespread in the sense of involving large numbers of union members; but the complaints were genuine, they had high publicity value, and were sometimes supported by sensational testimony.

In 1959 Congress passed the Labor–Management Reporting and Disclosure Act, usually referred to as LMRDA or the Landrum–Griffin Act. This legislation broadened the area of federal regulation to include most of the internal affairs of labor unions. This was not a totally new departure. Taft–Hartley was in effect a declaration of principle that government might regulate internal union affairs. Under it, a union that wished to use the facilities of the National Labor Relations Act, including National Labor Relations Board election procedures, was required to file with the secretary of labor a copy of its constitution and bylaws, an annual financial report, a list of its officers (including their salaries and allowances), and an affidavit by each officer that he was not a member of the Communist party or other subversive organization. This last provision was particularly offensive to the unions and a number of unions, including the vigorously anti-Communist United Mine Workers, declined to comply. A union that had its industry substantially organized could readily operate outside the protection of the act.

Several amendments to Taft–Hartley were written into the final version of the 1959 bill just before passage. One of these eliminated the non-Communist affidavit. Secondary boycotts were restricted, but the building trades' unions and clothing workers' unions were permitted to curb subcontracting in their respective industries by negotiating, if they could, "hot-cargo agreements" which controlled their employers' dealings with nonunion manufacturers, contractors, and jobbers. The union practice of advertising the names of secondary parties to a dispute, such as distributors selling goods produced by a manufacturer, in the hope of enlisting public support for boycott of such goods, continued to be legal. The closed shop, prohibited by Taft–Hartley, was in effect relegalized in the building industry. These amendments softened the opposition of some politically powerful unions sufficiently so that the leaders of organized labor, already deeply divided, were unable either to mobilize effective opposition or to unite on proposals for substitute provisions.

The main thrust of the Landrum–Griffin Act is an effort to increase the power of the individual union member vis-à-vis his officers. A "Bill of Rights" for union members, contained in Title 1, gives a guarantee of the right to vote in union elections and to oppose the incumbent leadership both in union meetings and by nominating opposition candidates. Provisions in union constitutions that fail to allow these freedoms can be challenged by individual members. This first part of the law also regulates the procedure by which union meetings are called and dues are assessed. Titles 2 through 6 create a new agency in the Department of Labor, the Bureau of Labor–Management Reports (BLMR), which has been given large responsibilities. The Secretary of Labor is given authority to investigate possible violations of the act as a whole; through the Bureau of Labor–Management Reports he must collect detailed reports from unions, which he is expected to analyze not merely for the discovery of violations but to compile statistics and to investigate the general operation of the law.

The reports required of unions are those formerly required by the Taft–Hartley Act's registration procedures, plus detailed information on the union's constitution and bylaws, its officers, procedures, membership qualifications, and day-to-day operation in imposing assessments, fines and fees, in disciplinary practices, and in election procedures. If the union has not had a constitution or bylaws, these must now be constructed and sent in. Annual financial reports on a uniform pattern determined by the Bureau of Labor–Management Reports are also required. No labor organization may declare itself outside the jurisdiction of the Bureau of Labor–Management Reports. All international unions, and every local no matter how small, are subject to the act, with the exception of unions representing government employees. State and other intermediate union bodies are assumed to be included in the data furnished by the international and local unions and are not required to file their own reports.

Officers and employees of unions (e.g. attorneys, research economists) are also required to report any financial dealings with employers or labor relations consultants if the union members' interests may be involved. Employers and labor consultants must report any payments made to union officers or expenditures on their account.

Title 3 of the act deals with trusteeships, requiring reports from the central body on any trusteeship established over a subordinate unit of the union. The law limits the conditions under which a trusteeship can be established and exercised, with enforcement either by the Secretary of Labor with criminal penalties for violation, or by union members filing civil suits in federal district courts. Complainants reporting violations to the Secretary of Labor are guaranteed anonymity.

Title 4 deals with union elections. The Bureau of Labor–Management Reports is responsible for establishing adequate procedures rather than for policing individual elections. Only if irregularities are reported will the Bureau of Labor–Management Reports actually supervise the conduct of an election. It is expected that the bureau will investigate complaints of election irregularities or inadequate procedures for removal of union officers charged with misconduct. Such complaints must be made within one month after the union member has exhausted the remedies available to him through the union's procedure, or within three months if his appeal to the union officers has been ignored. If a violation of the law is found, the Bureau of Labor–Management Reports must finish its own investigation and file suit in federal district court within an additional sixty days.

Title 5 establishes a fiduciary relationship of the union official to his union, enabling rank and file members to bring suit for improper monetary management, for conflict of interest situations, and possibly even for nonfinancial aspects of the union leader's work. Union officers must disclose any profit they receive from financial transactions. No conflict with the interests of the union is allowed. They cannot acquire personal interests that conflict, and if conflicts develop the union officer must act in the union's rather than his own personal interest. The law puts the union official in the legal position of a bank trust officer managing the estate of a client. Section 501(a) sets up a standard of ethical as well as legal conduct which is extremely high, and which makes the union official vulnerable to suit, both for financial mismanagement and for a wide range of activities where an honest mistake in judgment or the enmity of a political opponent brings the risk of severe legal penalties.

Altogether, the Landrum–Griffin Act created thirteen new federal crimes, with heavy penalties for violation; eight new civil remedies; and ten new enforcement procedures. This structure of government action does not reinforce but rather supplants the previous machinery, such as the Ethical Practices Committee of the AFL-CIO and the United Automobile Workers Public Review Board, which the unions themselves had created.

In union elections, where the law creates rigid formal requirements, the cost of holding elections has naturally risen. In general, compliance with the law has involved hiring more legal and administrative assistance. This has fallen most heavily on the grass-roots level of unionism, which the law presumably set out to strengthen and protect; yet in a large union, a corrupt leadership would not be greatly burdened either by the expense of hiring legal advice or the formalities of reporting and routine action which keep the officers within the letter of the law. In the use of trusteeships to bring recalcitrant locals into line, the "due process" requirements of the law tend to slow down and formalize the process of imposing centralized control but not necessarily to end abuses.

Perhaps the most lasting contribution of the Landrum–Griffin Act will be the collection of a mass of data about the structure and operation of unions across the United States. These data are open to the public, and the Board of Labor–Management Reports is eager to assist students of labor problems in compiling statistics and analyzing union reports. If this mountain of information is successfully mined, in the next decade or two we may know more about union structure and government than we know today.

But answers to the most important questions about the operation of the law will have to be sought elsewhere. Will the law make internal union government less stable? More conservative and cautious in bargaining? More dependent on employers than on the union rank and file? In the first ten years of operation there is little evidence that collective bargaining has been adversely affected. But neither is there any evidence that the law has eliminated corruption in those segments of organized labor where illegal practices existed before 1959. The most clear-cut effect has been the bureaucratization of the American labor movement. All the lessons of history, however, suggest that good elected leaders come from good electorates, and that electoral procedures are less important.

The concepts and vocabulary of the long period of judicial, rather than statutory, control of industrial relations have continued into the present era. The underlying logic of the use of economic pressure gained gradual recognition by the legal profession and the courts and was subsequently written into law by Congress and the state legislatures. The goals of industrial peace, of limiting the area of conflict when conflict occurred, and of limiting the impact of hostile action to those immediately involved, partially supplanted the common law rules. The unstated but overriding goal of policy is, as it has been for over half a century, to ensure continued growth of the economy by improving the status, earnings, and productivity of the industrial worker.

ADMINISTERING PUBLIC POLICY

The basic statute controlling the conduct of industrial relations today is the amended National Labor Relations Act (NLRA). The administrative structure created in 1935 has been continued by successive Congresses, with amendments added in 1947 by the Taft–Hartley Act and in 1959 by the Landrum–Griffin Act.

The National Labor Relations Board

The agency charged with administering the law is the National Labor Relations Board, usually abbreviated to NLRB, or "the board."

The prime responsibility of the National Labor Relations Board is rule making, and its rulings have the force of law. Its functions are half administrative, through its authority to make investigations, and half judicial, through its power to adjudicate disputes. The Board's rules and decisions taken together have established a line of precedents through which there has come into being a "common law of industrial relations." Across the United States unions and employers conduct negotiations on a relatively uniform pattern. Orderly procedures and settled precedents make it possible for both sides to know what to expect in most situations.

The Board consists of five members, appointed by the president but not removable by him, with a five-year term of office. This arrangement, which is typical of federal regulatory commissions, tries to combine elements of responsiveness to public opinion expressed through presidential elections with elements of stability and independence of political controls. The board will usually include individuals of different political views, and the expectation is that they will consult reasonably on cases coming before them. The president designates one member of the board as its chairman.

The board acts as a group in the hearing and disposition of cases. These are of two types: (1) those arising from disputes over "unfair labor practices" as defined in the act, and (2) those arising from representation disputes under the act's election procedures. A case may be heard by all five board members, or by three members. Majority agreement is needed for decision.

The administrative powers of the board are concentrated in the office of the general counsel. He is appointed by the president, with senate consent, for a four-year term. He is also removable by the president, but only for malfeasance, and this provision has not been used to date. Day-to-day administration of the act is carried out by regional offices, established at key industrial centers throughout the country, under the direction of the general counsel.

The duties of the general counsel are impressive. He has final authority over investigations; complaints in unfair practice cases issue only over his signature; he is responsible for all litigation involving the board; and his office supervises the regional offices across the country, with their large staffs of attorneys and other employees.

In addition to these statutory responsibilities, the general counsel has certain duties assigned him by the board. These include the conduct of all elections and all matters of personnel administration. The general counsel has a large administrative staff. Trial examiners, who are appointed from the register of the Civil Service Commission, conduct hearings and issue decisions called "Intermediate Reports." Their decisions become the final order of the National Labor Relations Board unless one of the parties carries an appeal to the board within twenty days. They have broad powers in hearings, and can rule on all motions and questions raised by attorneys for the disputing parties. Heading up this structure is a chief trial examiner and two associate trial examiners.

The regional offices, each a replica of the national, are headed by a regional director who is assisted by a chief law officer and a staff of field attorneys. In the larger regional offices there are field examiners; and in some regions there are subregional offices headed by an officer-in-charge.

National Labor Relations Board procedure in unfair labor practice cases involves three stages: (1) complaint; (2) hearing; and (3) issuance of a board order. The board cannot initiate a complaint but must wait until a charge has been filed. The regional office will then schedule a hearing before one of the trial examiners. The rules of court procedure apply in general to these hearings, but the aim is to collect facts as expeditiously as possible and any party can introduce evidence, or request evidence to be produced under subpoena. The trial examiner files his report with recommendations, which the board can accept, reject, or modify. It can also require the case to be reopened for further evidence. But in most cases the trial examiner's report is approved and becomes the basis for an order issued in the name of the board. In form this will be a "cease-and-desist" order, including a requirement of affirmative action (legally, a "remedy"). If the order is issued against an employer, there will also be a requirement of posting in the plant so that employees can be informed of the board's action.

At this point the board's authority ceases. It has no enforcement powers of its own. If either party to the dispute ignores or refuses to comply with the order, an action must be brought in the U.S. Court of Appeals in whichever of the eleven federal judicial circuits the dispute originated. Legal action may be started by the board; or the respondent may ask the court to review the board's order. The court can enforce, modify, set aside, or order further evidence to be taken; but it cannot simply substitute its own judgment. The board's findings of fact "if supported by substantial evidence" are conclusive. Only questions of law are reviewable.

The weapon of enforcement is a contempt-of-court proceeding. The officers of a corporation can be held personally responsible for obedience to a National Labor Relations Board order upheld by court review. The board has another weapon, the temporary injunction, which can be sought in a federal district court as a means of freezing the dispute pending a decision. If this is used in a strike or boycott case where the dispute concerns assignment of work between two unions, the board need only show a prima facie case. If the strike or boycott has been called to force the employer to recognize an uncertified union, or in violation of the board's prior certification, the board is obliged under the law to ask the district court for an injunction.

When a dispute has been appealed to the courts, the issue can go eventually to the Supreme Court. Reviewability is limited; otherwise the volume of appeals could clog the Court calendar and frustrate enforcement of the act. For example, the board's certification of elections has been defined by the Supreme Court as not within the meaning of "final orders" under the act, and hence not reviewable.[13] Other rulings that fall short of being final orders include negative decisions by the general counsel in unfair labor practice complaints; i.e. the general counsel cannot be compelled to issue a complaint. His discretion on this point is final.

Court review aims to ensure a balance between forceful support of National Labor Relations Board decisions on the one hand, and protection of constitutionally guaranteed individual rights on the other. Ruling by ruling, the board's decisions hammer out a pattern which holds industrial conflict within predictable lines of action. To the extent that the contestants feel they cannot expect a better deal by appealing to the board, or by appealing from the board to the courts, they are encouraged to reach agreement through private collective bargaining.

As a piece of social machinery, the National Labor Relations Board can be given a good rating on both purpose and structure. It is reasonable that the courts should have given the board wide latitude and support over the years. Recent cases suggest, however, an increasing judicial concern to protect private rights against arbitrary board action. Indeed, after more than thirty years of operation, there remain basic unsettled questions about the board's role in making national labor policy. The Supreme Court, confronted with the necessity of deciding substantive issues on which Congress has remained silent, does not always show a high degree of confidence in the National Labor Relations Board. Instead of accepting the board's expertise and authority, the Court sometimes appears to limit the board's role to fact finding. Final decisions on substantive policy come down to a battle of Court precedents versus board precedents. As one authority has said, "Who's in charge here?" [14]

Why should there be, after three decades, so much oscillation and apparent inconstancy of purpose? Partly because Congress defaults by its silence. But the trouble stems too from lack of data about the Board's effectiveness; also, from its infrequent use of formal rule-making for the clear articulation of settled policies. There are statistics on the number of cases "settled" at various levels of the board. But

---

[13] *AFL* v. *National Labor Relations Board,* 308 U.S. 401 (1940).

[14] Clyde Summers, "Labor Law in the Supreme Court: 1964 term," *Yale Law Journal,* Vol. 75 (November, 1965), 59.

there have been hardly any empirical studies of the *impact* of board policies.

One such study was an investigation of nine cases in the Chicago area. All were discrimination cases, on which the issue and the remedy were quite clear, but the investigators found it impossible to obtain data about what had happened following the board's decision. The employers were reluctant even to discuss the cases. The union officials, due partly to the high turnover of union personnel, could not or would not identify the official who had been directly involved in the cases. The employees themselves, who had been the subject of the controversy, simply could not be located. Thus the study could not answer such a simple query as how many individuals had returned to work as a result of the board's decision. The investigators concluded that in most substantive fields the difficulty would be still greater.[15] For example, the most flagrant cases of secondary boycotts may escape the board's procedures because of an imbalance of power between union and employer, which deters the employer from bringing a complaint.

The board, seeking flexibility in developing its policies, has made little use of its power to announce rules after formal notice and hearing; and in its adjudications, written opinions often do not accompany the decision. Thus uncertainty about the *grounds* for board decisions is common. Sometimes an issue is raised twice before two differently constituted boards and a complete reversal occurs. Such reversals occur also in the courts; but when they do, and especially in Supreme Court cases, the reasons are stated carefully in the Court's opinion. Development of a line of *reasoned* precedents, and more courageous rule making, might cause the Supreme Court to give greater weight to board decisions.

At any rate, despite the declared purpose of Congress that the expertise of the board should be considered, the courts continue to grant entirely new trials. The National Labor Relations Board has more "business" in the appeals courts than all other federal administrative agencies combined. So long as the board and the lower courts do not regard each other's decisions as in any way binding, there are many areas in which it is not possible to say exactly what can be done and what cannot be done under the act.

The National Mediation Board and
National Railroad and Airlines Adjustment Boards

The transportation industry operates under a regulatory system different from the rest of American industry. This is partly because

---

[15] Douglas V. Brown, "The Impact of Some N.L.R.B. Decisions," Industrial Relations Research Association, *Proceedings,* 1960, pp. 18–26.

the government regulates fares and other matters through the Interstate Commerce Commission and the Federal Aviation Commission; but this fact cannot fully explain the separate treatment. The Railway Labor Act, with its amendments, sets up machinery altogether different from that provided in the National Labor Relations Act. The act classifies disputes as "major" and "minor," and separate but related procedures are followed for each type. Minor disputes are those arising under an existing contract or from unforeseen circumstances— in effect, grievance cases. Major disputes are those arising in contract negotiations. The statute requires in both cases that the parties first negotiate with each other. If the parties cannot agree, in disputes under existing contracts the dispute is submitted to the National Railroad Adjustment Board, whose award is binding.

If the parties are unable to agree in a major dispute, the next stage is mediation by the National Mediation Board. The National Mediation Board may also move into the case without waiting for a request by the contending parties. If the National Mediation Board cannot settle the dispute, it requests the parties to submit the case to arbitration. If the patries reject arbitration (as they almost invariably do), and if the National Mediation Board certifies the dispute as threatening to deprive the country of essential transportation, the president appoints an emergency fact-finding board. Meanwhile, the dispute is frozen for thirty days from the date of formation of the emergency board, which means that a strike during this period can be enjoined by the courts.

The act's provisions go no further. After the cooling-off period, the parties are free to engage in a trial of strength. Experience shows, however, that when the statutory procedures fail there will be rapid intervention, by the president and possibly also by Congress.

The National Railroad Adjustment Board is made up of thirty-six members, eighteen selected by the carriers and eighteen by the unions. They are paid by the parties they represent and are organized in four divisions, each with jurisdiction over a stated group of transportation employees. When the act was extended to air transportation in 1936, Title 2 created a four-member National Air Transport Adjustment Board on the same pattern as the Railroad Adjustment Board.

The National Mediation Board, at the apex of the structure, consists of three members appointed by the president, with senate approval, and removable only for cause. Not more than two may be of the same political party. Their term of office is three years, with the terms overlapping so that one new appointment is made annually. One member of the board is chosen by the others to act as chairman.

The Railway Labor Act of 1926 was drafted after long consultation with the railroad brotherhoods and representatives of the carriers. This may help to explain the success of its grievance arbitration machinery. Arbitration of major disputes, however, has been consistently resisted by the unions; and the issues have often been passed on to Congress for settlement. Presidential requests for Congressional action were made by Wilson in 1916 and 1919, by Roosevelt in 1944, by Truman in 1946 and 1952, and by Kennedy in 1963. Three of these resulted in special legislation that sought to avert specific work stoppages, two of them nationwide. Most recently, in a dispute over use of firemen on diesel locomotives, Congress in the Railroad Arbitration Act of 1963 made arbitration of the dispute compulsory for a period of two years. In all three cases the threatened strike was postponed, but within a year there followed renewed presidential intervention. In no case has Congressional action really resolved the dispute.

Awards in arbitration cases have frequently been set aside by federal districts courts, new trials often being granted where money awards were claimed. In June, 1966, amendments to the Railway Labor Act for the first time prescribed specific standards for judicial review. The district court may now set aside an arbitration award only for failure to comply with the requirements of the act, for exceeding the scope of the board's jurisdiction, or for fraud or corruption. These standards still leave considerable scope for judicial review. In particular, "failure to comply with the requirements of the act" opens the door to judicial intervention.

Collective Bargaining: A Multistage Process

State and federal statutes have established a pattern of self-organization and majority rule, closely resembling the political process, as the basis for economic relationships in American industrial life. This means that the terms of making one's living, which are matters central to most people's lives, are determined by group action rather than by individual negotiation. A whole class of contracts, those of employment, have been removed from the application of the traditional law of contracts. Negotiations remain private, however, and the signed agreement that determines the conditions of employment for a whole plant, industry, or other bargaining unit, is a contract enforceable in the courts. Although it is no longer an individual contract, it is a *private* contract, in contrast to countries where the terms of employment are determined by a government ruling.

The process goes through a predictable series of stages, beginning with the confrontation of union officials and employer representatives in bargaining negotiations. In theory, the two sides are free to negotiate as they see fit, about any subject either side wishes to bring up. In practice, both sides know that previous rulings of the National Labor Relations Board and the courts have defined certain limits of action. They may abide peacefully within these limits or they may decide to test the limits by doing something just somewhat different. Out of previous contests have come scores of rulings which, taken together, make up a kind of "common law of industrial relations." The vast majority of negotiating sessions operate within the framework of this new common law and proceed to the writing of a contract.

Beyond the private negotiations, however, is the possibility of appeal by one side to the National Labor Relations Board, or to the equivalent state tribunal, or to the Railroad Adjustment Board, for an interpretation of the basic law as it applies to a particular set of facts. The final stage, and one in which it is sometimes possible to bypass the National Labor Relations Board, is appeal to the courts.

This multistage process has created a legal structure of great diversity. Perhaps diversity is a source of strength in our circumstances, for the structure of American industry scarcely permits of simple, uniform solutions to employment problems. What is appropriate for electronics manufacturing may be unsuitable for the trucking industry, or for longshoring, or automobile manufacturing. Legally, of course, it is untidy. Indeed, the most remarkable aspect of the system may be that there are so many areas of what the experts call "settled law," areas in which the parties are willing to accept previous rulings and to do things as they have been done by an earlier generation of negotiators. In the next chapter we explore the main issues and areas of action, both settled and unsettled, in contemporary collective bargaining.

Discussion Questions

1. "Until recently there were practically no statutes affecting labor relations; yet public control over labor relations is as old as trade unions themselves." Explain, giving examples.

2. Why have unions taken strong exception to the injunction procedure? How did the Norris–LaGuardia Act alter the use of this device?

3. Explain why union organization was easier after passage of the Wagner Act than before that time.

4. Compare the philosophy and objectives of the Taft–Hartley Act with those of the Wagner Act.

5. Recalling the discussion of union government in Chapter 13, would you expect federal regulation to have much effect on the internal operations of trade unions?

6. Does it make sense to have a special set of rules for industrial relations in the railroad and airline industries? Explain.
7. "Experience since 1933 proves that it is impossible to legislate good labor relations. The best thing that could be done would be to repeal all federal and state statutes on the subject and turn the matter back to the regular courts." Discuss.
8. Suppose the National Labor Relations Act had been passed *without* creating a National Labor Relations Board. Would the act have been equally effective? Explain.

Reading Suggestions

References on current labor law are given at the end of the next chapter. Studies with a historical orientation include Bernstein, Irving, *The New Deal Collective Bargaining Policy*. Berkeley and Los Angeles: University of California Press, 1950; Frankfurter, Felix, and Nathan Greene, *The Labor Injunction*. New York: The Macmillan Company, 1930; Killingsworth, Charles C., *State Labor Relations Acts*. Chicago: The University of Chicago Press, 1948; Millis, Harry A., and Emily C. Brown, *From the Wagner Act to Taft–Hartley*. Chicago: The University of Chicago Press, 1950; and Turner, Marjorie S., *The Early American Conspiracy Cases; Their Place in Labor Law*. San Diego: San Diego State College Press, 1967.

There are a number of useful general discussions dealing with the problems and institutions of American labor policy. Book-length studies include Evans, Robert, *Public Policy Toward Labor*. New York: Harper & Row, Publishers, 1965; McCloskey, Robert C., *The American Supreme Court*. Chicago: The University of Chicago Press, 1960; Ulman, Lloyd, ed., *Challenges to Collective Bargaining*. Englewood Cliffs, N.J.: Prentice-Hall, Inc., 1967; Shister, Joseph, Benjamin Aaron, and Clyde W. Summers, eds., *Public Policy and Collective Bargaining*, Industrial Relations Research Association Publication 27. New York: Harper & Row, Publishers, 1962; and *The Public Interest in National Labor Policy*. New York: Committee for Economic Development, 1961. Shorter general discussions include: Meltzer, Bernard D., "The Supreme Court, Congress, and State Jurisdiction over Labor Relations," in *Columbia Law Review*, Vol. 59 (1959), 6; Rutledge, L. C., "Justice Black and Labor Law," *U.C.L.A Law Review*, Vol. 14 (1967), 501; Wellington, Harry, "The Constitution, the Labor Union, and 'Government Action,'" *Yale Law Journal*, Vol. 70 (1961),

345; Cox, Archibald, "The Role of Law in Labor Disputes," *Cornell Law Quarterly*, Vol. 39 (1954), 592; Ziskind, David, "Standards for Evaluating Labor Legislation," *Cornell Law Quarterly*, Vol. 51 (1966), 502; and Aaron, Benjamin, "The Labor Injunction Reappraised," *Labor Law Journal*, January, 1963, pp. 41–81.

THE LAW
OF
COLLECTIVE
BARGAINING
TODAY

18

What are the main outlines of American labor law? What are the parties to collective bargaining required to do, what are they free to do, what are they prohibited from doing? As in other areas of law, the answers are not entirely clear-cut. We shall try to distinguish between what appear to be settled principles and frontier issues on which legal opinion is evolving and inconclusive.

The substantive issues to be examined fall into six groups:

1. The right of free and unrestrained organization.
2. The determination of bargaining representatives.
3. The duty to bargain in good faith.
4. The status of collective agreements and arbitration awards.
5. The individual's relation to his union.
6. The use of economic weapons—strikes, picketing, and boycotts.

THE RIGHT OF
FREE AND UNRESTRAINED
ORGANIZATION

The law governing the establishment of a new collective bargaining relationship looks first to the adoption of standards for union organizing-campaigns and elections. In principle, certain items are paramount: (1) The employees should have a free choice between competing unions, and the right of rejection of unionism. (2) The union campaign should be conducted with propriety, without undue attacks on the employer, or on rival union groups, or on those employees who wish to abstain altogether. (3) The employer is similarly restricted in the tactics he may use to combat the union campaign. (4) The personal and property interests of employers and employees alike should be respected. (5) The election process as administered by the National Labor Relations Board should be above reproach.

Election standards are set forth in the National Labor Relations Act. The employee is protected from coercion and from various forms of interference with his free choice [Sec. 8 (a) (1)]. He is protected from employer domination [Sec. 9 (c) (2)], and employer assistance to a company-dominated union is forbidden [Sec. 10 (c)]. The courts under these provisions have prohibited a wide variety of discriminatory actions. The act also defines certain unfair practices of unions in elections [Sec. 8 (b) (1) and (4)]; and the union winning the election may be certified by the National Labor Relations Board as exclusive bargaining representative [Sec. 8 (a) (5) and 9 (a)].

The National Labor Relations Board procedure in representation cases may be formal or informal. When there is no doubt about the scope of the bargaining unit and no dispute with the employer, a "consent election agreement" is prepared by the company and the union, specifying the name of the bargaining unit, the eligibility of voters, and the date of the election. On the other hand, if there is doubt as to whether the union has an actual majority, or disagreement over the bargaining unit, the regional director (through his agents) conducts hearings on these issues. A formal order is then issued ("direction of election"), ordering an election to be held in a specified unit within a certain period, usually very brief. The procedure from this point resembles in all respects a local political election. If votes are challenged when the ballots are counted and the challenges cannot be settled at once, the ballots will be set aside. If there are enough challenged votes to affect the outcome, the regional director will hand down a ruling on the disputed ballots.

The volume of elections is great and has been growing steadily. Final authority and responsibility rests with the National Board of Labor Relations in Washington, but has increasingly been delegated to the regional directors. Since 1961, appeal to the board occurs only where there are compelling reasons either for reconsidering a board policy or for believing that there as been a factual error.

The two principal issues in representation elections are (1) who is eligible to vote and (2) what constitutes majority choice. Eligibility of employees engaged in an economic strike has been a troublesome issue. The 1959 amendments to the National Labor Relations Act permit such employees to vote for a twelve-month period following the beginning of the strike, even if they have taken other jobs and are not entitled to reinstatement with the company.

What constitutes majority choice? As in other American elections, it is not necessary to have a majority of all employees but only a majority of the valid ballots cast. If more than one union is involved and no union wins a majority, a runoff election is conducted in which the employees choose between the two highest candidates, one of which may be the choice "no union."

The final count of ballots is not necessarily decisive. Elections may be set aside by the board, either on generalized grounds such as interference with employees' freedom of choice, or on allegations of specific union or employer unfair practices. There is also the possibility of judicial review of the board's certification, though this has been used rarely and on a limited basis. In a 1965 case the Supreme Court overruled the court of appeals and indicated that the courts must accept the board's discretion in appraising factual situations to determine the bargaining unit. The Supreme Court said, "For reviewing courts to substitute counsel's rationale or their discretion for that of the Board is incompatible with the orderly function of the process of review." [1]

The present law provides little control of tactics in union organizing-campaigns, and it is not uncommon to see bitter no-holds-barred contests. Under the Wagner Act, employer free speech was strictly limited. No matter how innocent his remarks, under the board's definition of "strict neutrality" they would be ruled coercive. In the Taft–Hartley amendments of 1947, the employer was allowed to make statements seeking to influence the election, provided they contained no threat of reprisal or promise of benefits. Subsequently the board adopted the concept of a framework of coercive behavior based on the "totality of conduct" by the employer. The courts have never fully accepted the board's rationale of this policy, however, and judicial rulings have allowed greater latitude to the employer in elections.

After 1961, with a change in membership of the National Labor Relations Board, there appeared more detailed restrictions on the content of employer campaign-statements. It became accepted practice that the employer might take various forms of action against the union, and might freely express his antiunion beliefs, provided he did not either threaten the employees or promise benefits as a condition of rejecting the union. In the *Dal–Tex Optical Company* case in 1962 the union lost by a vote of 101 to 96, and asked the board to set aside the election on the grounds that hostile speeches by the

[1] *National Labor Relations Board* v. *Metropolitan Life Insurance Company,* 380 U.S. 438 (1965).

employer had been coercive.[2] The speech complained of had included a statement that the employees' interests were not necessarily the union's interests, the employer was not afraid of a strike, the union had nothing to lose, and the ones actually hurt would be the employees. The board ruled this to be a misrepresentation of the consequences of unionism and thus to go beyond the free-speech privilege of the Taft–Hartley amendments.

In the same year, the board set aside a Mississippi election because the employer had circulated handbills containing appeals to racial prejudice. In the *Hollywood Ceramics* case, the board ruled that an election might be set aside because of statements that involved "a substantial departure from the truth" and that were circulated at a time when the other side could not reply effectively—that is, the action must have had a significant effect on the election. The Hollywood Ceramics election was invalidated because a leaflet distributed by the employer just before the balloting made a dramatic but erroneous comparison of the comparative wage situation between his plant and unidentified "other union plants." [3]

It is well settled that employers shall have access to relevant information and shall be free to act on it. The employer must furnish information about the company's operations when requested by the union; and the employer may not unreasonably limit either the employees or outside union organizers from meeting, even on company property, to discuss unionization. The employer cannot use plant rules against solicitation to bar union organizers from communicating with the employees. This principle was laid down in 1945 in the *Republic Aviation* case. It was reinforced in 1949, when the board ruled that a company cannot deny the union use of a meeting hall if this is the only public space available in a company town.[4]

The board, in short, has very considerable discretion. Unlike the situation in political campaigns, the burden of proof has been on the party making a speech to establish that it was truthful and relevant. There has also been a tendency toward inconsistency in applying the board's own precedents, particularly as turnover of membership has resulted from new political administrations in Washington. In 1953 the "Eisenhower board" had ruled that letters to employees could not be made the basis for setting aside an election; but in 1962 (the *Dal-Tex* decision) a "Kennedy board" ruled that hostile speeches by the employer, even though they contained explicit disclaimers of coercive intent, were not privileged as "employer free spech."

Three regulations of recent years have aimed at equal opportunity

2 *Dal–Tex Optical Company*, 137 NLRB 1782 (1962).

3 *Hollywood Ceramics, Inc.*, 140 NLRB 221 (1962).

4 *Republic Aviation Corp.* v. *National Labor Relations Board*, 324 U.S. 793 (1945); *National Labor Relations Board* v. *Stowe Spinning Co.*, 336 U.S. 226 (1949).

for the parties. First, the "equal opportunity rule" requires that the union must be given an opportunity to reply if the employer makes a speech on company time and property. In the *Elson Bottling Company* case in 1967, the employer was required to give the union space and time for a one-hour meeting to "redress the imbalance" following a preelection speech by the employer. Second, the "captive audience rule" requires that the employer refrain altogether from addressing the employees on company time in the twenty-four hours immediately preceding the election. Third, neither side may engage in "material misrepresentation."

Both employer and union statements in organizing campaigns are subject to the protection of free speech guaranteed by the First Amendment, as well as the standards set by the National Labor Relations Board. In political campaigns, the right of free speech has been jealously protected by the courts. In the late 1960s some fairly extreme expressions of employer views have been held to be privileged free speech. In a 1966 case, descriptions of violence and reference to "union goons who trampled a nonstriker to death in a tavern" were ruled noncoercive. In the same year it was held that a statement that unions "blew up homes and kidnapped children" was a mere expression of opposition to unionism.

In recent years, the free speech issue has been raised chiefly in a context of racial prejudice in organizing campaigns in the South. In the *Sewall Manufacturing* case the board set aside an election, lost by the union, on the grounds that the employer's literature had "inflamed and tainted the atmosphere." In two 1965 cases, where the employer had asked that an election be set aside because of union statements asking the employees not to act like "Uncle Toms," the board ruled that such statements were not prejudicial but rather an appeal to "racial self-consciousness," which was germane to the issue. But in a 1966 case involving far less inflammatory union statements than the "Uncle Tom" references, a National Labor Relations Board ruling was overturned by the circuit court on the ground that the union could have no other purpose than the inflammation of racial feeling.[5]

Misrepresentation designed to influence the election was the basis for setting aside an election in a case where the union had offered to waive initiation fees if the union won, at the same time stating that employees hired after the election would have to pay. There was an element of misrepresentation, the court ruled, in that the fee was rumored to be $300 without any union denial. But the crucial fact was the conditional nature of the offer, its dependence on union vic-

[5] *Sewall Manufacturing Co.*, 138 NLRB 66 (1962). For a review of these and other cases see Daniel H. Pollitt, "The NLRB and race hate propaganda in union organization drives," *Stanford Law Review*, Vol. 17 (1965), 373.

tory. A similar ruling against employer action came from the Supreme Court in 1964. Six days after the National Labor Relations Board had ordered an election, the employer offered a "floating holiday" and a "birthday holiday" for all employees, combined with a summary of past benefits and the suggestion that these might not be continued if the union won. The Court ruled that, to avoid the taint of misrepresentation, economic benefits must be "conferred unconditionally and permanently." [6]

DETERMINATION OF BARGAINING REPRESENTATIVES

To win certification as bargaining representative, a union must demonstrate that it is the choice of a majority of employees "in an appropriate bargaining unit." But what is the appropriate unit? There is frequently disagreement on this point between the employer and the union, and there may also be disagreement within the labor force. Groups of skilled workers may prefer to be represented by separate unions of their own craft, while semiskilled production workers may prefer a single plant-wide unit. Resolving such disputes is one of the board's important functions, both in terms of volume of work and the influence of board decisions in shaping the collective bargaining structure.

In most cases the appropriate bargaining unit is determined informally by a stipulation between the regional director and the parties. Where voluntary agreement cannot be reached, there is a formal hearing procedure. Since 1961, power to make unit determinations has been delegated to the regional director, subject only to limited review by the National Labor Relations Board.

The most controversial issue has been that of granting separate bargaining rights to particular groups of skilled workers. During the period of AFL–CIO rivalry in the thirties and forties, the board was under strong pressure from both sides, and there was considerable shifting of policy. In an early case (*Globe Machine Company*, 1937) the board ruled that the question of separate craft representation should be put to a vote of all employees in the plant. With low-skilled workers in a decided majority, this policy tilted the scales against craft unionism.[7]

---

[6] For a general discussion of the board's policies in regulating representation elections see Derek Bok, "The Regulation of Campaign Tactics in Representation Elections under the National Labor Relations Act," *Harvard Law Review*, Vol. 78 (1964), 38.

[7] Matter of *Globe Machine and Stamping Co.*, 3 NLRB 294 (1937).

A few years later, in the *American Can* case, the board ruled that a minority group could not have separate representation when a larger unit had already been established by board determination, and where bargaining had been carried on actively by the larger unit. But as pressures from powerful craft unions continued, exceptions to the *American Can* doctrine were made and "craft severance" was granted where certain conditions were met. These conditions were summed up in the board's opinion in the *General Electric* case of 1944. The essential elements were a demonstration that the group was truly a craft, not merely a dissident faction; that it had maintained its identity throughout the period of bargaining on the comprehensive unit basis and had protested being included in the larger unit; or that the comprehensive unit had been established without its knowledge and without previous consideration of the merits of a separate unit. In the 1946 *Allied Chemical* case, craft severance was granted even though the craft had not been in existence when the earlier determination was made and subsequently had not protested against inclusion in the larger unit.

The craft unions seemed to have won a victory when the Taft–Hartley Act in 1947 forbade the board to decide "that any craft unit is inappropriate . . . on the ground that a different unit has been established by a prior board determination." [sec. 9(b)(2)]. In the 1948 *National Tube* case, however, the board interpreted Section 9 (b)(2) as permitting prior history to be considered as long as it was not the only ground for preventing creation of a craft unit. A group of bricklayers asked severance from a long-established industrial unit in basic steel. The board examined the traditional bargaining pattern in basic steel and concluded that, for this reason and because of the highly integrated production process, a craft unit would be inappropriate. This precedent was later used to deny craft severance in the milling, lumber, and aluminum industries.

In summary, the board's rulings on separate craft representation take into account the past history of bargaining in the plant and industry, the degree of industrial integration and the company's organization for personnel management, the degree of skill involved in the work for which separate representation is asked, and finally but not solely, the expressed wishes of the employees. Where the group in question has a well-established craft skill, and where there is clear evidence of its desire for separate representation, this will usually be granted.[8]

The issue of single-employer versus multi-employer bargaining units has proven less controversial. Where multi-employer units have

[8] Development of the board's policy in making unit determinations is summarized in Archibald Cox and Derek Bok, *Cases and Materials on Labor Law,* 6th ed. (Brooklyn: The Foundation Press, Inc., 1965), pp. 346–48.

been established, this is usually because both parties prefer them for the reasons discussed in Chapter 15.

Once a bargaining unit has been defined and a bargaining representative certified, how long does the decision last? Can the employer or a rival union come in next month and demand a new election? The board early adopted a rule that certification of a representative bars any new election for at least a year, and this policy was confirmed by the Taft–Hartley Act. The board also requires an employer to continue bargaining with the certified union for a year even if employee sentiment has changed. In a 1954 case, an election had been won by the Machinists Union. A week after the election and before the union had formally been certified, the employer received a letter from nine of his thirteen employees stating that they did not wish to be represented by the union. The employer thereupon refused to bargain with the union, and the National Labor Relations Board declared the refusal an unfair labor practice. The Circuit Court of Appeals upheld the board's order, but in another district precisely the opposite ruling had been made. The Supreme Court thereupon made a comprehensive ruling that the employer may not refuse to bargain, though he may petition the board to revoke the certification, during a one-year period following the selection of the bargaining agent.[9]

The presence of an existing collective agreement will also bar a new election or certification until the old contract runs out. But in the course of time this rule has frequently been amended, and a substantial list of circumstances is now required to keep a contract in force against the apparent wishes of a majority of the employees. If it has no fixed duration, it will not be a bar for any period. If it has a fixed term of years, a petition may be filed by a rival union after only three years have passed. It may not contain provisions violating any section of the National Labor Relations Act; and in 1962 the board ruled that no contract could bar an election petition if it discriminated against employees on racial grounds. Procedural requirements also exist. The rival union must file its petition not more than ninety nor less than sixty days before termination of the existing contract. But if the bargaining representative has become "defunct" or if a "schism" is found to exist, or if changes in the employer's operations through merger or relocation have brought major changes in personnel, an existing contract will not bar a new election.

The Taft–Hartley Act, while it continued the Wagner Act certification procedures, established a new procedure for decertification, i.e. a way by which employees can get rid of a union that they no longer wish to represent them. If a "substantial number" (interpreted

---

[9] *Brooks* v. *National Labor Relations Board,* 348 U.S. 96 (1964).

as 30 percent) of the employees in a bargaining unit file a petition requesting decertification, the National Labor Relations Board must conduct a secret ballot to determine the wishes of the majority. More than a hundred such elections are held each year, most of which are lost by the union. This is not surprising, since the very filing of a decertification petition is an indication of serious dissatisfacton.

THE
DUTY TO BARGAIN
IN
GOOD FAITH

Once a bargaining representative is certified, the National Labor Relations Act places on both parties a legally enforceable duty to bargain. The reason is partly that without this the other provisions of the act would be meaningless. Organization is of no avail unless it leads to joint determination of conditions of employment. Further, it is believed that serious exchange of proposals and the reasoning behind them has an educational effect. Each side comes to understand the other's position better, ways may be found of bridging initially irreconcilable positions, and the chances of peaceful agreement are increased.

Refusal to bargain may be remedied by an affirmative order of the National Labor Relations Board; and if the board's order to bargain has been properly issued, the United States Courts of Appeals is required to compel enforcement under contempt-of-court penalties. Moreover, certain kinds of bargaining behavior may be held to constitute an unfair labor practice.

But what does this duty actually mean? Does it mean going through the motions, or does it mean serious bargaining? And what is "serious" bargaining? In Congressional debate on the Wagner Act it was stated that this provision "only leads the employees to the door of the employer . . . what happens behind those doors is not inquired into." But this view turned out to be untenable. As one party or the other did not like what was going on behind the doors and complained to the board, the duty to bargain began to be defined in depth by board and court decisions.

Some of these decisions were codified by the Taft–Hartley Act in 1947. The parties must meet at reasonable times. They must confer "in good faith" about terms of employment; and they must go beyond discussion to negotiation of an agreement. Points on which agreement has been reached must be put into a written contract. The obligation to bargain, however, does not compel either side to make concessions on specific points. Bargaining may be as hard as the economic power of the parties can make it.

The test of good faith is thus partly a procedural test. The board cannot look into the hearts of the parties and discern there a cooperative or antagonistic spirit. Nor can it require that the proposals put forward by one side or the other be "reasonable." This would go too far in the direction of government interference with the content of collective agreements. What it can do is to infer, from the behavior of the parties, whether they are trying to avoid agreement or whether their negotiating posture is sufficiently genuine to meet their legal obligation.

On mandatory bargaining subjects (to be defined in a moment) each party must listen to the other's proposals, make counterproposals, and advance facts and arguments in support of its position. The employer must furnish relevant data to the union on request. In the *Truitt* case the board held that: "It is settled law that when an employer seeks to justify the refusal of a wage increase upon an economic basis, . . . good-faith bargaining under the act requires that upon request the employer attempt to substantiate its economic position by reasonable proof." [10] The Supreme Court upheld this ruling.

The two sides do not have to agree, but they must "bargain to impasse." When both sides have exhausted their stock of proposals and arguments, and still no settlement has been reached, either party is free to break off negotiations and call a strike or declare a lockout.

A key case in this area involved the General Electric Company's use of the "boulwarism" technique described in Chapter 15. In 1960 the company opened negotiations with the International Union of Electrical Workers by bringing in a comprehensive three-year contract, with the announcement that this was both its first and last offer. There followed a professional public relations campaign, in which management sent 246 separate bulletins to employees in its Schenectady plant and 277 communications to the Pittsfield plant employees. Meanwhile, the company was prepared to go on talking indefinitely. It claimed that the proposed contract had been carefully researched and represented the very best that could be done. In effect, it relied on the ability of management to foresee all claims that the union could rationally make, and also on the workers being motivated more by a desire for uninterrupted work than by a desire to support their representatives in contract negotiations.

The National Labor Relations Board ruled against this take-it-or-leave-it technique.[11] Management, the board said, must fulfill the requirement of good-faith bargaining by affirmatively demonstrating its

---

[10] *Truitt Mfg. Co.*, 110 NLRB 856 (1954); *National Labor Relations Board* v. *Truitt*, 351 U.S. 149 (1956).

[11] *General Electric Company*, 150 NLRB 192 (1964).

willingness to resolve differences and reach common ground. Four types of actions were cited as evidence of bad faith: (1) failure to furnish information requested by the union; (2) attempts to deal separately with local unions on matters that were properly within the scope of national negotiations, while at the same time the local unions were solicited to refrain from supporting the threatened strike; (3) the take-it-or-leave-it presentation of proposals, with specific mention of a clause involving personal accident insurance; and (4) the company's general approach to the conduct of bargaining, which relegated the union to a merely advisory position.

The National Labor Relations Board did not prohibit any specific action by General Electric. Its complaint was that the General Electric policy "devitalized negotiations" and sought to discredit the union. In March of 1970 the Supreme Court refused to review the board's ruling on 'boulwarism', a decision which had little practical effect since the Company itself, following a 14-week strike in 1969, had backed away from the policy.

In the *Reed and Prince* case, negotiations were with the Steelworkers.[12] The company, which is family-owned, submitted a signed contract as a "final offer." Simultaneously, management sent all employees a letter calling the union's bargaining position "CIO sabotage of their wage-earning capacity." The National Labor Relations Board ruled this an unfair practice, interpreting the letter as evidence of a concealed determination to avoid agreement. Meanwhile, the union had called a strike. The company then hired a public relations consultant and carried through a publicity campaign aimed at discrediting the union. Subsequently, more than half the employees signed petitions authorizing acceptance of the company's contract offer, and the strike was broken. The National Labor Relations Board decided that in the "total context" the Reed and Prince communications to their employees were evidence of bad faith, and again ordered management to resume bargaining.

The local union collapsed without a contract having been signed. Five years later, the Steelworkers won an election by a vote of 449 to 304. Negotiations following certification proved fruitless and the National Labor Relations Board, by a divided vote, found a breach of the duty to bargain. This time, five specific grounds were given: (1) delay in scheduling the first negotiating session and delay in furnishing the union with data on the company's wage structure; (2) insistence on a stenotypist recording the sessions; (3) withholding agreement on "trivial" matters, such as permission for the union to post its notices on company bulletin boards; (4) giving a wage increase after the negotiations had broken down; and (5) refusing a checkoff

[12] *National Labor Relations Board* v. *Reed & Prince Mfg. Co.*, 205 F. 2d 131 (1st Circuit, 1953); certiorari denied, 346 U.S. 887 (1953).

of dues. None of these actions individually was declared an unfair practice. Rather, they were cited as a test of motive of state of mind on the part of management.

The company held off the union for thirty-nine months and finally signed an agreement which merely wrote into contract form the existing wage scales and company personnel policies. In fifteen years, this contract has never been renegotiated. The *Reed and Prince* case suggests that, if a weak union fails to secure its first contract, a stubborn management can avoid the burden of collective bargaining even though the National Labor Relations Board and the courts have ruled against the employer.[13]

The National Labor Relations Board and the courts would say that their function is not to strengthen one side or the other but only to assure fair play. Whether the unions can in fact compel good faith bargaining within this framework is still an unsettled question.

While the courts have emphasized, and would prefer to hold to, a procedural test of good faith, the board has edged into applying also a *substantive* test. The central issue here is what *subjects* the parties are obliged to bargain about. The act refers to "wages, hours, and other terms and conditions of employment," which the courts have ruled to be mandatory subjects for bargaining. But these concepts have considerable elasticity. Unions steadily try to enlarge the mandatory area by giving a broad interpretation to "terms and conditions of employment." Employers naturally contest this at every stage, claiming an area of "management prerogative" in which efficient operation requires unilateral decision.

Occasionally the shoe is on the other foot. One employer proposed a contract clause under which, before the union could call a strike, it must take a secret ballot of all employees on the employer's last offer. In the event of employees rejecting the offer, the company was to have seventy-two hours to present a new proposal. The union refused to bargain on this issue, on the ground that it related to internal union affairs, and this position was upheld by the board.

An issue on which the parties are not required to bargain is termed a nonmandatory or "permissive" issue.[14] Either party is free to raise such a subject, but the other party is under no obligation to discuss it, and his refusal to do so is not an unfair labor practice. Nor may the party who raised the subject insist on it to the point of a strike

13 J. Cross, D. Cullen, and K. C. Hanslow, "Good Faith in Labor Negotiations: Tests and Remedies," *Cornell Law Quarterly,* Vol. 53 (July, 1968), 1009. See also Herbert R. Northrup, "The Case for Boulwarism," *Harvard Business Review,* Oct., 1963, pp. 86–97.

14 In addition to *mandatory* and *permissive* subjects, there is a small category of *prohibited* subjects that may not be included in a collective agreement. The leading examples are the closed shop and the "hot-cargo clause," under which the union requires the employer to refrain from dealing with third parties.

or lockout. This is permissible only in the case of disagreement on mandatory subjects.

The board, and ultimately the courts, are responsible for drawing the line between permissive and mandatory subjects. The consequences are important. Matters that are ruled to be mandatory will be subjected to joint control through collective agreements, not only in the industry where the issue first arose, but in other industries that rely on the first as a precedent. A ruling that a subject is permissive only will tend to exclude it from collective agreements. The broad phrase, "other terms and conditions of employment," can be used either to restrict or to expand the scope of bargaining.

The most controversial area involves the employer's right to close down or relocate plants, to subcontract work previously done by company employees to an outside contractor, or to make other labor-displacing changes in production schedules and methods. Unions argue that such decisions directly affect the job security of their members, and should therefore be subject to joint control. Management replies that these matters have traditionally been reserved for management decision, and that without this orderly and efficient management becomes impossible.

A few cases may illustrate the variety of situations that arise. Can an employer cease operations and move without first consulting the union? The National Labor Relations Board in 1965 held that this constituted a denial of good faith bargaining when Garwin, a New York manufacturer of swimsuits, closed down and formed a new Florida corporation to produce the same items with funds and machinery from the defunct New York firm and under a management in which only the executive titles had been changed. The board's ruling required that the New York employees be offered jobs in Florida and be compensated for lost wages if they decided not to accept. Moreover, the employer must either return to New York or bargain with the old union at the new plant regardless of whether the union represents a majority of the Florida employees.

Can an employer threaten to close the plant and subsequently go out of business if the union wins an election? The National Labor Relations Board said "No," but the Supreme Court did not agree. In the *Darlington Mills* case, the board ruled that if the plant is one unit in a large business, and if closing results from antiunion animus, the employees must be compensated or put on preferential hiring lists. But the Supreme Court rejected this ruling in 1964, on the basis that the right to go out of business is an absolute right which cannot be ruled an unfair labor practice.[15]

---

[15] *Textile Workers Union* v. *Darlington Mfg. Co.,* 308 U.S. 263 (1965). For a discussion of the *Garwin* case see the Comment in *Harvard Law Review,* Vol. 79 (February, 1966), 855.

These cases again suggest that determined refusal to bargain can sometimes be successful. In the *Garwin Swimsuit* case, even assuming full enforcement of the board's order, the company would be able to resist the union more easily in a largely nonunion state like Florida. The *Darlington Mills* case suggests that threats to close the plant are still a powerful weapon against unionization, especially where executives and capital are readily transferable to other parts of the enterprise.

In the *Fibreboard* case, where the company had "contracted out" an operation without first consulting the union, the Supreme Court undertook to define those "terms and conditions of employment" that are as basic as wages and hours. In so doing, it had to balance management's function of adopting technical changes and increasing production efficiency against the rights of the workers to security and stability in their jobs. A narrow interpretation of the statutory phrase would give the company an unrestricted right to eliminate jobs through technological improvements. A broad or vague definition would give the union a veto on technical change. The ruling of the Supreme Court in effect included in the protected "terms and conditions of employment," the termination rights and posttermination pension rights of present employees. The Court requires that *all* management decisions representing a departure from prior practice that significantly impair (1) job tenure, (2) employment security, and (3) "reasonably anticipated work opportunities," must be negotiated as mandatory subjects before the management decision becomes effective.[16]

The board is not supposed to prescribe the outcome of the bargain; at times, however, it has come close to doing so. In the *Porter* case, the board ruled in 1963 that the employer must concede a proposal for checkoff of union dues, *in return for some reasonable but unspecified concession* by the union. The checkoff of dues was in this case a matter of life or death for the new union. The board's ruling, though upheld by the court of appeals in 1967, was struck down by the Supreme Court in March 1970 with a strong statement that any extension of the board's remedial powers to enforce mandatory bargaining must come from Congress. Meanwhile a similar ruling in the *Roanoke Iron and Bridge Works* case had also been upheld by the court of appeals.[17]

[16] *Fibreboard Paper Products Corp.* v. *National Labor Relations Board,* 379 U.S. 203 (1964).

[17] *United Steelworkers* v. *National Labor Relations Board,* D.C. Circuit, December 27, 1967. The Steelworkers reached their first agreement with Roanoke in 1951, with the checkoff of dues not included. During the term of this first contract the union lost its majority, and in 1961 the company negotiated an agreement with a local union that did not include the checkoff. This second union also disappeared by the time its agreement expired. In 1964 the Steelworkers returned and gained National Labor Relations Board certification. After lengthy negotiations and a

The legal and practical difficulties of establishing a group of subjects on which refusal to bargain would be prima facie evidence of bad faith are great, for it is hard to discern any inherent logic in the placement of specific contract provisions inside or outside the mandatory area. The principle of freedom of contract, which is the foundation of collective bargaining, requires the government to stay out of the terms of the contract; yet it has another mandate, sometimes conflicting, that requires the establishment of collective bargaining relationships to promote industrial stability. In applying this mandate the board has influenced both the scope of collective agreements and, by altering the relative strength of the parties, the outcome of the bargain. Some legal opinion holds that the board has intruded too far into the subject matter of bargaining, that the whole effort to distinguish mandatory from permissive subjects is misguided, and that the parties should be left to bargain about any issue which either side wishes to raise.[18]

PRIVATE AGREEMENTS
AND
PUBLIC POLICY

The collective agreement, in addition to regulating wages and other terms of employment, usually contains two procedural provisions. First, grievances arising during the life of the contract that the parties are unable to resolve by negotiation are usually referred to a neutral arbitrator, whose decision is final. Second, the parties agree that there will be no strike or lockout during the contract period.

---

strike, agreement was reached but with no provision for dues checkoff. The Steelworkers appealed to the National Labor Relations Board charging refusal to bargain in good faith; the board ruled that the company's purpose in denying the checkoff was the belief that this would break the union, and ordered bargaining resumed. This ruling was subsequently upheld by the court of appeals on the grounds that the checkoff is now the normal method of dues collection (83% of all contracts in 1967) and is not an arrangement affecting allocation of economic values between worker and employer.

[18] On this point, see the interesting discussion in Harry Wellington, *Labor and the Legal Process* (New Haven: Yale University Press, 1968), chap. 2. Wellington concludes that ". . . the totality of effects which stems from the mandatory–nonmandatory distinction makes law much too important in terms of the statutory goal of freedom of contract . . . The Borg–Warner rule, that insistence on hard bargaining over a nonmandatory subject is itself an unfair labor practice, is indefensible and should be rejected. It, more than any other rule, makes sharp the distinction between mandatory and nonmandatory subjects: the Borg–Warner rule keeps such subjects from collective bargaining and out of the contract. To this extent the institution of collective bargaining develops by governmental fiat; the terms of collective contracts through government intervention" (pp. 76–77).

Is this just a gentleman's agreement between the parties, enforceable only by private methods? Or can one party or the other go to court to compel enforcement? In practice, lawsuits are not likely to promote good industrial relations, and the parties will normally prefer to avoid them. But can they go to law as a last resort?

It appears that they can. Before 1947 there was considerable doubt in most states whether the trade union, which is an unincorporated association, could be sued for breach of contract. But Taft–Hartley included a specific provision on this point: "Suits for violation of contracts between an employer and a labor organization . . . may be brought in any district court of the United States having jurisdiction of the parties. . . ." The courts have shown themselves willing to entertain such suits, and so by this route also government has been projected farther into the details of industrial relations.

Both the National Labor Relations Board and the courts have taken a favorable view of grievance arbitration. The board generally will not accept an unfair labor practice change unless the contract procedures, including arbitration, have been exhausted. The Supreme Court has also held that, where there is an arbitration clause in the contract and the employer refuses to observe it, the union can bring suit to compel him to do so.

Suppose, however, the employer maintains that the issue in question does not fall within the scope of the arbitration clause. This question arose in a case [19] in which the company had contracted out some of its maintenance and repair work, causing a layoff of several of its employees. The union challenged this action and, when the dispute was not resolved through discussion, filed suit to compel arbitration. The company replied that contracting out was strictly a function of management, and that the agreement provided that "matters which are strictly a function of management shall not be subject to arbitration." The Supreme Court ordered that the case go to arbitration, explaining:

"An order to arbitrate the particular grievance should not be denied unless it may be said with positive assurance that the arbitration clause is not susceptible of an interpretation that covers the asserted dispute. Doubts should be resolved in favor of coverage . . ."

The arbitrator himself might rule that the issue in question was not arbitrable. The Court was saying, in effect, that a qualified arbitrator is better able to make this kind of technical judgment than a group of judges who are amateurs in industrial relations.

[19] *United Steelworkers* v. *Warrior and Gulf Navigation Co.,* 363 U.S. 574 (1960). For a critical review of the issues see Donald H. Wollett, "The agreement and the National Labor Relations Act: Courts, arbitrators and the NLRB—Who decides What?", *Labor Law Journal,* Vol. 14 (1963), 1041; and Dallas L. Jones and Russell A. Smith, "Management and Labor appraisals and criticism of the arbitration process: a report with comments," *Michigan Law Review,* Vol. 62 (1964), 1115.

A different situation arises after an arbitration award has been made. Can the losing party appeal to the National Labor Relations Board or the courts to upset the decision? Here again the tendency has been to rely on the arbitrator's judgment. In a 1955 case the National Labor Relations Board laid down a set of conditions under which it would accept an award as final: first, if the proceedings had been "fair and regular"; second, if the parties had made an advance agreement to accept the award as binding; and third, if the decision was not "clearly inconsistent" with the purposes of the National Labor Relations Act. The board in effect gave up its primary jurisdiction over arbitrable grievances involving breach of contract, and possibly to some extent over arbitrable grievances involving unfair labor practices.

The Supreme Court also has tended to hold that court review of arbitration awards is inappropriate. In one leading case [20] it stated that:

"The refusal of courts to review the merits of an arbitration award is the proper approach to arbitration under collective bargaining agreements. The federal policy of settling labor disputes by arbitration would be undermined if courts had the final say on the merits of the awards."

This judicial modesty is no doubt commendable. The effect, however, is to compel the sending of disputes to arbitration and to compel acceptance of the award without serious court review of the circumstances. Wellington has argued that it would be better to withhold legal enforcement of arbitration clauses, leaving this to the economic strength of the parties: ". . . under present law the major function of courts in the labor arbitration area . . . is blindly to approve and make official the actions of private decision-makers whose authority to decide is frequently itself the issue in dispute . . . It seems to me quite improper, where contempt of court and ultimate imprisonment may be at stake, for a court so to rubber-stamp the decision of a private arbitrator." [21]

---

[20] *United Steelworkers* v. *Enterprise Wheel and Car Corporation,* 363 U.S. 593 (1960). See also *United Steelworkers* v. *Warrior and Gulf Navigation Co.,* 363 U.S. 574 (1960); and *United Steelworkers* v. *American Mfg. Co.,* 363 U.S. 564 (1960). These cases are commonly referred to as the "Steelworkers Trilogy," and are a landmark in the law of arbitration. The case of *Warrior and Gulf Navigation* contains the fullest expression of the Court's viewpoint.

There has been widespread comment by students of labor law on the implications of these cases. See A. Bickel and H. Wellington, "Legislative Purpose and the Judicial Process," in *Harvard Law Review,* Vol. 71 (1957), 1; B. Meltzer, "The Supreme Court, Arbitrability and Collective Bargaining," *University of Chicago Law Review,* Vol. 28 (1960), 464; H. Wellington, "Judicial Review of the Promise to Arbitrate," *New York University Law Review,* Vol. 37 (1962), 471; and Benjamin Aaron, "Strikes in Breach of Collective Agreements: Some Unanswered Questions," *Columbia Law Review,* Vol. 63 (1963), 1027.

[21] Wellington, *Labor and the Legal Process,* pp. 122–23.

Finally, it is now clear that the courts will order enforcement of a no-strike clause. Indeed, the Supreme Court did this in one case [22] where the contract did not contain a no-strike clause but did provide for grievance arbitration. The reasoning was that a promise to settle all grievances through arbitration *implies* a promise to refrain from direct action. A union that violates the no-strike clause, then, can be sued for damages, though practical considerations may deter the employer from bringing suit. In the rarer case of an employer lockout during the life of the contract, the union could presumably bring a similar suit.

INDIVIDUAL RIGHTS
AND
UNION POWER

The union has traditionally been regarded as a voluntary organization, and as such outside the scope of public regulation. Like religious organizations and private clubs, the operation of trade unions has been in theory and largely in practice, the sole responsibility of the membership. But as unions increasingly took on powers conferred by state and federal laws, the groundwork for public regulation was laid. The growing size and financial strength of unions also invited regulation, for union officers increasingly controlled the economic destinies of members, while at the same time their dependence on the goodwill of the membership diminished. When such power was used in an arbitrary or discriminatory fashion, redress was sought first through the courts and finally through the legislature.

The Right to Fair Representation

The principle of majority rule, in industrial relations, first stated in the Railway Labor Act of 1926, is now firmly established.[23] The terms established by the collective agreement cannot be modified unilaterally by the employer to grant or deny certain benefits to individual employees.

In 1944 the Supreme Court invoked this principle to bar the J. I. Case Company from undercutting a recently certified union. The company had obtained from about 75 percent of its employees signed one-year individual contracts of employment. It then notified the union that these contracts had legal effect and refused to bargain on any matters covered by the individual contracts. The Supreme Court

[22] *Local 174, Teamsters* v. *Lucas Flour,* 369 U.S. 95. (1962).

[23] A leading case is *Order of Railroad Telegraphers* v. *Railway Express Agency,* 321 U.S. 342 (1944).

refused to permit this. In its decision, the Court defined the collective agreement as different from a contract of employment. "The negotiations between union and management result in . . . a trade agreement rather than a contract of employment." While there is still room for an individual contract, even in industries covered by the National Labor Relations Act, such contracts cannot be used to defeat or delay the law's procedures, nor to exclude the contracting employee from a properly established bargaining unit, nor to obtain individual advantages. "The practice and philosophy of collective bargaining looks with suspicion on . . . individual advantages. The workman is free, if he values his own bargaining position more than that of the group, to vote against representation, but the majority rules." [24]

If individuals can no longer bargain for themselves, it becomes important that the union bargain effectively and impartially on their behalf. The union in return for its position as sole bargaining representative, has a clear duty to represent fairly all workers within the bargaining unit. But this is not easy of accomplishment. The lines of resistance have been threefold: discrimination against nonmembers of the union; discrimination on racial grounds; and economic discrimination of various types.

Nonmembers. It is well settled that the bargaining agent cannot legally cause any disadvantage to workers who are not members of the union. This is true both in negotiating the contract and in handling grievances under the contract. The union cannot secure special advantages for its members to the disadvantage of nonmembers.

Questions of discrimination arise chiefly in industries where employees do not work regularly for any one employer, and where the union acts as an employment agency. The main examples are building construction, shipping, and longshoring.[25] In 1957 the National Labor Relations Board declared that a contract of construction workers with the Mountain Pacific Chapter of the Associated General Contractors, Inc., was invalid unless the contract explicitly provided that selection of applicants for referral to jobs would "not be based on, or in any way affected by, union membership, bylaws, rules, regulations, constitutional provisions, or any other aspect or obligation of union membership, policies or requirements." [26]

In several more recent cases the board has intervened to require that hiring halls be operated in a nondiscriminatory manner.[27] But it is unclear whether these rulings have had much practical effect. It

[24] *J. I. Case Company* v. *National Labor Relations Board,* 321 U.S. 322 (1944).
[25] See "Unilateral Union Control of Hiring Halls: the Wrong and the Remedy," Note, 70 *Yale Law Journal* 661 (1961).
[26] *Mountain Pacific Chapter, Assoc. Gen. Contractors, Inc.,* 119 NLRB 883 (1957).
[27] Wellington, *Labor and the Legal Process,* pp. 141–44.

is obviously easier to detect the presence of discrimination than to prescribe a workable remedy short of public operation of the dispatching service.

Minority Groups. Union membership is not always open, even to qualified applicants. In spite of the good record of the labor movement as a whole, and despite the efforts of most national union leaders, there remain pockets of racial discrimination. Here, the conflicting economic interests of white and black workers have resulted either in Jim Crow locals with no black members, or in discriminatory systems that give priority treatment to white union members at the expense of black members. As early as 1944, in a case arising under the Railway Labor Act, the Supreme Court declared these practices illegal. The majority union may not sacrifice the rights of the minority of a craft who are outside the union. "The use of the word representative," the Court said, "in all the contexts in which it is found plainly implies that the representative is to act on behalf of all the employees which, by virtue of the statute, it undertakes to represent."

The National Labor Relations Board did not move vigorously to apply this doctrine until 1964. In that year, in the *Hughes Tool Company* case, the board refused to certify a discriminatory union. The board's opinion said, "We hold that the board cannot validly render aid under Section 9 of the act to a labor organization which discriminates racially when acting as a statutory bargaining agent." [28] In the case of unions still struggling for recognition, the fact that the board will no longer certify a union guilty of racial discrimination is a rather strong weapon. But in areas where unions are already strongly entrenched, such as railroading and construction, this weapon loses most of its force.

A more direct approach was provided by the Civil Rights Act of 1964, when for the first time Congress declared racial discrimination to be contrary to national labor policy. Under this act, a court can now issue an order forcing a union to admit an employee to membership. But will the courts actually do this? Mere passage of the law, though an important step, may not be enough. Title 7 creates an Equal Employment Opportunity Commission as the enforcing agent, but the law gives this body only investigative and negotiating functions. The commission is not an adjudicating body like the National Labor Relations Board. If negotiation and publicity fail to eliminate discriminatory practices, the Equal Employment Opportunity Commission may refer cases to the attorney general for action; or the individual may bring suit on his own behalf in a federal district court, which is empowered to issue an injunction against the offending conduct.

[28] *Independent Metal Workers Union, Local No. 1, Hughes Tool Co.,* 147 NLRB 1573 (1964).

The root of the problem, however, is that few discriminatory systems are written into collective agreements. Most of them are informal
"understandings," which are made effective by manipulating the job
classification system or the seniority rosters. There may be separate
seniority lists for white and black workers, although both are doing
identical work. Or black jobs and white jobs may be classified differently without regard to job content. In some cases both black and
white workers are admitted to the lowest job classification, with provision that only white workers can bid for promotion to jobs at higher
levels. In another type of arrangement two or more groups of jobs
are organized in separate seniority districts, so that each group has
little or no functional relation to the other groups. Only black workers are hired for the district holding the least-attractive jobs, and only
white workers for the other district, with transfer prohibited and no
line of seniority existing between the districts although they are not
labeled "black" or "white." Although such policies are clearly discriminatory, they may be set up on paper so that bias is difficult to
prove. The employer can accomplish a good deal also by defining
"ability to do the job" as he sees fit, and the union has only to agree.[29]

Economic Discrimination. This will continue to be a problem so
long as there are conflicts of interest among employees. Public policy
has moved increasingly to protect the individual worker in this area
as well as in the area of racial discrimination; and the National Labor
Relations Board has asserted its power to rule a union guilty of an
unfair labor practice for violating the duty of fair representation.[30]

Opinion is still divided, however, on the precise boundaries of economic discrimination. The standards for what constitutes "fair representation" are not settled. They still have to be hammered out, case-
by-case. At one extreme is the view that any sort of unfairness or
injustice to an employee, committed by the union and acquiesced in
by the employer, may be examined by the board to discover whether
there has been a breach of the fiduciary duty to represent all employees fairly; and that, if such a breach is found, it can be ruled an
unfair labor practice by both the union and the employer under
Section 8 of the National Labor Relations Act. This view, held by
some members of the National Labor Relations Board and by some
members of the federal courts, considers the main goal of public policy to be protection against arbitrary union power. At the other extreme is the view that the unfair labor practice machinery is not
suited to the task of deciding general questions of private wrongs,

[29] "Seniority Discrimination and the Incumbent Negro," 80 *Harvard Law Review*
1260 (April, 1967).
[30] *Miranda Fuel Company*, 140 NLRB 181 (1963). "Labor Relations Act: The
Brave New World of Miranda," New York University Conference on Labor, Vol. 16
(1963), 3.

and that there is danger that the board would be inundated with charges of this character unless the line is sharply drawn. Congress, in this view, did not intend to outlaw all unfair treatment of employees by unions; it meant only to prevent economic discrimination based on union membership.

Since the passage of the Landrum–Griffin Act it has been possible for an individual employee to challenge union actions and, under Section 301, to sue the employer for positive enforcement of his contractual rights under the collective agreement. But the courts have not encouraged such challenges. The Supreme Court, on the contrary, has asserted the need to protect employer and union from frivolous or harassing legal action by individual employees. But opinion continues to be divided, and the lines of policy are not clear.[31]

Union Membership and Discipline

Since membership in a union can affect a worker's status in the plant or industry, the fact of membership itself takes on significance. Freedom to join, freedom not to join, and the status of workers dropped from union membership become important.

There has been a concern to control compulsory unionism of any kind. The closed shop, under which only union members will be considered for employment, was forbidden by Taft–Hartley, though it still exists in covert form in industries where it has long been traditional. The milder union shop, under which the employer may hire at will but employees must subsequently join the union, is legal under federal law. The Taft–Hartley amendments to the National Labor Relations Act however, expressly allowed the state legislatures to forbid collective agreements that make union membership a condition of employment. Some twenty states have passed such laws, usually termed "right-to-work laws." These are mainly in the south and west, and do not include the major industrial states.[32]

A variant of the union shop is the "agency shop," under which workers who choose not to become union members must nevertheless pay the regular monthly dues and initiation fee. The union argument for this is the "free rider" argument that no one should be able to obtain the benefits of collective bargaining without supporting the

[31] See Michael I. Sovern, "Section 301 and the Primary Jurisdiction of the N.L.R.B.," *Harvard Law Review,* Vol. 76 (1963), 529.

[32] See D. Gilbert, "A Statistical Analysis of the Right-to-Work Law Conflict," in *Industrial and Labor Relations Review,* Vol. 19 (July, 1966), 533. For contrasting views, see A. Erwin, "The Case for Right-to-Work Laws," and N. Goldfinger, "The Case Against Right-to-Work Laws," in *Labor Law Journal,* February, 1958, p. 8. For a comprehensive discussion of the conflict with national policy see Duane B. Beeson, "State Right-to-Work Laws and Federal Labor Policy," *California Law Review,* Vol. 52 (1964), 95.

organization that makes these benefits possible. The amounts paid to
the union by nonmembers are considered a fee for services rendered.
This reasoning has found favor with both legislatures and the courts.
The agency shop was held legal by the Supreme Court in 1963, in a
case involving General Motors and the United Automobile Workers.[33]
The status of the agency shop under state right-to-work statutes is not
entirely clear. In 1963 the Supreme Court ruled, in effect, that the
courts in each state can decide whether a specific agency-shop arrangement violates state law.[34]

A standard objection to the union shop used to be that, where
union membership is compulsory, a worker who is expelled from the
union for any reason is thereby deprived of his job. Taft–Hartley provided, however, that the employer shall not discriminate against a
nonmember if (a) he was denied membership on the terms and conditions open to other employees, or (b) if his membership was terminated for reasons other than his failure to pay the standard dues and
initiation fees. This latter provision, as Wellington points out, "means
that an employee can break every minor rule in the book . . . be expelled from the union, and under the statute retain his job if he
tenders his dues to the union. Good union membership . . . and job
rights are separated, or at least that is the statute's aim." [35] The union
may still pressure the employer in one way or another to get rid of
the offending worker; but if the employer yields, he is guilty of an
unfair labor practice.

From rules concerning expulsion from union membership, it is a
short step to regulating fines, suspensions, and other lesser penalties.
In recent years there has been increasing concern for the individual
member's ability to hold his own against a growing concentration of
union power. As unions have increased in size and wealth, there has
been less concern than before about maintaining the union's institutional strength. The pendulum has shifted toward attempted protection of the individual. As one federal judge said in a leading case,
"The union is not a political unit to whose disinterested tribunals an
alleged defamer can look for an impartial review of his "crime." It is
an economic action group, the success of which depends in large
measure on a unity of purpose and sense of solidarity among its members." Decision by decision, in cases arising under the Railway Labor
Act and the National Labor Relations Act, lines have been drawn
between permissible and nonpermissible forms of union discipline.

1. The union may not discipline employees who cross a picket line
to work during a strike, if the disciplinary action affects their job
rights. In the case of the *National Labor Relations Board* v. *Bell Air-*

33 *National Labor Relations Board* v. *General Motors,* 373 U.S. 734 (1963).
34 *Retail Clerks* v. *Schermerhorn,* 375 U.S. 96 (1963).
35 Wellington, *Labor and the Legal Process,* pp. 132–33.

craft Corporation, 300 employees who crossed picket lines during a strike were charged by the union with violating their union responsibilities. Under the contract, union members against whom charges were pending were ineligible for promotion. The union sent management a list of these employees and one of them, Finch, was denied promotion to a foremanship solely on the basis of the union's action. He appealed to the National Labor Relations Board, which upheld the union's position. But Finch was not in arrears on his union dues. The circuit court of appeals ruled that under the amended Section 7 of the National Labor Relations Act, protecting the employee's right to strike *or not to strike,* the job rights of Finch and the others could not be made an instrument of union discipline.[36]

2. But the union may use coercive discipline as long as it does not strike at the individual's job or working conditions. Fines have been the preferred method. In a Wisconsin case, the National Labor Relations Board upheld fines on members who had exceeded production ceilings set by a union rule designed to limit incentive earnings.[37] This form of discipline is permissible also in strikes. The United Automobile Workers, in 1964, was upheld in imposing fines on workers who had worked during an economic strike.[38] The board's majority opinion said, "Just as the First Amendment to the United States Constitution protects the right to speak but does not insulate the speaker against all consequences of having exercised the freedom of speech, in like fashion the act . . . protects the right of an employee either to support a lawful picket line or to refuse to do so, but does not insulate the employee from all consequences flowing from his choice." But the union may not exercise this power in "arbitrary" fashion. It must have procedures that do not deprive the member of his basic rights under the law, and that also give the individual a fair hearing and impartial treatment. For example, a union that had imposed a fine for filing charges with the National Labor Relations Board before the union's own remedies had been exhausted, was ruled in violation of the act.

3. Union discipline for intraunion political activities is restricted, though it is permissible under some circumstances. This was already true at common law, but previous provisions were codified and strengthened by the Landrum–Griffin Act.

The right to electioneer against the union officers, and to criticize their actions even to the point of libel, is apparently beyond the reach of union discipline. In the case of *Salzhandler* v. *Caputo,* the financial

---

[36] 206 F. 2d 235 (1953). For a detailed review of the issues and cases, see two articles by Clyde W. Summers: "Legal Limitations on Union Discipline," *Harvard Law Review,* Vol. 63 (1951), 1049; and "The Law of Union Discipline: What the Courts Do in Fact," *Yale Law Journal,* Vol. 70 (1960), 175.

[37] *Wisconsin Motor Corp.,* 145 NLRB 109 (1964).

[38] *Automobile Workers Union,* 149 NLRB 10 (1964).

secretary of a local union attacked the president, circulating election handbills accusing the president of fiscal malfeasance and even of larceny. The union district council, after a trial, found Salzhandler guilty of "acts inconsistent with the duties and obligations of a member of the brotherhood," removed him from the post of financial secretary and suspended him for five years from all participation in union affairs. The district court held that the circulated leaflet had been libelous and that the Landrum–Griffin Act was not designed to protect libel and slander. But the court of appeals rejected this view, and ruled that "although libelous statements may be made the basis of a civil suit between those concerned, the union may not subject a member to any disciplinary action on a finding . . . that such statements are libelous." [39]

4. The right of free speech, it appears, will be upheld by the courts against any provision of the union constitution. In a 1964 case involving removal of officers for electioneering against the incumbent union management, the court refused to allow their discharge although they had not been elected by the membership and had in fact been appointed by the union president whom they opposed.

In external political activity also, union discipline cannot infringe on the constitutional right of free speech. In 1964, however, a New York union with an anti-Communist provision in its constitution was upheld in a severe disciplinary action, a five-year suspension of a member who had arranged speeches and rallies for a well-known Communist party member.[40]

THE USE OF
ECONOMIC WEAPONS:
STRIKES, PICKETING, BOYCOTTS

Public control operates in this area as in others. Actions that are entirely legal as individual rights become a subject of state and federal regulation when they are part of a pattern of group action. The right to strike is based on the individual's freedom to work or to leave his job. Underlying the boycott is the principle that anyone is free to withhold his labor or his purchasing power. Picketing, insofar as it involves the communication of information about a labor dispute to potential employees or potential customers, involves the right of free speech. But it would be overcredulous to assert that an individual

[39] 316 F. 2d 445; certiorari denied 375 U.S. 946 (1963). See Benjamin Sigal, "Freedom of Speech and Union Discipline: The 'Right' of Defamation and Disloyalty," New York University Conference on Labor, Vol. 17 (1964), 367.

[40] *Rosen* v. *District Council No. 9, Brotherhood of Painters,* Southern District of New York (1964).

could or would undertake these activities by himself, as an individual, without the intention of persuading others to join him in "concerted activity." Thus concerted action by employees or employers is never free from government control absolutely and as a matter of right.

The Right to Strike

Before 1935 public policy was largely negative. The force of law operating through the courts was weighted on the employer's side. There was a shift toward neutrality with the Norris–LaGuardia anti-injunction Act of 1932, which restricted employer use of the federal courts in breaking strikes. Positive recognition of the right to strike came in 1935, when Congress declared in the National Labor Relations Act that employees have the right to undertake a concerted work stoppage, and that strikers retain their employee status. Subsequently the Supreme Court carried this statement of policy to its logical conclusion, ruling in the *McKay Radio* case that, if the strike has been called because of an employer's unfair labor practices, the strikers must be reinstated even if replacements have been hired.[41]

The National Labor Relations Board distinguishes between "unfair-practice strikers" and "economic strikers," i.e. workers involved in a normal contract dispute over wages and other terms of employment. Unfair-practice strikers have a right to reinstatement with back pay "so long as the labor dispute is current." Without this protection an employer determined not to deal with a union could readily bring on a strike, declare that the strikers had left his employ, and hire permanent nonunion replacements. In some cases where the union has remained officially on strike for years, and where the employer has eventually been judged guilty of an unfair labor practice, he has been faced with a large bill for back pay to the striking workers.

Economic strikers receive less protection. The employer is entitled to hire temporary strikebreakers to keep production going, even though he intends to take back the strikers after the end of the dispute. Moreover, he may hire a permanent replacement for a striking worker. This ends the worker's employment connection, and he is no longer entitled to reinstatement.

Replacement hiring raises both legal and practical problems. If the strike has been long, many workers will have given up and taken permanent jobs elsewhere. Those who lasted the course and who reclaim their old jobs will have to work beside some individuals who crossed the picket line during the strike. It is in the nature of the conflict that the employer will press for favored treatment of the newly hired replacements, and that the union will resist such action. Some em-

[41] *National Labor Relations Board* v. *McKay Radio and Telegraph Company,* 304 U.S. 333 (1938).

ployers have tried to give the replacements an automatic "bonus" of so many years' seniority as a reward for their cooperation with him during the strike. In the 1963 *Erie Resistor Corporation* Case, however, the Supreme Court ruled against granting such extra seniority rights.

Various qualifications have been added to the basic policy protecting the right to strike. Thus the Taft–Hartley Act amended Section 7 of the National Labor Relations Act to protect the right *not* to strike. Certain types of strike—notably strikes to short-circuit or upset the results of National Labor Relations Board elections—were declared unfair labor practices. The law also requires written notice by either party of intention to modify or terminate an existing contract at least sixty days prior to the termination date. During this period the party serving notice must inform the appropriate federal and state mediation agencies and must observe all terms and conditions of the existing contract without resort to strike or lockout.

Federal law dominates this field of policy. For interstate industries there can be no state regulation of peaceful strikes over wages, hours, or conditions, whether by legislative or judicial action. The Supreme Court has ruled that even local utilities are subject to federal policy if interstate commerce is affected. Employment in intrastate industries is under state control, and in most states the right to strike is protected either by state statute or at common law.

Unlawful Strikes

There is no absolute right to strike. This principle was first laid down by the Supreme Court in a Kansas case in which the strike, though orderly and peaceful, was ruled "illegal because of its purpose." [42] The Mine Workers had called a strike, not over terms of employment, but to compel the company to pay a claim for $180 due to one of the local union's members, Brother Mishmash. The claim had been pending for two years, there was no provision for arbitration, and in fact Brother Mishmash had changed jobs and left the company. Union discipline was so tight, however, that the strike succeeded in forcing payment of the claim. Criminal proceedings were brought against the union vice-president, Dorchy, on the basis of a Kansas antistrike law; Dorchy claimed as a defense that the Kansas law was unconstitutional as a denial of the liberties protected under the Fourteenth Amendment. The Supreme Court, in an opinion by Justice Brandeis, ruled that "to collect a stale claim due to a fellow member of the union who was formerly employed . . . is not a permissible purpose."

A strike may be "tainted" or ruled illegal either because of its pur-

[42] *Dorchy* v. *Kansas,* 272 U.S. 306 (1926).

pose or because of the way it is conducted. The "illegal purpose" doctrine most commonly means that the right to strike is in conflict with some other established policy, either state or federal. Thus a strike to obtain wage demands that would violate wartime wage-control legislation was held illegal. A strike creating a national emergency in coal mining was ruled illegal.[43] Strikes of public employees are normally held unlawful as conflicting with the sovereignty of the state. A strike in violation of a contract made under federal law was ruled illegal.[44] State law also can supersede the right of workers to strike, provided the state policy does not conflict with national labor policy. The leading example is a case in which a Missouri antimonopoly law was held to be a proper exercise of state authority. Union action that forced a company to violate the state law thereby became illegal. A union of ice peddlers picketed the Empire Storage and Ice Company to prevent the sale of ice to nonunion distributors. The company claimed that, under the state antimonopoly law, it was required to sell to all distributors alike. On this basis it obtained an injunction against the union's activities, in a decision later upheld unanimously by the Supreme Court.[45]

Most of the cases in which state law has been controlling have involved the *conduct* of a strike. Under the federal constitution, the states are responsible for the health and safety of their citizens. This is known as the states' "police power," and under it either individual actions in a strike or the entire strike pattern may be called to account in the state courts. Moreover, state labor laws control employer–employee relations as long as they do not conflict with applicable federal law. They may, and in most cases do, control the conduct of strikes and other union activities. These controls will be illustrated as we consider the definition and limits of "peaceful picketing."

Picketing

For a brief period after 1937, the Supreme Court took the view that picketing was almost exempt from state control by the free speech guarantees of the Fourteenth Amendment. A Wisconsin law authorizing peaceful "stranger" picketing by a union attempting to organize a nonunion shop was challenged by an employer, but was ruled constitutional by the Supreme Court on the grounds that the Fourteenth Amendment gives union members a constitutional right to "make known the facts of a labor dispute." [46] Picketing, in this view, is "com-

---

43 *United States* v. *United Mine Workers*, 330 U.S. 258 (1947). For an excellent discussion of this historic case, see John L. Blackman, Jr., "Presidential Seizure in Labor Disputes" (Cambridge: Harvard University Press, 1967), pp. 33–36.

44 *National Labor Relations Board* v. *Sands Mfg. Co.*, 306 U.S. 332 (1939).

45 *Giboney* v. *Empire Storage and Ice Co.*, 336 U.S. 490 (1949).

46 *Senn* v. *Tile Layers' Union*, 301 U.S. 468 (1937).

munication." A few years later an Alabama law that made every sort of picketing a misdemeanor was declared unconstitutional in a decision that broadly indentified peaceful picketing with free speech. Subsequently the Court applied this principle to strike down a state court's injunction against peaceful picketing, where no state law but rather a state policy based on common law forbade picketing if there was no immediate dispute between employer and employee.[47]

But the tide receded from this high point of the "free speech doctrine." The Supreme Court later ruled that picketing, even though peaceful, involved more than just communication of ideas and could not be totally immune from state regulation. "Picketing . . . involves patrol of a particular locality and . . . the very presence of a picket line may induce action of one kind or another, quite irrespective of the nature of the ideas which are being disseminated." Since 1957, the Court has relied increasingly on the facts of each case, balancing the competing interests of unions, employers, their employees, and the public at large. There is no abolute right of free speech in picketing any more than there is an absolute right to strike. In a Texas case,[48] an injunction had been granted under a state antitrust law against picketing of a restaurant by unions protecting the use of nonunion labor, not by the restaurant itself but by a contractor who had done some work for the restaurant. The contractor's dispute had nothing to do with the restaurant being picketed. The Supreme Court ruled that Texas was not violating the Fourteenth Amendment in "insulating" this neutral establishment from the dispute. In cases where picketing involved more than "publicity," or where the element of "communication" was less important than the element of pressure, the states might issue injunctions in support of valid state policy.

State policies thus upheld by the Supreme Court have included a common law policy against the union shop; a California policy against employment on racial lines, upheld against union picketing of a place of business solely to demand that employees be hired in proportion to the raical origin of customers; a statutory policy against employer coercion of employees' choice of bargaining representative, in an injunction against picketing a hotel with signs declaring the owner unfair to organized labor after an unsuccessful attempt at unionization; a state right-to-work law, upheld as the basis for an injunction against picketing a general contractor to eliminate nonunion men from the

---

[47] *AFL* v. *Swing*, 312 U.S. 321 (1941). For a comprehensive discussion of the "free speech doctrine" see Charles O. Gregory, *Labor and the Law*, 2d rev. ed. (New York: W. W. Norton & Company, Inc., 1958), chap. 11, "Rise and Decline of the Thornhill Doctrine."

[48] *Carpenters' and Joiners' Union* v. *Ritter's Café*, 315 U.S. 722 (1942).

job; and a Wisconsin statute prohibiting picketing "in the absence of a labor dispute," upheld against picketing a nonunion gravel pit in an effort by the Teamsters' Union to organize the company's drivers. The Wisconsin case,[49] decided in 1957, has become the leading case because the Court specifically restated the principles governing interpretation of the Fourteenth Amendment as applied to state regulation of picketing.

Control of strike violence is the commonest area of state regulation under the police power. A strike that occurs in a context of destruction of property and personal injury will be declared illegal, with consequent loss by the employees of their protection under the National Labor Relations Act. Individual strikers guilty of serious violence may be discharged,[50] and local laws against destruction of property can be applied. The employer may also refuse reinstatement to workers against whom violence on the picket line can be specifically proved.

The National Labor Relations Board is responsible for determining whether acts of violence are the responsibility of the union and thus an unfair labor practice. In a 1948 decision, the board made the union responsible for incidents of violence and misconduct even by unidentified pickets. When a strike against the Sunset Line and Twine Company followed the breakdown of contract negotiations, the company reopened the plant with nonstrikers, and called local law-enforcement officers to protect the cars transporting men across the picket line. In the presence of the first vice-president of the local union, the business agent of the local, and the regional director of the international, a crowd of 200 to 300 men succeeded in blocking off some of the cars and closed the plant down for that day. There was considerable jostling, and pickets crowded against the cars. The sheriff made arrests and threatened to use tear gas. The vice-president actively urged on the pickets, while the other officers stood by and said nothing. Nonstrikers were followed home by a parade of pickets shouting abuse and threats. The National Labor Relations Board ruled these acts illegal and held the union officers responsible.[51]

Misconduct by strikers, even if nonviolent, may be ruled "coercive" by the board and therefore a ground for removing National Labor Relations Act protection from the strike and for refusing reinstatement to individual employees. In a Massachusetts case, the circuit court of appeals held that visits to the homes of nonstrikers by several carloads of strikers were coercive in nature because they were calcu-

---

[49] *International Brotherhood of Teamsters, Local 695, AFL* v. *Vogt, Inc.,* 354 U.S. 284 (1957).

[50] *Berkshire Knitting Mills* v. *National Labor Relations Board,* 139 F. 2d 134 (1943).

[51] Matter of *Sunset Line and Twine Company,* 79 NLRB 1487 (1948).

lated to instill fear of physical harm.[52] But while the states may regulate the methods by which a strike is conducted, it is important to note that the National Labor Relations Act cannot be superseded by any form of state regulation. The state court's determination that a strike is an illegal breach of the peace will not necessarily deprive the strike of the protection of Section 7 of the National Labor Relations Act, nor the employees of their rights to reinstatement.

Disputes over Organization and Recognition

The recognition strike has presumably been made unnecessary by the certification procedures of the National Labor Relations Board. Where the union claims to represent a majority of the employees, it can file a representation petition with the board. Informational picketing is then permitted. The union's claim can be tested either by an election or by other evidence, such as signed authorization cards demonstrating to the satisfaction of the board that it is the free choice of the majority of the employees. Once a decision has been reached, a union that has failed to win certification, or a union that has lost out to another in an election, is barred from further picketing of the employer's premises.

There is some uncertainty over whether a union can picket for recognition where no election has been held. This might happen because the union has been unable to obtain enough signed authorization cards, or because it has not tried to do so. Such a situation was not covered explicitly by the 1959 Landrum–Griffin Act amendments. It is also unclear whether the union defeated in an election can continue picketing if the wording on the picket signs is changed from a demand for recognition to some other "informational" wording.

As a result of this ambiguity, unions have developed a tactic of picketing for "area standards." If the union's sole purpose is to advertise the fact that the company is paying wages below the standards prevailing in the area, or to publicize some other valid labor issue, it appears that picketing is permitted even though it may cause some employees to refuse to work. Picketing may also be aimed at the consumer public. In a 1961 case, the Hotel and Restaurant Employees' Union had been picketing a cafeteria with signs stating that the establishment was "nonunion." No election petition had been filed. The board at first ruled that since the evidence indicated that the cafeteria employees did not want to join the picketing union, the picket line, regardless of the wording of the signs, was "concealed recognitional picketing." But subsequently the board reconsidered this decision and ruled that "purely informational picketing cannot

[52] *National Labor Relations Board* v. *Thayer Co.,* 213 F. 2d 748 (1954).

be curtailed," even if it is done for the purpose of recognition or organization, provided that it does not cause a work stoppage.[53]

Secondary Pressures

An old and controversial union tactic is the "secondary boycott." This involves putting pressure on one employer so that he will exert pressure on another employer whom the union is really after. The carpenters' union, for example, has jurisdiction over factories making millwork and other lumber products. These plants are numerous, small, and often difficult to organize. One way to organize them is for the union carpenters on construction jobs to refuse to install millwork from nonunion factories. This forces the building contractors to buy from union plants only. The nonunion plants find their market reduced or even destroyed, and are forced to recognize the union.

The legitimacy of such "billiard-shot" tactics has been debated for decades. Boycott activities have usually been held illegal at common law. The Taft–Hartley Act reinforced this view by making it an unfair labor practice to encourage a strike or a concerted refusal to handle a company's goods when the purpose is to force the company to stop doing business with another company. This has led to complicated litigation over who is the "primary" and who is the "secondary" employer in a particular case, whether the secondary employer is actually neutral or whether he is in effect an ally, and so on. For example, construction unions trying to organize a subcontractor have taken the position that they are in fact engaged in a dispute with the general contractor. Is it possible to distinguish between different kinds of secondary boycotts, some more undesirable than others? Will collective bargaining be impaired by a restriction on the use of economic pressure to the detriment of third parties?

The traditional refusal of union workers to work on the same site with nonunion men was a central issue in the *Denver Building and Construction Trades' Council* case, which came to the Supreme Court soon after passage of the Taft–Hartley Act. The Court held that a strike to force the general contractor on a construction project to cancel its contract with a nonunion subcontractor was an unfair labor practice. Doose and Lintner, the general contractor, had given a subcontract for electrical work to a firm (Gould and Preisner) that for 20 years had employed nonunion workmen. The construction project was brought to a halt when the Denver Building Trades' Council placed a single picket at the site. The union claimed that its objective was to force Doose and Lintner to make the construction site an all-union job; and indeed, if Doose and Lintner themselves had employed nonunion labor, the union's right to strike would have been clear.

[53] *Crown Cafeteria,* 130 NLRB 570 (1961).

But the Court ruled that the existence of a business relationship between independent contractors restricted the union's use of economic pressure.[54]

Congress amended the basic act in 1959 to close loopholes that had been exposed by actions brought before the National Labor Relations Board and the courts. One change in the wording of the secondary boycott provisions made the prohibition applicable to refusals to work by workers who were not technically "employees." Another was intended to make clear that inducement to even a single individual to refrain from work was proscribed. General threats of "labor trouble" made to the secondary employer had previously been held to be outside the range of prohibited action. Now Congress made such conduct unlawful, if it could be shown to "threaten, coerce, or restrain" any person.

These provisions were interpreted by the Supreme Court in a 1964 case. A union of delivery drivers and salesmen was conducting a strike against Servette, Inc., a wholesale food distributor in California. The union sought to support the strike by picketing supermarkets that bought food from Servette. Handbills were passed out in front of the supermarkets asking customers not to purchase Servette's merchandise. The handbills were carefully limited to named products, and were not worded as an attack on the supermarkets themselves. When Servette complained to the National Labor Relations Board, the board dismissed the charges on the grounds that the managers were not being induced to refrain from performing their managerial duties. Rather, they were being asked to make a managerial decision to discontinue accepting merchandise from Servette, and they remained free to do so or to go on as before. The Supreme Court interpreted as informational and nonthreatening the union's warning to the supermarket managers that handbills would be distributed.[55]

The central issue in secondary boycotts, as in organizational disputes, has thus come to turn on the question whether the union's pressure on third parties is limited to a peaceful publicity campaign. The 1959 amendments specifically legalized publicity, other than picketing, for the purpose of truthfully advising the public about a labor dispute, so long as such publicity did not have the effect of inducing any individual to stop transporting goods or performing services for a secondary employer. In a 1964 case, the Supreme Court ruled that this mention of publicity other than picketing had not been intended to outlaw picketing itself in all circumstances.

---

[54] *National Labor Relations Board* v. *Denver Building and Construction Trades' Council*, 341 U.S. 675 (1951). For a general discussion of the effect of the Taft–Hartley Act on secondary boycotts see Howard Lesnick, "The Gravamen of the Secondary Boycott," *Columbia Law Review*, Vol. 62 (1962), 1363.

[55] *National Labor Relations Board* v. *Servette, Inc.*, 377 U.S. 46 (1964).

In this case, the Fruit and Vegetable Packers' Union sought to support a strike against fruit packers in Yakima, Washington, by instituting a consumer boycott against their apples in Seattle. The union picketed Safeway Stores and other supermarkets, with a carefully worded appeal to refrain from buying Washington State apples, which were only one of many food products sold in the stores. The limited nature of the boycott was explained in a letter to the store managers before the picket line was set up, and the pickets were expressly forbidden to request customers not to patronize the store, and also to avoid interfering with the Safeway employees or with deliveries or pickups. The National Labor Relations Board, ruling against the union, held that consumer picketing in front of a secondary establishment is prohibited by the 1959 amendments. But the Supreme Court, reviewing the legislative history of the act, rejected this view: "In the sensitive area of peaceful picketing Congress has dealt explicitly with isolated evils which experience has established flow from such picketing." Justice Black, in a concurring opinion, felt that if the statute had intended to prohibit such picketing it would be unconstitutional under the free-speech protection of the First Amendment.[56]

Hot-Cargo Clauses

Closely related to the secondary boycott is the "hot-cargo clause" by which an employer agrees with a union not to handle or use the goods of another employer. For a long time it was argued that a *voluntary* agreement not to handle nonunion goods was a valid expression of support for proper union objectives. The Supreme Court had ruled that an employer might voluntarily support a boycott, and hence might legally agree to do so. "The board has no general commission to police collective bargaining agreements," said the Court, "and to strike down contractual provisions in which there is no element of an unfair labor practice." [57] In reaction to this Supreme Court decision, Congress in 1959 amended the National Labor Relations Act to outlaw agreements to support secondary boycotts. Such action by an employer is now an unfair labor practice.

Exceptions were permitted, however, for the construction and clothing industries, in which refusal to handle nonunion work was deeply embedded in past practice. The first exemption applied only to agreements between union and employer relating to the contracting or subcontracting of work to be done at the site of construction.

---

[56] *National Labor Relations Board* v. *Fruit and Vegetable Packers Local 760,* 377 U.S. 58 (1964).

[57] *Local 1976, United Brotherhood of Carpenters and Joiners* v. *National Labor Relations Board,* 357 U.S. 93 (1958).

The second exemption permitted enforcement of agreements relating to both the premises of the manufacturer and the stages of an integrated process of production in the clothing industry. These exemptions were challenged as unconstitutional, but the circuit court of appeals accepted the argument that Congress was justified in not disturbing long-standing tradition in these industries.[58]

National policy is now clear. The National Labor Relations Act makes unenforceable and void any agreement, express or implied, by which one employer agrees to cease from handling, transporting, or dealing in the goods of another employer. It is an unfair labor practice for an employer to grant, or for a union to demand, such an agreement. Nevertheless, some powerful unions, such as the Teamsters, continue to have a working relationship with employers on this point. And in industries where hot-cargo clauses were a feature of collective bargaining in the years before they were outlawed by Congress, efforts have been made to write contracts that will give the union some measure of protection without coming under the Congressional ban.

The Amalgamated Lithographers union, for example, has negotiated agreements that contain a "struck work" clause, providing that the employer will not render assistance to any lithographic employer engaged in a strike with the union, and that the employees shall not be requested to handle any work not already begun for an employer whose plant was struck by any Amalgamated local. The struck work clause in this form embodies the "ally doctrine"—that employees cannot be compelled to handle work farmed out by another employer who is engaged in a strike with their union. It would be unreasonable to force one local to help break a strike by another local. The Supreme Court has held that such an arrangement by itself is not prohibited by the 1959 amendments.

Work Assignment Disputes

A common situation is the jurisdictional dispute where two unions —say, the Carpenters and the Machinists—each demand that the employer assign a certain type of work to their members under penalty of shutdown. The Taft–Hartley Act prohibited strikes in such situations and provided for decision by the National Labor Relations Board unless the parties could work out their own arrangements for a settlement. This has stimulated the growth of private settlement machinery, notably as between the various building trades' unions. It has also led to an increase in litigation before the National Labor Relations Board and the courts.

[58] *Employing Lithographers of Miami* v. *National Labor Relations Board,* 5th Circuit, 301 F. 2d, 20 (March, 1962).

A key case arose out of a dispute in the Columbia Broadcasting System in 1961. CBS had assigned the lighting work for a major telecast in New York City to the Stage Employees rather than to the "technicians" who were members of the Electrical Workers (IBEW). Both unions were certified bargaining agents for their respective CBS employee members, but neither the National Labor Relations Board certification nor the contracts subsequently negotiated had apportioned clearly the areas of work for each group. Particularly acrimonious was the question of "remote lighting," when telecasts away from the home studio took place. When the rival locals could not agree, CBS claimed the right to divide the disputed work on improvised criteria, keeping the peace on a day-to-day basis. This broke down when the technicians refused to operate the cameras unless the entire lighting assignment was given to their members. A major program had to be canceled, and CBS filed unfair practice charges claiming a violation of the amended National Labor Relations Act.[59]

The National Labor Relations Board held the strike illegal, not on the factual basis of the dispute, but on the ground that a strike over work assignment is illegal unless the union is entitled to the work under a board order, a board certification, or a collective bargaining agreement.[60] The union refused compliance, contending that this ruling was too narrow an interpretation of the board's statutory duty "to determine the dispute." The union claimed that the board's ruling should have been a final determination of the work assignment issue and should have been based on broad criteria derived from the practices and custom of the industry. The question of what kind of decision is required of the National Labor Relations Board under the law had come up also in other circuit courts, some of which had taken one view and some another.

When the CBS case reached the Supreme Court, the Court ruled that the board cannot limit its determination to a legalistic finding concerning the "guilt" of the parties. Rather, the board has the responsibility of actually allocating the disputed work on the facts and merits of the case before it. The board defended its narrow construction on a variety of grounds, which added up to a reluctance to assume loosely defined yet very broad powers, which had been given in the act without clear standards to govern their application. In such circumstances, the board felt, it would be exercising the functions of

[59] *National Labor Relations Board* v. *Radio & Television Engineers Union, International Brotherhood of Electrical Workers,* 364 U.S. 573 (1961).

[60] For a review of the issues, see James B. Atleson, "The National Labor Relations Board and Jurisdictional Disputes: The Aftermath of CBS," *Georgetown Law Journal,* Vol. 53 (1964), 93; and Guy Farmer and N. Thompson Powers, "The Role of the National Labor Relations Board in resolving jurisdictional disputes," *Virginia Law Review,* Vol. 46 (1960), 660.

an arbitrator rather than its proper function of rule making. The board obviously believed that this area would best be left to private settlement. The Supreme Court, however, was unsympathetic to this view, saying that with the board's long experience "and a knowledge of the standards generally used by arbitrators, unions, employers, joint boards and others in wrestling with this problem," the board could do the job.

Following the CBS decision, the board adopted criteria to be considered in making affirmative awards in jurisdictional disputes. "The board will consider all relevant factors in determining who is entitled to the work in dispute, e.g. the skills and work involved, certifications by the board, traditional practice in the company and the industry, agreements between unions and between employers and unions, awards of arbitrators, joint boards and the AFL-CIO in the same or related cases, the assignment made by the employer, and the efficient operation of the employer's business." [61] Subsequent decisions have been aimed mainly at encouraging the disputing unions to settle jurisdictional disputes by private agreement. Existing agreements between unions, or between employers and unions, have generally been given greater weight than other criteria.

Employer Behavior in Strike Situations

Where should the line be drawn between the right of the employer to operate his business and the right of the employees to strike? Under the National Labor Relations Act, the employer is prohibited from interfering with the right to strike. This ended a long period in which the employer could exact reprisals for striking or for other union activities. But this apparently clear-cut provision, like other sections of the act, has raised many problems of interpretation.

The employer is entitled to hire strikebreakers to keep the plant in operation. Moreover, he is entitled to promise them permanent jobs, so that, if and when the strikers return to work, the new men must be fitted into the work force. If, however, it can be shown that his real purpose is to get rid of some of the strikers because of their union activities, he may be held guilty of an unfair labor practice.[62]

May an employer lock up his plant when the union calls a strike? There appears to be no simple answer. The legality of the lockout, like that of the strike, will be judged on the factual situation rather

[61] *International Association of Machinists* v. *J. A. Jones Construction Co.*, 135 NLRB 1402 (1962). For a general review of the problem see Bernard D. Meltzer, "Organizational Picketing and the N.L.R.B.: Five on a Seesaw," *University of Chicago Law Review*, Vol. 30 (1962), 78.

[62] *National Labor Relations Board* v. *Mackay Radio and Telegraph Company*, 304 U.S. 333 (1938).

than on abstract principles. Generally, the Court has limited the right to lock out employees to situations in which, at the very least, the possibilities of settlement through collective bargaining have been exhausted.

The National Labor Relations Board rule, formulated in the *Quaker State* Case, is that a lockout does not violate the act when it is used "to safeguard against unusual operational problems or hazards or economic loss where there is reasonable ground for believing that a strike is imminent." Lockouts have been approved to prevent seizure of a plant by a sitdown strike,[63] to forestall repetitive disruptions of an integrated operation by quickie strikes,[64] to avoid spoilage of materials in case of a sudden work stoppage,[65] and to prevent the immobilization of customers' automobiles brought in for repair.[66]

The board approved the use of the lockout by a multi-employer bargaining unit as a response to a whipsaw strike against one of its members, in a ruling later upheld by the Supreme Court. Subsequently the lockout was used as a defensive measure against the whipsaw strike by four operators of retail food stores who locked out their employees when the local union struck a fifth employer during contract negotiations.[67] All five employers were able to operate with the help of temporary replacements and management personnel. This dispute reached the Supreme Court in 1965, where the hiring of temporary replacements during the lockout was ruled to be not discriminatory. The Court argued that the union could have returned its members to work by ending the strike, and that the employer motivation, a union shop being in effect, was only the protection of legitimate business interests. The first nationwide lockout occurred, in the trucking industry, in March, 1967.

The National Labor Relations Board has been reluctant to put the legality of the lockout on the same level as the legality of the strike, possibly feeling that this would tip the scales too far in the employers' favor and defeat the statutory purpose of ensuring equality at the bargaining table. In a 1965 case involving a Great Lakes shipbuilding company,[68] the board ruled a lockout illegal as an unfair practice. After extended negotiations, no agreement had been reached a week

[63] *Link Belt Co.*, 26 NLRB 227 (1940).

[64] *International Shoe Company*, 93 NLRB 907 (1951).

[65] *Duluth Bottling Association*, 48 NLRB 1335 (1944).

[66] *Betts* v. *Cadillac-Olds*, 96 NLRB 268 (1951).

[67] *National Labor Relations Board* v. *Brown*, 380 U.S. 278 (1965).

[68] *American Shipbuilding Company* v. *National Labor Relations Board*, 380 U.S. 300 (1965). The leading authority on lockouts is Professor Bernard D. Meltzer; see his review of the problems and cases in "Single Employer and Multi-employer Lockouts under the Taft–Hartley Act," *Univ. of Chicago Law Review*, Vol. 24 (1956), 70; and his discussion of the 1965 cases in *Supreme Court Review, 1965* (Chicago: The University of Chicago Press, 1965), p. 87.

after the old contract expired. The employer then proceeded to lay off most of his employees. Following these layoffs negotiations resumed and, after several more weeks of discussion, a two-year contract was signed. All employees were recalled the following day.

The union filed charges with the National Labor Relations Board on the ground that the shipyard closings had been due, not to lack of work, but to an effort to bring economic pressure to secure prompt settlement of the dispute on the company's terms. The board decided in favor of the union. The Supreme Court, in a unanimous decision, overruled the National Labor Relations Board, saying that the right to strike does not carry with it the right exclusively to determine the timing and duration of all work stoppages. To find a violation, the Court said, the board must show that the employer has acted for a proscribed purpose—that is, to discourage union membership, or to discriminate against the union. The tools of economic self-help available to the employer—replacement of strikers, stockpiling, subcontracting, maintaining his operations while the strikers go without pay, and especially the right to institute his own conditions unilaterally when his contract with the union has expired—also include the lockout, provided it is used in nondiscriminatory fashion.

Discharge and disciplinary measures are protected against board orders for reinstatement under Section 10(c) of the National Labor Relations Act if the individuals have been suspended or discharged "for cause." The employer's right to manage his business in his own interest has been a common defense to union charges of bias and discrimination. There is an important exception: Where a strike has been caused by the employer's unfair labor practices, National Labor Relations Board policy has usually prohibited discharge even to the point of requiring reinstatement at the expense of replacements hired during the strike.[69] Even "unfair labor-practice strikers," however, lose their protected status if violence or other misconduct occurs during a strike. The sitdown strikes and plant seizures of the late 1930s came within this category. In a Massachusetts case in 1954, the appeals court required the National Labor Relations Board to distinguish between employees in an unfair labor-practice strike who had restrained and coerced other employees, ruling that those who were guilty of misconduct might legally be discharged by the company.[70] The employer is free to refuse reinstatement to striking workers against whom violence on the picket line can be specifically proved.

Short of the strike, various intermediate forms of pressure, such as the slowdown, and "informational picketing," are available to the union. These and other forms of harassment, like violence on the

[69] Matter of *Brown Shoe Company,* 1 NLRB 803 (1936).

[70] *National Labor Relations Board* v. *Thayer Co.,* U.S. Court of Appeals, First Circuit, 213 F. 2d 748 (1954).

picket line, can be countered by disciplinary measures against individuals or by a lockout. The small number of cases that have come to the point of National Labor Relations Board ruling or court decision suggest that such activities are far less effective than the strike. But they pose important issues. The Supreme Court apparently considers that action short of a strike is beyond the reach of the National Labor Relations Board: The statutory list of unfair labor practices cannot be increased or reduced except by Congress. This reasoning may apply either to employee or to employer action. In a 1951 case the employees of a small, new TV station engaged in picketing without any work stoppage, seeking to force the employer to meet their demands by a publicity campaign attacking the quality of the station's broadcasts. Their handbills revealed that the station's programming came from tapes, and they criticized the management for not using any local material. The pickets responsible for the handbill were discharged on the ground of "disloyalty," the station owner arguing that the content of their propaganda had nothing to do with the labor dispute, but was intended to discredit the company at a time when it was having difficulty building up an audience. The discharges were upheld by the board and later by the Supreme Court.[71] Three dissenting justices, however, felt that the majority's interpretation of the law was too broad, and that such imprecise notions as "discipline" and "loyalty" should not be invoked in labor controversies.

Subsequently the Supreme Court reviewed the basic issues underlying concerted activities short of a strike. May union on-the-job tactics during negotiations be ruled illegal by the board solely because they seek to put pressure on the employer? This question reached the Court in 1960.[72] The Insurance Agents' International Union had informed the Prudential Insurance Company that, if agreement on the terms of a new contract was not reached when the old contract expired, the union members would engage in a "work-without-a-contract program." The tactics included refusal to solicit new business, refusal to comply with the company's reporting procedures, refusal to participate in sales campaigns, reporting for work but not performing customary duties, absenting themselves from business conferences, and meanwhile picketing and soliciting the support of policyholders. The National Labor Relations Board entered a cease-and-desist order, claiming that the union tactics were not a protected concerted activity. On this assumption, as the Supreme Court said, "the employer could have discharged or taken other appropriate disciplinary action against the employees participating in these 'slow-down,' 'sit-in,' and arguably

[71] *National Labor Relations Board* v. *Local 1229, International Brotherhood of Electrical Workers,* 346 U.S. 464 (1951).
[72] *National Labor Relations Board* v. *Insurance Agents' International Union,* 361 U.S. 477 (1960).

unprotected disloyal tactics." But the employer rather than the board had the legal right to take protective action. Discharge and disciplinary weapons were the proper countermeasures. Even if the tactics were reprehensible, this did not give the National Labor Relations Board a warrant to declare the union activity an unfair labor practice as a refusal to bargain. "It may be that the tactics used here deserve condemnation, but this would not justify attempting to pour that condemnation into a vessel not designed to hold it." The Court warned the board to stop short of picking and choosing which devices of labor and management should be branded as in themselves unlawful. Since Congress has specifically listed unfair labor practices, the list may not be expanded except by legislation.

Discussion Questions

1. What are the present ground rules for union and employer behavior in representation elections? Are these rules fair to both parties?
2. "The effort to distinguish between mandatory and permissive issues has produced undue government intervention in the substance of collective bargaining. This concept should be abandoned, and both parties left free to raise any issue they wish." Discuss.
3. What are a union's duties toward black workers employed in the bargaining unit that the union represents? What difficulties are involved in actual enforcement of these duties?
4. Does present law adequately protect the rights of workers who may dissent from and campaign against local or national union officials?
5. What are the main legal restrictions on the right to strike? What practical difference does it make whether a strike is ruled unlawful?
6. Under what conditions may picketing of an employer's premises be held unlawful? Are present rules governing picketing too lenient? Too severe? About right?
7. Which measures may an employer take, and which may he not take, against a striking employee? Are the rules reasonable?
8. What kinds of situation come under the heading of "secondary pressures"? Is the policy of treating such pressures as unlawful (a) reasonable? (b) effective?

Reading Suggestions

Case materials and general discussions of the substantive issues in labor policy can be found in Summers, Clyde W., *Cases on Labor Law.* Brooklyn: The Foundation Press, Inc., 1969; Cox, Archibald, and Derek C. Bok, *Cases and Materials on Labor Law.* Brooklyn: The Foundation Press, Inc., 1965; Gregory, Charles O., *Labor and the Law,* 2d rev. ed. New York: W. W. Norton & Company, Inc., 1958; and Wellington, Harry H., *Labor and the Legal Process.* New Haven: Yale University Press, 1968. A useful comparative survey will be found in Kahn-Freund, Otto (ed.), *Labour Relations and the Law.* Boston: Little, Brown and Company, 1965.

Among the many specialized studies, a few recent titles may help to focus the knowledge that the student has gained from Chapters 12 to 16. Good faith bargaining is discussed in Ross, Phillip, *The Government as a Source of Union Power.* Providence: Brown University Press, 1965. A detailed account of the problems of contracting out is Chandler, Margaret, *Management Rights and Union Interests.* New York: McGraw-Hill Book Company, 1964. A comprehensive study of the effect of industrialization on union organization and growth in the southern United States is Marshall, F. Ray, *Labor in the South.* Cambridge: Harvard University Press, 1967. A comprehensive survey of the Labor Management Reporting and Disclosure Act of 1959 is Estey, Martin S., Philip Taft, Martin Wagner, eds., *Regulating Union Government.* New York: Harper & Row, Publishers, 1964. See also the *Symposium on Labor Law* in *Northwestern University Law Review,* Vol. 63 (March–April, 1968), and the "Symposium on the LMRDA of 1959" in *New York University Law Review,* Vol. 43 (April, 1968).

FRONTIERS
OF
PUBLIC POLICY

19

Having set forth the legal framework of our industrial relations system, we proceed to examine some frontier issues that seem likely to be with us for the indefinite future. A first problem is how to avert or settle strikes that cause serious public inconvenience. A variety of techniques are now in use. None of them is very satisfactory. There is a continuing search for better methods of strike avoidance.

A second problem area, growing rapidly in importance, involves unionization and collective bargaining by public employees. What are the differences, legal and practical, between public employee bargaining and bargaining in the private sector? Are strikes of public employees ever permissible? If not, how are unsettled disputes to be resolved?

Third, the status of unions under the antitrust laws is both ambiguous and controversial. Is the multi-industry or economically conglomerate union a new power bloc similar to the combinations in restraint of trade that were outlawed by the antitrust machinery? Is there a case for clarifying, and perhaps extending, the application of antitrust to union activities?

GOVERNMENT'S ROLE
IN
MAJOR STRIKES

Most strikes cause little permanent loss of output, for reasons examined in Chapter 16. But it is equally clear that some strikes do cause serious economic damage. These are often called "emergency strikes," and there is a strong case for government intervention to avert or settle them.

What is an "emergency" strike? The common answer is: one that causes dangerous curtailment of a necessary service. But what services are "necessary"? At what point does curtailment of service become dangerous rather than merely inconvenient? At one pole, a strike in a toy-manufacturing plant would be recognized as minor. At the other pole, a nationwide railroad strike is clearly dangerous. But in between there is a continuum of situations, and the point at which danger sets in is a matter of judgment. It is probably better to speak of "major" strikes, recognizing that there will be differences of judgment on the proper content of this category.

One approach to a definition is to observe the kinds of cases in which government has intervened in the past. Rail and air transport are considered essential, and there is special statutory provision for disputes in these industries. (There are no comparable provisions for road transport, though a trucking strike could interrupt the flow of foodstuffs and other essential supplies.) The emergency dispute provisions of the Taft–Hartley Act were invoked twenty-eight times between 1948 and 1967. Twelve of these cases involved direct defense industries: atomic energy, aerospace, aircraft and aircraft engines, shipbuilding. Another nine involved longshoring or merchant shipping, which affect the overseas flow of military supplies as well as commercial exports and imports. Other scattered cases involved bituminous coal (three cases), basic steel, telephone service, and meatpacking. At the local level (excluding for the moment strikes of public employees), strikes in bus and subway service, electrical utilities, hospital services, and newspaper publishing have been held to require government intervention.

A common feature of all such disputes is that they generate political pressure. If the dispute has high visibility, either because it causes widespread inconvenience or because there is a dramatic potential for claiming danger to public health or safety, pressure will inevitably build up for government intervention. The president, the governor, or the mayor will be expected to settle the dispute—whether or not he actually has power to do so. Either of the contending parties may try to use government intervention to win concessions they could not gain by collective bargaining. Meanwhile the focus of public wrath may be shifted away from union or management representatives to a politically vulnerable elected official. The appeal for government intervention marks a shift of the dispute from the economic to the political arena, with the elected executive having willy-nilly a large personal stake in the outcome.

The trend has been for legislative bodies, state and national, to give the executive branch the authority to intervene in critical disputes, and for the executive to tread warily in using this authority. The governor or mayor who takes vigorous action in a strike knows that he stakes his political future on the outcome, and no sensible politician will do this. But it is politically dangerous also for a chief executive to have a long-drawn-out and damaging strike placed on his doorstep. To forestall this possibility there has been, especially since 1945, an increasing buildup of settlement machinery in the city, state, and federal governments.

Existing Settlement Machinery

Techniques of government intervention may be divided into *ad hoc* procedures versus *continuing* or *statutory* procedures. At the federal level, the Railway Labor Act and the Taft–Hartley Act authorize presidential intervention in certain circumstances. Several states have laws specifying the procedures to be used in emergency situations. But presidents, Congress, governors, and mayors have also improvised measures to deal with specific situations.

Under the Railway Labor Act, the National Mediation Board may intervene in "major" (new contract) disputes at the request of either party or on its own motion. If mediation is unsuccessful, the board must request the parties to submit the dispute to voluntary arbitration, which they almost always decline to do. The president may then appoint an emergency board to investigate the dispute and make recommendations concerning it. During the thirty days that the emergency board is allowed for its investigation, and for another thirty days after the board's report is filed, neither party may make any change in the conditions out of which the dispute arose. The parties are not obliged to accept the recommendations of the emergency board, however, and a strike at the end of the waiting period is entirely legal.

Before World War II labor disputes on the railroads seem to have been settled quite successfully within the framework of the act. Between 1926 and 1941 only sixteen emergency boards were appointed, most of these disputes were settled along the lines of board recommendations, and only two minor strikes occurred. Since 1941, however, few major disputes in the industry have been settled successfully through the procedures of the Railway Labor Act. In most cases the president has had to intervene to avoid a crisis. In 1941, for instance, the unions were dissatisfied with the recommendations of an emergency board and appealed to President Roosevelt, who negotiated a settlement which gave the unions more than the emergency board had proposed. In three cases, one from 1942 to 1943, one in 1947, and one in 1951, both the emergency board recommendations and the terms proposed by the president were repudiated by one of the parties, and service was maintained only by government seizure of the railroads under the president's emergency powers. In 1963 and again in 1967, special legislation by Congress was required to settle major railroad disputes.

The Taft–Hartley Act also provides a special procedure for cases in which "in the opinion of the President of the United States, a threatened or actual strike or lockout affecting an entire industry or a substantial portion thereof . . . will, if permitted to occur or to continue, imperil the national health or safety." In such cases the president, after preliminary investigation by a board of inquiry, may ask the Attorney General to seek an injunction against the strike. If the injunction is granted, strike action becomes unlawful for an eighty-day period, during which the parties may continue to negotiate. If no agreement is reached by the end of the period the injunction is dissolved and the strike may proceed.

There is considerable difference of opinion about the usefulness of this procedure. It was invoked twenty-eight times between 1948 and 1967. In twenty of these cases a strike was already in progress when intervention occurred. Injunctions were issued in twenty-four cases. Where a strike was already in progress, the injunction halted it in all except two cases, both involving the bituminous coal industry. Most significant is what happened during the compulsory waiting period. Here the record is mixed. Where a strike was halted by injunction, settlements were achieved without renewal of the strike in about three out of four cases. The act did fail to ward off a strike, however, in eight cases—a 1949–50 coal case in which a strike continued until President Truman threatened seizure, and seven disputes in longshoring and shipping, where union–management relations are unusually bitter and interunion rivalry is strong.[1]

Such statistics, of course, are not a conclusive test of the Taft–Hartley procedure. There is continuing controversy over such matters as: whether existence of this procedure leads to its being used more often than necessary; whether the injunction is really a neutral device;

[1] For a more detailed review, see Donald E. Cullen, *National Emergency Strikes* (Ithaca: New York State School of Industrial and Labor Relations, 1968), chap. 3.

whether likelihood that the procedure will be used in a particular case encourages union and management negotiators to stall in the earlier stages of bargaining; and whether the procedure could be improved by giving the boards of inquiry power to make recommendations for settling the dispute, which the act presently prohibits them from doing.

Where it is not considered desirable to invoke the statutory procedures, or where a strike continues after these procedures have been exhausted, or where (as in many states and most cities) there is no specific legislation, the executive is forced to improvise. He seeks a good solution by any means available, or by a combination of several techniques in sequence. For example, *ad hoc* intervention may begin with an announcement that mediation services have been offered to the parties, followed by appointment of a fact-finding board and distribution of press releases describing the board's assessment of the issues. There may follow conferences with the secretary of labor, persuasion to accept arbitration, and even dramatic meetings of the leaders of both sides with the chief executive. The essence of the *ad hoc* approach is that it looks neither backward nor forward. It attends only to the specific dispute at hand.

Although we think of this method of settlement as typical of executive action, Congress and state legislatures have also intervened in strikes on an *ad hoc* basis. In 1913 the Newlands Act set up a new voluntary arbitration procedure for railroad workers, thus settling a major wage dispute threatening to shut down the entire eastern railroad system. The Newlands Act, although passed by Congress after full consultation and approval by both railroads and railway brotherhoods, lasted only a short time and was bypassed when the next major dispute arose. In 1916 the Adamson Act was passed in response to a threatened rail strike over working hours. Congress settled the dispute by legislating the eight-hour day for railway employees. In 1963 Congressional intervention settled a threatened railroad strike over work rules by creating a special arbitration board with mandatory powers over the issues in dispute. Compulsory arbitration was imposed on an *ad hoc* basis. Again, in a 1967 railroad wage dispute where prolonged mediation had failed to produce a settlement, Congress ordered the men back to work and set up an arbitration board to decide the issues.

In other cases presidents have requested and been granted new powers to deal with specific disputes. Such action has been confined largely to periods of war or national emergency, indicating that national policy has retained the right to strike as a basic element in collective bargaining in all but the most threatening circumstances. Out of thirteen presidential proposals for Congressional action, eight requested seizure power and only five of these were granted. Of the six pieces of antistrike legislation actually passed, four authorized the use of seizure in wartime and all but one of these expired with the conclusion of the war emergency. The standards and policies applied by the president under their authority have varied from one incident to the next, have not always been consistent, and have borne little if any relation to presidential or Congressional action in past or future labor disputes.

The president's powers derive from his military authority as commander-in-chief, and from his administrative authority as chief executive, under Article II of the Constitution. Presidents have also improvised powers for handling major disputes from existing legislation, and have used the attorney general's power of criminal prosecution to punish individuals for strikes that the president deemed unlawful, or for defiance of antistrike injunctions. Presidential power to intervene with coercive force is, of course, always subject to review by the Supreme Court.

Dissatisfaction with existing statutes and with hastily improvised procedures has led to a continuing search for improved methods of dispute settlement. The policy objective is not just to prevent stoppages of production, which can always be done by use of force. The objective is rather to prevent strikes by methods that are orderly and uniform in their application, that involve a minimum of direct compulsion, that do not impose greater pressure on one party than on the other, and that leave maximum scope for settlements to be reached through direct negotiation between the parties. These subsidiary requirements make the problem extraordinarily difficult.

We proceed to review the main techniques currently in use, plus several others that have been proposed. The purpose is not to single out one technique as superior to all others, but rather to explore their strengths and weaknesses. Each has been used successfully on occasion. None of them works all the time.

Improving Voluntary Settlement Procedures

An obvious first step is to improve the regular collective bargaining machinery where possible. To the extent that this leaves fewer unsettled disputes, the need for emergency procedures is reduced.

The commonest proposals in this area are, first, greater use of the technique of "continuous bargaining" described in Chapter 15. This involves setting up joint union–management committees to work on especially thorny issues, such as work rules, production standards, and actual or threatened labor displacement. The crisis atmosphere of a contract expiration deadline is not conducive to resolving these technical issues. By calm discussion over a period of months or years, it may be possible to reach special agreements on these matters, or to have proposals ready well in advance for incorporation in the regular contract at its next renewal.

Second, the parties might be encouraged to submit unsettled disputes to neutral arbitration. This is already general practice for grievances under existing contracts. Both unions and companies have been reluctant to accept arbitration of new contract terms, where the stakes are higher, precedents less clear-cut, and the risks of an unsatisfactory decision greater. But this should not discourage continued exploration of this technique. A good number of agreements in public employment contain arbitration clauses. The sanitation strike of 1968 in New York City was settled by *ad hoc* resort to arbitration. This was also considered, though not used, in the 1968 steel-industry negotiations. Some unions and managements might well conclude on reflection that the risks of arbitration by an experienced neutral whom they have selected are less than the risks of intervention by less-experienced public officials in a politically charged atmosphere.

A further suggestion is continued improvement in government's mediation facilities. In the context of an emergency dispute, mediation is no longer entirely voluntary. In the background is the probability of more forceful government action if mediation is rejected or is unsuccessful. But of all the weapons of settlement, mediation seems to have been the most creative and fruitful in seeking out new possibilities of compromise. It is open-ended, flexible, and settlement-oriented. Its purpose is to guide but not to dictate terms. In the end, actual settlement of a dispute typically results from mediation, even when injunctions, plant seizure, or other forcible techniques have been used meanwhile to keep production going.

Specifically, it has been suggested that mediators should enter the picture earlier, or perhaps be in the picture continuously for discussion of complex issues that seem likely to give trouble in the next negotiation. This is often termed "preventive mediation," and is being emphasized increasingly by the U.S. Mediation and Conciliation Service.

A further possibility is the "partial strike," under which some services are continued in the event of a work stoppage. On the local level, it is common practice for hospitals and similar institutions to receive special treatment from striking utility workers, fuel delivery drivers, or building service employees. On the national level, defense materials have been moved during airline strikes, although nondefense transport came to a halt. In a 1967 strike an agreement for partial operation was made by the United Automobile Workers with the Ford Motor Company. The fact that most operations are shut down maintains pressure on the parties to reach an agreement. But maintenance of key services can defuse the dispute and remove it from the emergency category.

Compulsory Waiting Period

Under the Railway Labor Act and the Taft–Hartley Act, the president can require both parties to maintain the status quo for a specified period before strike action can be taken. This is also a common procedure in other countries. The compulsory waiting period is sometimes inaccurately termed a "cooling-off period," implying that strikes result from hot tempers, and that more time for reflection will produce a calmer attitude. There is little evidence, however, that sheer postponement of the issue has any beneficial effect. A waiting period is effective only if, during the period, additional steps are taken toward a settlement. Its main value lies in allowing more time for mediators to accomplish whatever they can, and for higher officials to lay out possible lines of action if mediation should fail.

A Board of Inquiry

It is often provided that during the waiting period a specially appointed board shall investigate the issues in dispute, report on the positions of the parties, and perhaps recommend terms of a settlement. The hope is that the report will focus public opinion, generate pressure on both parties to accept the recommended terms, and lay a foundation for such further executive action as may be required.

To let this procedure have maximum effect, it would seem that the board's report should be made public and that it should contain recommendations for a settlement. The Taft–Hartley prohibition against board recommendations apparently arose from employers' fears in 1947 that board members would have a prounion bias, and that any recommendations they might make would be to the disadvantage of employers. Most experts consider this provision unwise and favor its repeal.

The board of inquiry technique is useful in permitting neutral investigation of the facts of a particular dispute and in bringing these facts clearly before the public. Experience suggests, however, that public opinion is not very effective in forcing a settlement. If the recommended terms are seriously objectionable to one or both of the parties, they will be rejected and the dispute will continue.

Our longest and most intensive experience with boards of inquiry has been under the Railway Labor Act. Contrary to popular impression, many board recommendations are accepted. Between 1948 and 1967, for example, 121 boards were appointed and only sixteen strikes occurred after submission of a board report. The cases settled in accordance with board recommendations, however, were typically small disputes involving one railroad, or one issue, and a limited number of workers. In such cases both unions and management may find it expedient to "pass the buck" to government. But in major cases, involving key issues such as wages or work rules and many or all railroads in the country, board recommendations are almost invariably rejected. The dispute ends up in the East Wing of the White House, and is settled eventually by the kind of *ad hoc* action described earlier.

There is considerable agreement also that the emergency board procedure has undermined the bargaining process in major disputes. Knowing that the dispute will come before an emergency board, and probably go eventually to the White House, neither party makes a serious effort to reach a private settlement. Moreover, they are careful not to reveal their true positions, which might then be cited against them in later proceedings. Rather, they try to stake out and document a shadow position that they hope will impress the board members and other public officials.

Compulsory Arbitration

If the parties to a major dispute will not accept the recommendations of a public board voluntarily, why not provide that they must accept them? Unions have always been strongly opposed to compulsory arbitration, and most management officials regard it with almost equal distaste. On this account it used to be said that resort to compulsory arbitration in the United States is unthinkable. This can no longer be said with so much confidence. Following the wave of post-World War II strikes, several states enacted antistrike laws for public utilities, with settlement provisions that amount to compulsory arbitration. The same tendency is apparent in some states for disputes involving public employees, who are also forbidden to strike.

In 1963, Congress sent a major work-rules dispute on the railroads to compulsory arbitration and suspended the right to strike for two years. When the board award went seriously against the union position, the Locomotive Firemen announced their intention of resisting it by every lawful means, including a renewed strike. But the two-year protected enforcement of the compulsory award, which was tested and upheld in the courts, had shifted the balance of power against the union and no strike materialized. Again, in a 1967 railroad wage-dispute during which several "cooling-off periods" were laid end to end and stretched to the breaking point, leading finally to a two-day national strike, Congress created a board to conduct "mediation to finality," which seems indistinguishable from compulsory arbitration.

The main argument for compulsory arbitration is that, unlike the techniques described earlier, it *does* secure an adjudication of the disputed issues. It does prescribe terms of settlement. True, the terms may be rejected and a strike may still ensue, as has happened frequently in Australia despite its widespread arbitration system. But in this event the executive has a clear mandate to enforce the award by legal procedures and can expect strong support from public opinion.

The main argument on the other side is that compulsory arbitration, rather than serving as a supplement to collective bargaining, tends to supplant and eliminate any genuine bargaining. As in the case of board of inquiry proceedings, but even more strongly, the parties will decline to reveal their true positions or to compromise their shadow positions. Rather than make concessions on a disputed issue, they will "pass the buck" to the board in the hope of a favorable decision.

Compulsory arbitration is a legal procedure, a special kind of court trial. The outcome of a trial is a victory. The outcome of bargaining is an agreement. There is strong reason to believe that terms that have been agreed to voluntarily, rather than imposed by government, will be accepted with better grace and complied with more completely. In addition, the process of mutual persuasion is educational to both parties.

For these reasons most authorities would agree that compulsory arbitration, if used at all, should be confined to major disputes that cause serious public inconvenience. For such disputes, it is somewhat academic to compare the merits of compulsory arbitration with the (presumably greater) merits of free collective bargaining. Such disputes, when they reach the impasse stage, will not be left to private bargaining. The realistic comparison is between compulsory arbitration and other kinds of settlement procedure, all involving some degree of public pressure.

Plant Seizure

This device has been used seventy-one times since 1864, mainly but not entirely during war periods.[2] Five times in this century presidential action has taken over all the major railroads; the coal mines were seized three times between 1943 and 1947; the telephone and telegraph industry was seized in the first World War; and in the post-World War II period seizures of meat-packing firms, oil refineries, basic steel, and trucking firms took place. Principally the needs of national defense have called forth this extreme exercise of presidential power; but the *threat* of seizure has also been used, in five peacetime disputes by four presidents. Cleveland used this threat to force continued operation of the railroads during the Pullman strike of 1894;

---

[2] For a definitive analysis of seizure cases, see John L. Blackman, Jr., *Presidential Seizure in Labor Disputes* (Cambridge: Harvard University Press, 1967).

Theodore Roosevelt in 1902 considered the possibility of seizure and army operation of the Pennsylvania anthracite mines, successfully using this to back up his mediation and arbitration proposals. In 1914 Woodrow Wilson used the threat of seizure in a Colorado coal-mine dispute, and in 1916 he asked Congress (unsuccessfully) for authority to seize and operate the railroads if threatened by a strike or lockout. President Kennedy in 1963 contemplated seizure of the railroads when mediation failed to settle the work-rules disputes. Although seizure has not been used since 1952, when President Truman's seizure of the steel industry was overturned by the Supreme Court, it has since then been used successfully as a threat to forestall stoppages.

At the state level, Virginia and New Jersey have laws permitting plant seizure and compulsory arbitration of public utility disputes. (Several other states have compulsory arbitration laws that do not include provision for plant seizure.) Seizure and operation of facilities is also one of the courses open to the governor under the Massachusetts statute to be described in a moment.

The practical effect of seizure depends on what government does during the seizure period. In earlier times it was sometimes used simply as a strikebreaking device, as illustrated by a letter that Professor Blackman reproduces from the president of the Philadelphia and Reading Railroad on the termination of the 1864 seizure:

Philadelphia, July 18, 1864

Major Gen. Geo. Cadwallader
Sir:

Our difficulties having terminated by the complete submission of the men and the discharge of more than one half of them, I avail myself of the occasion to thank you for the prompt support which you rendered to me throughout—especially for your immediate compliance with my request that you should take military possession of the road.

Your action brought the strike at once to a crisis and hastened a result favorable to us.

Respectfully yours, etc.,

Charles E. Smith, President

The viewpoint represented by this letter has pretty well disappeared from American policy. In seizure cases during this century, the government has been extremely flexible in adapting its policy to the needs of the specific situation. There have indeed been cases of one-sided intervention, in which the "paper seizure" has left management in full control and in which the government's role has focused on either replacing the strikers or forcing them back to work. But there have also been cases in which the government has fully taken over the functions of management, bringing in its own accountants and administrators, making unilateral wage and other changes, and in effect running the business in the public interest until management and the union succeeded in reaching agreement.

Seizure is effective in maintaining production and, unlike the waiting-period procedure described earlier, it has no fixed expiration date. It can continue as long as necessary. But by itself it does not settle the issues in dispute. Government mediation efforts typically continue, and in most cases the parties eventually agree to accept certain terms (which have sometimes been instituted by government on an interim basis). Mediated settlements were reached in forty of the seventy-one cases reported by Blackman, after an average of about two months of government operation. Where one or the other of the parties remains obdurate, seizure usually continues until the end of the national emergency. In World War II, for example, twenty-two facilities were still under government operation at V-J Day. These were released almost immediately, but in many of them strikes broke out again during the reconversion period and several were reseized.

Have the settlements worked out by government had any marked bias? Apparently not. Blackman concludes that in forty of the seventy-one seizures neither side made any appreciable gain in bargaining power; and the fifteen cases in which the union seems to have gained at the expense of management are balanced by sixteen in which management appears to have gained.

The Statutory Strike

This ingenious proposal, developed by academic experts, has not been adopted anywhere, nor does it seem very likely of adoption. The central idea is to keep production going while imposing on the parties the economic losses associated with a strike and thus maintaining pressure for a negotiated settlement. When an impasse was reached in negotiations, a "strike" could be declared by either party. Production would continue. But part or all of the workers' wages, and part or all of the company's net income, would be deposited in a special fund, which could be released only after agreement on a new contract. This would exert enough financial pressure on both sides to stimulate active search for a negotiated solution. Economic pressure is difficult to measure, however, and it might be hard to get agreement on a formula that would exert *equal* pressure on the parties, or that would reproduce the (possibly unequal) pressures arising from an actual work stoppage.[3]

[3] For a review of these proposals see David B. McCalmont, "The semi-strike," *Industrial and Labor Relations Review,* January, 1962, p. 191; and Stephen H. Sosnick, "Non-stoppage strikes: a new approach," *Industrial and Labor Relations Review,* October, 1964, p. 73.

The Arsenal-of-Weapons Approach

This approach, also termed the "choice-of-procedures" approach, was devised originally by a tripartite committee headed by the late Professor Sumner Slichter, and subsequently enacted into law in Massachusetts. The Massachusetts law applies to production and distribution of food, fuel, water, electric light and power, gas, hospital care, and medical services. It does not cover local transportation or telephone service. When the governor finds that a dispute in these industries threatens public health and safety, he may take any or all of the following steps:

1. Require the parties to appear before a moderator to show cause why they should not submit the dispute to arbitration. The moderator may also perform mediation functions. If he fails to get a settlement or a submission to arbitration, he makes a public report on responsibility for the failure but may not comment on the merits of the case.

2. Request the parties voluntarily to submit the dispute to a tripartite emergency board empowered to recommend terms of settlement. If a submission is arranged, the board must submit its findings and recommendations to the governor within thirty days.

3. If the governor finds these procedures inappropriate or if the dispute remains unsettled after using them, he may declare an emergency and arrange with either or both parties for continuing production to the degree necessary for public health and safety.

4. He may also seize and operate the plant or facilities. During the seizure period he may at his discretion put into effect the recommendations of the emergency board if there has been one, or he may appoint a special commission to recommend terms of employment and may put these into effect at his discretion. Seizure ends when the parties notify the governor that the dispute has been settled, or he may terminate it when he considers it no longer necessary even though the dispute remains unsettled.

This law seems to have yielded broadly satisfactory results, partly because the governor has wisely refrained from intervening in every situation. Where intervention has occurred, the eventual settlement has usually been reached either through continuation of collective bargaining or through a submission to voluntary arbitration. The settlements do not appear to have been biased consistently in favor of labor or of management.

Some experts have urged that the arsenal-of-weapons approach be adopted at the federal level. No one settlement technique, it is argued, can be equally effective in all situations. Moreover, the very specific procedure under the Railway Labor Act and the Taft–Hartley Act lets the parties know precisely what to expect, and enables them to outwit or outsit the government. Instead, policy should aim to keep the parties guessing as to what will happen next. Holding over their heads a variety of possibilities, most of them distasteful, will generate maximum pressure on them to settle their own disputes.

There is not universal agreement, however, on the virtues—or even the feasibility—of uncertainty. Cullen quotes one expert as saying that "any labor or management leader who could not find out what the president was going to do in a given emergency probably was not operating in the big-strike leagues." [4]

A Summary Word

The nature of sound policy concerning emergency disputes has been well stated by Cox: ". . . ideal legislation dealing with national emergency disputes would avoid any built-in bias affecting the relative bargaining power of the parties, but would nevertheless allow the administration to preserve neutrality or exert limited pressure in either direction according to economic conditions and the merits of the issue, while at the same time securing an essentially private voluntary settlement." [5]

It is easier to specify objectives than to embody them in effective legislation. The approaches described above are steps toward a comprehensive policy for handling emergency disputes, but they do not yet constitute such a policy. This will doubtless continue to be one of the most controversial and difficult areas in industrial relations.

COLLECTIVE BARGAINING
IN
PUBLIC EMPLOYMENT

Public Employees and Their Unions

In Chapter 3 we noted the rapid expansion of government employment, both absolutely and as a percentage of total employment. It is estimated that by 1975 government employees will total 15 million, or almost one-fifth of the labor force. About four-fifths of these will be employed by state and local government.

Unionism has recently been expanding much faster in public than in private employment. The number of government workers in unions rose from 915,000 in 1956 to 1,500,000 in 1967 and must be substan-

[4] *Emergency Strikes,* p. 111.

[5] Irving Bernstein, Harold L. Enarson, and R. W. Fleming, eds., *Emergency Disputes and National Policy* (New York: Harper & Row, Publishers, 1955), p. 233.

tially larger today. In addition, there are professional bodies such as the National Education Association, with its 1½ million teachers, that are acting increasingly like unions in their day-by-day activities.

Traditionally, salaries and other terms of public employment have been determined by legislatures, civil service commissions, and administrators of government agencies. Unions of public employees adapted to this structure by concentrating heavily on lobbying activities. Collective bargaining was viewed as inapplicable to public employment, as somewhat undignified, even as illegal. But this view is rapidly changing. The substantial gains won by unions in private employment, the backwardness of personnel administration in the public service, the continuing pressure of inflation on living standards, the tendency for public sector wages to lag behind the general advance have combined to produce a new spirit of militancy. Unions of government employees have turned increasingly to direct bargaining. They are winning a growing number of formal agreements incorporating most of the provisions found in private industry, including the union shop and the dues checkoff. Strikes, slowdowns, and similar activities have occurred with increasing frequency in schools, publicly owned utilities, hospitals, sanitation departments, fire departments, local transportation systems, and other state and municipal services.

The total number of unions including some government workers is very large. In 1967, federal employees were organized in more than seventy unions. Of these, forty-one were national unions including both private and public sector employees. Of the unions containing only government workers, some twenty-odd were affiliated with the AFL-CIO, while five were independent.

Unionization of postal employees dates from 1890. Virtually all postal workers now belong to the United Federation of Postal Clerks or the National Association of Letter Carriers, which have a combined membership of about 250,000. The American Federation of Government Employees, chartered by the AFL-CIO in 1932, has more than 300,000 members in the classified federal service. Blue-collar workers in federal employment tend to join the unions of their respective trades. Craftsmen in arsenals and navy yards, for example, have long been organized in District 44 of the Machinists' Union, which reported 44,000 members in 1966.

At the state and local level, the oldest and strongest union is the International Association of Fire Fighters, AFL-CIO, which dates from before 1900. In 1964 it claimed 115,000 members, or 90 percent of all eligible employees. The largest and most rapidly growing group, however, is the American Federation of State, County, and Municipal Employees (AFSCME), chartered in 1937 and reporting 237,000 members in 1965.

The AFSCME is an unusual union in several respects.[6] It is perhaps the most loosely organized federation of locals in the country. The constitution permits withdrawal of individual members or entire locals on very short notice, and places unusual emphasis on members' rights to challenge the leadership and control internal union affairs. This loose-structure, low-pressure approach is a source of strength in applying unionization to the extraordinary variety of local government units in the United States. From the beginning the AFSCME has emphasized collective bargaining rather than lobbying as its central function. It is mainly responsible for widespread development of collective bargaining in local governments, without benefit of statutory authorization and with very little use of the strike weapon. As early as 1962 it had 284 formal agreements in thirty-five states, plus 115 "unilateral" agreements that the union had negotiated and that were then issued by the employing agency as an executive order or ordinance. These collective agreements cover the whole range of wages, hours and conditions found in private industry, including union security. Most of them confer exclusive bargaining rights, and many provide one form or other of union shop. Checkoff of union dues has also been won by more than 1,000 locals including about 80 percent of AFSCME members. The AFSCME has discouraged strikes except when faced with a denial of recognition or refusal to bargain. Such cases are rare. The number of AFSCME strikes, and the loss of man-hours per year, remain insignificant.

The rapid growth of union activity among the nation's 2 million school teachers was noted in Chapter 12. This is associated with a growing percentage of male teachers, who now form 35 percent of all teachers compared with 17 percent in the 1920s; with a tight labor market for teachers, which strengthens their bargaining power; and with the failure of many local governments to raise salary schedules as rapidly as market conditions would warrant.

The two leading organizations in the field are the American Federation of Teachers, AFL-CIO, which in 1966 had 120,000 members, and the much larger National Education Association, with some 1½ million members. The two groups have quite different traditions. The American Federation of Teachers has advocated and practiced collective bargaining from its formation in 1916, while the National Education Association did not sanction use of economic pressure to improve working conditions until 1961. The National Education Association is a professional organization, which seeks to improve the status of education and the level of professional accomplishment. The American

[6] Leo Kramer, *Labor's Paradox: The American Federation of State, County and Municipal Employees, AFL–CIO* (New York: John Wiley & Sons, Inc., 1962), pp. 1–3, 31–46, 84–86, 153–54.

Federation of Teachers is frankly an employee organization. The National Education Association is a loose confederation, with teachers having direct membership as individuals in the local, state, or national organizations, or in all three. In practice, the state organizations have been strongest. The American Federation of Teachers is organized on typical trade-union lines, individuals joining a local that claims jurisdiction over all teachers in a school district or city system.

One result of these structural differences is that the National Education Association typically is most effective in the state legislatures, while the American Federation of Teachers finds its greatest strength in confronting local school district administrations. The National Education Association membership includes supervisory personnel and school administrators, while American Federation of Teachers locals are usually restricted to nonsupervisory personnel. The National Education Association membership has a larger proportion of women, and the American Federation of Teachers a much larger percentage of men; and the American Federation of Teachers has a larger proportion of junior and senior high school teachers, where the ratio of men is higher than in the primary grades.

The American Federation of Teachers has actively supported the strike as a weapon for improving teachers' conditions, and has in general taken a vigorous and militant attitude. The New York City teachers' strike of 1962, led by the United Federation of Teachers (an American Federation of Teachers affiliate), resulted in the first comprehensive collective agreement covering teachers. This was followed by an organizing drive in which the American Federation of Teachers received important support, both financial and organizational, from the AFL-CIO. By 1965 representation elections had been won by the American Federation of Teachers in a large number of school systems, including such important cities as Detroit, Cleveland, Philadelphia, and Boston. In a substantial number of other cities the American Federation of Teachers achieved such a high degree of organization that its power was clearly demonstrated.

The National Education Association, in response to this militant advance, began to act like a traditional union where local memberships demanded it do so. In some cities the National Education Association stole a march on the American Federation of Teachers, demanding representation elections before the latter had built up its strength. The National Education Association also became, *nolens volens,* the exclusive bargaining agency for groups of teachers and negotiated comprehensive agreements in Rochester, Newark, New Haven, and New Rochelle, among other cities. As a result, the climate of opinion in the teaching profession has undergone a profound transformation, with widespread acceptance of the life style of organized unionism, its "demands," bargaining, negotiation, and general militancy. By 1965, the National Education Association convention had dropped its former condemnation of the strike weapon. In 1966 the local National Education Association in Newark engaged in a stoppage over a salary dispute; in Michigan, four National Education Association affiliates were out on strike at the same time. Mass resignations were threatened elsewhere when local boards failed to grant concessions. In states where teachers were included in a general statute permitting public employees to organize and bargain, National Education Association affiliates were steadily winning representation elections in 1966. In Michigan, forty-eight out of sixty-eight elections were won by the National Education Association, representing 51,900 teachers as against 15,770 represented by the American Federation of Teachers. In Wisconsin in the same year, the National Education Association won eighteen out of twenty-three elections, and was designated as exclusive bargaining representative in an additional 100 cases.

The American Federation of Teachers has rejected invitations to merge with the National Education Association on terms that would have meant breaking its affiliation with the labor movement; but merger at some future time remains a possibility. Meanwhile competition between the two organizations continues, probably to the economic benefit of teachers, with varying effects on school systems in different localities, and in an environment of rising public alarm.

Some Peculiarities of Public Sector Bargaining

Collective bargaining in the public sector has several distinctive features, which derive from the nature of public employment. There is first the legal tradition that the sovereign cannot be bound against his will. The sovereign—in this country, a legislative body acting on behalf of the people—may delegate part of its authority to executive agencies of government, but these agencies may not further delegate any part of their authority to private parties. On a strict interpretation, a public agency could not even bargain with its employees over a wage increase, since this would be giving up part of the budgetary authority that belongs ultimately to the legislature. Even where terms of employment are in fact determined by negotiation with a union, public employers sometimes insist that these terms shall be *announced* as unilateral actions of the employer, thus preserving the forms of sovereignty.

The common law view, sometimes reinforced by statute, that a strike of public employees is unlawful derives from the same source. Such a strike is a rebellion against the sovereign, which cannot be allowed. This view raises several problems. Is it sensible to forbid all strikes by public employees? How can a union have any bargaining power when deprived of this normal economic weapon? If deadlocks in bargaining cannot be resolved through a strike, how are they to be resolved? What sanctions can be invoked when a strike occurs despite the legal prohibition?

A second peculiarity is that the employer negotiators often do not have final authority to strike a bargain. For example, some school boards have power to levy taxes to cover school operating costs; but most boards do not. Additional expenditures must be approved by the city budgetary authorities and sometimes, if they involve a tax increase, by a public referendum. Moreover, since school costs are usually financed partly from state grants, the governor and state legislature are involved. This affects the *timing of negotiations,* which to be effective must be concluded before the state and city budgets go to the legislative bodies for action; and it affects the *ratification of agreements,* which on the employer side often requires approval by numerous officials at various levels of government.

Third, there is the economic circumstance that public services are usually provided free and financed from tax revenues. This affects the parties' costs of agreement and disagreement, and hence their relative bargaining power. If production is shut down by a strike, there is no loss of revenue to the employer, hence no economic cost of disagreement. But if the public is seriously inconvenienced, there are political costs, which will be visited on the officials deemed responsible. The cost of agreement to a higher salary schedule will not be a price increase, but may well be a tax increase, which again involves political risks.

Where a price is charged, say by a locally owned public utility, much depends on whether the enterprise is required to be self-financing. If it is, the bargaining situation is similar to that in a privately owned utility; but it is not identical, because public employers are usually more subject to political pressures than private employers. If subsidies are allowed, the situation is still more fluid and "political." The New York subway fare is a classic illustration. The system has long operated at a deficit. A union demand for higher wage scales confronts city officials with the unpleasant alternatives of a fare increase or an increased subsidy from the city budget. The supposed employer, the Transit Auhority, is something of a bystander in these negotiations.

An interesting question is whether the peculiarities of public sector employment tend systematically to raise union bargaining power. One might rather ask, *under what conditions* will this result occur? Hildebrand has speculated that union bargaining power will be relatively high, and wage costs will be distorted upward, if one or more of the following conditions exist:

1. If the agency with which the union deals has the power to assess taxes to cover deficits or increased costs.

2. If the agency with which the union deals has continuing access to subsidies from other jurisdictions.

3. If a union of strategically situated public employees covers only a small fraction of the municipal labor force and is the only government union in the community. (The "importance of being unimportant" operates in public as well as private employment.)

4. If the labor movement is relatively large in a given community, and the public employees are also highly organized.[7]

These and similar hypotheses could be submitted to statistical tests, but this has not yet been done.

Bargaining Arrangements: Federal Level

The growth of public sector unionism has raised much the same issues as were faced earlier with respect to private employment. Should employees have the right to organize and designate their own representatives? Should public employers be required to negotiate with such representatives? Should negotiations cover the full range of "wages, hours, and other conditions of work" found in private sector bargaining? If public employee strikes are prohibited by law, what alternatives can be provided for the resolution of a bargaining impasse? These questions have been faced, with varying success, at all levels of government in the United States over the past twenty years or so. Coming through the back door, collective bargaining has become a working reality in the public service in the United States, as it has been for many years in most European countries.

Federal authorities long took a negative if not hostile view of employee organization. Federal employees, along with state and local employees, were excluded from the coverage of the Wagner Act, while the Taft–Hartley amendments of 1947 specifically outlawed strikes by federal employees: ". . . Any individual employed by the United States or any such agency who strikes shall immediately be discharged from his employment, and shall forfeit his civil service status, if any, and shall not be eligible for reemployment for three years . . ."

The first positive statement of policy came in two executive orders issued by President Kennedy in 1962, after investigation by a task force under the chairmanship of Arthur Goldberg. These laid down a "Code of Fair Labor Practices" in federal employment, and also "Standards of Conduct for Employee Organizations." Agencies excluded from these orders include those which had already set up their own labor relations programs, such as the Tennessee Valley Authority, and those involving national security, such as the Central Intelligence Agency,

[7] George H. Hildebrand, "The Public Sector," in John T. Dunlop and Neil W. Chamberlain, eds., *Frontiers of Collective Bargaining* (New York: Harper & Row, Publishers, 1967), pp. 153–54.

FBI, and Atomic Energy Commission. But the "old line agencies," the regulatory commissions, and the "independent" agencies are now covered.

The orders guarantee the right of federal employees to join unions, though this right is defined to exclude the right to strike. Unfair labor practices by unions or employing agencies are prohibited in much the same terms as in the National Labor Relations Act. A union that receives a majority of votes in an election participated in by at least 60 percent of the employees eligible to vote is to be granted exclusive recognition. Disputes over the scope of the "appropriate unit" are to be resolved by the secretary of labor, who may resort to advisory arbitration for this purpose. There is provision also for two lower levels of recognition: formal recognition, where the union includes at least 10 percent of the employees in a unit where no other union has been granted exclusive recognition; and informal recognition, for organizations with less than 10 percent membership.

Unions with exclusive recognition have the right to negotiate agreements. (Formal recognition confers a right to be consulted on personnel matters, while informal recognition gives a union the right to be heard on matters affecting its members.) The subjects of bargaining, however, are severely restricted by a provision reserving certain matters for management decision. These include the right to hire, transfer, promote or demote, suspend, lay off, discipline, or discharge employees; and to determine the methods and personnel by which operations are to be conducted. The order also provides that the obligation to negotiate "shall not be construed to extend to such areas of discretion and policy as the mission of an agency, its budget, its organization and the assignment of its personnel, or the technology of performing its work." A grievance procedure is established, with provision for appeal of administrative decisions adversely affecting employees.

The limited scope of collective bargaining reflects the contrasting philosophies of the two federal agencies most closely concerned with the subject. The Department of Labor believes in encouragement rather than mere toleration of collective bargaining, and supports extension of bargaining rights to the fullest extent compatible with law. In this view, people work better if they exercise genuine control over their conditions of work. The Civil Service Commission, on the other hand, supports the hierarchical view of the public service in which responsibility for efficient performance is fixed in the agency head, authority is delegated to subordinates, and daily tasks are set and performed under duly established rules. In this view the work relationship is to be judged primarily by criteria of efficiency in performance rather than job satisfaction, and the existence of a merit system for hiring and promotion is regarded as a fully satisfactory substitute for employee representation and collective bargaining. Thus, on the one hand, the Code of Fair Labor Practices invites federal employees to organize and try to bargain with their supervisors. But the broad definition of "management prerogatives," reflecting the traditional Civil Service Commission attitude, at the same time holds bargaining within a narrow range of subjects; and the absence of impasse-resolving machinery, along with the Congressional prohibition against striking, tends to keep the union representatives in the position of petitioners rather than allowing them to bargain on equal terms.

Since the 1962 executive orders there has been a marked increase in union activity in the federal service. Postal employees, who have the longest tradition of unionism within federal employment, have achieved "exclusive recognition units" covering 90 percent of the ¼ million postal workers. Elsewhere, exclusive representation rights have been achieved in some 800 units, covering some 835,000 employees, or about one-third of all federal employees. Some 430 agreements have been negotiated, about half of which are with the Department of Defense, covering 750,000 workers. The Department of Labor has processed over 150 requests for advisory arbitration to define bargaining units.

The unions of federal employees, however, are by no means satisfied with the operation of the system. The commonest grounds of complaint are: that top personnel managers in each agency have been unwilling to delegate enough authority to local management to permit meaningful negotiation; that agencies restrict the scope of bargaining even more narrowly than the executive order requires; that too many matters are excluded from the grievance procedure, and that few agencies have been willing to submit unsettled issues to advisory arbitration; that only 10 percent of agreements provide for outside mediation, and only 25 percent for fact finding and referral to higher authorities in the agency when an impasse occurs in bargaining—an important matter where the strike is forbidden; and that unfair practice charges are usually heard by hearing officers from within the agency itself, who tend to rubber-stamp management decisions.[8]

The lack of a central agency to administer the code means that each agency has developed its own rules and procedures. Legislation has been proposed to create a board comparable to the National Labor Relations Board, which would administer the code impartially and uniformly in all departments to which it applies. But Congress has shown little inclination to pass such legislation.

[8] See Jack Stieber, "Collective Bargaining in the Public Sector," in Lloyd Ulman, ed., *Challenges to Collective Bargaining* (Englewood Cliffs, N.J.: Prentice-Hall, Inc., 1967).

Bargaining Arrangements: State and Local Levels

The most striking advances in public employee unionism in the United States have taken place in state and local government. Municipal governments competing with private employers in a tight postwar labor market were the first to face problems of employee discontent in school systems, police, fire, and sanitation departments, and other municipal services. Collective bargaining developed in several large American cities without specific authorization. The state legislature, however, is the ultimate authority for all units of government within the state, and any restrictions on public employee activity in state law apply automatically to all municipal and local government programs. Since there is a marked divergence of interest between the large city and the small-town agricultural constituency, there have been frequent jurisdictional conflicts between state and municipal authorities in handling threatened or actual strikes. A typical response by state legislatures has been passage of a repressive antistrike law for public employees, under penalty of discharge or even fine and imprisonment. Notwithstanding such attempted repression and the absence of enabling legislation, union activity has in fact increased.

Who are the "employers" who face these problems? In the state capital there will be a dozen or so traditional departments of government, under the direction of the governor through his appointees. This is only the beginning. All the states now have a large number of quasi-independent agencies, such as the state university, state housing authorities, turnpike authorities, state hospitals, prisons, and other welfare institutions. These are administered sometimes by independently elected state officials, sometimes by appointed boards or executives more or less independent of the governor, responsible through statute and financial control to the state legislature. The city governments, county governments, towns, villages, and school districts are all substantial employers of varying kinds of labor. They face the same problems as private industry in competing for sufficient labor to man the services which city dwellers take for granted. In many states, special districts have been created under legislative authority to extend such services to suburban and rural areas. And in all the states the separate school districts exercise a high degree of independent control of education through the hiring of teachers. Taken together, the number of separate governmental employing entities in any state runs into the thousands. This complex structure produces wide variation in policy and practice within the same legal jurisdiction.

Only a few states today attempt to prohibit organized activity by public employees, and then only in selected occupations. Arkansas and

Georgia prohibit participation in any labor organization by members of the police force. North Carolina has forbidden police and firemen to join labor unions. Alabama prohibits almost all categories of public employees from joining labor organizations and has invalidated contracts made between governmental units and unions within the state.

Most commonly, there is either statutory or tacit recognition of the right of public employees to join unions and negotiate with their employers. A number of states have passed legislation permitting public corporations, municipalities, and other local authorities to establish bargaining relations on a local option basis. Alaska, for example, authorizes its subdivisions to make agreements with labor organizations and otherwise leaves the subject open. In some cases the larger cities have not waited for specific approval by the state legislature to set up a labor relations program, but have assumed that this power is implied in their general responsibilities for hiring and determining working conditions. When such action by a municipal executive has resulted in signed agreements with a labor organization, the validity of the agreement has sometimes been challenged in the courts, with varying results. Depending on the strength of public employee organizations in the state, and also on the degree of harmony or conflict between political leaders at the state and municipal levels, enabling legislation may then be sought either piecemeal or in general terms. In contrast to other countries, where public employees in local governments have been represented by their own unions for many years, in the United States such developments have occurred mainly since 1960.

By 1968, about one-third of the states had enacted comprehensive labor relations programs for state and municipal employees. These states are: Alaska, California, Connecticut, Delaware, Florida, Maine, Massachusetts, Michigan, Minnesota, Missouri, New Hampshire, New York, Oregon, Rhode Island, Washington, Wisconsin, and Wyoming.[9] In these states, the pattern of public employee relations looks much like its counterpart in private industry. A comprehensive law usually contains an explicit declaration of the right of public employees to organize, to be represented by associations of their own choice, and to negotiate with their employers. In some states the hiring agencies are required to set up procedures for recognizing of, and negotiating with, employee organizations; in most states they are merely permitted to do so. The most important feature of the comprehensive law is its provisions for dispute settlement. The possibility of a dispute over recognition is usually settled by providing some form of supervised ballot. Issues of interpretation and application of work rules, whether

[9] For details, see R. S. Rubin, *A Summary of State Collective Bargaining Law in Public Employment*, Public Employee Relations Reports, No. 3 (Ithaca: New York State School of Industrial and Labor Relations, 1968).

or not these are set down in a formal agreement, are customarily handled by a grievance procedure that will move through informal stages to an appeal with formal hearing. Unlike the practice in private industry, however, the procedure often terminates at the top level of the agency instead of going to an outside arbitrator.

More serious are disputes over contract terms, which are the source of most work stoppages in public as well as in private employment. The techniques written into state statutes are basically similar to those in private industry, including mediation, fact finding by neutral boards or individuals, and voluntary or binding arbitration. But here the similarity ends. In all states, as in the federal government, a strike of public employees is unlawful and unacceptable, and a strike prohibition is usually written into the law.

Enforcement of such a comprehensive statute is usually entrusted to an administrative agency. This may be the state Labor Relations Board where one exists, as in Connecticut and Wisconsin, or a special Board for Public Employee Relations may be created, as in New York. In California, on the other hand, no central agency is charged with enforcement of the obligations stated in the law.

Even where a "comprehensive" statute has been passed, it does not necessarily cover all public employees in the state. Maine in 1965 passed a law with broad provisions covering the whole employment relationship, but limited its coverage to municipal firefighters. Michigan, as required by its state constitution, excludes from its otherwise comprehensive industrial relations program all state and local employees who are covered by civil service. Connecticut also provides that civil service and merit systems are not subject to collective bargaining. Wisconsin has passed separate laws, all with comprehensive provisions, for state employees and for local government employees; but police, sheriff's deputies, and county traffic officers are excluded from collective bargaining. Teachers are covered by separate enabling legislation in five states that have comprehensive laws for other employees—California, Connecticut, Rhode Island, Oregon, and Washington—and also in New York City.

The Strike Issue

Strikes of public employees are not supposed to happen, but they do happen.[10] In 1970 occurred a major strike of postal employees. There are also devices that, while technically not strikes, can slow down production and bring pressure on the public employer. Teachers have sometimes resigned or threatened to resign en masse, knowing that the school board could not replace them all, and that in the

10 Nor is this a recent development. See David Ziskind, *One Thousand Strikes Against the Government* (New York: Columbia University Press, 1940).

end the resignations would not be accepted. In other disputes, teachers have appeared and performed their classroom duties, but have declined to perform such auxiliary but customary duties as supervising lunchrooms and playgrounds or attending P.T.A. meetings. Air traffic controllers, transit employees, and other groups have used the device of "working to rule," which can tie up traffic without involving any illegal action.

Strike activity among public employees was particularly high from 1942 to 1953, and after a ten-year lull has been high again since 1964. Most of these strikes occur at the local level, fewer at the state level, very few at the federal level. The reasons for them are unclear. Unwillingness of public employers to bargain, or inexperience in bargaining on one or both sides, may be partly responsible. In some cases the strike may be a way of bringing pressure on higher budgetary authorities whose approval is needed for wage increases. War and inflation, accompanied by a deterioration in the relative economic position of public employees, may be conducive to a high level of strike activity.

Reduction in the incidence of strikes depends mainly on development of alternative procedures for resolving disputed issues. Statutory recognition of the right to organize, plus certification and election procedures administered by a labor relations board, can largely eliminate strikes over union recognition. Unsettled grievances should probably be handled through binding arbitration, as they normally are in private industry, despite legal qualms about government sovereignty.

For the more difficulty category of contract disputes, mediation is normally the first line of defense. Beyond this, the most commonly used technique is "fact finding" and recommendations by a publicly appointed individual or board. Of the seventeen states which have exacted comprehensive labor relations laws for public employees, nine provide for this method. "Fact finding" in this connection does not mean academic research, and what it actually means varies widely in different circumstances.[11] In many cases the fact finders function as mediators, and are able to settle the dispute without filing a formal report. Where a report is filed, indicating settlement terms that the neutrals consider reasonable, this may strengthen the hand of top legislative and executive officials in imposing a settlement. Alternatively, where the union and the employing agency are in substantial agreement but the legislature is the bottleneck, the report may generate pressure on the legislature to provide additional funds or take other necessary actions.

While experience with fact-finding procedures varies from state to

[11] See the analysis in Jean T. McKelvey, "Fact Finding in Public Employment Disputes: Promise or Illusion?" *Industrial and Labor Relations Review*, July, 1969, pp. 528–43.

state, it is on the whole encouraging. In Wisconsin, which passed one of the earliest laws in 1962, there were over the next six years 135 petitions for fact finding in municipal and county employment. Over half of these cases were resolved by informal mediation. Formal fact-finding reports were issued in fifty cases, in 90 percent of which the parties accepted the report in whole or in part. Only three strikes occurred after a fact-finding report, one involving rejection of the findings by the union, and two resulting from rejection by the employer.

In New York State, the Taylor Act of 1967 provides two alternative routes for resolving impasses over contract terms. First, the parties are encouraged to negotiate their own procedures and write these into the contract. Some public employers in the state have done this, sometimes providing for voluntary arbitration as the final step. Second, where an impasse is reached and mediation has failed, the Public Employee Relations Board is directed to appoint a fact-finding board of not more than three members. If the fact-finding report is rejected by one or both parties, the law directs the chief executive officer of the government involved to submit to the appropriate legislative body within five days his own recommendations for settling the dispute, together with a copy of the report. The union is also permitted to submit its views and recommendations to the legislative body, which is regarded as the final forum. Special procedures are operative in New York City, which has its own Office of Collective Bargaining.

In the first year after passage of the Taylor Act, some 316 impasses were referred to the Public Employee Relations Board, 80 percent of them involving teacher disputes with local school boards. Half of these were resolved by mediation, but 150 were referred to fact-finding boards. Of these cases, 22 percent were settled by further mediation and 45 percent by acceptance of the fact finders' report; but in one-third of the cases the report was not fully accepted. In most of these cases the dispute was finally resolved by "supermediation" after issuance of the report; but nine strikes occurred, two in New York City and seven elsewhere in the state.

What happens where mediation and fact finding have been tried and a strike still occurs? On one view, strikes in public employment should not be treated differently from strikes in private employment. They should be prohibited only when they cut off an essential community service, and otherwise should be allowed to continue. The preponderant view among experts, however, is that it would be difficult to get agreement on the boundary line between essential and nonessential services. Moreover, in public employment the strike does not have the constructive functions that it serves in private employment, where market pressures operate to force the parties toward agreement.

Unsettled disputes might be referred to compulsory arbitration as the final stage. This raises the legal problem that it places a private arbitrator in the position of dictating budget requirements to the sovereign legislative body. Despite this, Wyoming provides for binding arbitration of disputes involving firemen, while Pennsylvania and Rhode Island provide for compulsory arbitration of police and firemen's disputes. The final step of the New York State procedure amounts, in a sense, to compulsory arbitration by the legislature itself.

So long as public employee strikes are considered illegal, penalties will presumably be provided; but there is little indication that they are an effective deterrent. Here the experience of New York State is illuminating. In 1947 the state legislature passed the Condon–Wadlin Act that applied sanctions against the individual employee. Any striking employee was to be discharged immediately and, if reemployed, was to be in probationary status for five years and to forego any pay increase for three years.

These penalties were applied in five strikes in upstate New York. In New York City, however, the law was deliberately not invoked in thirteen cases, and the penalties were scaled down in two others. In no case was it applied against a strong and politically powerful union. After the New York City transit strike of January, 1966 had been settled, but it was clear that application of the legal penalties would bring a renewed strike, the legislature hastily passed a law exempting the transit workers from the provisions of the Condon–Wadlin Act.

Political difficulties apart, to discharge all employees in a particular industry in a tight labor market is not a very practical procedure. So the Taylor Committee recommended, and the Taylor Act of 1967 provided, that instead of discharge of employees sanctions be applied to the union organization. A union striking illegally could be fined up to $10,000 or one week's dues, whichever is less, for each day of the strike, with a minimum fine of $1,000 and loss of checkoff privileges for up to eighteen months. (The New York Teachers' Union subsequently had its checkoff privileges revoked on two separate occasions under this act.) These deterrents failed to prevent several serious strikes. After the New York City teachers' strike of 1968, Governor Rockefeller reconvened the Taylor Committee, which recommended further improvement of the impasse-resolving procedures and further stiffening of the strike penalties by removing any ceiling on the amount of daily fines or on the length of the period for which dues checkoff might be revoked. These proposals have not been acted on by the legislature at this writing.

While it may be easier to punish organizations than individuals, it is still difficult to act against a strong union in a strongly unionized city. In the end, main reliance must be placed on the impasse-resolving procedures discussed earlier.

LABOR RELATIONS
AND THE
ANTITRUST LAWS

Congress created the National Labor Relations Board as the prime interpreter of national labor policy, and this mandate has repeatedly been reinforced. Yet there remains on the books, in competition with the National Labor Relations Act, an alternative statutory framework for regulation of collective bargaining. This is the Sherman Act, as amended by Section 20 of the Clayton Act and modified by the Norris–LaGuardia Act. Continued existence of these overlapping sets of legal rules endangers the hard-won stability and the degree of industrial peace that the national labor policy has achieved. The record of the past decade indicates that this will be a problem of continuing urgency.

The Wagner Act asserted the positive role of law in labor relations, this time in support of unionism, with enforcement by a federal regulatory agency, the National Labor Relations Board. The Taft–Hartley amendments of 1947 created specific legal obligations that restricted union activity, but the basic authority of the National Labor Relations Board was reinforced. It appeared that the courts had effectively lost their power to apply the antitrust laws to union action, since machinery now existed for handling the full range of problems, including abuse of union power.

Congressional action was reinforced by judicial action. Shortly after the Supreme Court had approved the constitutionality of the Wagner Act, it virtually removed the possibility of either damage suits or criminal proceedings under the antitrust laws being applied to lawful union activities. The first case involved a suit by the *Apex Hosiery Company* against the *Hosiery Workers' Union,* which had sought to organize the company by a sit-down strike in which all shipments of hosiery out of the plant had been blockaded for seven weeks. The strike had been accompanied by violence and other organized activities, which could have been restrained by the application of criminal sanctions under local law; but instead the employer chose to sue the strikers for illegal restraint of trade under the Sherman Act. The Supreme Court ruled in 1940 that the union's action had a valid purpose, the organization of the company. Since the union had not intended to control the price of hosiery (and in fact the seven-week embargo on shipments had had no effect on hosiery prices) there had been no violation of the Sherman Act. Limitation of the employer's competitive freedom in the product market might be an incidental and even inescapable result of the strike; but as long as the purpose was sanctioned by Congress, such side effects would not make the strike illegal.[12] Unless the union had acted with the purpose of restraining price competition in the product market, union activities would not violate the antitrust laws.

In the following year, 1941, the Court declared in the *Hutcheson* case that the antitrust laws were "wholly unsuited" for the regulation of labor relations. The Carpenters had traditionally been in conflict with the International Association of Machinists for certain jobs involving erection and dismantling of machinery. In agreements between these two unions and the Anheuser-Busch Brewing Company, it was provided that disputed jobs should be submitted to arbitration. In 1939 the Carpenters' officers refused to accept arbitration of a specific dispute and called on the membership to enforce their demands by a strike and secondary boycott against Budweiser beer. The Justice Department charged that these activities violated the Sherman Act. But the Supreme Court's opinion, delivered in 1941 by Mr. Justice Frankfurter, ruled that the only test of legality is whether the union was acting out of self-interest and without combining with nonlabor groups. This was a broad and sweeping reading of the Norris–La-Guardia and Clayton Acts. A dissenting opinion noted that, in spite of continuing pressure, Congress had refused to legislate explicitly complete exemption of unions from the antitrust laws. The effect of the *Hutcheson* decision, however, was a complete exemption for the coercive self-help activities of national unions.[13]

Five years later a case reached the Supreme Court that for the first time raised the issue of unions controlling the product market in collusion with nonlabor groups. In New York City, Local 3 of the International Brotherhood of Electrical Workers had greatly enlarged the employment opportunities of its members by first obtaining closed shop contracts (at this time not illegal) with local concerns manufacturing electrical equipment, and then using the pressures of strike and boycott to persuade contractors to purchase equipment only from these manufacturers. Subsequently these agreements were expanded from individual contracts into an industry-wide "understanding" covering New York City, in which a committee of union, manufacturer and contractors' representatives acted to exclude from the metropolitan area all electrical equipment manufactured elsewhere—indeed,

[12] *Apex Hosiery* v. *Leader,* 310 U.S. 469 (1940).

[13] *United States* v. *Hutcheson,* 312 U.S. 219 (1941). The case arose out of a drive by the Department of Justice, under the direction of Assistant Attorney General Thurman Arnold, for vigorous enforcement of the antitrust laws against all combinations, including any labor groups whose actions were considered to be in restraint of trade. The government's position was defined in a public statement, which is reproduced with comment in "Antitrust Labor Problems: Law and Policy," *Law and Contemporary Problems,* Vol. 7 (1940), 82. For a discussion of the issues see Harry Shulman, "Labor and the Antitrust Laws," *Illinois Law Review,* Vol. 34 (1940), 769.

excluding even the output of factories with contracts with other International Brotherhood of Electrical Workers' locals. Allen–Bradley Inc., a Milwaukee manufacturer of electrical equipment, brought suit in federal court against the New York union. The district court found Local 3 in violation of the Sherman Act and issued an injunction; but this was reversed by the Court of Appeals on the grounds of the *Hutcheson* case—that is, that activities not forbidden to Local 3 if it were acting alone could not be prohibited merely because other groups had joined with the union to accomplish the same purpose.

But now the Supreme Court took a different view. It held that the Sherman Act had indeed been violated and that an injunction could be issued, provided it were limited to activities in which the union had combined with nonlabor groups to control the product market. The opinion, written by Mr. Justice Black, reasoned that the immunity claimed by Local 3 could not be found in any language of Congress, nor could it be inferred from the union's undoubted right to make bargaining agreements with employers. Standing alone, the contract of Local 3 was not a violation of the antitrust laws; but it did not stand alone. On the contrary, the facts of the case showed such collective agreements to be only one element in a larger program to monopolize all the business in New York City and to charge prices above a competitive level. "When the unions participated with a combination of businessmen who had complete power to eliminate all competition among themselves and to prevent all competition from others, a situation was created not included within the exemptions of the Clayton and Norris–LaGuardia Acts." [14]

For twenty years no sequel to the *Allen–Bradley* case appeared. Public opinion meanwhile had backed away from labor's sweeping claims of immunity from regulation, and the pendulum had swung toward mistrust of growing union power. In 1965 two Supreme Court cases once again raised the issue of private agreements versus public policy. Areas of union power continue to exist that cannot be reached by the regulatory machinery of the National Labor Relations Board if both parties agree to avoid it. If product price is adversely affected by such actions, do they nevertheless remain outside the control of antitrust policy? Students of labor had recognized the existence of a gray area, where challenges would arise only from great economic pressures and only when the challenger had effective power to carry the contest through a test of strength in the courts.

In the first case, *United Mine Workers* v. *Pennington*, the union and the major coal producers were alleged to have conspired to drive out of business the smaller and less-efficient coal producers by establishing a uniform, industry-wide wage rate set deliberately at a level

[14] *Allen–Bradley* v. *Local 3, International Brotherhood of Electrical Workers*, 325 U.S. 797 (1945).

higher than the small companies could afford to pay. The union claimed that an antitrust action could not be brought against a wage agreement; as a mandatory bargaining subject, the companies' "duty to bargain" was paramount. But the Supreme Court declined to ignore the purpose of the wage pact. Legality under the antitrust laws becomes an issue, said the Court, when as a precondition of the wage bargain the union agrees to "secure the same wages, hours or other conditions of employment from the remaining employers in the industry." In making a multiemployer agreement, the union may indeed attempt on its own to get the same terms from employers outside the unit. But the duty to bargain exists only on a unit-by-unit basis; there can be no compulsion to negotiate about standards outside the unit. "We think a union forfeits its exemption from the antitrust laws when it is clearly shown that it has agreed with one set of employers to impose a certain wage scale on other bargaining units." The Court ruled the Mineworkers guilty of conspiracy, but allowed reargument and in 1967 the union won its case; but meanwhile, in an identical case, a jury awarded triple damages of $1.5 million to the Tennessee Consolidated Coal Company. Using the *Pennington* rationale the Supreme Court upheld this award in March 1970, and the door was clearly opened to control of union activities under the antitrust laws.[55]

A companion case, *Amalgamated Meat Cutters* v. *Jewel Tea Company*, was decided on the same day. Jewel Tea, a retail chain, had sued the Meat Cutters' union under the Sherman Act, alleging a conspiracy between seven unions and 9,000 retailers to prevent the sale of meat in the Chicago area after 6:00 P.M. The union's defense was that hours of operation were so intimately connected with hours of labor that regulation was preempted by the National Labor Relations Act. The disputed clause of the union's 1957 contract read: "Marketing and operating hours shall be 9:00 A.M. to 6:00 P.M., Monday through Saturday inclusive. No customer shall be served who comes into the market before or after the hours set forth." Jewel Tea asked the union for Friday night operation and was refused. On threat of a strike vote, Jewel Tea finally signed the contract but then brought suit under the Sherman Act against both the unions and the Associated Food Retailers, a trade association. The complaint stated that 174 of the 196 Jewel Tea stores were equipped for a prepackaged self-service system, and that a butcher need not be on duty when purchases were actually made. An injunction and triple damages were asked.

15 *United Mine Workers* v. *Pennington*, 381 U.S. 657 (1965). For a discussion of the issues, see Theodore St. Antoine, "Collective bargaining and the antitrust laws," Industrial Relations Research Association, *Proceedings*, 1966, p. 66, and Archibald Cox, "Labor and the Antitrust Laws: Pennington and Jewel Tea," *Boston University Law Review*, Vol. 46 (1966), 317. The 1970 decision was one of four damage suits which reached the Supreme Court; see *The New York Times*, March 3, 1970, p. 22.

The union argued that the matter was entirely within the regulatory powers of the National Labor Relations Board and therefore outside the court's jurisdiction. But the court of appeals ruled that a conspiracy in restraint of trade had been shown, the marketing hours clause being classified as a product-pricing provision. The conspiracy ruling was rejected by the Supreme Court, but they also rejected the union argument that the case was exclusively a matter for the National Labor Relations Board. Exemption of the union's actions from the antitrust laws was held to depend not on the form of the agreement—the fact of bargaining on wages, hours, or working conditions—but on its relative impact on the product market balanced against the interests of union members in labor standards. The Court said in part: "Weighing the respective interests involved, we think the national labor policy expressed in the National Labor Relations Act places beyond the reach of the Sherman Act union–employer agreements on when, as well as how long, employees must work. An agreement on these subjects between the union and employers in a bargaining unit is not illegal under the Sherman Act, nor is the union's unilateral demand for the same contract of other employers in the industry." [16] On its reading of the facts, the Supreme Court ruled that the marketing hours provision was intimately related to a subject about which employers and unions must bargain. But the decision would apparently have gone the other way if the Court had believed that the self-service markets could actually operate without substantially increasing the workload of butchers during working hours. Then the restraint on the product market—exclusion of self-service stores from the evening market for meat—would stand alone. There would also have to be proof of intention to monopolize and actual attempts to frame a conspiracy.

So the application of antitrust to labor agreements, which on several occasions in the past has seemed to be settled, is once more in dispute. The courts seem to be saying that, wherever a collective agreement encroaches on product market competition, it may be held unlawful unless the effect is outweighed by the union's legitimate interest in wages, hours, and conditions. And who is to say which effect outweighs the other? Naturally, the courts. The door thus seems open to extensive judicial intervention in the substance of collective bargaining.

Most students of labor law agree that the problems are so complicated and technical that the courts should not attempt to rule on them without statutory guidance. But would it be possible to frame a

---

[16] *Local 189, Amalgamated Meat Cutters* v. *Jewel Tea Company*, 381 U.S. 676 (1965). For a detailed empirical study of the problems underlying the case, see Herbert R. Northrup, *Restrictive Labor Practices in the Supermarket Industry* (Philadelphia: University of Pennsylvania Press, 1967), chaps. 5 and 6.

statute delimiting the area in which the consumer interest in free competition is predominant, and separating protected union activity from undue control of the product market? At this point the experts profess doubt. Professor Cox suggests that we need much more information than we now have "on the extent or economic importance of union efforts to shelter employers from competition in the product market." Professor St. Antoine, emphasizing the technical complexity of these issues, believes that in the absence of "predatory purpose" there should be no substantive violation of the antitrust laws even if the contract covers labor standards outside the specific bargaining unit and thus loses its immunity under the Supreme Court's new doctrine.

Proposals for clarification of union activity affecting *product markets* should be distinguished from more sweeping proposals to reduce union power in *labor markets*. Some of the latter proposals would abolish multi-product or multi-industry unions, and probably industry-wide unions as well. The argument runs that labor monopoly is justifiable, if at all, only at the local level in order to correct employer monopsony. Reducing union bargaining power, it is thought, would reduce monopolistic distortion of the wage structure and also alleviate the problem of cost-push inflation. Whether these results would actually follow is doubtful. There is no hard evidence that fragmentation of national unions into company-sized unions would in fact reduce wage pressure, while in some industries it might increase it. Meanwhile the stabilizing role of the national union would be destroyed, with a predictable increase in industrial increase and (probably) a substantial increase of government intervention in industrial relations.

Those who propose disruption of national unionism are saying, in effect, that the adverse effects of collective bargaining as currently practiced outweigh the beneficial effects. This is an arguable position. But the reader might do well to suspend judgment until the final chapter, where the pros and cons of the present system are reviewed at length.

Discussion Questions

1. In what industries would you consider a stoppage of production serious enough to warrant special treatment by government? Give your reasons in each case.
2. Why is a national railroad strike a very uncommon event in the United States?

3. Review the main arguments for and against compulsory arbitration of major disputes.
4. Suppose you were asked to draft a new federal statute to replace the "emergency" provisions of the Taft–Hartley Act. What would you include in the statute?
5. In most of the Western democracies, the percentage of workers in unions is higher in the public sector than in the private sector. Would you expect that this will in time become true in the United States? Why, or why not?
6. "There is no reason for any legal distinction between union activities in the public sector and in the private sector. In both sectors, strike activity should be limited only where it interrupts production of an essential good or service." Discuss.
7. Are the determinants of bargaining power the same for a union of government employees as for a union of private employees? Explain.
8. What procedures would you recommend for dealing with impasses over contract terms in public employment? Do these differ from those you would recommend for "emergency disputes" in private employment? Explain.
9. In what ways might collective agreements serve, either deliberately or inadvertently, to restrict competition in product markets?
10. Draft an amendment to the antitrust laws specifying the kinds of bargained agreements that shall be considered unlawful because of their effect on product market competition.

Reading Suggestions

On the subject of national policy toward major strikes, the student may consult the following titles. Bernstein, Irving, Harold L. Enarson, and R. W. Fleming, eds., *Emergency Disputes and National Policy.* New York: Harper & Row, Publishers, 1955; Cullen, Donald E., *National Emergency Strikes.* Ithaca: New York School of Industrial and Labor Relations, Cornell, 1968; Chamberlain, Neil, "Strikes in Contemporary Context," *Industrial and Labor Relations Review,* Vol. 20, No. 4 (July, 1967), 602; Smythe, C. V., "Public Policy and Emergency Disputes," *Labor Law Journal,* October, 1963, p. 827; and Marshall, A. P., "New Perspectives in National Emergency Disputes," *Labor Law Journal,* Vol. 18 (August, 1967), 451. The definitive study of the use of presidential power in major disputes is Blackman,

John L., Jr., *Presidential Seizure in Labor Disputes.* Cambridge: Harvard University Press, 1967. On compulsory arbitration and settlement machinery, see Cole, David L., *The Quest for Industrial Peace.* New York: McGraw-Hill Book Company, 1963; also Northrup, Herbert R., *Compulsory Arbitration and Government Intervention in Labor Disputes.* Washington, D.C.: Labor Policy Association Inc., 1966.

For material on public employee unionism, see the symposium "Collective Negotiations in the Public Service," in *Public Administration Review,* Vol. 28 (March–April, 1968); and the symposium "Labor Relations in the Public Sector," in *University of Michigan Law Review,* Vol. 67, No. 5 (March, 1969). A comparative study that includes empirical data on the United States and selected foreign countries is Sturmthal, Adolf, ed., *White-Collar Unions.* Urbana: The University of Illinois Press, 1966. See also Kramer, Leo, *Labor's Paradox—The American Federation of State, County and Municipal Employees, AFL-CIO.* New York: John Wiley & Sons, Inc., 1962; State of New York, *Governor's Committee on Public Employee Relations, Final Report.* Albany: March, 1966.

On collective bargaining in education, two recent studies are Doherty, Robert E., and Walter E. Oberer, *Teachers, School Boards, and Collective Bargaining.* Ithaca: New York School of Industrial and Labor Relations, Cornell, 1968; and Moskow, Michael H., *Teachers and Unions.* Philadelphia: University of Pennsylvania, Wharton School, 1966. Two interesting short studies are Hazard, W. R., "Collective Bargaining in Education: The Anatomy of a Problem," *Labor Law Journal,* Vol. 18 (July, 1967), 412; and Garbarino, J. W., "Professional Negotiations in Education," *Industrial Relations,* Vol. 7 (February, 1968), 93.

On the application of antitrust laws to collective bargaining, see Cox, Archibald, "Labor and the Antitrust Laws; a Preliminary Analysis," *University of Pennsylvania Law Review,* Vol. 104 (1955), 252; Meltzer, Bernard D., "Labor Unions, Collective Bargaining and the Antitrust Laws," *Journal of Law and Economics,* Vol. 6 (1963), 152; Hildebrand, George, "Collective Bargaining and the Antitrust Laws," in Shister, Joseph, Benjamin Aaron and Clyde W. Summers, eds., *Public Policy and Collective Bargaining.* New York: Harper & Row, Publishers, 1962, pp. 152–82; St. Antoine, Theodore, "Collective Bargaining and the Antitrust Laws," *I.R.R.A. Proceedings,* 1966, p. 66; and Winter, Ralph, "Collective Bargaining and Competition: The Application of Antitrust Standards to Union Activities," *Yale Law Journal,* Vol. 73 (1963), 14.

COLLECTIVE BARGAINING: ECONOMIC IMPACT

In Part I we examined how labor markets allocate the labor force among thousands of specialized occupations and determine wage rates for these occupations. But in the unionized sector of the economy terms of employment are set by the union–management negotiation described in Part II. The results may differ from those that would be reached in a nonunion market. The purpose of Part III is to explore how far collective bargaining actually does alter market results. It thus serves as a capstone to the two preceding Parts.

Who is first in line for a vacant job? What are the tenure rights of an employee in his job? Under what conditions may he be transferred, demoted, laid off, or discharged? Chapter 20 examines union contract rules on these points and their possible effects on worker satisfaction and production efficiency. We consider also the union shop and other devices for union security, a subject that falls more logically here than at any other point.

Working conditions and work methods are regulated partly through contract rules, partly through the grievance procedure. Physical conditions of work often become a matter of dispute. Work speeds are usually regulated by formal or tacit agreement. This issue takes different forms, depending on whether workers are paid on an hourly basis, an output basis, or some combination of the two; and so we review union policies toward piece rate or "incentive" payment. Unions in such industries as building construction, printing, and railroading have often required hiring of unnecessary labor ("featherbedding") or insisted on time-consuming methods ("make-work rules"). Unions in manufacturing have usually not opposed mechanization, but have tried in various ways to cushion its labor-displacing effects. Issues in these areas, which typically involve both production efficiency and worker welfare, are discussed in Chapter 21.

The wage effects of collective bargaining are so extensive that we devote two chapters to them. Chapter 22 examines the main issues that arise at the company level: general wage changes in the company, rate setting for individual jobs, and the size of supplementary or "fringe" payments. Chapter 23 looks more broadly at the national wage structure, and examines how far union pressure alters relative rates of pay in different industries, occupational groups, and geographic areas. Finally, we ask whether unionism has a significant effect on the behavior of the money wage level, the rate of increase in real wages, and labor's share of national income.

The concluding chapter attempts an overview of the effects of unionism and collective bargaining on our political economy. These effects are numerous, complex, and often uncertain. Even where an effect is clear, its desirability often remains a matter of judgment. Thus when one seeks an overall judgment of the social utility of unionism, reasonable men may reach different conclusions. The writer has tried not to impose his own scale of preferences on the reader, but to provide the raw materials from which the student can fashion his own conclusions.

JOB TENURE AND JOB SECURITY

20

The matters regulated by the collective agreement or "union contract" vary greatly from one situation to the next, depending on the age of the agreement, the nature of the industry, the structure and policies of the union, and the attitudes and objectives of management. Speaking generally, unions attempt to regulate every kind of managerial action that directly affects the welfare of the membership or the strength and security of the union itself. Almost every aspect of personnel administration, and many aspects of production management, eventually become matters of collective bargaining. A list of the subjects covered in the more than 100,000 union contracts in the United States would include hundreds of items; and with respect to each of these, many different contract provisions have been worked out to meet differing circumstances.

To do justice to this wealth of issues and variety of solutions would require a separate book.[1] In the limited space available here it is

[1] For a survey of the detailed issues that arise in collective bargaining and the alternative methods of handling them, see Neil W. Chamberlain, *Collective Bargaining* (New York: McGraw-Hill Book Company, 1955); and John T. Dunlop and James J. Healey, *Collective Bargaining: Principles and Cases*, rev. ed. (Homewood, Ill.: Richard D. Irwin, Inc., 1953).

necessary to concentrate on a few key issues and, with respect to each issue, to discuss the general objectives and attitudes of the parties rather than detailed differences in contract arrangements. The student who wishes to examine the variety of contract provisions currently existing on any subject can find this information in a number of convenient sources.[2]

Union contracts normally contain a number of procedural provisions, designed to set the general framework of relations between the parties. These include provisions concerning recognition and status of the union, rights and prerogatives of management, duration of the agreement and method of extending or renewing it, prevention of strikes and lockouts during the life of the agreement, and handling of grievances arising under the contract.

The substantive provisions of the contract may be organized into three broad groups:

1. *Job Tenure and Job Security.* This includes all provisions concerning hiring, training, assignment to work, promotion and transfer, layoff and recall, and discharge. Since length of service (seniority) is an important criterion in some of these decisions, the contract must specify how seniority is to be calculated and applied.

2. *Work Schedules, Work Speeds, and Production Methods.* This includes determination of the standard workday and workweek, and payment for work in excess of the standard schedule. It covers also the determination of proper work speeds—size of machine assignments, proper speed of assembly lines, time standards and work quotas under incentive systems, and similar matters. Working conditions of every sort including health, safety, sanitation, heating and lighting, and ventilation are included. Finally, the agreement may touch on certain aspects of production methods—methods of work that may be used, number of workers to be used on a particular job, and introduction of new machinery and production processes.

3. *Amount and Method of Compensation.* This includes provisions concerning the basic wage schedule and general changes in this schedule; the method of wage payment and, if a piece rate or incentive system is used, the extent of union participation in the administration of the system; setting of wage rates on new or changed jobs; wage increases for individual workers on a seniority or merit basis; and a wide variety of indirect or supplementary wage payments to workers, including pension funds, health and welfare funds, and supplementary unemployment benefit plans.

In this and the next three chapters, we shall examine these three groups in turn. Note that they are increasingly economic, in the

[2] Notably the file of current union contracts maintained by the Bureau of Labor Statistics of the Department of Labor, and the current labor services issued by Prentice–Hall, Inc., and others.

sense of affecting labor costs per unit of output. Methods of hiring, promotion, and layoff doubtless affect costs, but the effect is indirect and hard to estimate. Work speeds and production methods have a clearer effect, since they determine how much output the worker delivers in exchange for his wage. The wage itself, including supplementary or "fringe" benefits, bears directly on costs. So all three groups are of concern to the employer; and for different reasons, each is important to the worker as well. The first affects his employment opportunities and job security, the second affects the pleasantness of his daily life on the job, while the third sets limits to his standard of living.

CONTROL OF HIRING:
APPRENTICESHIP;
THE CLOSED SHOP

Economic reasoning suggests that it is natural for unions to take an interest in the supply of labor. Reducing the supply of a particular kind of labor is one way of raising its price. Or, if the union simply demands and wins a wage above the market equilibrium, the result will be more workers seeking jobs at that wage than employers are willing to hire. The union is then likely to take an interest in *which* workers get hired for the available jobs.

Control over labor supply might be exercised at various levels. A union might try to control the number of persons who secure training for a particular occupation. If it cannot do this, it might restrict the number admitted to the union and make membership in the union a prerequisite for employment. Or it might admit to the union everyone who applies and still control the distribution of work among the members.

Training is important mainly for a limited number of skilled trades. Semiskilled jobs can be learned quickly and are normally learned on the job. The skilled crafts require longer training and experience, and are often learned in advance of employment either through vocational school courses or apprentice training programs. Control of the number admitted to such programs could conceivably be used to restrict the supply of labor.

This has not happened in practice, partly because there are so many other ways in which one can learn a skilled trade. Many men learn trades during service in the armed forces. Semiskilled workers are often trained and upgraded to skilled jobs within the plant. Many people simply pick up a trade by getting a smattering of it, finding someone willing to hire them, and improving their competence as they go along. Every farm boy naturally becomes something of a carpenter, painter, and auto mechanic. Between 1965 and 1975, the American economy will need about 600,000 new skilled craftsmen each year—some 400,000 to replace losses through death, disability, retirement, and shifts to other occupations, and 200,000 for net expansion. The total number of young people enrolled in registered apprentice programs, however, is only about 200,000, and many of these drop out before completion. The number completing apprenticeship programs has varied recently between 25,000 and 30,000 per year.[3] Since apprenticeship provides only a small part of the supply of new craftsmen, it can scarcely form an effective method of restricting labor supply.

Unions have nevertheless taken an active interest in apprenticeship programs for several reasons. Skilled workers have pride in their craft and would like to see the next generation get a thorough training. They want to make employers pay high enough wages to apprentices so that they do not become a source of cheap labor that could undercut the union scale. There is usually a contract provision that the apprentice shall start out at, say, 40 per cent of the journeyman's rate, and work up to this rate by steps over his period of training. Craftsmen also want adequate opportunity for their sons to gain admission as apprentices. It is as customary for a plumber's son to become a plumber as for a doctor's son to become a doctor.

The Machinists, Electrical Workers, Typographers, Plumbers, and Boilermakers have been particularly active in developing apprenticeship programs in cooperation with employers in their respective industries. The Bureau of Apprenticeship and Training in the U.S. Department of Labor has national responsibility for fostering such programs and setting minimum standards for their operation. The main problem is not union reluctance to permit more apprentices to be trained, but rather employer reluctance to take on as many apprentices as union regulations allow. The employer puts considerable investment into each apprentice, but has no assurance that the boy will stay with him beyond the apprenticeship period. So it is to each employer's interest to persuade *other* employers in his industry to train apprentices whom he will later be able to hire away from them. Heavier investment in training, with each employer bearing his proper share of the cost, might well benefit employers as a group; but to sell this idea and work out an acceptable program is often difficult.

Granted that a union can rarely control the number of persons who learn a particular trade, it might still control the number admitted to the union. Then if it could get employers to hire only people who are already union members (a *closed shop* arrangement), it

[3] *Manpower Report of the President* (Washington, D.C.: Department of Labor, January, 1969), pp. 235, 251.

would have effective control of labor supply. Admission to the union could be regulated either by closing the books when the number of union members equals the number demanded by employers at the union wage rate, or by charging an initiation fee high enough to reduce applications to the desired level.

Suppose the demand and supply curves for a particular craft are shown by the solid lines in Figure 1. The wage rate in a competitive

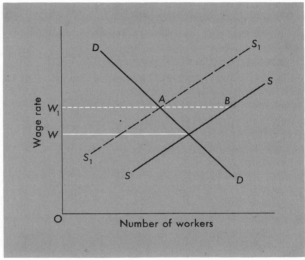

Figure 1

METHODS OF CONTROLLING LABOR SUPPLY

labor market would be OW. The number seeking employment just equals the number desired by employers, and the market is cleared. The union is strong enough, however, to secure a wage of OW_1 and to insist on a closed shop rule. At this wage, the number seeking work in the trade exceeds the number employers will hire by the distance AB. The union might do one of two things. It might say: "We will admit only W_1A people to the union, and the rest must remain outside." This requires some way of selecting the lucky people to be admitted. Alternatively, it might charge a stiff initiation fee for admission to the union. A charge for admission, by reducing the net returns from the occupation, will reduce the number seeking employment at a given wage, i.e. it will shift the labor supply curve to the left. The union could discover by experiment an initiation fee just high enough to shift labor supply from SS to S_1S_1. Then the number spontaneously seeking employment would once more equal the number desired by employers. This self-selection through the market mechanism would remove any political embarrassment to the union, while at the same time enabling it to turn a tidy profit.

Unions actually do not make much use of either method. That they do not use the second method is shown by the moderate level of union initiation fees. Out of 39,000 local unions filing reports under the Landrum–Griffin Act, only 342 reported initiation fees of more than $250, and the highest fee reported by any local was $1,400. This must be well below the value of union membership in many cases. "Becker reports that New York City taxicab medallions have sold for about $17,000 in recent years, and San Francisco papers in 1959 reported a figure of $16,000 for the transfer of licenses to operate a taxicab in that city. The value of entry to a union with a 20 percent effect on relative earnings would be of this order of magnitude even at fairly high interest rates." [4] One reason for not using high fees as a job rationing device is doubtless that it would outrage public opinion and publicize the monopolistic level of the union wage.

One finds occasional cases of arbitrary closing of the union books to exclude labor and buttress a high wage scale.[5] But these cases are exceptional. To leave a surplus of eager applicants (shown by *AB* in Figure 1) outside the union is a standing invitation for employers to hire these people at less than union wage rates. It is safer to take into the union everyone who applies, and this also brings in more dues revenue. Then, if there is less than enough work to go around, the union can devise rules for allocating this work among the membership.

Where there is an exceptional rise in labor demand, which is expected to subside in the near future, a local union sometimes decides to meet this not by enlarging its regular membership, but by allowing outsiders to work temporarily under a *permit card* system. This is a legitimate way of covering seasonal peaks of employment in irregular industries such as food processing or construction, or of meeting labor needs on a large construction project in a remote locality

---

[4] Albert Rees, *The Economics of Trade Unions* (Chicago: The University of Chicago Press, 1962), p. 128. Professor Rees adds in a footnote: "Membership in a union with an effect of 20 percent on annual earnings would increase earnings $1,000 a year for a man whose alternative earnings were $5,000. The present value of an annuity of $1,000 a year for 40 years is over $15,000 at an interest rate of 6 percent."

[5] An example of a closed union is the Newspaper and Mail Deliverers' Union of New York, which for years has maintained an illegal closed shop in violation of the Taft–Hartley Act. Memberships in it are reported to have sold for as much as $5,000, although about $500 is said to be the usual price. Sumner H. Slichter, James J. Healy, and E. Robert Livernash, *The Impact of Collective Bargaining on Management* (Washington, D.C.: The Brookings Institution, 1960), p. 41.

where the regular labor force is small. Some locals, however, have abused the permit system by refusing admission even to regularly employed workers, and then charging them high fees for the right to work. National unions almost invariably discourage such practices, and they are also regulated by legislation. Landrum–Griffin requires local unions to report on their permit fees, and Taft–Hartley prohibits the charging of fees higher than the union's normal dues.

The main examples of labor supply restriction occur in certain occupations covered by state licensing regulations. A law is passed providing that barbers, say, can be admitted to the trade only after passing an examination set by a state licensing board. (For "barbers" read also plumbers or electricians, or, for that matter, accountants, lawyers, or doctors.) To no one's surprise, the licensing board turns out to consist of representatives of the barbers' union and the master barbers' (employers) association. The number of candidates who "pass" is held down to a level that does not endanger the jobs or wage scale of those already employed in the industry. This is typically part of a broader pattern of monopolistic control over prices, wages, and admission of new employers as well as new workers.

If the closed shop is ordinarily not used to control the number admitted to an occupation, what is the point of the closed shop? First, it is traditional in many of the skilled trades. In Britain, the principle that a union craftsman will not work alongside a nonunion man is so well established that no formal closed-shop rules are necessary. Second, it strengthens the union organization. If nonunion men cannot even get hired, the employer has no opportunity to undermine and weaken the union. In addition to this defensive function, the closed shop enables the union to ration job opportunities among members of the craft on some equitable basis; and it often furnishes employers with a central employment agency.

The closed shop is typically accompanied by an arrangement under which the union acts as an employment agency for the industry and provides workers to individual employers on request. This is convenient where employers are small, as in clothing manufacture or job printing; or where jobs are of short duration and each employer's needs fluctuate widely, as in building construction. Central hiring is useful also in industries where there is a good deal of seasonal or casual unemployment, such as longshoring and merchant shipping. Where there is regular year-round employment, as in most manufacturing industries, the unions have taken little interest in closed shop clauses or central hiring facilities.

In 1946, just before passage of the Taft–Hartley Act, the closed shop appeared in about one-third of all union contracts. Taft–Hartley forbade the closed shop, and so it has almost vanished from union contracts; but this is not to say that the practice has disappeared. In building construction, the closed shop continued in open defiance of Taft–Hartley and was eventually (in effect) relegalized by Landrum–Griffin. In other cases the former contract provisions have been replaced by new clauses intended to have the same effect. For example, the contract may provide that the union shall have first opportunity to fill job vacancies, and that only if the union cannot provide workers within a certain period will the employer look elsewhere; or that preference in employment will be given to workers employed in the industry before a certain date, i.e. during the closed shop period, hence necessarily union members; or that preference will be given to graduates of a training program operated by the union; or simply that preference will be given to "experienced" or "qualified" workers. There are additional cases in which a bootleg closed shop has continued by tacit agreement between the union and employer with no contract provision. Where there is a long tradition that union members will not work alongside nonunion men, it is simpler for the employer to accept this tradition than to assert his rights and lose his labor.

The main practical problem associated with the closed shop is that of union admission requirements. Where there is a tacit closed shop, and where the union declines to admit certain kinds of workers— women, nonwhites, or whatever—these people are barred from employment in the industry. This has not been an important problem in industrial unions, since they rarely have the closed shop and rarely discriminate in membership. Some of the craft unions have followed discriminatory policies, however, and this has made it hard particularly for nonwhite workers to get into the building trades, railroad trades, and some other areas of employment. The situation is all the more difficult because employers and the union are usually in full agreement on this policy.

COMPULSORY MEMBERSHIP:
THE
UNION SHOP

More than four-fifths of all union contracts contain some provision for union security. Much the commonest provision is a straight *union shop*. This leaves the employer free to hire at will; but after the worker has served his probationary period and becomes a regular member of the plant labor force, he is required to join the union. If he declines to do so, or if he drops out of the union, the employer must discharge him. A variant of the union shop is the *maintenance-of-membership* clause. This does not compel any worker to join; but if he chooses to join, he must then remain in for the duration of the contract as a condition of employment. Another rather rare variant is the *agency shop,* under which a worker who declines to join is obliged to pay the union a fee—usually set at the level of the monthly dues—in return for the collective bargaining service that it is rendering him.

In earlier times the union shop gave union leaders a powerful disciplinary weapon over recalcitrant members. Anyone who fell foul of the existing leadership could be expelled from the union and would then be out of a job. This doubtless contributed to the growth of oppressive and corrupt practices in some unions. To correct this Taft–Hartley provided that the employer is not obliged to discharge a worker who has been expelled from, or denied admission to, the union on any ground other than failure to tender the regular dues and initiation fees.

The union shop itself is legal under Taft–Hartley. But the act contains a curious provision that, where any state has passed a law forbidding the union shop, the state law shall take precedence. This reverses the normal rule that federal law has precedence as regards workers in interstate commerce. Twenty states have laws (usually labeled "right-to-work laws") that prohibit both the closed and union shop. These states are almost all in the South and West (Indiana is the only major industrial state with such a statute), and include only about 15 percent of industrial employment in the country. Unions have fought these laws vigorously on the ground that they will destroy trade unionism, while employer and farm groups have hailed them as the Magna Charta of the working man. It is doubtful that either claim could be substantiated. Research studies suggest that the practical effect of these laws has been small.[6] Employers who want good relations with their unions have usually winked at the law, just as employers in traditional closed shop industries have winked at Taft–Hartley. Where relations are bad, however, and where the employer wants to mount a drive against the union, an antiunion-shop law may give him an additional weapon.

Some Pros and Cons of the Union Shop

The legitimacy of the union shop has been argued for generations, and the issue arouses strong emotion on both sides. Unionists argue that, since everyone in the bargaining unit benefits from the contract terms established by the union, everyone should be required to contribute to the union's support. If this is not the case, some workers will receive a "free ride" at the expense of their fellow workers. This

[6] See, for example, Frederic Myers, *"Right to Work" in Practice* (New York: Fund for the Republic, 1959.)

situation is as unfair as one in which citizens of a community could decide whether or not they wish to pay taxes.

A more powerful argument for the union shop is that only if the union's existence is secure can it afford to cooperate with management and play a constructive role in the operation of the enterprise. The union interprets management's denial of the union shop as a lack of complete acceptance of collective bargaining, an indication that management does not consider the union a permanent part of the enterprise and hopes in time to be rid of it. The union must, therefore, devote much of its energy to keeping its fences mended against employer attack. It must try to hem in the employer by contract restrictions at any point where he might try to discriminate against union men; it must limit his power to select, promote, transfer, lay off, and discharge. It must manufacture enough grievances to keep the workers convinced that the employer is a tricky fellow and that the union is essential for their protection. It must give good service on grievances to its members, and poor service or no service to nonmembers, in order to emphasize the practical advantages of union membership; this discrimination makes for unequal treatment and ill-feeling within the labor force.

Employer acceptance of the union shop, it is argued, would make all this unnecessary. The time of union officials could be put to constructive use in ironing out personnel problems and production difficulties, giving prompt attention to genuine grievances, performing educational functions, and cooperating with management in other ways. Freed of any necessity to stir up antagonism to the employer in order to hold their members in line, union leaders could afford to take a reasonable position on disputed issues.

This general point of view is supported by a number of careful students of the subject. Slichter, for example, concludes that the union shop is desirable for the contribution it can make to stable industrial relations. He points out that a union whose security is beyond question can afford to be more reasonable on other matters —notably promotions, layoffs, and other points at which discrimination might be practiced against union members. A union that fears for its life must necessarily try to restrict the employer at all these points. Slichter concludes, therefore, that the employer can secure a generally more favorable contract by conceding the union-shop issue at the outset.[7]

On the other hand, many management officials argue that the union shop is coercive and involves an undue encroachment on the liberty of the individual worker. In a free society, a worker should be able to seek and accept employment with any employer who is will-

7 See Sumner H. Slichter, *Union Policies and Industrial Management* (Washington, D.C.: The Brookings Institution, 1941), chap. 3.

ing to hire him, without paying tribute to a third party. The union shop forces him to join an organization of which he may not approve, and forces him to pay for the right to work, a right which he should enjoy as a citizen.

This argument that the union shop coerces workers into unionism against their will appears to have been overdone. Few workers seem to have any conscientious objection to unionism. Most of those who stay out of the union do so simply out of inertia or to avoid dues payments. The coercion involved in requiring them to join the union is mainly financial, and is no greater than that involved in levying payroll taxes on them for social security or other purposes. There is abundant evidence that where the union shop has been in effect in the past, the great majority of workers favor its continuance. The Taft–Hartley Act originally provided that a union-shop clause could not be included in a union contract unless a majority of the employees in the bargaining unit voted in favor of it in a secret ballot conducted by the National Labor Relations Board. During the first year of the act's operation, some 22,000 elections were held under this section. The union shop was upheld in more than 98 percent of these cases and secured more than 95 percent of all ballots cast. It soon became clear, in fact, that these union-shop referenda were simply an unnecessary expense to the government, and the act was subsequently amended to eliminate the referendum requirement.

Beneath the arguments over the union-shop issue lies the hard fact of a power struggle. A union security clause strengthens the union's position in the shop, renders it less vulnerable to attack by the employer or rival unions, and helps to make it a permanent institution. It also makes the position of union officials more secure and less arduous. Management opposition to the union shop is based mainly on a recognition of these facts. Most managements see no reason to go out of their way in helping the union to become a permanent fixture. This does not necessarily mean that they have any hope of breaking the union. Their strategy may be merely to fight an effective delaying action. If the union can be kept busy holding its membership together, it will be in a weaker position to press fresh demands on the employer.

One's attitude toward the union shop is bound to depend on how one answers the following question: Is it desirable to maintain strong, stable, and permanent unions in American industry? If one answers no to this question, the open-shop position follows automatically. If one answers yes, a strong case can be made for a union-shop clause. There seems little doubt that a union is better able to function in a peaceful and constructive way if it embraces most or all of the labor force. It is unreasonable to demand that unions be "responsible" while at the same time denying union officers the control over their membership that would make group responsibility effective.

An issue related to the union shop should be noted in conclusion. Union demands for a union- or closed-shop clause have usually been accompanied by a demand for the "checkoff." This is an arrangement by which the regular weekly or monthly dues of union members are deducted from their paychecks by the employer and transmitted in a lump sum to the union. Most unions prefer the checkoff, partly because it saves them a good deal of effort and unpleasantness in collecting dues from delinquent members, and partly because it still further regulates and entrenches the position of the union in the plant. Most managements oppose the checkoff because it involves the company in effort and expense for the primary benefit of the union.

In general, where one finds a closed-shop, union-shop, or maintenance-of-membership provision, one is likely to find the checkoff as well. About two-thirds of all union contracts contain this provision. There are many detailed variations in checkoff clauses. Under some contracts, dues are checked off automatically for all union members; under others, they are checked off unless the worker asks the company in writing not to deduct his dues; in still other cases, the dues are deducted only if the worker makes a positive request in writing that this be done. Taft–Hartley provides that a dues checkoff requires the written consent of each employee; but this consent is rarely refused. The whole issue, while presenting many possibilities for technical arguments, is subsidiary to the broader argument over the union shop. The outcome of that argument usually determines the outcome of the checkoff argument as well.

JOB TENURE:
SECURITY
AND
OPPORTUNITY

An important group of provisions in union contracts concerns the conditions under which individual workers shall have access to vacant jobs, the rules governing their tenure of the job, and the conditions under which they may be separated from employment. So important is this matter that Perlman and others have found in it the key to the growth and persistence of trade unionism. Workers are continually faced with a scarcity of available jobs, and consciousness of this scarcity molds union philosophy and tactics. The union is a method of controlling the job opportunities in a craft or industry and of distributing these opportunities among union members according to some equitable principle.

The union tries to introduce into industry a "civil service system" of job tenure. The worker ceases to be so many units of productive power, which can be shifted about in the plant or dispensed with altogether at the pleasure of the employer. He becomes an individual with a system of rights, which the employer is bound to observe and which can be defended through the grievance procedure. The different matters regulated by this system of rights will be examined briefly in this section.

The Seniority Principle

Over the past thirty years there has been increasing acceptance of the principle that a worker's job rights should be related to his length of service. Common-sense ideas of equity suggest that a man who has devoted more years to the company deserves more of the company in return. Seniority is objective, relatively easy to measure and apply, and easy to defend before workers and outside arbitrators.

Seniority appears in the union contract in two main ways. First, it usually governs eligibility for "fringe benefits": vacations, paid holidays, pensions, severance pay, sick-leave provisions, insurance and health services, profit sharing, supplementary unemployment benefits, and the rest. In bargaining over these issues employers have usually insisted, and unions have accepted, that a man's entitlement to benefits should vary with length of service. The 20-year man gets longer paid vacations, larger pension rights, more sick leave, and so on, than the 2-year-man. Slichter, Healy, and Livernash call this *benefit seniority.*

The second area they term *competitive status seniority.* Here the problem is one of ranking workers relative to each other. Several workers are in competition to get a promotion or avoid a layoff, and the seniority principle is used to resolve the competition. The most obvious applications are to layoff, transfer, and promotion; but there are also many others. The senior worker may be given first choice in picking vacation periods. He may be given first chance to earn more money through overtime work. He may lay claim to the newest of a group of machines, or to the machine in the pleasantest location. Spaces in the company parking lot may be allocated on a seniority basis. In one company the senior men are allowed to punch out first on the time clock at the end of the day, which has advantages in reducing the wild scramble which occurred previously.

Benefit seniority is almost always calculated from the date of first employment with the company; but competitive status seniority is harder to calculate and apply. Suppose Bill Jones has been with the company fifteen years, working five years in department *A,* five years in department *B,* and five years in his present job in department *C.*

Layoffs now become necessary in department *C*, and it is agreed that they should be in order of seniority. What is Bill Jones' seniority in department *C*? Is it fifteen years, or only five years? If he is laid off from department *C*, can he go back to his previous job in department *B* and displace ("bump") some less-senior worker? And how much seniority does he have in department *B*? The rules have to be spelled out in the contract; and the rules may be different for different problems—one principle for promotion, another for layoff, and so on. These fine details have important effects on employee security and on management's freedom to deploy its work force to greatest effect.

Sharing of Work Opportunities; Irregular Industries

In some industries, continuous attachment to a single employer is impossible by the nature of the industry. Seamen are often paid off at the end of each voyage and, after a shorter or longer period "on the beach," sign on with another vessel for a new voyage. In long-shoring, the amount of work coming into a particular pier is irregular, depending on what ships happen to arrive on a particular day. When a cargo comes in and has to be unloaded, it is necessary to hire a gang of longshoremen on the spot; when the vessel is unloaded, their job ends. In other industries, production is highly seasonal. Building construction tapers off in the late fall and revives in the early spring. Each worker naturally wants to be the last man laid off in the fall and the first man hired in the spring. The men's and women's clothing industries have two production seasons during the year, one for the spring trade, the other for the fall trade. During each of these seasons activity begins slowly, mounts to a peak of production and employment, and then declines. Again, each worker in the industry wants to be the first hired and the last laid off.

In the absence of contract rules concerning hiring, the bulk of the work in such industries would go to men who were of superior efficiency or who had special "pull" with foremen and hiring officials. Workers who got relatively little work would feel that the union was not serving them effectively, and would be tempted to drop out. Partly to preserve the organization, partly out of considerations of equity, the union attempts to ensure that the available work is shared more or less equally among the membership.

Where employers are numerous and small, this attempt may require union control over the referral of workers to jobs. It is no accident that the union office has been used as an employment agency in the building, printing, and clothing industries, or that the union "hiring hall" has developed in longshoring and merchant shipping.

The devices used to ensure something like equal division of work vary from one industry to the next. In the shipping industry, the man who has been longest "on the beach" gets the first opportunity to sign up for a new voyage; all job vacancies and referrals to work are cleared through the union hiring hall. In longshoring work in Pacific Coast ports, a regular list of "gangs" (work teams) is maintained at union headquarters, and gangs are dispatched to work in the order in which they appear on this list. When a gang comes off the job it must go to the bottom of the list and wait until its number comes up again before being dispatched to a new job.

The hiring-hall arrangement has traditionally been a closed-shop arrangement as well, and was therefore rendered unlawful by the Taft–Hartley Act. The maritime unions, however, have succeeded in developing formulas that have maintained the hiring hall relatively unchanged. In merchant shipping, preference in hiring is no longer given to union members as such, but is given to men who have sailed previously on the ships of members of the employers' association. Since the great majority of seamen had been unionized in the past, this amounts to almost the same thing. The new arrangement appears to have had little effect on hiring-hall practices. Taft–Hartley requires that, if nonunion workers do come to the hiring hall, they must be given the same service as union members and referred to work on a nondiscriminatory basis.

In the clothing industries, the unions have favored reduction in working hours rather than layoffs as work tapers off toward the end of a season. In this way all workers in a shop get an equal amount of work as long as work is available. In building construction, there has been some experimentation with "first off, first on" rules, under which the first man laid off in the fall would be dispatched to the first job opening in the spring. This sort of rule, however, presents certain difficulties. The first men laid off in the fall may be chronic drunkards or undesirable for other reasons. Experience has shown that, where the first employer who starts building work in the spring is forced to hire those undesirables, there is a good deal of jockeying among employers to avoid this unpleasant necessity. Whether for this or other reasons, the building trades have done less than most other unions to enforce formal work-sharing rules.

Sharing of Work Opportunities: Reductions in Production Schedules

Even in stable industries the labor requirements of a firm may vary somewhat from month to month. It may fail to secure a large order on which it has been counting, the sales of a new product line may be disappointing, or a general business recession may develop. This situation causes a reduction in production schedules and man-hours worked. Several questions then arise. Who is to bear the brunt of the reduction in employment? How shall the work that is left be distributed among those who want it?

A reduction in production schedules can be met either by laying off workers, by reducing the number of hours worked per week, or by a combination of these methods. One possibility is to keep everyone on the payroll but to work the plant fewer hours per week. This policy is beneficial to the short-service employees, since it gives them some work, whereas layoffs based on length of service would put them out of work completely. Even the long-service workers are likely to consider it equitable that work opportunities be shared among the entire labor force. A policy of work sharing also has certain advantages to management, since it enables the plant labor force to be held together and eases the problem of increasing production when demand revives.

It is necessary, however, to set some limit to a work-sharing policy. If hours fall below thirty per week, most workers will feel that they are sharing poverty rather than opportunity. They will in fact be earning little more than the unemployment compensation they would receive if totally unemployed. If the drop in demand is severe and prolonged, therefore, it will be necessary to go beyond hours reduction to layoff of workers. Many union contracts provide for something like the following combination of procedures to meet a decline in production: first, lay off all temporary and probationary employees; second reduce hours of work as required down to some minimum—say 32 hours per week; third, if these measures are insufficient, begin to lay off members of the regular work force.

Where layoffs have to be made, unions typically and successfully insist that they should be made on a seniority basis. They argue that the workers with greater length of service will, in general, be more efficient at their jobs and more valuable to the company. In addition, the long-service workers will usually be men with family responsibilities, whose incomes should be protected on social grounds. Primarily, however, unions like the simplicity and definiteness of a seniority system, which makes it impossible for the employer or the foreman to use layoffs as an occasion for "taking it out" on certain workers. In some industries, such as the railroads, the older men are dominant in union affairs, and this may have something to do with union adherence to the seniority principle. By the same token, a straight seniority rule runs the risk of alienating the younger men by forcing them to bear the brunt of cyclical unemployment. This situation may cause serious factional conflict between younger and older men in the union, as has happened more than once in the railroad trades.

It is easier to defend the seniority principle than it is to work out detailed regulations for applying it. A central issue here is the size of the "seniority district." Should seniority be considered as the man's length of service in a particular occupation, or in a particular department of the plant, or in the plants as a whole, or in all plants of a multi-plant company? Under plant-wide seniority a man laid off in one department may be able to shift over and bump a worker in an entirely different department whose seniority is less than his own, who in turn may bump someone in a third department. A single layoff may thus set off a chain of displacements throughout the plant. The more narrowly the seniority unit is defined, the smaller is the possibility of bumping and consequently the smaller the protection afforded to long-service employees. The union will typically argue for broad seniority units in order to achieve maximum employee protection, while management will argue for narrower units in order to minimize the disruption of work teams and the added training time that may result from excessive bumping. Arguments over the drafting of seniority clauses and their application to individual workers consume a good proportion of union and management time in collective bargaining.

Whatever procedure is chosen for layoffs normally applies also to rehiring. Workers are recalled to work in reverse order from that in which they were laid off—"last off, first in." The brunt of unemployment is thus borne by those with the shortest period of service.

Some agreements provide that "key men" may be exempted from the operation of the seniority rule. These men are designated by management, and it is usually provided that they may not exceed a certain percentage of the total labor force. The argument of management for this provision is that it is desirable during depression to hold together a skeleton force of men trained for strategic positions in the plant. If this force is broken up through strict application of a seniority rule, it may be difficult and costly to rebuild it. The union sometimes makes a similar argument that, if key union officials are laid off during depression, smooth administration of the union contract will be seriously hampered. On this ground they urge "super-seniority" for shop stewards and other union officials, i.e. that these men be placed automatically at the top of the seniority lists in their respective departments. Management frequently objects to this provision on the ground that it creates a privileged class and places too high a premium on running for union office. Despite the objections, super-seniority clauses appear in an increasing percentage of union agreements.

Promotions and Transfers

It is increasingly the practice in modern industry to fill "good" vacancies in the plant by promoting members of the present work force. New workers usually enter the plant in the least-desirable jobs and work their way up as vacancies arise. The concept of "promotion" has more dimensions than might occur to an outside observer. Most obvious is movement to a job involving greater skill and a higher wage. But movement from the night shift to the day shift on the same job would also be considered a promotion by most workers, as would transfer to a lighter but equally well-paid job, or even movement to the newest machine or the pleasantest location in a particular work group.

The nonunion employer is free to decide whether to fill a vacancy from the outside or from within and, in the latter case, to decide who should be promoted. Decisions are made unilaterally and without advance notice. A union typically insists, as a minimum, that notice of vacancies shall be posted and that present employees shall have opportunity to apply. This enables each worker to know about vacancies as they arise, to decide whether a particular job would be a promotion *for him,* and to make his bid for it if he wants to.

Most unions try to make length of service the dominant consideration in promotion as well as in layoffs. Employers naturally resist this demand, which they feel would hamper them in rewarding merit and in selecting the most efficient man available for each job. Few contracts outside the railroad industry specify seniority as the *sole* criterion for promotion. The usual outcome is a compromise providing that where ability is relatively equal the senior man shall be promoted, or that the senior man shall be promoted if competent to do the job, or simply that both ability and length of service shall be considered in making promotion decisions. The meaning of these general statements is then worked out through the grievance procedure in individual cases. The practical outcome is usually that seniority governs in the absence of marked differences of ability among the candidates, and that where management believes there is a marked difference of ability it must be prepared to prove its case. Emphasis on the seniority factor is increasing in the course of time.

The Economic Impact of Seniority

Increasing emphasis on seniority in both layoffs and promotions has caused some apprehension concerning the long-run economic consequence.

We rely heavily on free worker choice in the labor market both to get the right man to the right job and to correct serious discrepancies in the terms offered by different employers. Anything which reduces workers' ability to make a free choice among alternative employers hampers the market in performing these functions. Heavy emphasis on seniority, it is argued, ties the worker increasingly to his present employer, reduces actual and potential labor mobility, and thus interferes with the market mechanism. If new employees are hired only for the least-attractive positions while "good" vacancies are filled from within, the worker who seeks to change employers runs a serious risk. He may have to step down to the bottom of the occupational ladder and work his way up again slowly and painfully, meanwhile being subject to the risk of layoff as a short-service employee. The obvious moral is to stay where you are and accumulate as much seniority as possible, thus insuring yourself against layoff and strengthening your chances of promotion.

Seniority, however, is only one of numerous factors making for strong attachment of workers to their present jobs. Most people prefer stability to change in any event. Accumulated pension rights and other company benefits make it increasingly worthwhile to stay on with the same employer. Long service typically confers certain privileges even where strict seniority does not govern. It is questionable whether seniority does much more to reduce labor mobility.

Moreover, labor mobility can be too high as well as too low. It is not desirable that everyone in the labor force shuttle about constantly from job to job. Efficient operation of the market requires only a mobile minority, which may be made up largely of new entrants to the labor force plus the unemployed. For the bulk of the labor force, stability has advantages in terms of productive efficiency as well as personal satisfaction. Thus, even if it could be shown that seniority reduces labor mobility, one could not conclude that this result is necessarily harmful.

Seniority in promotions is often criticized on efficiency grounds. If capable young men find that promotion comes only through serving time and bears no relation to effort, they may decide to exert less effort and initiative. The efficiency of the economy will suffer also through failure to assign the most productive worker to each job.

There is a problem here, but it may not be as serious in practice as it may appear on paper. Many low-skilled, machine-paced jobs leave little scope for differences of ability or effort. There is likely also to be some positive correlation between length of service in a plant and ability to perform successively higher jobs. On many production operations one finds a natural promotion ladder within a work team, and it is reasonable for men to work up from one rung to the next as vacancies occur. The fifth hand on a large paper machine becomes a fourth hand, then a third hand, and finally a machine tender in charge of the crew. Promotions to foremanships and other supervisory jobs are almost always at the sole discretion of management and are made on a merit basis.

As regards seniority in layoffs, it is argued that to give a long-service employee complete job security may cause him to work less diligently than he would with the possibility of layoff hanging constantly over his head. This argument implies that fear, or at least uncertainty about the future, will stimulate maximum effort. On the other hand, it is argued that people work best when they feel secure about their future and that seniority protection will therefore increase efficiency instead of reducing it. This whole question reduces to a difference of opinion over why men work well, a matter on which there is little reliable evidence.

Seniority rules prevent employers from following the traditional practice of "weeding out" the labor force during depression periods. They may even compel an employer to keep relatively inefficient people on his payroll indefinitely. The union replies to this, however, that the employer had ample opportunity to weed out these people during their probationary period in the plant. If he chose to keep them on, he made a mistake and must abide by the consequences. Supporters of seniority argue further that inability of the employer to correct his hiring mistakes in later years will in time lead him to be more careful and make fewer mistakes, with benefit to all concerned.

It should be noted also that the employer retains the right, even after the probationary period, to discharge an employee for gross inefficiency, insubordination, or violation of plant rules. This is normally sufficient to prevent workers from abusing their seniority protection.

Even if it were decided that seniority rules make it more difficult for the individual employer to run his plant at minimum cost, this would not settle the matter from a social standpoint. The workers whom one employer "weeds out" in his search for efficiency must be hired by someone else or must become public charges. Seniority systems may be regarded as a method of distributing the less-efficient workers more or less equitably among employers. Slichter points out that if employers were allowed to make layoffs on a strict efficiency basis, men over forty-five or fifty would be laid off in large numbers and would have great difficulty in finding new jobs.[8] Seniority rules may prolong their working lives to the age of sixty or sixty-five, with benefit both to themselves and to the economy. Apart from this, the peace of mind engendered by seniority rules must be counted as a positive benefit, albeit one that cannot be measured in monetary terms. Even if seniority did lead to a reduction in total physical output, which is doubtful, this reduction might be more than offset by psychic gain to the workers.

With respect to seniority in layoff and rehiring, then, one may conclude that the positive advantages probably outweigh any ad-

---

[8] Slichter, *Union Policies and Industrial Management,* pp. 160–61.

verse effects. One cannot speak so confidently about seniority in pro-motions, and employers are probably wise in resisting this principle as regards skilled jobs, where unusual ability can really show itself.

Discipline and Discharge

One of the most delicate areas of day-to-day administration is the application of discipline, including use of the ultimate weapon of discharge. Because seniority now carries so many accumulated rights, discharge is a drastic economic penalty that requires careful con-sideration. The union is forced to defend its members against dis-charge except in the most flagrant circumstances. Yet management must retain reasonable latitude to apply discipline and to enforce minimum standards of efficiency.

The union contract normally recognizes management's right to dis-cipline the work force and to take the initiative in applying penalties "for just cause." What constitutes just cause may be spelled out in the contract itself or in supplementary rules issued by the company. Standard grounds for discipline include continued failure to meet production standards, disobeying instructions of the foreman, per-sistent absence from work without excuse, participating in wildcat strikes or slowdowns, fighting, gambling, drinking, smoking in pro-hibited areas, and other personal misdemeanors. For each kind of offense there is usually a graduated series of penalties, which may begin with an oral reprimand by the foreman for the first offense, and then go on to written reprimand, a brief suspension from work with-out pay, a longer suspension from work, and finally discharge. The worker has thus usually had a number of warnings before incurring the ultimate penalty. Some offenses, however, may be considered so serious that suspension or discharge follows immediately.

If a worker contends that he is not guilty of the offense with which he is charged, or that the penalty imposed was too severe, the case is taken up through the grievance procedure. Discharges, because of their serious consequences for the worker, are invariably appealed and a large percentage of them are carried all the way to arbitration. Arbitrators have been reluctant to uphold discharges, especially for long-service workers, unless the offense is serious and the evidence clear. The box score of discharge arbitrations shows that in a substan-tial majority of cases the arbitrator has either reversed management's decision or scaled down the penalty to a temporary suspension from work.[9]

The union check on management's unfettered right of discipline

---

[9] For a detailed analysis, see Orme W. Phelps, *Discipline and Discharge in the Unionized Firm* (Berkeley and Los Angeles: University of California Press, 1959.)

has doubtless improved plant administration in addition to benefiting employees. In preunion days the right of discharge was often grossly abused. The foreman could take out his temper on those under him without recourse, and favoritism and bribery were common. This produced much injustice without necessarily promoting efficiency. Protection against arbitrary discipline and discharge is probably the most important single benefit that the worker derives from trade unionism. More than anything else, this serves to make him a free citizen in the plant.

Discussion Questions

1. Explain the main ways in which a union might try to restrict the supply of labor. Why is there little use of these methods in practice?
2. What are the advantages and disadvantages of a closed shop to the worker, the employer, and the union?
3. "The Taft–Hartley prohibition of the closed shop has had little practical effect and has simply encouraged law violation. It would be better to repeal this section of the act." Discuss.
4. What are the main arguments for and against the union shop?
5. Is there a conflict between the goal of stable collective bargaining, which is furthered by union-shop agreements, and the goal of maximum freedom for the individual worker? If so, how do you think the conflict might best be resolved?
6. What is the difference between *benefit seniority* and *competitive status seniority?* What are some of the difficulties in measuring seniority for the latter purpose?
7. What are the advantages and limitations of the seniority principle in making (a) temporary layoffs? (b) permanent layoffs? (c) promotions?

Reading Suggestions

In addition to general works on collective bargaining, the issues discussed in this chapter are examined in Phelps, Orme W., *Discipline and Discharge in the Unionized Firm*. Berkeley and Los Angeles: University of California Press, 1959; Rees, Albert, *The Economics of Trade Unions*. Chicago: The University of Chicago Press, 1962; Slichter, Sumner H., *Union Policies and Industrial Management*. Washington, D.C.: The Brookings Institution, 1941; Slichter, Sumner H., James J. Healy, and E. Robert Livernash, *The Impact of Collective Bargaining on Management*. Washington, D.C.: The Brookings Institution, 1960; Sultan, Paul, *Right-to-work Laws*. Los Angeles: Institute of Industrial Relations, U.C.L.A., 1958.

WORK SCHEDULES, WORK SPEEDS, AND PRODUCTION METHODS

21

Unions are less directly concerned with production management than with personnel management. Their concern is limited to points at which production decisions affect the security or satisfaction of workers on their jobs. Unions are concerned that hours of work should be reasonable, that work speeds and work loads should be moderate, and that physical working conditions should be safe and comfortable. They are interested in avoiding sudden and large-scale displacement of labor as a result of technological change. They have sometimes encouraged the use of relatively expensive production methods in order to create additional employment.

The points at which union objectives impinge on production management are the subject of this chapter. The issues discussed have only one thing in common: all involve some aspect of production management, and all have a direct effect on production costs.

WORK SCHEDULES

The Fair Labor Standards Act establishes a normal forty-hour week for most industries, and prescribes time-and-a-half payment for over-

586

time work. Union contracts, however, often go beyond this legal requirement. First, the contract regulates daily as well as weekly hours: for example, it may specify an eight-hour day and a five-day week. Thus a worker who put in forty hours during a certain week, but who worked ten hours on one day of that week, would not be entitled to overtime under the Fair Labor Standards Act but is entitled to two hours overtime under the union contract. Second, the union contract may set a weekly limit of less than forty hours. A number of unions now have standard workweeks in the thirty-two to thirty-seven hour range, and even lower hours are encountered occasionally. Third, the contract may impose heavier overtime penalties. Double time is often required for work on weekends and on specified holidays, and even triple time is not unheard of.

The intent of these provisions is to prevent overtime work by making it unduly expensive. The statistics of actual working hours suggest that this intent is usually realized. Weekly hours worked in manufacturing and most other industries have hovered around the forty-hour level since World War II. In contract construction, however, the average week is about thirty-seven hours, while in retail trade it has fallen gradually to below thirty-five hours.

During periods of peak demand, such as the years from 1965 to 1969, many employers face the question of whether to lengthen working hours or hire additional workers. Lengthening the workweek beyond the limit prescribed by the Fair Labor Standards Act or by union contract requires overtime payment. But recruiting, screening, and training new workers also involves costs, usually estimated at several hundred dollars per man. So, if the abnormal demand is expected to continue for only a short time, some employers will find it less expensive to offer overtime to the existing work force.[1] In the years from 1965 to 1969, the average workweek for all plants in durable goods manufacturing was about forty-two hours. This means that some plants were working substantial amounts of overtime.

We noted in Chapter 2 that some workers prefer a longer workweek than others. Those with low hourly earnings, or high consumption goals, or large family responsibilities, may be unable to meet their income requirements in forty hours. So, when overtime is available, they are eager to apply for it. Indeed, the demand for overtime typically exceeds the amount available, requiring some method of rationing. Union contracts usually specify seniority as the basis for rationing, though some attempt to ensure an equal division of overtime, and some give weight to family responsibilities.

Strong unions have occasionally demanded a short workweek, not

---

[1] For an analysis of this choice problem, see W. Oi, "Labor as a Quasi-Fixed Factor," *Journal of Political Economy*, December, 1962, pp. 538–55.

to reduce actual working hours, but to raise members' incomes. The New York local of the International Brotherhood of Electrical Workers, for example, has established a basic twenty-five hour week on construction jobs. This presumably does not mean that electricians will sit idle the rest of the week. Some of them will continue to work longer hours on their regular job, drawing time and a half for the hours beyond twenty-five. Others may devote time to private electrical repair work or other sideline activities. The twenty-five hour week is mainly an income-raising rather than a work-spreading device.

A special scheduling problem arises in continuous-process industries where plants must operate around the clock. Such a plant may work a day shift from 8:00 A.M. to 4:00 P.M., a second shift from 4:00 P.M. to midnight, and a third or "graveyard" shift from midnight to 8:00 A.M. Even where continuous operation is not essential, two- or three-shift operation produces more output from the same plant, thus lowering overhead costs put unit. Against this must be set the fact that labor cost per unit is likely to increase. Workers on second shifts typically produce somewhat less than on the day shift, while third-shift output is substantially lower.

Where two or three shifts are operated, the question arises of who will man the later shifts, which most workers consider less attractive because they interfere with sleep, recreation, and family life. The contract usually provides a premium of so many cents per hour for second-shift workers, and a still higher premium for those on the third shift. The contract also typically provides that, as vacancies occur on the more desirable shifts, workers may apply for transfer to them on a seniority basis.

Shift differentials under collective bargaining are probably not much larger than the employer would have to pay anyway to induce workers to accept the less-desirable shifts. If they were, one would find a surplus of workers applying for second- and third-shift jobs, and this one usually does not find.

Another group of contract provisions relates to payment for time not worked. In coal mining, for example, it may take considerable time to travel from the pithead to the coal face. Miners used to be paid only for time spent actually working at the face. In the 1940s, however, the United Mine Workers negotiated a "portal-to-portal" clause, under which men are paid from the time they enter the mine until they leave it. There is often provision for paid lunch periods, and for "wash-up time" at the end of the day's work. Another common provision is for "call-in time" under which, if a man reports for work and is not needed on that day, he must be paid for a minimum number of hours.

In some industries, such as trucking, the worker may lose working time for reasons beyond his control. Over-the-road drivers are usually paid on a mileage basis; but to protect men assigned to short runs, they are normally guaranteed payment for a minimum number of hours per day, regardless of distance driven. Drivers paid on a trip basis are sometimes guaranteed a certain number of runs per week. The Teamsters' contracts also protect against numerous contingencies inherent in trucking, such as: payment for layover time and lodging, while waiting for a truck in which to return home; deadheading, when a man returns as a passenger; equipment breakdown; and impassable highways.

Union influence on work schedules raises two main questions. First, are working hours today shorter than they would be in the absence of trade unionism? The answer is not self-evident. With the sustained rise of real wages over the past century, workers would have preferred to "buy" more leisure as well as more goods and services. Evidence on this point was presented in Chapter 2. Even without unions, there would have been pressure for reduction of hours. It is probable, however, that unions helped to crystallize this sentiment and to speed up the reductions, which employers usually opposed. Unions of skilled craftsmen were in the forefront of the ten-hour movement of the 1860s and the eight-hour movement of the 1880s and 1890s. Labor provided the main political support for the Fair Labor Standards Act of 1938, which generalized the forty-hour week. Extension of paid vacations and holidays, which has brought a continued reduction of annual hours, has also been speeded by union pressure. It seems likely, then, that unionism has reduced total labor supply, i.e. the number of man-hours of labor available to the American economy.

A second question is whether unions tend to press for shorter hours than their members would prefer. Are leaders' preferences biased toward leisure as against income, compared with the average preference of the membership? There is little evidence on this point at present, though one study cited in Chapter 23 suggests that such a bias may exist. The belief that hours reduction is a remedy for general unemployment, and that hours reduction can be costless if accompanied by offsetting wage increases, is deep-rooted in union ideology. The history of union agitation for shorter hours produces strong institutional momentum in this direction; and so does the desire of union officers to take care of unemployed members in industries where labor demand is declining. The employed members, who may stand to lose by hours reduction, are apt not to see the issue clearly or to put up effective opposition.

The high employment level of the 1960s, however, has muted the pressure for hours reduction. Resolutions favoring a thirty-hour week are still passed at union conventions. The AFL-CIO has proposed that the overtime premium under the Fair Labor Standards Act be increased from time and a half to double time, to reduce overtime work.

But such proposals do not have much steam behind them at present, and probably will not have unless the economy enters a prolonged period of underemployment, or until real wages rise to a level at which most workers favor further reduction of hours.

WORK SPEEDS
AND
WORK ASSIGNMENTS

Workers have an interest in how much they must produce in return for their wage. In addition to the desire to avoid "working themselves out of a job," workers enjoy a moderate work speed for its own sake. Too rapid a pace not only robs the worker of any pleasure during the day but leaves him drained of energy and incapable of enjoyment after working hours. But what is a "moderate" pace of work in a particular situation? The workers may have one conception, while supervisors and top management may have quite another. Where there is disagreement over proper work speeds, the union is bound to get involved in bargaining over the issue.

Speed under Piecework

The problem of work speeds takes a somewhat different form depending on whether the worker is paid solely on a time basis or whether his earnings are related to the amount produced. Suppose that a plant is operating under the simplest type of piecework system, in which a worker's earnings vary directly and proportionately with his output. Suppose also that it has been decided that a worker of average proficiency on a certain job should earn four dollars per hour. This is a wage decision, the basis for which will be examined in the next chapter. It is necessary next to make a work-speed decision. How many units of output should the worker be required to produce per hour in order to receive four dollars? If it is reasonable to require twenty pieces in an hour, the piece rate will be twenty cents; if the worker should turn out twenty-five, the piece rate will be sixteen cents. Thus, this question amounts to asking how many seconds or minutes should reasonably be allowed for the worker to produce a unit of output. At this point the time-study man and the stopwatch enter the picture.

Ideal time-study procedure, not always adhered to in practice, is about as follows. The first step is to standardize conditions on the job and to determine the best way of doing it through a methods' analysis, including a study of workers' motions on the job. Operators on the job are then trained to use the proper methods until they do so naturally and automatically. This first step is essential to accurate time study, and can often by itself yield large increases in productivity. The next step is to select an operator who appears to be of average speed and ability, and to time his production over a long enough period so that variations in his speed of work can be averaged out. The worker will hardly ever take exactly the same time for two successive units of output. The only way to eliminate these irregular fluctuations in work speed is to time a considerable number of units and take an average.

The actual work of timing jobs is a good deal more complex than this brief statement suggests. The timer does not simply measure the time required for the whole process of turning out a unit of output. He breaks the production process down into each separate movement of the worker's hands and body. The time required for each of these movements is recorded separately. This enables the observer to determine whether the worker is using the proper methods, whether he is using them consistently, whether certain motions are taking more time than they should normally take, and even whether the worker is deliberately "holding back" during the time study.

After the time-study man has determined the average time required to turn out a unit of product, certain adjustments must be made in this result. If it seems that the operator was above or below "normal" ability, or that he was working above or below "normal" speed during the study, an adjustment must be made on this account. In addition, allowances are usually added for fatigue, unavoidable delays, necessary personal time, and other possible interruptions to production. At the end of the process one obtains a total of, say, three minutes per unit. This indicates a normal hourly output or "task" of twenty units. If expected earnings on the job are $4.00, the piece rate must be 20 cents.

It is clear that this process is not mathematically precise and that it involves numerous judgments by the time-study observer. Was the man timed actually of average ability? Was he using the best methods available? Was he working at the right rate of speed? There is an almost unavoidable tendency for workers to slow down while being timed, even when they do not mean to do so, and the time-study man must correct for this as best he can. Again, what allowance should reasonably be made in the circumstances for fatigue, personal time, unavoidable stoppages of production, and other factors?

The greatest difficulty is that the question of what constitutes a proper speed of work is incapable of any strictly scientific answer. Industrial engineers tend to think of the proper or "normal" work speed as the highest rate that a man can maintain week after week without physical deterioration. This is a mechanistic concept that takes account only of physical wear and tear on the worker, analogous to the wear and tear on a machine owing to the speed at which it is operated. A worker may well ask, however, "Why should I work that fast? The job will be pleasanter for me if I work at a slower rate. Why is my interest in a pleasant job not as important as the employer's interest in greater output?" These are pertinent questions. Who is to say just how fast a man should work for the benefit of the employer or the consumer? It seems unavoidable that there will be differences of opinion between production and engineering officials on the one hand, and workers and their union representatives on the other hand, and that actual work speeds must be a matter of bargaining and compromise rather than of scientific measurement.

Unions naturally insist that work speeds cannot be left to the sole judgment of management, and that the union must have a voice in the setting of time standards and piece rates on individual jobs. The procedure under most union contracts is that management has the right to make the initial time study of a job and to set a temporary piece rate on it. The temporary rate automatically becomes permanent unless protested by the union within a certain length of time. If the rate is protested by the union, the job is usually retimed, and the dispute can be carried up through the regular grievance procedure. Some union contracts provide that a piece rate cannot be put into effect at all until it has been approved by the union, but such provisions are rather rare.

In a few industries, the union sets the piece rate and management has the right to protest rates that it believes are unfair. This is the usual procedure in the men's and women's clothing industries, and is due to the special characteristics of those industries. Employers in the clothing industries are usually small, and many of them are transient. They could scarcely afford the engineering staff necessary to determine new piece rates on a great variety of styles and types of clothing. The union, being much the largest organization in the industry, can afford to maintain a staff of rate-setting experts. Piece-rate determinations are made in the first instance by the union rate-setters, with the employer having the right to appeal any decision within a certain period of time.

Piece-rate Changes

The other main problem in the administration of an incentive system is to determine the conditions under which management shall be entitled to retime a job and alter the piece rate. The generally accepted principle, written into most union contracts, is "no change in the rate without a change in the job." It is not easy, however, to get agreement on the application of this principle to specific cases. Where management has the upper hand, it will frequently try to take away from the workers the benefit even of their own greater effort or increased skill. A strong union, on the other hand, will often take the untenable position that piece rates cannot be changed unless there is a complete reengineering of the job. This stand produces inequities in the wage structure because of differing rates of technical progress on different jobs. A job on which management has made many minor improvements or the workers have discovered numerous shortcuts may gradually come to yield earnings twice as high as those on another job that requires the same skill and effort but which has undergone no changes in method. When these discrepancies have become sufficiently glaring, even the union will frequently agree to a general overhaul of piece rates. It is politically difficult, however, for a union to subscribe to a step that reduces the earnings of any of its members. The rank-and-file worker regards anything that reduces his earnings as a "rate cut," and he holds the union leaders responsible.

The difficulty of getting agreement on piece-rate changes leads to a good deal of tactical maneuvering by workers and management. Management tries to "sneak up" on jobs where it believes earnings have got too high, and to make just enough changes in the job to justify a new time study. Workers try to hold down their rate of production while a time study is in progress. The time-study man tries to guess how much they are holding back and to correct this in his results. Determination of time standards thus becomes to some extent a battle of wits between the worker and the engineer, in which the latter does not always come out victorious.

There is also a strong tendency for incentive workers to hold down their production at all times, and for different workers on a job to maintain about the same rate of output. Workers who rise much above the accepted rate are called "speed artists," "rate busters," and other uncomplimentary names. Unless they desist from their high rate of production, they are likely to find that things happen to their machines, that wrenches fall accidentally on their heads, and that they are ostracized by their fellows. The result is that incentive systems usually fail to obtain maximum effort from the faster workers. Their rate of production is limited by social pressures exerted by their fellow workers, while an incentive system requires completely individualistic behavior to produce its full effects.

The agreed rate of output on a job is usually set slightly below the level which the workers think would cause management to retime the job and cut the piece rate. Workers with long experience under incentive systems develop a keen sense of what is a "safe" amount to earn on a particular job, and are careful not to exceed this amount. If too much work is done one day, part of it is hidden overnight and turned in the next day, during which the worker takes it easy. Some workers prefer to work rapidly for several hours, produce their "quota," and then take it easy for the rest of the day. The most serious aspect of these output standards is that they become fixed by custom and persist even after improved methods have made a higher level of output appropriate. Where this happens, the main effect of improvements in methods is to increase the amount of leisure which workers have on the job rather than to increase their output.

Restriction of output by incentive workers is not due specifically to union organization, and seems to be as prevalent in nonunion as in union plants. It is not at all certain, therefore, that unionism results in slower work than would prevail without it.

Speed under Timework

The oldest form of wage payment, and still a very common one, is at a flat rate of so much per hour. It has often been pointed out that under timework the employment contract is incomplete. There is an understanding as to how much the worker shall be paid, but no understanding as to how much he must produce. It is left to the foreman to get as much work out of him as he can after the wage agreement has been made. Where the job is essentially a hand operation, the foreman has to rely on instruction, admonition, example, cajolery, sarcasm, and the ultimate threat of discharge. In a unionized shop, however, the foreman must stay within limits generally acceptable to the workers under him. Anything that the workers regard as undue "driving" or "pushing" by the foreman is likely to be raised as a grievance by the union.

Where the work is machine-paced, and the worker is mainly a machine-tender, the problem becomes: how fast should the machinery run, or how many machines should one worker be expected to tend? Two examples may be cited. In preunion days, automobile assembly lines were run at a speed determined solely by management and that many workers regarded as too fast. When the United Automobile Workers was organized, one of its first actions was to seek determination of assembly-line speeds by the company and the union together. The companies first contended that determination of these speeds was a "management prerogative" that should not be made subject to collective bargaining. The matter was of such great importance to the workers, however, that the union kept pressing the issue and gradually succeeded in bringing assembly-line speeds under joint control in most plants.

Another illustration is the size of machine assignments in the cotton textile industry. A weaver, for example, usually tends a considerable number of looms. As looms have become more nearly automatic, and as improved production methods have been developed, textile companies have tended to increase the number of looms assigned to each worker—sometimes on the basis of systematic engineering studies, sometimes without such studies. The workers usually object on principle to any "stretch-out" of their work assignment, and many spontaneous strikes have occurred over the issue even in nonunion plants. Management usually contends that machine assignments should be made and altered in the sole discretion of management. The unions in the textile industry have never conceded this right, and the size of work assignments has become a major issue in collective bargaining.

The problem of work speeds is intrinsically difficult, because there is no way of determining the proper pace of work with anything like mathematical precision. A faster pace of work means more discomfort to the worker, but lower unit production costs and lower prices to consumers. At some point there must be a proper balance between the interest of workers in a pleasant job and the interest of consumers in high production at low prices. Determination of this optimum, however, seems inevitably to be a matter of judgment. It is neither fully determined by market forces nor is it capable of scientific measurement. Unions may press for a pace of work below the socially desirable optimum, just as management is likely to set a work pace above the optimum point. The outcome in a particular case depends on the relative strength and bargaining skill of the parties, and actual achievement of the optimum work speed would appear to be only a lucky accident.

Incentive Work versus Timework

Because of these difficulties the basic question of whether workers are to be paid on an hourly or an incentive basis is an important feature of the union contract. Union policy on this point is variable. A few unions, which have experienced employer abuse of incentive systems or have found them unsuited to the conditions of their industries, have refused to work under any sort of incentive plan. The outstanding example among the older unions is the International Association of Machinists, which has long had a constitutional provision against introduction of an incentive system in any shop where it has not previously been used. The building trades' unions have also refused flatly to work under piece rates. Among the newer industrial unions, opposition to incentive payment has probably been strongest in the United Automobile Workers, which has succeeded in abolishing this type of payment throughout most of the automobile industry. Some unions that at one time opposed piece-rate payment, such as the International Ladies' Garment Workers' Union, later reversed themselves and now favor this type of payment. The reversal occurred when the union became strong enough to control the employers' administration of wage incentives, so that its members could enjoy the benefit of higher incentive earnings without risking a "speed-up" of their work.

Unions have frequently opposed the use of particular incentive formulas, such as the original Bedaux system and other plans under which the amount paid for extra units of output decreases as the worker's output rises. In addition to being inequitable from the workers' point of view, these plans have often been remarkably complicated. It is hard to see how a worker can be motivated to greater output by a system that makes it impossible for him to understand the basis of his paycheck.

Employer preferences also vary considerably. In the heyday of "scientific management" many companies were enthusiastic about the potential output gains from incentive payment. It was not fully understood that realization of these gains depends on careful day-to-day administration of the incentive system, and that without this the company may quickly find itself in a difficult position. Time standards that were set correctly in the first instance become looser over time as a result of technical progress, and this happens at differing rates on different jobs. The general level of earnings is inflated, and relative earnings on different jobs get seriously out of line. Yet workers resist retiming of jobs, and a strong union may succeed in blocking it for long periods.

From 1940 until about 1955 most manufacturing companies were operating in a sellers' market, in which the main thing was to get out production, and costs were a secondary consideration. Rather than arouse union opposition, many companies allowed their incentive systems to deteriorate. In the tougher economic climate of the late fifties and earlier sixties, these loose standards and high costs could no longer be afforded. Some companies underwent long strikes to regain control over production standards. And some decided that the gains from incentive payment are not worth the difficulties it creates, and tried to shift back to hourly payment.

The use of incentive payment varies widely from industry to industry. A Labor Department study [2] found that in some manufacturing industries (basic steel, men's suits and coats, women's outerwear, boots and shoes) more than 60 percent of production workers are paid on an incentive basis. There is moderate use of incentive payment—30 to 40 percent of production workers—in textiles, carpet manufacture, pottery works, steel foundries, electrical apparatus, and industrial machinery. Industries in which less than 10 percent of production workers are on an incentive basis include chemicals, scientific instru-

[2] Robert B. McKersie, Carroll F. Miller, Jr., and William E. Quartermain, "Some Indicators of Incentive Plan Prevalence," *Monthly Labor Review*, March, 1964, pp. 271–76.

ments, aircraft and parts, cigarettes, cement, and commercial printing.

In some cases, such as motor vehicles and equipment (13 percent on incentives), one can see a clear effect of union policy. In general, however, there is no statistical relation between the percentage of workers in an industry covered by collective bargaining and its use of incentive payment. The significant determinants appear to be: (1) the nature of the work. Where quality rather than quantity is important, as in diamond cutting or instrument manufacture, piecework is not appropriate. (2) The ratio of labor cost to total cost. Where the labor cost ratio is high, as in clothing and footwear, incentive payment may be preferred as a way of standardizing unit labor cost throughout the industry. Where labor cost is a minor factor—as in cigarettes, chemicals, cement, oil refining—there is little interest in incentives. (3) Age of the industry. Incentive payment is "old-fashioned" in the sense that it was developed in an era of primitive management and little knowledge of worker motivation. Many of the newer industries, such as aircraft manufacture, have never resorted to it because of the availability of other motivational techniques.

PRODUCTION METHODS
AND
EMPLOYMENT OPPORTUNITIES

An important reason for union interest in production methods is their effect on employment opportunities. Most workers are convinced that jobs are always scarce; it is important, therefore, to protect existing jobs and to create new ones if possible. This belief leads unions to combat technical changes that threaten to displace labor and to seek opportunities for the employment of additional workers.

These practices are particularly likely to develop in industries in which the total number of jobs is declining, such as railroading and "live" musical performances. In such industries, rising unemployment leads the union to seek desperate means of providing a livelihood for its members. Industries with rapidly increasing employment opportunities are less likely to suffer from restrictive practices. Craft unions are also more likely than industrial unions to resist technical change and to adopt make-work rules and policies. Skilled workers stand in particular danger of having their skill undermined, their job opportunities reduced, and the very basis of their craft whittled away by new production methods. An industrial union is less likely to be concerned over whether a particular operation is done by skilled men in one way or semiskilled men in a different way, since in any event the work will be done by members of the same union.

Make-work Rules and Policies

The effort to create employment, or to prevent a shrinkage of employment, takes many forms. The practices described in this section, however, all have the intent of increasing the number of man-hours of labor that employers must hire. For this reason they are often termed *make-work policies*.

a. Limiting daily or weekly output per worker. This is a widespread practice in both nonunion and union shops, particularly where the workers are paid on a piecework or incentive basis. The motive for limitation of output is partly to make work, partly to avoid rate cutting and speeding up by the employer.

The output limitations are frequently reasonable at the time they are set, but tend rapidly to become obsolete. It is natural for the output of a work group to rise gradually in the course of time, as a result of improvements in machinery, materials, and methods. If workers continue to produce at a rate determined years in the past, the gap between actual and potential output becomes larger and larger with the passage of time. The consequence is an ever greater volume of unnecessary labor and a progressive inflating of production costs.

b. Limiting output indirectly by controlling the quality of work or requiring time-consuming methods. These techniques are best illustrated in the building trades. While the unions have done a useful service in combating shoddy construction by the less-reputable contractors, they have frequently insisted on needlessly high quality in order to justify spending more time on the job. The gradual decline in the number of bricks laid per hour by bricklayers, for example, is usually justified by the union in terms of the care which must be taken to ensure perfect accuracy and soundness in the product. It would seem, however, that this argument has been overworked. Plastering, lathing, painting, and other processes are often done more thoroughly than necessary in order to create additional work.

Another frequent device of the building trades is to require that work be done on the construction site rather than in the factory. Painters often require that all window frames and screens be primed, painted, and glazed on the job. Plumbers in many cities prohibit the cutting and threading of pipe in the factory, and refuse to install toilets and other fixtures that have been assembled at the factory. There has recently been a growing movement toward prefabrication of plumbing fixtures, kitchen cabinets, and even whole kitchen units as a means of reducing production costs. This movement has been resisted by the organized construction workers. The prefabrication of the whole house structure has been resisted even more vigorously.

The restrictiveness of union policies in the building trades, however, should not be exaggerated. Haber and Levinson point out that many new techniques and materials have been introduced into the industry over the past generation. Union opposition to new methods was not nearly so strong during the high-employment fifties as it was during the depressed thirties. The trades in which restrictive practices are mainly concentrated—painting, plumbing, electrical work, and sheet metal work—represent only about 20 percent of on-site labor costs on a typical house. Haber and Levinson estimate that the total effect of opposition to new techniques, make-work rules, and other restrictive practices is to raise on-site labor costs by from 8 percent under favorable conditions to as much as 24 percent in areas where all union regulations are severely applied. Since labor costs form approximately 30 percent of the selling price of a house, this means that house prices are raised by from 2 to 7 percent.[3]

The difficulty of drawing general conclusions, however, is illustrated by another study of two Michigan cities.[4] The author found that the number of man-hours required to build a standard house was considerably *lower* for union than for nonunion contractors. True, the wage bill for the union-built houses was higher; but this was due entirely to the higher union wage scale, which more than offset the saving in man-hours. The author surmises that the higher man-hour output of the union contractors may have been due to some combination of higher labor force quality, use of more or better equipment, greater cost-consciousness of employers in an effort to offset the high wage scale, and (in the case of the strongly unionized Ann Arbor area) potential competition from nearby contractors in Detroit.

c. Requiring that unnecessary work be done, or that work be done more than once. Switchboards and other types of electrical apparatus, for example, were in the earlier days always wired on the job. The recent tendency has been to have this equipment wired in the factory, where the work can be done at considerably lower cost. The New York City local and certain other locals of the International Brotherhood of Electrical Workers have refused to install switchboards and other apparatus unless the wiring done in the factory was torn out and the apparatus rewired by union members.

Another example is the "bogus" rule of the International Typographical Union. This provides that when a newspaper uses ready-made plates or matrices, as is often done when the same advertisement is run in several papers, the copy must nevertheless be reset, read, and corrected in each paper's composing room. The reset copy is known as "bogus." Although this is mainly a make-work rule, it is

[3] William Haber and Harold M. Levinson, *Labor Relations and Productivity in the Building Trades* (Ann Arbor: University of Michigan Bureau of Industrial Relations, 1956), particularly chaps. 7–9.

[4] Allen B. Mandelbaum, "The Effects of Unions on Efficiency in the Residential Construction Industry: a Case Study," *Industrial and Labor Relations Review*, July, 1965, pp. 503–21.

sometimes used for bargaining purposes. A publisher may be exempted from the bogus rule in exchange for an outsize wage increase or a guarantee of a certain number of jobs.

d. Requiring stand-by crews or other unnecessary men. This practice is often termed *featherbedding*. The Musicians' Union, for example, attempted to enforce a rule that radio stations that broadcast recorded music or that rebroadcast programs originating elsewhere must employ a stand-by orchestra to be paid for doing nothing. This led eventually to passage of the Lea Act of 1946, which made it unlawful to compel a licensee under the Federal Communications Act to employ unnecessary people, or to refrain from using unpaid performers for noncommercial programs, or to limit production or use of records.

The theater is especially vulnerable to featherbedding because picketing can so easily interfere with attendance. The stagehands' union requires a minimum crew to be hired for any theatrical performance, regardless of whether their services are actually needed, and so does the musicians' union, the electricians', and other groups. The resulting inflation of production costs and ticket prices has contributed to the disappearance of commercial theaters in many cities.

The Motion Picture Projectors' Union has tried for years to require two operators for each projection machine, and has succeeded in some cities. The Operating Engineers asserts jurisdiction over all machines and engines used in building construction, regardless of their source of power. Even if the power is purchased from an electric company, a union member must be there to push the button or turn the switch, which may constitute his whole day's work.

e. Requiring crews of excessive size. This is a common practice among the printing pressmen, longshoremen, musicians, and a number of other unions. By far the most ambitious and successful efforts, however, have been made by the railroad-running trades. They have worked through the state legislatures to get full-crew laws and train-limit laws. The full-crew laws usually provide that the crew shall consist of an engineer, fireman, conductor, and a number of brakemen varying with the length of the train. Seventeen states had such laws in 1960. The train-limit laws limit the number of cars per train, and are intended to make more jobs for engineers and firemen. The Arizona train-limit law, however, was invalidated by the U.S. Supreme Court as having no reasonable relation to safety; [5] and while several states have train-limit laws on the books, they are not enforced.

The most recent controversy in this area, which is still continuing, concerns the use of firemen on diesel locomotives. On high-speed passenger trains, one can make a case for having a fireman in the cab with the engineer at all times. But the unions have been inclined to

[5] *Southern Pacific Company* v. *Arizona*, 325 U.S. 761.

insist also on use of firemen in local passenger, freight, and yard service. The railroads contend that many of these jobs are unnecessary and should be eliminated. This and other issues of train manning were at the heart of the 1963 rail dispute, which came to the point of a strike and led Congress to pass an act sending the dispute to compulsory arbitration.

f. Requiring that work be done by members of a particular occupational group. The object is to enlarge the job territory of the group so that there will be the maximum amount of work available to be divided among its members. Pursuit of this objective takes various forms. A common rule is that prohibiting employers or foremen from working at the trade. This prevents supervisors from reducing the amount of work available to employees by doing it themselves, and from acting as pacesetters by working alongside the men. Another common rule requires that skilled men be used for semiskilled or unskilled work. The Typographical Union frequently requires that proof be read and revised by union members before going to anyone outside the composing room. The building trades often require that material handling be done by craftsmen rather than laborers.

Some Teamsters' locals, on the other hand, prohibit drivers from assisting helpers in unloading their trucks. This does not make more work for drivers, but creates more jobs for helpers, so that total employment is increased. Longshoremen in some ports refuse to shift from ship to dock work, or even from one ship to another of the same company, thus compelling use of multiple crews. In this, as in other respects, the railroad unions "have gone to unbelievable extremes in restricting duties, taking the position that every item of work *belongs* to some employee. If that employee is deprived of the opportunity to do the work, he is entitled to compensation first. In addition, the one who does the work is entitled to compensation. In many instances the amount of compensation given to both is a day's pay. The result is that two days' pay may be given as compensation for a trivial amount of work." [6]

What can one say about the economic effects of make-work rules and policies? Pressure for them arises mainly from the threat of unemployment, but they are clearly not a desirable method of coping with unemployment. Seasonal and intermittent unemployment can best be dealt with through efforts to regularize production, supported by adequate public employment services and unemployment compensation systems. Cyclical fluctuations must be countered by fiscal policy and other types of governmental action. A long-run decline in the demand for a product requires that workers be transferred out of the declining industry.

It may be said that this is a harsh view. Why not cushion a drop

6 Slichter, Healy, and Livernash, *Impact of Collective Bargaining*, p. 319.

in the demand for labor by creating additional jobs? Why not have everyone in an industry somewhat underemployed, instead of some workers totally unemployed? If the expedients adopted were temporary, and were used only until more basic remedies could be devised, one might make out a case for their use. The difficulty is that restrictive work rules and practices are scarcely ever discarded. They persist even during periods of full employment, when they are clearly inappropriate. They tend to freeze in each industry the maximum number of people ever employed there in the past. In the long run, therefore, they create all sorts of anomalies in the structure of employment and production.

It is by no means clear that make-work policies are beneficial even to the group imposing them. There is a limit to the costs that a union can impose on an industry, set by the demand curve for the industry's products. If the union adds to the industry's costs through excessive employment, it must accept a lower level of wages. If restrictive practices were abandoned and excess employment eliminated, employers could be obliged to pay higher wages to the workers remaining in the industry.

It is easier to point out the undesirability of make-work rules than it is to do anything effective about them, particularly since the issue is often not as clear-cut as it seems at first glance. As Slichter points out:

> It is not always easy to determine when a union is "making work." There are some clear cases, such as those in which the union requires that the work be done twice; but the mere fact that the union limits the output of men or controls the quality of the work (with effects upon output), regulates the size of crew or the number of machines per man, or prohibits the use of labor-saving devices, does not in itself mean that the union is "making work." In such cases it is necessary to apply a rule of reason and to determine whether the limits are unreasonable. Opinions as to what is reasonable are bound to differ, but failure to apply a rule of reason would be to accept the employer's requirement, no matter how harsh and extreme, as the proper standard.[7]

The Industrial Unions and Technical Change

The quickened pace of mechanization and automation[8] since World War II has reduced employment opportunities in coal mining, basic steel, automobiles, and numerous other industries, and has

[7] Slichter, *Union Policies and Industrial Management,* pp. 165–66.

[8] The meaning of "automation" is discussed in chapter 3, in connection with trends in labor demand and employment. The writer is inclined to regard it as complex mechanization, differing in degree, but not in kind, from mechanization in earlier decades.

caused unions in these industries to be concerned for the job security of their members. In general, their reaction has not taken the form of trying to block technical change, a policy which would have had little chance of success. The new equipment in these industries is so labor-saving and cost-reducing that employers have a powerful incentive to install it, and the unions could at most fight a delaying action for a limited period. So they have concentrated instead on ways of cushioning the impact on their members.

In bituminous coal mining, mechanization has proceeded very rapidly both through mechanization of underground mines and acceleration of strip mining. The amount of mechanical equipment per worker has more than doubled, and so has output per man-hour. Since demand for coal has been declining, employment has dropped sharply. The United Mine Workers did not oppose the mechanization movement. Indeed, the union encouraged mechanization by raising wages rapidly even in the face of severe unemployment. It also secured substantial employer contributions for medical and hospital care, insurance, and pensions. But coal miners did not retire nearly fast enough to keep pace with the shrinkage of employment opportunities; unemployment rates in the coal fields have continued well above the national average.[9]

In automobile production, too, technical change has not been a disputed issue. The industry has a tradition of annual model changes, rapid technical innovation, and wide management flexibility in production methods. The fact that the industry operates on time payment rather than incentive payment eliminates the need for bargaining over new time standards as production methods change. Disagreements are focused on the speed of the assembly line, which has been subjected to joint control.

The record of certain other industries is less tranquil. The rubber industry operates mainly on incentive payment. During the forties and fifties this industry developed traditions of considerable autonomy by work gangs in the plant, loose incentive standards protected by deliberate restriction of output, and resistance through slowdowns and quickie strikes to management pressure for greater efficiency. As Killingsworth points out, "the syndrome of loose incentive standards, informal limitation of output, some excessive manning, and slowdowns and wildcat strikes may be considered a subterranean approach to job security." [10] In this industry there has often been a question whether,

[9] For a thorough analysis of mechanization in this industry, see C. L. Christenson, *Economic Redevelopment and Bituminous Coal* (Cambridge: Harvard University Press, 1962).

[10] Charles C. Killingsworth, "Cooperative Approaches to Problems of Technological Change," in G. G. Somers, E. L. Cushman, and N. Weinberg, eds., *Adjusting to Technological Change* (New York: Harper & Row, Publishers, 1963), pp. 61–94.

if new equipment were introduced, the workers would allow it to operate at anything like full capacity. In some cases the companies have had to threaten to build, or actually build, a new plant in a new location to break through restrictive practices and secure maximum benefit from new equipment.

The basic steel industry has a contract provision (clause 2B in the agreement with U.S. Steel and other major companies), that restricts the right of management to change established local work rules. This is an old and conservative industry, and many of these practices are of long standing. They relate to such things as crew size on various machines, seniority, distribution of overtime, work assignments, shift scheduling, contracting out, layoffs, wash-up time, and lunch periods. The clause does not interfere with automation or other forms of technical change. Indeed, since change in equipment is a recognized basis for changing work practices, the clause may serve to encourage technical change. But it does contribute in some cases to overmanning and other forms of inefficiency. A company demand in 1959 for elimination of this clause was taken by the union as a prelude to wholesale elimination of jobs and displacement of workers, and led to a record 115-day steel strike. The strike ended inconclusively, and the issue is not really resolved. In 1962, however, the union won substantially increased provisions for job security, which will probably make it more willing to accept reasonable changes in work methods.

The Kaiser Steel Company of California broke away from the other companies during the 1959 strike and reached its own agreement with the union. Among other things the agreement established a nine-man tripartite committee, including three eminent neutrals, to recommend "a long-range plan for equitable sharing between the stockholders, the employees, and the public of the fruits of the Company's progress." The plan recommended by the committee and put into effect by the company early in 1963, is rather complicated [11] but has two essential features. First, it provides that no worker shall be laid off as a result of technical change. Displaced workers go into a work reserve, pending reassignment to another job in the company. Workers may be laid off on the usual seniority basis in the event of a drop in production. But shrinkage in the number of workers required for a given production volume as a result of technical progress will be taken care of through normal attrition of the labor force.

Second, savings in labor and materials costs per unit of product over the levels prevailing in 1961 are to be shared between workers and the company in agreed proportions. The employee share is set at 32.5 percent, this being the average relation between labor cost and

[11] For a detailed description, see *The Kaiser–Steel Union Sharing Plan* (New York: National Industrial Conference Board, 1963), Studies in Personnel Policy, No. 187.

total cost that has prevailed in the past. Wage and benefit increases given by other major companies in the industry are offset against this fund, and the balance is distributed each month as a cash bonus. If the gain-sharing fund falls below the increases given by other companies, Kaiser undertakes to make up the difference so that its employees cannot lose under the formula. One object of the plan is to get rid of incentive payment, which covers about 40 percent of plant employees and has led to inflated and inequitable earnings on many jobs. Incentive workers can choose to remain on incentive or to go over to hourly payment. In the latter case they receive a lump-sum cash bonus equal to about $2\frac{1}{2}$ years incentive earnings, and they also come under the gain-sharing formula. If they remain on incentive, they do not participate in gain sharing, and management has the right to retime the jobs. No new incentive jobs are to be created in the future.

In meat-packing, the Armour Company maintains a joint program with the union, under a neutral chairman who has usually been a labor economist. The program includes research on the company's future manpower requirements, advance notice of plant closings or cutbacks in employment, preferential hiring rights for displaced workers in other plants of the company, assistance with moving and relocation costs, and assistance in finding other work for those who prefer to remain in their home community.

In the mass-production industries, then, things have moved in the direction of a trade, in which management gets reasonable flexibility in changing production methods while the union gets provisions to cushion the impact on its members' jobs. The cushioning devices include pension plans, with emphasis in some cases on early retirement; severance pay for workers released permanently; supplementary unemployment benefits, beyond those provided by the social security system, for workers laid off for shorter periods; elaborate in-plant seniority and work-sharing systems; and arrangements under which workers in a plant that is closed down permanently can "follow the work" to other plants of the same company, with preferential hiring rights. The assumption is that the number of production jobs in these industries will continue to decline; and the object is to ensure that the shrinkage of employment will be orderly and will do minimum damage to the present labor force.

While this sort of trade involves costs for the employer, these may be much more than repaid by the opportunity to introduce productivity-raising improvements. A dramatic case in point is the West Coast longshore industry. From the recognition of the union in 1934 until the late fifties this industry was marked by poor union–employer relations, chronic guerilla warfare, and a host of inefficient work practices designed to use as much labor as possible. These included overmanning, dual handling of cargo, limitation of sling loads, and resistance to containerization and bulk cargo handling methods. Eventually, however, union leaders became convinced that this delaying action could not succeed indefinitely, and that they would do better to make a trade. In 1960 they negotiated an agreement that gave employers virtually a free hand in overhauling work rules, installing labor-saving devices, and increasing efficiency generally. The *quid pro quo* for the union was a promise that no registered longshoreman would be laid off as a result of the changes, a guaranteed annual wage, and a pension fund permitting voluntary retirement at sixty-two. These guarantees are underwritten by a fund to which employers will contribute 4 to 5 percent of longshore payrolls. "But their savings are considerably greater. During negotiations, an estimate was presented showing that the elimination of *only* the multiple-handling rules, in Los Angeles *alone,* would save the employers more than their total fund contributions." [12] The agreement was renewed with some revisions in 1966.

This was a special arrangement to meet an aggravated problem and is not necessarily repeatable elsewhere. But it illustrates the possibilities of peaceful accommodation and mutual gain.

PHYSICAL CONDITIONS
OF
WORK

Union officials spend much time negotiating with management over various aspects of physical working conditions—heating, lighting, ventilation, and cleanliness of the plant; safety arrangements; sanitary facilities; dangerous or objectionable features of particular jobs; provision of adequate cafeterias and rest rooms; and many other matters. Most of these matters are discussed informally in the plant from day to day, since they are usually too small to arise as issues in contract negotiations. Taken as a whole, these matters are very important to the workers; but they are so varied and heterogeneous that it is difficult to find any way of generalizing about them.

The nearest one can come to generalizing is to distinguish three kinds of improvement in working conditions. The first involves plant improvements that produce an increase in labor productivity more than sufficient to cover the cost of making the improvements. It is usually assumed that management will be alert to such opportunities and will seize them of its own accord, but this is not always the case.

---

12 Killingsworth, *Technological Change,* p. 83.

Unions can do valuable work by pointing out improvements that perhaps should have been obvious to management but were not, and that, once discovered, can be installed with a net gain to the company as well as the workers.

Second, one may distinguish improvements that are a matter of *degree,* and where beyond a certain point the additional cost outweighs the gain in labor productivity. Consider a plant using very hot processes, the natural temperature of which would be 130 degrees Fahrenheit. By installing an air-cooling system the plant can be cooled to any desired temperature. The lower the temperature, however, the greater the cost of the system. Suppose also that worker productivity increases steadily as the temperature falls. It will pay the employer to reduce the temperature of the plant down to the point at which the additional cost of cooling just equals the additional revenue obtained from increased output. If this point turns out to be 95 degrees, this is the optimum plant temperature from the employer's standpoint.

The workers, however, might feel happiest at a temperature of 70 degrees. There is a divergence here between the interest of workers and management. In a perfectly competitive labor market, management would presumably have to pay a higher wage rate to compensate for the unpleasant working conditions. In practice, however, competitive forces are not fully effective, for reasons explored in Chapter 5. One cannot be sure, therefore, that unpleasant conditions will actually be offset by a wage premium.

Suppose now that a union comes on the scene and compels the employer to reduce the temperature of the plant from 95 degrees to 80 degrees. Depending on the circumstances of the case, the added cost of doing this might or might not be absorbed out of existing profit margins. For the sake of argument, however, suppose that the cost is entirely transferred to buyers of the product through higher prices. The union, in effect, has taxed consumers a certain amount in order to improve the daily lives of its members in the plant. Is this action economically beneficial or harmful?

The problem appears even more clearly in a third type of case, where there is no effect on productivity, and the only consequence of the improvement is pleasanter "plant living-conditions" for the workers concerned. The money cost of the improvement is felt initially by the employer, later by buyers of the product. The social cost consists in the economic resources that were used in making the improvement. How can one say whether, in a particular case, the benefit to the workers was worth the expenditure of resources? How far should consumers be taxed in order to pay for improved working conditions? How far should the satisfaction of man as consumer be reduced in order to increase that of man as producer?

There seems no way of giving any general answer to these questions. One is certainly not entitled to assume that all plant improvements of this type are economically harmful, or that all are beneficial. A separate decision must be made in each case on the basis of informed judgment.

Discussion   Questions

1. What would be the main economic consequences of reducing the standard workweek in manufacturing from forty hours to thirty hours?
2. What would be the effect of amending the Fair Labor Standards Act to require double time rather than time and a half for overtime work?
3. Suppose you were asked to design a research study to determine whether union leaders prefer a shorter workweek than their members, on the average, would prefer. How would you proceed?
4. How much would you estimate that make-work rules and policies reduce the potential output of the economy? Can anything be done to reduce the frequency and impact of such rules?
5. Why is it difficult for unions to resist technical changes in mass-production manufacturing? What provisions have unions negotiated with employers to cushion the labor-displacing impact of such changes?
6. "Work speeds and work assignments are a matter for management decision. Union interference in these matters is fatal to productive efficiency and harmful to the public interest." Discuss.
7. "Time study is a scientific procedure that leaves no possible room for argument or bargaining over work speeds." Discuss.

Reading   Suggestions

Classic early studies include Barnett, George, *Chapters on Machinery and Labor*. Cambridge: Harvard University Press, 1926; Mathewson, Stanley B., *Restriction of Output among Unorganized Workers*. New York: The Viking Press, Inc., 1931; Palmer, Gladys L., *Union Tactics and Economic Change*. Philadelphia: University of

Pennsylvania Press, 1932. For more recent studies of union policy, see Christenson, C. L., *Economic Redevelopment in Bituminous Coal.* Cambridge: Harvard University Press, 1962; Somers, G. G., E. L. Cushman, and N. Weinberg, eds., *Adjusting to Technological Change.* New York: Harper & Row, Publishers, 1963. There is a large literature on time study and incentive wage systems, references to which will be found in any standard text on personnel management. For specific discussion of union attitudes and policies, see Gomberg, William A., *A Trade Union Analysis of Time Study,* 2nd ed. Englewood Cliffs, N.J.: Prentice-Hall, Inc., 1955; Kennedy, Van Dusen, *Union Policy and Incentive Wage Methods.* New York: Columbia University Press, 1945.

WAGES AT THE COMPANY LEVEL 22

There has been more research and writing on wage issues in collective bargaining than on nonwage issues. This does not necessarily mean that wage issues are more important; but they tie in more directly with the main body of economics, and there is more quantitative information suited to statistical analysis.

Collective bargaining might have a variety of wage effects. It might alter (1) the wage level of a particular firm relative to other firms; (2) the relative rates of pay for specific jobs within the firm; (3) the division of workers' compensation between direct wage payments and supplementary or "fringe" benefits. Such effects at the plant or company level are the subject of this chapter.

Looking more broadly at the national economy, unionism might affect (4) the rate of increase in money wages at various levels of unemployment, i.e. the location of the Phillips curve; (5) the general level of real wages; (6) interindustry wage differences; (7) occupational wage differences; (8) geographic wage differences. Evidence on the size of such effects will be reviewed in the next chapter. But since any large-scale effects must result from the aggregation of individual wage bargains, the two parts of our discussion are closely related.

UNION
WAGE
POLICY

We must first consider how unions approach the problem of wage determination. A union is usually said to be a "monopoly." If by this we mean that it has some power over wages, the statement is correct. But it is misleading if it connotes that union decision making closely resembles that of the monopolistic seller of a commodity. The union does not sell labor and receive the proceeds. Rather, union–management negotiations establish the framework of rules within which the employer may buy labor from individual workers.

It is nonetheless natural to start from the established principles of business monopoly. Given a monopolistic firm's cost and revenue schedules, we can define the price and output that would maximize profit; and the firm is often assumed, as a first approximation, to aim at maximum profit. So it is natural to ask whether a union tries to maximize any monetary quantity and, if so, what this quantity is.

Consider a union bargaining over wages in a locality (for local-market industries) or on a national scale (for national-market industries). There will be a demand curved for union labor, its elasticity depending partly on the degree of union organization in the industry. In cotton textiles, for example, only about 20 percent of total employment is under union contract. There are many producers, selling their products under conditions approaching those of pure competition. In this situation, it is not feasible to push the wage level of union mills much above that of nonunion mills. At anything above the nonunion wage, the demand for union labor will be highly elastic. This is the prevalent situation in textiles, garment manufacture, and numerous other light manufacturing industries.

Let D and S in Figure 1 be the general supply and demand curves for labor in a particular industry; and suppose that employers at the outset are paying the competitive wage OW. A union coming into this industry may be able to raise wages of union plants moderately above OW. The unionized mills may be able to increase efficiency somewhat to offset the wage pressure, or they may be willing in the short run to accept lower profit margins. But as the gap between the union and nonunion wage widens, more and more of the unionized companies will have to suspend operations. The demand for *union labor*, then, is shown by the dashed line D_1. The scope for union wage policy is limited.

Suppose on the other hand that the industry is fully unionized. The

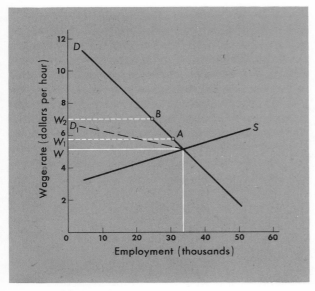

Figure 1
THE DEMAND FOR UNION LABOR
IN INDUSTRY *A*

demand curve for union labor is then identical with the demand curve
for all labor, i.e. it is simply *D*. Suppose further that union officials
know the location of this demand schedule. What will they do? The
quantities that they might conceivably try to maximize include *the
wage rate, the wage bill,* and *the level of employment.* Let us consider
the plausibility of these various targets.

The Wage Rate

In the situation shown, wages could be raised to $10 an hour or
even higher, while still retaining *some* employment for union members. Rational pursuit of this target might consist in pushing up the
wage rate, and reducing the level of employment, at precisely the rate
at which people retire from the industry. Eventually there would be
a single employee left, working at an astronomically high wage! It is
sometimes said that the policy of the United Mine Workers has tended
in this direction. Although demand for coal has been declining since
the late forties and the industry has been relatively unprofitable, the
union has raised wages rapidly and tolerated a rapid decline in employment.

The difficulties of a rate-maximizing policy are clear. If pushed too aggressively, it could displace prime-age workers as well as those ready to retire. Since union members are interested in having a job as well as in how much they earn on the job, displacement would produce grass-roots dissatisfaction and bring pressure on union leaders to modify their policies. Moreover, the success of a rate-maximizing policy depends on an assumption that the industry can be kept organized. But as the union rate is pushed higher and higher, there is increased incentive for employers to break away from the union and for new firms to set up on a nonunion basis. In any industry to which entrance is easy, this possibility acts as a constraint on union wage policy.

The Wage Bill

The union might conceivably try to maximize the total payroll of the industry, i.e. the wage rate multiplied by the number employed. But there is no particular reason why it should do this, since the wage bill goes to the workers rather than the union. Moreover, this principle could lead to odd results. Over any section of the labor demand curve in which demand is elastic, the wage bill can be increased by *cutting* the wage rate. Union members would probably consider this rather odd and would not be consoled by a lecture on elasticity of demand.

The demand schedule in Figure 1 was drawn deliberately so that the upper portion (to the left of Point A) is elastic, while the portion to the right of A is inelastic.[1] A wage of OW_1 corresponding to the point of unit elasticity A, would maximize the wage bill. If the union had somehow established or inherited a higher wage, say OW_2, it would have to cut wages in order to follow this maximizing principle.

Employment

Pursuit of this goal would require a wage of OW, the same wage that would exist under competitive conditions. At any wage below OW, the number of workers willing to enter the industry would fall short of the number that employers wish to hire. The wage OW thus

---

[1] As one moves down a linear demand curve from the X-axis, the curve will at first be elastic, will pass through a point of unit elasticity, and will be inelastic thereafter. The reason is explained in most elementary economics texts, or can be reasoned out from the formula for demand elasticity, which here is

$$e = - \frac{\% \text{ change in } E}{\% \text{ change in } W},$$

where W represents the wage rate and E is employment. As one moves down D, the numerator of this expression decreases steadily while the denominator increases, so that e falls continuously.

yields maximum employment and (again assuming that the industry can be kept fully organized), maximum union membership of *OE*. But while union officials have some interest in the size of their membership, there seems no reason why they should take this as their *sole* objective.

The maximizing approach thus turns out not to be very helpful. So most writers, in the end, fall back on rather vague formulations: a union will try to set wages above the competitive level (how much above?), but at the same time it will take some interest in employment (how much interest?). There is no mechanical rule comparable to the profit-maximizing formula for a business concern.

Union policy is formulated by the leadership, subject to varying degrees of consultation and potential veto by the membership. We may gain additional insight by considering the main pressures impinging on the leaders as they go about their task. The most important of these are rank-and-file sentiment, the wage increases currently being won in "neighboring" occupations and industries, and the constraints imposed by the economic environment.

Union members at any time have some notion of whether they should be getting more, and how much more. If the cost of living is rising, their wives will remind them of the inadequacy of the paycheck. If other workers in their area are getting increases, they will feel that their own wages should keep pace. Thus during a general economic expansion, there will be persistent membership pressure, which may be alleviated for a time after each wage settlement, but will then recur. On the downswing, however, few workers will concede that wages should be reduced. They are not impressed by the argument that, if the cost of living is falling, they can take a money wage cut and still have the same real wage. The principle of "no backward step" is firmly grounded in membership sentiment.

Members' opinions are brought home to the leadership through the normal processes of union government. Wage demands are discussed in local union meetings before negotiations begin. Rank-and-file members or lower-level officials in close touch with the membership, usually sit on the negotiating committee. The terms tentatively agreed on with management must usually be submitted to a membership vote before final ratification. This used to be regarded as a formality, since the members almost invariably voted to accept the settlement. But in recent years, this view has been less valid. During the sharp inflation of the years from 1965 to 1969, union members frequently rejected the terms recommended by their officers, forcing continued negotiations and often a continuation of strike action.

A second important consideration is interunion rivalry for members and prestige. Such rivalry is clearest where unions are competing for membership in the same industry. Thus some West Coast airframe plants are organized by the United Automobile Workers, others by the International Association of Machinists. Sailors on the East Coast belong to the National Maritime Union, those on the West Coast to the Sailors Union of the Pacific. East Coast and West Coast longshoremen also belong to separate organizations, which keep a close watch on each other. In the basic aluminum industry, some plants are organized by the United Steelworkers, others by the United Aluminum Workers. In such situations neither union can afford to settle for less than the other.

Political pressures may be important even within a single union. In the Teamsters' Union, for example, James Hoffa succeeded between 1940 and 1955 in building a firm power base in the Midwest, culminating in the negotiation of a uniform wage agreement with over-the-road truckers throughout the central states and most of the South. He then moved on to the East Coast and eventually to the Pacific Coast where, sometimes over the opposition of local officials, he attracted membership support by promising and delivering terms equivalent to those in the Central States' Agreement. This brought him the Teamsters' presidency in 1958, and unchallenged domination of the union thereafter.

In some cases two unions have an unusually close relation because of the physical proximity of their members. Longshoremen and sailors mingle on the docks. Truck drivers and warehousemen meet at freight terminals. Lumbermen and sawmill employees work close to papermill workers in the forested regions of the country. In centers of heavy manufacturing, the Automobile Workers, Steelworkers, Electrical Workers, and Machinists usually have sizable memberships in close proximity. The importance of interunion rivalry and imitation was first pointed out by Professor Arthur Ross, who coined the term "orbits of coercive comparison." More recently several cases of this sort have been documented by Professor Harold Levinson.[2]

A third factor that the union leader must consider is the economic situation of the industry at the time. If profits are high and the business outlook is good, he can afford to make large demands. If business is declining and profits are falling, he may have to be content with holding the present wage level. Most union presidents have a shrewd knowledge of the structure and financial prospects of their industry. This knowledge is derived from frequent discussions with employers throughout the country and long experience in negotiating with them, supplemented by the work of the union's research department and by governmental and trade reports. In many cases the union president knows more about the industry and has a broader view of its problems than does any single employer.

[2] Arthur M. Ross, *Trade Union Wage Policy* (Berkeley and Los Angeles: University of California Press, 1948); Harold M. Levinson, *Determining Forces in Collective Wage Bargaining* (New York: John Wiley & Sons, Inc., 1966).

Although union leaders realize that there is an upper limit to what a company or industry can pay at a particular time, they do not necessarily take employers' statements about ability to pay at their face value. They believe that ability to pay is somewhat flexible; within limits, a company can pay more if it has to pay more. Any experienced union leader has had numerous experiences of wage increases that, according to the company's claim during negotiations, would cause bankruptcy but that the company later managed to bear. Employers have cried "wolf" so often that the union hesitates to believe them even when their plight is serious.

In the light of these various pressures, the union negotiators must decide on their (genuine) demands. The decision involves intuition and judgment, rather than application of a simple formula to clearly perceived economic data.

EMPLOYER
WAGE
POLICY

Management is freer than the union to think primarily in economic terms. In large companies, direct stockholder pressure is not likely to be important. Rivalry with other employers is important, but mainly in the economic sense that company *A*'s wage must be high enough, relative to that of other companies, to attract a labor force of the desired size and quality. Some of the largest companies may have to consider public relations and possible pressures from Washington, but these companies are a small proportion of the total.

This does not mean that formulation of company wage-policy is easy or automatic. The multidimensional nature of the employment "package" poses complications that were examined in Chapter 5. The employer cannot read off the correct wage from a supply–demand diagram. He has some discretion in wage policy, and the question is how this discretion will be exercised.

The typical manager seems to think of his company as occupying a certain rank in the wage hierarchy of the area. It "pays the best wages in town," or it is about at the area average, or it is toward the bottom of the area range. Management may simply try to maintain this position, moving up with the area average but not trying to move any faster. Or at times management may conclude that the company could gain by lagging behind or getting ahead of general wage movements, thus changing its relative position. Why do different companies occupy these different positions? And why may a company sometimes decide to change, or be forced to change, its relative ranking? These questions come close to the heart of wage policy as viewed from the operating level.

The company's position in product and labor markets sets outside limits, sometimes narrow, sometimes wide, within which management must navigate. There is at any time a maximum and a minimum feasible wage level—a minimum below which it could not hold enough labor to meet production schedules, a maximum above which it could not go for budgetary reasons. If all other items in the estimated budget for the year—sales receipts, raw material costs, and so on—are given, there is some maximum wage bill above which the company would suffer operating losses. The fact that these limits exist does not mean that they are always clearly defined in management's thinking. Management will not work hard to discover their precise position unless it feels that the company is close to one or the other limit and in danger of being pushed beyond it. Management may also work harder to marshal the facts if confronted by union demands than it would under nonunion conditions.

The position of the maximum and minimum points depends on the period of time that is taken into account. The plant may be able to maintain a very low wage level for a few weeks or months, particularly if there is serious unemployment. Over a longer period this wage level would cause it to lose too many workers, and a higher wage level is necessary. Similar considerations apply to the maximum point. Wage rates could be set very high for a short time, since the company could temporarily neglect maintenance and repairs on the plant, pass dividends, and even draw on its cash reserves to meet the wage bill. The firm cannot do these things, however, if it wishes to continue in operation year-in and year-out. It must at least break even in the long run. If it wishes to expand its operations in future, a positive rate of profit will be necessary, and the wage maximum will be still lower.

The longer the period considered, the lower will be the wage maximum and the higher the wage minimum, and consequently the smaller will be the distance between them. The controversy between "economic" theories of wage determination and "administrative" or "bargaining" theories turns in good measure on this point. Bargaining theorists assert correctly that over short periods the gap between the maximum and minimum points may be so wide that economic theories focused on determination of these points are not very helpful, and one needs some explanation of where the wage rate will settle within the range of discretion. Economic theorists assert, equally correctly, that over longer periods the limits set by economic forces lie closer together and are thus more compelling on the parties. The time factor is also an important reason for differences between union and management positions in collective bargaining. Union officers are apt to lean heavily on what the company could afford to pay in the short run under optimistic assumptions about future sales and profits. Management will usually have a genuinely lower estimate of its wage maximum, partly because it makes conservative estimates of future profits for safety reasons, and partly because it gives greater weight to the long-run expansion needs of the enterprise.

The minimum and maximum wage levels are influenced by different sets of forces—the minimum by conditions in the local labor market, the maximum by conditions in markets for the company's products. We are back, in short, to supply and demand in modified form. The wage minimum will be influenced by such things as the rates paid by other companies in the area for comparable work, the level of unemployment in the area, the increasing or declining needs of other companies for labor, the possible plans of the company to increase its employment and the speed of this increase, and the company's customary wage position in the area. A company that has long been a wage leader in a community is under greater pressure to continue paying high wages than a company that has customarily been near the bottom.

The maximum wage that the company can afford is influenced by industry characteristics such as elasticity of demand for the industry's products, rising or falling product demand, importance of labor costs relative to other costs, and pricing that is either competitive or controlled by tacit agreement. A second important factor is the relative efficiency of the company within its industry. In any industry one usually finds substantial differences in the unit production costs of different companies. An efficient, low-cost company has a higher wage maximum and greater latitude for wage policy than a high-cost company barely able to survive.

The fact that the company's wage minimum and wage maximum are determined by different sets of forces means that there is no necessary connection between them. One finds situations in which the maximum is so far above the minimum that the minimum is of no practical importance. A modern, efficient steel-fabricating plant located in a Southern town where it is the sole or leading employer might be in this position. At the other extreme, the minimum and maximum points may virtually coincide, leaving management with very little discretion. A shoe or furniture factory located in Detroit or Pittsburgh might find itself in this position. In practice, industries with low wage-paying ability would avoid these high-wage areas. If a company's wage maximum actually falls below its minimum for any considerable period, it is on its way to extinction.

The more interesting cases are those in which the company's wage maximum is well above the minimum because it is in a profitable and expanding industry, or because it is particularly efficient within its industry, or because it is located in a relatively low-wage area. A company in this happy position will often set a wage level considerably higher than the minimum at which it could just "get by." Possible reasons for such a policy were noted in Chapter 5. A high-wage policy reduces recruiting and turnover costs, increases labor force quality, and may enable supervisors to insist on a higher level of job performance. It also contributes to good employee relations and good community relations.

Even under nonunion conditions, however, employers are not completely free to make their own judgment of proper wage level. They will usually be under pressure from other companies in the industry not to pay too little, and from other companies in the area not to pay too much. Adam Smith commented that "masters are always and everywhere in a sort of tacit, but constant and uniform combination, not to raise the wages of labor above their actual rate. To violate this combination is everywhere a most unpopular action, and a sort of reproach to a master among his neighbors and equals." An employer who gets too far above the area wage level is accused of "upsetting the market," "pirating labor," and so on. One employer told the writer that if he got more than 15 percent above the area wage level he was in trouble with other employers, while if he fell more than 15 percent below the area level he was in trouble over labor supply.

It is also regarded as faintly unethical to fall too far below the wage level of other companies in the same industry. A company that is much below the industry wage level is in a position to undercut others on prices, unless its lower wages are offset by obsolete plant, managerial inefficiency, or other disadvantages. Leaders of the industry, sensitive to this competitive threat, will urge low-wage companies to come up to the industry level and not to engage in "unfair competition."

A company in a high-wage industry but located in a low-wage community is often caught between these two fires. If it conforms to the indusry it will be far out of line with the area, and vice versa. Different managements will reach different compromises on this point, depending a good deal on the structure of the industry in question. In oligopolistic industries where each producer is highly visible and cooperation in pricing and other competitive practices is essential, the industry wage level will have dominant influence. Steel, automobile, tire, glass, and petroleum plants are high-wage plants everywhere, and if this puts them above the area wage level, so much the worse for the area. In small-scale, highly competitive, and relatively anonymous industries, on the other hand, each company may hew closer to the area wage level and gain whatever advantage it can by so doing.

Long-term Agreements and Wage Formulas

With management and union positions thus established, the wage issue is bargained out through the procedures described in Chapter 15. Depending on the severity of the pressures impinging on the two parties, on their relative economic strength and staying power, on the stage of the business cycle, and on the tactical skill of negotiators, the bargain may come out closer to the union's or to the employer's figure.

Until recently wages and other issues were fought out every year in annual contract negotiations. Since 1950, however, there has been a marked trend toward longer agreements. Most of the major agreements [3] in the United States now run for three years or longer, and only about 10 percent are still on an annual basis. The reasons include growing employer acceptance of unionism as a permanent institution; the fact that on many nonwage issues—union security, seniority rules, grievance procedures, and arbitration—standard practices have been developed that both parties are willing to live with and that do not need to be renegotiated frequently; and the desire of employers to avoid the turmoil, expense, and uncertainty of annual negotiations. A major negotiation can tie up most of top management's time for an extended period. More and more companies have become convinced that this is not necessary, and have tried to stabilize their contract arrangements on a longer-term basis.

Most workers, however, have come to expect that their wages will rise at least once a year. For a long-term contract to be feasible, therefore, it must contain provisions for adjusting wages during the life of the contract. One possibility is a *wage-reopening clause.* This permits wages to be renegotiated, normally once a year, during the life of a multi-year contract, but other issues cannot be reopened until the contract expires.

Another common provision is the *cost-of-living escalator clause.* This provides that wages shall be reviewed frequently, usually every three months or every six months, and shall be adjusted if the Bureau of Labor Statistics' Consumers' Price Index has risen by a certain amount. Wages also escalate downward with price declines; but this provision is rather academic, since there has been no appreciable decline in consumer prices since 1940.

A third common provision is the *deferred wage increase,* under which subsequent wage increases are built into the contract at the

---

[3] A major agreement is defined by the Bureau of Labor Statistics as one covering 1,000 or more workers. In 1961 there were 1,733 such agreements in the country, with a total coverage of 8.3 million. ("Major Union Contracts in the United States, 1961," *Monthly Labor Review,* October, 1962.)

time it is signed. The first instance of this was the "annual improvement factor" negotiated by General Motors with the United Automobile Workers in 1948 as part of the price of a three-year agreement. Similar agreements were negotiated by the other major automobile companies in 1950. Beginning in 1955, the practice spread to basic steel, electrical equipment, rubber, meat-packing, trucking, railroading, and numerous other industries. By now more than half the workers under major agreements have this sort of provision.

The most recent survey of contract clauses [4] in major agreements shows the following prevalence of these various formulas:

		PERCENT OF	
		Agreements	*Workers*
(1)	DEFERRED WAGE INCREASE ONLY	39.3	27.5
(2)	WAGE REOPENING ONLY	17.4	24.1
(3)	COST-OF-LIVING ESCALATOR ONLY	1.8	1.3
	(1) + (2)	7.1	9.1
	(1) + (3)	18.6	24.2
	(2) + (3)	1.3	0.6
	(1) + (2) + (3)	1.8	3.3

These provisions affect the short-run timing of wage changes. A cost-of-living escalator may shorten the lag of wages behind prices during an inflationary period. A deferred wage increase, scheduled two or three years in advance, may turn out to be larger or smaller than if it had been negotiated under the actual economic circumstances of the year in question. But if either party finds that the formula has worked to its disadvantage over the contract period, it is free to seek redress at the next triennial negotiation. There is no evidence that the use of one or another adjustment formula causes a company's wage level to behave differently in the long run than it would have done under a regime of annual negotiations.

INTERCOMPANY DIFFERENCES
WITHIN
AN INDUSTRY

How does collective bargaining affect the relative wage levels of companies competing in the same product market? Where an industry is partially organized, are wages of unionized companies typically

[4] Bureau of Labor Statistics, Bulletin 1353, *Major Union Contracts in the United States, 1961.* These data are now unfortunately some distance in the past, but it appears that there has been no comparable recent survey.

above those of nonunion companies? Within the unionized sector, does the union try to enforce the same wage level on all companies? Or does it tailor its demands to the individual company's ability to pay?

Statistical studies of partially unionized industries usually show a wage differential between union and nonunion establishments. Vernon Clover found that Bureau of Labor Statistics studies of thirty-one manufacturing industries during the years 1960 to 1965 showed an average earnings differential of 18 percent between union and non-union plants. These differences were not fully explained by community size, region, or ratios of men and women employed. When the surveys were broken down by region, the average union–nonunion differential was still 12 percent, and appeared in seventy-one out of seventy-six cases.[5]

Such results must be interpreted with caution, however, because of the difficulty of controlling for all the variables affecting a company's wage level. For example, wages are normally higher in large plants and companies than in smaller ones. But large establishments are also more susceptible of unionization. So a new union coming into an industry may first organize the large establishments, which already had higher wages in preunion days. The specific impact of unionism cannot be inferred without controlling for plant size, labor force quality, and other relevant variables.

Moreover, the bargained wage in union establishments will probably affect the wage policies of nonunion companies. They may set a higher wage than otherwise in the hope of avoiding unionization. This has been termed the "threat effect" of unionism. To the extent that this effect is important, the observed wage differential between union and nonunion plants will *understate* the true impact of the union.[6]

There is clear evidence that unions try to reduce wage differences *among unionized companies* in the same industry, and that they in good measure succeed. The principle of "the standard rate" for men doing comparable work is firmly grounded in trade union history. It stems partly from considerations of equity and from political pressures within the union, but economic considerations are also important. If some companies in an industry are allowed to pay less than others, there is a danger that the low-wage companies will un-

[5] Vernon T. Clover, "Compensation in union and nonunion plants, 1960–65," *Industrial and Labor Relations Review*, January, 1968, pp. 226–33.

[6] For an interesting analysis, see Sherwin Rosen, "Trade Union Power, Threat Effects and Extent of Organization," *The Review of Economic Studies*, April, 1969, pp. 185–96. Rosen surmises that the threat effect is strongest in the early stages of unionization, and tapers off when the percentage of unionization passes a certain point. This might help to explain the fact that some unions seem to have raised the relative wage level of their industries most rapidly during the early stages of unionization.

derbid their competitors in the product market, forcing down prices and wages throughout the industry. A uniform wage level for firms selling in the same product market is regarded as a way of "putting a floor under competition" or "taking wages out of competition."

Application of this principle, as we noted in Chapter 15, varies with the geographic scope of the product market. In local-market industries there is a tendency toward wage equalization within the city, though there may be considerable variation in wage levels from one city to the next. In manufacturing industries where employers compete on a regional or national basis, there is a tendency toward leveling up of wages throughout the country. We shall be concerned in this section mainly with the economic effects of national wage equalization in manufacturing industries.[7]

It should be noted at the outset that "wage equalization" has several possible meanings: equality of the *lowest wage rate* in each plant, often termed the "common labor rate"; equality of all *job rates* in each plant; equality of *piece rates* in each plant; and equality of *labor cost per unit of output*. Each of these objectives has been pursued by one or another union at various times. Equalizing wages in one of these senses, however, will not produce equality in the other senses; and pursuit of these differing objectives will clearly have different economic consequences. Imposition of uniform hourly rates, for example, may work serious hardship on a plant with relatively inefficient workers, equipment, or management; its lower output per man-hour means that its unit labor costs are above the remainder of the industry. Uniform piece rates work no such hardship; if the workers in a particular plant produce little, by the same token they are paid little. This does not mean that the latter arrangement is necessarily preferable, but it is certainly different.

Since it is not possible to discuss each type of wage equalization in the space available here, we limit ourselves to a few remarks on the effects of installing a uniform scale of hourly job rates throughout an industry. This is in some ways the clearest case, and it is probably the most important in practice.

Effects of Wage Leveling

The effects of wage leveling will depend on why wage rates formerly differed in different plants of the industry. The reasons are

[7] See the chapter on "The Standard Rate" in Sidney and Beatrice Webb, *Industrial Democracy* (London: Longmans, Green & Co. Ltd., 1902); D. A. McCabe, *The Standard Rate in American Trade Unions* (Baltimore: The Johns Hopkins Press, 1912); R. A. Lester and E. A. Robie, *Wages under National and Regional Collective Bargaining* (Princeton: Princeton University Industrial Relations Section, 1946); and Thomas Kennedy, *Significance of Wage Uniformity,* Industry-wide Collective Bargaining Series (Philadelphia: University of Pennsylvania Press, 1948).

usually complex and vary from one industry to the next.[8] Two factors, however, are of outstanding importance:

1. The wage-paying ability of plants may differ because of variations in technical efficiency. Some plants may be newer, closer to optimum size, better designed, better located relative to materials and markets, or have other advantages. Managerial capacity also varies, and two managements may get different results from very similar plants.
2. Plants may be located in different areas with different local wage levels. Large cities typically have higher wage levels than smaller cities in the same region, the northeastern states have higher wages than the southeastern states, and so on.

The first effect of union pressure for wage equality is to test whether the low-wage firms are actually paying as much as they are able to pay. Allegations of inability to pay are not always well founded, and the union requires convincing evidence. Second, union pressure frequently forces management to step up efficiency and increase the firm's ability to pay. It may be objected that this "shock effect" works only the first few times it is applied, but a few times may be sufficient to raise the firm's efficiency substantially.

But what happens when everything possible has been done in this direction and the union comes up against irremovable differences in plant efficiency? Continued pressure for wage equalization will then tend to eliminate some of the less-efficient plants from the industry. Elimination of these plants will make more business available for the more efficient plants and encourage them to expand their operations. In the end, there may be little change in total output and employment in the industry, but there will be considerable redistribution of employment. Jobs will disappear at some places and new jobs will open up at other places, possibly far distant from the first. The long-run effects may be economically beneficial; the immediate effects will be disturbing to the employers who are shut down and to their workers. Indeed, if union members in a particular plant become convinced that to bring their wages up to the national level will cost them their jobs, they will usually vote to accept a lower wage and keep the plant in operation. This is particularly true where the plant is geographically isolated and the members would have to travel some distance to find new employment. In such cases even the national union officers may be willing to tolerate some departure from wage equality.

This is one reason why, even in a strongly organized industry, one

---

[8] For a more thorough analysis than can be given here, see Lloyd G. Reynolds and Cynthia H. Taft, *The Evolution of Wage Structure* (New Haven: Yale University Press, 1956), chap. 7.

rarely finds complete uniformity of wage scales. Most plants will cluster closely around a single wage level, but one will usually find that the union has left a few plants at lower levels because these plants are unable to pay the standard rate and yet it seems expedient to keep them in operation. One may also find that in some of the most efficient plants the union has yielded to the temptation to extract a little more than the prevailing scale. In general, however, unions hew closer to the principle of "the standard rate" than to the principle of "ability to pay." [9]

Where plants are located in different communities with different wage levels, wage equalization may have some effect on the geographical location of industry. The fact that some communities have lower wage levels than others acts as an inducement to new plants to establish themselves in those communities. Specifically, there is an inducement for new plants to spring up in small towns rather than large cities, and in the southern states rather than in the North. The effect of wage leveling is to remove this inducement. If the union insists on the same wage level in all parts of the country, there is no longer any reason for employers to prefer one locality *on grounds of labor cost,* though they may still have preferences based on access to raw materials or markets. The effect is to reduce, if not eliminate, movement of industry from North to South and from large cities to small towns. Whether this effect is desirable is certainly debatable, and the factors to be considered are not all economic.

The most celebrated issue is that of the "North–South wage differential." The reasons for the development of this differential were explored in Chapter 9. Suppose now that unionism should become sufficiently strong in the South to eliminate the differential entirely —at least as regards manufacturing industries operating in a national market. What will be the consequences? The incentive for workers to move North and industry to move South will certainly be reduced, but it will not be entirely eliminated. The pressure of population growth in the South will still force many people to move North in search of job openings. Many industries will still find better natural resources and other locational advantages in the South. This is true, for example, of the pulp and paper industry, which is learning to make efficient use of the quick-growing southern pine.

If labor should turn out to be less efficient in the South than in the North under identical conditions, wage equalization would work a hardship on southern industry. There is no clear evidence, however, that this is the case. In industries where substantial equality of wages

---

[9] For a good analysis of the ways in which a union may make concessions to firms with low wage-paying ability, see David H. Greenberg, "Deviations From Wage-Fringe Standards," *Industrial and Labor Relations Review,* January, 1968, pp. 197–209.

has already been established, such as the paper and basic steel industries, there is no indication that the southern plants are less profitable than the northern, or that they are losing out in the competitive struggle.

The effects of a wage equalization program thus depend a great deal on the factors responsible for the previous wage differentials. They depend also on what it is that the union is trying to equalize—plant minima, hourly base rates, piece rates, or labor costs. For reasons explained earlier, equalization of piece rates places less of a burden on the less-efficient employers than does equalization of hourly base rates. The effects of wage equalization also depend on how rapidly the leveling is carried out, how high the level is set, and how many exceptions are permitted.

THE
INTERNAL
WAGE STRUCTURE

Thus far we have concentrated on the *average* wage level of a company. Most companies, however, hire dozens or hundreds of different types of skill. Each of these jobs has its own wage, varying from the entrance rate or "common labor rate" to the highest-skilled job in the plant. How does management determine proper relative wage rates for these many kinds of work? And how does the presence of a union alter the process?

Some kinds of labor may be in general demand throughout the area and hence have an "outside market." This is apt to be true for jobs at the bottom and top of the skill ladder, for unskilled labor on one hand and skilled maintenance craftsmen on the other. It seems also to be true of standard office occupations. Turnover of women in these occupations is rather high, a new crop comes into the market each year through high school graduation, and the new graduates are able to get good information about company salary levels from high school vocational advisers, the public employment service, and shopping around. This puts pressure on each employer to remain within a reasonable distance of prevailing area rates.[10]

But the outside market impinges only at certain points in the company wage structure. There is a great array of semiskilled and skilled production jobs that are specific to a particular industry or even a particular company. Workers are usually not hired into these jobs

---

[10] For an interesting analysis of competition and salary determination for certain clerical occupations in Boston, see George P. Shultz, "A Nonunion Market for Whitecollar Labor," in *Aspects of Labor Economics,* pp. 107–46.

from the outside, but work up from within the company on a seniority basis. It is not easy for them to transfer to other companies, since the same job may not exist elsewhere, and since other companies also prefer to promote from within. Thus there is an "inside market" for these jobs, but no outside market. The precise ranking of jobs, and the determination of proper wage differences between them, becomes a matter for administrative discretion and collective bargaining.

A pattern of job rates develops in the first instance through shop custom. Certain jobs come to be regarded as related to each other on the basis of physical contiguity, sequence of production operations, or a learning sequence in which workers progress from lower to higher rank in a work team. Workers and foremen develop ideas about how much more one of these jobs should pay than another. Once established, these wage relationships tend to persist through custom. When asked to explain why their wage schedule looks as it does, most plant managers will say, "We have always done it that way," or "It just grew up that way."

Reliance on custom alone, however, is not always satisfactory. It is particularly unsatisfactory as an answer to workers or union officials who contend that a particular rate is too low and should be raised. During the past twenty years or so, therefore, management has turned increasingly to systems of "job rating" or "job evaluation" that purport to provide a scientific basis for determining the relative worth of different jobs. There are several reasons for the popularity of these systems. Some managers believe that they provide an absolutely fair and incontrovertible basis for determining relative wage rates. Even those who recognize that no wage scale can presume to absolute justice seek the definite standards provided by job evaluation, because they make for administrative uniformity and simplicity in handling wage matters. Job evaluation provides a yardstick by which management can judge the merit of complaints by workers or the union; at least, it enables management to answer these complaints and to provide a rational explanation of its wage decisions.

Job Evaluation Procedures

Job evaluation procedures cannot be discussed in any detail here and the student interested in them should consult the standard works on the subject.[11] In general, however, the procedure is as follows:

One must first select a set of "factors" or criteria to be used in rating jobs, and set a maximum point score for each factor. An example is the widely used rating scale of the National Metal Trades'

[11] See, for example, C. W. Lytle, *Job Evaluation Methods* (New York: The Ronald Press Company, 1946); F. H. Johnson, R. W. Boise, Jr., and Dudley Pratt, *Job Evaluation* (New York: John Wiley & Sons, Inc., 1946).

Association. The factors used and the maximum possible score for each are as follows: education (70), experience (110), initiative and ingenuity (70), physical effort (50), mental and visual effort (25), responsibility for equipment and processes (25), responsibility for material or product (25), responsibility for safety of others (25), responsibility for work of others (25), working conditions (50), and work hazards (25). More briefly, these factors may be summarized as: education, experience, and skill (250), responsibility (100), effort (75), and working conditions (75). This relatively heavy weighting of skill and light weighting of effort is characteristic of most of the other rating scales in current use.

The next step is to make a careful description of each job in the plant, and to rate each job in terms of the selected factors. The rating applies to *the job itself,* not to the workers who happen to be doing the job at the time. The result is a total point score for each job, which enables one to rank all jobs in the plant in order of importance. The next step is usually to group the different jobs into a limited number of brackets or "labor grades." Thus, jobs with a score of 450 to 500 may be put in labor grade 1, jobs with a score of 400 to 450 in labor grade 2, and so on down. In some systems the numbering is the other way round, so that the *lowest* jobs are in labor grade 1.

The actual work of job rating is more complex and controversial than this simple outline would suggest. Many different people have an interest and a voice in the evaluation of each job—the workers on the job, their foremen, the shop steward (in unionized plants), the plant superintendent, the industrial engineers making the survey, personnel officials, and others. There may be marked differences of opinion among these people. If the rating of a job comes out very much above or below its present position in the plant wage-structure, there is likely to be criticism and argument. If the rating of a job puts it on the borderline between two labor grades, which may mean a difference of several cents an hour in pay, the workers and even the foreman will try to add a few points on somewhere to push it over the line into the higher grade. The final rating of each job is not a mathematical measurement, but a practical compromise among the judgments of the different people concerned.

It is necessary next to decide what shall be the highest and lowest wage rates in the plant.[12] What rate shall be paid for, say, class 1 toolmakers, and what shall be paid for sweepers, laborers, and jan-

----

[12] The company may also select several intermediate jobs that exist in other plants in the area, so that there is an "outside market" for them. A survey is made of the wage rates being paid by other companies for these jobs, and the average wage for each job determined. These averages, or "peg points," can then be used as a guide in determining the company's own rate structure.

itors? In a nonunion plant, this decision is usually made on a comparative basis, i.e. by surveying the rates currently paid for class 1 toolmakers and laborers by other plants in the area or industry. Under trade unionism, of course, determination of the high and low rates becomes a matter of bargaining, though rates in other plants will probably still be used as data for bargaining purposes.

It must be decided, finally, how rapidly the rates for intermediate labor grades shall rise, i.e. what shall be the shape of the "rate curve." Two very different rate curves are shown in Figure 2. Employers tend

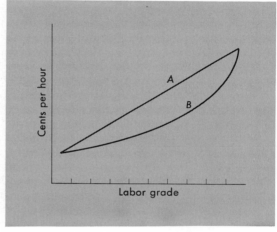

Figure 2

OCCUPATIONAL RATE CURVES FOR A PLANT

to favor a schedule similar to curve *B,* under which rates rise rather slowly for the first few labor grades in which the bulk of the labor force is concentrated, and then more rapidly in the higher labor grades where there are few workers.

As a practical matter, the decision will be influenced a good deal by the shape of the existing wage schedule of the plant. At some stage in the procedure, it is usual to take the existing rate for each job, chart it against the point score for the job, and fit a curve to the scatter diagram thus obtained. The rate curve finally adopted under the job evaluation system will not necessarily have just the same shape as this empirical curve, but is likely to resemble it rather closely. Custom and established wage relationships provide a powerful argument; and if the present wage structure of the plant resembles curve *B,* management is unlikely to agree to a new schedule resembling curve *A.*

Whatever the shape of the new rate curve, it will turn out that some jobs are currently receiving less than they are entitled to under the new schedule, while other jobs are being paid more than they should be. The accepted way of adjusting existing job rates to the new schedule is as follows: workers on jobs that are currently underpaid are raised immediately to the rate provided for the job in the new schedule; the rates of workers now on overpaid jobs are left unchanged, but new workers on these jobs must be hired at the lower rates provided in the new schedule. As the old workers leave, retire, or are transferred to higher-rated jobs, the earnings of all workers in the plant are gradually brought into alignment with the new wage schedule.

It is clear from this brief description that rate setting based on job evaluation is not "scientific" in the sense of mathematical precision. Judgment must be exercised at each step in the procedure—the choice of rating factors, the assignment of the point weights to each factor, the actual description and rating of jobs, the determination of the top and bottom of the wage structure, and the determination of the shape of the rate curve between these points. The judgments of different individuals on each point are bound to differ somewhat, and the final outcome is a working compromise. Job evaluation does, however, make the exercise of judgment more deliberate and systematic than it might be without definite rules of procedure.

Some of the most interesting problems of job evaluation arise in the course of administering an evaluated wage structure after it has been installed. A particular kind of worker becomes scarce, and the market rate for this job rises above the rate provided by the evaluated system. Shall the company continue to adhere to the evaluated rate, or shall it pay whatever is necessary to get workers? Again, a key worker threatens to leave the company unless his rate is raised, which can be done only by reclassifying his job into a higher labor grade. Shall this be done, in violation of job evaluation standards, or shall the company adhere to principle and lose the worker? The industrial engineers in charge of installing and managing the job evaluation system will usually urge that the evaluated rates be adhered to at all costs. Unless the purity of the system is maintained, they argue, it will soon become riddled with exceptions and its original advantages will be lost. Production officials, however, are inclined to regard this argument as "theoretical" and to pay whatever rates are necessary to attract and retain workers.

Another difficulty in the day-to-day administration of job evaluation is the fact that the characteristics of jobs in the plant are continually changing. This makes it necessary to rerate certain jobs from time to time. Since the tendency of modern industry is to make most jobs simpler and easier with the passage of time, usually more jobs are rerated downwards than upwards. The workers on the jobs that are to be downgraded naturally resent such action and resist it to the best of their ability, and management sometimes takes the easy course of overlooking the new ratings and leaving the previous wage rates intact. The result is a gradual accumulation of exceptions to the system.

Unions have usually been skeptical of job evaluation. They feel that it tends to freeze the wage structure too rigidly, to reduce the role of collective bargaining, and to restore the setting of job rates to unilateral management control. Unions typically resist the introduction of new job evaluation plans. Where a plan already exists, however, they will usually work under it while at the same time insisting on their right to bargain over the structure of the system and the rating of specific jobs. In a few cases the union has cooperated actively with management in designing a new evaluation program. The outstanding example is the rationalization of wage rates in basic steel, carried out jointly by the United Steelworkers and the major steel companies during the late forties.[13] Here the union secured reduction of an unmanageable load of grievances over wage inequities, some overall increase in earnings for its members, a standard wage structure applicable throughout the industry, and a gradual phasing out of regional wage differences.

Even where there is no formal job evaluation system, the wage agreement normally classifies jobs into a number of "labor grades," and specifies a wage rate or a range of rates for each grade. The structure of this list is naturally of major concern to the union. Should the top craftsman be paid 30 percent more than the laborer, or 50 percent more, or 100 percent more? And where should intermediate jobs be located within this range? Wage differences that appear small to higher management may be significant to workers in terms of status as well as income.

The form that this issue takes in collective bargaining depends partly on union structure. Where the skilled craftsmen are organized in one or more unions and the less-skilled workers in another, there may conceivably be either collaboration or rivalry among the groups as regards occupational differentials. Where all employees belong to a single industrial union, there is a difference of interest within the union membership. The interest of the less-skilled workers is to reduce occupational differentials, while the interest of the craftsmen is to maintain or widen them.

One might expect, therefore, that the impact of collective bargaining on occupational differentials would vary from industry to indus-

---

[13] For a detailed analysis of this case, see Jack Stieber, *The Steel Industry Wage Structure* (Cambridge: Harvard University Press, 1959).

try. Evidence on the actual impact in specific cases will be reviewed in the next chapter.

SUPPLEMENTARY
INCOME
PAYMENTS

The modern union agreement has been described as "a contract with a fringe on top." But the term "fringe benefits," coined in a period when such provisions were minor, is no longer appropriate. These items now constitute a large and growing proportion of workers' incomes and employers' payroll costs. We comment first on the size and makeup of supplementary income payments, and then on the specific effects of unionism.

A survey of 1,150 large companies by the U.S. Chamber of Commerce reports that in 1967 employee benefit payments averaged 26.6 percent of payroll, or 82.2 cents per payroll hour, or $1,719 per year per employee.[14] There was substantial variation, however, among companies. Ten percent of firms had benefits of less than 18 percent of payroll, while another 10 percent had benefits of 36 percent or more. On an industry basis, textiles had lowest benefits (20.6 percent), while banks and insurance companies were highest (32.5 percent).

In interpreting these figures one must remember that the sample consisted of large companies, and that fringe benefits are positively related to size of company. An average for all companies in the country would be lower than that shown by the chamber of commerce survey. On the other hand, the chamber survey includes paid rest periods, vacations, and holidays *in the payroll base.* If the base is defined to include only pay for time actually worked, then the ratio of supplementary income payments to payroll averaged almost 30 percent.

Whatever the correct figure for the current year, there is no doubt that the trend has been upward. The chamber of commerce survey reports that benefit payments for a sample of seventy-nine identical companies increased from 16.1 percent of payroll in 1947 to 24.2 percent in 1957, and to 29.9 percent in 1967.

Quantitatively most important are:

1. *Retirement Pensions.* Virtually all wage and salary earners are now covered by the Social Security system. In addition, about 75 percent of plant workers and 80 percent of office workers are covered

---

14 U.S. Chamber of Commerce, *Employee Benefits 1967* (Washington, D.C., 1968), p. 5. A similar survey is conducted and published every year.

by company pension programs.[15] Employer contributions to Social Security and to company retirement plans averaged 7.9 percent of payroll in 1967, for companies included in the chamber survey.

2. *Paid Vacations and Holidays* are now enjoyed by more than 80 percent of plant employees and 90 percent of office employees, and cost 6.8 percent of payroll in 1967 for companies covered by the chamber survey. Paid holidays have increased from four or five per year some time ago to an average of eight per year at present. In addition to the standard national holidays, there has been increasing use of "floating holidays"—for example, to provide a long weekend when a national holiday falls on a Thursday or Tuesday, or to give each employee a holiday on his own birthday.

Vacations are almost invariably linked to length of service. A common formula at present is one week after one year of service, two weeks after five years, three weeks after ten years, and four weeks after twenty years. Such formulas can be, and in fact have been, liberalized gradually in the course of time by reducing the years of service required for each length of vacation.

3. *Insurance and Health Programs.* More than 90 percent of both plant and office employees have company-financed life insurance, hospitalization insurance, and surgical insurance. A majority also have illness and accident insurance. About a third of plant employees and two-thirds of office employees have specified periods of sick leave on part or full pay. These programs cost 4 percent of payroll in 1967 for companies included in the chamber of commerce survey.

These are only the more important items. The chamber of commerce survey identifies and costs twenty-one types of fringe payment. The list includes such things as: employer contributions to state unemployment compensation and (in a few industries) to union-negotiated private unemployment benefit funds; paid rest periods, lunch periods, wash-up time, travel time, and other time not actually worked; and various types of profit-sharing and bonus arrangements.

The rapid growth of supplementary benefits has been attributed variously to: (1) their preferential treatment under the personal income tax. A dollar that the employer contributes to a pension, health, or insurance fund is a full dollar, while a dollar increase in direct wage payments may yield the worker only seventy to eighty cents after taxes. (2) The fact that life insurance or health protection is cheaper when purchased on a group basis. Again, a dollar spent by the employer in this way yields more benefit than if the dollar were paid to the worker and he had to purchase his own protection. (3) A

---

[15] James N. Hoff, "Supplementary wage benefits in metropolitan areas," *Monthly Labor Review,* June, 1968, pp. 40–47. This survey is more comprehensive than the chamber of commerce survey, so we rely on it to estimate the coverage of various benefit programs.

belief among employers that benefits whose value increases with length of service will attach workers more firmly to the company and reduce costly turnover. (4) Union pressure for larger supplements.

An analysis of manufacturing industries by Robert Rice [16] revealed a consistent positive relation between benefit levels and (a) level of direct wage payments, (b) size of company. The wage level alone explained more than 70 percent of the variance in benefit levels. Not only do supplementary payments vary positively with earnings, but the *ratio of supplements to earnings* also varies positively. This means that wage differentials progressively understate the differentials in total compensation as one moves up from lower-wage to higher-wage companies.

There was no significant relation between turnover rates and the level of supplementary benefits, which suggests that the turnover-reducing effect of benefits may have been exaggerated. Neither was there any significant relation between benefit levels and extent of unionization. This suggests that much of the increase, particularly in areas such as pensions and insurance, can probably be attributed to voluntary employer action.

At one stage employers contended that pensions, insurance, health programs, and similar matters were within the sole discretion of the company, and that the union was not entitled to bargain about them. But the National Labor Relations Board and the courts held otherwise, and bargaining on fringe payments is now regularly included in contract negotiations. In addition to arguing over the size of the increase in the employer's labor costs, the parties argue over the *allocation* of the increase between direct wage payments and supplementary items. At the end of the road the press reports a "package" settlement of, say, fifteen cents an hour, comprising nine cents in wage increases and six cents as the cost of fringe improvements.

This suggests several questions. First, does the fact that the union is bargaining on two fronts rather than one—for wage increases *and* fringe increases—enable it to get more than if it were bargaining on wages only? This seems rather unlikely. The cents-per-hour cost of a particular fringe improvement is readily calculated, and the employer is likely to regard this as highly substitutable with wage increases.

Unionism may have affected the *allocation* of increases in compensation as between wages and fringes. The total compensation of union workers may have risen over the past generation by about the same amount that it would have if fringes had never been invented. Yet, because of union policy, more of the increase may have gone into

16 Robert G. Rice, "Skill, Earnings, and the Growth of Wage Supplements," *American Economic Review Proceedings,* May, 1966, pp. 583–93.

fringes and less into direct wage payments than would have happened otherwise. It would be difficult, however, to test this surmise statistically. Because of a variety of social currents, including union pressure, both nonunion and union companies have shifted their compensation package toward a higher proportion of supplementary payments; but the specific influence of unionism is hard to determine.

A further question is whether union officers accurately reflect their members' preferences as between wage increases and fringe increases. Is there any systematic bias in the officers' perception of members' wishes? An analysis of this issue by Edward Lawler III and Edward Levin is interesting as an example of method. For each of two plants they endeavored to test (1) union officers' personal preferences as among various items, (2) union officers' perception of their members' preferences among these same items, and (3) the actual preferences of the members. The technique was to give each officer and member a hypothetical increase of $200 and allow him to allocate this among ten items, including a reduction in the workweek.

The members gave heaviest weight to protective and security items. Pensions, medical and dental insurance, disability insurance, and sick-leave pay received an average allocation of $111. Direct wage increases received $43, an increase in vacations and paid holidays $35, and a shortening of the workweek only $9.

Officers' estimates of members' preferences correlated reasonably well with actual member preferences.[17] But there was a systematic overestimate of members' desire for direct wage increases ($84 versus $43) and for a shorter workweek ($19 versus $9), and a corresponding underestimate of members' desire for most fringe items. Exceptions were pensions and medical care, where officers' and members' preferences coincided almost exactly.

Another operational approach would be to give union members the option of voting on two or more "packages," with a different benefit mix but the same total cost. This could be done in the course of formulating the union's contract demands; or, after negotiations, union and management officials might agree to submit alternative contract proposals rather than a single proposal to the membership for ratification.[18] The results would indicate the "revealed preference" of the members.

---

[17] The correlation coefficient was 0.58 in one plant and 0.85 in the second, both significant at the 1 percent level. For detailed results, see Edward E. Lawler III and Edward Levin, "Union Officers' Perception of Members' Pay Preferences," *Industrial and Labor Relations Review,* July, 1968, pp. 509–17.

[18] One case of this sort, involving the United Automobile Workers and the Ford Motor Company, is reported in B. M. Selekman, S. K. Selekman, and S. H. Fuller, *Problems in Labor Relations,* 2nd ed. (New York: McGraw-Hill Book Company, 1958), pp. 370–80.

Discussion Questions

1. How does a union's wage-setting problem differ from the price-setting problem of a business monopolist?
2. Describe the process by which union leaders typically formulate their wage demands. What are the main considerations that they must take into account?
3. Why will the maximum and minimum feasible wage levels for a company lie closer together in the long run than in the short run?
4. Give several examples of situations in which you would expect that:
    (a) the company's (long run) maximum and minimum wage levels would lie very close together;
    (b) there would be a large gap between the maximum and minimum levels.
5. What would be the main consequences of an effort by a national union to establish uniform schedules of hourly wage rates in all companies in an industry?
6. Company *A* maintains that, unless it is allowed to pay 10 percent less than the average wage level in its industry, it will have to go out of operation. Members of the local union in company *A* are willing to accept the company's position. What would be your position as national union president?
7. "Job evaluation provides a firm scientific basis for determining correct wage rates for each job in the plant, and removes any need for bargaining on this issue." Discuss.
8. The allocation of increases in compensation between direct wage payments and supplementary benefits is an important issue in any company. What are the main things to be considered by (a) management officials, and (b) union officials, in formulating a position on this issue?

Reading Suggestions

For analysis of union wage policies, see Dunlop, John T., *Wage Determination Under Trade Unions.* New York: The Macmillan Company, 1944; Lewis, H. Gregg, ed., *Aspects of Labor Economics.*

Princeton: Princeton University Press, 1962; Phelps Brown, E. H., *The Economics of Labor*. New Haven: Yale University Press, 1962; Rees, Albert, *The Economics of Trade Unions*. Chicago: The University of Chicago Press, 1962; Ross, Arthur M., *Trade Union Wage Policies*. Berkeley and Los Angeles: University of California Press, 1948; Shultz, George P., *Pressures on Wage Decisions*. New York: John Wiley & Sons, Inc., 1951. Company wage policies are discussed in Lester, Richard A., *Company Wage Policies*. Princeton: Princeton University Industrial Relations Section, 1948; Slichter, Sumner H., *Basic Criteria Used in Wage Negotiations*. Chicago: Association of Commerce and Industry, 1947; Slichter, Sumner H., James J. Healy, and E. Robert Livernash, *The Impact of Collective Bargaining on Management*. Washington, D.C.: The Brookings Institution, 1960. Other useful sources on wage determination at the company level include Garbarino, Joseph W., *Wage Policy and Long-term Contracts*. Washington, D.C.: The Brookings Institution, 1962; Stieber, Jack, *The Steel Industry Wage Structure*. Cambridge: Harvard University Press, 1959; Taylor, George W., and Frank C. Pierson, eds., *New Concepts in Wage Determination*. New York: McGraw-Hill Book Company, 1957.

WAGES
IN THE
NATIONAL **23**
ECONOMY

We turn now to the question of how collective bargaining has affected the national wage level and structure. Are there indications of significant effects on interindustry differentials, occupational differentials, and geographical differentials? Is there evidence that union pressure has altered the general level of real wages and labor's share of national income?

INTERINDUSTRY
DIFFERENCES

The commonest question asked by both laymen and scholars is this: does unionization of an industry tend to raise the industry's wage level relative to nonunion industries? Many consider this *the* key question about the wage impact of collective bargaining.

The nature of this effect is illustrated in Figure 1. Consider an economy consisting of two industries, A and B, with identical labor supply and demand curves. (This assumption is not necessary, but

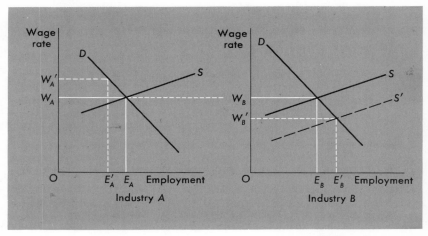

Figure 1

A POSSIBLE WAGE-EMPLOYMENT EFFECT
OF COLLECTIVE BARGAINING

simplifies the exposition.) If we assume a competitive labor market, both industries will pay the same wage, OW.

Industry A now becomes unionized. The union compels employers to pay a higher wage, OW'_A. At this wage, employers find it profitable to hire only OE'_A workers. So some of those previously employed in the industry, shown by the distance $E'_A E_A$, are out of work.

These workers would presumably rather work in industry B than remain unemployed. So labor supply to industry B increases from S to S'. The wage level of industry B falls to OW'_B, while employment rises to OE'_B. This increase just equals the decrease of employment in industry A, and everyone is once more employed.

Note that the allocation of labor between the two industries is no longer optimal. The marginal product of labor in industry B ($= OW'_B$) is substantially below that in industry A ($= OW'_A$). So national output is reduced. This effect is similar to that of monopoly power in product markets.

How is the wage effect of unionism to be measured? At first glance, the answer might seem to be $OW'_A - OW$. This is the wage increase in industry A *relative to the wage rate in that industry before unionization.* But this overlooks the fact that wages in the nonunion sector have at the same time been *reduced.* The significant measure, then, is $OW'_A - OW'_B$, the size of the "wage gap" between the union and nonunion sectors. It is useful to reduce this to a *percentage* of the average wage level for the economy, i.e. to calculate $OW'_A - OW'_B/$

$(OW'_A + OW'_B)$ /2. Alternatively, one could use the nonunion wage level, OW'_B, as the base.

So far we have been discussing *possibilities*. But what about actualities? Is there evidence that unions in the United States have raised the relative wage level of their respective industries? There have by now been about two dozen research studies aimed primarily at this issue.[1] They are of two kinds:

1. *Cross-section Studies at a Point in Time.* Take an industry such as hotels and restaurants, barber shops, or men's clothing manufacture, in which the degree of unionization in different areas ranges from zero to one hundred percent. Suppose one has data for 1970 on percentage of unionization and on average hourly earnings, area by area. One can then examine whether there is a systematic relation between unionization and earnings. It is of course necessary to control for other variables that have an influence on earnings, such as labor force characteristics (age, sex, color, education), region of the country, and size of community.

A variant of this method is to use some other group of workers as a reference group. In one study of construction wages, for example, the wage rate for carpenters in each area was divided by the average wage of common laborers in the area (excluding laborers employed in the construction industry). The problem then becomes: is the carpenters' premium over the common laborer, area by area, related systematically to the degree of unionization among carpenters?

2. *Studies of Change over Time.* Suppose we have data on average hourly earnings and percentage of unionization in fifty industries, year-by-year over the period 1950 to 1970. We then examine whether industries with a higher degree of unionization have had a more rapid rate of wage increase. Again, it is necessary to control for changes in other variables that may have influenced an industry's wage level, notably labor force quality, geographic location, profit level, and rate of increase in employment.

Alternatively, one can examine a single industry, using one or more other industries as a reference point. A study of bituminous coal mining, for example, used the average wage level in all manufacturing industries as its base. The question then was whether the ratio of coal mining wages to manufacturing wages was related systematically to changes in coal mine unionization.

Both types of studies face serious difficulties. First, as we emphasized in Chapter 9, there are many economic reasons for wage differences, and for changes in wage relations over time. An industry's relative wage level may change because of changes in the skill-mix of the labor force, shifts in geographic location, changes in the ratio of men and

[1] For a review of such studies, a reestimation of some of their findings, and an effort to draw general conclusions, see H. Gregg Lewis, *Unionism and Relative Wages in the United States* (Chicago: The University of Chicago Press, 1963).

women workers or of white and nonwhite workers, and a variety of other factors. Careful studies try to measure and adjust for all such influences, so as to isolate the independent effect of unionism. But this can never be done with perfect precision.

Further, it is usually assumed for statistical convenience that union power is a linear function of percentage of workers organized. A union with 100 percent coverage of its industry is assumed to have twice as much wage influence as one with 50 percent coverage, and four times as much as one with only 25 percent membership. But the actual relation is probably more complex. A union with 25 percent coverage may have zero influence on wages, because the nonunion firms have a dominant effect on price and wage levels in the industry. At some point in its expansion, however, the union "gets over the hump" and itself becomes the dominant force in the industry, with the remaining nonunion firms as the tail on the dog. Suppose this occurs at around 60 percent unionization. Then over the range of 0 to 50 percent the increase in wage influence will be less than proportionate to the increase in unionization, over the range of (say) 50 to 70 percent it will be much more than proportionate, and from 70 to 100 percent it may again be less than proportionate. Testing such a complex hypothesis is more difficult than testing a supposed linear relation and has rarely been attempted.

Recognizing these limitations, it is still interesting to look at the general drift of the statistical studies. As analyzed and summarized by Lewis, they suggest three conclusions:

1. Looking broadly at the economy, the "wage gap" created by union pressure seems normally to be of the order of 10 to 15 percent. Lewis' summary of past studies concludes: "These figures imply that recently the average wage of union workers was about 7 to 11 percent higher relative to the average wage of all workers . . . than it would have been in the absence of unionism. Similarly, the average wage of all nonunion workers was about 3 to 4 percent lower relative to the average wage of all workers than in the absence of unionism." [2]

It should be noted, however, that other economists have arrived at different estimates. Weiss concludes that "unions that organize their entire jurisdictions seemed to raise earnings by 7 to 8 percent for craftsmen and 6 to 8 percent for operatives, compared with poorly organized industries." [3] Throop estimates that the average union–nonunion differential was 22.3 percent in 1950 and 26.0 percent in 1960, but concedes that there is probably an upward bias in his results.[4] Reder, in a careful review of the Lewis volume, finds the basic data so faulty

[2] *Unionism and Relative Wages*, p. 5.

[3] Leonard W. Weiss, "Concentration and labor earnings," *American Economic Review*, March, 1966, pp. 96–117.

[4] Adrian W. Throop, "The union–nonunion wage differential and cost-push inflation," *American Economic Review*, March, 1968, pp. 79–99.

that "one cannot reject the null hypothesis that the relative wage effect of unionism has been zero for most of the period since 1920." [5] Despite these differences of judgment, there is more consensus today than there would have been twenty years ago that unionism has a significant, though moderate, effect on interindustry differentials.

2. The average effect of unionism has varied considerably in the course of time, and particularly as between periods of inflation and deflation. Union influence is felt most strongly in depressions, when unions maintain wages or even keep them moving upward, while nonunion wages stagnate or decline. Lewis estimates that at the bottom of the Great Depression in 1932 to 1933, the relative wage effect of unionism may have been above 25 percent. During an inflationary period, such as from 1940 to 1948 or from 1965 to 1969, on the other hand, nonunion wages are pulled up rapidly by rising labor demand, while the fact that union wages are set by contract for a fixed period may actually retard their advance. Lewis estimates that in the late forties the relative wage effect of unionism fell below 5 percent. In some unionized industries, including basic steel, there were sizable labor shortages at this time. This demand–supply gap suggests that the union contract rate was below the rate that would have prevailed in a competitive market.

3. Some unions have had more success in raising wages than others; and the same union has had differing degrees of success at different times.[6] Bituminous coal miners seem rather consistently to have earned 35 to 50 percent more than they would have in the absence of unionism. Commercial airline pilots and East Coast merchant seamen seem to have gained 35 percent or thereabouts. The relative gain of skilled construction workers has been estimated at around 25 percent. While there have not been comparable studies of the teamsters or the railroad operating crafts, their relative wage gain has probably been substantial. On the other hand, groups for which unionism seems to have produced wage gains of less than 10 percent include building construction laborers, employees of year-round hotels, and production workers in a wide range of manufacturing industries including cotton textiles, footwear, furniture, hosiery, women's dresses and (in recent years) men's clothing.

The same union has done better in some periods than in others. Thus in 1921 and 1922 bituminous coal miners are estimated to have earned more than twice what they would have earned without the union. Their wage advantage then declined as union strength declined, but recovered during the thirties; by the late fifties it was esti-

---

[5] Melvin W. Reder, "Unions and wages: the problem of measurement," *Journal of Political Economy,* April, 1965, pp. 188–96.

[6] See the summary table in Lewis, *Unionism and Relative Wages,* pp. 184–86.

mated at 48–58 percent. Less happy is the experience of the men's clothing industry, where the union is estimated to have secured a wage advantage of 20 to 30 percent for its members during the 1920s. This advantage has now almost completely disappeared, partly because of the difficulty of maintaining union organization throughout this small-scale and highly migratory industry.

These research findings suggest two questions. First, why has the overall impact of unionism apparently been rather moderate? Considering that elasticity of demand for labor varies widely among industries, and that some industries are much more expansive and profitable than others, one might have expected the most favorably situated unions to run away with their industry wage level, leaving the others far behind. Why has this apparently not happened?

The answer is not entirely clear, but several possible reasons may be suggested. One reason may be that many union officials function as "lazy monopolists" rather than aggressive monopolists. The politics of unionism compels them to keep up with the wage procession, but not necessarily to forge much ahead of it. They would prefer to keep out of trouble both with employers and with their members, and this dictates a certain conservatism in wage demands.

Further, even in an organized economy ideas of equity and reasonable wage relationships retain considerable force. If wages for a particular group, instead of being 20 percent above the competitive level, came to be 50 or 75 percent above it, other groups of workers might be resentful. Employers would feel on strong ground in resisting such demands and would have public support in doing so.

Finally, during periods of high employment the labor market limits the wage differences that can exist among industries for similar types of work. If certain industries fall too far below the level of the highest-wage industries, they will no longer be able to recruit and hold an adequate labor force. When this limit has been reached, the unions in the high-wage industries, while they may continue to push up their absolute wage rates, will no longer be able to improve their relative positions. Instead, they will simply pull up the wage levels of the low-wage industries at the same rate at which their own wages are rising. It is as though one had two men tied together by a rope in which there is at the moment a certain amount of slack. If one of the men decides that he wants to go in a certain direction, he can walk forward until the rope is pulled taut. After that he can go no farther unless the man on the other end of the rope moves in the same direction at the same rate.

Because of these various checks, the tendency toward wage distortion under collective bargaining may not be so serious as some have feared.

A second question arises from the observation that some unions have raised the relative wages of their members considerably more than others. What explains these differences in union success?

The economic environment is clearly important. An industry in which productivity is rising sharply, product demand curves are moving rapidly to the right, and profits are high and rising presents a favorable situation for outsize wage increases. Since profit margins are tending to widen, employers can concede large increases without cutting into profit, and this may weaken their resistance to union demands. Moreover, the tendency of wage increases to reduce employment, which might normally give the union pause, is cushioned by the rapid rightward shift of the labor demand curve.

One cannot say, however, that a favorable economic climate is *essential* to wage gains. Witness the large gains won since 1945 by the maritime unions and the bituminous coal miners, despite severe competitive pressure, low profits, and a rapid decline of employment in these industries.

A familiar hypothesis is that industrial concentration is favorable to a high wage level. A monopolistic or oligopolistic product market, a high degree of unionization, and a relatively high wage level tend to go together. But this does not reveal the chain of causation. Two separate issues are involved. First, is industrial concentration favorable to a high degree of unionization? Second, given the same degree of unionization, is a competitive or monopolistic market structure more conducive to union wage gains? [7]

The answer to the first question seems to be positive. Segal has argued that large-scale, highly concentrated industries (basic steel, automobiles, aluminum, heavy electrical equipment, aircraft manufacture, and so on) are especially susceptible to organization for several reasons. There are economies of scale in an organizing campaign. Where establishments are large, organizing costs *per capita* will be low. Workers in large establishments are likely also to be more alienated from management and hence more union prone. These industries are much in the public eye, and thus vulnerable to criticism if they engage in overt antiunion activity. Having a heavy investment in fixed plant, they cannot run away to escape the union. Barriers to entrance are high, so that once the union is ensconced in the industry it is relatively safe from new, nonunion competitors.

In relatively small-scale industries with numerous firms (textiles,

---

[7] There is a large literature in this area. Recent contributions include Harold M. Levinson, "Unionism, Concentration, and Wage Changes: Toward a Unified Theory," *Industrial and Labor Relations Review*, January, 1967, pp. 198–205; Martin Segal, "The Relation Between Union Wage Impact and Market Structure," *Quarterly Journal of Economics*, February, 1964, pp. 96–114; and Leonard Weiss, "Concentration and Labor Earnings," *American Economic Review*, March, 1966, pp. 96–117.

clothing, leather goods, furniture, and so on), the opposite conditions prevail. The multiplicity of small producers presents organizing difficulties. There is greater turnover of firms and, since all new firms are nonunion at the outset, the task of organization is never finished. Firms with little fixed plant are freer to move about the country in search of low-wage, nonunion locations. Even if the nonunion sector constitutes only a minority of employees, it imposes a critical limit on wage and price levels.

Why, then, does one sometimes find a high degree of unionization even in industries with a multiplicity of employers, such as longshoring, merchant shipping, and over-the-road trucking? Levinson has suggested that the basic factor is not industrial concentration per se, but rather "the ease of entry of new firms into production outside the jurisdictional control of the union." In oligopolistic manufacturing industries, the barriers to entrance take the form of large optimum scale of plant, heavy selling costs, patent protection of products or processes, and so on. But in other cases the barrier may lie in "the spatial limitations of the physical area within which new entrants could effectively compete." [8] Shipping and longshoring firms must have access to the docks. Long-distance trucking concerns must use certain terminals to make local deliveries and interchange freight with other lines. So once the union has effective control of these locations, the operation of nonunion firms can be prevented. By similar reasoning, Segal suggests that a union is in a stronger position in a competitive local-market industry than in a competitive national-market industry. Organizing is less costly when all potential recruits are in the same area, and geographic movement of firms to escape the union is no longer a possibility.

The second question remains: given the same degree of unionization in two industries, is there any independent relation between wage level and structure of the product market? A priori, one can argue this issue either way. In a concentrated industry, the fact that the price level is controlled by tacit agreement may reduce downward pressure on wages during recession and may enable wage increases to be translated more smoothly into price increases during expansion. This should be favorable to union wage gains. But on the other side one can argue that the managerial expertise and financial staying power of large oligopolistic concerns puts them in a better position to resist union demands. Where the industry includes scores or hundreds of relatively small firms, no one company or group may be able to stand up effectively against the union.

There is difference of opinion also on the statistical evidence. Re-

---

[8] Harold M. Levinson, *Determining Forces in Collective Wage Bargaining* (New York: John Wiley & Sons, Inc., 1966), pp. 265–66.

cent research findings suggest that when degree of unionization, labor force characteristics, and other relevant variables are held constant, the "pure" relation between concentration and wage level is either insignificant or slightly negative. The significant relation, in other words, is between concentration and ease of union penetration. But a 100-percent union is *not* likely to achieve greater wage gains under monopoly or oligopoly than under competition. A further complication is that increasing concentration is accompanied by increasing average size of plant, while large plants tend to pay higher wages than smaller ones. The wage effects sometimes attributed to concentration, therefore, may in fact be due to the plant-size variable.[9]

Proceeding from economic to other considerations, it has been suggested that strong interunion or intraunion political rivalry may accelerate the rate of wage increase. Interunion rivalry (between the Atlantic and Pacific coasts, and among rival unions on each coast) has probably contributed to the rapid increase of longshoring and maritime wages since 1945 despite adverse employment and profit trends. In the West Coast lumber industry, intense rivalry between AFL and CIO unions seems to have produced outsize wage increases in the immediate postwar period. There seems also to have been a spill-over effect from lumber to the paper unions on the West Coast, whose wage level rose faster than might have been expected on other grounds. In trucking, Hoffa's campaign to achieve national control of the Teamsters' Union almost certainly accelerated the rise of wages in previously low-wage sectors of the industry.

From his study of six Pacific Coast industries, however, Levinson concludes that the operation of political variables is not independent of other environmental factors: ". . . while the presence of strong political pressures provided, in several instances, a greater *motivation* to the unions . . . the ability of any union to translate these motivations into effective action depended upon the 'permissiveness' of the basic economic or pure power environment within which the union was functioning. Where the underlying economic or power environment was unfavorable, as in airframe from 1945 to 1949 and from 1953 to 1962, or in lumber and paper after 1952, the mere presence of political rivalry was not sufficient to generate any strong relative upward movement of benefits . . . But in those situations where *both* factors were operative—where political pressures were strong and the basic economic and/or power factors favorable—the rate of increase in benefits was exceptionally high, as in maritime, in lumber and paper from 1945 to 1949, and in trucking after 1952. Thus . . . political

[9] See in this connection Stanley H. Masters, "Wages and Plant Size: An Interindustry Analysis," *Review of Economics and Statistics,* August, 1969, pp. 341–45.

variables . . . represented an ancillary rather than a primary source of wage advantage." [10]

OCCUPATIONAL
DIFFERENCES

We concluded in the last section that unionism may have raised the average earnings of union members, relative to nonunion workers, by 10 to 15 percent. Union membership consists predominantly of blue-collar workers in manufacturing, mining, transportation and public utilities, and construction. It would seem to follow that unionism has raised earnings of unionized blue-collar workers relative to those of clerical, professional, and managerial workers. But since the rising level of education and other factors discussed in Chapter 9 has been working in the same direction, the *independent* influence of unionism is not easy to judge.

One must remember also that the bulk of the least-skilled and lowest-paid workers are nonunion: farmers and farm laborers, domestic servants, store clerks, hotel and restaurant employees, laundry workers, and other low-skilled workers throughout the service sector. The wages of these people are presumably *lower* relative to those of the unionized groups than they would be in the absence of unionism. Overall, then, it is not clear whether unionism has increased or decreased occupational differences in wages.

A more limited question concerns the effect of unionism on occupational differentials *within* the unionized sector. What might one expect to have happened? Is there satisfactory evidence as to what actually has happened?

Two preliminary comments are in order. First, how do we measure occupational differentials? Should the premium of one group over another be measured in *cents-per-hour,* or in terms of *percentage* relations? Suppose that in 1950 laborers in industry *A* earned $1.00 an hour and skilled men $1.50. In 1970 we observe that laborers in this same industry earn $2.00 an hour and skilled men $3.00. Do we say that the differential of the skilled men has *widened* from fifty cents an hour to $1.00 an hour? Or do we say that it has *remained unchanged* at 50 percent in both years? The second statement seems more nearly correct. The worker is concerned mainly with how well he can live on his earnings relative to other groups in the community. In this illustration, the skilled man in 1970 can live 50 percent better than the laborer, just as he could in 1950.

[10] *Determining Forces,* pp. 270–71.

The behavior of occupational differentials over time depends on how general wage increases are made in a company. If all workers receive a 5 percent increase, then occupational differentials (measured, as they should be, in percentage terms) will remain unchanged. But if all workers receive an increase of ten cents per hour, this will be a larger *percentage* increase for the laborer than for the craftsman. Occupational differentials will narrow. Thus the issue of whether differentials should be narrowed or maintained often takes the form of an argument over how general wage increases should be applied.

Our second preliminary comment is that collective bargaining is not the only determinant of occupational differentials. We saw in Chapter 9 that market forces have been tending to reduce the percentage premium for high-skilled jobs over low-skilled ones. So if we find that differentials have narrowed in an industry where rates are set by collective bargaining, we cannot conclude that union pressure was responsible. It is difficult to distinguish the impact of unionism from that of other factors in the situation.

Where skilled, semiskilled, and unskilled workers are employed in the same enterprise, one can assume that demand for the skilled men will be more inelastic. Their wages form a small proportion of total cost; it is less easy to replace skilled men with semiskilled men than vice versa; and skilled men are also less easily replaced by machinery.

One might expect this economic fact to be reflected in bargained wage structures; but the outcome will depend also on the form of organization. For example:

1. If the skilled men organize in one or more craft unions, while the others are unorganized, one might expect the skilled men to exploit their demand curves and to widen their differential over the other groups. To test this hypothesis, however, one would have to go back to the period before 1930, when craft unionism was dominant and most low-skilled workers were unorganized.

2. A common situation is that in which the skilled men have one or more craft unions, which bargain separately from another union of the lower-skilled workers. Thus in building construction the carpenters, bricklayers, and so on, are organized separately from the laborers and hod carriers. In the railroad industry, the train-operating crafts are organized separately from the shop crafts and the maintenance-of-way workers. In paper manufacturing, the skilled machine tenders usually belong to the Papermakers' Union, the maintenance men to craft unions of their respective trades, and everyone else to an industrial union, the Pulp, Sulphite, and Paper-Mill Workers.

In this case, too, one might reason that the skilled groups will exploit their demand curves and raise differentials to some equilibrium level beyond which, barring major changes in technology or labor supply, differentials would remain stable. But maximizing models may not yield correct predictions. One can find cases, such as the printing industry, where the premium of compositors over bindery workers and other low-skilled groups has been well maintained. But there seem to be more cases, including building construction, railroading, and paper, where differentials have fallen substantially over the past several decades despite the prevalence of craft organization.

One can argue, of course, that this reflects simply the *general* tendency toward narrowing of occupational differentials throughout the economy. But in some cases it has been furthered by union policy. The skilled Papermakers, who normally bargain jointly with the Pulp, Sulphite, and Paper Mill Workers, have collaborated with the latter group to raise the common labor rate rapidly, even though this meant a narrowing of occupational differentials. They seem to have reasoned that the labor rate is a protective floor underneath their higher rate structure, and that raising this floor improves their own long-run position.

3. Perhaps the most interesting case, and the one most frequently studied, is that of the industrial union including all levels of worker from laborer to craftsman. If the union behaved as a monopolist—trying, for example, to maximize the wage bill—it might still exploit the demand situation by establishing a relatively higher wage for the skilled men than would exist under nonunion conditions. It is a familiar principle that a monopolist selling in two or more distinct markets will maximize profit by charging the highest price in the market whose demand is least elastic.

On the other hand, the union is a political body, whose leaders must be responsive to membership sentiment. Since the bulk of the members are low-skilled, they might be expected to press for policies which would bring them closer (percentagewise) to the skilled wage level. On the basis of this "democratic" reasoning, it has often been assumed that industrial unionism makes inevitably for a narrowing of occupational differentials.

But this view is also rather simplistic. The skilled men will certainly feel that their "traditional" differential over the less skilled is right, proper, and should be perpetuated; and since custom has considerable weight in workers' thinking about wages, many of the less skilled will accept this reasoning. The skilled men also, because of their standing in the plant hierarchy and their personal qualities, will usually carry more than proportionate weight in union discussions and furnish more than their share of the union leadership. Finally, the skilled men can exert leverage by threatening to form their own union and bargain separately if their views are not given sufficient weight.

So while speculative reasoning might lead one to expect a narrowing of differentials under industrial unionism, in fact the pressure in this direction has not been strong. In the basic steel industry, for example, some narrowing did occur during the 1940s (as happened in virtually every industry during this period). During a period of rapid price inflation, which put particular pressure on the living standards of low-paid workers, equal cents-per-hour increases for all seemed equitable. This was also the formula favored by the National War Labor Board, whose rulings had extensive influence on the wage structure from 1941 to 1946. Since the late forties, however, percentage differentials in the industry have been fairly stable. General wage increases have taken the form of roughly equal *percentage* additions throughout the wage structure.

One of the most thorough investigations of union impact on an industry's wage structure is Robert Macdonald's study of the automobile industry.[11] In its early years the United Automobile Workers attached great importance to raising the bottom of the wage structure and insisted on equal cents-per-hour raises for all workers. The effect was to reduce the *percentage* differential between various grades of labor.

By the mid-fifties this trend had produced considerable restiveness among the skilled toolroom and maintenance workers, who constitute about one-quarter of automobile employment. They argued that they should receive larger cents-per-hour increases to restore their relative wage position, and some craft groups threatened to withdraw and bargain separately if their demands were not met. During the 1950s thirty-eight craft severance petitions involving the United Automobile Workers were filed with the National Labor Relations Board, one of which covered eighty-three General Motors' plants in the industry.

This pressure led to several shifts in union policy: (1) In 1955 a new wage-increase formula was adopted that combined the cents-per-hour and percentage principles as follows: "each employee . . . shall receive an . . . increase of $2\frac{1}{2}$ percent of his straight-time hourly wage rate . . . or 6 cents per hour, whichever is the greater." The number in this formula are larger today, but the principle is the same. For men toward the top of the wage structure, the percentage option will yield the larger result, so this will be applied and will yield larger cents-per-hour increases than those received by the less skilled workers. (2) Several special cents-per-hour increases were negotiated for the skilled workers, which did not apply to other groups. (3) Special representation procedures, described in Chapter 15, were established that gave craft representatives a direct voice in wage negotiations and an opportunity to vote separately on issues involving the crafts only.

The outcome in terms of relative occupational earnings is indicated by Table 1. The relative earnings position of the skilled men

[11] Robert M. Macdonald, *Collective Bargaining in the Automobile Industry* (New Haven: Yale University Press, 1963).

Table 1

AVERAGE HOURLY EARNINGS,
SELECTED OCCUPATIONS, AUTOMOBILE INDUSTRY,
1934–57
(material handler = 100)

	1934	*1940*	*1950*	*1957*
JANITOR, SWEEPER	—	91	93	95
LABORER, MATERIAL HANDLER	100	100	100	100
ASSEMBLER, MOTOR AND TRANSMISSION	122	111	108	105
MACHINE OPERATOR, II	123	113	109	106
SPRAYER, PAINT	128	119	113	110
ELECTRICIAN	—	121	125	129
TOOL- AND DIEMAKER	147	140	133	136
PATTERNMAKER, WOOD AND METAL	—	144	142	157

SOURCE: Macdonald, *Collective Bargaining in the Automobile Industry*, p. 138.

declined from 1934 to 1950, but this tendency was checked and reversed during the 1950s. The most striking development, however, was the decline of the assemblers and other semiskilled operatives relative to *both* the unskilled and the craftsmen. The custom of flat cents-per-hour increases in the lower ranges of the wage structure had by the late fifties brought laborers' rates very close to the semiskilled level.

A study by Sherwin Rosen [12] suggests that this may have happened in other industries as well. Using cross-section data for 1960, he analyzed union–nonunion differentials for major occupational groups. He concluded that the relative wage effect of unionism was largest for laborers, probably somewhat less for craftsmen, and decidedly less for semiskilled operatives. Put differently, unionism may have narrowed the laborer–craftsman differential slightly. The really significant effect, however, was a reduction in the position of the semiskilled relative to both the other groups. This conclusion was tested for several industries by using the regression equations to predict earnings in the industry and then comparing with actual earnings. Good results were obtained for automobiles, steel, farm machinery, rubber, clothing, electrical equipment, and textiles, indicating that these industries conform well to the model described above.

To sum up: a decline in the earnings of skilled and semiskilled workers relative to laborers has been a general tendency in the United States and other industrial countries over the past half century. Unionism may have accentuated this tendency. But the impact of union policy is not very striking—certainly less than would be de-

[12] Sherwin Rosen, "Unionism and the Occupational Wage Structure," *International Economic Review* (forthcoming).

duced from an economic model in which each skill-group maximizes its own wage bill. The impact has also varied considerably from industry to industry.

GEOGRAPHIC
DIFFERENCES

We saw in Chapter 9 that wage levels in the South are considerably lower, and those on the Pacific Coast somewhat higher, than in the North-Central states. There are also considerable differences among communities of varying size within each region.

Union efforts to apply "the standard rate" should have tended to reduce geographic differentials; but this depends on the market structure of the industry and the scope of the collective agreement. Where competition is limited to a locality, as in house building and repair, retailing, and the service industries, and where bargaining is conducted locally with little supervision by the national union, there is no reason to expect wage equalization among localities. On the contrary, it may well be that unionism, by entrenching itself first in the high-wage regions and communities, has for the time being widened differentials in such industries. This may be one reason why building-construction wages in the South today are further below the northern level than they were forty years ago.

In manufacturing industries selling in a national market, on the other hand, geographic differentials have usually been reduced and in some cases virtually eliminated. In addition to the economic pressures for wage equalization, there is usually political pressure from union members. Bargaining is typically on a national basis, and delegates from all parts of the country serve on the wage-policy committee. Delegates from lower-wage areas are bound to feel that their members should receive as much as workers in the highest-wage plants of the industry; and national union leaders are under pressure to effect a gradual leveling-up of area differences.

Employers, on the other hand, tend to feel that wages in a particular plant should be in line with the *community* wage level. If a company has been lucky or astute enough to locate in a low-wage area, it should be entitled to reap the benefit.[13] So where geographic leveling has occurred under collective bargaining, it must be attributed to union pressure overriding employer resistance.

[13] This is true, at any rate, in heavily capitalized and hard-to-enter oligopolistic industries, where wage differences do not threaten the price level. It is not necessarily true of more footloose and competitive industries such as textiles and clothing. Northern employers in such industries often urge the union to make a maximum effort toward raising southern wage levels.

Where differentials have been eliminated, as in basic steel and flat glass, there has typically been a combination of favorable circumstances: a high degree of unionization, a high degree of industrial concentration, and a situation in which the southern plants were subsidiaries of northern companies. It is easier in such a situation for the union to force acceptance of wage equalization, and for the industry to adjust to it, than in an industry with many small, independent producers.

The case of basic steel is interesting because of the size and diversity of the industry. When the union entered the industry in the late thirties, it found a chaotic wage structure resulting from a long historical development. Different plants of the same company operated at decidedly different wage levels. The relative ranking of specific jobs varied substantially from plant to plant. Geographic differentials were large. A 1938 Bureau of Labor Statistics' survey found that average hourly earnings in the Pittsburgh–Youngstown area were 17 percent higher than the southern average for skilled jobs, 31 percent higher for semiskilled jobs, and 47 percent higher for unskilled jobs. Mills on the Atlantic Coast were about 10 percent below the Pittsburgh level, while those on the Pacific Coast were 10 percent above it.

These large interplant differences, combined with the absence of a clear rationale for job rates within each plant, caused political unrest within the union and accumulation of a large number of unsettled grievances. By the early forties, the companies themselves found these grievances a considerable nuisance and were ready to consider a program of wage rationalization. The impetus toward rationalization was strengthened by a 1944 order of the National War Labor Board, which denied any general wage increase in the industry, but permitted the parties to use up to five cents per hour per employee for correction of wage inequities. A joint committee of the union and the major steel companies was established to conduct the first thorough analysis and ranking of jobs in the industry's history. The outcome was a 1947 agreement establishing a system of thirty-two "labor grades," with a uniform classification of jobs into these grades. A fixed cents-per-hour differential was established between grades, so that once a plant's common labor rate was determined the appropriate rate for any higher job could be read off from the scale.

The agreement did not in the first instance equalize common labor rates—and hence overall wage levels—among plants and areas, to which the employers were strongly opposed. They wanted wage rationalization *within* each plant, while at the same time preserving traditional geographic differences *among* plants. But the new standard job-classification obviously provided a powerful instrument for wage equalization. In the previous chaos of individual job rates, "equalization" could not even be defined. Now, if the common labor rates in all plants

654   *Wages in the National Economy*

could be brought into line, equalization above that level would be compelled by the standard scale. The union naturally hammered away at this objective, which was substantially achieved in 1954 when the "Birmingham differential" favoring the southern mills was finally eliminated.[14]

The course of events in the automobile industry is documented by Macdonald.[15] Here the union soon succeeded in substantially eliminating geographic differentials among Ford and Chrysler plants. General Motors, however, remained devoted to the community-wage principle, and put up a stubborn and largely successful resistance. By 1960 the union had still made only limited progress toward reducing interarea differences among General Motors' plants. The overall average wage level of the three major companies, however, was very nearly the same. In some of the smaller companies, notably Nash and Willys, a combination of aggressive local union leadership and management laxity on incentive standards, had produced average hourly earnings considerably *above* the major company level. Relatively high labor costs, together with the ferocious competition in the product market, helps to explain the elimination of Studebaker and other smaller "independents" from the industry, and the merger of others into the American Motor Company.

The difficulty of generalizing even about manufacturing is illustrated by the different experience of the pulp and paper industry. This is only in a limited sense a "national market" industry. There is a wide variety of paper products, differing in production location and market characteristics. The Pacific Coast mills are largely insulated from eastern markets by transportation costs. The Pacific Coast and southern mills have substantially lower production costs for most products (and hence higher wage-paying ability) than mills in the Northeast and Midwest. This is partly because the mills are newer, with larger and faster machines, and a higher capital–labor ratio; and partly because wood costs are considerably lower in the South and Pacific Coast regions.

In this context the unions seem to have followed a policy of exploiting each region's wage-paying ability independently. The southern mills, which in the 1930s had wages about 15 percent below those in the Northeast, have now been brought up to well *above* the northern level. (An ancillary factor here has been the rapid expansion of employment, which necessitated migration of skilled papermakers from North to South, which in turn required some wage inducement.) The Pacific Coast mills, which were already 10 percent above the Northeast in the thirties, have been brought up to 25 percent above. In short,

14 For a detailed examination of the union impact in steel, railroad transport, pulp and paper, and cotton textiles, see Lloyd G. Reynolds and Cynthia H. Taft, *The Evolution of Wage Structure* (New Haven: Yale University Press, 1956).
15 Macdonald, *Collective Bargaining in the Automobile Industry*.

wages in the two low-cost and expanding regions have been raised substantially relative to those in the high-cost, static northern region.

Within each major region there has been an effort to bring all union mills to a common wage level. In the South and the Pacific Coast region, virtually full equalization has been accomplished. In the Northeast and Midwest, however, there is still considerable variation, reflecting the cost and profit position of individual mills. The old and conservative paper unions have been reluctant to force closing down of mills, many of which are in isolated areas with few alternative employment opportunities. High-cost companies have usually been allowed to stay in business at a below-average wage level.

In some industries the union has not been able to control geographic differentials because of unevenness in its own strength from region to region. In cotton textiles, for example, the North–South differential is considerably smaller today than in the 1920s and 1930s. But this must be attributed mainly to economic forces—the great expansion of the industry in the South and the shrinkage of textile employment in New England, and the movement of new high-wage industries into the South, forcing textile producers to compete more actively for labor. The successive minimum wage increases under the Fair Labor Standards Act have probably raised common labor rates in the southern mills faster than they would have risen otherwise, exerting some pressure also on rates above the minimum. Union influence has been exerted mainly through legislative pressure rather than through collective bargaining. The industry wage level is dominated by the large, nonunion southern producers. The minority of union mills, located mainly in the North, cannot be made to pay much above this level without being forced out of operation.

The "textile model" can be generalized to hosiery, clothing, furniture, leather goods—indeed, to most of light manufacturing industry. We saw in Chapter 12 that unions have been relatively unsuccessful in organizing these industries in the South. Their influence on geographic differentials is thus necessarily small.

Finally, we may note the interesting case of the trucking industry. This is not a "national" industry in the true sense. Some over-the-road truckers, to be sure, operate routes across the country. But most confine their operations to a particular state or region, while local truckers operate within a single city. From the product-marketside, then, there is no reason for interregional wage equalization. The pressure came rather from within the union, and was associated particularly with Hoffa's drive for national leadership of the Teamsters and a single nationwide trucking contract.

Hoffa developed his initial power base in the Midwest, where by 1950 his Central States' District Council had established uniform (and favorable) contract terms over a large area. From here he moved during the 1950s on to the southern states, bringing outsize wage increases in his wake. Between 1950 and 1957, average hourly earnings of truck drivers in the South rose by 91 percent, compared with 62 percent in the Central States' District Council region. In absolute terms, the South was above the Central States' District Council from 1957 onwards. Finally, in the early sixties, Hoffa intervened in key-bargaining situations on the Atlantic and Pacific Coasts, winning membership backing and dethroning local leaders on the promise that he could do in their area what he had already done elsewhere. Outsize increases were used as a "demonstration effect" to consolidate his national leadership. Between 1959 and 1961, while teamsters' earnings rose twenty cents an hour in the older Central States' District Council area, they rose thirty-six cents on the West Coast, thirty-four cents in the mid-Atlantic area, and twenty-eight cents in New England. The ripples left by Hoffa's passage show up clearly in the wage statistics.

When the dust had settled, it turned out that city-wide rates for local truck drivers had been brought much closer together. In 1949, average hourly earnings varied from $1.04 in Atlanta to $1.75 in New York—a range of about 70 percent. By 1964 this range had been reduced to about 10 percent, from a low of $3.02 (Atlanta, Knoxville, Minneapolis) to a high of $3.34 in San Francisco. Wage scales in several of the southern cities tripled over this period, a result that can scarcely be attributed to market forces.

For over-the-road truck drivers, a uniform *basis of payment* was established throughout the country. Previous wage systems had varied from area to area, embracing a bewildering variety of hourly rates, mileage rates, and trip rates (a flat amount for a specified intercity run). Hoffa's preference was for a simple mileage rate, accompanied by a minimum hourly guarantee to protect the driver on slow and congested routes, and this system has now been generally established. A uniform wage system, of course, is almost essential for effective wage equalization. The *level* of mileage rates and hourly guarantees has been brought much closer together. The California and Central States' District Council levels are identical, though some areas in the East retain higher mileage rates to offset slower driving conditions. Because of variations in driving conditions, not fully offset in the wage scale, actual earnings of drivers in different regions have not been fully equalized. Earnings on the West Coast, where roads are seldom blocked by snow or ice, continue somewhat above those in the Midwest despite rate equality. Earnings in the New England and the Middle Atlantic region are slightly below the national average, presumably because of poorer road facilities and greater urban congestion.[16]

[16] For a more detailed account of wage developments over the period 1950 to 1965, see Ralph and Estelle James, *Hoffa and the Teamsters* (Princeton: D. Van Nostrand and Company, 1965), particularly chap. 22.

These differing experiences cannot be summarized in any simple formula. Most unions in the majority of industries have probably had little effect on geographical differentials, either because of the local-market character of the industry, or because of union weakness in one or more regions, or because the union (as in the paper case) has not found it expedient to aim at geographic equality. On the other hand in truck driving, coal mining, basic steel, automobiles, and some other branches of heavy manufacturing, geographic differentials have been reduced and in some cases eliminated.

Where differentials have been reduced, this might be expected to exert some influence on the location of industry. The fact that some communities have lower wage levels than others is an inducement for new plants to locate in those communities. Specifically, there is an inducement for new plants to spring up in small towns rather than in large cities, and in the southern states rather than in the North. Wage leveling reduces this inducement. If the union insists on the same wage level in all parts of the country, and if labor quality is substantially the same, there is no longer any reason for employers to prefer one locality on *grounds of labor cost,* though there may still be tax, marketing, or other advantages. The effect is to discourage movement of industry from North to South and from large cities to small towns. Or, to put the point in reverse, the effect is to increase congestion in established manufacturing centers.

This point may be less important in practice, however, than it appears in principle. It applies most strongly to small-scale, labor-intensive, footloose industries, in which labor costs are a large part of total costs. The "runaway garment shop" is the classic example. But these are precisely the industries in which unionism has had greatest difficulty in penetrating the low-wage areas. So where unionism might conceivably have had significant locational effects, it has in fact had relatively little influence. At the other pole, it seems unlikely that national wage uniformity wil have much effect on the location of steel mills, oil refineries, auto assembly plants, and so on.

THE GENERAL LEVEL
OF
REAL WAGES

We have found reason to believe that unionism usually raises the wages of union members, relative to what these members would have received under nonunion conditions. But are these gains canceled out by the losses of nonunion workers, whose numbers are increased and whose relative wages are lowered? Is there any reason to think that unionism raises the *average* level of real wages in the economy? Or that it increases the labor share of national income?

Let us begin with the neoclassical world of Chapter 8, in which all product and factor markets are fully competitive, and in which a factor's marginal product governs its rate of return. In this world the real wage rate depends on the size of the labor force and the height of labor's marginal productivity schedule, and unionism could influence the wage level only via one or both of these routes.

The height of labor's marginal productivity schedule is itself a complicated matter, depending on such things as: (1) the quantity of buildings, machinery, and other capital goods available, which depends on the percentage of national income saved and invested in previous years; (2) the rate of technical progress in developing new or improved products or lower-cost production methods, which depends partly on the resources devoted to scientific research; (3) the quality of managerial effort and the efficiency of business organization; (4) the quality of the labor force, including physical stamina, motivation, training, and skill.

How is the spread of unionism and collective bargaining likely to affect each of these factors? The effect on capital accumulation could be in either direction, depending on the determinants of business investment. If investment is constrained by companies' retained earnings, and if unions succeed in reducing business profits, investment will be reduced. But if borrowed funds are readily available, and if investment decisions are influenced by relative factor costs, then union wage pressure should increase investment by stimulating capital–labor substitution. Since the evidence on investment behavior is still unclear, we cannot say which line of reasoning is more plausible.

As regards technical progress, union wage pressure should stimulate more intensive research on production methods, designed to hold down unit costs in the face of rising wages. It may also help to give this research a labor-saving bias.

The effect on business management is quite conjectural. On one hand, it can be argued that union pressure provides a continuing stimulus to managerial efficiency. This can be supported by numerous cases in which the sudden necessity of meeting a higher wage bill has startled management into making economies that might otherwise have been postponed indefinitely. On the other hand it can be argued that if the union stands always ready to take away higher profits through wage demands, management is likely to lose interest in setting up targets at which the union can shoot. It will no longer have an incentive to raise profits by improving methods and expanding the enterprise. The tendency of unionism to strengthen monopolistic arrangements in product markets may also react adversely on managerial efficiency.

Unionism probably has significant effects on worker effort and efficiency, but again the effects run in both directions. Union emphasis on public education, trade training, reasonable hours, and other conditions may increase the quality and efficiency of the labor force. On the other hand, make-work rules, restrictions on work speeds, and other union policies may reduce output per man. An important effect of collective bargaining is to protect workers against arbitrary discipline and make them feel more secure in their jobs. On an armchair basis, one can reason either that this will make men work better or that it will lead to a slackening of effort. In this as in so many other matters of industrial relations, the only course at present is an honest confession of ignorance.

Concerning the supply of labor we can speak with greater confidence. It seems likely that unionism in the United States has produced a considerable reduction in labor supply. The labor movement was influential in the enactment of restrictive immigration laws in the 1920s, which reduced immigration from a flood to a trickle. Trade unions have also been in the forefront of movements to raise the school-leaving age, to limit the occupations in which young people and women may engage, and to encourage earlier retirement through private and public pension systems. These things all make for a smaller supply of labor from a given population. While the great reduction in weekly hours of work over the past century cannot be attributed entirely to union activity, the unions have played a prominent role. More recently, they have secured sizable reductions in annual hours of work through provision for longer vacations and more paid holidays. It is impossible to measure the total effect of these policies, but it would not be surprising to find that the present labor supply of the United States is 10 percent lower than it would have been in the absence of union activity.

Where does this bring us out as regards the impact of unionism on real wages? Since the effects on the productivity schedule are so difficult to appraise, and since they run in opposite directions, it is perhaps most plausible to assume that collective bargaining leaves this schedule unchanged. On this assumption, unionism in a competitive economy appears to (1) reduce the supply of labor at any point in time, (2) reduce national output because of the reduction in labor inputs, and (3) raise the level of real wages. The increase in the real wage level may raise labor's share of national income, but will not necessarily do so. This depends on the elasticity of capital–labor substitution, as explained in Chapter 8.

Let us consider next the implications of monopoly power in product markets and monopsony power in labor markets. It might be thought that a union dealing with a monopolistic employer could, by forcing up wage rates, "capture" a larger share of his monopoly profit and thus alter the distribution of income.

It is not established, however, that unions succeed in enforcing a higher wage level in monopolistic industries than in competitive ones, given the same degree of organization in the two cases. Even if they did so, labor's income share would not necessarily rise. On the ordinary monopoly diagram, a wage increase will shift the marginal cost curve upward. Demand and marginal revenue remaining unchanged, and assuming that the firm always seeks to maximize profit, this will (1) reduce output, (2) reduce employment, (3) raise the price of the product, (4) reduce profit, since the firm was presumably maximizing profit before the wage rise. With the wage rate higher but employment lower, the *wage bill* may or may not rise, and labor's share of value added in the company may increase or decrease. This depends on the shape of the demand and cost curves in a particular case. In general, however, raising wages is not a dependable method of capturing monopoly profit.

The case of monopsony is different. Here the employer has an incentive to restrict employment in order to lower the wage rate. The effect (as compared with what would happen in a perfect labor market) is to reduce the wage rate, employment, and the wage bill; to increase the employer's profit margin per unit and his total profit; and to reduce labor's share of value added. A minimum wage enforced by law or collective bargaining restores the conditions of a perfect labor market in the sense that labor supply becomes perfectly elastic at the prescribed wage. Up to a point, wages can be raised with a simultaneous *increase* in employment, hence in the wage bill, and also in labor's share of value added. Here, then, is a case in which unionism clearly can alter the distribution of income in labor's favor.

What we do not know is the practical importance of this case. How extensive is monopsony in nonunion labor markets? How fully do employers recognize and exploit their monopsony power? Differences of opinion on these points can lead to widely differing estimates of the union impact. The writer's hypotheses would be that (1) monopsony is important for large firms in towns of, say, 10,000 or less located at some distance from a metropolitan center; (2) many employers do take advantage of their monopsony position; (3) a union entering such a situation for the first time can often secure a large initial wage increase, which wipes out part or all of the previous monopsony gain; (4) this is a once-for-all increase, wages thereafter moving in line with regional or industry trends; (5) for the economy as a whole, it seems unlikely that such transfers could total more than a small percentage of the wage bill. The *direction* of the impact, however, is toward an increase in labor's income share.

Finally, one can develop a macroeconomic theory of distribution under which the labor and capital shares depend on the behavior of certain "grand aggregates" of the economy. In the Kaldor model described in Chapter 8, the outcome depends on investment as a percentage of national income, workers' savings as a percentage of wage income, and capitalists' savings as a percentage of profit income. It is hard to formulate plausible hypotheses about how collective bargaining might alter national investment levels and savings propensities. One might speculate that the *direction* of the effect is (1) to discourage investment, lowering the I/Y ratio; (2) to shift a modest amount of income from profit to wages; (3) on the basis of result (2) since the propensity to save out of wages is certainly less than that out of profit, to lower the S/Y ratio, possibly by about the same amount as the reduction in I/Y. One would thus have a picture that is at least internally consistent. But there is little evidence at present to support such speculations, and it seems unlikely that the global effect of collective bargaining is large, particularly in a partially unionized economy such as the United States.

A consideration of these possibilities leaves the impression that unionism probably has increased the *real wage rate* per man-hour of labor, mainly through a reduction in labor supply, but that this effect has not been very large. Labor's *share of national income* has probably not been significantly effected. If this is true, labor's *total real income* may be reduced along with the reduction of labor supply and national output, but with some offsetting gain in leisure. Evidence is scanty, however, and other economists might well disagree with these judgments.

Discussion Questions

1. You are asked to design a research study to determine whether wages in the automobile industry are higher than they would have been in the absence of unionism. Outline at least two ways in which you might approach this problem.
2. Some unions seem to have had a much larger effect than others on the relative wage level of their industries. What are the possible reasons for such differences?
3. You are national president of an industrial union, whose membership consists of 25 percent skilled workers, 60 percent semiskilled workers, and 15 percent unskilled workers. What policy would you pursue as regards occupational wage differentials?
4. You have data on average earnings in each occupation in an industry, year by year from 1940 to 1970. The industry has been unionized throughout this period, and you have full records of

the union's internal discussions. How would you proceed to estimate the impact of union policy, relative to the effect of economic
forces, on occupational differentials?

5. What conditions are most conducive to reduction of geographic
   wage differences through collective bargaining?
6. What are the probable effects of eliminating geographic wage
   differences in a national market industry where such differences
   were previously substantial?
7. The man in the street would probably say that unions have had
   a large effect on the average wage level in the economy. This
   chapter suggests that the effect has been quite moderate. Why this
   difference of opinion?

Reading Suggestions

In addition to the references listed in Chapter 22, see Lewis, H.
Gregg, ed., *Unionism and Relative Wages in the United States.*
Chicago: The University of Chicago Press, 1963; Levinson, Harold M.,
Determining Forces in Collective Wage Bargaining. New York: John
Wiley & Sons, Inc., 1966; Macdonald, Robert M., *Collective Bargain-
ing in the Automobile Industry.* New Haven: Yale University Press,
1963; and Reynolds, Lloyd G., and Cynthia H. Taft, *The Evolution
of Wage Structure.* New Haven: Yale University Press, 1956.

THE
BALANCE SHEET
OF
TRADE UNIONISM

24

We have had much to say
in earlier chapters about the effects of particular union policies. It is
now time to put the pieces together into an overall evaluation.
The effects of union activity may be classified conveniently under
eight headings: (1) the structure of labor and product markets; (2) the
level of money wages and prices; (3) the level of real wages; (4) relative
wage rates for different industries and occupations; (5) nonmonetary
terms of employment; (6) the social structure of the plant; (7) the
status of the individual worker; and (8) the balance of political power
in the community.

The picture to be painted here is an intricate one. Some union
gains have been achieved through political channels, others through
collective bargaining. An adequate appraisal must include both. Some
effects of unionism are reasonably certain, others are rather conjectural. Some of the effects may be rated as beneficial, others as harmful
from a public standpoint. Whether a particular effect is considered
beneficial, and whether the pros are regarded as outweighing the cons,
depends partly on one's political outlook and beliefs. Any sweeping
judgment of unionism, whether favorable or unfavorable, is certain
to be wrong.

STRUCTURE OF LABOR
AND
PRODUCT MARKETS

Perhaps the commonest statement about trade unions is that they are "monopolies." In both economic theorizing and popular writing this is usually meant as a term of reproach. What precise meaning can be given to this term? In what sense do unions exert monopoly power? Are the effects necessarily and automatically harmful?

It is necessary here to distinguish between product markets and labor markets and, as regards labor markets, to distinguish between wage determination and the processes of job choice and labor mobility. Wage determination and labor mobility are obviously related but they are not the same thing, and unionism affects the former considerably more than the latter.

Job Choices and Labor Mobility

Unionism seems to have had little direct effect on the *number of workers* admitted to particular industries and occupations. Most unions have not worked very hard to restrict entrance, and where they have tried they have not been very successful.

Union contract provisions have greater effect on *which* workers shall be employed in a particular industry or occupation. The general use of seniority in rehiring laid-off workers, plus frequent use of the closed shop, means that workers previously attached to an industry have first chance at employment opportunities. Newcomers can break into the industry only when experienced workers are fully employed, whereas in the absence of union restrictions employers might often prefer to substitute a highly competent newcomer for a less-competent former employee.

Unionism might tend in several ways to reduce interplant movement of labor. The grievance procedure makes it possible for workers to correct unsatisfactory conditions without resorting to the old expedient of quitting the job. Seniority protection, pension rights, and other benefits that accrue with length of service place a substantial premium on staying with the same employer for a long period. Emphasis on internal promotion based on length of service increases the height of the walls around each employing unit and makes it harder for workers to make an advantageous shift between employers.

It is questionable, however, whether collective bargaining has produced any major change in the pattern of labor turnover. Labor market studies ranging from 1900 to the present agree that the great bulk of voluntary quits occur during the first year of employment, indicating either that the worker was poorly selected and did not work out on the job, or that the job did not live up to the expectations that the worker held when he took it. Quitting is an intrinsic part of the process of job shopping in an imperfect labor market. Voluntary quit rates are also highly correlated with the business cycle, that is, with objective opportunities to change jobs. Quits rise sharply during boom years when jobs are plentiful and fall sharply during depression.

In addition to these cyclical swings, there has been a tendency for voluntary quit rates to decline gradually in the long run. Quit rates in American manufacturing were markedly lower in the 1920s than in the 1910s, and were still lower in the fifties and sixties. Unionism, seniority rules, and pension plans have probably had something to do with this. But other factors have also been at work, including more careful selection of new employees and better personnel management in general, tapering off of the rate of increase in total manufacturing employment and consequent stabilization of the manufacturing work force, and aging of the labor force in the nation as a whole.

A recent study by John F. Burton, Jr. and John E. Parker concludes that there is no significant relation between unionization and voluntary quit rates when other relevant variables are included in the analysis. A simple correlation of percentage of workers unionized in an industry with the voluntary quit rate for the industry shows a negative relation—stronger unionism, lower quit rate. But this is adequately explained by the fact that unions are strongest in high-wage industries, and that high-wage industries have relatively low quit rates. The wage level is the most important explanatory factor, as one might expect from economic analysis.[1]

Wage Determination

Unions can and do influence the wage levels of particular occupational groups, companies, and industries. This is often expressed by saying that unionism substitutes "monopoly" for "competition" in wage determination. It is questionable, however, whether this terminology clarifies the issues more than it confuses them. The market for manual labor is notoriously imperfect. There is no effective central clearinghouse; there is much ignorance and misinformation on both

[1] John F. Burton, Jr., and John E. Parker, "Interindustry Variations in Voluntary Labor Mobility," *Industrial and Labor Relations Review*, January, 1969, pp. 199–216. On this range of issues see also Arthur M. Ross, "Do We Have a New Industrial Feudalism?" *American Economic Review*, XLIX (December, 1958).

sides of the market; job hunting is haphazard; mobility is low; and most workers do not really have a "market outlook." Many employers are large relative to the local labor market in which they operate, and can alter wage rates rather than taking them as given by the market. They have some degree of monopsony power in buying labor.

Trade unions do not intrude into a situation in which wage rates have been perfectly aligned by competitive forces. They come into a situation in which relative wage rates have already been distorted by various types of market imperfection. Trade unions may thus *either* correct previous distortions of the wage structure or perpetuate and accentuate these distortions. How far unions actually do either or both of these things is a factual question about which we shall have more to say in a moment.

The disadvantage of the "monopoly" terminology is that it pre-judges the issue before the evidence has been examined, and condemns any bargained wage rate by applying to it a term of ill repute. It would be more neutral and more accurate to say that unionism *strengthens* the workers' bargaining position. Unionism does not necessarily *equalize* the bargaining position of the parties. In some cases union strength remains inferior to employer strength under collective bargaining, while in other cases it is markedly superior. In all cases, however, one can say that the workers' relative position is stronger than before.

Competition in Product Markets

It is probably safe to conclude that unionism strengthens monopoly tendencies in product markets. Most unions are firm believers in "orderly" or quasi-collusive price determination, and will line up with established producers against new competition from at home or abroad. In industries with a few large companies who are able to control competition effectively, unions simply insist on a share of the proceeds. In industries with many producers, where control of competition is difficult, unions may take the lead in forming and policing restrictive agreements. Unionism also makes it harder for new firms to break into an industry by preventing them from operating even temporarily at a lower level of labor costs while getting established. Unions are unenthusiastic about antitrust and other procompetitive policies, and fall in naturally with legalized cartel arrangements, such as those established by the National Recovery Administration codes in New Deal days.

As between any one industry and the remainder of the economy, the union lines up with employers and strengthens their hand against outside competition and against the consuming public. Unions are just as interested as employers in maximizing the industry's total "take" from the public,[2] and come to blows with them only over the division of the proceeds. Unionism thus tends toward a "syndicalist" economic structure, in which organized industry groups try to extract maximum gains from the economy under a regime of fixed prices, fixed wages, and controlled entrance.

MONEY WAGES
AND
THE PRICE LEVEL

Does unionism cause the level of money wages and prices to rise faster in the course of time than would happen under nonunion conditions? Does it produce or strengthen an "inflationary bias" in the economic mechanism? If so, what are the economic consequences? Do workers gain anything in real purchasing power through a more rapid advance of money wages, or are the wage increases simply canceled out by price increases?

There are several reasons for believing that unionism does strengthen inflationary tendencies in the economy. Perhaps most important is its influence on government's monetary and fiscal policies. Belief in full employment is now as firmly established as belief in motherhood and the home. But how full is "full"? Should one be content with 5 percent unemployment or should one insist on no more than 3 percent, or even 2 percent? Unions tend to set the employment target high and the unavoidable minimum of unemployment low. Whenever unemployment rises above this level they insist that the federal government leap into aggressive action on all fronts—lower interest rates, easier credit, increases in government spending, reductions in taxes. Too aggressive action, however, may raise aggregate demand at a rate that will pull up prices along with production. Beyond a certain point, the objective of higher employment conflicts with that of price stability. Unions give heavy weight to employment objectives and do not worry so much about increases in the price level. To the extent that they have political influence, this outlook is reflected in government policy.

On the collective bargaining front, the effect of unionism shows up most clearly in recession. In modern times, wage cuts are rare even

---

[2] An occasional exception should be noted. President Reuther of the United Automobile Workers has proposed on several occasions that automobile company profits should be reduced by lowering prices to consumers as well as raising wages to employees. This may have been merely a public relations gesture or may have been intended more seriously. In any event it was treated as a utopian idea, both by the companies and by most outside commentators, and nothing came of it.

under nonunion conditions. But in a serious recession some cuts will be made; and even without wage cuts, unit labor costs can be reduced by laying off inefficient workers and tightening up production standards. Unions not only resist wage cuts but also resist tightening of production standards and require that layoffs be made on a seniority basis. Under the predominant practice of multi-year contracts, with wage increases scheduled two or three years in advance, union scales continue moving upward right through a recession period; and this raises the wage expectations of nonunion workers as well.

There is less agreement as to how unionism affects the rate of wage increase in periods of rising aggregate demand. Perry[3] found that (for the same values of unemployment rate, profit level, and cost-of-living change,) wages had risen faster from 1948 to 1960, a period of marked unionization, than during the 1920s when unionism was much weaker. It has also been argued on a priori grounds that unionism reduces the lag of wages behind prices during inflationary periods through automatic escalator clauses, frequent wage reopenings, and aggressive bargaining. But Lewis and others reach an opposite conclusion. They believe that the sluggishness of collective bargaining procedures, as compared wih unilateral employer decisions, slows down the advance of union wages during an inflation; and that in such periods the advantage of union workers is materially reduced. At the moment one can conclude only that the evidence is not clear.

Collective bargaining may tend to perpetuate a wage–price spiral even after the aggregate demand which initiated the process has receded. The late sixties provide a good illustration. During the height of the Vietnam war in 1966 to 1968, consumer prices rose about 4 percent a year. But because most of the wage increases in unionized establishments had been negotiated in years of price stability *before* 1966, wage increases continued rather moderate. There was virtually no increase in *real* wages in 1966, and less than a 1 percent increase in 1967 and 1968—well below the long-term trend. This tends to support Lewis' view that unions do not do very well during inflationary periods.

As one inflationary year succeeded another, however, the size of newly bargained wage increases stepped up sharply. It rose from 3.8 percent in 1965 to 4.8 percent in 1966, 5.7 percent in 1967, and 7.5 percent in 1968. Since these contracts are typically for three-year terms, there are now large wage increases scheduled for 1970 to 1972 regardless of the level of demand in those years. This will put continuing upward pressure on prices.

Overall, then, it seems likely that collective bargaining strengthens

---

[3] George L. Perry, *Unemployment, Money Wage Rates and Inflation* (Cambridge, Mass.: The M.I.T. Press, 1966).

the inflationary bias which has been evident in the United States (and in other western industrial countries) since World War II.

REAL WAGES
AND
INCOME DISTRIBUTION

Little need be added to what was said on this subject in the last chapter. There is little evidence that unions have been able to encroach materially on business profits by the collective bargaining route. In monopsony situations, the union can secure a once-for-all gain in a newly organized plant. But thereafter the employer seems able to keep his distance as the union chases him up the wage–price escalator. He can rely on rising productivity as a partial or complete offset to rising money wages. Moreover, conditions which are favorable to large wage increases also permit employers to pass these on to the buyer in higher prices. Workers can do little, either individually or through union action, to close this escape hatch of price increases. Clark Kerr has put the point in the following parable:

> Each of these types of unionism is engaged in a grand pursuit—a pursuit mainly of the employer. And the employer is always trying, with more or less success, to escape. Now I do not wish to conjure up a picture of poor Eliza being chased across the ice by bloodhounds. Our Eliza is by no means always poor; nor do the bloodhounds always pursue very aggressively (they are often quite gentle creatures). They may even agree to stay a certain distance behind her, or to care for and protect her if she will be nice to them, or they may help arrange for better ice so that both Eliza and they can run faster. However, they may also try to get somebody else to hold Eliza one way or another so that they can catch up with her, which does not, offhand, sound very fair, though it may be quite effective. And, in our little drama Eliza does not always get across the river in time, although she usually does remarkably well and at times even turns around and chases the bloodhounds back again. Beyond that, the bloodhounds sometimes catch somebody else while chasing Eliza. They may even, inadvertently, catch themselves.[4]

Kerr concludes that wage bargaining alone can have little effect on distributive shares. Labor's share can be increased only if the unions are powerful enough to bargain about prices and profits as well as wages, or if the government will agree to "hold Eliza" by price

[4] Clark Kerr, "Labor's Income Share and the Labor Movement," in George W. Taylor and Frank C. Pierson, eds., *New Concepts in Wage Determination* (New York: McGraw-Hill Book Company, Inc., 1957), p. 267.

control measures, or if government will rifle Eliza's purse through taxation and distribute the proceeds.

Two qualifications, however, must be added. We have found reason to think that unionism reduces labor supply in man-hours below what it would be in the absence of unionism. This must tend to raise the real wage level, though it will not necessarily raise labor's share of national income.

Second, there is now a substantial redistribution of income from higher to lower income brackets through government channels. Money raised through income taxation is used to provide free or subsidized public services for all citizens, and to make cash payments to the aged, the unemployable, and other dependent groups. The distribution of income after taking account of taxes and subsidies is substantially more equal than the pretax distribution. This is in some degree a transfer from the propertied to the wage-earning group, and unions provide part of the political support for it.

UNIONISM
AND
RELATIVE WAGE RATES

The clearest effect of unionism is to alter the relative wages of particular groups of workers. Since Chapters 21 and 22 were devoted mainly to this subject, we need do little more than restate the conclusions reached there.

1. At the plant level, unionism tends to reduce differences among people doing the same kind of work by establishing standard job rates or rate ranges. The economic effect of this depends on how far the workers concerned differ in personal efficiency, and on just *what* is equalized—whether hourly rates, rate ranges, piece rates, or whatever.

The members of a work group will usually differ somewhat in strength, speed, experience, and other personal characteristics. In a perfect labor market, these differences in output capacity would be reflected in differing rates of pay. The market would tend to equalize, not earnings per worker, but wage rates *per efficiency unit of labor.*

The individual wage differences that one typically observes in a nonunion establishment, however, are not necessarily related to efficiency. Other possible reasons for them include: favoritism by the foreman, including the possibility of bribery or kickbacks; the fact that one worker may have been hired in a tight labor market, another during depression; and differences in individual bargaining power or negotiating skill. To the extent that such factors are important, union efforts to eliminate personal discrimination do not necessarily conflict with efficiency criteria.

The union effort may take the form of a standard hourly rate for the occupation. Each worker now receives the same amount, but the wage per efficiency unit is unequal, being highest for the least-efficient workers. This effect is relaxed under a piece-rate system, which permits workers who produce at different rates to earn different amounts. In principle, it can be relaxed also by setting a rate range rather than a single rate for a job, so that superior workers can advance beyond their fellows. In practice, however, unions usually try to restrict the employer's discretion on this point, fearing that it may be used in a discriminatory way, and urge promotion through the rate range on a seniority basis.

A side effect of union pressure for wage uniformity is to make employers more conscious of, and more careful about, their hiring standards. An applicant will not be hired, or will not survive the probationary period, unless he can produce enough to justify the standard wage. Thus the "layering" of the wage structure, with some plants and industries paying more than others, leads to a corresponding "layering" of the labor force. High-productivity individuals tend to be allocated to high-wage industries. This makes the difference in wages per efficiency unit of labor somewhat less than the crude wage differences.

2. Unionism tends to equalize the wage levels of companies competing in the same product market. In the case of local-market industries, such as retailing, repair and service industries, job and newspaper printing, and most building construction, this usually means equalization within a city or metropolitan area. In the case of manufacturing and other industries that compete on a national basis, it usually produces efforts at national wage equalization. This is not always true, however, as witness the paper industry case. And even where the union tries, it cannot succeed unless it is able to maintain a high degree of organization in all parts of the country.

The effect of bringing competing employers to the same wage level depends partly on the reasons for the previous wage differences. To the extent that monopsony power was responsible, there is simply a transfer from profit to wages. (There is also an incidental benefit to the higher-wage employers, who are freed of the threat of low-wage competition.) To the extent that low wages reflected low productivity resulting from lack of managerial capacity or effort, there will probably be a "shock effect" leading to a rise in productivity and some reduction in employment. On the other hand, companies suffering from irremovable disadvantages of location or antiquated equipment and that were previously able to offset this by a lower wage level, will find their profit margin permanently reduced. Returns to capital may fall to the point at which the company cannot survive. Unions are reluctant to put a company out of operation, however, particularly where reemployment possibilities for their members are poor; and they often make concessions to firms with low wage-paying ability.

3. To the extent that unions reduce intercompany differentials in regional- or national-market industries, this means a reduction in geographic wage differentials. This might be considered desirable as a long-run goal. Existing geographic differences in real wages, however, presumably reflect a disequilibrium situation, a more abundant labor supply (relative to demand) in some areas than in others. This situation requires labor migration out of the low-wage areas and capital migration into them, which will gradually reduce geographic wage differences. "Premature" wage equalization under collective bargaining, which reduces the incentives to both types of movement, may thus be considered undesirable.

4. There is considerable evidence that unionism has raised the wage level of unionized industries relative to earnings of nonunion labor. The effect varies, however, as between inflationary and depression periods, as among industries, and within the same industry at different periods of time. Estimates by Lewis and others suggest that the overall effect is of the order of 10 to 15 percent, though there are occasional instances in which the union has gained a wage advantage of 25 percent or more.

This "monopolistic distortion" of the wage structure is an undesirable effect of collective bargaining. The size of the effect, however, is smaller than has often been alleged. Why unions have not achieved larger distortions by exploiting differing elasticities of labor demand is one of the more intriguing questions in the economics of collective bargaining.

5. The fact that collective bargaining establishes standard rates for each job means that unions are necessarily concerned with occupational wage differences. It is difficult to frame general hypotheses about the outcome, because this depends partly on the form of union organization in each industry. There has also been less study of this problem than of interindustry wage relations.

The most interesting hypothesis to emerge recently is that unionism may raise the relative wage level of *both* laborers and skilled craftsmen, with little effect on the percentage differential between them. On this view, the main effect would be a relative *decline* in the position of semiskilled workers. There is some statistical support for this hypothesis, but more investigation is needed to support any firm conclusions.

If one looks at the whole range of occupations in the economy, it appears that unions have raised the average earnings of organized manual workers relative to *both* the white-collar groups higher up in the wage structure *and* the lowest-paid, unorganized groups at the bottom. It is not clear whether this has increased or decreased the overall inequality of earnings from labor.

While all these effects are important, the total impact of unionism on relative wage rates should not be exaggerated. We noted in Chapter 9 that there are strong economic forces working toward a narrowing of most types of wage difference—between men on the same job, between occupational levels, between geographical areas, and so on. Wage equalization is in the nature of things in an advanced industrial economy. Unionism works in the same general direction and has speeded up the wage-leveling process in certain respects. It does not seem, however, to have materially changed the broad contours of the national wage structure. To a considerable extent unions have been given credit (or blame) for developments that were "in the cards" on economic grounds.

NONWAGE BENEFITS
AND
THEIR COST

Unions try to win for their members a wide array of benefits in addition to wages. Some of these involve little cost or may even reduce costs and add to productive efficiency. Others, however, do involve costs that must be weighed against the benefits provided.

In some cases the costs are borne mainly by the workers themselves. Shorter hours of work and supplementary income payments are two leading examples. Here it is pertinent to ask whether the benefits are worth the cost from the workers' standpoint. Would they be willing to "buy" the benefits included in the union contract through the necessary sacrifice in wages? Or may the terms worked out by the union differ considerably from what workers would have chosen on an individual basis? An answer to this question does not necessarily tell which set of terms is preferable from a welfare standpoint. Economists usually take individual preferences as the most reliable guide, on the ground that each person knows his own interests better than anyone else. Many terms of employment, however, have to be defined by organizational rules set either by management or through collective bargaining; and workers may not always be the best judge of their own interests in the long run.

Support of the union organization itself involves costs, typically amounting to something less than 1 percent of members' weekly earnings. This may be regarded as a service charge for the union's efforts in policing working conditions, processing grievances, and pressing contract demands. Many workers doubtless undervalue these services and would be reluctant to pay for them on a fully voluntary basis, just as most citizens undervalue the protective services of government and grumble over the necessary tax levies. Union dues may nevertheless be a "good buy" in terms of workers' long-run interests.

A substantial part of employers' total payroll cost now goes into insurance payments and reserve funds to protect workers against retirement, illness and disability, medical expenses, unemployment, and other risks. Union pressure has probably contributed to the spread of these "private social security" systems, as well as improvement of benefits under government programs. Union members welcome these types of benefit heartily, not altogether realizing that they are partly an alternative to higher basic wage rates. If an employer is willing to concede a ten-cent-an-hour increase in labor costs in a particular year, and if the union asks him to put five cents of this into enlarging supplementary benefits, the remainder for direct wage increases is only five cents. It is possible that if workers were aware of the alternatives and could conduct referendum votes on them, they would often prefer higher wage rates and smaller benefits than those urged by union leaders. This does not mean, however, that the workers' evaluation is correct. One can make a strong case that workers should be adequately protected against the income risks of modern industry, and that they should be obliged to "buy" this protection even though many would be too shortsighted to do so on an individual basis.

Reduction of working hours below a certain level, as was argued in Chapter 2, means a reduction of national output, and part of this will fall on workers in the form of lower real incomes and consumption levels. Here one encounters the problem of workers' valuation of income versus leisure. Up to the present there has probably been no serious discrepancy between union-established working hours and those which workers would have chosen voluntarily; but the problem of conflicting objectives may become more serious in the future.

The workweek and work year will probably continue to decline gradually in unionized industries. Workers will go along with a policy of hours reduction, partly because they do not understand the income costs involved, partly because shorter hours are plausibly urged as an unemployment remedy. Actually, hours reduction is not a suitable remedy either for general unemployment or for overstaffing of a particular industry. There is also reason to doubt whether a further substantial shortening of hours would be in accord with workers' preferences. Several million people are now holding more than one job, indicating that for them the standard workweek was already too short. The eagerness of many workers to put in overtime whenever possible testifies in the same direction. It is quite possible, therefore, that unions may force down hours faster than most workers prefer, and that what used to be counted a major benefit of unionism may turn into a disadvantage.

The cost of some union benefits falls partly or mainly on consumers, among whom workers are of course included. Union efforts to control work speeds increase production costs by increasing the amount of labor time required per unit of product. Improvements in physical working conditions usually cost money. Resistance to technical improvements, insistence that promotions be made strictly on a seniority basis, and insistence that the union's consent must be given before certain management decisions can be carried out—these and other things tend to reduce production efficiency and raise costs.

Critics of unionism sometimes imply that any union policy that reduces man-hour output or increases unit production costs is economically harmful. This is not a tenable position. The question that must be asked in each case is this: Do the benefits that workers obtain from a particular union policy outweigh the additional costs imposed on consumers of the product? This question can be answered only with respect to a particular situation; and the answer will usually depend not on the kind of policy involved, but on the degree to which it has been carried. Down to a certain point, for example, a reduction in work speeds does more good than harm; beyond that point it becomes undesirable. The problem in each case is to strike a proper balance between the interests of a particular producer group and of society at large.

There is strong reason to think that, in the absence of trade union organization, the balance is tilted too far in the direction of minimizing money costs of production, i.e. of sacrificing the interests of workers to those of employers and consumers. There is equally little doubt that unions, in attempting to redress the balance, sometimes overshoot the mark and saddle industry with unduly high costs. On the whole, however, it seems likely that one comes closer to a proper balancing of producer and consumer interests with collective bargaining than without it.

It should be recognized also that collective bargaining yields important benefits involving little or no addition to production costs. Many improvements in working conditions and personnel methods can be accomplished with little expense; yet unless workers point out the possibilities and are in a position to insist on them, the changes may not be made. The greatest single benefit that unionism brings the worker is protection against arbitrary discharge. This involves little direct cost and seems as likely to raise worker efficiency as to lower it. Seniority rules concerning layoff and retiring are also much appreciated by workers and may well have a neutral or even favorable effect on efficiency. Where benefits accrue to the worker at little or no social cost, they would seem to be advantageous from every point of view.

SOCIAL STRUCTURE

OF

THE SHOP

A major consequence of collective bargaining is to change the foreman from an absolute to a constitutional monarch, who must operate within the framework of the union agreement and whose decisions can be appealed to higher authority. To the worker, this appears as an unmitigated gain. To the foreman, it appears as an increase in the difficulty and a reduction in the attractiveness of his job. It is one thing to maintain production standards when the men under you are fully subject to your authority. It is quite another when your every decision, large or small, may be taken up as a grievance by the union and you may be forced into ignominious retreat. The foreman is part of management, yet he must live with the workers and with the union. Nor can he be sure that higher management will back him up in a grievance proceeding. Management must save its powder for crucial issues and must view each case in the light of overall strategy vis-à-vis the union. The individual foreman is expendable. The trying nature of the foreman's job under union conditions has created a real problem of persuading qualified men to accept promotion to foremanships. Many workers understandably reason, "Why should I have everybody hating me for an extra ten cents an hour?"

The degree of personal harmony and productive efficiency in the shop depends a good deal on the relations that the foreman is able to work out with the union steward in his department. A skillful foreman can use the steward as an aid to management, an informal consultant and go-between in dealing with the workers. Foreman and steward may work out flexible interpretations of personnel rules and may trade enforcement on some points for concessions on others. Carried too far, of course, this may lead to erosion of the foreman's authority. One finds situations in which the union steward is the *de facto* head of the shop and the foreman's position is secondary. The foreman's central problem is to maintain effective control while winning consent and cooperation.

Whatever difficulties the grievance procedure may pose for the individual foreman, it has important advantages from an overall management standpoint. It provides a channel through which complaints and problems arising in the plant can be transmitted rapidly up the line to top management. In theory, the regular management chain of command already provides a means for upward communication of information and problems as well as downward communication of directives and instructions. It was pointed out in Chapter 14, however, that upward communication is apt to be heavily censored with a view to passing on only favorable news to one's superiors. Top management may thus get the impression that everything is running smoothly in the plant, when in fact discontent may have risen almost to the point of explosion.

Under collective bargaining, pressures accumulating in the plant that do not find expression through regular management channels can travel up the line through the grievance procedure. This procedure provides a supplementary, and frequently more rapid, line of communication from the bottom to the top of the management structure. Selekman has advocated that management make full use of this method of keeping its finger on the pulse of the labor force.[5] Management, he contends, should adopt a clinical rather than a legalistic approach to the grievance procedure. The first question to be asked about a grievance should not be, "Is it a valid grievance under the contract and does the worker have a legal case for adjustment?" The question should be rather, "What does the filing of this grievance, whether valid or invalid, indicate about the state of human relations in the shop? What can be done to improve the situation?"

Finally, collective bargaining makes a fundamental difference in the determination and administration of personnel policies. Under nonunion conditions these can be regarded as analogous to any other group of management functions—marketing, finance, engineering, and so on. They are subject to unilateral management control, and the only question that arises is whether a particular procedure will contribute to greater efficiency of the business. Under collective bargaining, this is drastically changed. A few functions—notably the selection and training of new employees, and certain welfare activities —remain under primary control of management. With respect to the great majority of personnel functions, however, both the determination and execution of policy become a bipartisan matter. With respect to any policy, management must ask not only, "Does it contribute to efficiency?" but also, "Can it be sold to the union?" Skill in negotiation and personal contacts, rather than skill in engineering and other managerial techniques, becomes the primary requirement for an industrial relations officer. An incidental effect is usually to raise the status of the industrial relations group in the management hierarchy, and to bring about the hiring of better industrial relations personnel.

[5] Benjamin Selekman, *Labor Relations and Human Relations* (New York: McGraw-Hill Book Company, 1947).

We have dwelt a good deal in earlier sections on wage rates and other economic consequences of collective bargaining. One should never lose sight, however, of the effects just described. It is these that most directly affect the daily lives of everyone in industry, from laborers to corporation presidents. These effects must consequently bulk large in any overall appraisal of trade unionism.

STATUS
OF
THE INDIVIDUAL WORKER

In the long run, one of the most important effects of unionism is that it produces a different kind of man. The worker under a union contract is freed from the danger of arbitrary and unpredictable treatment by the employer, from the necessity of flattering or bribing the foreman to hold his job, from the fear of offending the employer by his political opinions or personal conduct. To this extent he comes closer to being a completely free man.

Unionism increases the worker's sense of participation in economic and political affairs. He is no longer an isolated individual, subject to forces that he can neither understand nor control. He is a member of a powerful movement, which can influence events not only in the plant but in the economy at large. The top officers of his union are courted by political leaders and sit in the high councils of the nation. The worker's union membership gives him a more direct sense of participation than he enjoys as consumer, voter, stockholder, or in any of his other capacities. It gives him "a stake in the system" and renders him less susceptible to proposals for revolutionary change.

Unionism also opens up to the worker additional possibilities of personal progress. Workers of unusual ability can rise to salaried positions in the union hierarchy. A few go all the way to the top and become national figures. Many more rise to lower positions in which they enjoy a modest but assured income, influence over considerable numbers of workers and employers, and prominence in state and local affairs. In addition to the direct satisfactions afforded by union office, it is frequently a stepping-stone to positions in industry or government. Workers can demonstrate their abilities in union affairs, rise vertically through the union hierarchy, and then move laterally to prominent positions in other types of organizations.

In all these ways—by liberating the worker from arbitrary employer discipline, by increasing his feeling of participation and influence in civic affairs, and by opening up to him new channels of vertical mobility—unionism tends to create greater freedom and opportunity. At the same time it imposes a new network of union regulations with penalties for violating them. This raises a problem of guaranteeing citizenship rights in the union, of ensuring that the worker's gains in freedom as against the employer are not too heavily offset by a loss of freedom as against union officials. Clark Kerr has argued cogently for the need to protect the individual against domination by every type of private association as well as by the political state:

> In the area of liberty, there are probably four imperatives. First, freedom of access of the worker, without discrimination, to corporation and union alike. Second, an opportunity for him to participate in setting the most important relationships between employer and employee on the one hand and union and member on the other—in the first case through the right to select bargaining representation and in the second through the right to vote freely in elections. Third, a right to judicial review of disciplinary action whether by employer or union.
>
> Fourth, and this is a much neglected consideration, freedom from control or even dominant influence by the corporation or union in the nonjob phases of life. . . . This means a rejection of both the all-embracing corporation of Mayo and the all-embracing union of Tannenbaum. The separation of power over job, politics, consumption patterns and so forth, has as much to recommend it as the separation of governmental power into the legislative, the executive, and the judicial.[6]

BALANCE OF
POLITICAL POWER
IN
THE COMMUNITY

The political problem in an industrial society is exceedingly intricate. It involves preventing the individual from being overshadowed by corporations, unions, and other private associations as well as by government. It also involves some reasonable balance among private power groups seeking to influence the conduct of government. Unionism, by organizing a powerful new pressure group, produces a different balance of forces in the political arena. Union pressure, while frequently aligned with business pressure on narrow issues of industry interests, typically runs counter to it on broader issues. The range of conflict is suggested by such labor objectives as improvement of the legal status of trade unions, minimum wages and maximum hours of work, social insurance and other protective labor legislation,

[6] Clark Kerr, "Industrial Relations and the Liberal Pluralist," *Proceedings of Seventh Annual Meeting of IRRA* (1954), pp. 2–16.

progressive income and inheritance taxation, full employment policies, and government subsidization of housing construction, medical care, and education.

The advance of social legislation is so remorseless that it seems on the surface to result from some sort of natural law. It is doubtful, however, whether the progress of social legislation results mainly from greater general enlightenment and greater middle-class sympathy with labor's objectives. It is more influenced by the growing membership and increasing political awareness of trade unions, and by the efforts of each political party to win enough labor votes to secure control of the government. A political party that can be labeled as hostile to labor's main objectives has no chance of survival. Since survival and power are the aims of a political organization, one can be sure that both of our major parties will try in future to look like "friends of labor"—even between elections!

It is no longer possible to have governmental policies of the sort followed by conservative administrations in Britain and the United States before 1930. This may be good or bad, depending on one's outlook. It is certainly a development of major importance. Unions have a large share of the responsibility for barring the door to the past.

**IS
UNIONISM
A GOOD IDEA?**

The reader should by now have plenty of facts, ideas, and arguments on which to base his own evaluation of trade unionism. For the author to lay down the law would be wrong and would serve no educational purpose. He may perhaps be permitted, however, to sound one word of warning.

This warning is that one's evaluation of unionism should not be too narrowly economic in character. It is a curious fact that both the critics and defenders of unionism have based their arguments mainly on the wage–employment effects outlined in the first few sections of this chapter. The prevalent opinion among economic theorists has been that unions can make only limited income gains for their members, and that these gains are likely to be outweighed by the harmful effects of "artificial" interference with economic forces. Defenders of unionism have pointed to gaps in the assumptions of economic theory, have argued that unions have a substantial positive effect on productivity, wages, and employment, and have asserted that these gains benefit society at large as well as union members. Much of their reasoning, however, rests on dubious economics—for example, the familiar union dogma that a general increase in the money wage level always raises employment, in good times or bad.

Actually, there is little evidence that unionism has any striking effects on productivity, money wage levels, real wage levels, or the distribution of industry's receipts between wages and profits. These subjects bulk large in textbook discussion mainly because we have theories of a sort about wages and employment, while we have no accepted theoretical framework for analyzing working conditions, social relations in the plant, personal freedom, or political power. But the fact that we have conceptual difficulty in grappling with these problems does not mean that they are less important than wage issues.

It is doubtful whether either the defenders or critics of unionism can hope for much more than a draw on the wage-employment front. The situations in which union manipulation of labor supply and wage rates has favorable effects can always be matched by others in which the effects are unfavorable. A positive case for unionism probably has to be made mainly under the last four headings listed above— nonwage benefits, the social structure of the plant, the status of the individual worker, and the balance of political power in the community. Negative points can be made here also, but they have less force, and the general case for unionism and collective bargaining appears strong. But there is no reason to support a good case with bad economics, as is done by many who seek to justify unionism on a narrow income basis.

Discussion Questions

1. Discuss the effects of labor unions on the mobility of labor. Would the absence of unions significantly alter hiring and job seeking?
2. "Unionism substitutes 'monopoly' for 'competition' in wage determination." Discuss.
3. What are the effects of unions on competition in product markets?
4. What are the determinants of productivity? Do labor unions, on balance, raise or lower labor productivity?
5. What are the main noneconomic consequences of collective bargaining in terms of the plant and the individual worker?
6. "When all is said and done, the chief sufferer from union economic activity is the consumer." Discuss.

INDEX

DATE DUE

APR 9 '73			
NOV 8 '73			
NOV 27 '73			
UG 21 '74			
AUG 16 '74			
AUG 21 '74			
NOV 11 '76			
NOV 24 '76			
GAYLORD			PRINTED IN U.S.A.